MO

USA
NATIONAL
PARKS

THE COMPLETE GUIDE TO ALL
63 PARKS

BECKY LOMAX

CONTENTS

THE SOUTH 609

ISLANDS 707

ESSENTIALS 749

Although every effort was made to make sure the information in this book was accurate when going to press, research was impacted by the Covid-19 pandemic and things may have changed since the time of writing. Be sure to confirm specific details, like opening hours, closures, and travel guidelines and restrictions, when making your travel plans. For more detailed information, see page 761.

1: THE NEEDLES, CANYONLANDS
2: SOUTH RIM, CRATER LAKE
3: NEVADA FALL, YOSEMITE
4: OXBOW BEND AT SUNSET, GRAND TETON
5: FRENCHMANS BAY, ACADIA NATIONAL PARK

EXPERIENCE THE NATIONAL PARKS

These 63 national parks are masterpieces spread across the United States. The artistry of nature paints their rainforests with mossy green, their lakes a vivid blue, and their canyons in shifting oranges and reds.

Their beauty is in their wildness. Cactus deserts bloom against the odds, and rugged mountains trap snow to feed rivers tumbling to oceans, where seascapes change with each tide. Wolves, grizzly bears, orcas, and eagles still rule the animal kingdom, much as they did when only Indigenous people occupied these lands.

The sights can only be described in superlatives: North America's highest peak, tallest waterfall, deepest lake, lowest elevation, biggest trees, and the world's first national park.

Our parks provide moments of connection: hearing birds chatter, smelling fragrant trees, feeling the spray of waterfalls, touching rocks smoothed over by the centuries, and staring up into dark skies. These are the moments that let nature wash through us; that offer renewal of the human spirit.

Your trip to any of these national parks can be the start of a longer, life-enriching journey. Let it begin here.

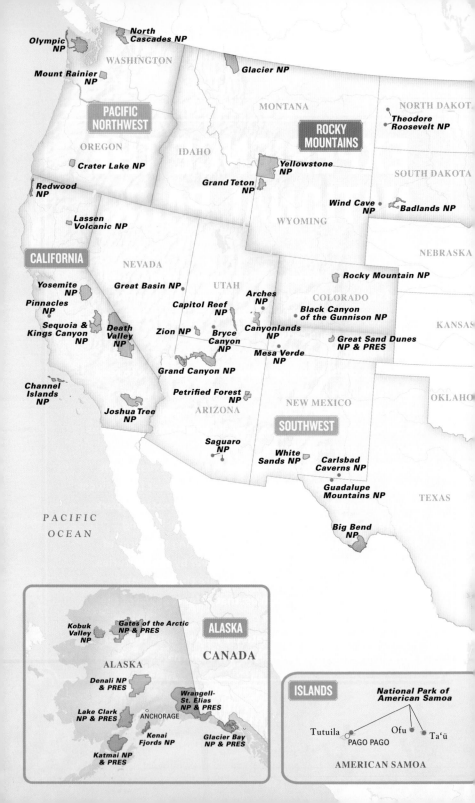

USA NATIONAL PARKS

Voyageurs NP

Isle Royale NP

Lake *Superior*

MAINE

Acadia NP

MINNESOTA

WISCONSIN

Lake *Huron*

VT

NH

Lake *Ontario*

MA

NEW YORK

CT RI

MICHIGAN

Lake *Michigan*

Lake Erie

GREAT LAKES AND NORTHEAST

PENNSYLVANIA

NJ

IOWA

ILLINOIS

Indiana Dunes NP

Cuyahoga Valley NP

INDIANA

OHIO

MD

DE

⊗ Washington DC

WV

Shenandoah NP

Gateway Arch NP

New River Gorge NP & PRES

VIRGINIA

MISSOURI

KENTUCKY

Mammoth Cave NP

Great Smoky Mountains NP

NORTH CAROLINA

ARKANSAS

THE SOUTH

TENNESSEE

SOUTH CAROLINA

ot Springs NP

Congaree NP

MISSISSIPPI

GEORGIA

ATLANTIC OCEAN

ALABAMA

LOUISIANA

FLORIDA

GULF OF MEXICO

Everglades NP

Biscayne NP

Dry Tortugas NP

Kaua'i

Ni'ihau

O'ahu

HONOLULU

Moloka'i

Maui

ISLANDS

VIRGIN ISLANDS

CHARLOTTE AMALIE

Haleakalā NP

HAWAII

Hawai'i

ISLANDS

Hawai'i Volcanoes NP

Virgin Islands NP

PUERTO RICO

Top ⑩ *Experiences*

① SEE VOLCANIC ISLAND-BUILDING AT HAWAI'I VOLCANOES

Kilauea spews lava into the ocean, expanding the Big island's footprint (page 721).

② MARVEL AT ICE-LADEN DENALI

Feast your eyes on the immense icy wonder of crevassed glaciers plunging from the highest point in North America (page 45).

3 TAKE A SCENIC DRIVE IN GREAT SMOKIES

Choose one of the many scenic drives in late fall to witness regal scarlets, oranges, and golds light up the forests (page 615).

4 HIKE THE NARROWS IN ZION

Plod upstream in the rocky water of the North Fork of the Virgin River through a deep, narrow slot canyon of vertical cliffs (page 317).

5 GO UNDERGROUND AT MAMMOTH CAVE

Explore this labyrinth—part of the longest cave system in the world—under electric lights, with handheld lanterns, or crawling through tight squeezes (page 642).

6 CATCH OLD FAITHFUL IN YELLOWSTONE

Set your watch to see Old Faithful, the famous geyser that erupts roughly every 90 minutes (page 463).

7 FEEL THE EXTREMES OF DEATH VALLEY

Drop to the lowest point in North America at Death Valley to experience the hottest temperatures and the driest climate (page 153).

8

8 RAFT THROUGH THE GRAND CANYON

Synch with the rhythm of the Colorado River during 7-21 days of crashing white water and flatwater floats below the immense canyon walls (page 275).

9 TOUR ANCIENT CLIFF DWELLINGS IN MESA VERDE

Visit the wondrous cliffside homes of the Ancestral Pueblo people on ranger-led tours (page 384).

10 GAZE UP AT GIANT TREES IN SEQUOIA AND KINGS CANYON

Stand in awe at the base f giant sequoia trees—including the largest tree by volume in the world (page 140).

Where TO GO

ALASKA

Alaska contains some of the most rugged and wildest parks. In **Denali**, bus tours carry visitors deep into the park to see wolves, bears, moose, and the tallest peak in North America. Flightseeing gets visitors even closer to Denali mountain. See tidewater glaciers in **Glacier Bay** and **Kenai Fjords**, or fly above the Arctic Circle to **Gates of the Arctic and Kobuk Valley.** Watch brown bears fishing in **Katmai,** go fishing in **Lake Clark,** and hike to glaciers in **Wrangell-St. Elias.**

CALIFORNIA

The California parks span unique extremes: the marine environment of the **Channel Islands,** the desert badlands of **Death Valley,** and the bubbling mud pots of **Lassen Volcanic.** Two deserts collide in **Joshua Tree,** rocky spires shoot skyward in **Pinnacles,** and giant redwoods and sequoias pack into **Redwood** and **Sequoia-Kings Canyon.** The crowning park, **Yosemite,** shows off waterfalls in Yosemite Valley, far-reaching views from Glacier Point, and a cabled climb up the steep Half Dome.

PACIFIC NORTHWEST

Every one of the Pacific Northwest parks centers on mountains—from the volcano holding **Crater Lake** to high **Mount Rainier** spilling with glaciers to the icy peaks dominating the **North Cascades.** In **Olympic National Park,** you can drive into the alpine at Hurricane Ridge or go west to plunge into the lush Hoh Rain Forest and stroll rugged Ruby Beach.

SOUTHWEST

The parks of the Southwest show off nature's sculpture in the cliffs, fantastical hoodoos, and arches of **Bryce,** **Arches, Canyonlands,** and **Capitol Reef.** Belowground, the artistry continues with stalactites in **Carlsbad Caverns.** Even vegetation contains a rare beauty, with stately cacti in **Saguaro** and ancient bristlecones in **Great Basin.** Colors run rampant in the Painted Desert in the **Petrified Forest,** cliff dwellings of **Mesa Verde,** giant dunes of **Great Sand Dunes,** glittering gypsum of **White Sands,** the Chisos Mountains of **Big Bend,** and the desert peaks of **Guadalupe Mountains.** Two parks stand out as Southwest royalty: **Zion** features the Narrows, Zion Canyon, and the Zion-Mount Carmel Highway. **Grand Canyon** has overlooks of the gaping chasm along Hermit Road and at Desert View Watchtower, while the inner canyon lures hikers and boaters.

ROCKY MOUNTAINS

In the Rocky Mountains, the large famous parks often overshadow the smaller ones. But these modest parks enchant in their own right—the narrow slot of **Black Canyon of the Gunnison,** colorful erosion of **Badlands,** boxwork of **Wind Cave,** and beloved badlands of **Theodore Roosevelt.** The large parks have earned fame for their iconic attractions. **Rocky Mountain** has its elk, Longs Peak, and Trail Ridge Road, the highest paved road in the country. **Glacier** has the scenic Many Glacier area, and the cliff-hugging Going-to-the-Sun Road. **Grand Teton** has wildlife and Teton Park Road. And **Yellowstone** has wildlife-watching, the Grand Canyon of the Yellowstone, and the incomparable Old Faithful Geyser.

GREAT LAKES AND NORTHEAST

In the northeast is **Acadia** with its Park Loop Road, Jordan Pond House, and historic carriage roads.

Like no other region, the Great Lakes contain parks that focus on water. In **Cuyahoga Valley,** Ohio, the canals preserve one of the nation's early water highways. In **Voyageurs,** Minnesota, the lake acreage rivals the amount of land. Lake Superior holds the isolated **Isle Royale,** while **Indiana Dunes** anchors Lake Michigan.

THE SOUTH

From the Appalachian mountain parks such as **Shenandoah,** Virginia, to the coastal marine parks of **Biscayne** and **Dry Tortugas** in Florida, the national parks of the South include the subterranean world of **Mammoth Cave,** Kentucky; the free-standing **Gateway Arch,** Missouri; the swamps of **Congaree,** South Carolina; one of America's oldest waterways in **New River Gorge,** West Virginia; and the mineral springs of **Hot Springs,** Arkansas. Two jewels stand out: **Great Smoky Mountains,** with Cades Cove, Cataloochee Valley, and Newfound Gap Road; and **Everglades,** for wildlife-watching, paddling, and the Ten Thousand Islands.

ISLANDS

The Pacific Ocean and Caribbean Sea hold islands with lovely beaches. The **Virgin Islands** flank white-sand beaches with coral reefs and turquoise water. Located south of the equator, **American Samoa** likewise harbors impressive coral reefs. But in Hawaii, the national parks climb to great heights far above the beaches at **Haleakalā** and **Hawai'i Volcanoes.**

KEEPSAKE STAMPS ▼▼▼

Visitors can collect free cancellation stamps for each national park they tour. Each park has an individual stamp that serves as a record of your visit. A few stamps feature a park icon; most name the park, the month, and the year. More than 400 properties in the national park system, including historical parks, monuments, and historical trails, have stamps. You can usually get your stamp at the park's visitors centers.

You can use the space provided on the opening page of each chapter in this book to collect the stamp for each national park you visit. A passport-like booklet for collecting your park stamps is also available from the National Park Service (www.eparks.com).

Happy collecting!

Acadia National Park
OCT 2024
Schoodic Peninsula

Kings Canyon National Park
JUN 2024
Kings Canyon Visitor Center

Know BEFORE YOU GO

NATIONAL PARKS PASS

Most national parks charge an entrance fee that is valid for seven days. To get the most bang for your buck, consider buying the **Interagency Annual Pass** ($80), which is good for all national parks and federal fee areas. Interagency passes are free for fourth graders in the United States, disabled persons, and military personnel. Seniors have two interagency pass options: Annual ($20), which is valid for one year, and Lifetime ($80).

FEE-FREE DAYS

Some national parks recognize several fee-free days annually. During fee-free days, the entrance fee for the park is waived. Most fee-free days include Martin Luther King Jr. Day (Jan.), the first day of National Park Week (Apr.), the anniversary of the Great American Outdoors Act/National Park Service birthday (Aug.), National Public Lands Day (Sept.), and Veterans Day (Nov. 11).

HIGHLINE TRAIL, GLACIER

NATIONAL PARKS APP

The **NPS smartphone app** has information on each national park: road conditions and closures, alerts, weather, ranger programs, maps, trails, activities, and campgrounds. Some parks include driving tours, self-guided walking tours, geyser eruption predictions, and parking lot status. **Download the app before you leave home.** Select the parks you'll be visiting and download information to use when cell service is not available, which is common in many parks.

RESERVATIONS

ROADS AND PARKING

Many uber-crowded parks are now requiring reservations (www.recreation.gov, fees vary) to drive certain **roads** or park at **trailheads.** The reservations costs are in addition to entry fees. Acadia, Arches, Glacier, Haleakalā, Rocky Mountain, and Yosemite require reservations to access certain roads at certain times. Great Smoky Mountains may require a parking pass for Laurel Falls. While each park's reservations open at different times, most offer two windows: 60-120 days in advance and 1-7 days in advance. Several other parks are considering reservations for over-crowded areas; check the alerts on the individual park websites or the NPS app when you begin planning your trip.

LODGES AND CAMPGROUNDS

Reservations book up fast for national park **lodges and campgrounds.** Plan to book as soon as reservation windows open. Book any lodge dinners, tours, or activity reservations concurrently.

To stay overnight at **lodges** inside the parks, make reservations through

BEST MEALS IN THE PARKS

Here are the top restaurants in the parks. Each offers something special: dining with a view, a historic setting, a unique experience—or all of the above.

ACADIA: Enjoy afternoon tea at the rustic recreated 19th-century **Jordan Pond House.**

CRATER LAKE: Feast on Pacific Northwest cuisine at the 1915 **Crater Lake Lodge.**

GLACIER: Enjoy lake and mountain views from the **Ptarmigan Dining Room** at the Many Glacier Hotel.

GRAND CANYON: Dine at the rustic but elegant **El Tovar** hotel on the lip of the South Rim.

GRAND TETON: See historic art and mountain views while dining in the Mural Room at **Jackson Lake Lodge.**

SHENANDOAH: Dine on the terrace at **Big Meadows Lodge** for sweeping views.

YELLOWSTONE: The 1904 **Old Faithful Inn** epitomizes "parkitecture" even in its high-ceiling dining room.

YOSEMITE: Even the elegant dining room at **The Ahwahnee** can't compete with the stellar valley views.

individual operators for peak seasons (usually summer) **12-13 months in advance.** This is especially true for Great Smoky Mountains, Grand Canyon, Yosemite, Yellowstone, Grand Teton, Glacier, Zion, Olympic, and Acadia.

Many **campgrounds** accept reservations (www.recreation.gov) up to **six months in advance.** Every year, more parks are converting campgrounds from first come, first served to the reservation system. When planning your trip, check on the park website to see whether reservations have been added.

ACTIVITIES

Some parks require advance reservations (www.recreation.gov) to hike certain **trails:** Angels Landing in Zion and Half Dome in Yosemite. Most **boat, bus, and recreation tours** are booked through individual operators with varying windows for reservations. Although you can get last-minute spots for 1-2 people, make reservations for May-September as soon as possible. For commercial **river trips** in the Grand Canyon, book **1-2 years in advance.** For **ranger-led tours,** such as cave tours, book tickets (www.recreation.gov) **six months in advance.**

LOTTERIES

Some activities require **lotteries** instead of reservations. Each lottery operates differently; most occur in winter or spring for the upcoming season. Lottery events include the **synchronous fireflies** in **Great Smoky Mountains and Congaree;** hiking **Half Dome** and backpacking to the **High Sierra Camps** in **Yosemite;** driving a private vehicle on the **park road in Denali; snowmobiling** in **Yellowstone;** and private **rafting trips** in the **Grand Canyon.**

SEASONS

High Season

Summer is often the best time to visit the national parks. As the winter snows disappear and temperatures begin to warm, the crowds thicken and visitor services are in full swing. Park roads start to open, though snow may bury high-elevation roads into **July** and often returns to dust mountain peaks at the end of **September.**

The parks of the Southwest, however, are best in **spring** and **fall;** time your visit then to avoid the triple-digit temperatures of summer.

Low Season

Winter is often the low season, when park lodges, campgrounds, and restaurants **close for the season,** leaving minimal services for visitors. Some national parks enjoy better weather and temperatures in winter thanks to their more moderate climates or tropical locales.

EATING IN THE PARKS

Before visiting a national park, check on food services first, so you can plan accordingly. Many parks have minimal or no food services. At parks with restaurants, expect to wait in line around mealtimes (very few accept reservations).

Packing picnic meals gives you more flexibility. Collapsible soft-sided **coolers** keep lunches and water bottles cold. They pack well whether you're driving to the parks or flying into the nearest airport.

Take **snacks** and **water** while hiking and traveling inside the parks. Food service locations are few.

WHAT'S NEW

DOWNLOAD THE NPS SMARTPHONE APP. It covers each national park with maps, alerts, activities, ranger programs, self-guided tours, and more. You can save some park information offline for areas where cell service is sketchy.

BUY YOUR PASS AT HOME. Multiple parks offer entry passes online (www. recreation.gov), which means you can zip through entrance stations faster.

VISIT THE NEWEST NATIONAL PARK. New River Gorge became the 63rd national park in 2020. It celebrates one of the oldest rivers in the country.

During peak season, Acadia, Arches, Glacier, Rocky Mountain, and Yosemite have added **RESERVATIONS FOR ENTRY** into certain portions of the parks to help alleviate overcrowding.

Many campgrounds are available via the parks' **CAMPING RESERVATION SYSTEM** (www.recreation.gov) during peak season. This makes planning ahead imperative, especially at parks like Yellowstone and Grand Teton, where all campgrounds are now reservable.

Due to an influx of backcountry use, more parks require **PERMITS FOR ACTIVITIES.** Some of the new permits include **HIKING** Angels Landing in Zion and Old Rag in Shenandoah, **TRAILHEAD PARKING** for Laurel Falls in Great Smoky Mountains, **BACKPACKING** in Sequoia and Kings Canyon and Mount Rainier, **SUNRISE** on Haleakalā, and **OVERNIGHT CLIMBING** in Yosemite and Mount Rainier. Many parks are releasing permit reservations online (www. recreation.gov).

Natural disasters have impacted several parks, causing access to some areas to be limited. Effects on trails, roads, and visitor services may linger for several years. In 2021, these included massive **WILDFIRES** in Lassen Volcanic, North Cascades, and Sequoia and Kings Canyon. A **LANDSLIDE** from melting permafrost destroyed Denali's main road; another landslide in North Cascades impacted access to the park's best hiking trail.

For paddlers, Mammoth Cave has a new designated **NATIONAL RECREATION TRAIL** on the Green and Nolin Rivers Blueway.

The busy **WEST ENTRANCE** of Joshua Tree is being **EXPANDED** to reduce waiting lines.

Channel Islands has added a **NEW CAMPGROUND** on Santa Cruz Island.

AVOID THE CROWDS

Our national parks are popular, and rightly so. As visitation increases, however, so do the crowds. Here are some tips to avoid the mayhem.

VISIT IN SHOULDER SEASON

Summer is often peak season, when crowds are at their largest. Time your visit for **spring** or **fall** instead, or consider visiting the park in **winter** when snowy solitude offers a quiet respite. If you must tour in summer, opt for some of the **least-visited parks** for a less harried experience. Visit on **weekdays** to avoid the influx of locals on weekends and holidays.

ARRIVE EARLY MORNING OR LATE AFTERNOON

Rush hour at park entrance stations is 10am-4pm. To claim a coveted parking spot at prime sights and trailheads, arrive **before 9am** (in the busiest and most visited parks or on weekends, arrive before 7am).

Tour the most popular sights and the best-loved trails in early morning or late afternoon, which avoids the crowds common during the busiest part of the day. Aim first for park areas that may require more time or energy to reach.

SPEED THROUGH ENTRANCE STATIONS

To get through entrance stations faster, buy an **annual park pass.** You can also purchase an entrance pass to select parks **online in advance** (www.recreation.gov).

HAVE AN ALTERNATE PLAN

Be flexible with your itinerary and forgo a stop or hike if it is too crowded. Always have a second trailhead or sight in mind to visit instead.

SUSTAINABILITY TIPS

USE A WATER BOTTLE

Bring your own **refillable water bottle** or buy one from a park gift shop. Don't needlessly add disposable plastic to the park refuse collection and recycling infrastructure.

STAY ON PATHS

Staying on designated paths and trails prevents erosion. This is especially crucial in alpine meadows and sensitive wildflower zones. Take photos with your feet on a trail.

CARRY OUT YOUR TRASH

Bring a small bag or container to corral your trash to pack out rather than letting tidbits drop along a trail or road. Think ahead and bring food with little to no packaging.

GET OUT OF THE CAR

When possible, get around by walking, biking, or taking shuttles. Turn off your vehicle's engine rather than idling for short stops.

▼ SCHOODIC PENINSULA, ACADIA

Best of THE NATIONAL PARKS

Best HIKING

ACADIA

A bit of scrambling and aid from iron rungs, steps, and handrails on exposed segments gets you straight up to the apex of the **Beehive Loop Trail** for views of ocean and mountains.

ARCHES

Hike to the free-standing **Delicate Arch,** a natural work of art sculpted by wind and erosion.

GLACIER

This tiptoe along the top-of-the-world **Highline Trail**—full of wildflowers and mountain goats—goes to historic Granite Park Chalet for panoramic views.

KENAI FJORDS

The trail snuggles up to several viewpoints of **Exit Glacier** as it plunges from the Harding Icefield to melt into braided streams.

GRAND CANYON

From the rim to canyon depths, the **Bright Angel Trail** descends through eons of geology to the Colorado River.

GREAT SMOKY MOUNTAINS

Wooden steps, stone staircases, and elevated boardwalks make short work of the climb to **Andrews Bald,** a mountaintop meadow where views encompass the southern Smokies.

MOUNT RAINIER

At Paradise, the **Skyline Trail** climbs through subalpine wildflower meadows and past waterfalls to vistas of Nisqually Glacier tumbling from the ice cap of Rainier.

OLYMPIC

Wildflowers pave the path to the summit of **Hurricane Hill,** perched perfectly for views north of the Strait of Juan de Fuca into Canada and south into the icy Mount Olympus.

SHENANDOAH

The switchback climb up **Old Rag** (permit needed) finishes by following blue

▼ DELICATE ARCH, ARCHES

markers with a hands-and-feet scramble under, over, and between boulders to reach the rocky summit.

YOSEMITE

Expect to be showered by waterfall mist on the **Mist Trail**'s scenery-laden ascent to thundering Vernal and Nevada Falls.

ZION

Get a permit to zigzag your way up a series of short switchbacks to **Angels Landing,** where fixed chains assist you on the skinny shimmy between immense drop-offs to reach the summit.

FIND YOUR PARK

Which park is for you? If you want . . .

ACCESSIBILITY: Take the wheelchair-accessible shuttle and paths along the South Rim of **Grand Canyon.**

BACKPACKING: Hike the Teton Crest Trail in **Grand Teton** and circle the Wonderland Trail in **Mount Rainier.**

BIKING: Pedal the historic canal towpath in **Cuyahoga Valley.**

BOULDERING: Scale the rock piles at Hidden Valley in **Joshua Tree.**

CAVES: Tour the self-guided Natural Entrance to the Big Room in **Carlsbad Caverns.**

DIVING: Explore sunken wrecks off **Dry Tortugas.**

FALL FOLIAGE: Take an autumn drive along Skyline Drive in **Shenandoah.**

GLACIERS CALVING: Cruise on a boat into **Glacier Bay.**

HORSEBACK RIDING: Saddle up at Glacier Creek Stable in **Rocky Mountain.**

HOT SPRINGS: Soak your worries away at Buckstaff Baths in **Hot Springs.**

HOUSEBOATING: Rent a houseboat to tour the lakes at **Voyageurs.**

NORTHERN LIGHTS: Go aurora-watching at **Denali.**

PADDLING: Kayak the miles of inlets and islets around **Isle Royale** in Lake Superior.

RAFTING: Splash through big white water on the New River in **New River Gorge.**

RAIN FORESTS: Sink into the lush greenery at the Hoh Rain Forest in **Olympic.**

REDWOODS: Walk amid old-growth giants in **Redwood National and State Parks.**

SAND: Sled or sandboard down dunes at **Great Sand Dunes** or **White Sands.**

SNORKELING: Swim through the coral reefs of the **Virgin Islands** or **American Samoa.**

SOLITUDE: Fly into **Gates of the Arctic** for the ultimate in wilderness.

SUNRISE: Catch the earliest dawn in the United States at Cadillac Mountain in **Acadia.**

SUNSET: Camp overnight on the **Channel Islands** to watch the sunset across the Pacific.

SWIMMING: Lounge on the sandy beaches of Lake Michigan at **Indiana Dunes.**

WATERFALLS: Get doused by waterfall spray in **Yosemite Valley** in spring.

Best FOR WILDLIFE

BIRDS IN BIG BEND

With year-round **birding,** Big Bend avians burst into song in spring, when tropical birds such as the Colima warbler arrive to nest.

BATS AT CARLSBAD CAVERNS

At dusk, sit in the amphitheater at the Natural Entrance to the caverns to watch thousands of **bats** take flight.

FIREFLIES AT CONGAREE AND GREAT SMOKY MOUNTAINS

In late spring, catch the mating ritual of **synchronous fireflies** in the evening as they light up together.

MARINELIFE IN THE CHANNEL ISLANDS

On these California islands in summer, **sea lions** and **northern fur seals** rear pups while **blue** and **humpback whales** surface offshore.

CARIBOU IN DENALI

From the bus tour on Denali Park Road, see a lone **wolf** cruising or a pack out hunting along river bottoms among herds of **caribou.**

CROCODILES AND ALLIGATORS IN THE EVERGLADES

You can bicycle or take a tram to see **crocodiles** and **alligators** in Shark Valley, plus scads of **egrets, ibis,** and **storks.**

▼ FIREFLIES, GREAT SMOKY MOUNTAINS

DARK SKIES

City lights drown out the stars for more than three-fourths of the U.S. population. Designated International Dark Sky Parks offer places where you can still see the Milky Way. Moonless nights are best, and you'll need red flashlights to help your eyes adjust. Some parks offer telescopes for viewing the starry skies. In August, watch for the annual Perseid meteor shower.

International Dark Sky Parks

All International Dark Sky Parks have dark skies for astrophotography and self-guided night sky viewing in addition to public programs.

ARCHES: Stargazing and ranger telescope programs at Panorama Point

BIG BEND: Stargazing ranger programs

BLACK CANYON OF THE GUNNISON: June astronomy festival; weekly astronomy ranger programs

BRYCE CANYON: June astronomy festival; evening ranger talks and telescope viewing

CANYONLANDS: Night-sky programs with telescope viewing

CAPITOL REEF: September Heritage Starfest and ranger programs

DEATH VALLEY: Night-sky events in winter and spring; February astronomy festival

GLACIER: Logan Pass stargazing programs; after-dark telescope viewing at Apgar and St. Mary Visitor Centers

GRAND CANYON: June Star Party; night sky programs

GREAT BASIN: Star trains; astronomy programs; full moon hikes; September astronomy festival

GREAT SAND DUNES: Night sky programs

JOSHUA TREE: September night sky festival

MAMMOTH CAVE: night sky programs

MESA VERDE: annual star party in October; ranger-led programs that highlight the importance of the night sky to Ancestral Puebloans

PETRIFIED FOREST: wildlife-centric astronomy programs

VOYAGEURS: Junior Ranger Night Explorer activities; stargazing; seeing the northern lights from remote lakeside campsites

ZION: Junior Ranger Night Sky activities

MILKY WAY OVER BRYCE CANYON

OTHER PARKS WITH NIGHT SKY FESTIVALS:
Acadia (Sept.), Lassen (Aug.), Rocky Mountain (every two years), and Badlands (July)

PARKS WITH SPECIAL NIGHT SKY PROGRAMS: Pinnacles (spring night hikes), Carlsbad Caverns (ranger-led star walks and full-moon hikes), Olympic (Hurricane Ridge astronomy programs)

BISON COW AND CALF IN YELLOWSTONE

WHALES IN GLACIER BAY

On a summer boat tour in Glacier Bay, catch a **humpback whales, orcas,** or **bald eagles** drawn to the waters rich for feeding.

MOOSE IN ISLE ROYALE

With willows galore, Isle Royale is home to giant awkward-looking **moose** barely kept in check by **wolf** populations.

BEARS IN KATMAI

From special viewing platforms, watch **brown bears** capture fish in the tumbling waters at Brooks Camp.

CONDORS AT PINNACLES

Use telescopes near the visitors center or hike the High Peaks Trail in early morning or evening to view **condors.**

ELK IN ROCKY MOUNTAIN

In spring, newborn **elk** follow cows, and in fall, the park resounds with bugling as large-antlered bulls round up harems during the rut.

WILD HORSES IN THEODORE ROOSEVELT

Through noisy **prairie dog** towns, **wild horses** run free. Visit in spring to see newborn colts prance.

BISON IN YELLOWSTONE

In spring, **bison** give birth to baby calves, known as "red dogs." See how the West once appeared with vast herds interspersed with **pronghorns.**

▼ WILD HORSES, THEODORE ROOSEVELT

BEST PARKITECTURE

National park lodges often reflect the architecture of their surrounding landscape with stone and log work. Many are National Historic Landmarks not to be missed.

The Ahwahnee, Yosemite: This wood and granite palace features stained-glass windows, two glorious stone fireplaces, Native American designs, and a three-story beamed ceiling in the dining room with floor-to-ceiling views of Yosemite Valley.

Grand Canyon Lodge, Grand Canyon: Perched on the North Rim, the lodge's dining room and sunroom offer dramatic overlooks of the immense canyon.

Many Glacier Hotel, Glacier: Restored to its former glory, Many Glacier boasts mountain views, a large fireplace in a four-story lobby, and a double spiral staircase.

Old Faithful Inn, Yellowstone: The five-story lobby is ringed with knob-by-wood balconies centered on a stone fireplace equal in height.

Paradise Inn, Mount Rainier: The inn features a steep-pitched roof and an immense lobby flanked by stone fireplaces.

Bryce Canyon Lodge, Bryce Canyon: The stone-and-wood edifice sports an expansive porch that invites a long look at the surrounding woods.

Crater Lake Lodge, Crater Lake: The lodge's first story is built of stone, then topped by wood and a shingled roof. The Great Hall and the back porch both overlook deep-blue Crater Lake.

Lake Crescent Lodge, Olympic: A glass-paned sunroom and dining room nearly pull Lake Crescent inside this lodge.

▼ OLD FAITHFUL INN LOBBY, YELLOWSTONE

SANDBOARDING DOWN GREAT SAND DUNES

Best PARKS FOR KIDS

The National Park Service's **Junior Ranger Program** is one of the best activities for kids. The program includes a booklet, which children complete as they learn about each park and engage in fun activities (parents can participate). Kids then turn in their completed booklets at a visitors center to be sworn in as Junior Rangers and receive a national park badge or patch.

In addition to the Junior Ranger Program, specialty **naturalist programs** are great for kids. Look for **Wildlife Olympics** programs, where kids can test their physical skills in comparison to animals. Check out **explorer backpacks** from the park visitors centers; each pack comes equipped with equipment for activities. The park visitors centers are filled with kids rooms, hands-on exhibits, and touchable learning programs.

ARCHES

Take the whole family on a **guided walk** through the rock-scrambling maze of the Fiery Furnace.

GREAT SMOKY MOUNTAINS

Join rangers to **catch salamanders** in Hen Wallow Falls.

ACADIA

Poke around **tide pools** to see the variety of creatures.

GREAT BASIN

Gaze through special **telescopes** that let you look right at the sun.

GREAT SAND DUNES

Sandboard down the majestic dunes in this giant sandbox.

PETRIFIED FOREST

Touch **fossilized plants and animals** in the Junior Ranger Paleontologist program.

BISCAYNE

Don a mask and **snorkel** to be enchanted by this watery park.

Indigenous Peoples
TRADITIONS

Many national parks are rooted in historic Native American lands. Some offer ways to con nect with Indigenous people and their culture. These are some of the best places to enrich your experience.

AMERICAN SAMOA

What better way to immerse yourself in an Indigenous culture than staying with its people! This national park works with local people to provide **homestays** where you participate in daily activities of fishing, gardening, or preparing meals.

TLINGIT HUNA HOUSE, GLACIER BAY

GLACIER

Blackfeet drivers of **Sun Tours** buses share their heritage with visitors along Going-to-the-Sun Road. Campground amphitheaters also host **Native America Speaks,** with local Blackfeet and Kootenai people sharing stories.

GLACIER BAY

The **Tlingit Huna House,** the Xunaa Shuká Hít, is a tribal house with daily interpretive programs that share traditional woodcraft and art, including dance and carving demonstrations.

GRAND CANYON

Inside **Desert View Watchtower,** Hopi artist Fred Kabotie painted murals incorporating Hopi symbols and stories.

▼ INTERIOR OF DESERT VIEW WATCHTOWER, GRAND CANYON

BEST FOR SOLITUDE

For crowd-free experiences and immersion in nature, consider adding these parks to your itinerary.

BLACK CANYON OF THE GUNNISON: Take the long drive to the North Rim for trails to overlooks where you might be the only visitor.

CHANNEL ISLANDS: Plan to camp overnight and you'll have nearly your own private island, especially on Anacapa (which has only seven campsites).

GATES OF THE ARCTIC: Access this remote arctic park by air to float or paddle a Wild and Scenic River or backpack through the trail-less wilderness.

GREAT BASIN: Climb the crowd-free trail to Wheeler Peak to see ancient bristlecone pines.

GUADALUPE MOUNTAINS: Stand alone on the highest summit in Texas as you overlook the Chihuahuan Desert.

HALEAKALĀ: Visitors flock to the summit of this volcano to watch the sun rise. After that, parking spots open up and crowds dissipate. Come instead for sunset, when there are fewer people.

ISLE ROYALE: This park is set in the midst of Lake Superior, where only canoes and sea kayaks can reach its private bays tucked around the island's 337 miles of shoreline.

NORTH CASCADES: Pick up a backcountry permit and stay overnight in a shoreline camp on Ross Lake, or backpack into the mountains to log some solitary miles.

THEODORE ROOSEVELT: Find secluded nooks in the badlands of the North Unit or at Roosevelt's favorite, the Elkhorn Ranch Unit.

VOYAGEURS: Boat in to shoreline campsites spread across this largely water park to watch the Northern Lights.

WRANGELL-ST. ELIAS: The largest national park in the United States is home to millions of acres of solitude, especially along its less traveled Nabesna Road.

Today, the tower hosts cultural demonstrations by Hopi, Havasupai, Hualapai, and Navajo artisans. It is also the first Inter-Tribal Cultural Heritage Site for the National Park Service.

HALEAKALĀ

Native Hawaiians from **Kīpahulu 'Ohana** lead cultural interpretive hikes with stops at a living farm, historic sites, and natural features like the Pools of 'Ohe'o.

HAWAI'I VOLCANOES

Visit the **Volcano Art Center Gallery** on **Aloha Fridays** for demonstrations of traditional Hawaiian arts like ukulele, hula, and lei-making. Other programs include cultural forest walks and "talk stories."

MESA VERDE

This park preserves more than 5,000 archaeological sites that include surface and cliff dwellings from **Ancestral Puebloans,** the forebears of today's Puebloan people.

PETRIFIED FOREST

Local Indigenous artisans demonstrate traditional creative skills inside the **Painted Desert Inn.**

TIOGA ROAD, YOSEMITE

CAPITOL REEF

The **Fremont people** chipped and etched **petroglyphs** into the sandstone canyon wall to tell stories of their lives.

REDWOOD

The Tolowa and Yurok groups perform dance demonstrations periodically, including the annual **renewal dance,** called **Ne'-dosh,** in July.

Best SCENIC DRIVES

TRAIL RIDGE ROAD

The country's highest paved road climbs to a dizzying 12,183 feet (3,713 m) into alpine tundra among granite peaks that define **Rocky Mountain National Park.**

SKYLINE DRIVE

Skyline Drive winds through **Shenandoah**'s lush forests and across long ridgelines, surrounded by spring cherry blossoms or the golds, oranges, and reds of fall.

GOING-TO-THE-SUN ROAD

Amid glaciated peaks and deep valleys, this National Civil Engineering Landmark cuts through **Glacier**'s cliffs to climb to its high point at Logan Pass.

BADLANDS LOOP DRIVE

In a landscape chiseled by water and wind, this scenic drive through the **Badlands** crawls between spires and sharp canyons banded in varied colors.

RIM DRIVE

This undulating loop circles the rim of **Crater Lake** to take in the intense blues of the deepest lake in the United States.

PAINTED DESERT RIM DRIVE

In **Petrified Forest National Park,** this road curves along the rim of pastel-hued badlands in the Painted Desert.

PARK LOOP ROAD

From rocky coast to forested lakes, this loop around **Acadia**'s Mount Desert Island stacks up scenery from sunrise to sunset.

BADWATER BASIN

Take in colorful and stark landscapes on **Death Valley**'s scenic road, which drops below sea level to the lowest elevation in North America.

NEWFOUND GAP ROAD

Bisecting **Great Smoky Mountains,** this ridgetop route provides epic views of the Smokies, roadside stops, spring wildflowers, and autumn colors.

TIOGA ROAD

Lined with subalpine lakes and granite peaks, **Yosemite**'s high-elevation road crests the Sierra through Tuolumne Meadows and Tioga Pass, with one of the best views of Half Dome.

SHARE THE LOVE:
COLORFUL PICS IN THE PARKS

Looking for the most eye-catching photos to share on social media? Visit these colorful spots to show off nature's best side. Bring a telephoto lens for close-up photography, and leave the drones home, as they are prohibited in the parks. Share your pics with other national park fans on Instagram at #nationalparks, #wildernessculture, #nps, and #travelwithmoon.

Cadillac Mountain, Acadia: Get a permit to drive to the summit to capture the orange flames of sunrise with the golden glow glinting off water amid pink granite slabs.

Watchman Overlook, Crater Lake: This overlook is the perfect spot for a top-of-the-world selfie backdropped by the acute blue lake.

Mather Point, Grand Canyon: For the best color of Vishnu Temple and the immensity of the Grand Canyon, capture the early-morning light at this promontory jutting above the abyss.

Zabriskie Point, Death Valley: Look like a total badass with a selfie taken in front of the craggy badlands. Go at sunrise to paint your pic with a depth of color.

Grand Prismatic Overlook, Yellowstone: This is the place to capture the radiant fiery arms rimming the turquoise hot spring from above.

Pa-hay-okee Overlook, Everglades: Catch the cypress trees and reflected colors that bounce off the watery expanse at sunset.

MATHER POINT, GRAND CANYON

SNOWCOACHES, YELLOWSTONE

Best BY
PUBLIC TRANSIT

Ditch the car. Hop a plane, train, bus, or shuttle for your park visit. Here are the parks most accessible by public transit.

INDIANA DUNES

The electric **South Shore Line train** runs daily between Chicago and South Bend, with four stops inside the park. Some trains permit bicycles, and one stop is near the campground.

GATEWAY ARCH

Catch the **MetroLink light-rail** from the St. Louis airport. It stops within a 10-minute walk from the park.

ACADIA

Bus services connect airports in Bar Harbor and Boston with the park and the **Island Explorer shuttle.** Public ferries go to the islands.

CUYAHOGA VALLEY

Greater Cleveland Transit and **Cuyahoga Valley Scenic Railroad** both serve the park from Cleveland.

GLACIER

Amtrak's Empire Builder goes to West or East Glacier where you can connect with **park shuttles** or tours.

YOSEMITE

From San Francisco or Sacramento, **Amtrak's San Joaquins train** connects with Merced, where **bus lines** cover the final stretch into the park. **Free shuttles** circle Yosemite Valley.

EVERGLADES AND BISCAYNE

Catch the local **Homestead Trolley** to these parks.

GRAND CANYON RAILWAY

ISLE ROYALE

Indian Trails bus service runs from Green Bay, Wisconsin, to Houghton, Michigan. **Ferry service** connects Houghton and other mainland towns to the island.

GRAND CANYON

Arizona Shuttles operates buses from Flagstaff, and **Grand Canyon Railway** goes from Williams. Then, use the **free shuttles** on the South Rim.

ROCKY MOUNTAIN

Buses run from Denver and Boulder to Estes Park, where you can transfer to **shuttles** into the park.

DENALI

Alaska Railroad runs a summer train between Anchorage and Fairbanks, stopping at Denali, where you can tour the park road on buses.

Best IN THE OFF-SEASON

Visiting parks in the off-season gives you the chance for extraordinary experiences, plus you'll encounter fewer people.

YELLOWSTONE

Take a **snowcoach** into the **Old Faithful** area to spend the night. You'll be one of few spectators there to see the famous geyser erupt in the morning.

DENALI

While much of the park road closes with snow, you can reach some areas by **cross-country skis.** You may witness the sky dancing with the **northern lights.**

YOSEMITE

Head up to **Glacier Point** on **cross-country skis** for big views, or opt for **downhill skiing** or **snowboarding** at Badger Pass.

OLYMPIC

Hurricane Ridge has it all: downhill skiing, snowboarding, cross-country skiing, snowshoeing, and sledding.

MAMMOTH CAVE, CARLSBAD CAVERNS, AND WIND CAVE

Caves maintain the same temperatures year-round, so they are great places to escape either summer heat or frigid winter temperatures on the surface.

DEATH VALLEY

February is one of the least visited months but yields pleasant temperatures and, in some years, rampant **wildflower blooms.**

GRAND TETON

Teton Park Road is groomed for **Nordic skiing** and **snowshoeing.**

VOYAGEURS

Drive ice roads on frozen lakes, where you can try **ice fishing.** Go **sliding** at **Sphunge Island.**

JOSHUA TREE

Moderate winter temperatures make for pleasant **hiking.** Opt for January or February to avoid the crowds.

HOT SPRINGS

Soaking in a hot bath is the perfect antidote to cold winters.

▼ JOSHUA TREE IN WINTER

The National Parks
AT A GLANCE

NAME	STATE	WHY GO	HIGH SEASON	FEE (PER CAR)	VISITATION RANK	PAGE
Acadia ★	Maine	seacoast	May-Oct.	$30	6	560
Arches	Utah	arches	Mar.-Oct.	$30	16	360
Badlands	South Dakota	prairie badlands	May-Sept.	$30	22	528
Big Bend	Texas	the Rio Grande	Feb.-May, Oct.-Dec.	$30	37	422
Biscayne	Florida	tropical waters	Mar.-June	none	33	694
Black Canyon of the Gunnison	Colorado	deep gorge	May-Sept.	$30	48	456
Bryce Canyon	Utah	hoodoos	Apr.-Oct.	$35	15	334
Canyonlands	Utah	canyon country	Mar.-Oct.	$30	28	370
Capitol Reef	Utah	cliffs, geology	Apr.-Oct.	$20	20	347
Carlsbad Caverns	New Mexico	caves	May-Sept.	$15 per person	44	409
Channel Islands	California	islands	June-Aug.	none	47	204
Congaree	South Carolina	old-growth forest	Mar.-June, Oct.	none	52	675
Crater Lake	Oregon	deepest lake	June-Sept.	$20-30	34	219
Cuyahoga Valley	Ohio	history	May-Nov.	none	13	576
Death Valley	California	sand dunes, desert scapes	Feb-Apr.	$30	23	153
Denali	Alaska	Denali, the mountain	May-Sept.	$15 per person	51	45
Dry Tortugas	Florida	coral and sand islands	Jan.-July	$15 per person	55	700
Everglades	Florida	subtropical wilderness	Nov.-Apr.	$30	27	680
Gates of the Arctic	Alaska	wilderness	June-Aug.	none	63	102
Gateway Arch	Missouri	history	Mar., May-Aug.	$3 per person	24	660

★ indicates one of the most-visited parks in the country.

NAME	STATE	WHY GO	HIGH SEASON	FEE (PER CAR)	VISITATION RANK	PAGE
Glacier ★	Montana	glaciers	June-Sept.	$25-35	10	505
Glacier Bay	Alaska	glaciers	May-Sept.	none	54	93
Grand Canyon ★	Arizona	mile-deep canyon	Apr.-Oct.	$35	4	275
Grand Teton ★	Wyoming	mountains	May-Sept.	$35	7	487
Great Basin	Nevada	caves	June-Sept.	none	53	310
Great Sand Dunes	Colorado	sand dunes	May-Sept.	$25	35	393
Great Smoky Mountains ★	Tennessee/ North Carolina	Smoky Mountains	May-Oct.	none	1	615
Guadalupe Mountains	Texas	fossil reefs	Mar.-May, Oct.	$10 per person	49	415
Haleakalā	Hawaii	volcanic summit	Feb.-Sept., Dec.	$30	29	711
Hawai'i Volcanoes	Hawaii	volcanic activity	Dec.-Aug.	$30	21	721
Hot Springs	Arkansas	hot springs	Mar.-Nov.	none	14	666
Indiana Dunes ★	Indiana	beaches	Mar., June-Sept.	$25	9	585
Isle Royale	Michigan	freshwater island	June-Sept.	$7 per person	57	593
Joshua Tree ★	California	Joshua trees	Oct.-Apr.	$30	11	164
Katmai	Alaska	brown bears	July-Aug.	none	58	76
Kenai Fjords	Alaska	fjords, glaciers	June-Aug.	none	42	62
Kings Canyon	California	scenic byways	May-Sept.	$35	38	140
Kobuk Valley	Alaska	caribou, sand dunes	June-Aug.	none	61	102
Lake Clark	Alaska	wilderness	June-Sept.	none	59	71
Lassen Volcanic	California	volcanic land	July-Sept.	$30	43	178
Mammoth Cave	Kentucky	cave	Apr.-Aug.	none	40	642
Mesa Verde	Colorado	cliff dwellings	May-Sept.	$20-30	39	384
Mount Rainier	Washington	glacial peak	June-Sept.	$30	18	246
National Park of American Samoa	American Samoa	tropical forests, coral reef	Mar.-May, Oct.-Nov.	none	62	740
New River Gorge	West Virginia	river rafting	May-Sept.	none	17	650

NAME	STATE	WHY GO	HIGH SEASON	FEE (PER CAR)	VISITATION RANK	PAGE
North Cascades	Washington	glacial scenery	June-Sept.	none	60	258
Olympic ★	Washington	rain forest	May-Sept.	$30	12	229
Petrified Forest	Arizona	petrified trees	Mar.-Oct.	$25	36	297
Pinnacles	California	volcanic peaks, talus caves	Mar.-May	$30	45	197
Redwood	California	coast redwoods	May-Sept.	varies	41	187
Rocky Mountain ★	Colorado	high peaks, wildlife	May-Sept.	$30-35	5	439
Saguaro	Arizona	saguaros	Feb.-Apr., Nov.-Dec.	$25	25	303
Sequoia	California	giant sequoias	May-Oct.	$35	26	140
Shenandoah	Virginia	Blue Ridge mountains	May-Oct.	$30	19	632
Theodore Roosevelt	North Dakota	wildlife, badlands	May-Sept.	$30	30	545
Virgin Islands	U.S. Virgin Islands	coral reefs	Apr.-June, Aug., Oct.-Dec.	none	46	731
Voyageurs	Minnesota	watery wilderness	May-Sept.	none	50	600
White Sands	New Mexico	gypsum dunes	Mar.-July	$25	31	401
Wind Cave	South Dakota	caves	May-Sept.	none	32	536
Wrangell-St. Elias	Alaska	largest national park	June-Aug.	none	56	83
Yellowstone ★	Wyoming	geysers, volcanic scapes	May-Sept.	$35	3	463
Yosemite ★	California	waterfalls, granite	May-Oct.	$35	8	117
Zion ★	Utah	canyons	May-Sept.	$35	2	317

▼ KENNICOTT GLACIER, WRANGELL-ST. ELIAS

ALASKA

Steep-walled fjords, charismatic bears, soaring eagles, and glaciers that creep down mountainsides into the sea: Alaska's national parks enchant with stunning scenery and wildlife. The eight parks may be a challenge to reach, with some only accessible by boat or air, but the reward of solitude amid stark beauty more than makes up for the effort.

Crowning the state, Denali bests all other mountains as the tallest summit in North America. Blanketed year-round in ice, the immense peak reflects in Wonder Lake. In many of Alaska's parks, visitors can spot wolves, grizzly bears, caribou, moose, and in the coastal parks, whales and sea otters. These animals figure prominently in the culture and survival of Indigenous peoples. Immense mountains, wildlife, and cultural experiences await in this Land of the Midnight Sun.

◀ ROOT GLACIER, WRANGELL-ST. ELIAS NATIONAL PARK

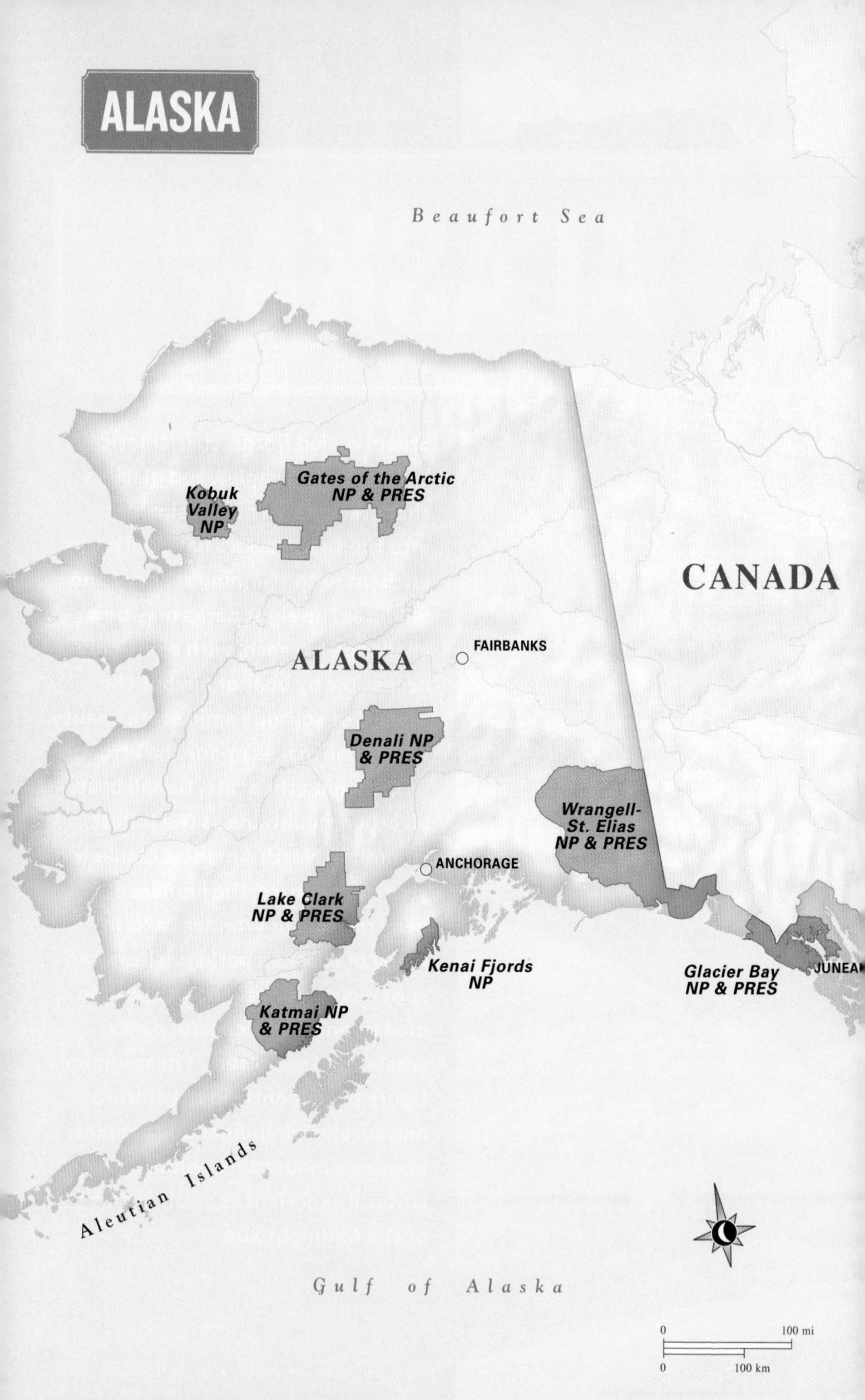

ALASKA

Beaufort Sea

CANADA

Kobuk Valley NP

Gates of the Arctic NP & PRES

ALASKA

FAIRBANKS

Denali NP & PRES

Wrangell-St. Elias NP & PRES

ANCHORAGE

Lake Clark NP & PRES

Kenai Fjords NP

Glacier Bay NP & PRES

JUNEAU

Katmai NP & PRES

Aleutian Islands

Gulf of Alaska

0   100 mi

0   100 km

The National Parks of ALASKA

DENALI

This sweeping wilderness has outstanding wildlife-viewing and the chance to spot the tallest peak in North America (page 45).

KENAI FJORDS

The immense Harding Icefield spills with over 30 glaciers, some that reach the sea in fjords (page 62).

LAKE CLARK

This roadless park defines wilderness, with brown bear-viewing and fly-fishing, plus large lakes that serve as floatplane highways (page 71).

KATMAI

Home to 2,200 brown bears, Katmai is the state's most iconic destination for bear-viewing (page 76).

WRANGELL-ST. ELIAS

It's a magnet for mountaineers, birders, wildlife-watchers, backcountry hikers, and ghost town fans (page 83).

GLACIER BAY

Ice only vacated much of the bays in the past 300 years, and glaciers still carve down rugged mountains through temperate rainforest into fjords (page 93).

GATES OF THE ARCTIC

This vast wilderness spans the Brooks Range with no established roads, trails, or campgrounds (page 102).

KOBUK VALLEY

Charter a small plane to staggering sand dunes and you may see an immense caribou migration (page 102).

1: CARIBOU, DENALI
2: CYLINDRICAL PINNACLES OF ICE, GLACIER BAY
3: GREAT KOBUK SAND DUNES, KOBUK VALLEY

Best OF THE PARKS

Flightseeing: Take a flightseeing trip around the highest peak in North America (page 49).

Exit Glacier and Harding Icefield: Hike to Exit Glacier or up a mountainside overlooking the Harding Icefield (page 66).

Bear-viewing: View bears at Brooks Falls in Katmai (page 80).

Valley of Ten Thousand Smokes: Tour the desolate ash-covered landscape created by the largest volcanic eruption of the 20th century (page 80).

McCarthy and Kennecott: Visit a quirky and isolated town that is joined by a neighboring "ghost mine town" (pages 87 and 89).

PLANNING YOUR TRIP

Because Alaska is so big and the logistics of transport are challenging, plan at least **three weeks** to tour the national parks. Make lodging and campground **reservations** for in-park lodges a year in advance.

High season is **mid-June** through **early September.** You'll have the best weather, the richest landscape, the most touring and wildlife-viewing opportunities, and the most services available—along with the highest prices.

While you can drive to Denali, Kenai Fjords, and Wrangell-St. Elias, touring them may require shuttles, buses, and boat transportation. To visit Katmai, Lake Clark, Kobuk Valley, and Gates of the Arctic, you'll need to fly. To see Glacier Bay, take a ferry or plane to Gustavus and then head into the park via boat.

Anchorage offers the most accessible airport to the Alaskan parks.

▲ BEARS AT BROOKS FALLS, KATMAI

Road Trip

Pound down some wild miles in this epic road trip that links Alaska's three road-accessible national parks. Fly into **Ted Stevens Anchorage International Airport** in Anchorage and **rent a car** capable of driving **gravel roads.**

In Anchorage, gain an understanding of Alaskan culture by visiting the **Anchorage Museum** (625 C St., 907/929-9200, www.anchoragemuseum.org, 9am-6pm daily May-Sept., shorter hours and days winter, $10-20) and the **Alaska Native Heritage Center** (8800 Heritage Center Dr., 907/330-8000, www.alaskanative.net, 9am-5pm Tues.-Sat. mid-May-mid-Sept., $19-29), which concentrates on the Indigenous people of Alaska through art, dance, movies, and game demonstrations.

Kenai Fjords

130 miles (210 km) / 2.5 hours

From Anchorage, drive south on the Seward Highway (AK 1) for 2.5 hours to the east side of the Kenai Peninsula.

NEAR HOLGATE GLACIER, KENAI FJORDS

At 90 miles (145 km), continue straight onto AK 9. In **Seward,** take Exit Glacier Road (aka Herman Leirer Rd.) to enter the park to see **Exit Glacier** and **Exit Glacier Nature Center.** Stay for two nights in Seward and hop a full-day **boat tour** to see a tidewater glacier in **Aialik Bay.** Depart the following

© MOON.COM

morning, unless you want to tack on the climb to the **Harding Icefield.**

Wrangell-St. Elias

380 miles (610 km) / 7 hours
From Kenai Fjords, the route to Wrangell-St. Elias retraces the drive to Anchorage on the Seward Highway (AK 1) before following the Glenn Highway (AK 1) east to the Richardson Highway (AK 4) and the **Copper Center Visitor Center.** Overnight at a motel on the Richardson Highway. The next morning, take the Edgerton Highway east to enter Wrangell-St. Elias on the unpaved **McCarthy Road.** At the bumpy road's terminus, walk into **McCarthy** to explore the funky town. Catch the shuttle and spend two nights at **Kennicott Glacier Lodge.** The next day, explore the **ghost mine** and hike to **Kennicott Glacier.**

Denali

335 miles (540 km) / 9 hours or 2 days
From Wrangell-St. Elias, regain the Richardson Highway (AK 4) north to the **Denali Highway (AK 8),** a mostly gravel 134-mile (216-km) trek through the Alaska Range. At Cantwell, turn north on Parks Highway (AK 3) to the park entrance at **Denali Visitor Center.** Plan to overnight at one of the entrance hotels, then catch your transport the next morning to relax at **Camp Denali** for several nights. En route, look for **wildlife** and explore **Eielson Visitor Center.** At the lodge, paddle **Wonder Lake,** hike, and gaze at the great mountain **Denali.** To return to Anchorage, drive south on Parks Highway for 240 miles (385 km, 4-5 hrs).

1: ROOT GLACIER (FOREGROUND) AND STAIRWAY ICEFALL, WRANGELL-ST. ELIAS
2: LYNX, DENALI
3: DENALI NATIONAL PARK NEAR EIELSON

DENALI NATIONAL PARK AND PRESERVE

Alaska

KEEPSAKE STAMPS ▼▼▼

WEBSITE:
www.nps.gov/dena

PHONE NUMBER:
907/683-9532

VISITATION RANK:
51

WHY GO:
See Denali, the highest peak in North America.

▲ ROAD TO POLYCHROME PASS

DENALI NATIONAL PARK AND PRESERVE

River

Lake Minchumina

Chilchukabena Lake

Kantishna

Creek

Moose

Minchumina ✈

DENALI NATIONAL PARK

SNOHOMISH HILLS

North Fork Kuskokwim River

Birch Creek

McKinley River

Slippery Cr.

Old Cache Lake

Spectacle Lake

Big Lake

DENALI NATIONAL PRESERVE

Wickersham Dome ▲

Kantishna ✈

RANGER STATION

Wonder Lake

WONDER LAKE

MCKINLEY BAR TRAIL

Highpower Creek

Castle Rocks 1,900ft ▲

Herron River

Wilderness Boundary

Birch

Muddy River

DENALI WILDERNESS within DENALI NATIONAL PARK

Swift

Fork

Creek

Slow Fork Hills

Foraker River

Straightaway

Foraker

Mount Koven ▲

North Peak 19,470ft ▲

DENALI

A L A S K A

Kahiltna Dome ▲

South Peak 20,310ft ▲

Tonzona River

Swift

Fork

Herron Glacier

Mount Crosson ▲

Mount Hunter ▲

Mount Foraker 17,400ft ▲

Mount Stevens ▲

Heart Mountain 6,500ft ▲

Chedotlothna Glacier

Mount Russell 11,670ft ▲

Avalanche Spire 10,105ft ▲

Glacier

Mount Goldie 6,315ft ▲

Surprise

Yentna Glacier

Lacuna Glacier

Kahiltna Glacier

Dall Glacier

Mount Dall 8,756ft ▲

DUTCH HILLS

PETER

DENALI NATIONAL PRESERVE

Chelatna Lake

KICHATNA MOUNTAINS

Cathedral Spires

West Fork Yentna River

East Fork Yentna River

Mount Kliskon 3,943ft ▲

Kahiltna

River

Fairview Mountain 3,266ft ▲

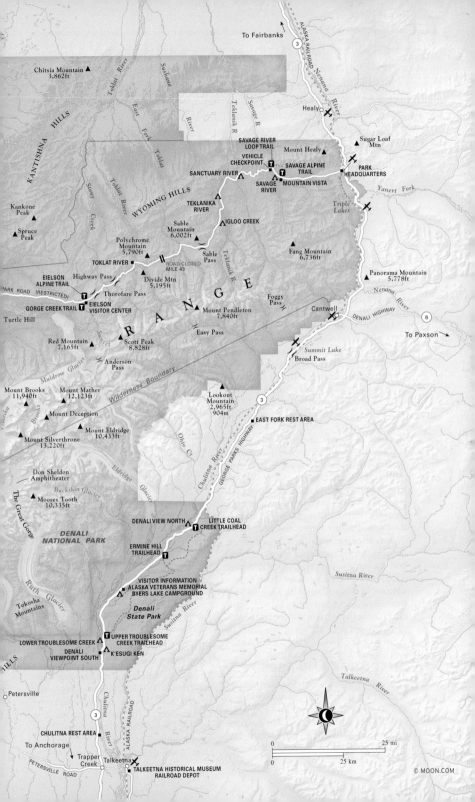

To Fairbanks

3

ALASKA RAILROAD · Nenana River

Chitsia Mountain ▲
3,862ft

Toklat River

East Fork · Toklat · River

Savage R

Teklanik R

Healy

Sugar Loaf
Mtn ▲

SAVAGE RIVER
LOOP TRAIL

VEHICLE
CHECKPOINT

SAVAGE ALPINE
TRAIL

SANCTUARY RIVER

Mount Healy ▲

MOUNTAIN VISTA

PARK
HEADQUARTERS

SAVAGE
RIVER

Yanert Fork

Triple
Lakes

Kankone
Peak ▲

Spruce
Peak ▲

WYOMING HILLS

Stony · Creek

Toklat River

TEKLANIKA
RIVER

Sable
Mountain
6,002ft ▲

IGLOO CREEK

Polychrome
Mountain
5,790ft ▲

Sable
Pass

Teklanik R

Fang Mountain
6,736ft ▲

Panorama Mountain
5,778ft ▲

TOKLAT RIVER

ROAD CLOSED
MILE 43

Divide Mtn
5,195ft

EIELSON
ALPINE TRAIL

Highway Pass

PARK ROAD (RESTRICTED)

Thorofare Pass

GORGE CREEK TRAIL

EIELSON
VISITOR CENTER

R · A · N · G · E

Mount Pendleton
7,840ft ▲

Foggy
Pass

Cantwell

Nenana River

DENALI HIGHWAY

8

To Paxson

Turtle Hill

Easy Pass

Red Mountain
7,165ft ▲

Scott Peak
8,828ft ▲

Anderson
Pass

Sunset · Glacier

Muldrow Glacier

Summit
Lake

Broad Pass

Mount Brooks
11,940ft ▲

Mount Mather
12,123ft ▲

Wilderness Boundary

Mount Deception ▲

Brooks · Glacier

Mount Eldridge
10,433ft ▲

Mount Silverthrone
13,220ft ▲

Ohio Cr.

Lookout
Mountain
2,965ft
904m

GEORGE PARKS HIGHWAY

3

EAST FORK REST AREA

Chulitna River

Don Sheldon
Amphitheater

Buckskin Glacier

Eldridge · Glacier

Mooses Tooth
10,335ft ▲

The Great Gorge

DENALI
NATIONAL PARK

DENALI VIEW NORTH

LITTLE COAL
CREEK TRAILHEAD

ERMINE HILL
TRAILHEAD

Susitna River

Ruth Glacier

Tokosha
Mountains

VISITOR INFORMATION
ALASKA VETERANS MEMORIAL
BYERS LAKE CAMPGROUND

Denali
State Park

Susitna River

HILLS

UPPER TROUBLESOME
CREEK TRAILHEAD

LOWER TROUBLESOME CREEK

DENALI
VIEWPOINT SOUTH

K'ESUGI KEN

Chulitna River

ALASKA RAILROAD

Talkeetna River

Petersville ○

3

CHULITNA REST AREA

To Anchorage

PETERSVILLE ROAD

Trapper
Creek

Talkeetna ○

TALKEETNA HISTORICAL MUSEUM
RAILROAD DEPOT

0   25 mi

0   25 km

© MOON.COM

Colossal **DENALI NATIONAL PARK AND PRESERVE** contains pristine lakes, braided rivers, and tundra set against the backdrop of the Alaska Range and 20,310-foot (6,191-m) Denali, the highest mountain in North America, whose name means "Tall One" in the Indigenous Koyukon language. This vast swath of wilderness is renowned for stellar opportunities to see bears, moose, caribou, and wolves in an intact, protected ecosystem. A single rough road runs just 92 miles (142 km) into a park that measures almost 9,500 square miles (24,605 sq km). Private vehicles are allowed on only the first few miles while buses tour the rest. Those looking to soak up an experience of a lifetime can overnight in the park's remote interior.

PLANNING YOUR TIME

The rugged, 92-mile (142-km) **Denali Park Road** is the sole entrance to the park. You can only drive the first 15 miles (24 km) of it. Beyond that, restricted access makes planning ahead imperative. Shuttles or tour buses require advance reservations. In 2021, melting permafrost caused a huge landslide that created a long-term road closure beyond mile 43. Repairs are scheduled for 2022-2023. Check ahead on the status of the road reopening.

Peak season (late May-mid-Sept.) is when services throughout the road system are fully operational. Once mid-September rolls around, many visitor-oriented activities and services—chief among them the "town" just outside the entrance to Denali National Park—shut down almost completely.

Advance reservations are required for shuttle, tour, camper buses, lodges, and campgrounds. For specific travel dates in peak season, make these reservations in December or January. If you have time and flexibility, you can book later. Do not wait to make shuttle reservations until your arrival at the park, as you'll be put on a two-day waiting list.

ENTRANCE AND FEES

There is only one entrance to Denali, located at mile 237 between Healy and Cantwell on George Parks Highway (AK 3). The entrance fee is $15 per person and good for seven days. You'll pay the fee when reserving bus tickets and campsites; if you're not riding the bus or camping, pay in person at the Denali Visitor Center.

VISITORS CENTERS
Denali Visitor Center

The **Denali Visitor Center** (mile 1.5, Park Rd., 8am-6pm daily mid-May-mid-Sept.) is the main welcome center, with ranger-led activities, an Alaska Geographic bookstore and gift shop, a luggage check, the only restaurant in the park, and exhibits showcasing Denali's landscapes, wildlife, and natural history. The Alaska Railroad train depot is just a short walk away.

Prior to reaching the visitors center, the **Backcountry Information Center** (mile 0.5, 8am-6pm daily mid-May-mid-Sept.) has permits. The **Denali Bus Depot** (mile 0.5, 5am-7pm daily mid-May-mid-Sept. for bus departures, 7am-7pm daily for tickets) sells bus tickets. It's the site of bus and shuttle departures, as well as check-in for the campgrounds. If you need tickets or to check into a campground after hours, you can do so at the **Riley Creek Mercantile** (mile 0.25) until 10pm.

Murie Science and Learning Center

The **Murie Science and Learning Center** (mile 1.4, 9:30am-5pm daily year-round) acts as the primary welcome center, except for summer, when it is only open for family programs (1pm-3pm daily). The science center also runs small-group interactive learning

Top ③

① TOUR THE PARK BY BUS

BUS TOURS IN DENALI

Private vehicles can only drive to mile 15 of the Park Road. Beyond that, you must take a bus. Both tour and shuttle buses travel the Park Road mid-May to mid-September; buses to the road's terminus at **Kantishna** usually start in June. Buy **tickets** (866/761-6629, www.reservedenali.com) online as early as December 1 of the preceding year. Prices, destinations, and schedules change through the season. Tickets are also sold in person at the **Denali Bus Depot.** Take a day pack with layers and rain gear for changeable weather.

Narrated tour buses (5-12 hrs, $100-240) are guided by naturalist drivers. They stop for photos but don't let people on or off the bus. Four tours go to different destinations; water and lunch or snacks are included.

Shuttle buses ($30-65) aren't narrated, but they stop for wildlife-viewing and to let people hop off along the road to explore or hike. The green shuttles run about every 30 minutes; double-check to make sure you don't miss the last bus back! Bring food, snacks, and water.

In 2021, a major landslide at Pretty Rocks (mile 43) closed the road beyond to destinations such as Eielson and Wonder Lake. Stabilizing the road and installing a bridge over the landslide are scheduled for 2022-2023; check online for details on reopening. Until reopening, tours will only go as far as mile 43.

② WATCH WILDLIFE

The park offers great opportunities to see wildlife. Many visitors treat the bus ride into the park as a photo safari and come back with scads of wildlife shots.

Spot **moose** on the first 15 miles (24 km) of the roadway, especially near streams; see **caribou** near mileposts 13-15; watch for **Dall sheep** on rocky areas above the tree line; and look for **grizzly bears** everywhere, but especially above the tree line. **Wolf** sightings are unpredictable, but this remains one of the best places in Alaska to spot them.

③ FLY OVER DENALI

To see much of the park—and Denali, the mountain—up close, take a **flightseeing** trip. You'll feel awe when "the High One" is front and center in the windshield. Many flightseeing operations also include a landing on a nearby glacier, so you can walk on ice that only the world's most intrepid explorers have ever reached. It's a worthy splurge.

FLIGHTSEEING IN DENALI

ONE DAY IN DENALI

If you only have one day in Denali, hop aboard the **shuttle bus** along Denali Park Road. The early morning bus takes four hours to travel to **Eielson Visitor Center,** stopping en route for wildlife-watching. Upon reaching the visitors center, tour the exhibits and then join a ranger on the **Eielson Stroll,** or opt for a more strenuous adventure on the **Eielson Alpine Trail.** If Denali is visible, you'll burn through plenty of photos before your evening return. For the trip, pack a few warm layers of clothing, lunch, snacks, water—and a camera.

opportunities. Many of those programs are intended for local students, but if you plan ahead, you might be able to send young visitors on an experiential field expedition through the **Alaska Geographic Field Institute** (www.ak-geo.org).

Eielson Visitor Center

With million-dollar views of Denali (when it is visible), the **Eielson Visitor Center** (mile 66, 10am-5:30pm daily June-mid-Sept.) offers services deep within the park, including daily ranger-led walks, interpretive exhibits, and a small art gallery. Many visitors make this their destination on the Park Road and hike one of the three nearby trails. Eielson Visitor Center has water but no food services.

SIGHTS

DENALI, THE MOUNTAIN

At a whopping 20,310 feet (6,191 m) in elevation, **Denali** is the tallest peak in North America. On clear days, it is visible from Anchorage, Fairbanks, and Talkeetna, although you can't see it from the park entrance because of the rolling hills in the way. Once you're past mile 9 of the Park Road, however, you have a chance of viewing the mountain—if it's "out." If you take a bus all the way to mile 66 of the Park Road and the Eielson Visitor Center, where there won't be any folds of land between you and *the* mountain, you might even get stunning vistas of Denali (weather permitting).

The skies around Denali are often clear during the winter, but the

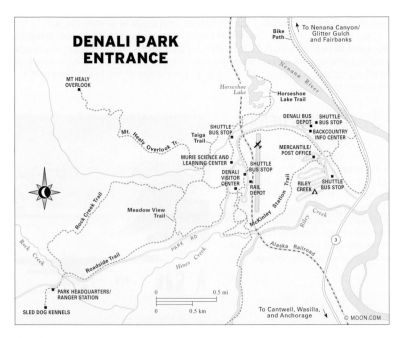

SLED DOG DEMONSTRATION

mountain generates its own clouds during the summer, so on average, it may only be fully visible one day out of three. Don't give up, though—it's worth taking a chance to see it, and you have a better than 50-50 chance of getting at least a partial view of the mountain peeking out of the clouds. Alaska's climate is changing, but you have a slightly better chance of seeing the mountain in the early summer than later in the year.

Here's one thing that you shouldn't do: Don't march up to the Denali National Park rangers and announce that you'd like to hike the mountain itself. Plainly put, most people can't; any trip up Denali is a high-level mountaineering expedition that requires technical skill, equipment, and physical fitness. If you don't have the requisite skills, you can enlist the aid of a professional guiding service like the locally run **Alaska Mountaineering School** (13765 E. 3rd St., Talkeetna, 907/733-1016, www.climbalaska.org)—but you need to be willing to work hard, put in a lot of preparation beforehand, and learn a new skill set that might just save your life or those of your fellow climbers.

WONDER LAKE

Wonder Lake is one of the most photogenic places for reflection pictures of Denali and the Alaska Range. The road that circles part of the 2.7-mile-long (4.3-km) lake allows you the closest view of the mountain. Even if clouds preclude seeing the reflection, the lake provides good wildlife-watching for moose and waterfowl. Even grizzlies swim across the lake. Swarms of mosquitoes cling to boggy ground in the area, so bring bug spray or head nets. To get to Wonder Lake requires an **11-hour round-trip shuttle ride.** The best views, made famous by photographs from the likes of Ansel Adams, are from the north end.

SLED DOG DEMONSTRATIONS

Denali is the only national park with a working kennel of sled dogs. You can **tour the park kennels** (30 min, June-Aug., limited schedule May and Sept., free), visit the working huskies, and see them demonstrate their work. Several tours are scheduled daily. There is no parking at the kennels; you must either walk 1.5 miles (2.4 km) mostly uphill or take the **Sled Dog Demonstration Shuttle** from the Denali Visitor Center bus stop (departs at least 40 min before each demonstration). You can also stop by the kennels (generally 9am-4:30pm daily year-round) to see the dogs, but in winter the dog teams may be out working. Do not bring your pets to the kennel.

SCENIC DRIVE
DENALI PARK ROAD

When snowplowing is complete (late Mar. or early Apr.), the 92-mile (148-km) **Denali Park Road** opens. In summer, rich patchworks of green forests and tundra flank broad braided rivers in gravel bars, while late August brings on yellows and reds. The road closes when winter returns (Sept.-Oct.).

Touring the first 15 miles (24 km) of paved road to Savage River Rest Area will take about an hour without stops. This is as far as cars can go, with the exception of those with reservations at Teklanika Campground. Even though the mountain Denali is 70-plus miles (113-km) away, you can still nab views through breaks in the taiga. When weather permits, you can spot it at **mile 9,** where the taiga breaks into tundra, again about 1.5 miles (2.4 km) farther, and around **Savage River.** Keep your eyes peeled for caribou and Dall sheep near the last 2 miles (3.2 km).

For those with **camping reservations at Teklanika Campground,** pass through the checkpoint at Savage River and continue another 14 miles (23 km) beyond the pavement on the bumpy gravel road. Stop in early summer to look at wildflowers at **Primrose**

Ridge (mile 16) and scan for sheep. The road parallels the Teklanika River for several miles before reaching Teklanika (mile 29).

For those lucky ones who won the **road lottery,** permits allow driving as far as conditions allow. The narrow and shoulderless gravel road includes washboards and potholes. After crossing Sable Pass, you'll reach mile 43, where the **road is closed** through 2023 to repair the damage from the Pretty Rocks Landslide. Check online for updates on reopening.

After the slide area, brilliant green and orange colors flank hillsides from **Polychrome Overlook** (mile 46). The braided **Toklat River** (mile 53) spreads wide across the valley floor, often home to herds of caribou, before the road climbs over Highway Pass to **Stony Dome** (mile 56) for a closer view of Denali. After popping over Thorofare Pass, the views of Denali only get bigger at **Eielson Visitor Center** (mile 66) and **Wonder Lake** (mile 85).

HIKING

Most of the maintained trails in Denali National Park are short, and the trails nearest the visitors centers are

▼ TOKLAT RIVER

WINNING THE ROAD LOTTERY

The 92-mile (148-km) road running into Denali National Park is only open to private vehicles until mile 15—unless you're lucky enough to win the annual road lottery. Anybody (including visitors from out of state or out of the country) can apply for the lottery. Winners can drive their own cars as far into the park as conditions permit on one day in September.

The **lottery entry period** runs May 1-May 31 every year (www.recreation. gov, $15 application fee) and the winning tickets are drawn in mid-June; if you win, the road permit costs $25. The driving period runs for four days, usually in September, and you're automatically assigned a day that your permit is valid. It's up to you to cover travel costs and logistics and to provide the car. The distance you can drive in 2023 will depend on completion of repairs at the Pretty Rocks Landslide closure; check online for the status.

Many rental car companies won't allow you to take their vehicles on gravel highways (including the Park Road), but **Alaska Auto Rental** (907/457-7368, www.alaskaautorental.com), based in Fairbanks with a second office in nearby Healy, will. They also rent to drivers under 25 years of age.

crowded. Rangers often lead hikes on the maintained paths and "Discovery Hikes" that go off-trail.

From Denali Visitor Center, **Horseshoe Lake Trail** (3 mi/4.8 km rt, 1.5 hrs, moderate) loops around a pretty lake of the same name and goes to an overlook before dropping steeply to circle the lake. An additional 0.5-mile (0.8-km) loop at the north end leads to the Nenana River.

You can drive the paved section of **Denali Park Road** or hop the free shuttle to Savage River for hiking. A family-friendly trail, the **Savage River Loop** (1.7 mi/2.7 km rt, 1 hr, easy) starts from the Savage River Day Use Area. Through the glacier-carved river valley, the tundra trail goes downstream, crosses the river on a bridge, and returns. By using the shuttle, you can hike point-to-point on the **Savage Alpine Trail** (4 mi/6.4 km one-way, 2 hrs, strenuous), which goes up and over tundra slopes to the Savage River Campground.

HIKING IN DENALI

Best Hike

EIELSON ALPINE TRAIL

DISTANCE: 1.6 miles (2.6 km) round-trip
DURATION: 1.5 hours
ELEVATION CHANGE: 1,010 feet (308 m)
EFFORT: strenuous
TRAILHEAD: Eielson Visitor Center; access via park shuttle to Mile 66

The views just get bigger and bigger on this trail that climbs Thorofare Ridge north from Eielson Visitor Center. Three long switchbacks ascend steeply to gain elevation. But soon, the trail departs the tundra to enter talus slopes and a seemingly barren alpine world, where tiny wildflowers such as pink moss campion thrive tucked in the rocks. When Denali is visible, hikers often forget to look elsewhere, but the ridge overlooks the giant McKinley River that widens along the valley floor. The high alpine tundra harbors Dall sheep and grizzly bears along with marmots. While you can zip up and down, exploring the wide-open summit with 360-degree views is worth the additional time.

RANGER WALK ON EIELSON ALPINE TRAIL WITH VIEW OF DENALI

Beyond the pavement on the Park Road, shuttle buses access other trailheads and let hikers hop off anywhere and flag another bus to hop on later. You can hike cross-country, but steer around delicate plants and wetlands. Also, spread out to avoid trampling the same route. At mile 85, near Wonder Lake Campground, the level **McKinley River Bar Trail** (4.8 mi/7.7 km rt, 2.5 hrs, moderate) goes through boggy meadows and spruce trees to terminate at the broad gravel expanse of the river bar.

RECREATION
BACKPACKING

Venturing off established trails and into the backcountry is one of the most glorious ways to see Denali. Due to the remote location and challenging terrain, which often involves crossings of swift glacier-fed creeks, backpacking is a serious backcountry expedition. The reward is sleeping in a tent somewhere off in the tundra, with the midnight sun or a spangle of stars and aurora borealis glimmering overhead.

BACKPACKING IN DENALI

Permits (first come, first served, free) are issued in person only at the **Backcountry Information Center** (mile 0.5, 8am-6pm daily mid-May-mid-Sept.) 24 hours before your departure date. A bear-resistant food container is required. Permits are assigned for specific unit areas rather than designated campsites. After you get your permit, buy maps and camper bus tickets.

CLIMBING

Extremes of altitude, weather, and remoteness make climbing the highest summit in North America a dangerous endeavor. **Denali** (20,310 ft/6,191 m) requires far more mountaineering skills, equipment, and experience than it takes to climb peaks in the Lower 48. Even to go with a guide service, you need to be in top physical condition and prepped for endurance amid rough conditions. Contact climbing rangers year-round at **Talkeetna Ranger Station** (907/733-2231) regarding required permits, information, and guide services.

FLIGHTSEEING

Only a few carriers are authorized to make glacier landings in Denali National Park. They are:

Fly Denali (907/683-2359, www. flydenali.com) is the only provider that can depart straight from the park entrance (they base their aircraft in Anchorage, Talkeetna, and Healy).

Talkeetna Air Taxi (departing from Talkeetna; 800/533-2219, www.talkeetnaair.com)

SAVAGE CANYON

TOKLAT RIVER

Sheldon Air Service (departing from Talkeetna; 907/733-2321, www.sheldonairservice.com)

K2 Aviation (departing from Talkeetna; 800/764-2291, www.flyk2.com)

Kantishna Air Taxi (departing from Kantishna; 907/644-8222, www.katair.com) provides air taxi services between Kantishna and the park entrance.

Temsco Air (907/683-0683, http://temscoair.com) also offers glacier landing tours to a glacier near the park and helicopter-supported hiking within the park. Small planes are an amazing adventure, but helicopters are even better: They can go closer, lower, and slower to terrain than a plane, and they can easily land in places that a plane pilot would never consider.

BIKING

Despite most vehicles being allowed to drive only to mile 15, bicyclists can ride all 92 miles (142 km) of the park road. You can rent a bike from most lodges near or inside the park. Bring proof that you paid your entrance fee or you may not get past Savage River checkpoint at mile 15. Be aware of the road closure lasting through 2023 after mile 43.

For day trips, some **shuttle buses** (by reservation) are equipped with racks for two bikes. Hop the bus in as far as you want, continue riding west for the best view of Denali, and then flag down a shuttle for the return.

To overnight, you can stay in **campgrounds,** which have bike racks and food storage containers. Or get a wilderness permit to camp off the road and carry a bear-resistant food container. You must also conceal your bike off the road; if you lose your bike in the bushes, rangers won't help you hunt for it.

RAFTING

At Denali, rafting is on the Nenana River, which borders the park. **Denali Raft Adventures** (888/683-2234 or 907/683-2234, www.denaliraft.com) offers trips all the way from calm Class I water to boiling Class IV rapids. You choose between oar rafts (only the guide paddles) and paddle rafts (everybody paddles following commands from the guide).

WHERE TO STAY

INSIDE THE PARK

There are only a few remote lodges at Kantishna at the western end of the Park Road. They offer all-inclusive rates (lodging, meals, activities), with no TVs, no phones, and limited satellite Wi-Fi (if any). People come here to unplug or to splurge on a base-camp experience that lets them hike, bike, or paddle deep in the park. To get here requires taking a bus or flying to the Kantishna airstrip. Due to the closure of the Park Road at mile 43 through 2023, access to lodges is only via air, but the benefit will be having the park almost to yourself.

Denali Backcountry Lodge (Mile 92 Park Rd., 800/808-8068, www.alaskacollection.com, early June-mid-Sept., from $575/night with bus transportation, from $1,750/3 nights with flights) has rooms with private baths in log cabins. A twice-daily shuttle runs to nearby Wonder Lake, and extra activities like gold panning, mountain biking, morning yoga classes, and lake fishing. Ask for a cabin room near the creek.

At **Camp Denali** (907/683-2290, www.campdenali.com, early June-mid-Sept., from $1,100 pp/night with bus transportation, flight transportation $500) you stay in one of 19 rustic cabins lit by propane lamps and heated by woodstoves, with outhouses. A modern shared bath and shower facility is available, but you'll have to walk five minutes to get there. The camp sits at the tree line and has amazing views,

including Denali when it's "out." It's a little more than 2 miles (3.2 km) from Wonder Lake. There's a fixed schedule for arrivals, with only three-, four-, or seven-night stays allowed.

Two other all-inclusive lodges are in Kantishna: **Kantishna Roadhouse Backcountry Resort** (907/374-3041 or 800/942-7420, www.kantishnaroadhouse.com) and **Skyline Lodge** (907/644-8222, www.katair.com).

There's just one real restaurant in Denali National Park. Near the visitors center, the **Morino Grill** (mile 1.5, Park Rd., 8am-6pm daily mid-May-mid-Sept., limited hours in shoulder season) offers boxed to-go lunches and coffee all day long, plus made-to-order lunch and dinner.

You can purchase a limited selection of snacks at the **Denali Bus Depot** (mile 1, Park Rd.), which also has a small coffee stand. The **Riley Creek Mercantile** (mile 0.25, Park Rd., 907/683-9246) sells sandwiches, snacks, and limited groceries, along with camp fuel.

Camping

There are six established campgrounds ($20-40) within Denali National Park. Make **reservations** (866/761-6629, www.reservedenali.com) usually starting December 1 for the next summer.

GRIZZLY BEARS

NAME	LOCATION	PRICE	SEASON	AMENITIES
Denali Backcountry Lodge	Kantishna	from $575	June-Sept.	lodge rooms, dining, shuttle
Camp Denali	end of Denali Park Rd.	from $2,025	June-Sept.	cabins, pit toilets, shared bath
Riley Creek	Mile 0.25	$17-49	May-Sept.	tent and RV sites
Savage River	Mile 13	$34-49	May-Sept.	tent, RV, and group sites
Sanctuary River	Mile 23	$17	May-Sept.	tent sites; camper bus
Teklanika River	Mile 29	$29	May-Sept.	tent and RV sites
Igloo Creek	Mile 35	$17	May-Sept.	tent sites; camper bus
Wonder Lake	Mile 85	$16	June-Sept.	tent sites; camper bus

Campgrounds include flush or vault toilets, picnic tables, but no hookups. Check-in for all campgrounds is at the Denali Bus Depot.

Three **vehicle-accessed campgrounds** accept reservations. These also have fire pits and potable water. Located right inside the park entrance, **Riley Creek** (mile 0.2, year-round, 142 sites, reservations accepted for early May-mid-Sept.) has an RV dump station in summer plus cell reception and seasonal internet availability. First-come, first-served winter camping (mid-Sept.-early May, free) has limited services. **Savage River** (mile 14, mid-May-early Sept., 32 sites) is reached by car or via the Savage River Shuttle. **Teklanika River** (mile 29, late May-mid-Sept., 53 sites) is one of the most coveted campgrounds, where you can drive yourself beyond mile 15 with a three-night minimum stay. Then use the shuttle to hike or sightsee farther up the Park Road. The campground can close temporarily for bear activity.

Three **tent-only campgrounds** (late May-mid-Sept.) can only be reached via the **camper shuttle bus** (reserve seats by calling 800/622-7275). **Wonder Lake** (mile 85, 28 sites) is the most popular due to stunning views of Denali reflected in the lake, but it has a healthy mosquito population. Due to the landslide in 2021, the campground won't be accessible until the road is reopened.

Check on status for 2023. **Sanctuary River** (mile 22, 7 sites, no water) and **Igloo Creek** (mile 35, 7 sites, no water) are both first come, first served with camper bus seats assigned upon check-in at Denali Bus Depot.

Basic camping items are available at **Riley Creek Mercantile** (mile 0.25, Park Rd., 907/683-9246). To rent or buy backpacking equipment, contact **Denali Mountain Works** (mile 239, Parks Hwy., 907/683-1542, http://denalimountainworks.com), 1.5 miles (2.4 km) north of the park entrance along the Parks Highway.

OUTSIDE THE PARK

Outside the park, on George Parks Highway (AK 3), a small community of seasonal visitor services and lodges clusters around the **entrance to Denali National Park.** Twelve miles (19 km) north, **Healy** is the closest year-round town to the park entrance.

GETTING THERE

AIR

Alaska Airlines (800/252-7522, www.alaskaair.com) offers daily flights to Anchorage and Fairbanks. In Anchorage, **Ted Stevens Anchorage International Airport** (ANC, 5000 W. International Airport Rd., www.dot.state.ak.us/anc) has year-round service from Alaska Airlines, Delta, United, Iceland

Air, and other airlines, with seasonal service from Condor.

RAIL

Unless you're planning to drive the Park Road or stay outside the park, taking the **Alaska Railroad** (800/544-0552, www.alaskarailroad.com) to Denali is one of the best rides in the state. The trip takes about 4 hours from Fairbanks or 7.5 hours from Anchorage.

CAR

Talkeetna, Anchorage, and Fairbanks are connected by the Parks Highway (AK 3), which merges into the Glenn Highway as it nears Anchorage. If you're coming to Denali by car, the trip is 240 miles (385 km) from Anchorage, 4-5 hours depending on Parks Highway traffic. The drive from Fairbanks is 124 miles (200 km) or just over two hours if you don't run into construction or slow RVs.

Year-round gas stations are available in Cantwell (30 mi/48 km south of the park entrance) and Healy (12 mi/19 km north of the entrance). During the summer, you can also get gas at a seasonal station 1 mile (1.6 km) north of the park entrance.

▼ TOUR DENALI BY BUS.

BUS

You can get to Denali on the **Park Connection** (800/266-8625 or 907/277-4321 www.alaskacoach.com), with service all the way from Seward and Anchorage to Denali.

GETTING AROUND

DRIVING

You can only drive to mile 15 of the Park Road. Fortunately, tours and shuttles can get you around and into the interior. Most lodging comes with a free shuttle that will pick you up from the train depot, airport, or bus stop, and if you're taking a tour, most tour operators will happily pick you up from your hotel or from one of the shuttle bus stops near the park entrance.

TOURS AND SHUTTLE BUSES

The **Denali Bus Depot** (mile 0.5, Park Rd., mid-May-mid-Sept., 5am-7pm for bus departures, 7am-7pm for tickets) is the launch point for all tours and shuttles. You can also buy **tickets** here if you haven't made advance **reservations** (866/761-6629, www.reservedenali. com, available online Dec. 1). The large parking lot at the bus depot can accommodate RVs and trailers.

SAVAGE RIVER AREA

Naturalist drivers guide four **narrated bus tours** (daily mid-May-mid-Sept., 5-12 hrs, $100-237) that stop only for photo ops. Schedules, rates, and destinations vary. Water and lunch or snacks are included.

Two types of non-narrated **shuttle buses** (daily mid-May-mid-Sept.) go into the Denali interior on the park road. Make reservations for the **green transit buses** (mid-May-mid-Sept., $30-65 rt) that run every 30 minutes along the park road to Eielson, Wonder Lake, or Kantishna. These stop for wildlife-viewing, and you can hop off to hike and flag down a later bus to board. Bring along food, snacks, and water. The **camper bus** (mid-May-mid-Sept., $60 rt) is available only to people who are staying at an established campground or in the backcountry.

FREE BUSES

Wheelchair-accessible **buses** (daily mid-May-mid-Sept., free) provide the way to shuttle hop around the park entrance area and up to mile 15 of the park road.

The **Savage River Shuttle** (2 hrs rt, starts July 1) runs four times daily between the visitors center, Denali Bus Depot, and the Savage River area (mile 15). It stops at trailheads at Mountain Vista and Savage River, plus the Savage River Campground.

The **Riley Creek Loop Shuttle** circles a loop every 30 minutes. It stops at all visitor service locations near the park entrance, Riley Creek Campground, and the Horseshoe Lake/Mount Healy Trailhead.

The **Sled Dog Demonstration Shuttle** leaves from the Denali Bus Depot, departing at least 40 minutes before each demonstration begins.

THE DENALI HIGHWAY

If you just can't get enough of Alaska's glorious alpine scenery, there is no drive better than the **135-mile (217-km) Denali Highway,** which runs east-west between the small community of Cantwell, on the Parks Highway, and the minuscule community of Paxson on the Richardson Highway. The road is mostly gravel and very rough in places, but tour buses navigate it—so if you're careful and go slow, it is almost always drivable in passenger vehicles. Because most of the road is above the tree line, you'll be treated to nonstop views of glaciers, lakes, and the skirts of dense green trees that are slowly creeping higher on the peaks as the state warms. Wildlife sightings include moose, bear, and waterfowl.

THE NORTHERN LIGHTS

Fairbanks, Alaska, is one of the very best places for viewing the northern Many visitors go to Alaska with the northern lights, the **aurora borealis,** high on their list of things to experience. These lights occur when electrically charged particles from the sun collide with earth's atmosphere. Summer may be the best time to visit Alaska for road trips, camping, and sightseeing, but it is the worst time for seeing the northern lights. In the Land of the Midnight Sun, the sky just doesn't get dark, especially May through mid-August. For the best chances to spot the aurora, visit September through April.

Denali has minimal light pollution, which helps for seeing the northern lights. Choose a vantage point where mountains do not block the northern sky, and look to the north when skies are clear and the darkest. The aurora also needs to be active. To assess potential for activity, check the University of Alaska Fairbanks Geophysical Institute's aurora forecast online (www. gi.alaska.edu/auroraforecast).

North of Denali is the **Aurora Oval,** where the northern lights happen overhead rather than on the northern horizon. Places around Fairbanks and Nome are under the oval. So are Gates of the Arctic and Kobuk Valley National Parks; however, they are extremely difficult to reach in winter. One study showed that if you spend three nights actively looking for the northern lights in Fairbanks from September to April, you have an 80 percent chance of success.

One of the best places to get away from the city lights of Fairbanks is **Chena Hot Springs,** 62 miles (100 km) northeast of Fairbanks. It has heated viewing areas where you can watch for the lights all night long. Most hotels under the Aurora Oval offer wake-up calls if the aurora comes out.

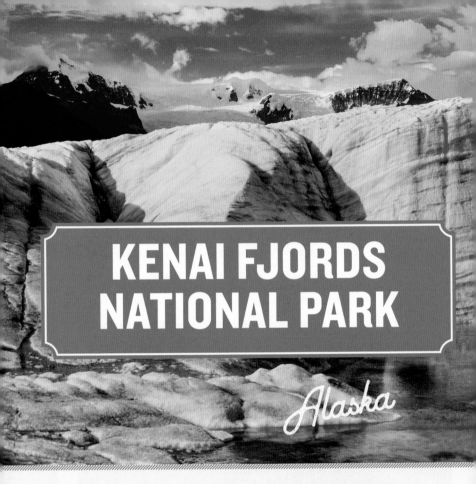

KENAI FJORDS NATIONAL PARK

Alaska

WEBSITE:
www.nps.gov/kefj

PHONE NUMBER:
907/422-0500

VISITATION RANK:
42

WHY GO:
Explore Alaskan
fjords and the
glaciers that
shaped them.

KEEPSAKE STAMPS ▼▼▼

▲ EXIT GLACIER

KENAI FJORDS NATIONAL PARK encompasses the traditional lands of the Sugpiaq or Alutiiq peoples, whose descendants still live along its coastline. It gets its name from the deep steep-walled inlets that were gouged by 35 glaciers, which now spill east and west from the immense Harding Icefield. These shrinking and thinning glaciers reveal the effects of climate change, despite the maritime weather that dumps 35 feet (11 m) of snow annually on the ice field.

The collision of the marine fjord and ice field environment makes this national park unique. Its marine zone bounces with wildlife that includes puffins, bald eagles, black oystercatchers, Dall's porpoises, Steller sea lions, and black bears. In the mountains above, creatures such as marmots, wolverines, moose, snowshoe hares, and mountain goats adapt to the cold. An added bonus are the humpback and gray whales that pass through during their March-mid-May migration period.

Taking to the water—or to the air—is the easiest way to absorb the high drama of this park.

PLANNING YOUR TIME

Kenai Fjords National Park is just outside the town of Seward on the Kenai Peninsula in south-central Alaska. There are three easy ways to explore the park: **by air** on a flightseeing or backcountry trip; **on foot,** via some of the state's most spectacular hiking trails; or **by tour boat** into the fjords. Most of the park is roadless wilderness, so you'll need to combine various modes of exploration.

June-August is the peak season for visiting. Services are reduced in May and September. Be prepared for cool rainy weather in summer, though temperatures can climb to the low 70s (21-24°C). October-April offers cross-country skiing on the Exit Glacier Road, but rough seas preclude boat tours of the fjords.

ENTRANCE AND FEES

From Seward Highway (AK 9), the main vehicle entrance is via **Exit Glacier Road** (signed as Herman Leirer Rd.), 3 miles (4.8 km) north of Seward. This is the only road that enters Kenai Fjords National Park. It takes about 20 minutes to drive to its end at the Exit Glacier Nature Center, where trails head to Exit Glacier, the closest glacier to reach on foot, and the Harding Icefield. There is no entrance fee.

VISITORS CENTERS

The **Kenai Fjords National Park Visitor Center** (1212 4th Ave., Seward, 907/422-0500, 9am-7pm daily Memorial Day-Labor Day, 9am-5pm daily mid-May-mid-Sept.) is in Seward, outside the park. It contains interpretive displays and an auditorium where many park films are shown.

The modest **Exit Glacier Nature Center** (Herman Leirer Rd., 9:30am-6:30pm daily summer) has a small selection of natural history displays. Ranger naturalists give daily talks and guide walks to Exit Glacier. Parking can be limited 10am-4pm; plan to arrive in the morning or late afternoon, when the light will make the glaciers appear bluer.

RECREATION

HIKING

When the weather is nice, strong hikers can tackle the **Harding Icefield**

KENAI FJORDS
NATIONAL PARK

TUSTUMENA
LAKE

5,720ft ▲

Indian Gl

**KENAI
NATIONAL
WILDLIFE
REFUGE**

Tustumena Glacier

5,269ft ▲

Truuli Glacier

Chernof Glacier

5,288ft ▲

5,873ft ▲

K
E
N
A
I

Chernof Gl

River

Sheep

Creek

Fox

Bradley

River

Glacier
Lake

6,340ft ▲

**KACHEMAK BAY
STATE PARK**

Kachemak Bay

Bradley Lake

Kachemak
Creek

Kachemak Gl

Dinglestadt

Glacier

Fjord

McCarty

Dixon Glacier

Nuka Glacier

Nuka

Nativ
Corpora

Portlock Glacier

**KENAI NATIONAL
WILDLIFE REFUGE**

Iceworm Peak
5,800ft ▲

Storm
Mountain
3,793ft ▲

Delight
Lake

Grewingk Glacier

Halibut

Creek

River

North Arm

Native
Corporation

McCarty
Lagoon

**KACHEMAK BAY
STATE PARK**

Yalik Glacier

Beauty Bay

Native
Corporation

West Arm

Roaring Cove

Ste
Poi

Wosnesenski Gl

4,540ft ▲

Petrof Glacier

Yalik Bay

Nuka Bay

McArthur

Pass

Bla
Ba

**PYE
ISLANDS**

Top 3

1 GAZE AT EXIT GLACIER

Exit Glacier is the only drive-to glacier in the park. Visit the **Exit Glacier Nature Center** to learn about glaciers, how they shape the landscape, and their retreat. Then follow the wheelchair-accessible pavement-and-gravel **Glacier View**

HIKER AT EXIT GLACIER

Loop (1 mi/1.6 km rt), where a spotting scope allows viewing the ice, 0.5 mile (0.8 km) away. As Exit Glacier has melted, it has retreated up the valley. Trail signs mark its size at various years. Since 2010, it has been receding at an average rate of 162 feet (49 m) per year. In early summer, some of the ice will still be covered with winter snow. To see the exposed blue ice and crevasses, plan a late-summer trip.

Exit Glacier is accessed via Exit Glacier Road (late May-mid-Nov.). In summer, avoid the clogged parking area and take the hourly **Exit Glacier Shuttle** from Seward. Rangers also lead daily walks in the area.

2 TOUR THE FJORDS BY BOAT

Kenai Fjords has more than 400 miles (645 km) of magical coastline, and boat tours are the best way to experience it. Tides, waves, winds, storms, and glaciers pummel the coast into a rugged work of art containing caves, arches, and standing rocks called stacks. As tectonic plates pull the Kenai Fjords landmass down into the sea, the coastline forests sink into the seawater. The half-day tour of **Resurrection Bay** (4-5 hrs) gives you the chance to spot whales, sea lions, and seals, plus noisy

HOLGATE GLACIER

seabird rookeries of cormorants, harlequin ducks, puffins, and kittiwakes. The full day tours tend to see more wildlife, particularly the bigger marine mammals, and get up near one of the tidewater glaciers in **Aialik Bay** (6-8.5 hrs).

All boat tours (late Mar.-late Sept.) depart from the harbor in Seward. Two popular day-cruise operators are **Major Marine Tours** (1302-B 4th Ave., Seward, 800/764-7300 or 907/274-8030, www.majormarine.com) and **Kenai Fjords Tours** (888/478-3346, www.alaskacollection.com). The latter is the only company that sets foot onto Fox Island in Resurrection Bay, where they have a day lodge.

3 STARE ACROSS IMMENSE HARDING ICEFIELD

Atop the Kenai Mountains, the Harding Icefield covers half of the park. You can see it in two ways. Strong hikers can grunt up the **Harding Icefield Trail.** From the Exit Glacier area, the steep route climbs up to a viewpoint overlooking the massive expanse of ice. **Flightseeing** with local air charters based at the Seward Airport allows for aerial viewing of the marine and mountain environments of fjords; you can see crevasses, icefalls, and arms of glaciers extending miles from the Harding Icefield.

ONE DAY IN THE KENAI FJORDS

With one day, you can squeeze in a visit to **Exit Glacier** and a **half-day boat tour.** Your own car makes the transfer between locales easiest, but hourly shuttles are available too. From Seward, drive early to Exit Glacier and hike the **Glacier View Loop Trail** to peer at the ice. Afterward, return to Seward to board the boat to **tour Resurrection Bay** to look for whales, sea lions, puffins, and other wildlife. If you'd rather see a tidewater glacier as well as wildlife, you'll need to spend the full day on the water to boat to **Aialak Bay** instead.

Trail (8.2 mi/13.2 km rt, 6-8 hrs). The path climbs above Exit Glacier to the ice field. Start on the Glacier View Loop to reach the signed junction for the Harding Icefield. The steep trail gains 3,300 feet (1,006 m) in elevation on its way to overlooks of the massive sheet of ice and snow that spawns 35 glaciers. Be ready for common black bear encounters, sun glare from the ice, and quick-changing weather.

If you want to hike on the ice, book a trip with the trained guides from **Exit Glacier Guides** (907/224-5569, www. exitglacierguides.com). They offer ice hiking and ice climbing, plus multiday and heli-assisted ice climbing and hiking adventures, peak summiting, and camping trips.

KAYAKING

With the proper guidance, almost anybody can manage a stable sea kayak in the waters of Resurrection Bay. One of the best outfitters for both tours and equipment rental is **Sunny Cove Sea Kayaking Co.** (1304 4th Ave., Seward, 907/224-4426, www.sunnycove.com). **Liquid Adventures** (1013 3rd Ave., Seward, 907/224-9225, www.liquid-adventures.com) offers both paddling and stand-up paddleboard adventures and rentals.

WINTER SPORTS

During winter, when the Exit Glacier Road closes (Nov.-early May), it is open

▼ HARBOR SEALS

Best Hike

EXIT GLACIER OVERLOOK TRAIL

DISTANCE: 2.2 miles (3.5 km) round-trip
DURATION: 1.5 hours
ELEVATION CHANGE: 470 feet (143 m)
EFFORT: moderately strenuous
TRAILHEAD: Exit Glacier Nature Center

From a junction at the west end of the Glacier View Loop Trail, the **Exit Glacier Overlook Trail** (also called Edge of the Glacier Trail) climbs a steeper path up bedrock to the Exit Glacier Overlook to the north side of the glacier. This closer overlook allows for photographing the blue ice and crevasses. You'll see **Toe of the Glacier** and the rubbled **Outwash Plain.** These are hazardous areas susceptible to falling ice slabs and flooding outbursts of ice, debris, and rushing water. The area within 0.5 mile (0.8 km) around the Toe of the Glacier is closed May-October, and no walking or climbing on the Toe of the Glacier ice is permitted.

for cross-country skiing, snowshoeing, fat biking, dogsledding, and snowmobiling. **IdidaRide Sled Dog Tours** (12820 Old Exit Glacier Rd., 907/224-8607, www.ididaride.com, mid-May-mid-Sept.) can take you on a 2-mile (3.2-km) dogsled ride.

WHERE TO STAY

INSIDE THE PARK

Set amid the Pedersen Lagoon Wildlife Sanctuary on Aialik Bay, **Kenai Fjords Glacier Lodge** (800/334-8730, www.alaskawildland.com, late May-early Sept., from $1,830 pp for 2 days and 1 night) is a modern eco-lodge with 16 private cabins featuring full baths, electricity, and heat. The cabins are connected via boardwalks to the main lodge, which houses a dining room and lobby overlooking Pedersen Glacier. Transportation is by boat from Seward to the lodge. Stays include all meals, activities, and lodgings.

Two rustic **public-use cabins** (late May-early Sept., $75/night, 3-night maximum) are secluded in Aialik Bay, requiring a boat (2 hrs) or seaplane (30 min) to reach. The cabins are equipped with a propane heater; there is no electricity and no running water (bring your own). Both cabins, rich in wildlife-watching and scenery, are surrounded by blueberries and salmonberries, which attract bears. Competition

BLACK BEAR

is keen for the **reservations,** so book in early January (877/444-6777, www. recreation.gov).

At the head of Aialik Bay in a spruce forest, the **Aialik Bay Cabin** sleeps four people in two wooden beds. Across the bay, Aialik Glacier plunges to the water. Below the cabin, you can explore the rocky beach at low tide. In Holgate Arm off Aialik Bay, the **Holgate Cabin** sleeps six people in three wooden bunk beds. From the deck, you can stare right at Holgate Glacier and listen to the sounds of calving ice.

The **Exit Glacier Campground** (12 sites, first come, first served, free) is a walk-in, tent-only campground located 0.25 mile (0.4 km) before the Exit Glacier Nature Center. It has drinking water, pit toilets, two accessible sites, and a central storage area for food and cooking items.

OUTSIDE THE PARK

Seward is just outside the park. It has the Kenai Fjords National Park Visitor Center motels, campgrounds, restaurants, boat tours, flightseeing, and visitor services. **Chugach National Forest** also has campgrounds.

GETTING THERE

AIR

The closest international airport is **Ted Stevens Anchorage International Airport** (ANC, 5000 W. International Airport Rd., www.dot.state.ak.us/anc), with year-round service from Alaska Airlines, Delta, United, and Iceland Air, and seasonal service from Condor. Car rentals are available at the airport.

BOAT

Many cruise lines use Seward as their port of call for Anchorage. If you're a ferry buff, you're out of luck; this is one of the few port cities the Alaska Marine Highway System does not serve.

RAIL

You can travel between Seward and Anchorage on the **Alaska Railroad** (800/544-0552, www.alaskarailroad. com, from $99 one-way).

CAR

The scenic drive from Anchorage to Seward is 127 miles (204 km, 2.5 hrs). From Anchorage, head southeast on

BEAR GLACIER

BEAR GLACIER

the Seward Highway (AK 1) to curve around Turnagain Arm, which separates the Kenai Peninsula from the mainland. In 87 miles (140 km), AK 1 exits right to Homer; continue straight, which becomes AK 9 to its terminus 39 miles (63 km) later in Seward. The year-round route is known as the Seward Highway, a National Scenic Byway.

BUS

Several bus services ply the roads up and down the Kenai Peninsula. The best deal is from **Seward Bus Lines** (888/420-7788 or 907/563-0800, www.sewardbuslines.net, May-mid-Sept., from $60 one-way to Anchorage or Whittier), with two departures from Seward to Anchorage daily.

GETTING AROUND

The only road in the park is **Exit Glacier Road** (signed as Herman Leirer Rd., closed Nov.-early May). The road departs AK 9 a short distance north of Seward, and terminates in 8.4 miles (13.5 km) at Exit Glacier Nature Center.

FLIGHT TOURS

Local air charters include **Seward Helicopter Tours** (2210 Airport Rd., 907/362-4354, www.sewardhelicopters.com), **Marathon Helicopters** (2210-B Airport Rd., 907/224-3616, www.marathonhelicopters.com), and **AA Seward Air Tours** (2300 Airport Rd., 907/978-3089, www.sewardair.com), which uses small planes. All tour operators are based at the airport in Seward.

SHUTTLES

From Seward, the **Exit Glacier Shuttle** (reservations 907/224-5569 or 907/224-9225, www.exitglaciershuttle.com, $15 rt) offers hourly trips to and from the Exit Glacier Nature Center. **Alaska Shuttle Service** (907/947-3349, www.alaskashuttleservice.com) offers taxi, shuttle, and tour service up and down the Kenai Peninsula, usually with a four-person minimum.

TAXIS

Land, air, and water taxis service the community of Seward. Air taxis licensed through the park service can get you to remote locations in Kenai Fjords, dropping you off one day and picking you up at a scheduled time and place. **Seward Air Taxi** (907/978-3089, www.sewardair.com) can do beach and glacier landings.

Water taxis vary according to season due to rough seas in winter. **Seward Ocean Excursions** (907/599-0499, www.sewardoceanexcursions.com) is the only water taxi that offers year-round service. **Alaska Coastal Safari/Seward Water Taxi** (907/201-0542, www.sewardwatertaxi.com) is a one-man operation with a three- or four-person minimum for each trip.

LAKE CLARK NATIONAL PARK AND PRESERVE

Alaska

KEEPSAKE STAMPS ▼▼▼

WEBSITE:
www.nps.gov/lacl

PHONE NUMBER:
907/781-2218

VISITATION RANK:
59

WHY GO:
Experience big wilderness.

▲ UPPER TWIN LAKE

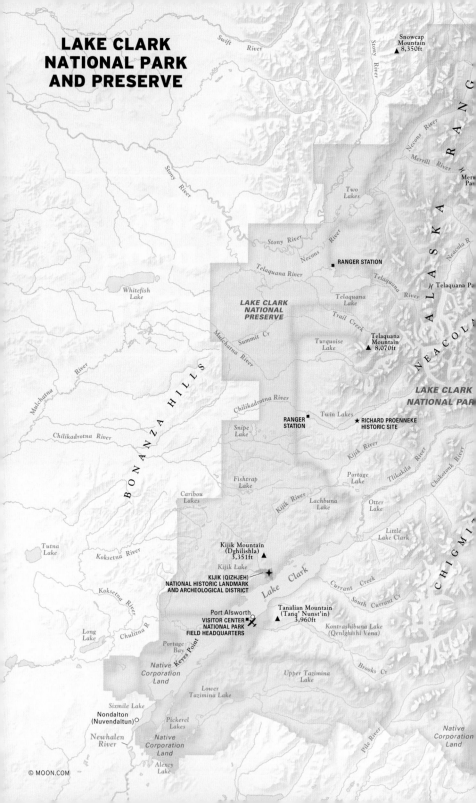

Rugged mountains, smoking volcanoes, and pristine waterways make up the roadless wilderness of **LAKE CLARK NATIONAL PARK AND PRESERVE.** The undeveloped park offers only back-country adventures for the hardy. It is famous for brown bear-viewing, fly-fishing, and the cabin of naturalist Richard Proenneke. But it also contains the Kijik National Historic Landmark, where more than a dozen archaeological sites, including villages, show 2,000 years of subsistence living by the Dena'ina Athabascan people. Many of their descendants live around the southern end of Lake Clark.

PLANNING YOUR TIME

Lake Clark has no roads, campgrounds, or services. Getting here requires a flight from Anchorage or Homer to **Port Alsworth,** the park entrance. The peak season is **June-mid-September.** There is no entrance fee.

The small **Port Alsworth Visitor Center** (907/781-2117, hours vary daily late May-mid-Sept.) in Port Alsworth has voluntary backcountry registration forms (no permit required), bear canister rentals (free), Alaska Geographic books and maps, and films.

BEAR-VIEWING

For top brown bear-viewing opportunities, charter a floatplane to fly to **Chinitna Bay, Crescent Lake,** or **Silver Salmon Creek.** Bear-viewing is best June-early September.

DICK PROENNEKE'S CABIN

Naturalist **Richard Proenneke** built this cabin (daily late May-Aug.) using only hand tools and lived in it for 30 years with no modern conveniences. He documented the building process in videos that have been collected in a DVD, *Alone in the Wilderness,* and his journals have been published in book form as *One Man's Wilderness.* Park rangers give cabin tours upon request. Getting here requires a 30-minute floatplane trip from Port Alsworth to Upper Twin Lake.

RECREATION

Hiking trails leave Port Alsworth for **Tanalian Falls** and **Kontrashibuna Lake** (5 mi/8 km rt, 2.5 hrs). At a trail junction midway, a strenuous climb shoots to the summit of **Tanalian Mountain** (5.2 mi/8.4 km rt, 2.5 hrs), with big-view rewards of Lake Clark and the surrounding mountains.

At 42 miles (68 km) long, Lake Clark offers plenty of shoreline for **kayakers** to paddle, and there are three National Wild and Scenic Rivers for skilled **white-water rafting** (Class III): the Tlikakila, Mulchatna, and Chilikadrotna. The rafting season

▼ KONTRASHIBUNA LAKE

TANALIAN RIVER

runs June-September; trips span 70-230 miles (113-370 km).

Crescent Lake and Silver Salmon Creek are the top fishing spots, where you may cast for salmon in the company of bears. For guided fishing trips, contact **Redoubt Mountain Lodge** (866/733-3034, www.redoubtlodge.com) on Crescent Lake or **Silver Salmon Creek Lodge** (907/252-5504, www.silversalmoncreek.com) at Silver Salmon Creek. Fishing season runs May-October.

In Port Alsworth, **Tulchina Adventures** (907/782-4720, www.tulchinaadventures.com) rents camping gear, paddling equipment, and motorized skiffs. It also maintains a campground and cabin rentals. For guided hiking, backpacking, kayaking, or rafting trips from Anchorage, contact **Alaska Alpine Adventures** (877/525-2577 or 907/351-4193, www.alaskaalpineadventures.com).

WHERE TO STAY

Lodges in Lake Clark are all privately owned and cater as much to fishing and kayaking as to bear-viewing. A full list is available online. **Silver Salmon Creek Lodge** (907/252-5504, www.silversalmoncreek.com, from $1,100) offers transport from Homer and Anchorage. **Redoubt Mountain Lodge** (866/733-3034, www.redoubtlodge.com, from $3,295, 2-night minimum) offers transport from Anchorage. Rates include use of gear.

Staying at two historic cabins on Lake Clark requires **reservations** (877/444-6777, www.recreation.gov, Feb.-Mar. and mid-May-mid-Oct., $45-65), available six months in advance, and an **air taxi.** The cabins have woodstoves and outhouses but no running water nor electricity. The **Priest Rock Cabin** has room for five people and the **Joe Thompson Cabin,** with room for two people, has the Portage Creek Trail nearby.

Backcountry camping is permitted throughout the park. Primitive campsites at **Hope Creek** (free) are first come, first served. Other backcountry sites include **Upper** and **Lower Twin Lakes.**

For accommodations and services, stay outside the park in tiny **Port Alsworth** on the shore of Lake Clark.

GETTING THERE AND AROUND

Alaska Airlines (800/252-7522, www.alaskaair.com) serves **Ted Stevens Anchorage International Airport** (ANC, 5000 W. International Airport Rd., www.dot.state.ak.us/anc). From Anchorage, take an air taxi to Lake Clark National Park and Preserve.

Air taxis require reservations. From Anchorage, contact **Lake Clark Air** (907/278-2054 or 888/662-7661, www.lakeclarkair.com) and **Lake and Peninsula Air** (907/345-2228, www.lakeandpenair.com). From Homer, contact **Adventure Airways** (907/299-7999, www.adventureairways.com), **Beluga Air** (907/235-8256, www.belugaair.com), or **Northwind Aviation** (907/235-7482, www.northwindak.com). **Lake Clark Air** (888/440-2281) and **Lake and Peninsula Air** (907/781-2228) maintain offices in Port Alsworth.

KATMAI NATIONAL PARK AND PRESERVE

Alaska

WEBSITE:
www.nps.gov/katm

PHONE NUMBER:
907/246-3305

VISITATION RANK:
58

WHY GO:
Watch brown bears
fish for salmon.

KEEPSAKE STAMPS ▼▼▼

▲ BEARS AT BROOKS RIVER

Stretching southwest from the bottom of the mainland, the Alaska Peninsula fractures into the volcanic Aleutian Islands. The biggest attraction here is bear-viewing at **KATMAI NATIONAL PARK AND PRESERVE.** While Katmai may be the best-known bear-viewing location in the world, this park also includes phenomenal sea kayaking, world-class fishing, and one of the most stunning sights: the Valley of Ten Thousand Smokes. An archaeological district contains hundreds of depressions along the Brooks River, where the Alutiiq people lived for thousands of years.

PLANNING YOUR TIME

Inaccessible by road, Katmai National Park requires **air travel** to reach its remote wonders. Flights from **Anchorage** go to **King Salmon,** the service community outside the park. From King Salmon, floatplanes head to Brooks Camp to watch bears catch fish in the river.

July and August are the nicest months to visit; limited travel and visitor services start in June and continue into September. Bear-viewing is best July and September, while fishing is better in the shoulder seasons.

ENTRANCE AND FEES

The town of King Salmon serves as the jumping-off point into Katmai. Floatplanes depart here for **Brooks Camp,** the point of entry for most visitors. No roads go into the park, and there is no entrance fee.

VISITORS CENTERS

The **King Salmon Visitor Center** (King Salmon Airport Bldg. 1, King Salmon, 907/246-4250, www.fws.gov/refuge/Becharof, 8am-5pm daily summer) serves as the park headquarters, with information, a bookstore, and educational displays on the Alaska Peninsula's Native cultures and traditions, wildlife, and fishing.

The **Brooks Camp Visitor Center** (June-mid-Sept.) serves as the campground check-in and provides backcountry information for those heading beyond Brooks Camp. Books and maps are available at the center's Alaska Geographic Association store. Rangers lead daytime and evening programs. All visitors to Brooks Camp are required to attend "Bear School," an orientation to safety in such a bear-rich place.

In the Valley of Ten Thousand Smokes, 23 miles (37 km) southeast of Brooks Camp, the small outpost of **Robert F. Griggs Visitor Center** (summer only) overlooks the ash and pumice valley, fallout from the 1912 eruption of Novarupta. Rangers lead daily hikes to the valley floor with a steep climb on the return.

SIGHTS

From Brooks Camp Visitor Center, ranger-led cultural walks (2pm daily early June-mid-Sept.) go to **archaeological sites** of the Alutiiq people. More than 900 depressions made by their ancient homes still remain. The program finishes at a partially reconstructed Alaska Native home.

MOUNT GRIGGS

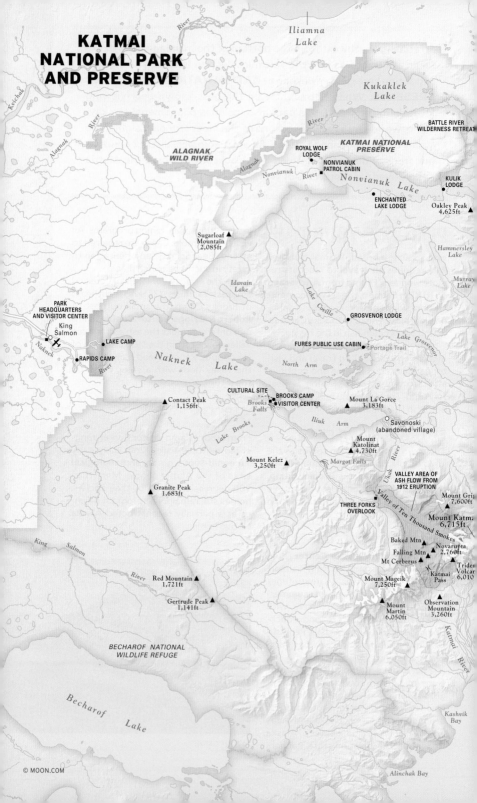

KATMAI NATIONAL PARK AND PRESERVE

Iliamna Lake

River

Kukaklek Lake

River

BATTLE RIVER WILDERNESS RETREAT

Alagnak River

ALAGNAK WILD RIVER

ROYAL WOLF LODGE

KATMAI NATIONAL PRESERVE

Nonvianuk

NONVIANUK PATROL CABIN

River

Nonvianuk Lake

KULIK LODGE

ENCHANTED LAKE LODGE

Oakley Peak
4,625ft

Kichak

Alagnak

River

Sugarloaf ▲
Mountain
2,085ft

Hammersley Lake

Idavain Lake

Murray Lake

Lake Coville

PARK HEADQUARTERS AND VISITOR CENTER

King
Salmon

GROSVENOR LODGE

Lake Grosvenor

FURES PUBLIC USE CABIN

Portage Trail

LAKE CAMP

Naknek

River

RAPIDS CAMP

Naknek *Lake*

North Arm

CULTURAL SITE

Brooks Falls

BROOKS CAMP VISITOR CENTER

Mount La Gorce ▲
3,183ft

Iliuk Arm

○ Savonoski
(abandoned village)

Contact Peak ▲
1,156ft

Lake Brooks

Mount
Katolinat ▲
4,730ft

Ukak River

Mount Kelez ▲
3,250ft

Margot Falls

VALLEY AREA OF ASH FLOW FROM 1912 ERUPTION

Granite Peak ▲
1,683ft

THREE FORKS OVERLOOK

Mount Gri
7,600ft

Valley of Ten Thousand Smokes

Mount Katma
6,715ft

Baked Mtn ▲

Falling Mtn ▲

Novarupta
2,760ft

King

Salmon

Mt Cerberus ▲

Trider
Volcar
6,010

Katmai
Pass

Red Mountain ▲
1,721ft

River

Mount Mageik ▲
7,250ft

Gertrude Peak ▲
1,141ft

Mount
Martin ▲
6,050ft

Observation
Mountain ▲
3,260ft

BECHAROF NATIONAL WILDLIFE REFUGE

Katmai River

Becharof Lake

Kashvik Bay

© MOON.COM

Alinchak Bay

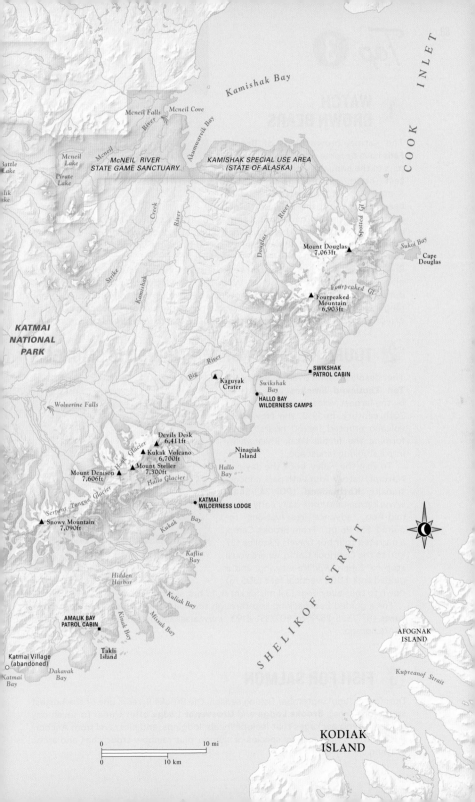

Top ③

① WATCH BROWN BEARS

The Katmai brown bears of **Brooks Falls** have become world famous, due in part to the annual online **Fat Bear Contest** (https://explore.org, usually late Sept.-early Oct.) to determine which bear has become the bulkiest before

BROOKS RIVER, KATMAI

denning for the winter. **Brooks Camp** includes the park visitors center, a campground, an auditorium where rangers lead nightly chats in addition to their daytime guided hikes, and, if you want to spend the night within four walls, **Brooks Lodge.** From here you can hike to Brooks Falls and the bridge crossing the Brooks River, where brown bears feed on sockeye salmon. Four viewing platforms allow places to watch the bears in action. When the Falls Platform maxes out with people during prime seasons in July and September, you may need to wait for space, and rangers limit viewing time to one hour per person. In summer, **webcams** (https://explore.org) catch the action above and underwater to let you watch from home.

② TOUR THE VALLEY OF TEN THOUSAND SMOKES

The desolate ash-covered **Valley of Ten Thousand Smokes** was created by the largest volcanic eruption of the 20th century. In 1912, the Novarupta volcano erupted for 60 hours, transforming the fertile Ukak River valley into a smoking landscape.

To visit the valley, book the daylong Natural History Tour with park concessionaire **Katmailand** (907/243-5448, www.katmailand.com, daily early June-mid-Aug., advance reservations required, $51-96 pp). From Brooks Camp, a narrated tour bus travels 23 miles (37 km) to the Overlook Cabin, where you'll stop for lunch, wildlife-viewing, and a guided trek 1,000 vertical feet (305 m)

VALLEY OF TEN THOUSAND SMOKES

down to the valley floor (3.4 mi/5.5 km rt, 1.7 hrs, strenuous).

For a guided backpacking trip through the valley, hire **Alaska Alpine Adventures** (877/525-2577 or 907/351-4193, www.alaskaalpineadventures.com), based in Anchorage.

③ FISH FOR SALMON

During the June-September fishing season, the Brooks River is one of the hottest spots for fishing. **Brooks Lodge** and **Grosvenor Lodge** offer three- to seven-day guided fishing packages that include meals, lodgings, and air travel from Anchorage. Cast your line for five species of salmon, plus rainbow trout, char, and arctic grayling.

VALLEY OF TEN THOUSAND SMOKES

RECREATION

A bewildering number of guide services are authorized to operate within Katmai. If you want to narrow it quickly and ensure a good experience, stick with **Brooks Camp** or **Brooks Lodge** (907/243-5448, www.katmailand.com) for right-at-the-camp lodging and fishing opportunities. From Anchorage, use **Alaska Alpine Adventures** (877/525-2577 or 907/351-4193, www.alaskaalpineadventures.com) for other activities such as hiking, backpacking, and paddling.

HIKING

Katmai has less than 5 miles (8 km) of maintained trails. From Brooks Camp Visitor Center, a wheelchair-accessible trail leads to **Brooks Falls** (2.4 mi/3.9 km rt, 1.2 hrs), where two viewing platforms provide a way to watch brown bears fishing for sockeye salmon. The third and fourth platforms are at the mouth of Brooks River. The more ambitious trail to **Dumpling Mountain** (3 mi/4.8 km rt, 1.5 hrs) climbs 800 feet (244 m) in elevation to views of Lake Brooks, Naknek Lake, the Brooks River, and Brooks Camp below.

KAYAKING AND CANOEING

At Brooks Camp you can canoe or kayak **Naknek Lake.** Experienced sea kayakers go for the inland **Savonoski Loop.** Starting and finishing at Brooks Camp, the 86-mile (138-km) route links two large lakes and two rivers. The route requires expert skills to paddle the swift-moving wave trains, avoid obstacles in the Savonoski River, and portage kayaks 1 mile (1.6 km). Most paddlers do the loop in 4-7 days. Fure's Cabin provides an overnight option in the Bay of Islands in the North Arm of Naknek Lake.

WHERE TO STAY

INSIDE THE PARK

Most visitors will want to stay in Brooks Camp, where **Brooks Lodge** (800/544-0551, www.katmailand.com, June-mid-Sept., from $850) has 16 modern guest rooms with baths. Breakfast, lunch, and dinner are served buffet-style in the lodge dining room, which overlooks Naknek Lake. Bear-viewing platforms are nearby. The lodge offers daily tours to the Valley of Ten Thousand Smokes. Lodge rooms may only be reserved by entering a lottery in December for stays during summer 1.5 years later. Rooms still available after the lottery can be reserved by phone or email in early February. July and September see the most demand for rooms due to salmon runs.

Grosvenor Lodge (800/544-0551, www.grosvenorlodge.com, June-mid-Sept., package rates apply, from $2,955 pp), a fishing lodge on Grosvenor Lake, accommodates up to six guests in three cabins (with heat and electricity), a separate bathhouse, and a kitchen

MCNEIL RIVER STATE GAME SANCTUARY AND REFUGE

Tucked outside the northern edge of Katmai National Park, **McNeil River State Game Sanctuary and Refuge** was established in 1967 to protect the highest concentration of wild brown bears in the world. As you can imagine, that leads to some amazing bear-viewing opportunities. Guides and researchers have counted more than 70 brown bears near the McNeil River at one time. Bear-viewing is best in July and mid-August, when chum salmon congregate at McNeil River Falls. A smaller number of bears swarm an early sockeye run up nearby Mikfik Creek.

A permit program limits visits to McNeil River Falls. Only 10 guided viewing permits are issued per day from early June to late August. **Permits** (907/267-2189, www.adfg.alaska.gov, $30 for lottery, $225-525 for permit) are assigned by lottery, which starts on March 2 of the prior year and ends on March 1 of the viewing year. Each permit is valid for four days. It's a four-mile (6.4 km, 2 hrs) round-trip hike to reach the falls.

If you don't win the permit lottery, apply for a **camp-standby permit** ($112-262), which is also valid for four days. The camp-standby permit allows you to stay in the sanctuary campground (tents only) and view bears from the campground and beach area. If somebody no-shows for a guided viewing trip, you can then take their spot.

This roadless sanctuary has no roads or modern amenities. Access is by chartered flight from Anchorage or Homer.

and dining area. The main lodge holds a lounge and bar.

Brooks Camp Campground (877/444-6777, www.recreation.gov, $12 June-Sept., $6 May and Oct.) accommodates 60 tent campers and fills quickly. Reservations open in early January for the summer; July and September reservations book fast for the peak bear-viewing periods. Facilities include cooking shelters, fire rings, food storage boxes, water, and vault toilets. The campground has no designated sites—the open grassy area is protected from bears by an electric fence.

Backcountry camping in the Valley of Ten Thousand Smokes can be arranged with a one-way drop-off from park concessionaire Katmailand; some sites fringe the valley. Alternatively, hike 12 miles (19.3 km, one-way) from Valley Road to the primitive **Baked Mountain Huts** (first come, first served, free). No permits are required, and there are no services.

In the Bay of Islands of Naknek Lake, rustic **Fure's Cabin** (877/444-6777, www.recreation.gov, June-Sept., $45) is a one-room wood-heated cabin with no electricity. It sleeps six. Make reservations starting in early January.

OUTSIDE THE PARK

Services are in the town of **King Salmon,** which has one hotel: the **Antlers Inn** (mile 1, Alaska Peninsula Hwy., 888/735-8525 or 907/246-8525, www.antlersinnalaska.com, from $225).

GETTING THERE AND AROUND

King Salmon sits 290 miles (465 km) southwest of Anchorage on the Alaska Peninsula, just off the west flank of Katmai National Park. You can only get here by plane. In summer, **Alaska Airlines** (800/252-7522, www.alaskaair.com) offers flights daily from Anchorage to King Salmon. **Ravn** (907/266-8394, www.ravnalaska) offers a couple of flights a day from Anchorage in summer.

Upon arrival in King Salmon, take an air taxi with **Katmai Air** (800/544-0551, www.katmaiair.com, reserve in advance) to the park's Brooks Camp. Katmai Air also provides floatplane charters to other locations in the park.

Katmai has no public transportation. To get around, you'll need a boat or kayak, or book a floatplane or tour bus to the Valley of Ten Thousand Smokes.

WRANGELL-ST. ELIAS NATIONAL PARK AND PRESERVE

Alaska

KEEPSAKE STAMPS ▼▼▼

WEBSITE:
www.nps.gov/wrst

PHONE NUMBER:
907/822-5234

VISITATION RANK:
56

WHY GO:
Visit the largest national park in the United States.

▲ GUIDED HIKE IN WRANGELL BACKCOUNTRY

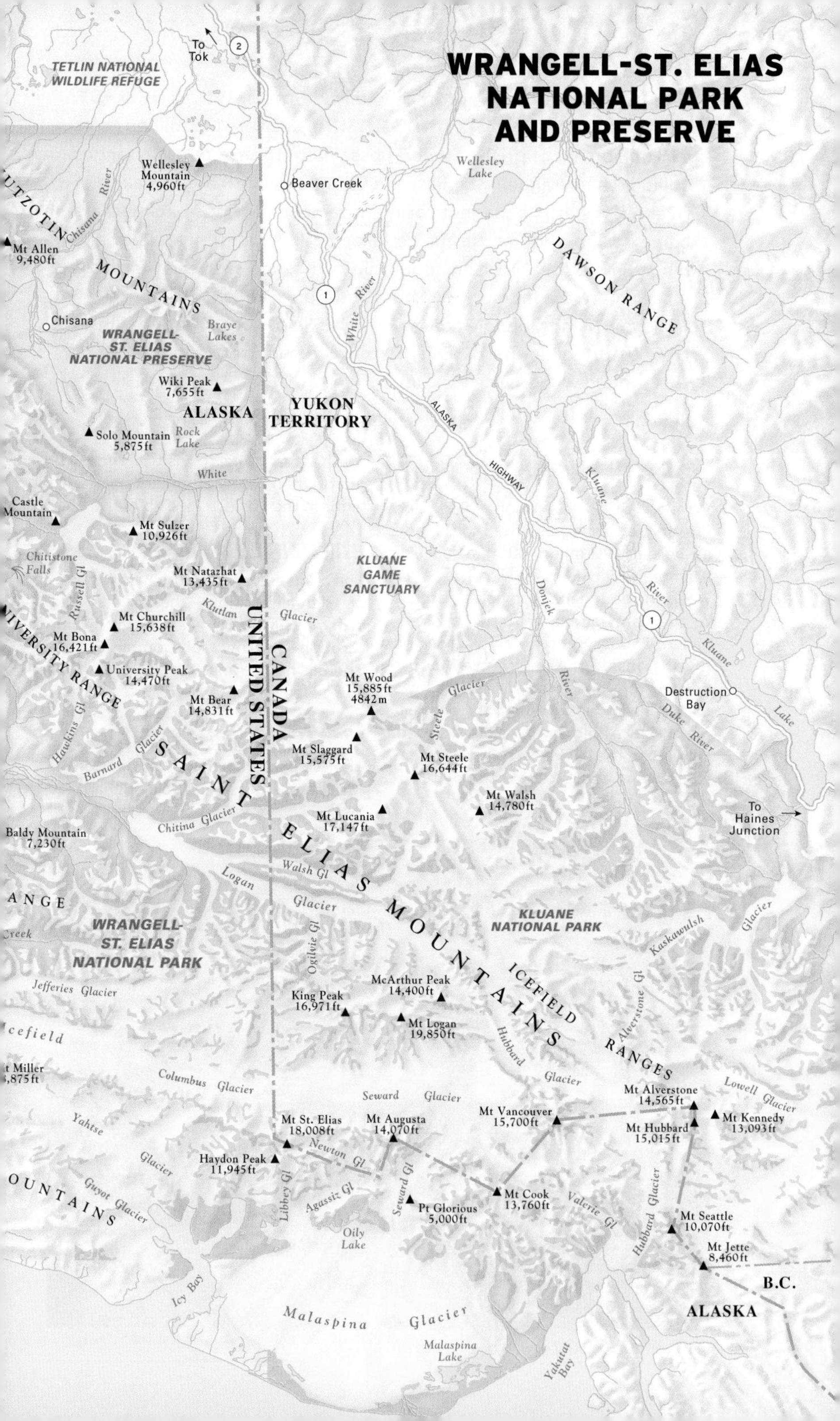

WRANGELL-ST. ELIAS NATIONAL PARK AND PRESERVE

TETLIN NATIONAL WILDLIFE REFUGE

To Tok
2

Wellesley Mountain 4,960ft

Beaver Creek

Wellesley Lake

DAWSON RANGE

Mt Allen 9,480ft

NUTZOTIN MOUNTAINS

Chisana River

Chisana

Braye Lakes

1

White River

WRANGELL-ST. ELIAS NATIONAL PRESERVE

Wiki Peak 7,655ft

ALASKA

YUKON TERRITORY

ALASKA HIGHWAY

Solo Mountain 5,875ft

Rock Lake

White

KLUANE GAME SANCTUARY

Kluane River

Castle Mountain

Chitistone Falls

Russell Gl

Mt Sulzer 10,926ft

Mt Natazhat 13,435ft

Klutlan Glacier

1

Donjek River

Destruction Bay

UNIVERSITY RANGE

Mt Churchill 15,638ft

Mt Bona 16,421ft

University Peak 14,470ft

Hawkins Gl

Mt Bear 14,831ft

CANADA

UNITED STATES

Mt Wood 15,885ft 4842m

Steele Glacier

Duke River

Kluane Lake

To Haines Junction

Barnard Glacier

Mt Slaggard 15,575ft

Mt Steele 16,644ft

Mt Walsh 14,780ft

Baldy Mountain 7,230ft

SAINT

Chitina Glacier

Mt Lucania 17,147ft

Logan

Walsh Gl

ELIAS

Glacier

KLUANE NATIONAL PARK

RANGE

WRANGELL-ST. ELIAS NATIONAL PARK

Creek

Jefferies Glacier

ELIAS

Ogilvie Gl

MOUNTAINS

King Peak 16,971ft

McArthur Peak 14,400ft

Mt Logan 19,850ft

ICEFIELD

Kaskawulsh Glacier

Alverstone Gl

RANGES

Glacier

Icefield

t Miller ,875ft

Columbus Glacier

Yahtse Glacier

Seward Glacier

Hubbard

Mt Alverstone 14,565ft

Lowell Glacier

Mt St. Elias 18,008ft

Mt Augusta 14,070ft

Mt Vancouver 15,700ft

Mt Kennedy 13,093ft

Haydon Peak 11,945ft

Newton Gl

Mt Hubbard 15,015ft

MOUNTAINS

Guyot Glacier

Glacier

Libbey Gl

Agassiz Gl

Seward Gl

Pt Glorious 5,000ft

Mt Cook 13,760ft

Valerie Gl

Hubbard Glacier

Mt Seattle 10,070ft

Oily Lake

Mt Jette 8,460ft

Icy Bay

Malaspina Glacier

Malaspina Lake

Yakutat Bay

B.C.

ALASKA

The largest national park in the United States, **WRANGELL-ST. ELIAS NATIONAL PARK AND PRESERVE** covers 13.2 million acres (5.3 million ha) of pristine wilderness where three mountain ranges collide (the Wrangell, St. Elias, and Chugach). With huge peaks and rivers of ice, it is a magnet for mountaineers. Serious backpackers come for solitude at turquoise lakes while wildlife-watchers aim binoculars at bears, bison, mountain goats, and wolves. It is also a place where the Indigenous Ahtna and Upper Tanana Athabascans, Eyak, and Tlingit peoples pass on the skills of subsistence living to their future generations. Only two roads penetrate the interior of this rugged wilderness.

PLANNING YOUR TRIP

Wrangell-St. Elias National Park and Preserve sits snug against the Canadian border, 190 miles (305 km) east of Anchorage. Paved roads skirt the park's western boundary, providing access to the gateway communities of Glennallen, Copper Center, Kenny Lake, and Chitina. Inside the park, most visitors beeline for the historic mining towns of **McCarthy** and **Kennecott,** accessible only by a long and difficult dirt road. Download the NPS smartphone app before leaving home to make use of its audio tours for the scenic drives.

The best time to visit is **June-August,** when balmy summers peak with highs in the 70s (21-26ºC) by July.

ENTRANCE AND FEES

The main entrance to the park is south of Glennallen along the paved **Richardson Highway** (AK 4), which runs through the town of Copper Center. There is no entrance station and no entrance fee.

VISITORS CENTERS

The **Copper Center Visitor Center** (Copper Center, mile 106.8, Richardson

CHUGACH MOUNTAINS SOUTH OF MCCARTHY

Top ❸

1 TAKE A SCENIC DRIVE ON MCCARTHY ROAD

McCarthy Road stretches 60 miles (97 km) from Chitina to McCarthy, taking three hours one-way on the rugged dirt road. Stop to marvel at the **Kuskulana Bridge** (mile 17.2), a 775-foot (236-m) expanse made even more impressive because it was built in 1910—and because you have to drive across it! Stop again at the huge **Gilahina Trestle** (mile 29) to admire its construction. Just before reaching the parking area, look for the Kennicott Glacier. The road terminates near the **McCarthy Road Information Station,** where you can get oriented, and at the **Kennicott River Footbridge,** where you can walk, bike, or take a shuttle to McCarthy.

The road is legendary for being narrow, rough, and full of sharp rocks just waiting to puncture tires. Before embarking, fill up on gas at Kenny Lake (AK 4) or Chitina, check on road conditions at Chitina Ranger Station, and download the audio tour (available online and on the NPS app).

2 EXPLORE ROOT GLACIER

Descending from Mount Blackburn, **Root Glacier** is one of Alaska's easiest glaciers to access. Join a guided day trek with **St. Elias Alpine Guides** (888/933-5427 or 907/231-6395, www. steliasguides.com, daily mid-May-mid-Sept., $95) to step out onto the ice to see brilliant turquoise pools, ice canyons, and crevasses. No experience is necessary for this adventure; you just need to be able to hike up to 6 miles (10 km), which includes the trail to get to the glacier. The company supplies the expert guide, crampons, and gear. It'll give you a taste of what mountaineers experience.

GUIDED TOUR ON ROOT GLACIER

3 EXPLORE KENNECOTT MINING TOWN

A 5-mile (8-km) road connects McCarthy with the ghost town of **Kennecott,** whose historic bright-red mine buildings are an eye-catching sight backdropped by the snowy Wrangell Mountains. In summer, **St. Elias Alpine Guides** (888/933-5427 or 907/231-6395, www.steliasguides.com) lead tours into the **Kennecott Mill** buildings, part of the Kennecott Mines National Historic Landmark. Most of the equipment is in surprisingly good condition and still works. With no private vehicle access, you must hike or bike to get here—or hop aboard the shuttle van from McCarthy.

KENNECOTT MINE

Best Hike

ROOT GLACIER

DISTANCE: 4-8 miles (6.4-12.9 km) round-trip

DURATION: 2.5-4 hours

ELEVATION CHANGE: 263-900 feet (80-274 m)

EFFORT: easy to moderate

TRAILHEAD: Kennecott Visitor Center

Favored by hikers and bears, this trail parallels the toe of Kennicott Glacier to reach the toe of **Root Glacier.** Both glaciers look like ice rivers coursing down from Mount Blackburn. The spectacular **Stairway Icefall** appears in the distance. The trail begins on a road to a fork where the left trail weaves through lateral moraines. At the junction past the Jumbo Creek Footbridge, turn left to drop to the toe of Root Glacier. Use caution: slick ice, collapsing ice bridges, frigid water, and falling ice can be dangerous. Return the way you came, or, back on the main trail, continue for another 2 miles (3.2 km), paralleling the glacier for more views.

Hwy., at Glenn Hwy., 907/822-7250, 9am-5pm daily mid-May-mid-Sept., reduced hours spring and fall, closed winter) is 10 miles (16 km) south of Glennallen. As the main park visitors center, it has exhibits, backcountry information, a bookstore, a theater, and ranger talks. Next door, the **Ahtna Cultural Center** (907/822-5778, hours vary, year-round) is an Indigenous heritage museum with a hand-built fish wheel. Outside, short paths visit scenic overlooks, and rangers lead guided walks.

McCarthy Road has several spots for obtaining visitor information. Outside the park, stop at **Chitina Ranger Station** (mile 33, Edgerton Hwy., Chitina, 907/823-2205, 9am-5pm daily mid-May-mid-Sept.) for an update on road conditions. At the upper end of McCarthy Road, the unstaffed **McCarthy Road Info Station** (mile 59) has an orientation kiosk. Five miles (8 km) north of McCarthy in a historic schoolhouse, **Kennecott Visitor Center** (907/205-7106, 9am-5pm daily summer) has ranger programs, exhibits, films, a bookstore, and backcountry information.

At the entrance to rugged Nabesna Road, stop at **Slana Ranger Station**

WRANGELL MOUNTAINS

(mile 0.5, 907/822-7401, 9am-5pm daily summer) to find out road conditions. The station also has exhibits, a film, ranger programs, and backcountry information.

SIGHTS
MCCARTHY

A remote Alaskan homestead miles from pavement, **McCarthy** once supplied the mining district with necessities and services. Today, you'll find lodgings, dining, a museum, and railroad memorabilia lining its 0.1-mile (0.2-km) main street. McCarthy is a launch point for backcountry exploration, flightseeing, and guided trips, with hiking trails to glaciers and mines. Visitors are restricted to one access point—a wide footbridge over the Kennicott River with a 0.5-mile (0.8-km) walk into town. Learn about the history of the area at the **McCarthy-Kennicott Historical Museum** (hours vary late May-early Sept.) in the old red depot building with the railcar outside.

SCENIC DRIVES

Two rugged gravel roads, about three hours apart, extend into the Wrangell-St. Elias interior. In summer, most 2WD vehicles work on them; however, check that your rental car company permits travel on gravel roads. Large RVs are not recommended. The slow-going roads can be full of potholes and washboards—if you drive too fast or have bald tires, expect a few flats. Fuel up in advance and bring a full-size inflated spare, jack, patch kit or Fix-a-Flat, and air compressor. Audio tours of both roads are available online for downloading and on the NPS app. The challenging **McCarthy Road** (60 mi/97 km one-way, 3 hrs) is the better of the two roads.

To drive rugged **Nabesna Road** (3 hrs rt), fuel up in Glennallen (76 mi/122 km south) for the 42-mile (68-km) drive into the north side of the park. Between miles 15 and 18, the massive Wrangell Mountains come into view and you may spot **Mount Wrangell,** the park's only active volcano. Many drivers turn around at **Kendesnii Campground**

POCKET GLACIER IN WRANGELL BACKCOUNTRY

(mile 27.8) because the remaining road demands high clearance and sometimes 4WD for stream crossings. Fuel up in Tok or Gakona before driving the road, and stop at the Slana Ranger Station for road updates, as washouts are frequent.

RECREATION
HIKING

To see the **Kennicott Glacier** (1.5 mi/2.4 km one-way, 50 min), hike the trail from the museum in McCarthy to the meltwater lake at the toe of the glacier. A lengthy river of ice, Kennicott Glacier carries mounds of debris: boulders, rocks, gravel, and silt. Most people expect to see white or blue ice, but much of the toe of the glacier is covered by brown and gray debris.

Two companies lead day hikes, ice climbing, backpacking, air-assisted hiking, and river rafting trips. **St. Elias Alpine Guides** (888/933-5427 or 907/231-6395, www.steliasguides.com) also offers mountaineering and skiing trips. **Kennicott Wilderness Guides** (800/664-4537 or 907/554-4444, kennicottguides.com) also leads packrafting trips.

FLIGHTSEEING

In McCarthy, air taxis offer expeditions into the park as well as drop-offs and pickups for backcountry adventures.

KAYAKING TO KENNECOTT GLACIER

Go flightseeing with **Copper Valley Air Day Tours** (866/570-4200 or 907/822-4200, www.coppervalleyairservice.com) or **Wrangell Mountain Air** (800/478-1160 or 907/554-4411, www.wrangellmountainair.com).

RAFTING

The silt-colored Kennicott River churns and boils beneath the footbridge toward McCarthy. **McCarthy River Tours & Outfitters** (907/302-0688, www.raftthewrangells.com, mid-May-mid-Sept.) specializes in these turbulent waters, with single-day and multiday trips in the Copper River Valley. They also offer calmer paddleboarding and kayaking trips in the lake at the toe of Kennicott Glacier. **Kennicott Wilderness Guides** (800/664-4537 or 907/554-4444, https://kennicottguides.com) leads packrafting trips.

WHERE TO STAY

INSIDE THE PARK

For those seeking solitude, the park maintains 12 fly-in or snowmobile-in **backcountry cabins** in remote locations. Four of the cabins require reservations. Obtain reservations by email (wrst_info@nps.gov) for Viking Lodge, Caribou Creek, and Nugget Creek two weeks to six months in advance. Reserve online for the Esker Stream Cabin (www.recreation.gov, $25).

McCarthy

The **Ma Johnson's Hotel** (101 Kennicott Ave., 907/554-4402, www.majohnsonshotel.com) has two lodging options: the old **boardinghouse** (from $225) and the **Lancaster Backpacker Hotel** (from $129). Baths are shared. The lodge bistro serves local yak meat and wild-caught Copper River sockeye salmon. The **Golden Saloon**, where the town goes to socialize, serves pub fare. The lodge store sells ready-made sandwiches, ice cream, liquor, hardware, and limited groceries. On the main street, **The Potato** (907/554-4504, www.theroadsidepotatohead.com, late May-mid-Sept.) serves breakfast and sandwiches.

Kennecott

The nicest accommodations are at the **Kennicott Glacier Lodge** (15 Kennicott Millsite, 800/582-5128, www.kennicottlodge.com, late May-mid-Sept., from $210). Guest rooms are in two buildings: 23 rooms in the lodge have shared baths and 20 rooms in the south wing have private baths. The dining room

KENNICOTT GLACIER LODGE

(907/554-1075, www.blackburncabins.com, year-round, from $169), which have two full beds, propane heaters, kitchens, and running water. Bike rentals, guided hikes and trips, and snow machine rentals are also available.

Camping

McCarthy Road has two private campgrounds before the footbridges at McCarthy. Only the aptly named **Glacier View Campground** (mile 58.9, McCarthy, 907/441-5737, www.glacierviewcampground.com, June-mid-Sept., $20) accepts reservations. It has a small open-air café and a bare-bones camp store.

At mile 27.8 on Nabesna Road, the primitive **Kendesnii Campground** (year-round, free) has 10 first-come, first-served campsites, but no drinking water. It is the only National Park Service-operated campground in the park. You can also camp at pullouts (free) along the road.

OUTSIDE THE PARK

The gateway communities of **Glennallen, Copper Center, Kenny Lake,** and **Chitina** have limited services. Small motels, cabins, and campgrounds dot **Richardson Highway** (AK 4), **Glenn Highway** (AK 1), and **Tok Cutoff Road** (AK 1).

serves family-style breakfast, lunch, and dinner fare that some term "wilderness gourmet." Common areas are lined with historical artifacts from the Kennecott copper mine.

For a cozier experience, reserve one of the five **Blackburn Cabins**

GUIDED HIKING TRIP IN WRANGELL BACKCOUNTRY

GETTING THERE

AIR

The closest international airport is **Ted Stevens Anchorage International Airport** (ANC, 5000 W. International Airport Rd., www.dot.state.ak.us/anc). Car rentals are available at the airport.

CAR

From Anchorage, it is a 180-mile (290-km) drive on **Glenn Highway (AK 1)** to Glennallen. Three miles (4.8 km) east of Glennallen, turn south onto Richardson Highway (AK 4); from there it's 10 miles (16 km) to the Copper Center Visitor Center.

To reach McCarthy and Kennecott, continue south on **Richardson Highway (AK 4)** from Copper Center for 23 miles (37 km). Turn left (east) onto **Edgerton Highway (AK 10)** and drive 33 miles (53 km) to the pavement's end at **Chitina,** the park entrance, and the **McCarthy Road.**

If **Slana** and **Nabesna Road** are your destination, follow Glenn Highway (AK 1) north from Glennallen for 76 miles (122 km).

SHUTTLE

From Anchorage, **Interior Alaska Bus Line** (800/770-6652, www.interioralaskabusline.com) travels to Glennallen.

GETTING AROUND

AIR

Wrangell Mountain Air (800/478-1160 or 907/554-4411, www.wrangellmountainair.com) operates once-daily flights in summer from Chitina to McCarthy.

CAR

Prepare for rough gravel roads inside the park (and be sure your rental car company will permit driving them). From the park entrance at Chitina, **McCarthy Road** (60 mi/97 km, 3 hrs one-way) goes to McCarthy and Kennecott. From the **Tok Cutoff Road (AK 1),** the rougher **Nabesna Road** (42 mi/68 km, 1.5 hrs one-way) leads north of the mountains.

SHUTTLES

The **Kennicott Shuttle** (907/822-5292, www.kennicottshuttle.com, summer only, reservations required) picks up guests outside the park in Glennallen, Copper Center, Kenny Lake, or Chitina with transportation to the footbridge crossing the Kennicott River.

At the footbridge, look for a sign listing shuttle companies that serve the zone between the footbridge, McCarthy, and Kennecott. They run about every 30-60 minutes; fares vary.

▼ FLIGHTS IN THE BACKCOUNTRY OF WRANGELL-ST ELIAS

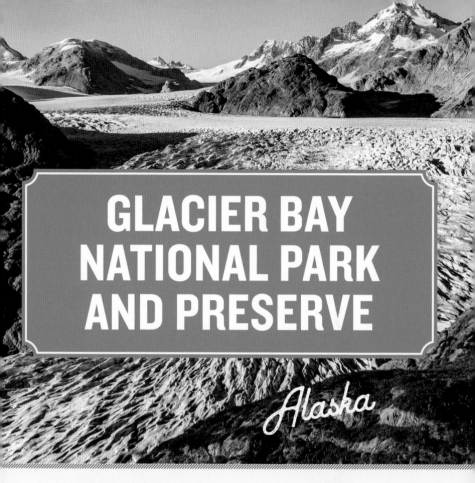

GLACIER BAY NATIONAL PARK AND PRESERVE

Alaska

KEEPSAKE STAMPS ▼▼▼

WEBSITE:
www.nps.gov/glba

PHONE NUMBER:
907/697-2230

VISITATION RANK:
54

WHY GO:
Watch tidewater
glaciers calve.

▲ GLACIER BAY NATIONAL PARK

GLACIER BAY
NATIONAL PARK
AND PRESERVE

© MOON.COM

GLACIER BAY NATIONAL PARK AND PRESERVE encompasses some 3.3 million acres (1.3 million ha) of land and water. Its craggy, snowcapped mountains, towering spruce and cedar trees, calving glaciers, and rich waters are hardly unique in Alaska, but this park is remarkable for several reasons.

The first is the pristine nature of the waters and lands; the waters, in particular, are some of the richest on earth, and Glacier Bay is one of the largest protected biosphere preserves in the world. Second, the solitude—cruise ships do visit the bay, but they never dock, and access is controlled during peak months.

Third, an enormous glacier covered most of the park until nearly 300 years ago, when a fast series of glacial advances and retreats melted out the bay. Today, active tidewater glaciers from the Little Ice Age still push into the bay, but warming temperatures are forcing them to recede at an alarming rate.

Finally, Glacier Bay is an integral part of the Tlingit Alaska Native tradition. In a collaboration between the park and the Tlingit clans, the new Xunaa Shuká Hít (Huna House) clan house became the first permanent clan house in the area since Tlingit villages were destroyed by a rapid glacier advance more than 250 years ago.

PLANNING YOUR TIME

Glacier Bay is virtually roadless. The park encompasses a 65-mile-long (105-km) saltwater bay with multiple fjords hunkering between ice-laden mountains draped with glaciers that plunge into the tidewater. To see the glaciers requires **travel by air or water,** plus the logistics of several trip legs to get here. From **Juneau,** getting to the park entrance requires a ferry or a flight to **Gustavus,** a service town just outside the park that is unreachable by road. From Gustavus, taxis travel the short distance to Bartlett Cove, inside the park. From Gustavus or Bartlett Cove, boat tours enter Glacier Bay.

May-September is high season, with services in Gustavus and Bartlett Cove open. Despite moderate summer temperatures, erratic maritime weather systems deliver pervasive rains, especially around Bartlett Cove, which sees up to 70 inches (178 cm) annually. Bring rain gear and warm, quick-dry layers, including a hat and gloves. For less rain, go in May or June.

ENTRANCE AND FEES

The park has no entrance station, but the official entrance is Bartlett Cove. There is no entrance fee.

VISITORS CENTERS

In Bartlett Cove, **Glacier Bay National Park Visitor Center** (Glacier Bay Lodge, 2nd Fl., 907/697-2661, 11am-8pm daily late May-early Sept.) contains an Alaska Geographic bookstore and exhibits, including a kids corner and an underwater listening station to hear whales. The theater has nightly educational programs, and ranger-guided walks depart for beachcombing or rainforest tours.

To go boating or camping in Glacier Bay, stop at the **Visitor Information Station** (Bartlett Cove, 907/697-2627, hours vary daily May-Sept.), adjacent to the public dock in Bartlett Cove. Pick up permits, maps, tide tables, and nautical charts, and attend an orientation covering the rigors of wilderness boating and camping.

Top ❸

1 CRUISE GLACIER BAY

Visitors can travel up the Main Channel or tour Glacier Bay's West Arm to view the tidewater glaciers. The only scheduled day tour in the park is the **Glacier Bay Tour** out of **Glacier Bay Lodge** (179 Bartlett Cove, 888/229-8687, www.visitglacierbay.com, daily summer). National Park Service rangers narrate the eight-hour tour on high-speed catamarans. The tour takes in wildlife and the tidewater **Grand Pacific and Margerie Glaciers.** Lunch is included.

Cruise ships depart from West Coast and Alaskan cities to tour Glacier Bay. Two ships per day are allowed up the West Arm to spend four hours in the glacier areas. Cruise ships do not

MCBRIDE GLACIER

dock; sightseeing is only from the boat. Tour operators in Gustavus also offer day trips and longer overnight expeditions into Glacier Bay.

2 GO WHALE-WATCHING

From mid-June through August, humpback whale-watching is phenomenal in the waters of Glacier Bay. Naturalists narrate two of the best half-day whale-watching tours. **The Taz Whale Watching Tours** (888/698-2726 or 907/321-2303, www.tazwhalewatching.com) also offers water-taxi services for kayakers and backpackers (the deck is large enough to handle large groups of kayaks). The more intimate **Wild Alaska Charters tour** (855/997-2704 or 907/697-2704, www.glacierbay.biz) is limited to six passengers at a time.

WHALE-WATCHING

3 KAYAK THE OPEN WATERS

Sea kayaking Glacier Bay is a bucket-list adventure. **Glacier Bay Sea Kayaks** (Bartlett Cove, 907/697-2257, www.glacierbayseakayaks.com) guides full- and half-day trips in the park and also provides gear rentals and trip-planning assistance to paddlers experienced enough to go without a guide. Two destinations are favored by kayakers: The **Beardslee Islands** have great beach camping and wildlife-viewing, and **Muir Inlet** restricts motorized boats, making this a prime place for quiet and solitude. Kayakers can use the daily Glacier Bay Tour boat as a water taxi to cut days off paddling time; they can also bring their own boats on the ferry from Juneau.

For longer multiday guided kayak tours, go with **Alaska Mountain Guides** (based in Haines, 800/766-3396 or 907/313-4422, www.alaskamountainguides.com) or **Spirit Walker Expeditions** (800/529-2537, www.seakayakalaska.com).

ONE DAY IN GLACIER BAY

If you must pack your Glacier Bay visit into one day, charter an early morning flight from Juneau to Gustavus. Spend that night at **Glacier Bay Lodge,** then take the **Glacier Bay Tour** into Glacier Bay—it's the only way to see the wildlife and tidewater glaciers. The eight-hour tour boat returns in time to catch a late afternoon flight back to Juneau.

SIGHTS

BARTLETT COVE

Bartlett Cove is Glacier Bay National Park's headquarters. Nestled at the south end of the bay, the enclave houses **Glacier Bay Lodge,** which contains the visitors center, hotel rooms, and a restaurant. The cove also has the **Huna Tribal House,** docks with boat services, kayak rentals, the **Visitor Information Station,** and a walk-in campground. Low tide is the perfect time to explore the intertidal zone around the cove, which is teeming with seaweed, algae, crabs, mollusks, and birds.

HUNA TRIBAL HOUSE

The **Huna Tribal House** (noon-5:30pm Mon.-Sat.) pays tribute to the Tlingit culture, which has a rich history in the lower bay. The building sports carvings and paintings that portray the history of Tlingit clans. Interpretive presentations are offered several times daily; weekly programs include guided walks and demonstrations on making dugout canoes. The house sits on the shoreline trail of Bartlett Cove, adjacent to Glacier Bay Lodge.

WHALE EXHIBIT

Stop at the outdoor pavilion near the Visitor Information Station to see the **Whale Exhibit,** home to the largest humpback whale skeleton on public display in the United States. Known as Snow, this humpback whale was a regular summer resident in the bay for 26 years. Her 3,729-pound (1,691-kg) skeleton is more than 45 feet long (14 m).

MARGERIE GLACIER

HIKER AND GLACIER

GLACIER BAY

There are three main areas to tour in Glacier Bay. The **Main Channel** contains the Marble Islands, where you might spot cliff-dwelling seabirds, sea lions, or summering humpback whales. At Tlingit Point, the waterways divide into two main arms.

The smaller **Muir Inlet** (sometimes called East Arm) contains multiple glaciers that are mostly terrestrial; McBride Glacier still reaches the tidewater, but Muir Glacier has melted with speedy recession back onto land.

The larger arm is **Glacier Bay,** known also as West Arm, where motorized boats and cruises can go. This arm holds the 35-mile-long (56 km) Grand Pacific Glacier and the smaller Margerie Glacier, which calve off icebergs into the bay. Johns Hopkins and Gilman Glaciers produce submarine calving, where ice breaks off underwater to explode to the surface.

RECREATION

HIKING

Glacier Bay has only 10 miles (16 km) of designated hiking trails, including an easy forested shoreline stroll on the **Tlingit Trail** (0.5 mi/0.8 km rt, 20 min) to the Huna Tribal House. A 0.25-mile (0.4-km, 15 min) trail goes along the beach to the Bartlett Cove Campground.

The **Forest Trail** (1 mi/1.6 km rt, 30 min) is a wheelchair-accessible boardwalk trail that leads to two viewing decks overlooking a pond. Past the pond, a dirt trail continues to the campground and the beach before looping back to the starting point. Park rangers lead daily hikes on this trail.

Bartlett River Trail (4 mi/6.4 km rt, 4 hrs) explores an intertidal lagoon, forest, and river estuary. The **Bartlett Lake Trail** (9.6 mi/15.4 km rt, 7-8 hrs) climbs over moraine and through spruce forests en route to Bartlett Lake.

BOATING

Glacier Bay has 700 miles (1,130 km) of shoreline for boaters to explore. June through August, private boat owners must secure a free permit (www.nps.gov/glba) to enter the waters of **Glacier Bay** and **Bartlett Cove.** Permits are good for up to seven days; apply within 60 days of your planned arrival date. Don't dillydally, though—permits often run out quickly from mid-June to early August. Only 25 motorized boats are allowed per day in Glacier Bay. The public dock at Bartlett Cove has boat services.

SEA LIONS

FISHING

The waters of Glacier Bay and Icy Straits are enormously productive—this is one of the best places in the world for fishing—and the isolated location means you won't have to battle crowds. Book an all-inclusive multiday fishing trip with **Glacier Bay Sportfishing** (907/697-3038, www.glacierbay-sportfishing.com, lodgings at the Annie Mae Lodge) or opt for a half-day to five-day trip with **Taylor Charters** (801/647-3401, www.taylorcharters-fishing.com). Glacier Bay Lodge rents fishing gear and sells licenses.

WHERE TO STAY

INSIDE THE PARK

The only accommodations inside the park are at **Glacier Bay Lodge** (179 Bartlett Cove, 888/229-8687, www.visitglacierbay.com, mid-May-early Sept., from $250). The facility has 48 small, rustic guest rooms with private baths. The lodge restaurant serves breakfast, lunch, and dinner; entrées specialize in Alaskan seafood. Bicycle rentals, fishing gear rentals, fishing licenses, and a laundry are available.

Bartlett Cove Campground (free, permit required, May-Sept.) offers serene tent camping with fantastic views over the water. It's a 0.25-mile (0.4-km) walk to the 33-site campground; facilities include bear-resistant food caches, outhouses, and a warming shelter. Register at the Visitor Information Station near the private docks, follow an orientation, and then pick up your free camping permit. Campers can shower at Glacier Bay Lodge.

OUTSIDE THE PARK

Accommodations and dining options can be found in the picturesque community of **Gustavus,** 8 miles (13 km) from the park entrance.

GETTING THERE

AIR

Alaska Airlines (800/252-7522, www.alaskaair.com, June-Aug.) offers a seasonal 40-minute flight from Juneau to Gustavus. From the airport in Gustavus, it's about 8 miles (13 km) to the entrance of Glacier Bay National Park.

▼ SUNRISE ON THE FAIRWEATHER RANGE

CRUISE SHIP APPROACHING MARGERIE GLACIER

Small planes, including seaplanes, hop between towns in southeast Alaska. They provide transportation plus flightseeing trips. **Alaska Seaplanes** (907/789-3331, www.flyalaskaseaplanes.com) is based in Gustavus and Juneau. **Admiralty Air Service** (907/321-3703, www.admiraltyairservice.com) and **Ward Air** (907/789-9150, http://wardair.com) are based in Juneau.

BOAT

Cruise ships enter the bay but don't dock. The **Alaska Marine Highway System Ferry** (800/642-0066, www.dot.state.ak.us/amhs) has 4-5 sailings per month June-September between Juneau and Gustavus, an approximately five-hour trip.

GETTING AROUND

Glacier Bay Lodge and most lodges in Gustavus provide shuttles from the airport or ferry terminal to the hotel. Taxis link the communities of Gustavus and Bartlett Cove; call **TLC Taxi** (907/697-2239, www.gustavusak.com/tlc-taxi) for service. The only road is the 10-mile (16-km) link between Gustavus and Bartlett Cove, but if you need to rent a car, contact **Bud's Rent-a-Car** (907/697-2403).

GLACIER BAY NATIONAL PRESERVE

Glacier Bay is a remote and special place—so much so that UNESCO recognized it as a World Heritage Site and a Biosphere Reserve. That designation is thanks in part to **Glacier Bay National Preserve,** a small portion of the park tucked in the northeast corner. Bounded by the Gulf of Alaska and the Alsek River, this unique area is rich in wildlife. Recreation includes fishing, hunting, river rafting, and 60 miles (97 km) of designated ATV trails.

To reach the remote preserve requires chartering an air taxi from Yakutat to one of two airstrips on the preserve. Visitors can camp in the wilderness (free) or reserve a small cabin rented out by the Yakutat Ranger Station (907/784-3295, $25). Three small lodges operate concessions.

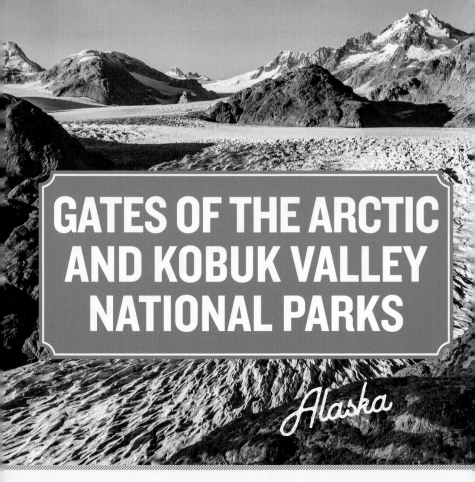

GATES OF THE ARCTIC AND KOBUK VALLEY NATIONAL PARKS

Alaska

GATES OF THE ARCTIC

WEBSITE:
www.nps.gov/gaar

PHONE NUMBER:
907/459-3730

VISITATION RANK:
63

WHY GO:
Visit a remote,
raw wilderness.

KOBUK VALLEY

WEBSITE:
www.nps.gov/kova

PHONE NUMBER:
907/442-3890

VISITATION RANK:
61

WHY GO:
See sand dunes and
migrating caribou.

KEEPSAKE STAMPS ▼▼▼

▲ WESTERN BROOKS RANGE

Two remote national parks claim places above Alaska's Arctic Circle. These roadless wildernesses see very few visitors. Most of the human footprints belong to the Inupiat people who still hunt caribou here as their ancestors did. The larger **GATES OF THE ARCTIC NATIONAL PARK AND PRESERVE** contains the wild Brooks Range, spilling with glaciers, huge rivers, tundra, and boreal forests.

The smaller **KOBUK VALLEY NATIONAL PARK** gains its fame from sand dunes made from ice age glaciers. Both have immense herds of caribou plus tundra swans, musk ox, moose, wolves, and grizzly bears. The weather and the animals still rule here; we are simply transient visitors.

PLANNING YOUR TIME

These wilderness parks are devoid of trails, roads, campgrounds, lodgings, visitors centers, and services. There are no entrance fees—or even entrances. All access is on foot or by bush plane. It's this very wildness that is the draw.

Winters are unforgivingly harsh and long. The best months to travel are **June-August.** Even during summer's short mild weather, temperatures can drop well below freezing. Expect high winds, mosquitoes, and changeable weather.

Fairbanks is the jumping-off point for driving the Dalton Highway (AK 11), a rough dirt-road trek to the small service towns east of Gates of the Arctic. Fly-in guided trips depart from Anchorage, Fairbanks, Kotzebue, or Bettles. For visitors aiming to check off all U.S. national parks, the right outfitter can get

NOATAK RIVER

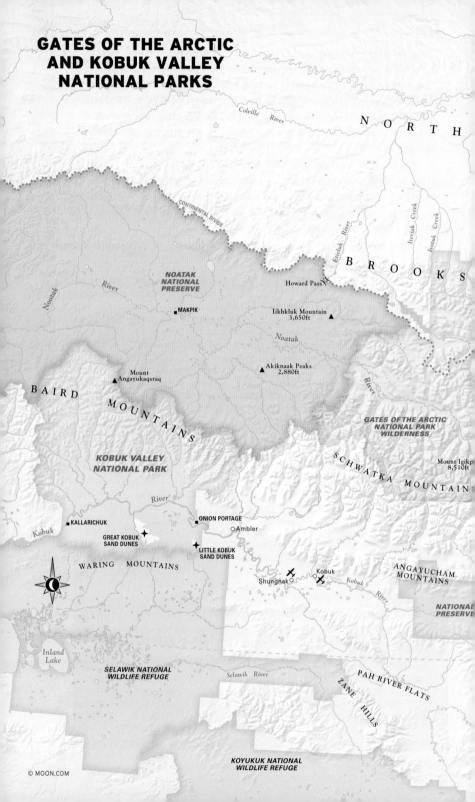

GATES OF THE ARCTIC AND KOBUK VALLEY NATIONAL PARKS

N O R T H

Colville River

CONTINENTAL DIVIDE

B R O O K S

Etivluk River

Ieriak Creek

Ivotak Creek

NOATAK NATIONAL PRESERVE

Noatak River

Howard Pass

■ MAKPIK

Iikhkluk Mountain
3,650ft ▲

Noatak

▲ Mount
Angayukaqsraq

Akiknaak Peaks
2,880ft ▲

River

B A I R D

M O U N T A I N S

GATES OF THE ARCTIC
NATIONAL PARK
WILDERNESS

S C H W A T K A   M O U N T A I N S

KOBUK VALLEY
NATIONAL PARK

Mount Igikp
8,510ft ▲

River

■ KALLARICHUK

Kobuk

■ ONION PORTAGE

○ Ambler

GREAT KOBUK
SAND DUNES

✦ LITTLE KOBUK
SAND DUNES

ANGAYUCHAM
MOUNTAINS

WARING   MOUNTAINS

Shungnak ○

Kobuk

Kobuk River

NATIONAL
PRESERVE

Inland
Lake

SELAWIK NATIONAL
WILDLIFE REFUGE

Selawik River

PAH RIVER FLATS

Z A N E   H I L L S

KOYUKUK NATIONAL
WILDLIFE REFUGE

© MOON.COM

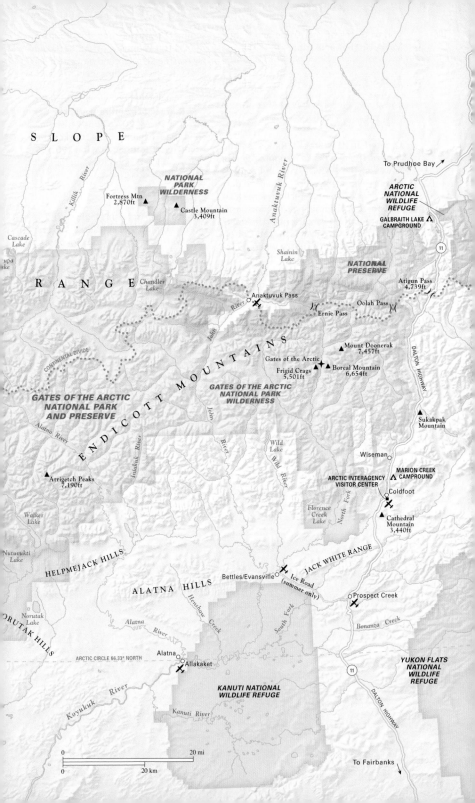

you to Gates of the Arctic and Kobuk Valley on the same trip.

GATES OF THE ARCTIC NATIONAL PARK AND PRESERVE

Located in the Brooks Range at the foot of the needlelike Arrigetch Peaks, Gates of the Arctic National Park and Preserve is a vast untouched wilderness that spans 8.4 million acres (3.4 million ha). Containing the northernmost mountain range in North America, it stretches west from the Dalton Highway through country where wildlife far outnumbers humans. Dense vegetation, marshes, frequent water crossings, glacial lakes, and soaring granite peaks make travel very challenging but beautifully remote.

PLANNING YOUR TIME

The closest "town" is the tiny hub of Bettles (population 10), accessible only by air or snow machine on the winter ice road.

Outside the park are three visitors centers. The **Arctic Interagency Visitor Center** (mile 175, Dalton Hwy., Coldfoot, 907/658-5209, hours vary daily summer) updates road conditions on the Dalton Highway, offers backcountry trip registration, and rents bear canisters. It also has films, exhibits, and a bookstore with maps.

Reachable only by air, the small **Bettles Ranger Station and Visitor Center** (in Bettles, 907/692-5494, summer only) has exhibits. The backcountry **Anaktuvuk Ranger Station** (907/661-3520, summer only) has an outdoor information kiosk.

RECREATION

Gates of the Arctic has flightseeing, remote camping, backpacking, packrafting, river float trips, paddling, photography, fishing, and hunting; hire a guide for all activities. In addition to guides licensed for both parks, two companies provide guide services from Anchorage into Gates of the Arctic:

Alaska Alpine Adventures (877/525-2577 or 907/351-4193, www.alaskaalpineadventures.com) guides hiking, backpacking, and rafting trips.

Expeditions Alaska (770/952-4549, www.expeditionsalaska.com) owner Carl Donohue guides photography, backpacking, and packrafting trips.

▼ ARCTIC DIVIDE NEAR ANAKTUVUK PASS

GATES OF THE ARCTIC NATIONAL PARK AND PRESERVE

WHERE TO STAY

Outside the park, **Bettles Lodge** (Bettles, 907/692-5111, http://bettleslodge.com, year-round) has guest rooms, dining, flightseeing, guided backpacking and fishing, aurora viewing, and dogsledding.

On the Dalton Highway, small communities such as **Coldfoot** also have a few lodging and outfitter options.

GUIDE SERVICES

For most visitors, access is by bush plane. Professional guide services offer a safe (although pricey) way to experience the wonder of these Arctic parks.

Bettles Lodge (907/692-5111, http://bettleslodge.com) books flightseeing in both parks.

From Bettles airstrip, **Brooks Range Aviation** (800/692-5443 or 907/692-5444, http://brooksrange.com) offers flightseeing in both parks and guides backpacking, river floating, remote camping, hunting, and fishing trips.

From Fairbanks, **Arctic Wild** (907/479-8203, www.arcticwild.com) guides backpacking, packrafting, hiking, and remote camping in Gates of the Arctic.

Campgrounds are at Galbraith Lake and Marion Creek.

GETTING THERE

From Fairbanks or Anchorage, **Ravn Alaska** (907/266-8394, www.ravnalaska.com) flies air taxis via Kotzebue to Bettles or Anaktuvuk Pass. **Wright's Air Service** (907/474-0502, www.wrightairservice.com) flies from Fairbanks to Bettles and Coldfoot.

KOBUK VALLEY NATIONAL PARK

The 1.75-million-acre (708,000-ha) Kobuk Valley National Park gains its fame from its 30 square miles (78 sq km) of massive **sand dunes** made by glaciers that ground their way through the land. Some dunes tower 100 feet (30 m) high. More than a half-million caribou migrate through the dunes, many crossing the Kobuk River at Onion Portage, where Indigenous people still gather to harvest the animals much as their ancestors did 8,000 years ago.

PLANNING YOUR TIME

Kotzebue is the gateway for visiting Kobuk Valley. The multiagency **Northwest Arctic Heritage Center** (171 3rd Ave., 907/442-3890, 9am-6:30pm Mon.-Fri., 10am-6:30pm Sat. June-Aug.) serves as the visitors center, nature center, and museum, plus headquarters for the park. Educational programs include classes in traditional native crafts. Spend an hour taking in the exhibits to learn about the parks.

RECREATION

Kobuk Valley has the largest active dunes in the North American Arctic. These wind-shaped relics show how the grinding power of ancient glaciers continues to change, even as grasses gain footholds in the sand. **Flightseeing** is the easiest way to see the dunes—on a flyover or landing to walk the sand.

CAMPING IN KOBUK VALLEY

GREAT KOBUK SAND DUNES

To see the **Onion Portage caribou migration,** plan a trip around Labor Day to the Kobuk River. Charter a bush plane to get there, set up camp, and climb a hill to watch the show.

From Kotzebue, fly with **Arctic Backcountry Flying Service** (907/442-3200, www.arcticbackcountry.com) for flightseeing or guided fishing, backpacking, and float trips.

WHERE TO STAY

Outside the park, Kotzebue houses the modern European-inspired **Nullaġvik Hotel** (306 Shore Ave., 907/442-3331, www.nullagvikhotel.com, from $279), whose name means "a place to sleep" in Inupiaq. Guest rooms have private baths and touches of Alaska Native art. One of the upper floors has an observation room overlooking Kotzebue Sound.

GETTING THERE

To reach Kobuk Valley, book a flight from Anchorage or Fairbanks to Kotzebue (there is no road access). From Kotzebue, charter a flight into the park. In summer, **Alaska Airlines** (800/252-7522, www.alaskaair.com) has daily flights from Anchorage. From Fairbanks or Anchorage, **Ravn Alaska** (907/266-8394, www.ravnalaska.com) flies to Kotzebue and then connects with Bettles. From Bettles, charter flights into Kobuk Valley are available from Ravn or **Bering Air** (800/478-3943 or 907/442-3943, www.beringair.com).

ARCTIC NATIONAL WILDLIFE REFUGE

Established in 1960, the **Arctic National Wildlife Refuge** (ANWR, U.S. Fish and Wildlife Service, Fairbanks, 800/362-4546 or 907/456-0250, www.fws.gov/refuge/arctic) includes 19.64 million acres (7.9 million ha) of land and water, more than 200,000 caribou, an unthinkable horde of mosquitoes, and one human settlement—the Inupiat village of **Kaktovik** (population 178).

Bordered by Canada to the east, the Arctic Ocean to the north, and the Dalton Highway to the west, ANWR is so large that it spans varied ecological regions: boreal forest, alpine, coastal plain tundra, and coastal marine. It is home to grizzly bears, polar bears, musk oxen, and the highest concentration of nesting golden eagles in Alaska.

Only 1,500 people visit the refuge annually. ANWR remains a vast, largely trackless wilderness, an undisturbed spectrum of Arctic ecosystems that most human beings will never see in their lifetime.

CALIFORNIA

From redwood forests to snowcapped mountains, the California landscape is filled with overwhelming natural beauty and wide-open wilderness. The national parks here excel in superlatives: the tallest mountain in the continental United States, the lowest point in North America, and one of the highest waterfalls in North America. They are a testament to powerful earth-shaping forces that left their diverse handiwork across the region.

In Yosemite, waterfalls feather down faces of granite. Groves of giant sequoias tower above the trails in Sequoia and Kings Canyon. Along the Pacific coast, lush forests fill with coastal sequoias and islands harbor endemic marinelife. In between, active volcanoes, bone-dry deserts, and craggy alpine peaks beg for exploration.

◄ YOSEMITE NATIONAL PARK

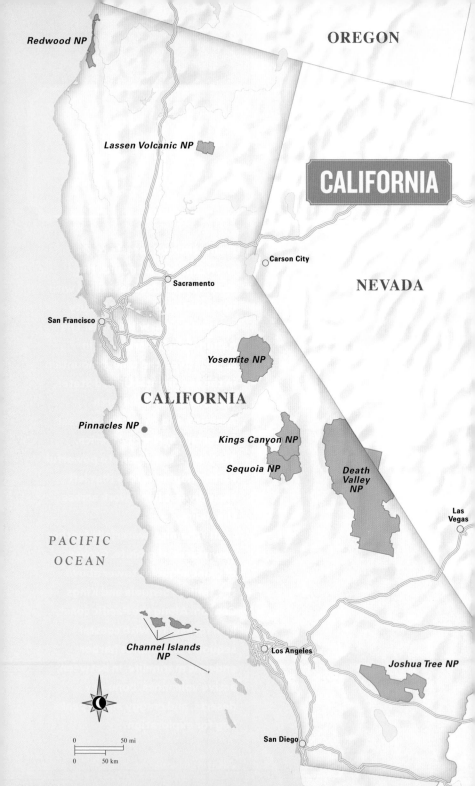

OREGON

Redwood NP

Lassen Volcanic NP

CALIFORNIA

Carson City

NEVADA

Sacramento

San Francisco

Yosemite NP

CALIFORNIA

Pinnacles NP

Kings Canyon NP

Sequoia NP

Death Valley NP

Las Vegas

PACIFIC OCEAN

Channel Islands NP

Los Angeles

Joshua Tree NP

San Diego

0   50 mi

0   50 km

© MOON.COM

The National Parks of
CALIFORNIA

YOSEMITE

Granite monoliths and plunging waterfalls are the hallmarks of this Sierra park that lures hikers, backpackers, and big-wall climbers (page 117).

SEQUOIA AND KINGS CANYON

These joined parks boast giant sequoia groves, numerous hiking trails, and smaller crowds than their more famous neighbor (page 140).

DEATH VALLEY

Sculpted sand dunes, crusted salt flats, and rugged canyons pervade this park, which has both the western hemisphere's lowest and hottest spots (page 153).

JOSHUA TREE

The park's namesake trees and surreal appeal draw wildflower hounds, serious hikers, and hard-core rock climbers (page 164).

LASSEN VOLCANIC

Geologic wonders include boiling mud pots, fumaroles, and a 10,457-foot (3,187-m) volcano (page 178).

REDWOOD NATIONAL AND STATE PARKS

A series of state and national parks line the California coast, filled with groves of primordial giant redwoods (page 187).

PINNACLES

Climbers, hikers, and campers can't get enough of the huge rock formations, deep caves, and vertical topography in this smaller treasure (page 197).

CHANNEL ISLANDS

This series of islands has undeveloped beauty, stellar coastal views, and stunning sea caves for exploring by kayak (page 204).

1: BRIDGE OVER WOODS CREEK, KINGS CANYON
2: CINDER CONE, LASSEN
3: CLIMBING HIGH PEAKS TRAIL IN PINNACLES NATIONAL PARK

Best OF THE PARKS

Yosemite Valley: Go to Yosemite's heart for El Capitan, Half Dome, and Bridalveil Fall (page 121).

General Sherman Tree: Admire the largest tree known on earth (page 144).

Badwater Basin: Drive this scenic road for the best of Death Valley, including North America's lowest elevation (page 157).

Hidden Valley: Scramble on rock formations along trails or challenge yourself with a technical climb (page 169).

Lassen Peak: Take a scenic drive to see the summit of this active volcano (page 182).

GENERAL SHERMAN

PLANNING YOUR TRIP

California's best feature is its all-season appeal. Time your trip for **summer** and **early fall,** when Tioga Pass opens across the Sierra between Yosemite and Death Valley, but that's also the season when the heat spikes in the desert. Be aware that summer brings the most visitors, which will not only add to the crowds but also to the traffic. To avoid the crowds, visit in **spring** when Yosemite's waterfalls are at their peak and fewer people populate the trails. In **winter,** some of Yosemite's roads are closed, including CA 120 and the Tioga Pass. Snow can blanket the California mountains anytime between November and April.

The easiest places to fly into are **San Francisco** and **Los Angeles.** Book **hotels** and **rental cars** in advance for the best rates and availability, especially in the high season of summer. Reservations are essential for **lodges** and **campgrounds.**

1: GENERAL SHERMAN TREE, SEQUOIA
2: LASSEN PEAK

Road Trip

YOSEMITE, DEATH VALLEY, AND SEQUOIA & KINGS CANYON

Start your trip in the Bay Area, where you can fly into **San Francisco International Airport and rent a car. Oakland International Airport** may be a cheaper alternative. This route is best traveled **June through October** when Yosemite's Tioga Road (CA 120) is open; however, temperatures at Death Valley climb to sizzling at that time of year. If Tioga Road is closed (usually Nov.-May), drop south from Yosemite along the west side of the Sierra to visit Sequoia and Kings Canyon first before traveling south and east to experience Death Valley.

BRIDALVEIL FALL, YOSEMITE

Yosemite

170 miles (275 km) / 4 hours

Leave San Francisco at 8am to reach Yosemite by noon. The drive to the **Big Oak Flat Entrance** takes at least four hours; however, traffic, especially in summer and on weekends, can make it much longer. From San Francisco International Airport, take US 101 south followed by CA 92 east. Merge onto I-880 north, then I-238 east. Continue on to

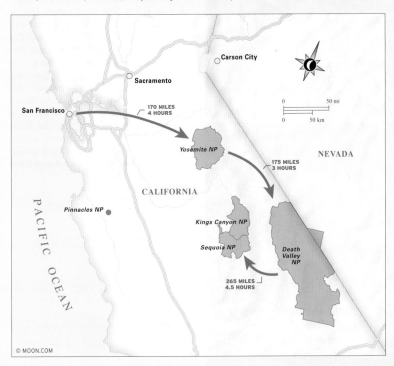

© MOON.COM

I-580 east, then I-205 east followed by I-5 north. Then, take CA 120 east, CA 99 north, and CA 120 east.

Spend a day touring **Yosemite Valley,** seeing **Half Dome, El Capitan,** and **Yosemite Falls,** and then hike the **Mist Trail** to Vernal Fall. Spend a night under the stars at one of the park's campgrounds or indoors at **The Ahwahnee Hotel** (make reservations well in advance). In summer, go higher on the scenic Tioga Road and plan a hike at **Tuolumne Meadows** before overnighting there at the lodge or campground. Exit the park over Tioga Pass.

Death Valley

175 miles (280 km) / 3 hours
Cross Yosemite's **Tioga Pass** heading east on CA 120, then onto US 395 south. Just south of **Lone Pine,** veer southeast on US 136, which joins US 190 to enter Death Valley National Park. Cruise through **Panamint Springs.** An hour east is the aptly named park hub of **Furnace Creek,** a perfect base for touring **Badwater Road** and **Zabriskie Point.**

Sequoia and Kings Canyon

265 miles (425 km) / 4.5 hours
Cross Death Valley on US 190 west and drive US 395 south, then CA 14 south, and CA 58 west to Bakersfield. From there, take CA 99 north and CA 65 north to the **Ash Mountain Entrance** of **Sequoia National Park.** Enjoy the scenic drive north on Generals Highway, stopping at **Moro Rock,** the **General Sherman Tree,** and the **Giant Forest Museum** (pick up tickets for **Crystal Cave**). Bed down at the **John Muir Lodge** in Kings Canyon, where you're primed for visits to **Grant Grove** and the winding drive down **Kings Canyon Scenic Byway.**

1: ZABRISKIE POINT, DEATH VALLEY
2: MORO ROCK, SEQUOIA
3: REDWOOD CREEK AT KINGS CANYON SCENIC BYWAY

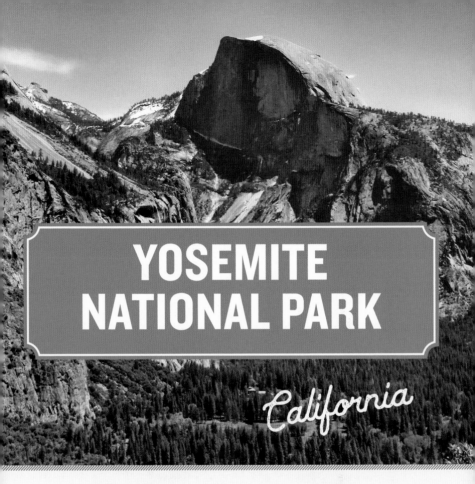

YOSEMITE
NATIONAL PARK

California

KEEPSAKE STAMPS ▼▼▼

WEBSITE:
www.nps.gov/yose

PHONE NUMBER:
209/372-0200

VISITATION RANK:
8

WHY GO:
Admire waterfalls
and granite
cathedrals.

▲ HALF DOME OVER YOSEMITE VALLEY

YOSEMITE
NATIONAL PARK

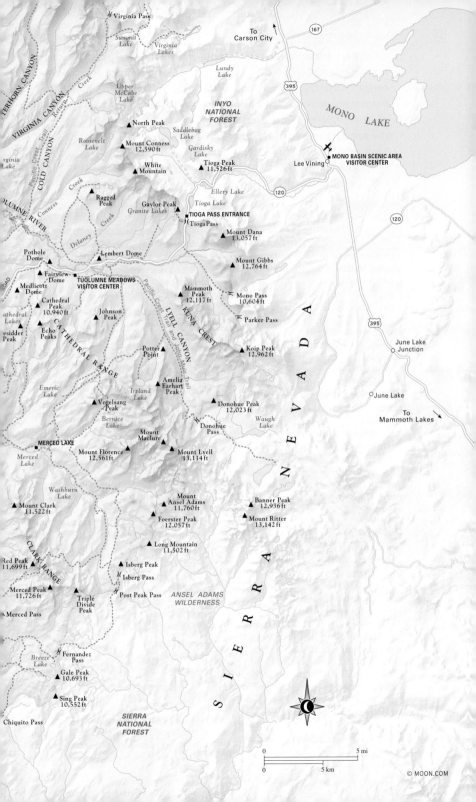

Of all the natural wonders California has to offer, few are more iconic than this national park nestled in the Sierra Nevada and the historic lands of the Miwok people. **YOSEMITE NATIONAL PARK** is a natural playground that has been immortalized in the photographs of Ansel Adams. Naturalist John Muir called it "the grandest of all the special temples of Nature I was ever permitted to enter." It was Muir who lobbied for national park designation in 1890 and then introduced its wonders to President Theodore Roosevelt in 1903. If this is your first visit, prepare to be awed.

PLANNING YOUR TIME

The first place most people go is **Yosemite Valley** (CA 140, Arch Rock Entrance), the most crowded region in the park, filled with sights, hikes, and services. Plan at least 2-3 days just in Yosemite Valley, with an excursion to Glacier Point. With a week or more, add on Tuolumne Meadows (summer only) or Wawona.

You will need to make **advance reservations:** 12 months for lodges and 5.5 months for campgrounds. Last-minute options are Curry Village tent cabins or first-come, first-served campgrounds. You may also need to get advance **permits** for some activities: rock climbing, hiking Half Dome, and backpacking. To visit Yosemite Valley May-September, you may need an **entrance reservation** (good for 3 days, www.recreation.gov, $2). Check online well ahead of your visit to confirm.

Summer is high season, when traffic jams and parking problems plague the park. Plan to arrive before or after peak traffic congestion (11am-2pm and 4pm-7pm), park in the Yosemite Village day-use lot, and use the **park shuttle** (7am-10pm daily year-round, free) or bicycle to get around. Tuolumne Meadows and the Eastern Sierra are less congested, making them good summer options. **Spring** is best for waterfalls and wildflowers, and crowds thin slightly, as in **fall.** In **winter,** roads close and crowds are minimal. Chains may be required on any park road at any time.

ENTRANCES AND FEES

The entrance fee is $35 per vehicle ($30 motorcycle, $20 individual) and is valid for seven days. You can **buy your pass online** (www.recreation.gov) from home to speed through entrance stations faster. There are **five park entrances**:

Arch Rock (CA 140): The main entrance accesses Yosemite Valley from the west (San Francisco, Sacramento). Once inside the park, CA 140 becomes El Portal Road. Long lines with two-hour waits form at this busy entrance station May-October; plan to arrive before 9am or after 5pm.

Big Oak Flat (CA 120): This entrance accesses Yosemite Valley and Tuolumne Meadows (summer only) from the north (San Francisco, Sacramento). Inside the park, CA 120 becomes Big Oak Flat Road.

South (CA 41): This entrance goes to Wawona from the south (Fresno, Los Angeles). Inside the park, CA 41 becomes Wawona Road, which eventually reaches Yosemite Valley.

Tioga Pass (CA 120): This High Sierra route is on the east side of Yosemite, 12 miles (19 km) west of US 395. Tioga Road accesses Tuolumne Meadows and the Eastern Sierra in summer. Tioga Pass is **closed in winter** (usually Oct.-May or early June).

Hetch Hetchy (off CA 120): This is the only access to the Hetch Hetchy Reservoir and region. The entrance and Hetch Hetchy Road are open 7am-9pm year-round.

To visit **Yosemite Valley,** you may need an **entry reservation** (www.recreation.gov, late May-Sept., $2) for day use in addition to park entrance fees. Each reservation is good for one vehicle

Top ❸

① SCALE HALF DOME

One of Yosemite's most recognizable features rises high above the valley floor—**Half Dome.** This granite ridge was polished to its smooth dome-like shape millions of years ago by glaciers. Rock climbers scale its vertical Northwest Face, and hikers summit the dome

HALF DOME

via a cable route first installed in 1919; it's terrifying to some and has been deadly for a few. You can also view the iconic granite dome by taking the shuttle and hiking to **Mirror Lake** to admire the giant from its base. Outstanding road viewpoints include **Stoneman Meadow, Tunnel View** (CA 41), and **Glacier Point.**

The nontechnical climb on **Half Dome** (14-16 mi/23-25 km rt, 10-12 hrs, late May-mid-Oct., shuttle stop 16) requires a monumental day. The route follows the Mist Trail to Nevada Fall and then is signed for Half Dome. Its 4,800-foot (1,463-m) gain and descent are grueling. The final ultra-steep 400-foot (122-m) ascent is via metal hand cables that see a lineup of climbers (use leather gloves on the cables). At the top, an expanse of stone offers a resting spot on which to enjoy the scenery with other climbers.

Do not attempt this trail lightly! It is not for young kids, anyone out of shape, or those unaccustomed to long, strenuous, high-altitude hikes. You must begin *before sunrise* and turn around by 3:30pm. Do not climb the dome when the cables are down, when the trail is closed, or during thunderstorms.

A **permit** (877/444-6777, www.recreation.gov, $10 lottery plus $10 pp) is required. The park distributes permits through an online lottery in March and a second lottery two days in advance.

② TOUR YOSEMITE VALLEY

Yosemite Valley is the most visited spot in the park. It houses the towering granite walls of **El Capitan** and **Half Dome** and the plunging **Bridalveil Fall** and **Yosemite Falls.** Many hikes, including the popular **Mist Trail,** launch from the valley floor. You can check out the visitors center, theater, galleries, museum, hotels, and outdoor historical exhibits. Tour it by car, shuttle, bicycle, or foot, although the last three are best in summer. To visit May-September, you may need an entrance reservation (good for 3 days, www.recreation.gov, $2).

③ VIEW THE VALLEY FROM GLACIER POINT

In 1903, naturalist John Muir brought President Theodore Roosevelt to **Glacier Point,** igniting the president's passion for Yosemite. A **drive** (arriving before 9am to get a parking spot) or **shuttle bus** up Glacier Point Road (16 mi/26 km one-way, June-early Nov., exact open dates vary pending snow) leads to a short, paved, wheelchair-accessible path with epic vistas across Yosemite Valley and the High Sierra. Pose for a photo op in the footsteps of Muir and Roosevelt, then return to the valley floor via the Four-Mile Trail (4.8 mi/7.7 km one-way, 3-4 hrs). Be aware that Glacier Point Road will have construction delays in 2023. When the road is closed or snowbound, you can still hike up and back from the valley floor or cross-country ski (10.5 mi/16.9 km one-way) from Badger Pass Ski Area to Glacier Point and back. Rangers lead interpretive programs at Glacier Point, including star-gazing events.

ONE DAY IN YOSEMITE

With only one day, concentrate on the sights in Yosemite Valley, which is accessible year-round. Enter Yosemite National Park through the **Big Oak Flat** or **Arch Rock Entrances.** Once in Yosemite Valley, hop aboard the **Valley Shuttle** for a scenic exploration of **Bridalveil Fall, El Capitan,** and **Half Dome.** Then, enjoy a leisurely stroll around **Mirror Lake,** scale a waterfall on the **Mist Trail,** or test your powers of endurance on the way to **Upper Yosemite Fall.**

for three days. Check online for current requirements and reservation windows. Day-use reservations are already included with lodging and campground reservations, commercial tours, YARTS buses, and permit holders for Half Dome and backpacking.

VISITORS CENTERS

Valley Visitor Center

The **Valley Visitor Center** (Yosemite Village, 209/372-0299, shuttle stops 5 and 9, 9am-5pm daily year-round) has an interpretive museum in addition to exhibits, information, books, maps, and schedules of ranger-led walks and talks. The complex includes the **Yosemite Museum** (9am-5pm daily, free), the **Ansel Adams Gallery** (9am-6pm daily summer, 10am-5pm daily winter), and public restrooms. Behind the museum is the recreated **Indian Village of the Ahwahnee,** home to structures made by Miwok people.

Behind the visitors center, the **Yosemite Theater** (Northside Dr., 7pm daily Apr.-Oct., adults $10, under age 13 free) presents programs and films, including the **John Muir Performances** starring Lee Stetson, Yosemite's resident actor.

Construction is underway on a new visitors center in Yosemite Village, slated to open in 2023. It will be southwest of the current visitors center and closer to the main parking area, next to the Village Store.

Wawona Visitor Center at Hill's Studio

The **Wawona Visitor Center at Hill's Studio** (Wawona, 209/375-9531, 8:30am-5pm daily May-Oct.) is housed in the former studio and gallery of Thomas Hill, a famous landscape painter from the 1800s. You can see his floor-to-ceiling paintings, gather information, and get wilderness permits.

Tuolumne Meadows Visitor Center

The **Tuolumne Meadows Visitor Center** (Tioga Rd., 209/372-0263, 9am-6pm daily late May-late Sept.) is in a rustic building near the campground and Tuolumne Meadows Store. Ranger talks are held in the parking lot through summer. Pick up permits at the **Tuolumne Meadows Wilderness Center** (8am-5pm daily mid-May-mid-Oct.) along the road to Tuolumne Meadows Lodge (shuttle stop 3).

SIGHTS

YOSEMITE VALLEY

Bridalveil Fall

Bridalveil Fall (0.5 mi/0.8 km rt, 20 min) is a 620-foot (189-m) cascade running year-round. Accompanied by a roar, its mist sprays most powerfully in the spring—expect to get wet. By autumn, the waterfall thins. The trailhead area features boardwalks, interpretive signs, wheelchair accessibility, and viewing areas. The main parking area is at the east end of the Wawona Road, accessible from Southside Drive.

Cook's Meadow

Soak in quintessential Yosemite Valley scenery on wheelchair-accessible and strolling boardwalks. From the trailhead at the visitors center or shuttle stops 5, 6, 9, or 11, **Cook's Meadow Loop** (1 mi/1.6 km rt, 30 min, easy) goes to Sentinel Bridge for Ansel Adams's famous view of Half Dome and gazing up at Upper Yosemite Falls, Royal Arches, and Glacier Point. Trail signs

EL CAPITAN AND BRIDALVEIL FALL

make it easy to navigate and extend into a bigger loop by circling **Sentinel Meadows** (2.25 mi/3.6 km rt, 1 hr). Bicycles, strollers, and leashed pets are also permitted.

Yosemite Falls

Yosemite Falls (shuttle stop 6, Northside Dr.) is actually three separate waterfalls—Upper Fall, Lower Fall, and the middle cascades. This dramatic formation together creates one of the highest waterfalls in the world. The best time to visit is in **spring,** when snowmelt swells the falls and the thundering water throws mist like rain (bring rain gear). Walk to **Lower Yosemite Fall** (1 mi/1.6 km rt, 30 min, easy) to enjoy the wondrous views of both Upper and Lower Yosemite Falls.

El Capitan

The province of world-class climbers, **El Capitan** (Northside Dr., west of El Capitan Bridge) rises as a massive hunk of Cretaceous granite soaring in vertical cliffs nearly 3,600 feet (1,100 m) above the floor of Yosemite Valley. Most big-wall climbers use ropes and technical gear, but Alex Honnold free-soloed the face, the only person to do so. From **El Capitan picnic area** or roadside pull-outs, most visitors prefer to gape with binoculars at climbing teams and the portaledges where they sleep. You can also hear climbers call back and forth.

Be cautious about walking to the base without a helmet as rockfall can be dangerous.

WAWONA

The tiny village of **Wawona,** 4 miles (6.4 km) from the South Entrance, is home to a historical district with a hotel and restaurant, outdoor exhibits, and even a golf course.

UPPER AND LOWER YOSEMITE FALLS

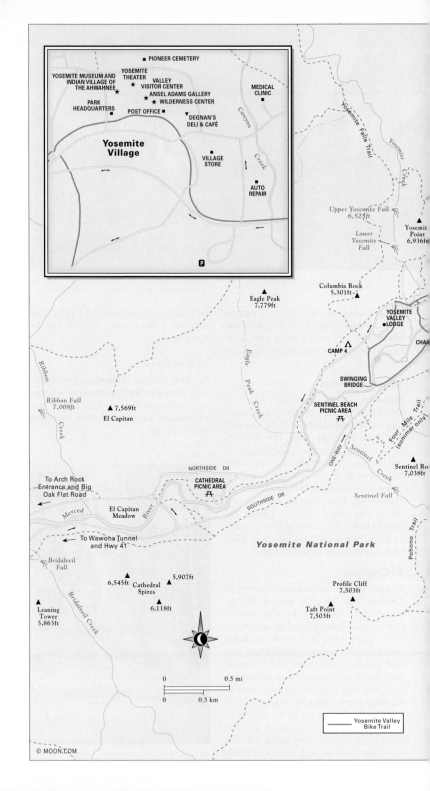

PIONEER CEMETERY

YOSEMITE MUSEUM AND
INDIAN VILLAGE OF
THE AHWAHNEE

YOSEMITE
THEATER

VALLEY
VISITOR CENTER

ANSEL ADAMS GALLERY

WILDERNESS CENTER

MEDICAL
CLINIC

PARK
HEADQUARTERS

POST OFFICE

DEGNAN'S
DELI & CAFÉ

**Yosemite
Village**

VILLAGE
STORE

AUTO
REPAIR

Canyon

Creek

P

Yosemite Falls Trail

Yosemite Creek

Upper Yosemite Fall
6,525ft

Lower
Yosemite
Fall

Yosemite
Point
6,936ft

Columbia Rock
5,301ft

Eagle Peak
7,779ft

Eagle

Peak

Creek

YOSEMITE
VALLEY
●LODGE

CHA

CAMP 4

SWINGING
BRIDGE

SENTINEL BEACH
PICNIC AREA

Four Mile Trail
(summer only)

Ribbon

Ribbon Fall
7,008ft

Creek

▲ 7,569ft
El Capitan

Sentinel

Creek

Sentinel Ro
7,038ft

To Arch Rock
Entrance and Big
Oak Flat Road

NORTHSIDE DR

CATHEDRAL
PICNIC AREA

SOUTHSIDE DR

ONE-WAY

Sentinel Fall

Merced

El Capitan
Meadow

River

To Wawoha Tunnel
and Hwy 41

Yosemite National Park

Pohono Trail

Bridalveil
Fall

Bridalveil Creek

6,545ft Cathedral
Spires

5,907ft

6,118ft

Profile Cliff
7,503ft

Taft Point
7,503ft

Leaning
Tower
5,863ft

0   0.5 mi

0   0.5 km

Yosemite Valley
Bike Trail

© MOON.COM

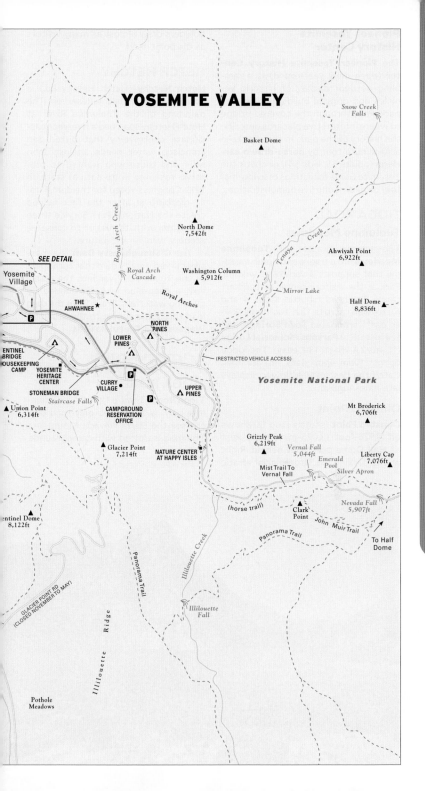

YOSEMITE VALLEY

Snow Creek Falls

Basket Dome ▲

Royal Arch Creek

North Dome ▲
7,542ft

Tenaya Creek

Ahwiyah Point ▲
6,922ft

Royal Arch Cascade

Washington Column ▲
5,912ft

Royal Arches

Mirror Lake

Half Dome ▲
8,836ft

SEE DETAIL

Yosemite Village

THE AHWAHNEE ★

NORTH PINES ⌂

LOWER PINES ⌂

(RESTRICTED VEHICLE ACCESS)

Yosemite National Park

ENTINEL BRIDGE
OUSEKEEPING CAMP

YOSEMITE HERITAGE CENTER

CURRY VILLAGE ●

UPPER PINES ⌂

STONEMAN BRIDGE

Staircase Falls

CAMPGROUND RESERVATION OFFICE

▲ Union Point
6,314ft

Mt Broderick ▲
6,706ft

Glacier Point ▲
7,214ft

NATURE CENTER AT HAPPY ISLES

Grizzly Peak ▲
6,219ft

Vernal Fall
5,044ft

Emerald Pool

Liberty Cap ▲
7,076ft

Mist Trail To Vernal Fall

Silver Apron

entinel Dome ▲
8,122ft

(horse trail)

Clark ▲ Point

Nevada Fall
5,907ft

John Muir Trail

To Half Dome

Panorama Trail

Illilouette Creek

GLACIER POINT RD (CLOSED NOVEMBER TO MAY)

Illilouette Ridge

Panorama Trail

Illilouette Fall

Pothole Meadows

Pioneer Yosemite History Center

The **Pioneer Yosemite History Center** (open daily year-round) is a rambling outdoor display of historic vehicles and original buildings from the park. Pass through the covered bridge to where interpretive placards describe the history of the park. In summer, take a 10-minute tour by **horse-drawn carriage** (adults $5, kids $4), or check the *Yosemite Guide* for listings of living-history programs and live demonstrations.

TIOGA ROAD

Tuolumne Meadows

The waving grasses of **Tuolumne Meadows** are a fragile subalpine meadow that supports a variety of wildlife. Park at the visitors center or Lembert Dome Trailhead (shuttle stops 4 and 6) to walk across the Tuolumne River, past carbonated **Soda Springs,** and see historical **Parsons Memorial Lodge** (1.5 mi/2.4 km rt, 1 hr, easy). The lodge opens 10am-4pm daily in summer. Catch the best of wildflower displays late June-August.

Olmsted Point

Olmsted Point (shuttle stop 12) shows off 9,926-foot (3,025-m) Clouds Rest as Half Dome peeks out behind. Right at the parking lot, large glacial erratic boulders draw almost as many visitors as the point itself.

HETCH HETCHY

Hetch Hetchy (Hetch Hetchy Rd.) is home to Hetch Hetchy Reservoir. The damming of the Tuolumne River at Hetch Hetchy spawned a five-year passionate controversy that pitted San Francisco water needs against John Muir and those who wanted to preserve Yosemite in its natural state. In 1913, Congress voted for the dam. Public disapproval after the fact helped create the National Park Service three years later with its mission to conserve scenery, wildlife, and nature.

The **O'Shaughnessy Dam** is a massive curved gravity dam that turns part of the Tuolumne River into the reservoir, a deep-blue lake surrounded by gushing waterfalls. Trails from the dam lead through a tunnel to the stunning **Wapama** and **Tueeulala Falls.**

SCENIC DRIVE

TIOGA ROAD

Tioga Road (39 mi/63 km, CA 120, summer only) is Yosemite's only road that crosses the Sierra Nevada Mountains. The road is dotted with campgrounds,

▼ HETCH HETCHY RESERVOIR

TUOLUMNE MEADOWS

trailheads, and scenic overlooks as it climbs into the High Sierra, through Tuolumne Meadows, and crosses Tioga Pass to exit the park and drop through the Eastern Sierra. Along the way, stop to take in the vista at **Olmsted Point,** stroll along the sandy beach at **Tenaya Lake,** and scramble atop **Pothole Dome.**

Anchoring the drive is **Tuolumne Meadows,** a subalpine meadow with fragile summer wildflowers and wildlife, including bears. Across the road is the Tuolumne Meadows Visitor Center, a large campground, a camp store and grill, and a wilderness center.

From the west, CA 120 becomes Big Oak Flat Road at the Big Oak Flat park entrance. In 9 miles (14.4 km), at the left fork to Crane Flat junction, it becomes Tioga Road. The Tuolumne Meadows Visitor Center is 39 miles (63 km) farther east. To get to Tioga Road from Yosemite Valley, take Northside Road to Big Oak Flat Road. At the Tioga Road junction, turn east.

HIKING

YOSEMITE VALLEY

Upper Yosemite Fall

One of the most strenuous, yet most rewarding, treks is **Upper Yosemite Fall** (7.2 mi/11.6 km rt, 6-8 hrs, strenuous, shuttle stop 7). From the trailhead at Camp 4, the climb steepens right away—2,700 vertical feet (823 m) in just three miles. For a shorter climb with plenty of switchbacks, you'll reach **Columbia Rock** (2 mi/3.2 km rt, 1,000 vertical ft/305 m, 2-3 hrs), with plummeting views of the valley below. Continuing farther up about 0.75 mile, you can grab a good view of Upper Yosemite Fall after two downhill switchbacks lead to a traverse along a sparsely treed ledge that heads toward the fall's base. Turning north and climbing back into the forest, the wet, slippery trail assumes a stack of relentless stone-step switchbacks with occasional railings to reach the lip of the fall. Bring plenty of

HIKING IN YOSEMITE'S HIGH SIERRA

Best Hike

MIST TRAIL

DISTANCE: 2.4-5.4 miles (3.9-8.7 km) round-trip
DURATION: 3-6 hours
ELEVATION CHANGE: 1,050-2,000 feet (320-610 m)
EFFORT: moderate
TRAILHEAD: Happy Isles

From the Happy Isles Nature Center (shuttle stop 16), the moderately strenuous **Mist Trail** climbs over steep, slick granite—including more than 600 stairs, most of which are wet with mist—to the top of **Vernal Fall** (2.4 mi/3.9 km rt, 3 hrs). In spring and June, bring rain jackets and pants to avoid getting drenched. From lip of the fall, views take in the valley below, where mist can create a rainbow. Climb another 2 miles (3.2 km) of switchbacks to the top of **Nevada Fall** (5.4 mi/8.7 km rt, 5-6 hrs) and return via the **John Muir Trail.** The trail is **closed in winter** due to ice and snow and can be dangerous when the river peaks in spring. Park in the Curry Village day-use parking lot to board the free Yosemite Valley shuttle bus to Happy Isles. Expect crowds.

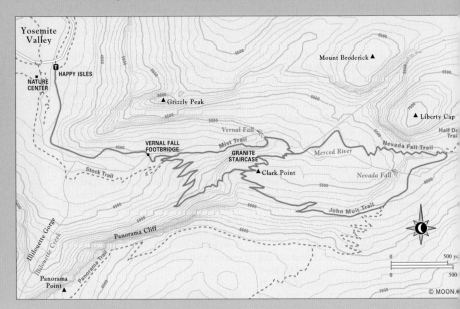

water and snacks to replenish energy for the potentially tricky climb down.

Mirror Lake

Best in spring and summer when water fills the shallow seasonal lake, **Mirror Lake Loop** (shuttle stop 17, end of Southside Dr., no vehicles) offers a stunningly clear reflection of Tenaya Canyon and Half Dome. A short, gentle **hiking path** (5 mi/8 km rt, 2.5 hrs, easy-moderate) circles around the valley, crossing Tenaya Creek on a footbridge at the northeast end. Use caution on snow or ice in winter.

GLACIER POINT

The road to Glacier Point opens late May-November, depending on snow. For one-way hikes from Glacier Point to the valley floor, make shuttle reservations with **Glacier Point Tour** (888/413-8869, www.travelyosemite.com). Strong hikers can climb from the valley floor to Glacier Point and back down.

VERNAL FALL, MIST TRAIL

MIRROR LAKE

Sentinel Dome and Taft Point

A choice of two spectacular viewpoints 2,000 feet (610 m) above the valley floor await from the trailhead 1 mile (1.6 km) west of Glacier Point. At the junction shortly after starting, turn right through the forest to **Sentinel Dome** (2.2 mi/3.5 km rt, 2-3 hrs, moderate). Below the dome, a spur trail departs left for a steep but quick climb to the top. To reach **Taft Point** (2 mi/3.2 km rt, 1 hr, moderate), go left at the first junction to pop over a small hill and descend to the point. You'll see unusual rock formations en route and fissures at the

point, and stare straight across at El Capitan.

Panorama Trail

The **Panorama Trail** (8.5 mi/13.6 km one-way, 6-8 hrs, strenuous) runs from the Glacier Point Trailhead to Yosemite Valley, with a 700-foot (213-m) ascent and a 3,200-foot (975-m) descent. The trail passes Illilouette Fall and Panorama Point, with views of Half Dome, Upper and Lower Yosemite Falls, and a sweeping vista of Yosemite Valley. The route finishes on the Mist Trail, picking up at Nevada and Vernal Falls.

Four-Mile Trail

The **Four-Mile Trail** (4.8 mi/7.7 km one-way, 3-4 hrs, strenuous) connects the valley with Glacier Point. The climb down affords views of Yosemite Falls and the valley that grow more impressive with each switchback.

WAWONA

Mariposa Grove of Giant Sequoias

From the Mariposa Grove parking area near the South Entrance, hop the free wheelchair-accessible shuttle bus (8am-8pm daily mid-Mar.-Nov., shorter hours spring and late fall, depending on

▼ FALLEN MONARCH IN MARIPOSA GROVE

TENAYA LAKE

weather) to reach the trailhead for this famous grove of giant sequoias. Parking usually fills by midmorning, but cars are allowed in as spaces free up. Bicyclists can ride and drivers with disability placards can drive up to the grove trailhead where **Big Trees Loop** (0.3 mi/0.5 km rt, 45 min, easy) is wheelchair accessible. **Grizzly Giant Loop** (2 mi/3.2 km rt, 1.5 hrs, moderate) climbs to the famous California Tunnel Tree and 3,000-year-old Grizzly Giant. The **Guardians Loop** (6.5 mi/10.5 km rt, 4-6 hrs, strenuous) takes in parts of the lower loops and climbs farther to Telescope Tree and Wawona Tunnel Tree. You may see some of the 15 sequoias that were toppled in 2021 during high winds; one was more than 1,000 years old.

TUOLUMNE MEADOWS AND TIOGA PASS

When Tioga Road opens (late May-June, depending on snow), the **Tuolumne Meadows Hikers Bus** (mid-June-mid-Sept., $2-23) offers car-free access to some trailheads.

Tenaya Lake

You can see the water from Tioga Road, but the loop trail around **Tenaya Lake** (2.5 mi/4 km rt, 1.5 hrs, easy, shuttle stop 9) takes you to sunny beaches on the east end and possibly the most picturesque views in all of Yosemite. The only difficult part is fording the chilly and sometimes deep outlet stream at the west end of the lake.

May Lake and Mount Hoffman

May Lake (2.5 mi/4 km rt, 1 hr, moderate, shuttle stop 11) sits peacefully at the base of the sloping granite of Mount Hoffman. The trail up to the lake gains a steady and steep 500 feet (153 m). For energetic hikers, a more difficult trail grunts 2,000 feet (610 m) higher to the top of **Mount Hoffman** (6 mi/9.7 km rt, 3-4 hrs, strenuous). Much of this walk is along granite slabs and rocky paths, but you'll have clear views of Cathedral Peak, Mount Clark, Half Dome, and Clouds Rest.

North Dome

For an unusual look at a Yosemite classic, take the **North Dome Trail** (8.8 mi/14.2 km rt, 4-5 hrs, strenuous) from the trailhead at Porcupine Creek through the woods and out to the dome. Getting to stare right at the face of Half Dome and Clouds Rest at what feels like eye level makes the effort worth it.

CLIMBING EL CAPITAN

Clouds Rest

Strong hikers often prefer **Clouds Rest** (14.5 mi/23 km rt, 7 hrs, strenuous, shuttle stop 10) to Half Dome due to fewer people, no permits, less elevation gain, and a higher summit. The 1,775 vertical feet (540 m) packs into switchbacks about 30 minutes into the hike. At Clouds Rest, stupendous 360-degree views take in the plunge to Yosemite Valley surrounded by North Dome, Sentinel Dome, and Half Dome. You can focus your binoculars on climbers on the cables.

Cathedral Lakes

The trail to **Cathedral Lakes** (7 mi/11.3 km rt, 4-6 hrs, strenuous, shuttle stop 7) climbs more than 800 feet (244 m) to picture-perfect lakes that show off crystalline waters, surrounding lodgepole pines, and dramatic alpine peaks. You'll encounter backpackers, as the route is part of the John Muir Trail. These high-elevation lakes may test your lung capacity but will reward with Instagram-perfect scenery.

Gaylor Lakes

From the Tioga Pass Entrance, the less crowded **Gaylor Lakes Trail** (3 mi/4.8 km rt, 2 hrs, easy) starts at a thin-air 10,000 feet (3,048 m) and climbs a steep 600 vertical feet (180 m) up the pass to the Gaylor Lakes valley. Once in the valley, you can wander around five lovely lakes, stopping to admire the mountain views or visit the abandoned 1870s mine site above Upper Gaylor Lake.

HETCH HETCHY

Wapama and Tueeulala Falls

Begin the hike to thundering **Wapama Falls** (5 mi/8 km rt, 2 hrs, moderate) by crossing O'Shaughnessy Dam, then following the Wapama Falls Trail through a tunnel and along the shore of the reservoir. Along the way, the ribbon **Tueeulala Falls** plunges from cliffs above.

RECREATION

BACKPACKING

Yosemite has bucket-list backpacking routes, including the north end of the 210-mile (340-km) **John Muir Trail** and 70 miles (113 km) of the **Pacific Crest Trail.** Before venturing out, you'll need a park-approved bear canister (rentals at all permit centers, $5/week plus $95 deposit) and a **wilderness permit** ($10 plus $5 pp). Reserve permits through the weekly **permit lottery** (www.recreation.gov, mid-Nov.-mid-May) 24 weeks in advance. After the lottery is completed, the remaining permits are released online about 22 weeks in advance. **First-come, first-served permits** (year-round) are available in person at 11am one day in advance at permit centers; arrive early May-October to get in line. Backpackers with wilderness permits may spend one night before and after their trip in backpacker campgrounds ($8 pp) at four front-country locations in the park.

Yosemite's **High Sierra Camps** (888/413-8869, www.travelyosemite.

THE AHWAHNEE

com, July-early Sept.) offer tent cabins with amenities, breakfast and dinner in camp, and a sack lunch. Stay at **Merced Lake, Vogelsang, Glen Aulin, May Lake,** or **Sunrise Camp**—or visit all the camps in one 49-mile (78.8 km) loop. Reservations are by lottery; applications are accepted in October for the following summer.

ROCK CLIMBING

El Capitan boasts a reputation as one of the world's seminal big-face climbs, a challenge that draws experienced rock climbers. But Yosemite also has other significant rock faces for climbers, including Half-Dome Northwest Face, Cathedral Peak, and North Dome. **Wilderness climbing permits** (4-15 days in advance, free) are required for all overnight climbs. For gear rental and guided rock climbing, use **Yosemite Mountaineering School** (209/372-8344, www.travelyosemite.com, 8:30am daily Mar.-Nov.). They also have beginner, intermediate, and advanced rock-climbing classes for adults and children.

BICYCLING

Yosemite Valley has 12 miles (19 km) of paved bike trails, mostly scenic areas on the Valley Loop Trail. Bicycles can also use the road, especially routes closed to cars at the east end of the valley. **Rentals** (www.travelyosemite.com, 10am-6pm daily, last rental 4:45pm) are available at **Yosemite Valley Lodge** (209/372-1208, mid-Apr.-mid-Nov.) and **Curry Village** (209/372-8323, mid-Apr.-Oct.). Glacier Point Road allows bicycles for a few days each May before opening to vehicles.

HORSEBACK RIDING

Wawona Stable (Wawona Rd., 209/375-6502, www.travelyosemite.com, 7am-5pm daily mid-May-Sept.) has sedate two-hour horseback rides on a historical wagon trail. More strenuous trips go into the mountains. Reservations are recommended.

WINTER SPORTS

Badger Pass Ski Area (Glacier Point Rd., 209/372-8430, www.travelyosemite.com, 9am-4pm daily mid-Dec.-Mar.) has rentals, lessons, and plenty of beginner downhill ski runs with enough intermediate runs to keep it interesting. The **Cross-Country Ski School** runs classes, rents gear, and guides cross-country ski tours, including an overnight trip to **Glacier Point Ski Hut.** A free **shuttle** runs between Yosemite Valley and the ski area twice daily in season.

CURRY VILLAGE

Curry Village has an outdoor ice-skating rink (Southside Dr., 209/372-8333, 3:30pm-9pm Mon.-Fri., noon-9:30pm Sat.-Sun. mid-Nov.-mid-Mar.) in winter with skate rentals.

WHERE TO STAY

INSIDE THE PARK

All Yosemite lodgings book up quickly, one year in advance. Lodging **reservations** (888/413-8869, www.travelyosemite.com) for overnight accommodations are essential. Rates vary seasonally.

Yosemite Valley

Yosemite Valley is where everyone wants to be: It has the most services, lodging options, campgrounds, and restaurants.

Yosemite Valley Lodge (shuttle stop 8, year-round, from $278) has motel-style rooms and lodge rooms with king beds and balconies looking across the valley. Enjoy the heated pool in summer and free shuttles to the Glacier Point ski area in winter. Food services include the **Mountain Room Restaurant** (5pm-8pm daily), **Mountain Room Lounge** (5pm-9pm daily), and **Base**

Camp Eatery (7am-10am, 11am-2pm, and 4pm-8pm daily).

Built as a luxury hotel in the early 1900s, **The Ahwahnee** (shuttle stop 3, year-round, from $518) includes cottages and hotel rooms dripping with sumptuous appointments and Native American decor. A bonus is the elegant **dining room** (7am-10am, 11:30am-3pm, and 5:30pm-8:30pm daily) with expansive ceilings, wrought-iron chandeliers, and stellar views. Make reservations for all meals; dinner attire is resort style (long pants, collared shirts or blouses, dresses).

Curry Village (shuttle stop 13, Mar.-Nov. and Dec.-Jan., Sat.-Sun. only Jan.-Mar., from $137) has more rustic options. Canvas tent cabins come with or without heat and shared baths. The **Yosemite Cabins** and **Stoneman Cottage** rooms have heat, private baths, and daily cleaning service. The three-sided tent cabins at **Housekeeping Camp** have cement walls, white canvas roofs, and a white canvas curtain separating the bedroom from a covered patio and shared baths.

In Curry Village, the **Seven Tents Pavilion** (7am-10am and 5:30pm-8:30pm daily mid-Apr.-Oct.) serves breakfast and dinner. Other eateries include the **Coffee Corner** (6:30am-11am daily

Apr.-Nov.), **Bar 1899** (noon-8pm daily May-Oct.), **The Deck** (noon-8pm daily Apr.-Nov.), and **Meadow Grill** (7am-10am and 11am-6pm daily summer).

Yosemite Village has no lodgings, only dining options. **The Loft at Degnan's** (11:30am-9pm daily year-round) serves pizza, Mexican fare, and Asian rice bowls. **Degnan's Kitchen** (10am-5pm daily year-round) has sandwiches, salads, and baked goods. The **Village Grill Deck** (11am-6pm daily Mar.-Oct.) has standard burgers and grilled food.

Wawona

The **Wawona Hotel** (Apr.-Nov. and mid-Dec.-early Jan., from $145) opened in 1879 and still maintains its white-washed look and historic charm. Rooms (with bath and without) come with Victorian wallpaper, antique furniture, and a lack of in-room TVs and telephones. In summer, the lodge runs shuttles to the Mariposa Grove Trailhead for guests.

The **dining room** (209/375-1425, 7am-10am, 11am-3pm, and 5pm-9pm daily) serves upscale California cuisine. Reservations are not accepted, so expect to wait for a table on weekends and in summer. The common area offers seating, drinks, and live piano (Tues.-Sat.).

Tuolumne Meadows and Tioga Pass

White Wolf Lodge (White Wolf Rd. off Tioga Rd., June-Sept., from $125) rents 24 heated canvas tent cabins and four wood cabins. The wood cabins include a private bath, limited electricity, and daily cleaning service, while the tent cabins share a central restroom and shower facility; all cabins include linens and towels.

Tuolumne Meadows Lodge (Tioga Rd., early June-mid-Sept., from $125) offers charming wood-frame tent cabins with no electricity in a gorgeous subalpine meadow setting. Central facilities include restrooms, hot showers, and a **dining room** (209/372-8413, breakfast and dinner daily early June-mid-Sept.); dinner reservations are required.

Camping

Select campgrounds accept **reservations** (877/444-6777, www.recreation.gov), which are imperative, especially for Yosemite Valley. At 7am Pacific Time on the 15th of each month, campsites become available for booking five months in advance. Most book up within minutes. In 2022, the park piloted a lottery (mid-Jan.-early Feb., $10) for peak season reservations (mid-July-early Sept.) at North Pines. Check the park website for updates to the lottery system and applicable campgrounds.

All campgrounds ($26-60) have picnic tables and toilets but no hook-ups. Water is available at all campgrounds except where noted. Some

1: HALF DOME FROM SENTINEL BRIDGE
2: SEQUOIAS IN MARIPOSA GROVE
3: TAFT POINT

NAME	LOCATION	PRICE	SEASON	AMENITIES
Camp 4	Yosemite Valley	$10 pp + $10 lottery fee	year-round	tent sites
Upper Pines	Yosemite Valley	from $26	year-round	tent and RV sites
North and Lower Pines	Yosemite Valley	from $26	Apr.-Nov.	tent and RV sites
Curry Village	Yosemite Valley	from $137	year-round	motel rooms, wooden cabins, tent cabins, dining
Housekeeping Camp	Yosemite Valley	$108	Apr.-Oct.	duplex camp units, showers
Yosemite Valley Lodge	Yosemite Valley	from $278	year-round	hotel rooms, dining
The Ahwahnee	Yosemite Valley	from $518	year-round	hotel rooms, cottages, suites, dining
Bridalveil Creek	Wawona	from $26	July-Sept.	tent and RV sites
Wawona Campground	Wawona	from $26	year-round	tent and RV sites
Wawona Hotel	Wawona	from $150	Apr.-mid-Jan.	hotel rooms, dining
Tamarack Flat	Tuolumne Meadows	$12	June-Oct.	tent sites
Yosemite Creek	Tuolumne Meadows	$12	July-Sept.	tent sites
Porcupine Flat	Tuolumne Meadows	$12	July-Oct.	tent sites
White Wolf	Tuolumne Meadows	$18	July-Sept.	tent and RV sites
Hodgdon Meadow	Tuolumne Meadows	from $26	year-round	tent and RV sites
Crane Flat	Tuolumne Meadows	from $26	July-Oct.	tent and RV sites
Tuolumne Meadows	Tuolumne Meadows	from $26	July-Sept.	tent and RV sites
White Wolf Lodge	Tuolumne Meadows	$125	June-Sept.	wooden cabins, tent cabins, dining
Tuolumne Meadows Lodge	Tuolumne Meadows	$125	June-Sept.	tent cabins, dining

ARCH ROCK ENTRANCE

campgrounds have group, family, horse, or double sites.

Yosemite Valley has four campgrounds. Reservations are accepted for **Upper Pines** (year-round, 235 sites) and **Lower Pines** (mid-Apr.-late Oct., 73 sites). Reservations are also accepted for **North Pines** (mid-Apr.-late Oct., 80 sites), but this campground is on a lottery system ($10 fee) for peak season stays (late July-mid-Sept.). The lottery runs from mid-January to early February; winners are notified in mid-February and can book reservations over the next few weeks. Any leftover lottery sites are then released on the regular reservation system. If you don't have a campsite reservation, call the **campground status line** (209/372-0266) for a recording of what's available that day. Competition for sites at **Camp 4** (year-round, 61 shared walk-in sites, tents only, $10 pp/night) is heavy from spring to fall. For first-come, first-served sites, a long line forms at the registration kiosk (opens 8:30am daily). During peak season (late May-early Sept.), you must enter a lottery ($10, enter midnight-4pm one day in advance) to get a campsite; results are emailed soon after 4pm.

Two campgrounds (RV limit 35 ft/10.7 m) are south of Yosemite Valley. Midway up Glacier Point Road, **Bridalveil Creek** (mid-July-early Sept., 115 sites, first come, first served) sits along Bridalveil Creek, making it an appealing spot. North of Wawona, the forested **Wawona Campground** (year-round, 97 sites) has scenic sites along the Tuolumne River with reservations accepted for peak season (Apr.-early Oct.) and first-come, first-served sites off season (mid-Oct.-Mar.).

Tioga Road has six campgrounds. Near the Big Oak Flat entrance, **Crane Flat** (year-round, 166 sites) and **Hodgdon Meadow** (year-round, 105 sites) accept reservations for peak season (early Apr.-mid-Oct.); otherwise, they are first come, first served. The most coveted and largest campground, **Tuolumne Meadows** (July-Sept., accepts reservations, 304 sites) is closed for reconstruction until 2024 or 2025. The remaining campgrounds ($12-18) are first come, first served with opening and closing dates snow-dependent: **White Wolf** (July-Sept., 74 sites, RV limit 27 ft/8.2 m) has water; boil creek water at **Tamarack Flat** (June-Oct., 52 sites), **Yosemite Creek** (July-Sept., 75 sites), and **Porcupine Flat** (July-Oct., 52 sites). RVs and trailers are not recommended at the latter three campgrounds.

OUTSIDE THE PARK

Gateway towns offer accommodations, campgrounds, dining, and services: **El Portal** and **Mariposa** on CA 140, **Groveland** on CA 120, **Oakhurst** on CA 41, and **Fish Camp** on CA 41.

The resort town of **Mammoth Lakes** (U.S. 395) has upscale lodging 40 minutes south of Yosemite's east entrance. YARTS shuttles run from Mammoth into the park.

GETTING THERE

AIR

The closest international airports are **San Francisco International Airport** (SFO, US 101, San Mateo, 650/821-8211 or 800/435-9736, www.flysfo.com), **Oakland International Airport** (OAK, 1 Airport Dr., 510/563-3300, www.

◄ DOGWOOD IN SPRING, YOSEMITE VALLEY

CLIMBER ON NORTH DOME

oaklandairport.com), **Sacramento International Airport** (SMF, 6900 Airport Blvd., 916/929-5411, www.sacramento.aero/smf), and **Reno-Tahoe International Airport** (RNO, 2001 E. Plumb Ln., Reno, NV, 775/328-6400, www.renoairport.com). Car rentals are available at all airports.

CAR

From the San Francisco Bay Area, it takes 4-5 hours to drive to the park's west entrances of Arch Rock and Big Oak Flat for the quickest access to Yosemite Valley. Take I-580 east and continue east to I-205 and I-5 near Manteca. From Manteca, follow CA 120 east through Groveland and the **Big Oak Flat Entrance** on the west side of the park. From Big Oak Flat, it's a 45-minute drive to Yosemite Valley.

Alternatively, from I-5 south, take CA 140 east through Merced to reach the **Arch Rock Entrance.** From Arch Rock, it's a 30-minute drive to the valley. This is the **most popular and most crowded entrance** to Yosemite Valley. Plan to arrive before 9am or after 5pm to avoid long entrance lines.

From points south, enter the park through the **South Entrance** via CA 41, a 1.5-hour drive north from Fresno. In 4 miles (6.4 km), CA 41 becomes Wawona Road. From Wawona, it's another 1.5 hours to Yosemite Valley.

TRAIN AND BUS

From San Francisco or Sacramento, **Amtrak** (www.amtrak.com) connects with Merced and Fresno, where **buses** with the **Yosemite Area Regional Transportation System** (YARTS, 877/989-2787, www.yarts.com) travel the final stretch into the park. You can buy tickets on the bus; no reservations are necessary. Buses run more frequently in summer. From **Merced,** YARTS buses goes to Yosemite Valley, where free shuttles circle the valley. From **Fresno,** YARTS buses go to the South Entrance of Yosemite.

GETTING AROUND

DRIVING

Driving in **Yosemite Valley** can be a crowded, congested experience. Parking lots and roadside pullouts fill early. Plan to arrive before 9am and leave your car in one of the three major parking lots (Yosemite Village, Yosemite Falls, Curry Village) and then navigate the valley via the park's free shuttle.

There are no **gas stations** in Yosemite Valley. The closest stations are in El Portal and at Crane Flat.

RVs and **trailers** have restrictions on several roads: Wawona, El Portal, Big Oak Flat, Glacier Point, Mariposa Grove, and Hetch Hetchy. Tioga Pass poses challenges for hauling trailers, and Yosemite Valley has limited parking for RVs and trailers. Check online for detailed restrictions and seasonal concerns.

Glacier Point Road

Glacier Point is about an hour's drive from Yosemite Valley. From the Valley Visitor Center, drive 14 miles (23 km) south to Chinquapin junction and turn left onto **Glacier Point Road** (closed Nov.-May, no trailers or RVs over 30 ft/9.1 m allowed) for 16 miles (26 km). In winter (Dec.-Mar.), the first 5 miles (8 km) of the road are plowed up to Badger Pass Ski Area; chains may be required. Construction from Badger Pass to Glacier Point will cause delays in 2023.

Tioga Road

Tioga Road (CA 120) stretches from Crane Flat east to Tioga Pass, the east entrance to the park, where it becomes Tioga Pass Road. **The road is open only in summer.** To check weather conditions and road closures, call 209/372-0200. When the road is closed, there is no access to Tuolumne Meadows.

SHUTTLE BUS

In summer—especially on weekends—traffic and parking in Yosemite Valley can be stressful. Park your car at the Yosemite Village day-use lot, Curry Village, or near Yosemite Falls; then use the **Yosemite Valley shuttle** (7am-10pm daily year-round, free) to get around. Shuttles run every 10-20 minutes, stopping at Yosemite Valley Lodge, Valley Visitor Center, Curry Village, all campgrounds, and Happy Isles Trailhead.

The **Glacier Point Tour** (888/413-8869, www.travelyosemite.com, 8:30am and 1:30pm daily May-Nov., $28.50-57) meets at Yosemite Valley Lodge to travel up Glacier Point Road when the road is open.

The summer-only **Tuolumne Meadows Hikers Bus** (209/372-1240, mid-June-Sept., $2-23) runs along Tioga Road between Olmsted Point and the Tuolumne Meadows Lodge. Service varies seasonally.

The **Mariposa Shuttle** (8am-8pm daily mid-Mar.-Nov., hours shorten spring and late fall, depending on weather, free) goes from the Mariposa parking area to the grove trailhead.

EL CAPITAN

SEQUOIA AND KINGS CANYON NATIONAL PARKS

California

WEBSITE:
www.nps.gov/seki

PHONE NUMBER:
559/565-3341

VISITATION RANK:
26 (Sequoia) and
38 (Kings Canyon)

WHY GO:
Explore giant sequoias,
underground caves,
and scenic byways.

▲ GIANT SEQUOIAS, SEQUOIA
NATIONAL PARK

KEEPSAKE STAMPS ▼▼▼

SEQUOIA AND KINGS CANYON NATIONAL PARKS preserve some of the tallest and oldest trees on earth, some more than 3,000 years old. Unfortunately, wildfires in 2020 and 2021 destroyed thousands of mature sequoias and damaged others, to the point where they may not survive the next few years. But many of the easily accessed famous sequoia groves survived.

Much of the landscape is remote Sierra Nevada backcountry, which tops out at the snow-capped Mount Whitney, the highest peak in the contiguous United States. From the Sierra Crest on the eastern park border, alpine peaks plunge into deep glacier-carved canyons, crossed only by hiking paths, including the John Muir Trail and Pacific Crest Trail. When combined with their shared boundary, the two parks stretch across an acreage larger than Yosemite but with the benefit of smaller crowds. Their unique granite and sequoia ecosystem—the historic lands of the Monache, Yokuts, and Tubatulabal peoples, among others—extends into Sequoia National Forest and Giant Sequoia National Monument.

PLANNING YOUR TIME

Located in central California, Sequoia and Kings Canyon are accessed by road only from the west side of the Sierra. *No roads enter the park from the Eastern Sierra, and there is no way to drive across the Sierra from either park.*

Exploring the large parks takes time and requires long drives. Plan to stay 3-4 days to enjoy some of the many walks through scenic sequoia groves. In the main campgrounds, vacationers often set up a tent for one or two weeks and use the camp as a base for exploring the parks.

Due to vast elevation differences, weather varies with extremes. **Summer** is high season, when snow melts from cooler high-elevation trails and hot temperatures pervade the foothills. Winter dumps snow on the mountains, often closing park roads and making driving treacherous. Other than periodic road closures for snow, Grant Grove, Giant Forest, and Foothills areas stay open year-round. Roads to Cedar Grove (Kings Canyon) and Mineral King open late spring to early fall but close in winter. If you plan to visit Mineral King, check into the construction schedule for the Mineral King Road. Starting in 2023, the road could see some closures over the next few summers.

You will see impacts from the 2021 wildfire along the Generals Highway, among other places. Be aware that the National Park Service may be stabilizing soils and slopes as well as removing hazard trees in the next few years; check online for trail and road closures that may be in effect, as fire recovery can last several years.

ENTRANCES AND FEES

The entrance fee is $35 per vehicle ($30 motorcycle, $20 individual). You can **buy your pass online** (www.recreation. gov) from home to speed through entrance stations faster.

There are two main entrances. From the west and north, the **Big Stump Entrance** (CA 180) is the most direct route with the closest access to Kings Canyon National Park, Grant Grove, and Generals Highway. From the south, the **Ash Mountain Entrance** (CA 198) enters Sequoia National Park, where CA 198 becomes Generals Highway. On the Mineral King Road, the **Lookout Point Entrance** (May-Oct., gate locked Nov.-Apr.) has a self-pay kiosk.

SEQUOIA AND KINGS CANYON NATIONAL PARKS

OWENS VALLEY

Owens River

River

Los Angeles Aqueduct

Independence Creek

To Bishop

Big Pine

Big Pine Creek

S I E R R A   N E V A D A

Independence

Split Mountain
14,058ft

Tahoose Pass
11,400ft

Striped Mountain
13,160ft

Pinchot Pass
12,050ft

Colosseum Mountain
12,473ft

Sawmill Pass
11,347ft

Mount Baxter
13,125ft

Baxter Pass
12,320ft

Diamond Peak
13,126ft

Kearsarge Pass

RAE LAKES

Woods Lake

UPPER BASIN

Bishop Pass
11,972ft

PALISADE CREST

Mather Pass
12,100ft

North Palisade
14,242ft

Middle Palisade
14,040ft

South Fork Kings River

Bench Lake

Arrow Peak
12,958ft

Pyramid Peak
12,777ft

MURO BLANCO

Mount Clarence King
12,905ft

Mount Gardiner
12,907ft

Glen Pass
11,978ft

Woods Creek Trail

PARADISE VALLEY

Mist Falls

Marion Peak
12,719ft

Granite Pass
10,673ft

ROADS END
PERMIT STATION

The Sphinx

Mount Goethe
13,264ft

South Lake

Lake Sabrina

Mount Powell
13,361ft

Black Giant
13,330ft

LE CONTE CANYON

Windy Peak
8,867ft

KINGS CANYON NATIONAL PARK

KINGS CANYON

CEDAR GROVE VISITOR CENTER

Mount Darwin
13,830ft

GLACIER DIVIDE

McCLURE MEADOW

ENCHANTED GORGE

SIMPSON MEADOW

Kennedy Pass
10,900ft

Pavilion Dome
11,846ft

Mount Goddard
13,568ft

Mount Reinstein
12,604ft

Finger Peak
12,404ft

Tunemah Peak
11,894ft

Burnt Mountain
10,608ft

Kings River

LE CONTE DIVIDE

Hell for Sure Pass
11,297ft

KETTLE RIDGE

Kettle Dome
9,446ft

Middle Fork Kings River

Wren Peak
9,450ft

KINGS CANYON SCENIC BYWAY

Kings River

KINGS CANYON LODGE

Mount Henry
12,196ft

San Joaquin River

South Fork

Spanish Mountain
10,051ft

Obelisk
9,700ft

KINGS CANYON LODGE

Wishon Reservoir

Courtright Reservoir

Kings River

Top ❸

GENERAL GRANT TREE, KINGS CANYON

❶ GAZE UP AT THE "GENERALS"

By sheer volume of wood, the Generals are the two largest trees on earth. At 275 feet high (84 m) and 106 feet (32 m) in circumference at the base, the 2,200-year-old **General Sherman Tree** (Wolverton Rd., off Generals Hwy.) is the largest. From the parking lot or shuttle stop at Wolverton Road, a 1-mile (1.6-km) round-trip trail with interpretive signs leads down stairs and walkways to the viewing area, where summer crowds swarm to see the giant. Visit on a weekday or early in the morning for a quieter experience. A wheelchair-accessible trailhead with a shorter trail is on Generals Highway (south of Wolverton Rd.).

The **General Grant Tree** (north of Kings Canyon Visitor Center) may be the second-largest tree and the nation's only living war memorial. The 1,700-year-old giant sequoia is 268 feet (92 m) tall with a diameter of 33 feet (10 m). The paved **General Grant Tree Trail** (0.3 mi/0.5 km rt, 20 min, easy) leads to its namesake tree and the **Fallen Monarch,** an immense hollowed-out tree lying on its side. It also passes the 1872 **Gamlin Cabin,** the former living quarters of the grove's first ranger, and the **Centennial Stump,** which once hosted whole Sunday school classes on top of it.

❷ LEARN ABOUT SEQUOIAS AT THE GIANT FOREST MUSEUM

The **Giant Forest Museum** (Generals Hwy., 9am-6pm daily summer, shorter hours fall-spring) has touchable and interactive exhibits that provide context to these fast-growing trees. Learn about the importance of fire in the life of a giant sequoia, how the park used to look, and why many of the buildings have been removed to make way for more trees. This is a great stop for families. From the museum, numerous hikes branch out into the surrounding Giant Forest Sequoia Grove, which contains 8,000 of these special trees. The paved, wheelchair-accessible **Big Trees Loop** (0.75 mi/1 km rt, 1 hr, easy) circles Round Meadow.

❸ GO UNDERGROUND AT CRYSTAL CAVE

Crystal Cave (Cave Rd., near Giant Forest, May-Sept.), one of 275 natural caves in the park, has immense underground rooms. They fill with fragile limestone stalagmites and stalactites that have metamorphosed over time into marble.

Access to the cave is by **guided tour only** (877/444-6777, www.recreation.gov, adults $16-25, kids $5-8). Tours range from 45 minutes to two hours, with longer adventures for serious spelunkers ($140, six hours). Tickets are not sold at the cave entrance; purchase them in advance at the visitors centers or online. Day-of tickets go quickly; pick them up early in the morning.

The long, winding drive to the cave parking lot can take more than an hour, and reaching the cave requires a steep and strenuous 0.5-mile (0.8-km) walk. Bring a warm layer for the 50-degree temperatures (10°C) inside. Crystal Cave will be closed until spring 2023 for cleanup from the KNP Complex Fire of 2021.

ONE DAY IN SEQUOIA & KINGS CANYON

Those short on time should head for the giant trees. Start with a walk around **General Grant Grove.** Then drive down Generals Highway to the **General Sherman Tree** and tour the **Giant Forest Museum.** If time permits, drive **Kings Canyon Scenic Byway** to Cedar Grove. Stop at canyon overlooks and hike the short **Zumwalt Meadow Trail.**

VISITORS CENTERS

Five visitors centers have maps, information, weather conditions, and road closures. They also have bookstores that sell maps, educational books, and gifts. All have wilderness permit desks.

Kings Canyon Visitor Center (83918 CA 180 E., 559/565-3341, 8am-5pm daily summer, 10am-3pm Jan.-mid-Mar., 9am-4pm daily mid-Mar.-mid-May) is in Grant Grove Village near the Big Stump Entrance. It has a movie and exhibits that illustrate the local ecosystems. Rangers offer interpretive programs, including snowshoe walks in winter.

Near Cedar Grove Village in Kings Canyon, the **Cedar Grove Visitor Center** (CA 180, 559/565-3793, 9am-5pm daily summer) has exhibits covering the natural and human history of Cedar Grove.

At the **Lodgepole Visitor Center** (Generals Hwy., 559/565-4436, 8am-4:30pm daily summer), you can watch a park film, join a ranger talk or walk, and buy Crystal Cave tour tickets. It's about an hour's drive to Lodgepole from either park entrance.

The **Foothills Visitor Center** (Generals Hwy., 559/565-3341, 8am-4:30pm daily mid-Mar.-Sept., 9am-4pm daily Oct.-mid-Mar.), just north of the Ash Mountain Entrance, serves as the park headquarters and has exhibits covering the area's human history. Rangers lead talks and walks. You can also buy Crystal Cave tickets.

Near the end of Mineral King Road, the **Mineral King Ranger Station** (559/565-3768, 8am-4pm daily summer) has small exhibits about the area.

SIGHTS

GIANT SEQUOIA NATIONAL MONUMENT

Divided in two sections 25 miles (40 km) apart, **Giant Sequoia National Monument** (www.fs.usda.gov) abuts the west and south sides of the two national parks. The monument protects groves of giant sequoia trees that grow only on the western slopes of the Sierra Nevada in California, between 4,000 and 8,000 feet (1,219-2,438 m) elevation.

Along Kings Canyon Scenic Byway east of Grant Grove, the **Converse Basin Grove** may have once held the largest grove of sequoias before being logged in the late 1800s. A wheelchair-accessible loop path goes to the 20-foot-high (6-m) **Chicago Stump** (0.5 mi/0.8 km, easy). It's all that remains from the 3,200-year-old General Noble Tree that was cut down in chunks to ship to the 1893 Chicago World's Columbian Exposition. **Boole Tree Loop** (2.5 mi/4 km rt, moderate, 1 hr) tours immense stumps and a post-logging second-growth forest that includes the Boole Tree.

SCENIC DRIVE

KINGS CANYON SCENIC BYWAY

Beginning at the Hume Lake Ranger Station in the foothills west of the park, CA 180 becomes spectacular **Kings Canyon Scenic Byway** (50 mi/81 km). After entering the park and reaching Grant Grove Village, the road continues north and east through Sequoia National Monument and Converse Basin on its way to Cedar Grove and Roads End. From the start at Grant Grove, at 6,500 feet (1,981 m), the road weaves down several thousand feet before climbing back up along the South Fork Kings River. Ample roadside pullouts make it easy to stop for views of the canyon and surrounding peaks.

At **Canyon View** (1 mi/1.6 km east of Cedar Grove Village), you can see the distinct U-shape of a glacier-carved

Best Hike

MORO ROCK

DISTANCE: 0.5 mile (0.8 km) round-trip
DURATION: 30 minutes
ELEVATION CHANGE: 300 feet (90 m)
EFFORT: strenuous
TRAILHEAD: Moro Rock/ Crescent Meadow Road

Moro Rock, a granite dome poised above the landscape, provides stunning views of the Great Western Divide and western part of Sequoia. Park in the lot at the base of the rock and climb the 380 concrete and stone steps to reach the top. Handrails line much of the route, which has steep drop-offs in some sections. In summer, the access road is closed to vehicles weekends and holidays, so take the free shuttle (9am-6pm). Do not climb Moro Rock if thunderstorms loom or if snow or ice cover the route. When the weather is good, Moro Rock is a popular spot for watching sunsets.

canyon, lodged between the soaring peaks flanking the Kings River. One mile (1.6 km) farther east, walk a short path to the small picturesque **Knapp's Cabin,** built in the 1920s by businessman George Knapp. The wheelchair-accessible **Roaring River Falls Trail** (0.5 mi/0.8 km rt) travels under a cool canopy of trees to water gushing through a granite chute.

Tucked between North Dome and Grand Sentinel, **Roads End** marks the end of driving in Kings Canyon. From here, hikers begin their exploration of the high Sierra forests, lakes, and mountain passes.

RECREATION

HIKING

Grant Grove

General Grant Grove is home to dozens of giant sequoias, the largest of which is the General Grant Tree. From the parking lot, take the **North Grove**

▼ TRAIL UP MORO ROCK

HIKER IN KINGS CANYON

Loop Trail (1.5 mi/2.4 km rt, 1 hr, easy) along an old park road through the sequoia forest.

North of the Big Stump Entrance, the **Big Stump Trail** (1.5 mi/2.4 km rt, 1 hr, easy) travels through a grove that was heavily logged in the late 19th century and is slowly regrowing. The route passes the **Mark Twain Stump,** the remains of a 16-foot-wide (4.8-m) tree that was cut in 1891. A set of wood stairs lets you stand on top of the stump.

Redwood Mountain Grove (in Redwood Canyon) is home to the largest grove of giant sequoias in the world. Walk down a short old roadbed to a trail junction and turn left to begin the **Hart Tree and Fallen Goliath Loop** (7.3 mi/11.7 km rt, 3-4 hrs, moderate) across Redwood Creek and past the former logging site of Barton's Post Camp. About halfway around the loop, you'll come to a short spur trail that takes you to the **Hart Tree,** the largest in the grove and the 25th largest known in the world. **Fallen Goliath,** a little farther along, is another impressive sight. To reach the trailhead from Grant Grove, drive five miles (8 km) south on Generals Highway to Quail Flat; turn right and drive 1.5 miles (2.4 km) to Redwood Saddle. Turn left at the fork for the trailhead.

The trail to **Buena Vista Peak** (2 mi/3.2 km rt, 2 hrs, moderate) makes a 450-foot (137-m) ascent to the peak for views of the Western Divide, Mineral King, and Farewell Gap. The Buena Vista Trailhead is 6 miles (9.7 km) south of Grant Grove.

The **Big Baldy Ridge Trail** (4.4 mi/7.1 km rt, 2.5 hrs, moderate) climbs 600 feet (183 m) to the granite summit of Big Baldy for views into Redwood Canyon. The trailhead is 8 miles (13 km) south of Grant Grove.

Cedar Grove

Kings Canyon Scenic Byway leads to trailheads for family-friendly hikes and big mountain adventures. One mile (1.6 km) west of Roads End, the **Zumwalt Meadow Trail** (1.6 mi/2.6 km rt, 1 hr, easy) leads through the lush meadow and continues through a grove of heavenly smelling cedar and pine trees along the Kings River.

From the Roads End Trailhead, the **Mist Falls Trail** (8 mi/13 km rt, 4-5 hrs, moderate) begins with a sandy, dusty path along the rapids of Bubbs Creek. It then turns north to climb steep switchbacks 600 vertical feet (183 m) to one of the largest falls in the parks.

RAE LAKES

Giant Forest and Lodgepole

Along the Generals Highway, short trails lead to big views and giant trees. From the Little Baldy Trailhead, the 790-foot (241-m) ascent up 8,044-foot (2,452-m) **Little Baldy** (3.4 mi/5.5 km rt, 2-3 hrs, moderate) reaches the top of the granite dome to look down into the Giant Forest.

From the General Sherman Tree Trailhead, the wheelchair-accessible **Congress Trail** (2.7 mi/4.5 km rt, 1.5 hrs, easy) passes many of the park's most famous giant sequoias—the eponymous General Sherman, Chief Sequoyah, and President McKinley—as well as the House and Senate Groups.

From Crescent Meadow parking lot, the **Crescent Meadow-Log Meadow Loop** (1.6 mi/2.6 km rt, 1 hr, easy) leads hikers through forest groves encircling several meadows. The trail passes Tharp's Log, the park's oldest cabin. The trail to **Tokopah Falls** (3.4 mi/5.5 km rt, 2 hrs, easy) starts just beyond the Marble Fork Bridge in Lodgepole Campground. The trail follows the Marble Fork of the Kaweah River to the 1,200-foot (3,656-m) waterfall.

Foothills and Mineral King

At the southern entrance of Sequoia National Park, the Foothills area offers vigorous adventure with a big payoff. The **Marble Falls Trail** (7.8 mi/12 km rt, 4 hrs, strenuous) starts from Potwisha Campground on a forest road before winding upward through the woods 2,150 feet (655 m) to sweeping views of the canyons and the water below. At a large slab that looks like white marble, you see the dramatic Marble Falls.

Hikes in the remote Mineral King area (Lookout Point Entrance, May-Nov.) are demanding and strenuous. The exception is the **Cold Springs Nature Trail** (2 mi/3.2 km rt, 1 hr), an easy walk from the campground along the Kaweah River.

BACKPACKING

The premier backpacking trip in Kings Canyon is the **Rae Lakes Loop** (42 mi/68 km rt, 5-7 days). From Roads End, the trail varies from flat and pleasant to mettle-testing steep grades, rock scrambling, rugged switchbacks, and stream crossings. Along the way, you'll gain about 7,000 feet (2,134 m) of elevation to reach the sparkling blue Rae Lakes and **Glen Pass** (11,978 ft/3,651 m elevation, snow-covered until July). Many hikers spend at least two nights at the lakes. The loop also takes in a portion of the John Muir and Pacific Crest Trails.

Wilderness permits are required. During the **quota season** (late May-late Sept.), make **reservations** (www.recreation.gov, $15 fee plus $5 pp) online six months in advance; competition is tough, so be ready to reserve as soon as your desired dates are released. A limited number of first-come, first-served permits are available at permit stations, including the **Roads End Permit Station** (7am-3:30pm daily late May-late Sept.). During the **non-quota season** (late Sept.-late May), free permits may be picked up at open visitors centers.

Bear canisters are required; limited rentals (from $5/3 days) are available from some permit stations (Kings Canyon, Foothills, Lodgepole, and Mineral King).

HORSEBACK RIDING

In summer, saddle up with **Grant Grove Stables** (559/335-9292) or **Cedar Grove Pack Station** (Cedar Grove Village, 559/565-3464 summer, 559/802-7626 winter). Cedar Grove also guides customized backcountry overnight trips.

SEQUOIA TREE

WHERE TO STAY
INSIDE THE PARK

All park lodgings and campgrounds fill on weekends, holidays, and May-September. Make reservations in advance: 12 months ahead for peak times at lodges and 6 months in advance for camping.

Grant Grove

Grant Grove Cabins (866/944-1572, www.visitsequoia.com, year-round, from $110) offer rustic timber structures and tent cabins with private baths or a shared central facility with public showers. The attractive yet simple **John Muir Lodge** (866/944-1572, www.visitsequoia.com, year-round, from $210) is cedar lodges with motel-style rooms built in 1999. Nearby, **Grant Grove Restaurant** (Grant Grove Village, 7am-10am, 11:30am-2:30pm, and 5pm-8pm daily) serves meals.

Montecito Sequoia Lodge (63410 Generals Hwy., 559/565-3388 or 800/227-9900, www.mslodge.com, year-round, from $199) is a rustic full-service resort with lodge rooms and cabins. In summer, Montecito operates primarily as a family camp, but rooms are available to noncampers. Rates are all-inclusive. The dining room (hours vary daily year-round) serves breakfast, lunch, and dinner; reservations are accepted for hotel guests.

Cedar Grove

Cedar Grove Lodge (Cedar Grove Village, 866/944-1572, www.visitsequoia.com, May-Oct., from $150) has 21 guest rooms with private baths and air-conditioning. Services include a **snack bar** (7:30am-9pm daily May-Oct.), a gift shop, a mini-mart, laundry, showers, and an ATM.

Lodgepole

The **Wuksachi Lodge** (64740 Wuksachi Way, 866/944-1572, www.visitsequoia.com, year-round, from $238) offers upscale accommodations with facilities built in 1999. The on-site **Peaks Restaurant** (559/625-7700, 7am-10am, noon-2pm, and 5:30pm-8pm daily year-round) features sweeping forest views and serves three meals daily, plus the lodge has a pizza deck.

HIGH SIERRA OF KINGS CANYON

Lodgepole Village contains a large visitors center, market, the **Lodgepole Café** (8am-8pm daily May-Oct.) with a full menu or grab-and-go, a gift shop, coin laundry, an ATM, shuttle services, and a post office. Many facilities close in winter.

The **Sherman Shack** (11am-5pm daily summer, weather dependent), a solar-powered food cart in the General Sherman Tree parking lot, has grab-and-go snacks and lunches.

Mineral King

At Mineral King, the **Silver City Resort** (559/242-3510, www.silvercityresort. com, May-mid-Oct., from $195) has chalets and cabins. Reaching the Mineral King area (Mineral King Rd., no trailers or RVs, 25 mi/40 km east of CA 198) requires driving a narrow 22-mile (35-km) road that takes at least 1.5 hours in good weather.

Camping

The parks have 14 campgrounds, 3 of which are open year-round. This area is black bear habitat, which makes proper food storage in campgrounds essential. Campsites have picnic tables, fire rings, and food storage boxes but no hookups.

For **campground reservations** (877/444-6777, www.recreation.gov,

$22-60), book six months in advance. Azalea, Sunset, Sentinel, Lodgepole, Dorst Creek, Potwisha, and Buckeye take reservations; a few others take reservations only for group campsites.

Three campgrounds cluster near Grant Grove Village: **Sunset** (158 sites, May-Sept.), **Azalea** (40-88 first-come, first-served sites mid-Apr.-mid-May; 110 reservable sites mid-May-early Nov.; 19 first-come, first-served sites early Nov.-mid-Apr.), and **Crystal Springs** (50 sites, late May-early Sept.).

Cedar Grove Village has **Sheep Creek** (111 sites, late May-mid-Sept.), **Sentinel** (82 sites, May-mid-Nov.), and **Moraine** (121 sites, late May-early Sept.). **Canyon View** (16 sites, mid-June-late Sept., $40-60) has group sites by reservation.

Near Lodgepole, **Lodgepole Campground** (214 sites, late-Mar.-late Nov.) is along the Kaweah River, and **Dorst Creek Campground** (222 sites, mid-June-Labor Day, $22-60) sits along Generals Highway north of Wuksachi Village. Shuttles stop at both campgrounds.

At Foothills, **Potwisha Campground** (42 sites, year-round) and tent-only **Buckeye Flat** (27 sites, late Mar.-late

▶ HIKERS ON THE WAY TO THE SUMMIT OF MOUNT WHITNEY

MOUNT WHITNEY

One of the most famous backpacking trips in Northern California is the trek to **Mount Whitney.** At 14,494 feet (4,418 m), Whitney is the highest peak in the continental United States, and this must-do trek draws intrepid hikers and climbers from around the world. Whitney also marks the southern end of the **John Muir Trail** and makes for a dramatic end or beginning for hikers doing the whole route.

Mount Whitney is at the far eastern edge of Sequoia National Park, just west of the town of Lone Pine. You can see the impressive peak from a few places in the backcountry of Sequoia and Kings Canyon, but you can't drive there from within the parks as **no road crosses the parks from west to east.** If you're coming from the west, you have to drive around the parks and enter from the eastern side.

Although Mount Whitney is a very challenging climb, with an elevation gain of more than 6,100 feet (1,859 km), it is not technical. You can climb the 10.7 miles (17.2 km) of switchbacks all the way to the top of Mount Whitney and back in one day if you're in good shape and prepare properly for the journey. It's important to plan ahead, start early, and bring all the right safety gear for extreme weather.

Permits (760/873-2483, www.fs.fed.us/r5/inyo) are required for anyone entering the Mount Whitney Zone—even day hikers. Permit reservations are issued by lottery application (submitted Feb.-mid-Mar., 877/444-6777, www.recreation.gov).

The nearest campground is **Whitney Portal** (end of Whitney Portal Rd., 6 mi./9.7 km west of Lone Pine, 47 sites, late Apr.-late Oct., $26-80) in the Inyo National Forest 7 miles (11 km) from the trailhead. Make reservations (877/444-6777, www.recreation.gov). If you're planning to climb the summit, stay even closer at 25 walk-in sites located near the **Mount Whitney Trailhead** (first come, first served, one-night limit) to wake up in the wee hours and start your ascent.

Sept.) sit on the Kaweah River. The primitive **South Fork Campground** (South Fork Dr., 10 sites, year-round, $6) is 13 miles (21 km) off CA 198 near Three Rivers. There are pit toilets but no drinking water.

Two tent-only campgrounds (May-Oct., $22) are at Mineral King: **Atwell Mill** (21 sites) and **Cold Springs** (40 sites).

OUTSIDE THE PARK

Visalia and **Three Rivers** have visitor services, lodgings, and a summer shuttle into the park. **Sequoia National Forest/Giant Sequoia National Monument** (www.fs.fed.us) has seven nearby campgrounds, some that take reservations. Stony Creek Village has the **Stony Creek Lodge** (Generals Hwy., 877/828-1440, www.sequoia-kingscanyon.com, May-early Oct.).

GETTING THERE

AIR

The closest international airport is **Fresno Yosemite International** (FAT, 559/621-4500, www.flyfresno.com), a one- to two-hour drive to either park entrance. Rental cars are available. From **Los Angeles International Airport** (LAX, 1 World Way, 424/646-5252, www.flylax.com), it's a four- to five-hour drive to the park, most of it on I-5.

CAR

From Fresno, take **CA 180** to enter Kings Canyon National Park at Big Stump Entrance. For the south entrance to Sequoia, take **CA 99** south to Visalia and turn east onto **CA 198.** Both park entrances are linked by the slow, winding Generals Highway, which may close in winter due to snow.

GETTING AROUND

DRIVING

Park roads may require chains at any time due to snow. Check online or call the park for road conditions (559/565-3341).

Grant Grove is in Kings Canyon National Park, 3 miles (4.8 km) east of the Big Stump Entrance on CA 180. **Cedar Grove** is 30 miles (48 km) northeast of Grant Grove on Kings Canyon Scenic Byway (CA 180); only the first 6 miles (10 km) of the road are open in winter (Oct.-Apr.).

Lodgepole is on Generals Highway, 22 miles (35 km) north of the Ash Mountain Entrance and 27 miles (43 km) south of the Big Stump Entrance, about an hour's drive from either entrance. Wuksachi Village is 3 miles (4.8 km) northwest of Lodgepole.

From CA 198, the Ash Mountain Entrance accesses the **Foothills** area. To reach **Mineral King,** turn right onto Mineral King Road (2 mi/3.2 km before the Ash Mountain Entrance) and drive 25 miles east (40 km, 1.5 hrs). The narrow and winding road does not permit RVs or trailers. Pass through the Lookout Point Entrance (May-Oct., gate locked Nov.-Apr.) and pay the entrance fee at a self-serve kiosk.

No **gas** is sold in the national parks, but **Stony Creek Village** (Generals Hwy., 24 hours daily summer only) has gas pumps and accepts credit cards.

SHUTTLES

Sequoia National Park provides free summer **shuttle service** (8am-6:30pm daily late May-Sept.), stopping at Giant Forest Museum, Lodgepole Visitor Center, and Moro Rock, plus Dorst and Lodgepole Campgrounds. The **Visalia Shuttle** (reservations required, 877/287-4453, www.sequoiashuttle.com, late May-early Sept., $20 rt) runs from Visalia and Three Rivers to Giant Forest Museum; the park entrance fee is included.

COOLING OFF IN WOODS CREEK, KINGS CANYON

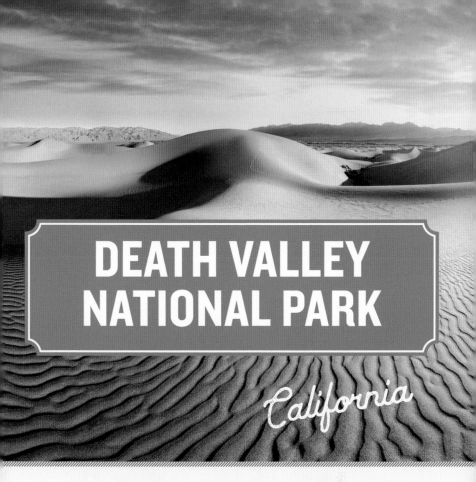

DEATH VALLEY NATIONAL PARK

California

KEEPSAKE STAMPS ▼▼▼

WEBSITE:
www.nps.gov/deva

PHONE NUMBER:
760/786-3200

VISITATION RANK:
23

WHY GO:
See sculpted sand dunes, hidden oases, and geologic discoveries.

▲ MESQUITE FLAT DUNES, DEATH VALLEY NATIONAL PARK

DEATH VALLEY
NATIONAL PARK

10 mi

10 km

To Las Vegas

Lathrop Wells

Amargosa Valley

Winters Peak

95

VALLEY VIEW RD

AMARGOSA FARM ROAD

A M A R G O S A   D E S E R T

Beatty

374

Rhyolite (ghost town)

DAYLIGHT PASS ROAD

A M A R G O S A

FUNERAL MOUNTAINS

Nevares Peak

190

Daylight Pass 4,316ft

TITUS CANYON RD

Thimble Peak 6,381ft

Corkscrew Peak 5,804ft

▲ HELLS GATE

Scottys Junction

To Tonopah and Reno

95

Wahguyhe Peak 8,629ft

Leadfield (ghost town)

Red Pass

BEATTY CUTOFF

SCOTTY'S CASTLE RD

Salt

HISTORIC STOVEPIPE WELL

SALT CREEK

Grapevine Peak 8,738ft

Creek

STOVEPIPE WELLS VILLAGE

267

Mount Palmer 7,979ft

D E A T H

Mesquite Flat Sand Dunes

MOSAIC CANYON

Gold Point

SCOTTY'S CASTLE VISITOR CENTER AND MUSEUM

GRAPEVINE

Death Valley National Park

P A N A

White Top Mountain 7,607ft

NEVADA
CALIFORNIA

MESQUITE SPRING

Tin Mountain 8,953ft

DEATH VALLEY / BIG PINE ROAD

UBEHEBE CRATER

RACETRACK ROAD

THE RACETRACK

Magruder Mountain 9,046ft

Dry Mountain 8,674ft

HOMESTAKE DRY CAMP

Hunter Mountain 7,454ft

CRANKSHAFT JUNCTION

Last Chance Mountain 8,456ft

L A S T   C H A N C E   R A N G E

TEAKETTLE JUNCTION

Ubehebe Peak 5,678ft

To Big Pine

Steel Pass

Eureka Dunes

S O U T H   E U R E K A   V A L L E Y   R O A D

WARM SPRINGS

Cerro Gordo Peak

N   E U R E K A   V A L L E Y   R O A D

Chocolate Mountain 11,123ft

E U R E K A   V A L L E Y

S A L I N E   R A N G E

Saline Valley Dunes

S A L I N E   V A L L E Y

SALINE VALLEY ROAD

New York Butte 10,668ft

To Big Pine

Waucoba Mountain 11,123ft

Mount Inyo 11,107ft

I N Y O   M O U N T A I N S

Lone Pine

Located within the northern Mojave Desert, **DEATH VALLEY NATIONAL PARK** boasts extremes as the hottest, the driest, and lowest national park in the United States. From the glaring salt flats below sea level to its tallest peak, this arid park reveals a complex geologic history of seas, volcanoes, tectonic forces, and fault lines.

Battered by wind or watered by secret oases, the landscape is flecked with hidden springs, mining camps, ghost towns, petroglyphs, and sacred spots of the Indigenous Timbisha Shoshone people who call the valley home. Get out of the car to walk its twisting canyons, feel the heat, and listen to its wilderness.

PLANNING YOUR TIME

Death Valley National Park is in southeastern California, with a small slice crossing the border into Nevada. Most of the park is accessible year-round. **CA 190** bisects it east to west, passing through the main park hub of Furnace Creek, 190 feet (57 m) below sea level.

Spring, fall, and **winter** are the best times to visit. Make reservations for the few accommodations starting 13 months in advance; book campsites 6 months in advance. Summer is the off-season, with temperatures topping out at 130°F (54°C). Winter brings snow to the higher elevations, and some roads may close, but the valley areas are pleasant and cool. In spring (Feb.-Apr.) the desert explodes with **wildflower blooms.** The park sees the biggest crowds Friday-Sunday, holidays, and during spring.

Services are limited at Furnace Creek, Stovepipe Wells, and Panamint Springs. Before entering the park, stock up on food, gas, and supplies. When venturing away from developed areas, carry water (1 gal/3.8 l pp/day).

ENTRANCES AND FEES

CA 190 is the most efficient way to enter the park from east or west, and it accesses the most popular sights. The entrance fee is $30 per vehicle ($25 motorcycle, $15 individual) and valid for seven days. Pay the entrance fee at self-pay kiosks or at ranger stations. You can buy passes in advance online (www.recreation.gov).

VISITORS CENTERS

The **Furnace Creek Visitor Center** (Furnace Creek, CA 190, 8:30am-4:30pm daily) has exhibits, drinking water, information on park sights and activities, ranger programs, camping, and hiking. Outside, a thermometer shows the temperature; an adjacent mosaic shows how temperatures change at different elevations. Buy park passes, permits, and park books from the on-site **Death Valley Natural History Association** (http://dvnha.org).

Stovepipe Wells has a small ranger station with general park and backcountry information.

SIGHTS

DANTE'S VIEW

Dante's View (Dante's View Rd.) provides spectacular panoramic views of Death Valley. The Panamint Range rises dramatically from the stiflingly low Badwater Basin salt flats 282 feet (86 m) below sea level to 11,049-foot (3,368-m) Telescope Peak, which is snowcapped much of the year.

FURNACE CREEK

On the east side of the park, the main park hub of **Furnace Creek** (CA 190) has a visitors center and a small cluster of visitor services: lodging, restaurants, a general store, a gas station, and a golf course.

The **Borax Museum** (760/786-2345, www.oasisatdeathvalley.com, 9am-9pm daily, donation), housed in the park's oldest structure, dating to 1883,

Top ③

① SPY HIGH FROM ZABRISKIE POINT

Zabriskie Point (CA 190, 5 mi/8 km south of Furnace Creek) overlooks otherworldly and eroded badlands from a high vantage point. A popular stop for photographers and other visitors, the colors kindle at sunrise and sunset, capturing the magnificent desolation of the valley with the Panamint Mountains towering above.

ZABRISKIE POINT

② SINK LOW AT BADWATER BASIN

Badwater Basin (Badwater Rd., 15 mi/ 24 km south of Furnace Creek) is the lowest point in North America at 282 feet (86 m) below sea level. These unforgiving vast salt flats of sodium chloride, borax, calcite, and gypsum stretch across 200 square miles (518 sq km), the remnants of an ancient lake with no outlet that evaporated. Stroll the boardwalk to a pool with aquatic and plant life. Walk out onto the salt flats (not advised in summer after 10am) to look for delicate salt-crystal formations; you find salt polygons about 1.5-2 miles (2.4-3.2 km) out. The blinding glare, emanating heat, and scale of humans next to the surrounding Black Mountains put our existence into perspective.

BADWATER BASIN

③ GAZE AT NIGHT SKIES

As an **International Dark Sky Park,** Death Valley has places with minimal light pollution that elsewhere impedes night views of stars and the Milky Way. The park holds frequent ranger-led night sky viewing programs in winter and spring. The annual Dark Sky Festival (late Feb.) includes multiple days of NASA speakers and ranger programs. The Ranch at Death Valley hosts star parties. All of these programs have telescope-viewing and astronomers to tell you what you are seeing.

On your own, you can also go out to stargaze on moonless nights around Harmony Borax Works, Ubehebe Crater, Mesquite Flat Dunes, or Badwater Basin, although the latter has mountains that shrink the size of the sky. Bring binoculars and flashlights with red light, as white prevents your eyes adapting to night vision, which takes 30 minutes. The park may also convert the Stovepipe Wells airstrip into a night-sky viewing location; ask about the status at visitors centers.

On full moon nights, you won't need a flashlight for walking, but bring one for safety. Badwater Basin or Mesquite Flat Dunes make perfect places to stroll under the full moon with minimal walking obstacles.

ONE DAY IN DEATH VALLEY

CA 190's paved route along **Badwater Road** makes for a perfect tour of the park. Stop at **Badwater Basin, Mesquite Flat Dunes,** and **Zabriskie Point.** Leave time for a short hike off **Artists Drive** or to **Darwin Falls.** Take water with you and plan in advance for overnight accommodations in the Furnace Creek area.

provides the history of borax mining, the "white gold" of the valley. Other exhibits cover Indigenous people and prospectors in Death Valley. Wander outdoors to view historic artifacts, including a 60-ton oil-burning locomotive that hauled borate.

Two miles (3.2 km) north of Furnace Creek, a short paved path leads to the site of **Harmony Borax Works.** A 20-mule-team wagon, the remains of a borax refinery, and interpretive signs tell the history of the site as a base for the 1883-1888 borax mining and processing operations. Faint eroded remains of **borax haystacks** flank a 1.5-mile (2.4-km) walk across the salt pan.

TWENTY MULE TEAM CANYON

The graded dirt **Twenty Mule Team Canyon Road** (CA 190, east of Furnace Creek, 2.5 mi/4 km one-way) loops through a mudstone canyon past badlands and the site of historical mining prospects at **Twenty Mule Team Canyon.** When the road veers to the right, look to the left to see the site of the **Monte Blanco assay office,** a large wooden house built in 1883 to serve miners.

ARTISTS DRIVE

Named for its shifting palette of colors, the one-way loop **Artists Drive** (Badwater Rd.) rises along an alluvial fan fed by the Black Mountains. The colors, caused by the oxidizing of different metals on the volcanic rock, proffer a chaotic jumble of green, rose, yellow, purple, and red hues. Stop midway at **Artists Palette** for a scenic viewpoint. The lovely paved 9-mile loop (15 km, one-way) starts on Badwater Road, 5 miles (8 km) south of Furnace Creek.

DEVIL'S GOLF COURSE

Admire the controlled chaos of the **Devil's Golf Course** (Badwater Rd., 10 mi/16 km south of Furnace Creek) on the northern end of the eerie stark salt flats of Badwater Basin. Devil's Golf Course is filled with spiky salt crystals—as groundwater seeps to the surface, it prompts the jagged pinnacles. Drive the graded dirt road to a small parking lot, where you can see the formations at closer range.

STOVEPIPE WELLS

Stovepipe Wells (CA 190, www.death-valleyhotels.com), a tourist outpost built in 1926, still sits on the former toll road that brought tourism to Death Valley. The story goes that a stovepipe was used as a marker when sand covered the area. The road was originally built to join Stovepipe Wells with Lone Pine in the Sierra Nevada and now serves as a park hub with a campground, hotel, restaurant, and gas station.

East of Stovepipe Wells on the unpaved Sand Dunes Road, the wind-sculpted **Mesquite Flat Dunes** rise above the desert floor in linear, star-shaped, and crescent dunes. Sandboarding is allowed, and these dunes are outstanding for sunrise, sunset, and night-sky photography.

At **Devil's Cornfield** (CA 190, east of Stovepipe Wells, 8 minute-drive east of Stovepipe Wells) mounded clumps of arrowweed plants stretch in neat rows along the sandy desert floor. The carefully plotted lines of salt-tolerant evergreen plants look surreal against the backdrop of the Funeral Mountains. In the spring, the haystack tops blossom in blue.

Salt Creek (CA 190, 18-minute drive east of Stovepipe Wells) holds a unique ecosystem in Death Valley, with pale eroded mud hills and an expanse of pickleweed. A weathered wheel-

MESQUITE FLAT DUNES

chair-accessible interpretive **board-walk loop** (0.5 mi/0.8 km rt, 20 min, easy) follows the seasonal Salt Creek. This tiny riparian environment supports the endemic **Salt Creek pupfish.**

SCOTTY'S CASTLE

Millionaires Albert and Bessie Johnson built **Scotty's Castle** (Scotty's Castle Rd. at CA 267), a Spanish colonial-style mansion, in 1922 at the urging of Walter Edward Scott. Known as Death Valley Scotty, he was infamous for his wild tales of gold deposits to lure investors. The elaborate complex features a two-story house, 1920s furnishings, a Spanish tile roof, tiled walkways, and a clock tower.

Located one hour from Furnace Creek and Stovepipe Wells, Scotty's Castle closed in 2015 after a flash flood caused significant damage to the buildings and road. Access is allowed only to ticketed participants on ranger-led **Flood Recovery Tours** (www.dvnha. org, 9:30am and 1pm Sun. early Dec.-mid-Apr., 2 hrs, $25). Scotty's Castle is slated to reopen in 2023.

UBEHEBE CRATER

A powerful volcanic explosion about 2,000 years ago created this colorful crater that measures 600 feet (183 m) deep and 0.5 mile (0.8 km) across. Park at the end of the paved access road to see **Ubehebe Crater** (Scotty's Castle Rd., 75-minute drive from Furnace Creek). The rim hike (1.5 mi/2.4km rt, moderate) allows you to peer down into the colorful depths of Ubehebe Crater, Little Hebe Crater, and other smaller craters.

THE RACETRACK

Despite its remoteness, many visitors make the long and difficult drive to **The Racetrack** (Racetrack Valley Rd.), a dry mud-cracked lakebed scattered with the faint trails of rocks that sometimes move across its surface. After rain, if the lake freezes, thin ice sheets act as conveyer belts, carrying rocks across the surface, leaving the mysterious tracks.

From Ubehebe Crater, scenic **Racetrack Valley Road** (28 mi/45 km one-way, 2 hrs) jounces on a long, rutted, rocky washboard road, where flat tires are common. At **Teakettle Junction** (19.4 mi/31 km), turn southwest to reach Racetrack Valley. A high-clearance vehicle is usually adequate, but a 4WD vehicle may be necessary due to flooding and washouts.

EUREKA DUNES

Isolated in the park's remote north, the beautiful and pristine **Eureka Dunes** (South Eureka Rd., no sandboarding permitted) rise from the valley floor as the tallest sand dunes in California, towering more than 680 feet (207 m). From their base, a climb into the dunes goes 0.5-2.5 miles (0.8-4 km) and ascends 300-600 feet (91-183 m). Upon reaching the ridgeline, you are rewarded with sculpted dunes and sweeping views of the valley.

WILDROSE CHARCOAL KILNS

From the dune tops, when the sand is dry, sometimes you can hear the sand "singing" as it slides down the steep faces of the dunes, sounding like low notes of an organ or the droning of an airplane. The dunes make for outstanding photography locations at sunrise and sunset.

From Ubehebe Crater Road, drive the graded dirt Death Valley/Big Pine Road (44 mi/71 km) north and turn south onto the South Eureka Road (10 mi/16 km); it's about 2.5 hours from Furnace Creek. Check conditions before driving it with a standard vehicle.

AGUEREBERRY POINT

Aguereberry Point (Aguereberry Point Rd., 40-minute drive south of Stovepipe Wells off Emigrant Canyon Rd.) yields a 360-degree view of Death Valley. Along **Aguereberry Point Road,** you can explore the remains of a camp, cabins, and the Eureka Mine that prospector Pete Aguereberry worked in 1905.

WILDROSE CHARCOAL KILNS

The 10 historic **Wildrose Charcoal Kilns** (Charcoal Kiln Rd., 70-minute drive south of Stovepipe Wells) stand in a line, looking like beehives. Made of local cut limestone, they are cemented with gravel, lime, and sand to stand approximately 25 feet (7.6 m) tall. Built in 1877, they provided charcoal to fuel nearby lead-silver smelters for about two years. Open arched doorways lead to the interior of the kilns.

SCENIC DRIVE
TITUS CANYON ROAD

From CA 374 (Daylight Pass Rd.), 6 miles (10 km) south of Beatty, Nevada, the dirt-and-gravel **Titus Canyon Road** (27 mi/43 km one-way, 3 hrs) sweeps through rugged rock formations, hangs over canyon views, skirts past **petroglyphs,** and rolls through a **ghost town,** eventually passing through the grand finale: the canyon narrows. The narrows tower overhead, barely letting cars squeeze through before they open wide to reveal the barren Death Valley floor. A **high-clearance** vehicle is usually fine, but a 4WD vehicle may be needed in inclement weather.

RECREATION
HIKING

Off Badwater Road, **Golden Canyon** (3 mi/4.8 km rt, 1.5 hrs, easy) has gentle

▼ TITUS CANYON ROAD

Best Hike

DARWIN FALLS

DISTANCE: 2 miles (3.2 km) round-trip
DURATION: 1.5 hours
ELEVATION CHANGE: 220 feet (67 m)
EFFORT: easy
TRAILHEAD: off CA 190; turn onto gravel road 0.9 mile (1.4 km) west of Panamint Springs and drive 2.5 miles (4 km) to the trailhead

The marvel of **Darwin Falls** is that they exist at all. A short gravelly walk in a wash leads to a high-walled canyon with unexpected vegetation, water, and birds. The unmarked trail's stream crossings and large slick rocks require caution. As the canyon narrows, you come to a sight to behold: a 20-foot (6-m) waterfall that flows year-round. Protect this fragile resource by hiking only where a previous route exists. There is no swimming; it's the drinking water source for Panamint Springs Resort.

grades that lead to sheer red walls with majestic creases. The mouth of the canyon begins along a gravel wash through short narrows with sedimentary and volcanic rock walls. Then the canyon opens to a gold corridor of badlands, both bright and desolate. At a signed fork, go left for another 0.25 mile (0.4 km) to the **Red Cathedral.** Go right at the fork all the way to **Zabriskie Point** (6 mi/9.7 km rt, 3 hrs, moderate) and loop back down via **Gower Gulch.**

Farther south on Badwater Road, go early to avoid crowds on the trail to **Natural Bridge** (1 mi/1.6 km rt, 1 hr, easy). The bridge spans a red-wall canyon that contrasts with the bright sky above. Look back toward Badwater Basin to see Telescope Peak in the distance.

Wildrose Canyon Road goes to two peak-bound trailheads. Near Wildrose Charcoal Kilns, a signed trail leads to **Wildrose Peak** (8.4 mi/13.5 km rt, 6 hrs, moderate). The trail is intermittently steep up to the saddle and sweeping views of Death Valley.

Near Mahogany Flat, the hike up the highest peak in Death Valley—**Telescope Peak** (14 mi/23 km rt, 7-8 hrs, strenuous)—is worth every switchback. The path climbs to 11,049 feet (3,368 m) above Badwater Basin. Expect sweeping views of Death Valley to the east and Panamint Valley to the west. Snow covers the peak in winter (ice ax and crampons needed); it is usually snow-free early May to mid-November.

BIKING

A paved bicycle path (2 mi/3.2 km rt) travels from Furnace Creek to Harmony Borax Works. More difficult rides include the hilly paved loop of **Artists Drive** (9 mi/14.5 km one-way) and the exposed gravel loop of the **West Side Road** (up to 40 mi/64 km) running along the valley floor. Mountain bikers can ride all 4WD roads. **Furnace Creek Ranch General Store** (760/786-3371, www.oasisatdeathvalley.com) rents mountain bikes; pickup and drop-off are at the gas station.

GOLF

At 214 feet (65 m) below sea level, **Furnace Creek Golf Course** (CA 190, 760/786-3373, www.oasisatdeathvalley.com) claims to be the lowest-elevation golf course in the world. Dotted with water, this 18-hole course is lined with palm and tamarisk trees.

WHERE TO STAY

INSIDE THE PARK

In Furnace Creek, lodgings (CA 190, Death Valley, 800/236-7916, www.oasisatdeathvalley.com, year-round) are at **The Inn at Death Valley** (from $389), with new casitas built in 2018, and the **Ranch at Death Valley** (from $149), both with outdoor swimming pools. Make reservations for either starting 13 months in advance. The **Inn Dining Room** (760/786-3385, dinner daily

SCENIC FOUR-WHEEL DRIVES

Hundreds of miles of unmaintained 4WD roads provide access to remote destinations in Death Valley. **Farabee's Jeep Rentals** in Furnace Creek rents 4WD vehicles and has up-to-date backcountry road information. Backcountry drivers should plan carefully. Take basic tools, a shovel, extra water (for you and your vehicle), and food. **Permits** (free) are required for dispersed camping along dirt roads; get them from Furnace Creek Visitor Center or Stovepipe Wells Ranger Station when open.

The best times are spring and fall. Summer sees blazing temperatures; in winter, rain or snow can render some roads impassable. Stay on roads at all times to preserve fragile desert flora and biological soil crusts.

Cottonwood Canyon Road: West of Stovepipe Wells, this 8.5-mile (14-km) primitive road crawls into the Cottonwood Mountains. Starting off with a slog through sand, the road becomes more solid on washboard and gravel but much rougher in Cottonwood Canyon wash.

Echo Canyon to Inyo Mine: Between Furnace Creek and Zabriskie Point, this 20-mile (32-km) round-trip road tours a winding canyon to mining camp ruins. To the canyon mouth (3 mi/4.8 km) requires a high-clearance vehicle, but 4WD is required beyond.

Warm Spring Canyon to Butte Valley: The lower canyon follows a well-graded road the first 10 miles (16 km) to Warm Springs Camp near talc mines. The upper canyon requires 4WD into the Jurassic quartz monzonite granite of Butte Valley (21 mi/34 km).

Racetrack Valley Road: 4WD adventures to **The Racetrack** can turn into multiday trips by overnighting at Homestake Dry Camp at the south end of Racetrack Valley. You can add on **Ubehebe Peak, Hidden Valley,** and remote mining camps like **Ubehebe Mine, Lost Burro Mine, Lippincott Mine,** and the **Goldbelt Mining District.**

Saline Valley Road: This rough yet graded dirt road travels 78 lonely miles (126 km) from Death Valley-Big Pine Road near Big Pine to CA 190, west of Panamint Springs. Although a high-clearance vehicle is suitable during good weather, 4WD is preferred to access the remote **Saline Valley** that contains sand dunes and Salt Lake. To drive the road takes the better part of a day without stops; for time to explore, allow at least three days, and camp at the centrally located, primitive **Warm Springs Camp.**

May-Sept., breakfast, lunch, and dinner daily Oct.-Apr.) takes advance dinner reservations for hotel guests and requires resort attire. A few minutes away, the **Ranch 1849 Buffet** (7am-7pm daily) rotates self-serve options for breakfast, lunch, and dinner, and the **Last Kind Words Saloon** (760/786-3335, breakfast, lunch, and dinner daily), a steakhouse, takes reservations. The Ranch also has a general store with convenience foods.

Stovepipe Wells Village (51880 CA 190, Death Valley, 760/786-7090, www.deathvalleyhotels.com, from $179) has a hotel with an outdoor swimming pool. Dining is in the **Toll Road Restaurant** (7am-10am and 5:30pm-9pm daily) and **Badwater Saloon** (11:30am-close daily). The RV Park (from $40) has hookups.

Panamint Springs Resort (40440 CA 190, Panamint Springs, 775/482-7680, www.panamintsprings.com) has motel rooms (from $160), camping (tents $10, RV hookups $40, tent cabins from $55), a restaurant, and a general store.

There are **nine national park campgrounds.** All campgrounds can get very windy at night. If tent camping, stake all gear properly. If relying on RV electrical hookups, expect power surges and outages.

Furnace Creek (136 sites, including group and RV electrical hookups, year-round) is the only park campground that accepts **reservations** (877/444-6777, www.recreation.gov, Oct. 15-Apr. 15, $22-60) six months in advance. From mid-April to mid-October, sites are first come, first served ($16-60).

All other campgrounds are first come, first served. Along CA 190, find **Texas Springs** (92 sites, Nov.-May, $16), **Sunset** (270 sites, Nov.-May, $14), **Emigrant** (10 tent sites, year-round, free), and **Stovepipe Wells** (190 sites, mid-Sept.-mid-May, $14). **Mesquite Spring** (30 sites, year-round, $14) is nearest Scotty's Castle. **Thorndike** (6 sites, Mar.-Nov., free), **Wildrose** (23 sites, year-round, free), and **Mahogany Flat** (10 sites, Mar.-Nov., free) are on Emigrant Canyon Road (no vehicles over 25 ft/7.6 m, high-clearance needed for Thorndike and Mahogany Flats).

OUTSIDE THE PARK

The gateway towns of **Lone Pine, Big Pine, Ridgecrest,** and **Beatty, Nevada,** have limited accommodations and restaurants.

GETTING THERE AND AROUND

AIR

The closest international airports are **Los Angeles International Airport** (LAX, 1 World Way, Los Angeles, 855/463-5252, www.flylax.com) and **McCarran International Airport** (LAS, 5757 Wayne Newton Blvd., Las Vegas, 702/261-5211, www.mccarran.com). Both airports have car rentals.

CAR

From **Los Angeles,** take I-5 north toward Palmdale and Lancaster to CA 14. Drive 120 miles (193 km) north on CA 14 to Indian Wells to join US 395. Continue north on US 395 for 42 miles (68 km) to the town of Olancha. Turn right (east) onto CA 190 and continue 45 miles (72 km) to Panamint Springs. Stovepipe Wells lies 29 miles (47 km) east of Panamint Springs; Furnace Creek is 53 miles (85 km) east of Panamint Springs.

From **Las Vegas,** I-15 intersects with US 95 north of the airport. Take US 95 north for 74 miles (119 km) to Lathrop Wells, Nevada. Turn left (south) onto NV 373 and drive 24 miles (39 km) southwest. NV 373 becomes CA 127 when it crosses into California. At the tiny outpost of Death Valley Junction, turn right (west) onto CA 190 and continue west for 30 miles (48 km) to the park hub at Furnace Creek.

The park has no shuttles or public transportation—**bring your own vehicle.** For back-road excursions, rent 4WD rigs through **Farabee's** (Furnace Creek, 760/786-9872, http://farabee-jeeps.com, mid-Sept.-mid-May); advance reservations are recommended.

Gas is sold inside the park at Furnace Creek and Stovepipe Wells, but prices are expensive. Fill up at one of the gateway towns instead.

JOSHUA TREE NATIONAL PARK

California

WEBSITE:
www.nps.gov/jotr

PHONE NUMBER:
760/367-5500

VISITATION RANK:
11

WHY GO:
Explore a desert
landscape filled with
jumbled boulders
and Joshua trees.

KEEPSAKE STAMPS ▼▼▼

▲ BARKER DAM HIKING TRAIL AT
JOSHUA TREE NATIONAL PARK

JOSHUA TREE NATIONAL PARK's seemingly desolate landscape startles and charms. Powerful forces molded the rocks into twisted shapes and scrambled boulder piles. The namesake Joshua trees, which can live up to 150 years, form spiked angles against blue skies. But long-term drought is inhibiting the saplings from sending deep roots to water, thereby dwindling the population of these icons of the Mojave Desert. Farther south, the landscape changes in the Colorado Desert to austere and arid, with wide alluvial fans of creosote bushes and spindly ocotillos guarding mountain canyons.

The park lures spring wildflower seekers, birders, serious hikers, and hard-core rock climbers. For many first-time visitors, the landscape initially looks empty; for the Indigenous people—the Cahuilla, Chemehuevi, Serrano, and Mojave—who traditionally relied on what the land provided, it is ripe with fruits, seeds, berries, and animal life.

PLANNING YOUR TIME

Joshua Tree is in Southern California, east of Los Angeles and northeast of Palm Springs. Its location near these major urban centers brings scads of day-trippers. Most visitors arrive via CA 62 to enter the park on the west side near the town of Joshua Tree. From town, Park Boulevard winds through the park, connecting with Twentynine Palms just outside the north entrance on CA 62. Short spurs from CA 62 take in additional park sights.

Visit during the cooler, but crowded, months of **October-April;** weekdays draw fewer people. Spring wildflower season (late Feb.-May) draws the biggest crowds of the year. Large lineups of cars enter the park 10am-2pm and exit around sunset. When parking lots fill to capacity, the main park road may become drive-through only. Always have an alternate hiking plan, in case your intended trailhead lot is full.

The weather is gorgeous in spring and fall, but brutal in summer, with average temperatures topping 100°F (38°C). In winter, the park is dusted by snow.

Camping is the only overnight option inside the park; make reservations six months in advance. You'll need a **car,** a full tank of gas, **water** (at least 1 gal/3.8 l pp/day), and food. There are no services and no cell service inside the park.

ENTRANCES AND FEES

The entrance fee is $30 per vehicle ($25 motorcycle, $15 individual), which is good for seven days. Buy a pass in advance online (www.recreation.gov) for quicker access.

All roads and entrance stations are open year-round. The park has three entrance stations:

West Entrance (CA 62 and Park Blvd.) is in the town of Joshua Tree, south of the Joshua Tree Visitor Center. It sees the heaviest visitation. Lines extend nearly 2 miles (3.2 km) midday during peak season. In 2023, a larger fee station with more lanes will open, moving the entrance 0.5 mile (0.8 km) farther into the park.

North Entrance (CA 62 and Utah Trail) is in the town of Twentynine Palms about 4 miles (6 km) from the highway.

South Entrance (exit 168 off I-10) accesses the park's Colorado Desert and the less visited Cottonwood Spring.

VISITORS CENTERS

The park's four visitors centers have information, exhibits, maps, water, and restrooms. On-site bookstores sell maps, guidebooks, and gifts. Rangers lead patio talks and chats; you can

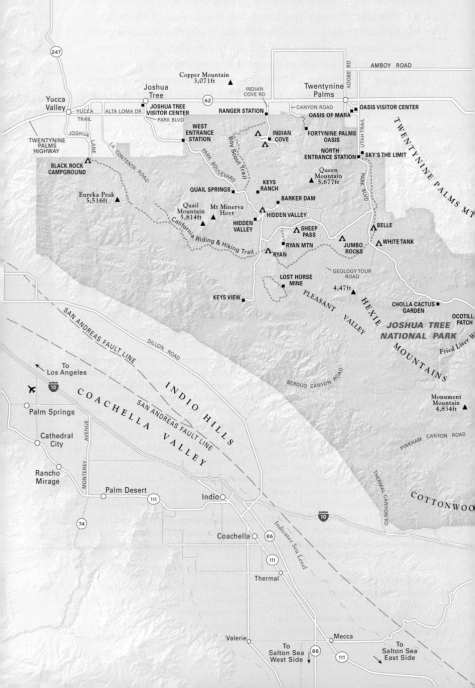

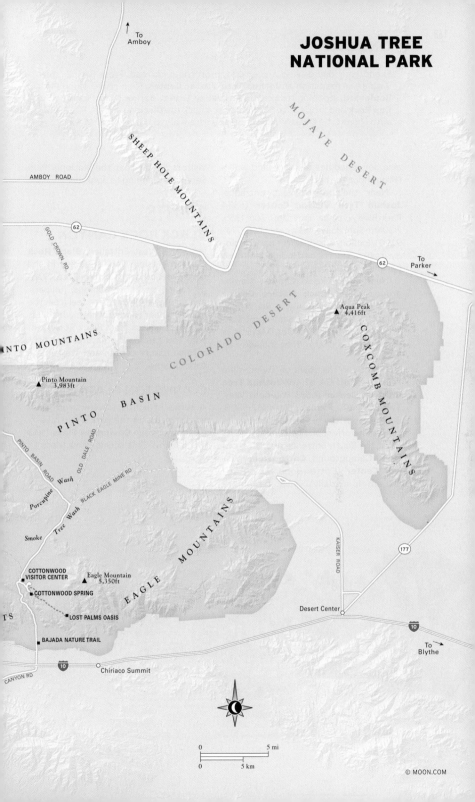

To
Amboy

MOJAVE DESERT

SHEEP HOLE MOUNTAINS

AMBOY ROAD

62

GOLD CROWN RD

62

To Parker

NTO MOUNTAINS

COLORADO DESERT

▲ Aqua Peak
4,416ft

COXCOMB MOUNTAINS

▲ Pinto Mountain
3,983ft

PINTO BASIN

OLD DALE ROAD

PINTO BASIN ROAD

Porcupine Wash

BLACK EAGLE MINE RD

Smoke Tree Wash

EAGLE MOUNTAINS

KAISER ROAD

177

COTTONWOOD
VISITOR CENTER

■ COTTONWOOD SPRING

▲ Eagle Mountain
5,350ft

■ LOST PALMS OASIS

■ BAJADA NATURE TRAIL

TS

Desert Center

10

To
Blythe

10

CANYON RD

Chiriaco Summit

0   5 mi

0   5 km

© MOON.COM

ONE DAY IN JOSHUA TREE

Spend your day driving a scenic loop on the park road. From CA 62, start with an introduction at **Joshua Tree Visitor Center.** Then cruise along **Park Boulevard,** stopping to hike **Hidden Valley Trail** or **Barker Dam.** Picnic below **Cap Rock** and stop to see **Skull Rock** and walk the **Discovery Trail.** Finish your auto tour at the **Oasis Visitor Center** with a walk to the **Oasis of Mara.**

also get schedules of ranger-led walks throughout the park.

Near the park's West Entrance, **Joshua Tree Visitor Center** (6554 Park Blvd., Joshua Tree, 760/366-1855, 7:30am-5pm daily) has a café (760/974-9290). Exhibits inside cover park geology, its two deserts, and Indigenous people and historical sites.

Near Black Rock Canyon Campground, **Black Rock Nature Center** (9800 Black Rock Canyon Rd., Yucca Valley, 760/367-3001, 8am-4pm Sat.-Thurs., 8am-8pm Fri. Oct.-May) is a small visitors center that includes an art gallery.

Directly in the town of Twentynine Palms, just off CA-62, the **Joshua Tree Cultural Center** (6533 Freedom Way, Twentynine Palms, 760/367-5500, 8:30am-5pm daily) houses a visitors center and offers plentiful parking.

At the South Entrance near Cottonwood Campground, **Cottonwood Visitor Center** (Cottonwood Spring Rd., 8:30am-4pm daily) is a temporary

visitors center that the National Park Service is planning to upgrade.

SIGHTS
BLACK ROCK CANYON

Near the West Entrance, **Black Rock Canyon** (Joshua Lane) huddles in the northwest corner of Joshua Tree. Craggy rolling peaks and piñons, junipers, and oaks give it a different feel from the more popular Hidden Valley, which has no direct access from Black Rock Canyon. You can walk a nature trail, tour a small nature center, and stay at the campground.

COVINGTON FLATS

A series of lightly traveled and graded dirt roads in the park's northwestern corner tour **Covington Flats** (10.3 mi/16.5 km). This scenic drive leads to

▼ COVINGTON FLATS

Top ③

① CRUISE ALONG PARK BOULEVARD

From the West Entrance near the town of Joshua Tree, **Park Boulevard** delves deep into the Hidden Valley to emerge in the town of Twentynine Palms 25 miles (40 km) later. This drive takes in iconic scenery of Joshua trees and jumbled rocks, with access to Hidden Valley's **campgrounds, trailheads,** and **sights.**

HIDDEN VALLEY TRAIL

② SEE THE DESERT WITH NEW EYES

To some, the desert looks barren and void. But it fills with wildlife. Birders spy resident, migrant, and nesting birds, including the occasional group of 200 or more turkey vultures overnighting near **The Oasis of Mara** during spring migration. Listen for the descending notes of canyon wrens and spot roadrunners, Gambel's quail, prairie falcons, and American kestrels. You may also see desert bighorn sheep around **Barker Dam** or **Lost Palm Oasis.** Places with vegetation and water are prime wildlife attractants, such as **Cottonwood Springs** and **49 Palms Oasis,** but keep your distance to allow them access to much-needed food and water.

③ ROCK CLIMB IN HIDDEN VALLEY

From beginners to rock stars, climbers of all levels seek the park's vast array of traditional-style crack, slab, and steep-face climbing. More than 400 climbing formations and more than 8,000 recognized climbs make it a world-class destination. Plenty of rock-climbing guides teach courses and lead private climbs, including for families with kids. Some good places to watch climbers in action are the **Quail Springs** picnic area, **Hidden Valley Campground,** the **Wonderland of Rocks, Cap Rock, Jumbo Rocks, Indian Cove, Ryan Campground, Split Rock,** and **Live Oak.**

CAP ROCK

DESERT QUEEN MINE

a sweeping overlook, several hiking trails, and some of the largest stands of Joshua trees, junipers, and piñons in the park. Access is off La Contenta Road.

EUREKA PEAK OVERLOOK

Follow signs to 5,521-foot (1,683-m) **Eureka Peak Overlook** for sweeping panoramic views. From the summit, the Coachella Valley, Desert Hot Springs, and the San Jacinto Mountains lie southwest, while views to the north take in the Morongo Basin.

HIDDEN VALLEY

Wonderland of Rocks

Dubbed the **Wonderland of Rocks,** this region contains a wildly eroded maze of striking granite rock formations studded with hidden basins, gorgeous views, and desert bighorn sheep. The Wonderland of Rocks covers the area between Indian Cove Campground and Hidden Valley Campground. From Park Boulevard, its compelling rock formations are visible to the northeast. To go into the heart of the area, walk the **Barker Dam Trail** (Park Blvd.) and stay at **Indian Cove Campground** (Indian Cove Rd.).

Ryan Ranch

The homestead ruins of the **Ryan Ranch** (Park Blvd. near Ryan Campground) date to 1896. An interpretive trail (1 mi/1.6 km rt, 30 min, easy) tours its adobe bunkhouse, windmill, and a pioneer cemetery. Evidence of grinding stones reveal the earlier presence of Indigenous people.

Keys View

The paved, wheelchair-accessible **Keys View** (Keys View Rd.) is a windswept observation point in the Little San Bernardino Mountains. An impressive panorama stretches to the Salton Sea, Santa Rosa Mountains, San Andreas Fault, Palm Springs, San Jacinto Peak, and San Gorgonio Peak.

Keys Ranch

Learn how ranchers once eked out a living in the Mojave Desert. From 1917 to 1969, homesteader and miner Bill Keys carved out a domain at his ranch. Rangers guide tours of the **Keys Ranch** (90 min, daily Oct.-May, adults $10, kids $5, under age 6 free), which includes a ranch house, schoolhouse, store, and workshop. **Reservations** (877/444-6777, www.recreation.gov) are required; make them up to 60 days in advance. Allow 40 minutes for the drive (22 mi/35 km) from the visitors center to the ranch gate.

QUEEN VALLEY

The **Queen Valley** is a cross section of Joshua Tree's greatest hits, with Joshua trees, mining ruins, Indigenous villages, scenic hikes, and views. Short dirt roads crisscross Queen Valley through one of the largest pockets of Joshua trees in the park. Mining ruins range from Desert Queen Mine, which was a large gold operation, to the humble rusty remains of tent encampments. Hiking trails follow old mining roads to **Desert Queen Mine, Lucky Boy Vista,** and **Wall Street Mine.** To reach the Queen Valley area, follow the unpaved Queen Valley Road or Desert Queen Mine Road east to Pine City.

CHOLLA CACTUS GARDEN

In the endless landscape of the Pinto Basin, the **Cholla Cactus Garden** (Pinto Basin Rd.) appears like an army of prickly planted teddy bears covered with barbed spines. Their sheer numbers impress in this surreal landscape. A 0.25-mile (0.4 km, rt, 15 min) trail tours one of the few teddy-bear cholla stands in the park.

COTTONWOOD SPRING

At the South Entrance, **Cottonwood Spring Oasis** (Cottonwood Spring Rd.), created by earthquake activity, was used for centuries by the Cahuilla people, who left mortars and clay pots, or ollas, in the area. Underground water

forced to the surface nurtures this fan palm oasis, one of five in the park, and a surprising crop of cottonwood trees.

NIGHT SKIES

Designated an **International Dark Sky Park,** Joshua Tree has minimal light pollution, letting moonless nights bring out the Milky Way. You can go out on your own to stargaze from campgrounds or road pullouts, such as those along Pinto Basin Road that have minimal light and traffic. Use a flashlight with red light; white lights impinge night vision. Year-round, rangers in tandem with park partners offer Night Sky Programs, with telescopes for viewing planets and nebulae. The **Night Sky Festival** (www.nightskyfestival.org) happens annually around the fall equinox. Tickets go on sale in June.

SCENIC DRIVE
GEOLOGY TOUR ROAD

The **Geology Tour Road** (18 mi/29 km) is a backcountry drive that descends south into the broad Pleasant Valley and an ancient dry lake. Enjoy views of the unique geologic phenomena, which

▼ BARKER DAM

Best Hike

BARKER DAM

DISTANCE: 1.1 mile (1.8 km) round-trip
DURATION: 1 hour
ELEVATION CHANGE: negligible
EFFORT: easy
TRAILHEAD: Wonderland of Rocks

The **Barker Dam Trail** gives a classic taste of the Mojave Desert with Joshua trees, piñon pines, and yucca. The trail loops through boulders to a small pond, a watering hole for migrating birds, and desert bighorn sheep. You'll pass the western edge of the Wonderland of Rocks, where climbers scale formations and plenty of boulders offer places to scramble. An Indigenous Cahuilla rock art site contains both pictographs and petroglyphs (help preserve it by viewing from the sign). Prepare for minimal shade.

include dramatic erosion and uplifts. Pick up a free interpretive pamphlet from the Joshua Tree Visitor Center, which details the route with 16 numbered points of interest (also listed on the NPS app).

The first 5 miles (8 km) of graded dirt road are passable by most cars (no RVs) in dry weather. After that, the road is **4WD only** due to deep ruts, sand,

SKULL ROCK

and steep grades. Then, the road completes a one-way loop clockwise along the Hexie Mountain foothills and through Pleasant Valley. You're committed to the two-hour drive once you start the loop.

RECREATION
HIKING

Joshua Tree has top-notch hiking in an otherworldly landscape. But watch for dehydration, the biggest danger. Always carry at least **1 gallon (3.8 l) of water per person per day** and balance water intake with salty snacks. During spring and fall, hike during cooler times of the day, such as sunrise to 10am or after 4pm. Hiking in summer is not recommended.

Black Rock Canyon

Hike clockwise on the interpretive **Hi-View Nature Trail** (1.3 mi/2.1 km rt, 1.5 hrs, moderate) for sweeping views of Yucca Valley, Black Rock Canyon, and the San Bernardino Mountains with the snowcapped 11,503-foot (3,506 m) San Gorgonio Mountain.

Hidden Valley

Trails around Hidden Valley are the **most popular in the park.** Arrive early as parking lots fill up.

The wheelchair-accessible, hard-packed sandy **Cap Rock Trail** (0.4 mi/0.6 km rt, 20 min, easy) leads through whimsically eroded boulder

LOST HORSE MINE

formations to an angled cap-like rock balanced on top of a larger formation.

Created by kids for kids, the loop **Discovery Trail** (0.8 mi/1.3 km, 30 min, easy) leads through desert washes near Jumbo Rocks. Local students designed trail placement and information placards, and the Youth Conservation Corps constructed the trail. Extend the loop by adding **Skull Rock** (1.7 mi/2.7 km rt, 1.5 hrs, easy), named for depressions that look like gaunt eye sockets. This trail winds through the boulder- and plant-strewn landscape to Jumbo Rocks Campground, then follows the campground road to cross Park Boulevard and loop back through more boulders with desert views.

The **Hidden Valley Nature Trail** (1 mi/1.6 km rt, 45 min, easy) passes through granite boulders to emerge in scenic Hidden Valley, a small enclosed valley with tempting bouldering opportunities.

The trail to **Ryan Mountain** (3 mi/4.8 km rt, 2.5 hrs, strenuous) climbs more than 1,000 feet (305 m) to ascend to this wind-scoured summit with panoramic views.

Start counterclockwise on the looping **Lost Horse Mine Trail** (4 mi/6.4 km rt, 2-3 hrs, moderate). The route climbs up Lost Horse Mountain, and below tours remains from a gold rush: a weathered stamp mill, rock house

foundations, equipment, and fenced-off mining tunnels.

Queen Valley

Starting from the Wonderland of Rocks Trailhead, the **Wall Street Mill Trail** (2.2 mi/3.5 km rt, 1.5 hrs, easy) veers east passing abandoned cars, mining

CHOLLA CACTUS

artifacts, and a well with a windmill. The trail terminates at the mill with a winch and tracks—the best-preserved gold mill in the park.

Northeast

A flinty landscape hides **49 Palms Oasis** (3 mi/4.8 km rt, 2-3 hrs, moderate), which nestles against jagged hills. The sometimes steep, arid path climbs over a ridge and drops through hills to the oasis of native fan palms secluded in a rocky canyon. Keep your distance to avoid disturbing wildlife seeking much-needed water.

Cottonwood Spring

Two trails depart from Cottonwood Spring parking area. **Mastodon Peak**

Loop (3 mi/4.8 km rt, 2 hrs, moderate) passes concrete foundations of the old **Winona Mill** before climbing toward the peak for sweeping views of the Cottonwood Mountains and the remains of the **Mastodon Mine.**

Lost Palms Oasis Trail (7.2 mi/11.6 km rt, 5-6 hrs, strenuous) undulates down an exposed trail to a secluded canyon and the largest collection of fan palms in the park. In the steepwalled boulder-filled canyon, maintain a distance from the oasis, a crucial water source for bighorn sheep and other wildlife.

BIKING

The paved **Park Boulevard** (25 mi/40 km) offers prime cycling through the

CLIMBER IN JOSHUA TREE

WILLOW HOLE TRAIL

park's most spectacular scenery between the West Entrance in Joshua Tree to the North Entrance near Twentynine Palms. **Pinto Basin Road** (30 mi/48 km), the other paved park road, cuts through the Pinto Basin's open desert with fewer vehicles but less scenic appeal.

Rent bikes at **Joshua Tree Bicycle Shop** (6416 Hallee Rd., Joshua Tree, 760/366-3377, www.jtbikeshop.com) outside the park's West Entrance.

ROCK CLIMBING

Joshua Tree's monzogranite jumbles are the perfect lure for trad-style rock climbers, boulderers, and highliners from around the world. Four trails (Barker Dam Loop, Boy Scout Trail, Willow Hole, and Wonderland Wash) knife into the **Wonderland of Rocks,** where climbing trails are signed and established.

The park is developing a plan to protect soils, vegetation, and cultural resources from destructive climbing practices; look online for updates that may affect access and procedures. **Permits** are required for some types of climbing in some locations. Be aware of permanent and seasonal closures to protect raptor nesting zones. To get updates and information, join a climbing ranger at **Climbers Coffee** (Hidden Valley Campground, 8am-10am Sat.-Sun. mid-Oct.-Apr.). Bring your own mug; hot beverages are provided. You can also glean beta from other climbers.

Joshua Tree has several guide companies to get beginners started or just up your game on rock:

Joshua Tree Rock Climbing School (760/366-4745, www.joshuatreerockclimbing.com) offers year-round classes and private guided climbs.

Cliffhanger Guides (760/401-5033, www.cliffhangerguides.com) specializes in custom guided climbs.

Vertical Adventures (800/514-8785, www.vertical-adventures.com) has one- to five-day courses, private instruction, and guided climbing.

Climbing Life Guides (760/780-8868, www.theclimbinglifeguides.com) teaches courses and guides private climbs.

To gear up for rock climbing, go to one of the outfitters on the main drag in Joshua Tree:

Nomad Ventures (61795 Twentynine Palms Hwy., Joshua Tree, 760/366-4684, www.nomadventures.com)

Coyote Corner (6535 Park Blvd., Joshua Tree, 760/366-9683, www.jtcoyotecorner.com)

WHERE TO STAY
INSIDE THE PARK

There are no accommodations or food inside the park. The park has 500 campsites ($15-30), most of which accept **reservations** (877/444-6777, www.recreation.gov). Make reservation sstarting six months in advance, especially for weekends, holidays, and spring (mid-Feb.-mid-May). Campgrounds start to fill by Thursday most weekends **October-May.** All campgrounds have picnic tables, fire pits, and vault toilets (some have flush toilets) but no hookups. Some have bicycle sites ($5).

Year-Round Campgrounds

All year-round campgrounds except Hidden Valley **require reservations late August-early June;** otherwise, they are first come, first served.

In the northwest corner of the park, with quick access to Yucca Valley for supplies, **Black Rock** (99 sites) has drinking water, flush toilets, and a dump station.

JUMBO ROCKS CAMPGROUND

On Park Boulevard are three campgrounds with no drinking water; bring your own. **Jumbo Rocks** (124 sites) is the largest campground in the park. **Ryan** (31 sites) sits among boulders and rock formations. **Sheep Pass** (6 group sites, by reservation only up to 12 months in advance) is a tent-only campground.

The Wonderland of Rocks area has two ultra-popular campgrounds without water (bring your own). Accessed from CA 62, **Indian Cove** (101 sites) is on the north edge of the Wonderland. **Hidden Valley** (44 sites) is a first-come, first-served campground at the south end of the Wonderland.

Near the South Entrance off I-10, **Cottonwood** (62 sites) has potable water, flush toilets, and a dump station.

Seasonal Campgrounds

Two seasonal campgrounds (early Sept.-May, $15-20) are on the north end of Pinto Basin Road where dark skies offer outstanding stargazing. Neither has water; bring your own. Both are first come, first served. RVs and trailer combos are limited to 25 feet (7.6 m). From the north, **Belle** (18 sites) is followed by **White Tank** (15 sites); both are set amid granite boulders.

OUTSIDE THE PARK

Outside the park, find lodging and dining in **Yucca Valley,** the town of **Joshua Tree,** and **Twentynine Palms.** Backcountry camping is permitted on BLM land, and the town of Joshua Tree has a private RV park.

GETTING THERE

AIR

The closest airport is **Palm Springs Airport** (PSP, 3400 E. Tahquitz Canyon Way, 760/318-3800, www.palmspringsairport.com). International travelers can fly into **Los Angeles International Airport** (LAX, 1 World Way, 424/646-5252, www.flylax.com) or Las Vegas's **McCarran International Airport** (LAS, 5757 Wayne Newton Blvd., 702/261-5211, www.mccarran.com).

▼ CACTUS FLOWER

NAME	LOCATION	PRICE	SEASON	SITES	AMENITIES
Black Rock	Black Rock Canyon	$25-30	year-round; reservations required late Aug.-early June	99	tent/RV and horse sites, flush toilets, drinking water, dump station
Hidden Valley	Hidden Valley	$15-20	year-round	44	tent/RV sites, vault toilets
Ryan	Hidden Valley	$20-25	year-round; reservations required late Aug.-early June	31	tent and horse sites, vault toilets
Sheep Pass	Hidden Valley	$25-50	year-round, reservation only	6	group tent sites, vault toilets
Jumbo Rocks	Hidden Valley	$20-25	year-round; reservations required late Aug.-early June	124	tent/RV sites, vault toilets
Belle	Hidden Valley	$15-20	early Sept.-May	18	tent sites, vault toilets
White Tank	Hidden Valley	$15-20	early Sept.-May	15	tent/RV sites, vault toilets
Indian Cove	Indian Cove	$20-25	year-round; reservations required late Aug.-early June	101	tent/RV sites and group sites, vault toilets
Cottonwood	Cottonwood Spring	$25-30	year-round; reservations required late Aug.-early June	62	tent/RV and group sites, flush toilets, drinking water, dump station

CAR

From **Palm Springs,** it's an hourlong drive to the park. Yucca Valley is the best place to fuel up before entering. The small town also has several major car rental agencies. From **Los Angeles,** it's roughly a two-hour drive east via I-10.

The **West Entrance** (CA 62) to Joshua Tree is 50 miles (81 km, 1.25 hrs) north of Palm Springs and 145 miles (233 km, 3-4 hrs) east of Los Angeles. From I-10 near Palm Springs, head north on CA 62 for 30 miles (48 km) to the town of Joshua Tree. Turn south on Park Boulevard and follow the road into the park.

The **North Entrance** (CA 62) is farther east, near Twentynine Palms. From the town of Joshua Tree, drive 16 miles (26 km) east along CA 62 then turn south on Utah Trail. From **Las Vegas,** the North Entrance is roughly a four-hour drive southwest via I-15.

The **South Entrance** (I-10) is about 65 miles (105 km, 1.25 hrs) east of Palm Springs along I-10 and 160 miles (257 km, 4 hrs) east of Los Angeles. From I-10, turn north on Cottonwood Spring Road to enter the park.

GETTING AROUND

No shuttles or public transportation are available. You'll need your own vehicle. Gas up before you go into the park.

LASSEN VOLCANIC NATIONAL PARK

California

WEBSITE:
www.nps.gov/lavo

PHONE NUMBER:
530/595-4480

VISITATION RANK:
43

WHY GO:
Explore a volcanic
landscape.

KEEPSAKE STAMPS ▼▼▼

▲ LASSEN PEAK

Due to rugged weather and geographic distance from California's urban centers, **LASSEN VOLCANIC NATIONAL PARK** is preserved as largely unspoiled wilderness, much as it was when four local Indigenous groups, the Atsugewi, Yana, Yahi, and Maidu, harvested and hunted through these valleys. Encased within the park is Mount Lassen, an active volcano with a history of eruptions, the last of which took place 1914-1917. As in Yellowstone, hydrothermals pushing to the surface still shape the landscape, which clusters with fumaroles, mud pots, and hot springs. A partial loop drive through the park follows the stark slopes and jagged rocks of the most recent eruption to an enormous volcano crater. Plentiful hiking trails, ponds, and campsites welcome visitors to enjoy the panorama.

PLANNING YOUR TIME

Located in Northern California, this high-elevation park is only accessible from **June** into **October** when snow melts and daytime temperatures rise to the 80s and 90s (upper 20s-lower 30s C). Snow chokes the area October-June, closing the main road through the park. Most visitors arrive **July-September.**

In 2021, the Dixie Fire burned 69 percent of Lassen Volcanic National Park. The main park road follows the western fringes of the fire, with most of the heavily affected areas to the east. Some trails, bridges, structures, hydrothermal areas, and campgrounds suffered damage, which may take several years to rehabilitate. Check with the National Park Service to verify the status ahead of your visit.

ENTRANCES AND FEES

There are two park entrances, both located on CA 89. The **northwest entrance** (summer only) is at the junction of CA 89 and CA 44 near Manzanita Lake. The **southwest entrance** (year-round) is accessed from CA 36 and travels north through the park from the Kohm Yah-mah-nee Visitor Center. In winter, the park road is closed after the visitors center.

The entrance fee is $30 per vehicle ($25 motorcycle, $15 individual) and good for seven days.

VISITORS CENTER

The **Kohm Yah-mah-nee Visitor Center** (21820 Lassen National Park Hwy., Mineral, 530/595-4480, 9am-5pm daily May-Oct., 9am-5pm Wed.-Sun. Nov.-Mar.) has interactive exhibits, a café, a souvenir shop, and a bookstore. Outside, strategically placed benches offer views of the mountains, and a short interpretive trail tours the paved walkways. Rangers lead programs, including snowshoe walks in winter.

SIGHTS

SULPHUR WORKS

For the most easily seen volcanic activity right on the main park road, **Sulphur Works** has a colorful mix of loud boiling mud pots, vents that hiss, a sulfur stench, and a small steaming stream that sends up occasional bursts of boiling water. From the Kohm Yah-mah-nee Visitor Center, drive north to the parking area.

SUMMIT LAKE

Lassen is dotted with tiny lakes. One of the most popular (and most easily accessible) is **Summit Lake.** It attracts paddlers, anglers, and campers to its two campgrounds. Easy paths stroll along the shore.

DEVASTATED AREA

When Lassen Peak erupted in 1915, boiling mud and explosive gases tore off

LASSEN VOLCANIC NATIONAL PARK

VOLCANO ADVENTURE YOUTH CAMP

LOST CREEK GROUP CAMP

LASSEN NATIONAL FOREST

Badg

Table Mountain 6,919ft

Nobles Emigrant Trail

To Redding

Dwarf Forest

Chaos Jumbles

Reflection Lake

CHAOS CRAGS AND CHAOS JUMBLES

ENTRANCE STATION

Manzanita Lake

Crags Lake

Lava

HOT ROCK

Raker Peak 7,483ft

Hat Creek

MANZANITA LAKE CAMPGROUND

Manzanita Creek

8,530ft

CHAOS CRAGS

Lava

Anklin Meadows

Lost Creek

DEVASTATED AREA

Hat Mountai 7,695ft

Crescent Crater 8,645ft

Devastated Area

HAT CREEK TRAILHEAD

Dersch Meadows

LASSEN VOLCANIC WILDERNESS

LASSEN NATIONAL FOREST

Paradise Meadows

SUMMIT LAKE TRAILHEAD

SUMMIT LAKE NORTH

Shadow Lake

Summit Lake

SUMMIT LAKE SOUTH

Loomis Peak 8,658ft

Crescent Cliff

LASSEN PEAK 10,457ft

North Fork Bailey Creek

Blue Lake Canyon

Eagle Peak 9,222ft

ROAD'S HIGH POINT 8,512FT

Cliff Lake

Reading Peak

Soda Lake

LASSEN PEAK TRAILHEAD

Pilot Pinnacle 8,886ft

Lake Helen

Emerald Lake

Upper Meadow

Kings Creek Falls

Mount Diller 9,087ft

BUMPASS TRAILHEAD

Bumpass Mountain 8,753ft

KINGS CREEK PICNIC AREA

KINGS CREEK TRAILHEAD

Kings

Ridge Lakes

Little Hot Springs Valley

Hydrothermal Areas

Diamond Pk 7,968ft

Sifford Lakes

SULPHUR WORKS

Brokeoff Mountain

Forest Lake

Mill Creek Falls

Bumpass Cr

Crumbaugh Lake

LASSEN VOLCANIC WILDERNESS

Devils Kitchen

KOHM YAH-MAH-NEE VISITOR CENTER

SOUTHWEST

Conard Meadows

Panther

ENTRANCE STATION

Mount Conard 8,204ft

Twin Meadows

Creek

Drake Lake

Mill Creek

Huckleberry Lake

Ridge Lake

Blue Lake

LASSEN NATIONAL FOREST

To Mineral

To Hwy 44

Butte Creek

Prospect Peak
8,338ft

Bathtub
Lake

BUTTE LAKE

Butte
Lake

Pacific Crest Trail

Soap
Lake

Sunrise Peak
7,139ft

Emigrant
Lake

Nobles Emigrant Trail

Cinder Cone
6,907ft

Lava

Widow
Lake

Big Bear
Lake

Cluster

Silver
Lake

Lakes

Fantastic Lava Beds

Little Bear
Lake

Feather
Lake

Fairfield Peak
7,272ft

Lava

Ash Butte
7,577ft

Snag
Lake

Teal
Lake

Lower Twin Lake

Rainbow
Lake

**LASSEN VOLCANIC
WILDERNESS**

Echo Lake

Upper Twin
Lake

Swan Lake

Hidden
Lake

Mount Hoffman
7,883ft

Red Cinder Cone
8,008ft

Grassy Creek

Cameron
Meadow

**LASSEN
VOLCANIC
NATIONAL
PARK**

Crater Butte
7,267ft

Jakey
Lake

Grassy Swale

Horseshoe
Lake

Inspiration Point

Crystal Cliffs
7,548ft

Corral Meadow

Pilot Mountain
7,175ft

Crystal
Lake

Flatiron Ridge

Saddle
Mountain
7,638ft

Indian
Lake

Juniper
Lake

Glen
Lake

Island
Lake

East
Lake

Kings

**DRAKESBAD
GUEST RANCH**

Creek

WARNER VALLEY

**WARNER VALLEY
TRAILHEAD**

Hot

JUNIPER
LAKE

Bonte Peak
7,777ft

Boiling
rings Lake

Pacific Crest Trail

Springs

Creek

**MOUNT HARKNESS
FIRE LOOKOUT TOWER**

Hydrothermal
Areas

Terminal
Geyser

Warner Valley

ford Mountain
7,408ft

Kelly Mountain

Little Willow
Lake

Willow
Lake

0   1 mi

0   1 km

To Chester   To Chester

© MOON.COM

Top ③

① TOUR LASSEN VOLCANIC SCENIC BYWAY

LASSEN PEAK

From the southwest entrance, the **park road** (CA 89, open June-early Oct. depending on snow) twists and turns for 30 miles (48 km) through a volcanic landscape. The stunning drive climbs to 8,512 feet (2,595 m) below the summit of 10,457-foot (3,187 m) **Lassen Peak,** presiding over the rocky landscape— the remnants of the 1915 eruption. Scenic pullouts offer places for viewing and photographing the scenery, including volcanic features. The Lassen Peak Parking Area and Viewpoint offers the closest look at the peak. The road, which roughly follows the western perimeter of the 2021 Dixie Fire, has multiple switchbacks south of Lassen Peak but fewer curves to the north. Bicyclists can ride the road car-free in spring during the period after plows clear the road of snow and before the road opens to motorized vehicles. In winter, cross-country skiers can also tour the route, but be aware of avalanche dangers.

② WALK THROUGH BUMPASS HELL

The colorful basin of **Bumpass Hell** is packed with hydrothermal activity in the park's largest and most active volcanic basin. Walk the boardwalks and paths along the **Bumpass Nature Trail** (3 mi/4.8 km rt, 2 hrs, moderate, open June-Oct.) to see boiling mud pots, fumaroles, steaming springs, and bubbling pools. The strong smell of sulfur proves that this volcano is far from extinct. If you can't get to Yellowstone, this is a close cousin. Stay on the trail for safety amid these hot hydrothermals. The parking lot, 7 miles (11 km) north of the Southwest Entrance, often fills 10am-2pm.

BUMPASS HELL

③ SOAK UP MANZANITA LAKE

On a windless day, **Manzanita Lake** may be the most picture-perfect locale in the park. Stroll the trail (1.7 mi/2.7 km rt, 1 hr, easy) circling the lake. Go early before breezes ruffle the water to the north shore for reflections of Lassen Peak and Chaos Crags, or to the western shore late in the day for sunset views with alpenglow lighting up the peaks. Start at the Manzanita Lake Day Use Area, where a boat launch also offers easy access for kayakers and canoers. Rent single and double kayaks from the Manzanita Lake Camper Store (https://lassenlodging.com, 10am-4pm daily late May-Sept.).

Best Hike

LASSEN PEAK TRAIL

DISTANCE: 5 miles (8 km) round-trip

DURATION: 3-5 hours

ELEVATION CHANGE: 1,957 feet (597 m)

EFFORT: strenuous

TRAILHEAD: Lassen Peak

The **Lassen Peak Trail** follows a loose rock cinder path to climb Lassen Peak (10,457 ft/3,187 m), one of the world's largest plug dome volcanoes and the highest peak in the park. Along the way, exhibits explain the scenery of volcanic remains, lakes, wildlife, and rock formations. As the forest thins, so does the air, making breathing more labored. The trail switchbacks up a ridge to the first summit, the end of the maintained trail, but you can continue on a steep path to the real summit. Views take in a 360-degree panorama and the Devastated Area, a testament to the powerful 1915 eruption from this vantage. Due to the high elevation, the trail can hold snow into July and can be cool even in summer heat; the weather can change fast. Prepare for this hike as you would for a full-day hike in rugged conditions.

the side of the peak, killing all the vegetation in the area. A hail of lava rained down, creating new rocks ranging in size from gravel to boulders across the mountain's north side. Today, the **Devastated Area** north of Summit Lake has an interpretive wheelchair-accessible path (0.5 mi/0.8 km rt) through a small part of the boulder field to see some of the world's youngest rocks, plus new vegetation.

CHAOS CRAGS AND JUMBLES

In the northwest corner of the park, a massive rock avalanche about 350 years ago created the broken **Chaos Jumbles.** It was so big and fast that it trapped a pocket of air beneath the rocks. Regrowth since has allowed a greater variety of plants to get a

▼ SULPHUR WORKS

ONE DAY IN LASSEN

Visitors short on time can enjoy most of the park's sights by cruising along the 30-mile (48-km) **Lassen Volcanic Scenic Byway.** Pick up the park's road guide from the visitors center, stop at interpretive pullovers, and marvel at the volcanic wonders.

foothold. Today, visitors can enjoy a variety of coniferous trees at the park road pullout.

LOOMIS MUSEUM

Near the northwest entrance, the **Loomis Museum** (530/595-6140, 9am-5pm Fri.-Sun. late May-mid-June and Oct., 9am-5pm daily mid-June-Sept., free) shows the history of Mount Lassen, focusing heavily on the 1914-1915 eruptions photographed by B. F. Loomis. The photos capture the devastation and regrowth on the volcanic slopes.

NIGHT SKIES

You can go **stargazing** on your own; find places for dark skies at trailheads, visitors centers parking lots, and on the shores of Summit and Manzanita Lakes. Rangers lead **Starry Night programs,** and the park's annual **Dark Sky Festival** takes place for two nights in early August. Check online or in visitors centers for details.

RECREATION
HIKING

Trailheads line the paved park road. The **Kings Creek Falls Trail** (2.3 mi/3.7 km rt, 2 hrs, moderate) treks downhill to waterfalls. Admire the small cascade and pool before beginning the 700-foot (213-m) climb back up. Find the trailhead 13 miles (21 km) north of the southwest entrance.

From the congested Summit Lake Trailhead, a gentle forested path passes Summit Lake en route to **Echo Lake** (4.4 mi/7.1 km rt, 2-3 hrs, moderate) and views of Lassen Peak. Be at the trailhead by 9am for parking.

The **Brokeoff Mountain Trail** (7.4 mi/11.9 km rt, 5-7 hrs, strenuous) grunts up a 2,600-foot (793-m) ascent from a more than mile-high starting point for one of the toughest hikes. But the reward is big panoramic views, including the ancient Mount Tehama caldera;

▼ BROKEOFF MOUNTAIN

Brokeoff Mountain was part of this volcano. Locate the trailhead south of the southwest entrance station.

For fewer people in the remote northeast corner of the park and a radical change of scenery, take the **Cinder Cone Trail** (4-5 mi/6.4-8 km rt, 3 hrs, moderate) that rises 800 vertical feet (244 m) to overlook dunes and lava fields. To lengthen the hike, walk down the south side of the cone. Geology and photography buffs will like this hike, which shows off some of the park's less seen volcanic features. Find the trailhead at Butte Lake at the end of a gravel road (CA 44).

BACKPACKING

Lassen offers backpacking routes through a volcanic landscape pockmarked with scenic lakes. Wilderness **permits** (free, self-registration at the visitors center and ranger stations) are required. NPS-approved **bear canisters** are also required April-October; rent them at the bookstore ($10 for 7 days plus $95 deposit), at Loomis Museum (summer only), or the visitors center (year-round).

For families and beginning backpackers, the **Cluster Lakes Loop** (11 mi/17.7 km, 2-3 days) from the Summit Lake Trailhead takes in seven lakes, but it will be crowded and full of mosquitoes in early summer; short side trips add more lakes. The **Pacific Crest Trail** also cuts through the park (from north to south), but it can only be accessed from other trails. Reach it from three trailheads on the park highway (Hat Creek, Summit Lake, or Kings Creek) or from three trailheads on the east side of the park (Butte Lake, Juniper Lake, or Warner Valley).

WHERE TO STAY
INSIDE THE PARK

Lassen has seven campgrounds (one with cabins) and a remote ranch for lodging. Make camping **reservations** (877/444-6777, www.recreation. gov) six months in advance for **Manzanita Lake Campground and Cabins** (late May-mid-Oct.), **Summit Lake** (late June-mid-Sept.), **Butte Lake** (early June-early Sept.), and **Warner Valley** (late June-early Oct.). After peak season, these campgrounds are first come, first served. The rest of the park's campgrounds are first come, first served year-round. Campgrounds have picnic tables, fire pits, and flush or pit toilets.

Main Park Road

Four developed campgrounds and two cafés are along the paved park road. **Manzanita Lake** (May-Oct., 179 sites, $26-72, RV limit 40 ft/12 m) has potable water, a dump station, and showers. Reservations go fast for 20 rustic cabins ($76-101) that line the north shore of the lake. The **Manzanita Lake Camper Store** (8am-8pm daily mid-May-Sept., hours vary seasonally) sells hot food and snacks.

Summit Lake North and South (late June-Sept., 94 sites, $22-24) are split on either side of the water, with scenery and prime hiking. Bring your own water for drinking.

Near the visitors center, **Southwest Walk-In** (year-round, 20 tent sites,

LASSEN VOLCANIC NATIONAL PARK

$10-16) has a short, paved trail from the parking area to campsites (RVs can park in the lot). It has drinking water in summer and reduced fees in winter when the water is shut off.

The **Lassen Cafe & Gift** (Kohm Yah-mah-nee Visitor Center, 530/595-3555, 9am-5pm daily mid-May-mid-Oct., 11am-2pm Sat.-Sun. mid-Oct.-mid-May) sells burgers, pizza, coffee, and ice cream.

East Side

Remote dirt roads reach the remaining primitive campgrounds near hiking trails on the east side. In the northeast corner, accessed from CA 44, **Butte Lake** (June-mid-Oct., 101 sites, $15-22, RV limit 35 ft/11m) has seasonal drinking water and a nearby boat launch. North of Chester in the southeast corner, **Juniper Lake** (late June-early Oct., 18 sites, $12) has a boat launch nearby; bring your own drinking water. **Warner Valley** (early June-mid-Oct., 17 sites, $21) has seasonal drinking water. Trailers are not allowed.

Near the southwest entrance station, the **Drakesbad Guest Ranch** (14423 Chester Warner Valley Rd., Chester, 877/622-0221, www.lassenlodging. com, June-mid-Oct., from $220) is an all-inclusive ranch with horseback riding, swimming, and fishing.

OUTSIDE THE PARK

The nearest lodgings are south in **Mineral** and in the tiny town of **Chester.**

GETTING THERE AND AROUND

AIR

The closest international airport is **Sacramento International Airport** (SMF, 6900 Airport Blvd., 916/929-5411, www.sacramento.aero/smf), where car rentals are available.

CAR

Lassen Volcanic National Park is 150-175 miles (242-280 km, 3 hrs) north of Sacramento. Take I-5 north to Red Bluff, then follow CA 36 east for 43 miles (69 km) past Mineral. Turn left onto CA 89, which leads to the southwest park entrance.

CA 89 becomes the main road through the park; the visitors center, campgrounds, trailheads, and lakes cluster along it. It is closed from late October to May, June, or July, depending on weather and snowfall.

The park has no public transportation; exploration requires a vehicle. Manzanita Lake Camper Store has the only **gas station.** Otherwise, gas up en route in Red Bluff, Chester, or Susanville.

MANZANITA LAKE

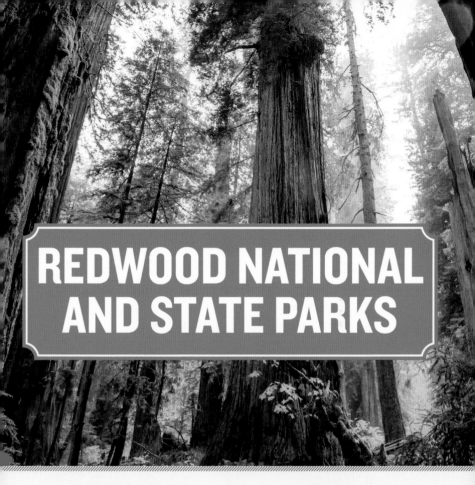

REDWOOD NATIONAL AND STATE PARKS

KEEPSAKE STAMPS ▼▼▼

WEBSITE:
www.nps.gov/redw

PHONE NUMBER:
707/464-6101

VISITATION RANK:
41

WHY GO:
Wander among towering coastal redwoods.

▲ REDWOOD FOREST AT REDWOOD NATIONAL PARK

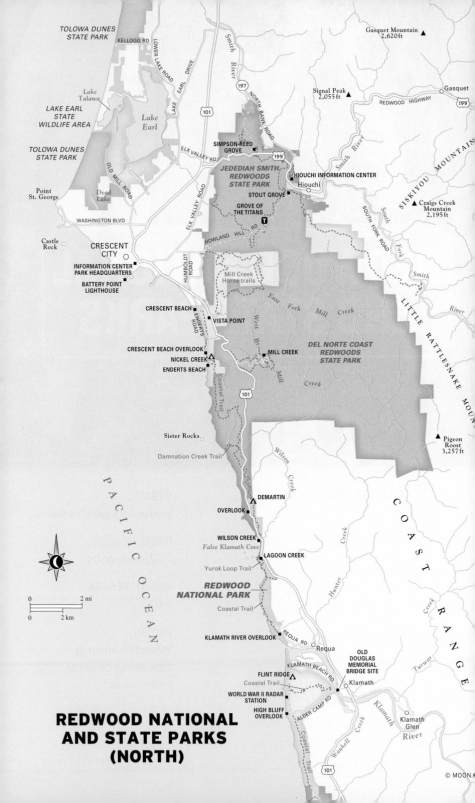

REDWOOD NATIONAL AND STATE PARKS (NORTH)

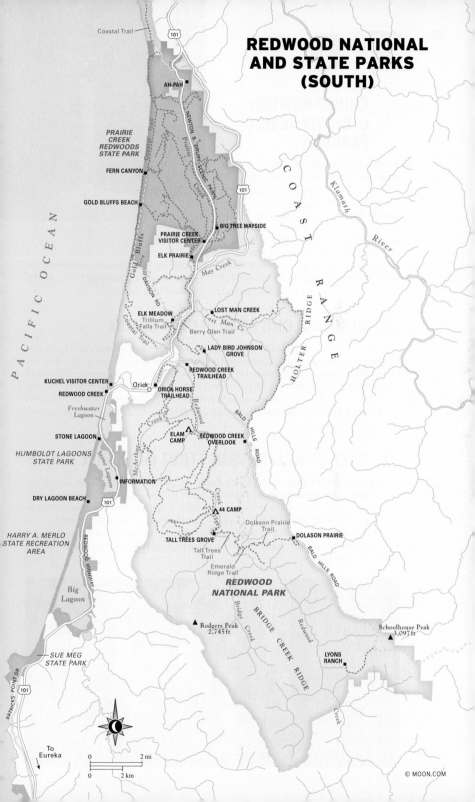

Top 3

1 CRUISE NEWTON B. DRURY SCENIC PARKWAY

Gorgeous **Newton B. Drury Scenic Parkway** (10 mi/16 km one-way) parallels US 101 through the redwoods. Along the parkway, old-growth redwoods line the road and offer an up-close view of the forest ecosystem, with frequent groves and trailheads inviting further exploration. The north

NEWTON B. DRURY SCENIC PARKWAY

entrance is 4 miles (6.4 km) south of Klamath off exit 765; the south entrance is 6 miles (9.7 km) north of Orick off exit 753. The road closes to all vehicle traffic on the first Saturday of the month (Oct.-May) for Bike and Hike Day.

2 STROLL ALONG GOLD BLUFFS BEACH

Miles of driftwood line **Gold Bluffs Beach,** a haven for sea mammals and birds. Sitka spruce groves top nearby bluffs, and herds of Roosevelt elk frequently roam the wide salt-and-pepper-colored beach. Look for whales migrating in early spring and late fall. Prospectors found gold flakes here in 1850, giving the beach its name. The beach, part of Prairie Creek Redwoods State Park, is accessible via Davison Road off US 101 at Elk Meadow. **Permits** (www.redwoodparksconservancy.org, free) are required May-September.

3 GAZE UP AT GIANTS IN STOUT MEMORIAL GROVE

In **Jedediah Smith Redwoods State Park,** old-growth redwoods sit along the Smith River. The **Stout Memorial Grove** (0.5 mi/0.8 km, 1 hr, easy) is home to ancient trees, including the Stout Tree, the biggest, which has a viewing platform. Located on the rough Howland Hill Road (RVs and trailers not recommended) off US 101, this grove is popular for its photogenic qualities. Trailhead parking is small, but you can walk a trail from Jedediah Smith Campground to cross the river on a summer-only hiker bridge.

STOUT MEMORIAL GROVE IN JEDEDIAH SMITH REDWOODS STATE PARK

Along California's rugged north coast, towering redwoods inspire pure awe. *Sequoia sempervirens* defines the verdant landscape. It's easy to imagine ancestors of the Tolowa Dee-ni' Nation and Yurok people collecting berries and hunting wild game here. You can explore the natural groves of these gargantuan treasures in the **REDWOOD NATIONAL AND STATE PARKS**, which line the coast from Eureka to Crescent City. Along US 101, this cluster of state and national parks are a World Heritage Site and International Biosphere Reserve. Numerous hiking trails, forested campgrounds, tide pools, sandy beaches, and some of the tallest and oldest trees on the continent await.

PLANNING YOUR TIME

Redwood National and State Parks meander 40 miles (64 km) along the Northern California coast between Crescent City in the north and the old logging town of Eureka in the south. In addition to **Redwood National Park,** this parkland includes three state parks—**Prairie Creek Redwoods, Del Norte Coast Redwoods,** and **Jedediah Smith Redwoods.** Combined, the region encompasses most of California's northern redwood forests.

May through September are the busiest months, with cool temperatures in the 40s-60s (4-16°C), fog, and damp weather. Fall, winter, and early spring (Oct.-Apr.) can deliver copious rain.

ENTRANCES AND FEES

US 101 connects the multiple park entrances. Redwood National Park has no entrance fee; however, Prairie Creek Redwoods, Del Norte Coast Redwoods, and Jedediah Smith Redwoods State Parks collect entrance and day-use fees.

VISITORS CENTERS

Four visitors centers offer information, exhibits, maps, ranger-led talks and walks, and restrooms.

Thomas H. Kuchel Visitor Center (US 101, Orick, 707/465-7334, 9am-5pm daily spring-fall, 9am-4pm daily winter) is the largest facility, with a ranger station, maps, advice, permits for backcountry camping, and books. In the summer, rangers lead talks and coast walks.

Prairie Creek Visitor Center (Newton B. Drury Scenic Pkwy., 707/488-2039, 9am-5pm daily summer, 9am-4pm daily fall-spring) includes a bookshop and a small interpretive museum that describes the history of the California redwood forests.

Hiouchi Visitor Center (US 199, Hiouchi, 707/458-3294, 9am-5pm daily summer, 9am-4pm daily winter) has backcountry permits, a park movie, and a picnic area.

Jedediah Smith Campground Visitors Center (US 199, Hiouchi, 707/458-3496, 9am-5pm daily June-Sept.) has information and materials about all of the nearby parks.

SIGHTS
REDWOOD NATIONAL PARK

This iconic park harbors old-growth groves of coastal redwoods. These sacred places spur the imagination with their verdant beauty and lush undergrowth of moss, ferns, and rhododendrons. On the coast, tide pools await exploration, and rangers lead tours to help spy the creatures in the tidal zone. Bring the binoculars to watch whales migrate (Nov.-Dec. and Mar.-Apr.).

PRAIRIE CREEK REDWOODS STATE PARK

Prairie Creek Redwoods State Park (Newton B. Drury Scenic Pkwy.,

ROOSEVELT ELK

707/488-2039, www.parks.ca.gov, sunrise-sunset daily, day use $10) has miles of wild beach, wildlife, and a popular hike through a one-of-a-kind fern-draped canyon. Prairie Creek offers a sampler platter of the natural elements of California's North Coast.

Stop at the **Big Tree Wayside,** home to the 304-foot-high (123-m) **Big Tree,** estimated to be 1,500 years old. Its life was almost cut short by a homesteader who wanted to chop it down to use the stump as a dance floor. Follow the short five-minute loop trail near the Big Tree to see other neighboring giants.

Look for a herd of **Roosevelt elk** at Elk Prairie, a stretch of open grassland along the southern end of the parkway. The best times to see the elk are early morning and around sunset. During the mating season (Aug.-Oct.), the bugling of the bulls fills the air as they round up harems and fend off other bulls.

DEL NORTE COAST REDWOODS STATE PARK

South of Crescent City, **Del Norte Coast Redwoods State Park** (Mill Creek Campground Rd., off US 101, 707/464-6101, www.parks.ca.gov, day use $10) encompasses a variety of ecosystems, including 8 miles (13 km) of wild coastline, second-growth redwood forest, and virgin old-growth forests. Del Norte State Park has no visitors center, but you can get information from

▼ DEL NORTE COAST REDWOODS STATE PARK

Best Hike

GROVE OF THE TITANS

The **Grove of the Titans** has 4 of the 30 largest coast redwoods in the world. Lost Monarch, the biggest, is estimated at 1,500 years old. The official trail (1.6 mi/2.6 km, 1 hr, moderate) through the grove was constructed after social trails caused extreme damage to the area. Hike north along Mill Creek to the elevated steel walkway that tours the grove. Turn around at the bridge to return the way you came.

DISTANCE: 2.5 miles (4 km) round-trip
DURATION: 1.5 hours
ELEVATION CHANGE: 123 feet (37 m)
EFFORT: moderate
TRAILHEAD: Mill Creek, 4 miles (6.4 km) up the rough Howland Hill Road (not recommended for RVs or trailers) in Jedediah Smith State Park

the **Crescent City Information Center** (1111 2nd St., Crescent City, 707/465-7306, 9am-5pm daily spring-fall, 9am-4pm Thurs.-Mon. winter).

JEDEDIAH SMITH REDWOODS STATE PARK

The **Jedediah Smith Redwoods State Park** (US 199, 9 mi/15 km east of Crescent City, 707/464-6101, www.parks.ca.gov, day use $10) is the northernmost of the redwood parks. It preserves a pristine forest of old-growth redwoods along the Smith River in the **Stout Memorial Grove.** Each July, the Tolowa Tribe provides a demonstration of the renewal dance at the campground.

RECREATION

HIKING

Redwood National Park

The most popular place to get close to the redwoods in Redwoods National Park is the **Lady Bird Johnson Grove Nature Trail** (Bald Hills Rd., 1.5 mi/2.5 km rt, 1 hr, easy). The trail, lined with lush ferns and mossy fallen logs, can feel otherworldly, with fog floating in from the ocean. Starting in late May, pink rhododendrons burst into bloom. Gradual uphills and downhills on a lollipop loop provide an intimate view of the redwood forests that define this region. Pick up an interpretive brochure at the trailhead.

The cool, dark **Trillium Falls Trail** (Davison Rd. at Elk Meadow, 2.5 mi/4 km rt, 1.5 hrs, easy-moderate) has striking redwoods and a small moss-flanked waterfall that is lovely anytime but best in spring when the water volume peaks. The trail is named for the spring-blooming white trillium.

The **Lost Man Creek Trail** (east of Elk Meadow, 1 mi/1.6 km off US 101, 1-22 mi/1.6-35 km rt, easy-difficult) has it all. The first 0.5 mile (0.8 km) is perfect for wheelchairs and families with small children. But as the lush redwood- and fern-lined trail rolls along, grades get steeper and more challenging. About 2 miles (3.2 km) from the trailhead, a stream crossing requires caution. Reaching the Lost Man Creek picnic grounds at 11 miles (18 km) requires ascending more than 3,000 feet (914 m) of elevation and crossing several streams. Bikes are permitted on this trail.

To sink into a full day of enchantment in this moist forest, hike the **Redwood Creek Trail** (Bald Hills Rd. spur off US 101, 8-15.4 mi/13-24 km rt, 7-9 hrs, strenuous), which follows Redwood Creek to the **Tall Trees Grove.** Two bridges over the river are installed in summer only (May-Sept.) along the route. A **permit** (www.redwoodparksconservancy.org) is required to visit the Tall Trees Grove.

Prairie Creek Redwoods State Park

South of the visitors center, the **Revelation Trail** (0.25 mi/0.4 km rt, 20 min,

PRAIRIE CREEK BRIDGE

easy) is designed for wheelchair accessibility and those with impaired vision. The interpretive trail focuses on all senses amid an old-growth forest.

Near Gold Bluffs Beach, **Fern Canyon Loop** (0.7 mi/1.1 km rt, 30 min, easy) runs through a narrow canyon carved by Home Creek. Ferns, moss, and other water-loving plants form a vertical carpet of greenery as they climb the sides of the canyon (scenes from *Jurassic Park 2* and *Return of the Jedi* were filmed here). **Permits** (www.redwoodparksconservancy.org, free) are required May-September.

The **James Irvine Loop** (12.4 mi/20 km rt, 7 hrs, moderate) starts from the Prairie Creek Visitor Center on the **James Irvine Trail** and reaches the beach. Return on the **Miners' Ridge Trail.** As you head out, bear right when you can, following the trail through enormous trees until it joins Fern Canyon Trail. Turn left at the coast and walk along Gold Bluffs Beach for 1.2 miles (1.9 km) to the campground, turning east to head back on the more demanding trail that returns to the visitors center.

Del Norte Coast Redwoods State Park

In summer, Mill Creek Campground is the trailhead for several trails (access is from US 101 when the campground is closed). The **Trestle Loop Trail** (1 mi/1.6 km rt, 30 min, easy) trots along a defunct railroad route from the logging era with trestles and other artifacts along the way. It's a good place to tour second-growth redwoods. A leisurely walk on the **Nature Loop Trail** (1 mi/1.6 km rt, 30 min, easy) offers interpretive signage about the unique redwood trees and their ecosystem.

Jedediah Smith Redwoods State Park

A shady hike beneath 1,000-year-old redwoods, the **Simpson-Reed Trail** (1 mi/1.6 km rt, 30 min, easy) descends to the banks of the Smith River, where fallen trees create pools for fish. Look for red-legged frogs on the damp forest floor.

From the Hiouchi Visitor Center and Jedediah Smith Campground, paths cross a summer footbridge over the turquoise Smith River to access several trailheads. To hike north along the river, take the **Hiouchi Trail** (2 mi/3.2 km rt, 1 hr, moderate) through old-growth redwoods into a streamside environment of wild berries and Pacific madrone.

The **Boy Scout Tree Trail** (5.6 mi/9 km rt, 3 hrs, moderate) is usually quiet, with few hikers, and its gargantuan forest will make you feel truly tiny. A spur at the end of the trail leads to a double-trunked redwood tree. The trail ends at Fern Falls. The trailhead is on the rough Howland Hill Road (not recommended for RVs or trailers).

BACKPACKING

Hikers can don an overnight pack in seven different areas with designated campsites and some dispersed sites. On the **Redwood Creek Trail** (8 mi/12.8

ONE DAY IN THE REDWOODS

A drive along US 101 on the Redwood Highway gets you up close to the towering trees. Make your first stop at the **Thomas H. Kuchel Visitor Center** to learn about the giant coast redwoods, then take a walk to the beach. Stroll the **Lady Bird Johnson Grove Nature Trail** in Redwoods National Park, then drive north to the otherworldly **Newton B. Drury Scenic Parkway** in Prairie Creek Redwoods State Park.

km one-way, 2-3 days), camp at **Elam Camp** (3 sites) or **44 Camp** (4 sites). Dispersed camping is possible on gravel bars on Redwood Creek. The northern section of the **California Coastal Trail** (CCT, www.californiacoastaltrail.info) runs through Redwood National Park and has 10 primitive backcountry sites. The trail is reasonably well marked with signs featuring the CCT logo.

Permits (free) are required for backcountry camping. Apply online (www. redwoodparksconservancy.org).

BIKING

The **Newton B. Drury Scenic Parkway** (10 mi/16 km one-way) offers pedaling fun on the first Saturday of the month October-May. The road closes to cars all day but allows cyclists and walkers.

A 19-mile (31-km) ride links trails and roadways into a loop. With easy and steeper sections, it combines the Ossagon Trail, Coastal Trail, Davison Road, Streelow Creek, and the Newton B. Drury Scenic Parkway. But watch for elk and hikers on the route. Pick up a bicycling flier at visitors centers or download from the park website.

WHERE TO STAY

INSIDE THE PARKS

Redwood National Park has no designated campgrounds, but several state park campgrounds take **reservations** (800/444-7275, www.reservecalifornia. com, $35). You can reserve campsites six months in advance for Gold Bluffs Beach (year-round), Elk Prairie Campground (year-round), and Jedediah Smith Campground (May-Sept.). Otherwise, campgrounds are first come, first served. Sites include picnic tables,

STOUT MEMORIAL GROVE, JEDEDIAH SMITH REDWOODS STATE PARK

FAMILY ENJOYING GIANT REDWOOD TREE

fire pits, flush toilets, showers, and food storage lockers, but no hookups.

Tucked under ancient redwoods, **Elk Prairie Campground** (Prairie Creek Redwoods, 127011 Newton B. Drury Scenic Pkwy., 75 sites, year-round, RV limit 28 ft/8.5 m, trailer limit 24 ft/7.3 m) has a campfire area with evening programs hosted by rangers and volunteers.

Gold Bluffs Beach Campground (Prairie Creek Redwoods, Davison Rd., 26 sites, year-round) sits on the ocean. RVs are limited to 24 feet (7.3 m); trailers are prohibited.

Mill Creek Campground (Del Norte Redwoods, US 101, 145 sites, mid-May-Sept., RV limit 28 ft/8.5 m, trailer limit 24 ft/7.3 m) spreads beneath young redwoods.

Jedediah Smith Campground (Jedediah Smith Redwoods, US 199, Hiouchi, 86 sites, year-round, RV limit 25 ft/7.6 m, trailer limit 21 ft/6.4 m) sits under old-growth redwoods on the banks of Smith River.

OUTSIDE THE PARKS

Small towns dot the coast along US 101. Look for accommodations and restaurants in **Crescent City, Trinidad, Garberville, Eureka,** and **Arcata.**

GETTING THERE AND AROUND

The Redwood National and State Parks line 40 miles (64 km) of US 101. There is no public transportation; a vehicle is required for exploration.

AIR

The closest airport is the small regional **Del Norte County Airport/Jack McNamara** (CEC, 1650 Dale Rupert Rd., Crescent City, 707/464-7288, http://flycrescentcity.com). The closest international airports are **San Francisco International Airport** (SFO, US 101, San Mateo, 800/435-9736 or 650/821-8211, www.flysfo.com) and **Sacramento International Airport** (SMF, 6900 Airport Blvd., 916/929-5411, www.sacramento.aero/smf), both a six-hour drive from the parks.

CAR

From **San Francisco,** take US 101 north to Leggett, where it meets with CA 1. Follow US 101 north to Orick, where you'll find the Thomas H. Kuchel Visitor Center. The 325-mile (525-km) drive takes about six hours.

From **Sacramento,** take I-5 north to CA 299 west, which ends in Arcata. Turn north on US 101 to Orick. The 330-mile (530-km) drive takes 5-6 hours.

Prairie Creek Redwoods is 6 miles (10 km) north of Orick on US 101. The Newton B. Drury Scenic Parkway parallels US 101 as an alternate route.

Del Norte Coast Redwoods is on US 101, about 19 miles (31 km) north of Prairie Creek Redwoods. The park entrance is on Hamilton Road, east of US 101.

To reach Jedediah Smith Redwoods State Park, continue north along US 101 to US 199. Turn right onto US 199 and continue east for 9 miles (15 km).

SIGHTS NEARBY

Three more California state parks await along US 101. **Humboldt Redwoods State Park** (17119 Avenue of the Giants, Weott, 707/946-2263, www.parks.ca.gov or www.humboldtredwoods.org) houses the **Avenue of the Giants.**

Sue-meg State Park (4150 Patrick's Point Dr., Trinidad, 707/677-3570, www.parks.ca.gov) is a rambling coastal park with campgrounds, trails, and beaches.

Richardson Grove State Park (1600 US 101, 707/247-3318, www.parks.ca.gov, sunrise-sunset daily) has a visitors center, a campground, and old-growth redwoods.

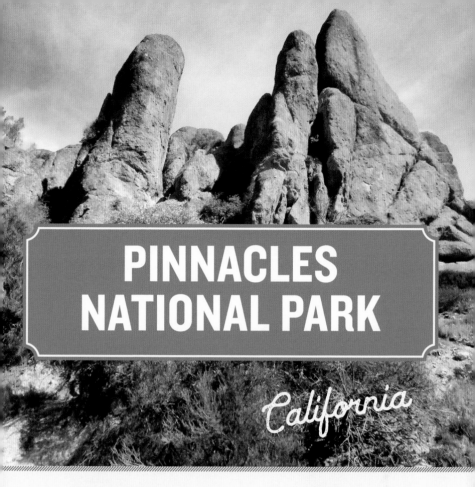

PINNACLES NATIONAL PARK

California

KEEPSAKE STAMPS ▾▾▾

WEBSITE:
www.nps.gov/pinn

PHONE NUMBER:
831/389-4485
visitors center,
831/389-4486 park
headquarters

VISITATION RANK:
45

WHY GO:
Scramble through
talus caves and up
volcanic peaks.

▴ PINNACLES NATIONAL PARK

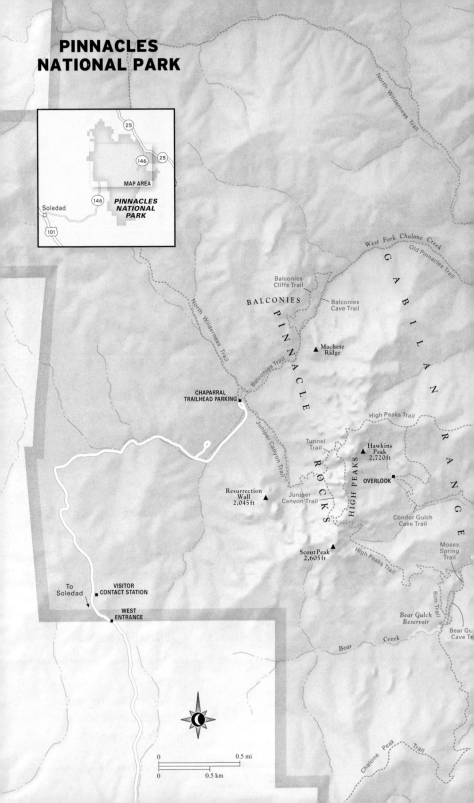

Rising above the Gabilan Mountains on the east side of the Salinas Valley, **PINNACLES NATIONAL PARK** is filled with the walls, spires, and towers of rock castles. A natural wonder created by volcanic activity, Pinnacles holds some of the world's largest talus caves, created when boulders became lodged in narrow canyons. Its intricate geology is best explored on hiking trails and along rock faces, where climbers ascend cracks and nubbins. After extinction in the wild, California condors have returned to Pinnacles, thrilling biologists, birders, and the Amah Mutsun people, whose mythology celebrates the condor as the escorts to the afterlife.

PLANNING YOUR TIME

East of the Salinas Valley, in the parched hills of the Gabilan Mountains, Pinnacles National Park attracts hikers, rock climbers, cave explorers, and birders. True to its name, the park is studded with huge rock formations jutting into the sky. Access the park via its west or east side. Crowds head for the east side, especially on weekends, holidays, and in spring. There are no services or campgrounds on the west side.

The weather is generally warm and dry throughout the year, but blazing hot in summer. **Spring** (Mar.-mid-May) is high season, when visitors flood the park for rare access to the upper and lower Bear Gulch Caves. Regardless of when you visit, it is essential to bring plenty of water with you on the trails.

ENTRANCES AND FEES

Pinnacles National Park has two entrances, both accessed via CA 146. No roads connect the entrances. The **east entrance** (24 hours daily) accesses the park campground and popular Bear Gulch Day Use Area, with multiple trail options. During spring and fall, plan on long lines 9am-3pm at the entrance. The **west entrance** is only accessible when the park gate is open (7:30am-8pm daily); it closes overnight.

The entrance fee is $30 per vehicle ($25 motorcycle, $15 individual).

VISITORS CENTERS

You can get information and maps at the **East Pinnacles Book Store** (831/389-4485, 9am-5pm daily), which also sells souvenirs. Inquire about the status of the caves here. The **Bear Gulch Nature Center** (10am-4pm Sat.-Sun. Jan.-May) in the Bear Gulch Day Use Area has wildlife and nature exhibits. On the west side, stop for information in the **West Pinnacles Visitor Contact Station** (10am-3pm Wed.-Mon.).

RECREATION

HIKING

One of the best ways to experience the geology of Pinnacles is via the west side's **Juniper Canyon Loop** (4.3 mi/6.9 km rt, 2-3 hrs, strenuous), which leads hikers through a steep, narrow traverse of the **High Peaks.** From the Chaparral Parking Area, begin on the Juniper Canyon Trail to climb 2,605-foot (794 m) Scout Peak, where you may spot a condor soaring overhead. The loop then swings through High Peaks before returning to the trailhead.

From the east side Bear Gulch Day Use Area (parking lot often fills before 8am), hikers can take the **Moses Spring to Rim Trail Loop** (2.2 mi/3.5 km rt, 1.5 hrs, moderate) to Bear Gulch Reservoir. For a longer hike, the **Chalone Peak Trail** (9 mi/14.5 km rt, 4-5 hrs, strenuous) continues from the reservoir to North Chalone Peak.

ROCK CLIMBING

Most of the park's best rock climbing is on the east side, where routes range from beginner to advanced, but the rock here is volcanic breccia and prone to weakness. The **Tourist Trap** and the

Top ③

1 SCRAMBLE UP BEAR GULCH CAVE

From the Bear Gulch Day Use Area, a series of well-signed connected trails leads to **Bear Gulch Cave** (2.2 mi/3.5 km rt, 1.5 hrs, moderate). The high rocky walls of this talus cave slope inward as the 0.7-mile (1.1-km) self-guided path meanders past lodged boulders and along Bear Creek. You'll need a flashlight or headlamp to see in the dark, and you may splash through a little water in places as the cavern route follows a tumbling creek. The climb through the cave goes up stairways and scrambles through a few slots, and you'll need to duck a few times to avoid hitting your head. Exiting the upper portion of the

BEAR GULCH CAVE

cave, the trail climbs to scenic **Bear Gulch Reservoir,** a convenient spot to catch your breath and enjoy a quick lunch.

To start, head out on the **High Peaks Trail;** turn left onto the **Moses Spring Trail** to reach the entrance to the **Bear Gulch Cave Trail.** The return loop follows the **Rim Trail** back to the High Peaks Trail; turn right to return to the day-use area or left to scale the High Peaks Trail.

Mid-May to mid-July, Bear Gulch Cave closes to protect the large colony of Townsend's big-eared bats raising young. Access to both upper and lower Bear Gulch Cave is open to hikers for only a few weeks in March and October. Otherwise, the lower part opens with the exit trail cutting back to the Moses Spring Trail. Check online or at the visitors center for closure schedules.

2 CRAWL THROUGH BALCONIES CAVE

Balconies Cave offers a fun, self-guided, 0.4-mile (0.6 km) scramble through a series of stacked boulders, the shorter but more tactile and hands-on exploration of the park's talus caves. Bring a flashlight or headlamp to see in darkness as you climb over stones, crawl under chockstones, and squeeze through slots. You may also wade through water.

Before planning a trip to the cave, check online or with the visitors center about its status. Rainstorms can close it, as does the annual spring-summer schedule to protect the maternity colony of Townsend's big-eared bats.

To get to Balconies Cave takes more work than Bear Gulch Cave. From the westside Chaparral Parking Area, the **Balconies Cliffs-Cave Loop** (2.4 mi/3.8 km rt, 1.5 hrs, moderate) is the shortest route. The trail ascends to the south junction, where you can opt to climb through the cave first or over the top on Balconies Cliff first. Either way, the loop returns to the junction. From the east side at the Old Pinnacles Trailhead parking area, hike the **Old Pinnacles Trail** (5.3 mi/8.6 km rt, 3-5 hrs, moderate) up the West Fork of Chalone Creek to the north junction of the Balconies Cliffs-Cave Loop. Opt for either way as the loop returns to the junction.

3 WATCH CONDORS

Impressive California condors inhabit Pinnacles year-round. The endangered species reached extinction in the wild, but Pinnacles National Park serves as the only National Park Service release site for transitioning captive birds back into the wild. With binoculars, you can see condors with radio transmitters and plastic identification tags, which help biologists monitor the birds. Watch for condors soaring on thermals near **High Peaks** and the ridge south of the campground. Look for them roosting in trees too. **Spotting scopes** are on the Bench Trail near the visitors center for looking for condors. Rangers often do 30-minute **Condor Talks** on weekends at Bear Gulch Day Use Area.

Discovery Wall are the closest climbs from the Bear Gulch Day Use Area. For more information, visit **Friends of Pinnacles** (www.pinnacles.org), an organization dedicated to climbing at Pinnacles.

WHERE TO STAY

INSIDE THE PARK

At the east entrance, the **Pinnacles Campground** (877/444-6777, www.recreation.gov, year-round, tents $37, RVs $49) has 99 tent sites, 36 RV sites with electrical hookups, and 14 group sites. Most are shaded by oaks, and all come with a picnic table, fire ring, and restrooms, with showers nearby. Make reservations six months in advance, especially for spring and fall weekends.

OUTSIDE THE PARK

Accommodations and dining options are located in **Salinas, Soledad,** and **King City.**

GETTING THERE

AIR

The closest international airports are **Mineta San Jose International Airport** (SJC, 1701 Airport Blvd., San Jose, 408/392-3600, www.flysanjose.com) and **San Francisco International**

HIGH PEAKS TRAIL

Best Hike

HIGH PEAKS TRAIL

DISTANCE: 6.7 miles (10.7 km) round-trip

DURATION: 5 hours

ELEVATION CHANGE: 1,425 feet (434 m)

EFFORT: strenuous

TRAILHEAD: Bear Gulch Day Use Area

The star loop trail in the park is the **High Peaks Trail,** a tough haul to the top of the park's volcanic pinnacles with views across multiple counties. At the top, a 0.7-mile (1.1-km) portion of the trail climbs across the steep rock-strewn ridgeline via steps carved into the rock with handrails for support, almost like a beginner version of Yosemite's famed Half Dome hike. Multiple trails connect with the High Peaks Trail. With more mileage and time, you can add on Bear Gulch Cave. For a shorter loop, link High Peaks with **Condor Gulch Trail** (5.3 mi/8.5 km rt, 4 hrs, strenuous). The parking lot usually fills at the trailhead before 8am.

Airport (SFO, US 101, San Mateo, 800/435-9736 or 650/821-8211, www.flysfo.com). From either airport, it's roughly a two-hour drive south to the park via US 101.

CAR

Pinnacles has two entrances, but no roads connect them—making the drive from one to the other a two-hour endeavor.

To reach the **east entrance** from the north, take US 101 to CA 25 through the town of Hollister. After another 30 miles (48 km), turn right on CA 146 to the park entrance. From San Francisco, the trip is more than 130 miles (209 km) and takes nearly three hours. From Monterey, it is 79 miles (127 km) and 1.5 hours.

For the **west entrance,** continue south on US 101 past Salinas to CA 146 in Soledad. Take CA 146 east for a very slow 14 miles (23 km). There are no services at this entrance. The trip from Monterey, via CA 68, is 54 miles (87 km), taking a little over an hour.

GETTING AROUND

There is limited parking in both the east- and west-side lots. A large overflow parking lot is next to the campground; on weekends, a **shuttle** (8am-5pm, free) runs from there to the Bear Gulch Day Use Area, with every other run stopping at the Old Pinnacles parking lot. Plan to board the shuttle before 10am to avoid the hour-plus wait on weekends.

CALIFORNIA CONDORS

With wings spanning 10 feet (3 m) from tip to tip, California condors are some of the area's most impressive natural treasures. The largest flying bird in North America, their presence here is a story of hope and testament to the success of conservation efforts. In the early 1980s the condor population had dropped to a low of 22 raptors due to their susceptibility to lead poisoning and through deaths caused by electric power lines, habitat loss, and hunting. A captive breeding program was initiated for this endangered species and, after more than 30 years, there are now more than 300 wild California condors.

As a recovery site, the jutting spires of Pinnacles are home to about 90 California condors bred in captivity and then released into the wild. The park also had its first chick fledged in the wild in 2016. If you're lucky, you might even spy a condor flying overhead on one of the park's rugged hiking trails. (Look for a tracking tag on the bird's wing to determine that you are actually looking at a California condor and not a big turkey vulture.)

CHANNEL ISLANDS
NATIONAL PARK

California

WEBSITE:
www.nps.gov/chis

PHONE NUMBER:
805/658-5730

VISITATION RANK:
47

WHY GO:
Paddle and hike an
island sanctuary.

KEEPSAKE STAMPS ▼▼▼

▲ SANTA CRUZ ISLAND IN
CHANNEL ISLANDS NATIONAL
PARK

Off the California coast, the remote **CHANNEL ISLANDS** are accessible only by air or sea. Boats travel routes once paddled in dugout canoes by the Indigenous Chumash people to reach the islands. Even the most visited islands reward hardy souls with uncrowded trails, isolated beaches, and an extensive marine sanctuary. Offshore, kelp forests sway in the ocean's surge as the California state fish, the pumpkin-colored garibaldi, swim past rocks dotted with multicolored sea urchins. Onshore, rare species, including the island fox and the island scrub jay, roam freely. Day-trippers can kayak, snorkel, and even scuba dive, while campers enjoy solitude and dark skies.

PLANNING YOUR TIME

The five Channel Islands lie off the central California coast, accessible by boat or plane from Santa Barbara and Ventura. The most visited islands are tiny **Anacapa,** a dramatic 5-mile (8-km) spine jutting out from the sea and closest to the mainland, and **Santa Cruz,** California's largest island at 24 miles (39 km) long and 6 miles (10 km) wide. The second-largest island, **Santa Rosa,** is difficult to access because of consistently strong winds. The smaller **San Miguel** is accessible spring-fall by permit only. **Santa Barbara** is the smallest and southernmost of the islands.

Day trips (boats depart roughly 8:30am-10am, return at 4pm) visit Anacapa, Santa Cruz, and to a lesser degree Santa Rosa. Trips to Santa Cruz and Anacapa are available year-round.

Summer (June-Aug.) is high-season for recreational activities such as snorkeling, diving, and kayaking. Wildlife migrations take place in **spring** and **fall.** Sailing to the islands takes 1-4 hours, and tough winds can crop up on the open water. While weather varies daily, summer daytime temperatures hang in the mid-60s (16-21°C) with nights dropping by only 10-15 degrees (6-9°C).

ENTRANCES AND FEES

There is no entrance fee to visit Channel Islands; however, you must buy a ticket on a boat or plane departing from Santa Barbara or Ventura (fee).

VISITORS CENTERS

There is no main visitors center. Instead, go to the **Robert J. Lagomarsino Channel Islands National Park Visitor Center** (1901 Spinnaker Dr., Ventura, 805/658-5730, 8:30am-5pm daily) in Ventura Harbor Village before heading to the islands. It has a bookstore, displays of marinelife, exhibits, and a 25-minute introductory film on the islands. The **Outdoors Santa Barbara Visitor Center** (113 Harbor Way, Santa Barbara, 805/456-8752, https://sbmm.org, 10:30am-4:30pm Thurs.-Sun.) also has information about the national park and the Channel Islands National Marine Sanctuary.

SANTA ROSA ISLAND

Fewer visitors reach the rugged and windy **Santa Rosa Island** (Apr.-early

MARINELIFE ABOUNDS IN THE CHANNEL ISLANDS.

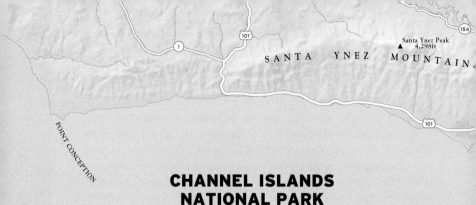

CHANNEL ISLANDS NATIONAL PARK

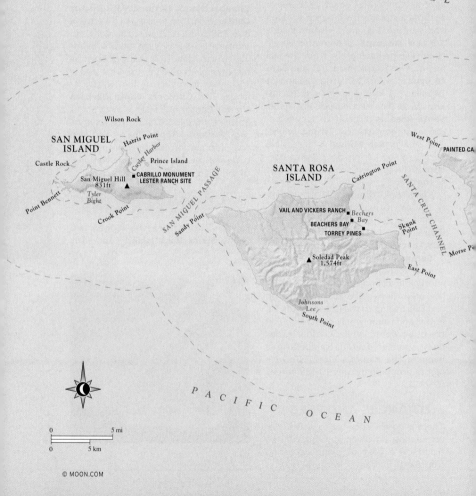

POINT CONCEPTION

SANTA YNEZ MOUNTAIN

Santa Ynez Peak
4,298ft

101

154

1

101

SANTA BARBARA CHANNEL

Wilson Rock

SAN MIGUEL ISLAND

Harris Point

Cuyler Harbor

Prince Island

Castle Rock

San Miguel Hill
831ft

CABRILLO MONUMENT
LESTER RANCH SITE

Point Bennett

Tyler Bight

Crook Point

SAN MIGUEL PASSAGE

Sandy Point

SANTA ROSA ISLAND

Catrington Point

West Point

PAINTED CA

SANTA CRUZ CHANNEL

VAIL AND VICKERS RANCH

Bechers Bay

BEACHERS BAY

TORREY PINES

Skunk Point

Morse Po

Soledad Peak
1,574ft

East Point

Johnsons Lee

South Point

PACIFIC OCEAN

0   5 mi

0   5 km

© MOON.COM

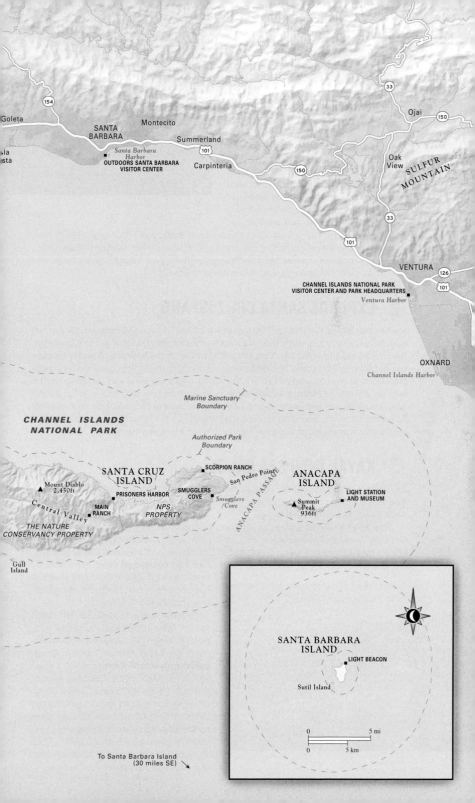

Top ③

1 DAY TRIP TO ANACAPA ISLAND

Tiny **Anacapa** has three islets on the east end of the main island, West Anacapa. Boats (year-round, 90 min) land on **East Anacapa,** an island with steep cliffs. Best explored by hiking, it houses the stunning Inspiration Point, **Anacapa Lighthouse,** and a small vis-

ANACAPA LIGHTHOUSE

itors center. From the island, you can see **Arch Rock,** a 40-foot-high (12-m) rock window in the waters offshore. During nesting season for Western gulls (Apr.-mid-Aug.), rookeries can be noisy and stinky, contain guano and bird carcasses, and birds may demonstrate aggressive territorial behavior.

2 EXPLORE SANTA CRUZ ISLAND

Santa Cruz Island (year-round, 90 min by boat), the largest and most popular of the islands, is the only place in the world to see endemic species such as the Channel Island fox and island scrub jay. A small visitors center at the **Scorpion Ranch Complex** has displays on threatened species, conservation, and the Indigenous Chumash people. Hiking is the top way to explore the island, and snorkeling and paddling are the best on water. The **Nature Conservancy** (www.nature.org, access by special permit only) owns 75 percent of the island, which it manages in collaboration with the National Park Service, aiming to restore the natural habitat from the impacts of ranching. Water is available at Scorpion Harbor but not Prisoners Harbor.

3 KAYAK INTO SEA CAVES

Santa Cruz Island has some of the world's largest sea caves, tucked in a diverse marine world best explored by kayak. To find easy-to-reach sea caves, paddle northwest out of **Scorpion Anchorage.**

Anacapa has outstanding sea kayaking, but due to rugged cliffs, East Anacapa's Landing Cove has the only water access. Paddle out to **Arch Rock,** the 40-foot-high (12-m) rock arch in the waters just east of the islet, or to **Cathedral Cove.** This scenic section of coast has **Cathedral Arch** as well as **Cathedral Cave,** reachable by kayak during higher tides. The cave has five entrances that lead into an impressive chamber.

Reserve kayak space on the boat to the islands (Island Packers Cruises, 805/642-1393, www.islandpackers. com). For kayak rentals, contact **Channel Islands Kayak Center** (3600 S. Harbor Blvd., Ste. 2-108, Channel Islands Harbor, 805/984-5995, www.cikayak.com). For guided kayak tours to sea caves on Santa Cruz, book through **Santa Barbara Adventure Company** (32 E. Haley St., Santa Barbara, 805/884-9283, www.sbadventureco.com), which also operates from Scorpion Anchorage.

ANAPACA ISLAND

Best Hike

INSPIRATION POINT

DISTANCE: 1.5 miles (2.4 km) round-trip
DURATION: 1 hour
ELEVATION CHANGE: 40 feet (12 m)
EFFORT: easy
TRAILHEAD: Landing Cove, East Anacapa

If you've seen a photo of the Channel Islands on a calendar or postcard, most likely it is the spectacular view from **Inspiration Point** on Anacapa Island. On the way, the loop trail includes stops at Pinniped Point and Cathedral Cove, where you can view sea lions stacked like sandbags on pocket beaches hundreds of feet below. At the point, a bench offers a place to soak in the view and the solitude of the Channel Islands. Middle Anacapa Island and West Anacapa Island rise out of the ocean to the west like a giant sea serpent's spine. In the distance, the larger Santa Cruz Island peers from behind them. Below, rust-colored kelp forests speckle the blue-green ocean waters while gulls perform aerial acrobatics. Stay on the trail to protect fragile vegetation and nesting seabirds.

Nov., 3 hrs by boat). Its mountainous spine rises to 1,592-foot (485-m) Radar Mountain, with views of neighboring Santa Cruz Island and the mainland coastline. The island's white-sand beaches and coastal lagoons seem untouched. Santa Rosa is also home to one of only two Torrey pine forests in the world.

SAN MIGUEL

The westernmost island in the chain, **San Miguel Island** (Apr.-early Nov., 4 hrs by boat) has abundant wildlife, especially at **Point Bennett,** where an estimated 30,000 seals and sea lions reside. Most visitors arrive at **Cuyler Harbor,** a large half-moon bay on the northeast side. Tide pools await at the east end of the scenic 2-mile-long (3.2-km) white-sand beach. Western gulls, California brown pelicans, cormorants, and Cassin's auklets nest on tiny Prince Island, which sits in the mouth of the harbor. San Miguel Island is under the jurisdiction of the U.S. Navy and is open only when National Park Service personnel are on the island.

SANTA BARBARA

At one square mile, **Santa Barbara** (Apr.-Oct., 3 hrs by boat) is the smallest of the islands and a rare stop. With currents bringing warmer water north, this southernmost of the Channel Islands is good for swimming, diving, snorkeling, and kayaking. It is home to huge seabird colonies, including one of the world's largest colonies of Scripps's murrelets.

RECREATION

HIKING

On Anacapa, the **Lighthouse Trail** (0.5 mi/0.8 km rt, 20 min, easy) climbs to a viewpoint.

Santa Cruz Island can't be beat for coastal scenery, cliff-top views to the mainland, and whale-watching. **Cavern Point Loop** (2 mi/3.2 km rt, 2 hrs, moderate) provides a vantage to spot whales. The **Smugglers Cove Trail** (7.5 mi/12.1 km rt, 4 hrs, strenuous) follows an old ranch road across the eastern interior to a south-facing beach. Even if you don't find the elusive island scrub jay on **Scorpion Canyon Loop** (4.5 mi/7.2 km rt, 3 hrs, moderate), you'll tour a unique canyon followed by a series of stunning vistas.

On Santa Rosa Island, the **Water Canyon Beach Trail** (3 mi/4.8 km rt, 1.5 hrs, easy) leads to a white-sand beach. The **East Point Trail** (16 mi/25.7 km rt, 8 hrs, strenuous) takes in the rare Torrey pine forest and beaches of Santa Rosa Island. The **Lobo Canyon Trail** (9.6 mi/15.4 km rt, 5 hrs, strenuous) goes to a water-sculpted canyon resembling those in the Southwest.

On San Miguel, hike inland from Cuyler Harbor through a canyon with

ANACAPA ISLAND

native vegetation to the **Lester Ranch Site** (2 mi/3.2 km rt, 1 hr, moderate) to see the remains of a cistern, a root cellar, and the living-room chimney in a rubble pile. Visitors must obtain a permit (including a liability waiver) to visit the island and must stay on the designated trails due to possible unexploded ordnance at this onetime bombing range.

On Santa Barbara Island, hike the **Arch Point Trail** (1 mi/1.6 km rt, 30 min, moderate) to view the 130-foot-high (40-m) arch on the island's northern tip. For wildlife, walk to **Elephant Seal Cove** (2.5 mi/4 km rt, 1.5 hrs, strenuous) or **Sea Lion Rookery** (2 mi/3.2 km rt, 1 hr, moderate), where steep cliffs overlook sea mammal colonies. To view the whole island, take the **Signal Peak Trail** (2.5 mi/4 km rt, 1.5 hrs, moderate) to the island's apex at 634 feet (193 m).

SNORKELING AND SCUBA DIVING

Santa Cruz Island offers outstanding snorkeling and scuba diving off the beach in Scorpion Harbor. The kelp east and west of the Scorpion Anchorage Pier are rich in sea life. The wreck of a World War II minesweeper lies 50 yards (46 m) off Scorpion Rocks in 40-60 feet (12-18 m) of water. Rent snorkel gear from **Santa Barbara Adventure Company** (805/884-9283 www.sbadventureco.com) in Scorpion Harbor.

To dive the island's other spots, you'll need your own boat or to charter a dive boat. Schedule diving trips from Ventura Harbor with **Peace Dive Boat** (1691 Spinnaker Dr., G Dock, 949/247-1106, www.peaceboat.com) or Santa Barbara Harbor with **Sea Landing** (301 W. Cabrillo Blvd., 805/963-2564, www.sealanding.net).

WHERE TO STAY
INSIDE THE PARK

There are no accommodations, food, or services on the Channel Islands. **Camping** (877/444-6777, www.recreation.gov, $15) is the only overnight option; reservations are required. All campsites have picnic tables, pit toilets, and food storage bins. Water is not available (bring your own), except where noted below.

On Santa Cruz Island, **Scorpion Ranch Campground** is a 0.5- to 1-mile (0.8- to 1.6-km) walk from the pier at Scorpion Anchorage. With drinking water, the lower campground (22 sites) sits in a eucalyptus-shaded canyon, while the upper loop (3 sites, 6 group sites) is spread in a meadow—but it's twice as far to lug your camping gear. From Prisoners Harbor, a strenuous 3.5-mile (5.6-km) hike goes to the **Del Norte Backcountry Campsite,** a remote spot in an oak grove. The shaded **Prisoners Harbor Campground** (6 sites, 1 accessible site, accessible vault toilet) is 0.25 mile (0.4 km) on a flat route from the landing.

A 0.5-mile (0.8-km) hike on East Anacapa includes 157 stairs to reach the sun- and wind-exposed **Anacapa Island Campground** (7 sites). A steep 1-mile (1.6-km) hike uphill reaches **San Miguel Island Campground** (9 sites). From the visitors center, a steep

0.25-mile (0.4-km) hike connects with the seasonal **Santa Barbara Island Campground** (10 sites). On Santa Rosa, a level 1.5-mile (2.4-km) hike accesses the **Water Canyon Campground** (15 sites, water available), and backcountry beach camping (mid-Aug.-Dec.) is allowed on the undeveloped coastline.

OUTSIDE THE PARK

Accommodations and restaurants are plentiful in **Ventura** and **Santa Barbara.**

GETTING THERE

AIR

The closest major airport is **Los Angeles International Airport** (LAX, 1 World Way, 424/646-5252, www.fly-lax.com). There are also regional airports in the Greater LA area. It's roughly a two-hour drive north via US 101 to reach Ventura, the gateway to the Channel Islands.

Channel Island Aviation (305 Durley Ave., Camarillo, 805/987-1301, www.flycia.com) has flights to Santa Rosa Island.

BOAT

Most visitors reach Channel Islands National Park via a boat run by **Island Packers Cruises** (1691 Spinnaker Dr., Ste. 105B, Ventura Harbor, 805/642-1393, www.islandpackers.com). Schedules change seasonally with crossing times ranging 1-4 hours, based on distance and conditions. Some landings require climbing steel ladders to docks and then stairs to reach the island tops. The company also offers a wildlife-watching cruise in the water surrounding the islands; this tour doesn't land on any of the islands.

Anacapa: By boat (year-round, 90 min), Anacapa requires debarking by climbing up a steel ladder and then ascending stairs to the island top.

Santa Cruz: The two primary points of entry onto Santa Cruz are at **Scorpion Anchorage** and **Prisoners Harbor.** After a 90-minute boat ride from Ventura, travelers off-load either by climbing a steel ladder to a short shore pier or via skiff landings.

Santa Rosa: Boats debark at Santa Rosa, where visitors must climb a 20-foot (6.1-m) steel-rung ladder to reach flat land. Year-round flights to the island take 25 minutes.

San Miguel: Boat trips can experience potentially rough seas and skiff landings require waterproof gear.

Santa Barbara: Boat travel requires a skiff transfer to a rocky ledge adjacent to the dock. Severe winter storms damaged the dock, with no repairs scheduled in the future. A 0.25-mile (0.4-km) set of steps crest the island top.

▼ SANTA CRUZ ISLAND

PACIFIC NORTHWEST

Rugged mountains define the Pacific Northwest. Massive volcanoes tower over the land, and glaciers gleam from mountainsides.

In Oregon, Crater Lake pits startlingly blue water against a rim of steep rock cliffs.

Washington's three national parks cluster close together. In the north, fjord-like lakes stretch below the jagged peaks of North Cascades National Park.

Around its mountainous interior, Olympic National Park contains rainforests, enormous old-growth trees, and rocky tide pools on the Pacific coast.

Looming above Seattle, 14,411-foot (4,392-m) Mount Rainier lures climbers to scale its glaciated summit while backpackers circle the peak on the Wonderland Trail.

◄ MYRTLE FALLS, MOUNT RAINIER NATIONAL PARK

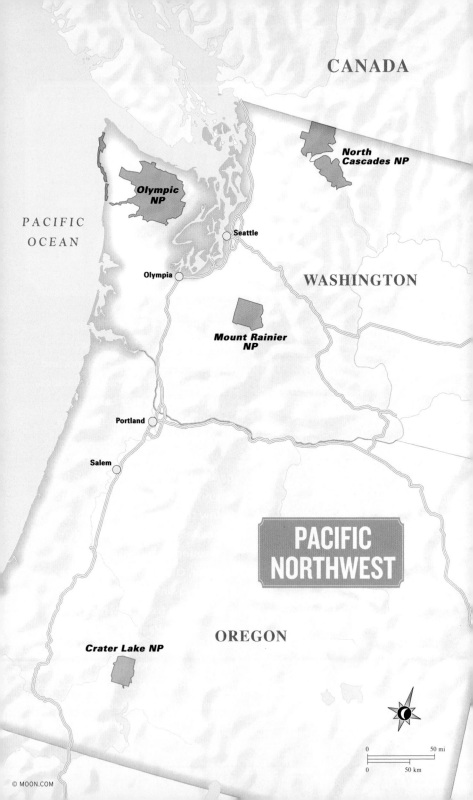

CANADA

North
Cascades NP

PACIFIC
OCEAN

Olympic
NP

Seattle

Olympia

WASHINGTON

Mount Rainier
NP

Portland

Salem

**PACIFIC
NORTHWEST**

OREGON

Crater Lake NP

50 mi

50 km

© MOON.COM

The National Parks of
THE PACIFIC NORTHWEST

CRATER LAKE, OR
The caldera from a catastrophic volcanic eruption 7,700 years ago now contains the nation's deepest and bluest lake (page 219).

OLYMPIC, WA
Wet, lush, and wild, the park fills with a rugged coastline, rainforests housing world-record trees, and a mountain range that begs hiking (page 229).

MOUNT RAINIER, WA
The king of the Cascades, this volcanic peak is crowned with the largest number of glaciers on any mountain in the Lower 48 (page 246).

NORTH CASCADES, WA
These jagged peaks are one of the wildest places in the Lower 48. Get a taste of the scenery on the beautiful North Cascades Highway (page 258).

1: JAMES ISLAND, RIALTO BEACH, OLYMPIC
2: MOUNT RAINIER SUMMIT
3: CRATER LAKE LODGE, CRATER LAKE

Best OF THE PARKS

Crater Lake Rim Drive: Circle the rim of this lake-filled caldera (page 223).

Hoh Rain Forest: Walk under some of the tallest trees in the world in this mossy rainforest (page 233).

Hurricane Ridge: Take in majestic alpine views that get even more impressive if you continue on one of several hiking trails (page 233).

Ruby Beach: Enjoy a winning combination of beauty and accessibility at this Pacific Ocean beach (page 233).

Wildflowers at Paradise: Relish icy Mount Rainier framed by fields of wildflowers in summer (page 250).

North Cascades Highway: Navigate the beautiful curves, reservoirs, forests, and peaks of this scenic mountain highway (page 263).

PLANNING YOUR TRIP

You'll need at least **two weeks** to tour all four parks or **7-10 days** for the Washington parks. To stay inside the parks, make advance **reservations:** one year for lodges, six months for campgrounds. **Winter** closes many of the roads in this region, with limited access to a handful of locations and services.

Summer is prime time for Washington and Oregon. From June to September, the days are long and the temperatures seldom climb above the mid-80s (upper 20s C). Snow melts from mountain passes and high-altitude hiking trails, usually by July. The sunny, mild days are great for kayaking.

Seattle provides the most central access to Olympic, Mount Rainier, and North Cascades National Parks.

1: SUNSET AT HURRICANE RIDGE
2: NORTH CASCADES HIGHWAY

Road Trip

MOUNT RAINIER, OLYMPIC, AND NORTH CASCADES

Launching from **Seattle,** this road trip makes a grand loop that includes a ferry ride across Puget Sound. The route spans the mountains to the coast for a rich taste of Washington's best.

BENCH LAKE, MOUNT RAINIER

Mount Rainier

80 miles (130 km) / 1.5 hours

From **Seattle,** get an early start for the two-hour drive to the **White River Entrance** in the northeast corner of Mount Rainier National Park. In Seattle, take I-5 south to exit onto WA 18 heading east to Auburn, where WA 164 heads east to Enumclaw. Go east and then south on WA 410 into the park, turning right onto Sunrise Park Road to reach the entrance station. A winding road climbs to **Sunrise,** a hub of park activity and the highest point on the mountain accessible by car. Get your bearings at the visitors center, have lunch at the cafeteria, and then head out for a couple of hours of alpine hiking.

Drive down Sunrise Park Road to WA 410, where a right turn follows the highway southward until it becomes WA 123. Turn right onto Stevens Canyon Road to climb through switchbacks up to Paradise for dinner and overnighting at **Paradise Inn.** In the morning, tour the visitors center, explore the wildflower meadows, and hike to **Bench Lake** or **Plummer Peak.** The next day, exit the park via **Longmire** and the **Nisqually Entrance.**

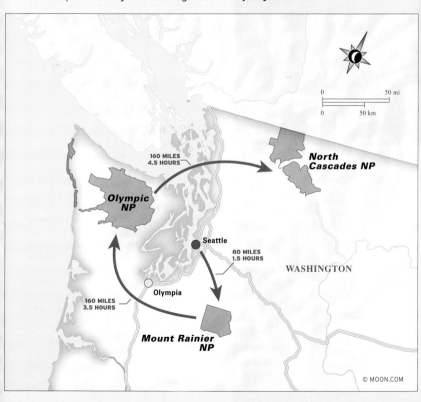

Olympic

160 miles (260 km) / 3.5 hours

Say good-bye to Rainier as you head west on WA 706 toward Olympic National Park. In Elbe, continue northwest on WA 7 to connect with WA 702 heading west. In McKenna, take WA 507 west to Yelm and continue northwest on WA 510 to reach I-5. Go southwest to reach Olympia, exiting onto US 101 going northwest. Take WA 8 west to Elma, then US 12 west to Aberdeen and then US 101 north.

Stop at **Lake Quinault,** at the southwestern end of the park, where you'll experience the lush primordial forest. Drive up the coast on US 101 to dine and overnight at **Kalaloch Lodge.**

In the morning, drive north to **Ruby Beach,** a classic example of Washington's misty pebble-strewn coastline. Continue north on US 101 to glacier-carved **Lake Crescent.** Spend the afternoon floating on its tranquil turquoise-green waters before overnighting at **Lake Crescent Lodge** or in Port Angeles.

The next morning, drive from Port Angeles up Hurricane Ridge Road to the only part of the Olympic Mountains accessible by car: **Hurricane Ridge.** Stop at **Hurricane Ridge Visitor Center** and walk to **Hurricane Hill** for expansive views. Depart the Olympics in the early afternoon to drive east on US 101 to Discovery Bay and then north on WA 20 to Port Townsend (1 hr) to catch the 35-minute ferry (fee, reservations required) across Puget Sound to Whidbey Island.

North Cascades

160 miles (260 km) / 4.5 hours

After debarking on Whidbey Island, drive north on WA 20 to cross Deception Pass Bridge to the mainland. Your next stop is **Marblemount,** two hours east on WA 20, where you'll spend the night. In the morning, follow the **North Cascades Highway** (WA 20) as it slices 30 miles (48 km) across the park. Stop at **North Cascades Visitor Center** before taking a boat tour of **Diablo Lake.** Back on the highway, head east to visit **Ross Lake Overlook.** Go as far as **Washington Pass** for views of Liberty Bell Mountain and Early Winter Spires. The next day, it's a 2.5-hour drive back to Seattle.

1: ROYAL BASIN, OLYMPIC NATIONAL PARK
2: DIABLO LAKE, NORTH CASCADES
2: KAYAKING ON CRESCENT LAKE

CRATER LAKE NATIONAL PARK

Oregon

WEBSITE:
www.nps.gov/crla

PHONE NUMBER:
541/594-3000

VISITATION RANK:
34

WHY GO:
Visit a sapphire-blue lake in the heart of a sunken volcano.

▲ CRATER LAKE

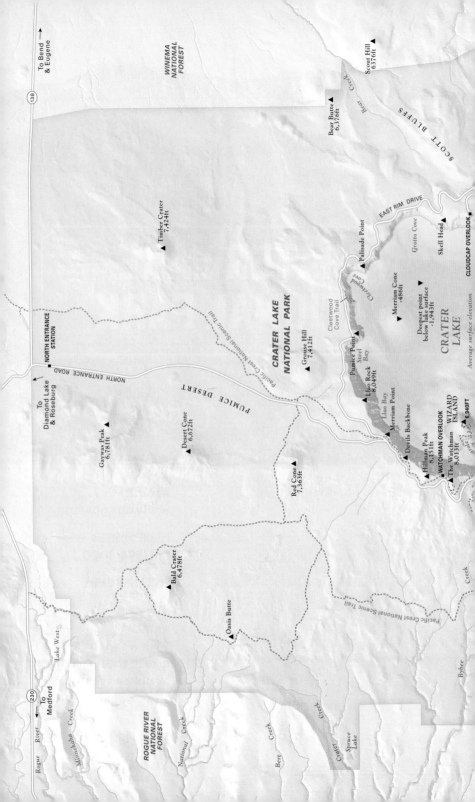

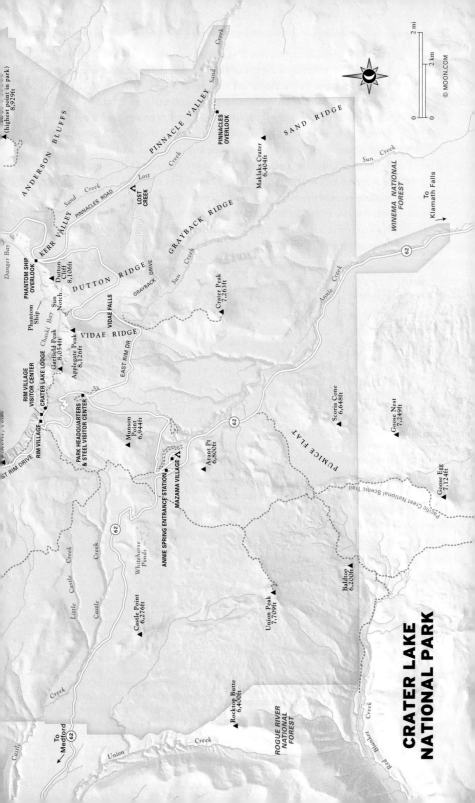

CRATER LAKE NATIONAL PARK

High in the Cascades lies the crown jewel of Oregon: **CRATER LAKE,** the country's deepest lake at 1,943 feet (592 m). Its surface glimmers like a polished sapphire. It's tucked inside a volcano that erupted then collapsed thousands of years ago—an event witnessed by the ancestors of the Klamath tribes and Cow Creek Umpqua people. Today, we know it as one of the first national parks in the country, preserving a pristine aquatic habitat.

Crater Lake's extraordinary hues are the result of the depth and clarity of the water, which absorbs all the colors of the spectrum visible to our eyes except the shortest wavelengths—blue and violet. As you crest into the crater for the first time and spot the lake, its immense azure expanse hits with a burst of stark beauty. "Wow" is an afterthought.

PLANNING YOUR TIME

Crater Lake National Park is southern Oregon's top destination. **Summer** (June-Sept.) is peak season, when the loop drive around the caldera clogs with traffic. Most visitors schedule their trip when the whole loop is open to drive; weather and snowpack dictate its opening (late May-late June) and closing (mid-Oct.-mid-Nov.), when winter snows bury the road.

Crater Lake is high in the Cascade Mountains and erratic weather is prevalent. July, August, and September see the warmest and sunniest days with highs in the 60s (over 16°C). Spring and fall yo-yo between rain and snow. In winter, wet snowstorms pelt the park—which averages 42 feet (13 m) of annual snowfall—and clouds can block your view of the lake. Check the park webcams to verify visibility.

ENTRANCES AND FEES

The park's **South** and **West Entrances** (OR 62) are open year-round; a pay station for both is at Annie Creek near Mazama Village. The **North Entrance** (OR 138) is open mid-June to mid-October. The entrance fee is $30 per vehicle ($25 motorcycle, $15 individual), valid for seven days. You can **buy a pass online** (www.recreation.gov) in advance to go through the entrance station faster.

In winter (fees reduced to $20 per vehicle, $15 per motorcycle), the South Entrance is the only way to reach the south rim to see the lake, as snow closes the North Entrance, East Rim Drive, and West Rim Drive.

VISITORS CENTERS

The tiny **Rim Visitor Center** (9:30am-5pm daily late May-late Sept., shorter hours spring and fall) is in Rim Village near Crater Lake Lodge. It has a few exhibits and a bookstore. A rock stairway behind the building leads to **Sinnott Memorial Overlook,** with one of the best views of the lake and daily ranger talks in summer.

The **Steel Visitor Center** (9am-5pm daily late Apr.-early Nov., 10am-4pm daily early Nov.-late Apr.) is below Rim Village near park headquarters. It has a film, exhibits, information, maps, backcountry permits, and a bookstore.

SIGHTS

THE LAKE

At 1,943 feet deep (592 m), **Crater Lake** is the deepest lake in the United States. It has no inlet or outlet; its water level is maintained by snow, rain, and evaporation. Although Crater Lake often records the coldest temperatures in the Cascades, the lake itself has only frozen over once since records have been kept. Deeper water in the lake stays around 38°F (3°C), although scientists have discovered hot spots 1,400 feet (427 m) below the

BICYCLISTS ON THE RIM LOOP

Top ❸

❶ CIRCLE THE LAKE ON THE RIM DRIVE

The **Rim Drive** (33 mi/53 km, July-Oct.), divided into a longer East Rim and a shorter West Rim, offers a scenic cruise around the glistening lake. If you're seeing Crater Lake for the first time, drive into the park from the north for the most dramatic perspective. After crossing through a pumice desert, the road climbs to higher elevations until it overlooks the blue lake.

From the North Junction, follow **East Rim Drive,** stopping at pullovers along the way. East Rim Drive finishes at the lake's south end at park headquarters and Steel Visitor Center.

From park headquarters, continue the tour on **West Rim Drive,** which takes in the historic **Crater Lake Lodge** and **Watchman Overlook,** for picture-perfect views of Wizard Island.

If you enter from the north, drive East Rim followed by West Rim; for entering from park headquarters, drive West Rim followed by East Rim. This clockwise circling of the lake makes pulling off at more than 30 viewpoints easier. Plan at least three hours for the curvy drive.

❷ TAKE A BOAT TOUR TO WIZARD ISLAND

Due to the caldera's steep, avalanche-pruned slopes, only one trail leads down to the lake itself, and it is the only way to reach the tour boat. **Crater Lake Hospitality** (866/292-6720, www.travelcraterlake.com, daily July-mid-Sept.) launches a narrated cruise to Wizard Island, with three hours of exploration on the tiny dot of land. A boat shuttle offers access for self-explorers as well. All boats depart from Cleetwood Cove, accessible only by the steep trail. Reconstruction of the marina is slated for 2024-2025, which will close the area for boat tours and shuttles.

❸ BIKE THE RIM

The paved **Rim Drive** (33 mi/53 km, summer and fall only) around Crater Lake is a cyclist's dream ride. But it's no lazy pedal nor family-friendly riding. Flying downhills swoop immediately into steep, long uphill climbs as the rolling road circles the lake. Elevation gain for the entire loop nearly reaches 4,000 feet (1,219 m), and minimal shoulders on the narrow road make the ride only for cyclists experienced with cars at their elbows. Most cyclists opt for a clockwise loop from park headquarters to get the monster climbs done first.

Two times offer prime cycling. September usually has two car-free days on the East Rim (registration recommended, https://ridetherimoregon.com), and cyclists are permitted to ride portions of the road still closed to cars in June after the plows have removed snow. Bring your own bicycle; the closest rentals are in Ashland, 89 miles (143 km) away.

ONE DAY IN CRATER LAKE

Thanks to the scenic **Rim Drive,** visitors who only have one day can circle the entire loop. Stop at overlooks to enjoy the lake from various vantages and squeeze in at least one short hike to **Sun Notch** or **Watchman Peak.**

lake's surface. Some types of mosses and green algae grow more than 400 feet (122 m) below the lake's surface, a world record for these freshwater species. See the lake from all sides via East and West Rim Drives.

WIZARD ISLAND

Wizard Island, a large cinder cone that rises 760 feet (201 m) above the surface of the lake, offers evidence of volcanic activity since the caldera's formation. The true crater at the top of the island is the source of the lake's name. See the island from overlooks on East Rim and West Rim Drives, or for up-close inspection, take the tour boat over to hike on it and see its 800-year-old trees.

BEST EAST RIM DRIVE OVERLOOKS

On the east side of **East Rim Drive,** check out three overlooks within about 4 miles (6.4 km) of each other just north of Pinnacles Road. **Cloudcap Overlook** has its own signed spur road (2 mi/3.2 km rt), one of Oregon's highest paved roads. Spotted with wind- and snow-battered whitebark pines, the overlook affords a panoramic view of the crater and lake. At the **Pumice Castle Overlook,** spot the bright orange "castle" on the cliff wall. It's especially vibrant in the early evening, when the sun lights it up. At the **Phantom Ship Overlook,** try to spy the tiny island in this big lake. Formed from lava, it is 170 feet tall (52 m).

BEST WEST RIM DRIVE SIGHTS

West Rim Drive has historic and scenic overlooks. At the junction above park headquarters, go right to visit the **Sinnott Memorial Overlook** and historic **Crater Lake Lodge.** Return to the junction to continue north on West Rim Drive. In about 1 mile (1.6 km), stop at **Discovery Point** (a great

sunrise location), where a gold prospector stumbled upon the lake while riding his mule. Farther along West Rim Drive, **Watchman Overlook** offers good views of Wizard Island and an outstanding sunset location.

RECREATION

HIKING

West Rim Drive

Just east of Crater Lake Lodge, the **Garfield Peak Trail** (3.4 mi/5.5 km rt, 2-3 hrs, strenuous) climbs an imposing ridge with wildflower displays of phlox, Indian paintbrush, and lupine, plus frequent sightings of eagles and hawks. The route, which is steep in places, tops out at Garfield Peak with a 360-degree view of the crater and the lake 1,888 feet (575 m) below.

GARFIELD PEAK TRAIL

Best Hike

WATCHMAN PEAK

DISTANCE: 1.4 miles (2.3 km) round-trip
DURATION: 1.5 hours
ELEVATION CHANGE: 420 feet (128 m)
EFFORT: moderately strenuous
TRAILHEAD: Watchman Overlook (3.8 mi/6.1 km northwest of Rim Village) on the West Rim

While **Watchman Peak Trail** yields a huge view any time of day, and crowds attest to its short climb with big rewards, it's a great place to catch the sunset on a ranger-led hike (daily in summer). From the trailhead, the route starts on the Pacific Crest Alternate Trail until the trail splits at a signed junction. Here, the Watchman trail bolts up a series of shadeless switchbacks to reach an active fire lookout. Crater Lake spreads out with Wizard Island in the foreground, almost at your feet.

East Rim Drive

A half mile east of park headquarters, **Castle Crest Wildflower Loop** (0.4 mi/0.6 km rt, 20 min, easy) is one of the best places to view summer flora. A short loop with lots of visual punch goes to **Sun Notch** (0.5 mi/0.8 km rt, 45 min, easy) on a trail that climbs 150 feet (46 m) through a meadow to overlook the Phantom Ship and Crater Lake. Find the trailhead 4.4 miles (7.1 km) east of park headquarters.

From Pinnacles Road, a dirt path goes through old-growth forest to **Plaikni Falls** (2 mi/3.2 km rt, 1 hr, easy), which rolls down a glacier-carved cliff. To view the falls at the end requires a short, steep grunt uphill.

Only the **Cleetwood Cove Trail** (2.2 mi/3.5 km rt, 1.5 hrs, strenuous) cuts through the rim to reach the lakeshore. You can swim in the lake, but be ready for frigid water and a return climb of about 700 feet (213 m). A hike to **Wizard Island Summit** (2.3 mi/3.7 km rt, 2 hrs, strenuous) requires a boat ride (fee) and a 770-foot (235-km) climb. Once at the top, you can peer into the crater while circumnavigating the rim on a flat trail. Drop-offs are steep, but the views go all directions. This area is slated for reconstruction starting in 2024 and may last two years. During this time, the cove trail will be closed and boat tours won't run.

From a trailhead 14 miles (23 km) east of park headquarters, a trail ascends to the top of 8,929-foot (2,721-m) **Mount Scott** (5 mi/8 km rt, 3 hrs, strenuous), the highest peak in the park. Lake

CLEETWOOD COVE

CRATER LAKE LODGE

views and perspectives on a dozen Cascade peaks are the rewards at the end of the trek that gains 1,152 feet (351 m).

WINTER SPORTS

When snow buries the park in winter, services and activities are cut to a minimum. However, many cross-country skiers, snowshoers, and winter campers enjoy this solitude. Park rangers lead **snowshoe hikes** (1pm daily mid-Dec.-mid-Apr., weather permitting). Ski and snowshoe rentals are available at Rim Village.

Winter trekkers must be prepared to blaze their own cross-country trails and contend with frequent snowstorms. Inquire about trail, avalanche, and weather conditions at the visitors center before embarking. Circling the lake takes two or three days, even in good weather; only highly skilled winter skiers should attempt this 33-mile (53-km) route, which requires a beacon, probe, and shovel for traversing avalanche paths.

WHERE TO STAY

INSIDE THE PARK

Lodging is concentrated on the southern edge of the lake at **Rim Village;** opening and closing dates vary. Most services are open mid-May to mid-October. Make lodging and camping **reservations** (866/292-6720, www.travelcraterlake.com) one year in advance.

Crater Lake Lodge (late May-mid-Oct., from $239) is hewn of local wood and stone with massive picture windows of the lake and decor echoing its 1915 origins. Many of the 71 rooms have expansive views of the lake, while less expensive rooms face Upper Klamath Lake and Mount Shasta. The lobby's large stone fireplace serves as a gathering spot on chilly evenings. The **dining room** (7am-10am, 11am-3pm, and 5pm-9:30pm daily, hours vary seasonally, dinner reservations advised) serves Pacific Northwest cuisine. A bar menu offers drinks and appetizers in the lobby or on the porch overlooking the lake. Also at the rim, **Rim Village Café** (10am-6pm daily mid-June-Labor Day, shorter hours fall-spring) is open year-round and sells grab-and-go sandwiches, salads, and rice bowls.

At Mazama Village (7 mi/11 km south of Rim Village), the **Cabins at Mazama Village** (late May-late Sept., $160) have rooms with 1-2 queen beds and a bath; there are no TVs, phones, or air-conditioning. The **Annie Creek Restaurant** (7am-10:30am, 11am-3pm, and 5pm-8:30pm daily mid-June-Labor Day, shorter hours spring and fall) serves American-style comfort food.

Mazama Campground (Mazama Village, June-late Sept., $22-42) accepts reservations for some of its more than

CRATER LAKE WITH WIZARD ISLAND

200 sites; all other sites are first come, first served. Facilities include drinking water, flush toilets, and showers (fee). **Lost Creek Campground** (Pinnacles Rd., July-Oct., first come, first served, $5) has 16 tent-only sites with drinking water and vault toilets.

OUTSIDE THE PARK

Accommodations, restaurants, and services are available in **Ashland.** Several national forests surrounding Crater Lake have campgrounds and lodges, including **Diamond Lake** in Umpqua National Forest north of Crater Lake.

GETTING THERE

AIR

The closest international airport is **Rogue Valley International-Medford Airport** (MFR, 1000 Terminal Loop Pkwy., Medford, 541/772-8068, www.jacksoncountyor.org), served by

United, Alaska Airlines, and Allegiant. Car rentals are available at the airport.

TRAIN

Amtrak (800/872-7245) has a station 70 miles east at Klamath Falls (KFS, 1600 Oak Ave., 541/884-2822). The **Crater Lake Trolley** (541/882-1896, www.craterlaketrolley.net) runs a shuttle from the Amtrak station to Rim Village (July-early Oct.).

CAR

The only year-round access to Crater Lake is from the south via **OR 62.** To reach Crater Lake from Grants Pass, head for Gold Hill and take OR 234 until it meets OR 62. As you head up OR 62, the road makes a horseshoe bend through the Cascades, starting at Medford and ending 20 miles (32 km) north of Klamath Falls.

The northern route via **OR 138** (Roseburg to US 97, south of Beaver Marsh) is usually closed by snow

TAKE A BOAT RIDE ON CRATER LAKE.

THE GEOLOGY OF CRATER LAKE

Crater Lake lies in a caldera, which is produced when the center of a volcano caves in on itself. The cataclysm occurred 7,700 years ago with the destruction of formerly 12,000-foot-high (3,657-m) Mount Mazama. Klamath Native American legend tells of a fierce battle between the chiefs of the underworld and the world aboveground causing explosions and ashfall. The story parallels the scientific explanation for Crater Lake's formation.

Following the volcanic activity, the caldera filled with water over thousands of years. The lake is self-contained, fed only by snow and rain, with no outlets other than evaporation and seepage.

This great eruption left huge, deep drifts of ash and pumice. The pumice deserts to the north of the lake and the deep ashen canyons to the south are the most dramatic examples. These reddish pockets of bleakness in the otherwise green forest are so porous that water percolates through too rapidly for plants to survive. In the southern canyons, hot gases bubbling up through the ash created the eerie gray hoodoos that hardened into rocklike towers to withstand centuries of erosion.

mid-October-July, as is the park's north entrance.

GETTING AROUND

There is no public transportation within the park. Most visitors tour the 33-mile (53-km) Rim Drive in private vehicles.

BOAT TOURS

Crater Lake Hospitality (866/292-6720, www.travelcraterlake.com, daily July-mid-Sept.) offers narrated tours on the lake. Tickets are sold up to 24 hours in advance via touch-screen kiosks in Crater Lake Lodge or Annie Creek Gift Shop in Mazama Village. Kiosk sales shut down two hours before departure; after that, you can pick up any remaining tickets at the Cleetwood Cove Trailhead until 45 minutes before departure. A limited number of tickets are available by **reservation requests** online. Choose between two boat tours:

Two-hour narrated excursions (6 departures daily, 9:30am-3:45pm, adults $44, kids $30) cruise counterclockwise around the perimeter of the lake and do not stop at Wizard Island.

Five-hour narrated cruises (departs 9:45am and 12:45pm daily, adults $55, kids $37) make a three-hour stop for hiking at Wizard Island.

If you just want to get to Wizard Island for three hours of self-guided exploration, take the **boat shuttle** (departs 8:30am and 11:30am daily, adults $28, kids $18).

Allow 90 minutes to drive the 12 miles (19 km) from Rim Village to the Cleetwood trailhead. Prepare to hike the **Cleetwood Cove Trail** (1.1 mi/1.8 km one-way, 30-45 min, strenuous) 700 feet (213 m) down to **Cleetwood Cove dock,** where boat tours depart. Reconstruction of the dock is slated for 2024-2025, which will close the area for boat tours and shuttles.

TROLLEY TOURS

The **Crater Lake Trolley** (541/882-1896, www.craterlaketrolley.net, 10am-3pm daily July-mid-Oct., tours vary June and Sept.-Oct., $26-29 adults, $18 kids) takes a two-hour tour along Rim Drive with stops at scenic viewpoints. The trolleys are ADA-compliant and feature commentary by a guide. Purchase tickets in advance from a trolley parked by the Community House at Rim Village, near the Crater Lake Lodge.

SIGHTS NEARBY

En route from Redwood National Park to Crater Lake, it's worth a stop at **Oregon Caves National Monument** (OR 46, 541/592-2100, www.nps.gov/orca, hours vary spring and fall) to see stalactites and stalagmites deep inside a mountain.

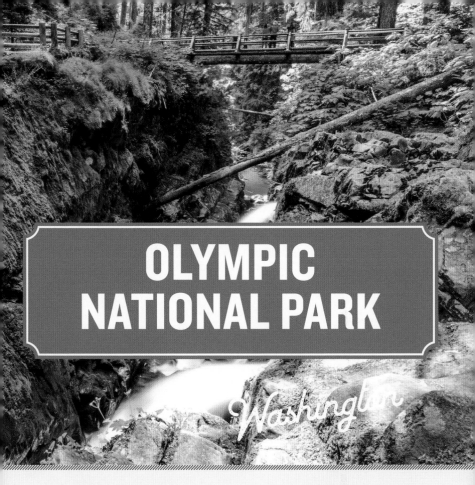

OLYMPIC
NATIONAL PARK

Washington

KEEPSAKE STAMPS ▼▼▼

WEBSITE:
www.nps.gov/olym

PHONE NUMBER:
360/565-3130

VISITATION RANK:
12

WHY GO:
Wander amid
old-growth
temperate rain
forests.

▲ SOL DUC WATERFALLS
OLYMPIC NATIONAL PARK

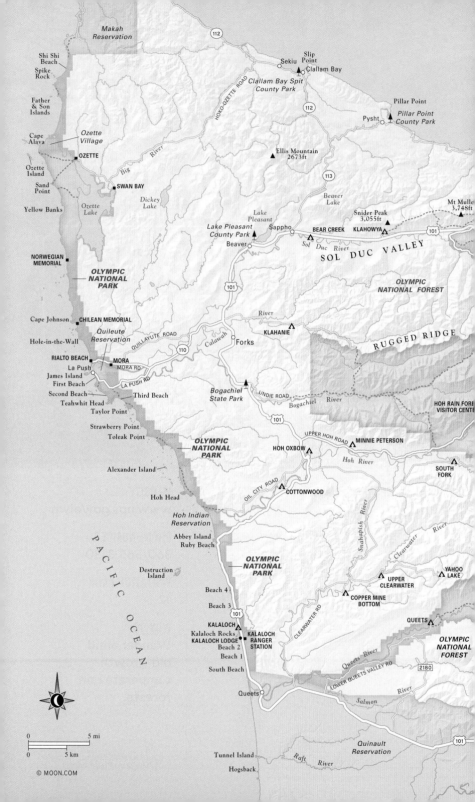

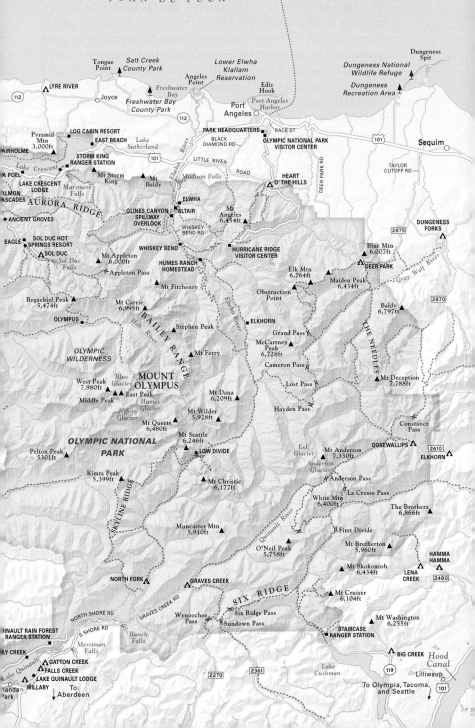

OLYMPIC NATIONAL PARK

STRAIT OF JUAN DE FUCA

Ferry to Victoria, British Columbia, Canada

Dungeness Spit

Dungeness National Wildlife Refuge

Dungeness Recreation Area

Tongue Point
Salt Creek County Park
Freshwater Bay
Angeles Point
Lower Elwha Klallam Reservation
Ediz Hook
Port Angeles Harbor

LYRE RIVER
(112)
Joyce
Freshwater Bay County Park
Port Angeles

Sequim
(101)
TAYLOR CUTOFF RD

Pyramid Mtn 3,000ft
LOG CABIN RESORT
EAST BEACH
FAIRHOLME
Lake Sutherland
PARK HEADQUARTERS
BLACK DIAMOND RD
RACE ST
OLYMPIC NATIONAL PARK VISITOR CENTER

A POEL
STORM KING RANGER STATION
(101)
LITTLE RIVER
ROAD
HEART O' THE HILLS
DEER PARK RD

LAKE CRESCENT LODGE
Lake Crescent
Mt Storm King
Mt Baldy
Madison Falls
DUNGENESS FORKS

SALMON CASCADES
Marymere Falls
AURORA RIDGE
ELWHA
ALTAIR
Mt Angeles 6,454ft
(2875)

ANCIENT GROVES
GLINES CANYON SPILLWAY OVERLOOK
WHISKEY BEND RD
HURRICANE RIDGE VISITOR CENTER
Blue Mtn 6,007ft

EAGLE
SOL DUC HOT SPRINGS RESORT
SOL DUC
Sol Duc Falls
WHISKEY BEND
Elk Mtn 6,764ft
DEER PARK
Gray Wolf River
(2870)

Mt Appleton 6,000ft
Appleton Pass
HUMES RANCH HOMESTEAD
Maiden Peak 6,434ft

Bogachiel Peak 5,474ft
Mt Fitzhenry
Obstruction Point
Baldy 6,797ft

OLYMPUS
Mt Carrie 6,995ft
BAILEY RANGE
ELKHORN
THE NEEDLES

OLYMPIC WILDERNESS
Hoh River
Stephen Peak
Grand Pass
McCartney Peak 6,728ft
Mt Deception 7,788ft

West Peak 7,980ft
Blue Glacier
MOUNT OLYMPUS
Mt Ferry
Cameron Pass
Lost Pass

Middle Peak
East Peak
Humes Glacier
Mt Dana 6,209ft
Hayden Pass

Jeffers Glacier
Mt Wilder 5,928ft
Constance Pass

Pelton Peak 5301ft
Mt Queets 6,480ft
Mt Seattle 6,246ft
LOW DIVIDE
Eel Glacier
Mt Anderson 7,330ft
DOSEWALLIPS
ELKHORN
(2610)

OLYMPIC NATIONAL PARK
Anderson Glacier
Anderson Pass

Kimta Peak 5,399ft
Mt Christie 6,177ft
White Mtn 6,400ft
La Crosse Pass
The Brothers 6,866ft

SKYLINE RIDGE
First Divide
Mt Bretherton 5,960ft
HAMMA HAMMA

Muncaster Mtn 5,910ft
Quinault River
O'Neil Peak 5,758ft
Mt Skokomish 6,434ft
LENA CREEK
(2480)

NORTH FORK
GRAVES CREEK
SIX RIDGE
Mt Cruiser 6,104ft
Mt Washington 6,255ft

NORTH SHORE RD
GRAVES CREEK RD
S SHORE RD
Six Ridge Pass
STAIRCASE RANGER STATION
(119)

QUINAULT RAIN FOREST RANGER STATION
Wynoochee Pass
Sundown Pass
BIG CREEK
Hood Canal

LY CREEK
Merriman Falls
Bunch Falls
Lilliwaup

Lake Quinault
GATTON CREEK
FALLS CREEK
LAKE QUINAULT LODGE
WILLABY
Lake Cushman
(2270)
(2361)
To Olympia, Tacoma, and Seattle
(101)

To Aberdeen

OLYMPIC NATIONAL PARK is an ecologically diverse place. Between its ocean coast and icy mountains, a massive rain forest stretches across the Hoh, Queets, and Quinault river valleys. Immense thousand-year-old trees create a thick canopy over a moist understory of ferns, mosses, and fungi. Walk among the giant spruce, cedars, and hemlocks in a landscape that looks like it hasn't changed in the past millennium. It's so lush it feels like if you took a nap by the side of the trail, you'd wake up covered in moss.

On the coast, a narrow strip of parkland provides access to mist-shrouded beaches where winter storm-watching is a recreational activity. Mountains dominate the center of the park where the glaciated summit of Mount Olympus climbs to 7,980 feet (2,432 m). These rich forests, mountains, and beaches provided plentiful food for the ancestors of eight Indigenous groups who are still connected to these lands.

PLANNING YOUR TIME

This more than 1,400-square-mile (3,734-sq-km) park lies in the center of the Olympic Peninsula and includes a 73-mile (118-km) stretch of the Pacific coastline. With multiple entrance points placed far apart, the easiest access is via US 101, which loops nearly around the park. Most of the park's interior is inaccessible by car, making it the province of hikers, backpackers, and climbers.

With a lot of driving, **four days** will get you to the main sights. Plan 7-10 days to soak up the area's riches. Lodging in the park is limited, so most visitors make use of the surrounding gateway towns: **Port Angeles, Port Townsend, Sequim,** and **Forks.** Book summer **reservations** in these areas one year in advance.

The park is open year-round. **May-September** is the most popular time to visit, when it's drier and temperatures range 75-85 degrees (24-29°C). Avoid the big summer crowds by visiting off-season or hiking in remote locations.

Fall-spring, some roads, campgrounds, and facilities close and the threat of rain is ever-present—bring rain gear. Come winter, low-elevation temperatures stay above freezing while upper elevations like Hurricane Ridge amass snow.

ENTRANCES AND FEES

The entrance fee is $30 per vehicle ($25 motorcycle, $15 individual) and good for seven days. Purchase a pass in advance online (www.recreation.gov) to go through the entrance station faster. There is no fee to enter parts of the park crossed by US 101, such as at Lake Crescent and along the coastline south from Ruby Beach.

Five entrance stations are staffed daily May-September: **Hurricane Ridge** (Hurricane Ridge Rd., weekends and holidays in winter), **Hoh** (Upper Hoh Rd.), **Ozette** (Hoko-Ozette Rd.), **Sol Duc** (Sol Duc Rd.), and **Staircase** (Staircase Rd.). Entrance stations are unstaffed in the off-season (Sept.-May); use the self-serve pay stations instead.

VISITORS CENTERS

Olympic National Park has four visitors centers with exhibits, information and ranger program schedules, maps, and bookstores. Kids can choose from two Junior Ranger booklets (free) or pick up a **Discovery Backpack** ($5 donation) for in-the-field explorations.

Olympic National Park Visitor Center

The **Olympic National Park Visitor Center** (3002 Mount Angeles Rd., Port Angeles, 360/565-3130, 7:30am-6pm daily summer, hours vary fall-spring)

Top ③

① STEP INTO THE HOH RAIN FOREST

The **Hoh Rain Forest** is the best place to explore the park's lush rainforest environment. A drive up the Hoh River weaves through the dark canopy and shaded understory, but walking through the rainforest yields a vastly different experience—damp woods, earthy scents, fields of moss, and every shade of green imaginable. Explore the short trails around the Hoh Rain Forest Visitor Center.

HOH RAIN FOREST

② GO HIGH ON HURRICANE RIDGE

Hurricane Ridge is the only car-accessible route to high vistas inside the Olympic Mountains. From Port Angeles, **Hurricane Ridge Road** (daily May-mid-Oct., Fri.-Sun. Nov.-Mar., chains required in winter) snakes up the mountainside for 17 picturesque miles (27 km) at an easy 7 percent grade. The road climbs amid big scenery to alpine trails, fields bursting with wildflowers, and shrieking marmots. As the road nears the summit, you'll reach the **Hurricane Ridge Visitor Center,** which has an observation deck for peak-gazing. To the south lie ice-draped citadels and Mount Olympus, the park's highest peak.

③ EXPLORE TIDE POOLS AT RUBY BEACH

Sea stacks and driftwood decorate **Ruby Beach,** which transitions from rocky ground to red sand as waves crash on the shore. From the parking area overlook, the paved **Ruby Beach Trail** (0.5 mi/0.8 km rt, 20 min) leads through woods and tall undergrowth down to the tidal zone. Come at low tide, when you have clear passage up and down the beach to explore tide pools full of mussels, sea stars, and urchins while sea otters frolic in the water. Look for the famous hole in a sea stack next to Cedar Creek.

SEA STAR, RUBY BEACH

Spend the night in **Port Angeles** for an early start for your one day in the park. Start with a drive up to **Hurricane Ridge,** followed by a stop for lunch at **Crescent Lake Lodge.** Then cruise through the **Hoh Rain Forest** and finish with a stroll along **Ruby Beach.**

has hands-on exhibits for kids and a park film. The **Wilderness Information Center** (360/565-3100, daily Apr.-Oct., hours vary by season) has weather updates, trail reports, permit information, and bear canisters for loan (subject to availability).

Hurricane Ridge

The **Hurricane Ridge Visitor Center** (Hurricane Ridge Rd., 360/565-3131, 9am-6pm daily late June-Sept., hours and days vary Oct.-May) has an observation deck, self-guided nature trails, and ranger-led walks in summer. It is located 17 miles (27 km) south of Port Angeles on the south slope of Hurricane Ridge.

Hoh Rain Forest

The **Hoh Rain Forest Visitor Center** (360/565-3000, 9am-5pm daily mid-May-Sept., hours and days vary May-Oct.)

has ranger-led interpretive walks and presentations. It is located at the end of the Upper Hoh Road, 31 miles (50 km) south of Forks.

Kalaloch

The small **Kalaloch Ranger Station** (156954 US 101, Forks, 360/962-2283, hours vary daily late June-Sept., Tues.-Sat. mid-May-late June) is the best resource for the Olympic coast.

SIGHTS
ELWHA VALLEY

The removal of two dams in 2011-2014 has transformed the **Elwha Valley** by returning the Elwha River to a free-flowing state. Now, water flows through its old channels, and salmon swim upstream.

HURRICANE RIDGE

KAYAKING ON LAKE CRESCENT

BULL ELK

From US 101 about 11 miles (18 km, 20 min) southwest of Port Angeles, follow Olympic Hot Springs Road (Elwha River Rd.) south into the park. Access terminates at a gate just inside the park boundary. Here, the paved, wheelchair-accessible 200-foot (61-m) path leads to **Madison Falls.**

To see the river transformation, you can hike or bike the closed road and bypass trail that goes around a road washout to get to **Glines Canyon Overlook** (6.8 mi/10.9 km rt, 3 hrs).

LAKE CRESCENT

Lake Crescent is the place to go for tranquil beauty. Follow US 101 south as it cuts into the park along the 12-mile-long (19-km) glacier-carved lake. Set in a trough of steep old-growth forest, Lake Crescent is more than 600 feet (183 m) deep. The translucent turquoise-green water is startlingly clear; at some points, visibility extends to 60 feet (18 m) deep, making it a popular spot for paddlers and anglers. Multiple locations rent kayaks, canoes, and paddleboards. Boat tours (888/896-3818, www.olympicnationalparks.com, 3-4 times Thurs.-Sun. mid-June-mid-Sept., 90 min, $13-27) cruise on Lake Crescent. The shoreline holds three picnic areas, a campground, **Crescent Lake Lodge, Log Cabin Resort,** and two **boat launches.**

An environmental education center with a facility near the lodge, **NatureBridge** (360/928-3720, www.naturebridge.org) has weekend family programs (spring-summer) and two-week science camps for teens (summer).

SOL DUC VALLEY

West of Lake Crescent on US 101, paved **Sol Duc Hot Springs Road** (pronounced "sole duck") leads into the park along the Sol Duc River. Old-growth forest looms on either side of the road, with beams of sunlight breaking through high tree branches to dapple the forest floor.

At 5 miles (8 km), **Salmon Cascades** has a viewing platform. Stop to watch steelhead trout in spring and coho salmon in fall as they struggle to migrate upstream.

Near the end of the road, **Sol Duc Hot Springs Resort** (12076 Sol Duc Hot Springs Rd., 888/896-3818, www.olympicnationalparks.com, Apr.-Oct., day passes $11-15 per 90-min session) has three cement soaking pools with temperatures ranging 99-104ºF (37-40ºC). One large nonthermal swimming pool offers shared space for sunbathers, swimmers, and kids.

LAKE OZETTE

Lake Ozette is the third-largest natural lake in Washington. The area from its eastern shore to the coastline is part of the national park and includes a picnic area, boat launch, and campground on the north shore.

KALALOCH

The name **Kalaloch** (CLAY-lock) derives from a Quinault term meaning "sheltered landing." This coastal portion of Olympic National Park stretches between the Hoh Indian Reservation and the Quinault Reservation, providing access to wild beaches.

Seven points along US 101 connect to the water. Stop first at the north-end viewpoint to overlook **Ruby Beach.** From here, six numbered points access the beach from south to north. **Beach Four** is good for tide-pooling, and in summer park rangers conduct guided tours of the tide pools. Next up is **Kalaloch Beach,** 7.6 miles (12 km) south of Ruby. Between Kalaloch Campground and Kalaloch Lodge, Kalaloch Creek enters the ocean where the **Kalaloch Rocks** sit offshore. **South Beach** is the southernmost beach in the park.

QUEETS RAIN FOREST

South of Kalaloch, the paved and gravel Upper Queets Valley Road leads 27 miles (43 km) into the **Queets Rain Forest.** This less crowded region of the park is the province of campers, hikers, and anglers casting into the Queets River. At the road's terminus is the huge **Queets Sitka Spruce**—the largest

WILLABY CREEK FLOWS INTO LAKE QUINAULT.

Best Hike

HURRICANE HILL

DISTANCE: 3.2 miles (5.2 km) round-trip

DURATION: 2 hours

ELEVATION CHANGE: 700 feet (213 m)

EFFORT: moderate

TRAILHEAD: Hurricane Hill Road parking lot, 1 mile (1.6 km) west of Hurricane Ridge Visitor Center

The **Hurricane Hill Trail** winds through summer fields of wildflowers before gaining elevation for immense views of mountains and waters as far as the eye can see. With interpretive signs, the paved, wide trail climbs out of the forest into high alpine meadows and mountain goat terrain. The path steepens the farther you go. At the ridge, immense views spread to the south, including glaciers flanking Mount Olympus, the highest peak in the park. To the north, look straight down on Port Angeles and the Strait of Juan de Fuca, which separates the United States from Canada. On a clear day, you can see Mount Baker rising in the Cascades to the east. Plan to arrive by 8:30am, as the parking lot fills quickly.

spruce in the world by volume. The 248-foot-tall (77.6-m) wonder is almost 15 feet (4.6 m) in diameter at its base.

QUINAULT RAIN FOREST

Frequent rains feed the **Quinault Rain Forest.** Walk the **Big Sitka Spruce Tree Trail** (0.6 mi/1 km rt, 30 min, easy), located on the South Shore Road, to see the **Quinault Lake Spruce,** the world's largest Sitka spruce by girth. However, the most impressive trees are on the North Shore on the **Big Cedar Trail** (0.4 mi/0.6 km rt, 20 min, easy).

At the center of the rain forest sits **Lake Quinault,** a glacier-fed natural reservoir of the Quinault River. The lake harbors **Lake Quinault Lodge** (on the South Shore), which is listed on the National Register of Historic Places. You can boat, fish, and swim in summer or hop on a boat tour (888/896-3818, www.olympicnationalparks.com, 3 times daily June-Sept., 90 min, $25-35).

The **Quinault Rain Forest Loop Drive** (31 mi/50 km) goes to trailheads and campsites. The road travels around the lake and up one side of the Quinault River and back down the other. The upper portions of North Shore and South Shore Roads are dirt.

HIKING

HURRICANE RIDGE AND THE NORTH SIDE

Opposite the visitors center, easy paths let you absorb the beauty. Two wheelchair-accessible paved trails go to **Big Meadow** (0.5 mi/0.8 km rt, 20 min) for mountain views and **Cirque Rim** (1 mi/1.6 km rt, 45 min, wheelchair assistance may be needed) to overlook the Strait of Juan de Fuca. The partly paved **High Ridge Loop** (0.5 mi/0.8 km rt, 30 min) climbs to Sunrise Point for views in all directions.

Klahhane Ridge

From the Hurricane Ridge Visitor Center, an out-and-back traverse to **Klahhane Ridge** (7.6 mi/12.2 km rt, 4 hrs, strenuous) packs in big views in both directions, lush wildflower meadows, and resident mountain goats and marmots. After passing the Switchback Trail, the last mile steepens to climb more than 700 feet (213 m) to the ridge.

Grand Valley

From the end of Obstruction Point Road, a trail descends into **Grand Valley** with four destinations. All demand a strenuous 1,800-foot (549-m) climb back up on the return. The route starts with a stunning high traverse south on Lillian Ridge before dropping into the valley cradling three lovely lakes—**Moose Lake** (8.2 mi/13.2 km rt, 4-5 hrs, strenuous), **Grand Lake** (7.9 mi/12.7 km rt, 4 hrs, strenuous), and **Gladys Lake** (9.2 mi/14.8 km rt, 5 hrs, strenuous), the last above the tree line. Talus and wildflower meadows line the trail that culminates at **Grand Pass** (13 mi/20.9 km rt, 7 hrs, strenuous) for big views.

Royal Basin

The Upper Dungeness Trail enters the park to reach **Royal Lake** (14.4 mi/23.2 km rt, 8 hrs, strenuous), tucked below the craggy Needles and Mount Deception. The trail follows Royal Creek into the rugged Royal Basin, a glaciated bowl of forest, meadows, talus slopes, and waterfalls. The **Upper Dungeness Trailhead** is located outside the park, south of Sequim. You'll need an America the Beautiful Pass or a one-day Northwest Forest Pass ($5, www.discovernw.org) and an early start to park at the crowded trailhead parking lot.

LAKE CRESCENT

Marymere Falls

From Storm King Ranger Station, a gentle walk in the woods culminates at the 90-foot (27-m) **Marymere Falls** (1.8 mi/2.9 km rt, 1 hr, easy).

Spruce Railroad Trail

From East Shore Road, the paved **Spruce Railroad Trail** (2-8 mi/3.2-12.9 km rt, 1-4 hrs, easy) takes a lakeside route along the north shore of Lake Crescent on a repurposed railroad track that goes through a tunnel. Bikes are allowed, and it is wheelchair accessible with some short inclines. For the shortest destination on the trail, **Devil's Punchbowl** (1 mi/1.6 km, 30 min, from the trailhead) is a calm cove surrounded by tall bluffs. A bridge with a postcard-worthy view of Mount Storm King crosses the deep blue cove waters, a popular swimming hole.

SOL DUC VALLEY

Drive to the terminus of Sol Duc Road to hike to roaring **Sol Duc Falls** (1.6 mi/2.6 km rt, 1 hr, easy) that makes a two-level, 50-foot (15-m) drop. Find the best viewing at the bridge, where you'll get spritzed with a gentle mist. From Sol Duc Hot Springs Resort, the **Lover's Lane Trail** (5.8 mi/9.3 km rt, 3 hrs, easy) follows Sol Duc River to the falls.

HOH RAIN FOREST

From the visitors center, follow the **Mini Loop Trail** (0.1 mi/0.2 km),

WATERFALL VIEWS INTO OLYMPIC NATIONAL PARK

HOH RAIN FOREST

a wheelchair-accessible loop with interpretive signage. The evocatively named **Hall of Mosses Trail** (0.8 mi/1.3 km rt, 30 min) arcs past giant firs, big-leaf maples festooned with moss, and licorice ferns that carpet the forest floor. The **Spruce Nature Trail** (1.2 mi/1.9 km rt, 45 min) goes through the forest to the Hoh River.

LAKE OZETTE AND THE COAST

Shi Shi Beach

Head through the Makah Reservation to **Shi Shi Beach** (4-8 mi/6.4-12.9 km rt, 2-5 hrs, easy, purchase $10 pass in Neah Bay), pronounced "shy shy." A partial boardwalk path cuts through damp woods to a steep rope-assisted descent to the sand and driftwood beach. The 2.5-mile (4 km) beach, best at low tide for tide pools of starfish and sea urchins, terminates at **Point of Arches,** massive intricate sea stacks.

To reach the trailhead, take Cape Flattery Road west of Neah Bay for 2.5 miles (4 km) and turn south onto Hobuck Beach Road. After crossing the Sooes River the road becomes Sooes Beach Road to reach the trailhead.

Cape Alava

From the Lake Ozette **Ranger Station** (360/565-3130, daily June-Sept.) at the end of Hoko-Ozette Road, two routes diverge to go to the coastline. **Cape Alava** (6.2 mi/10 km rt, 3.5 hrs, easy) plods on a cedar boardwalk through forest and wet prairie to the westernmost point of the Lower 48, passing the site of a **Makah village.** The **Sand Point Trail** (5.6 mi/9 km rt, 3 hrs, easy) travels mostly over boardwalk to reach the beach at a southern point.

The **Ozette Loop** (9 mi/14.5 km rt, 5 hrs, easy) connects the Cape Alava Trail to the Sand Point Trail, adding 3 miles (4.8 km) of beach walking. Rocks and driftwood litter the beach, and you'll see the **Wedding Rocks,** with Indigenous petroglyphs depicting whales, fertility figures, and a European ship.

EAST SIDE

Upper Lena Lake

The trail to Lena Lake crowds with weekend hikers, but those who go farther inside the park to **Upper Lena Lake** (14 mi/22.5 km rt, 7-8 hrs, strenuous) will find plenty of breathing room. The path climbs through subalpine wildflowers and huckleberries, with views of the Brothers, a pair of rugged peaks. From US 101 north of Hoodsport, take the Hamma Hamma River Road (Forest Rd. 25) to the trailhead.

Staircase Rapids Loop

From the Staircase Ranger Station, at the end of the twisting dirt road, the **Staircase Rapids Trail** (4 mi/6.4 km rt, 2 hrs, easy) combines with **North Fork of the Skokomish River Trail** to make a loop on both sides of the river, connected by a bridge. The route passes Pacific rhododendrons, vibrant mossy old growth, a big fallen cedar tree, and waterfalls.

RECREATION

BACKPACKING

Beaches, long forested valleys, and subalpine passes with a riot of colorful wildflowers are backpacker rewards. For trips of 2-3 days, head to the **Ozette Loop** (9 mi/14.5 km rt), **Royal Basin** (14.4 mi/23.2 km rt), or **Grand Valley** (8.2-13 mi/13.2-20.9 km rt). For a goat-trail traverse across Bogachiel Peak with spectacular views of Mount Olympus and Blue Glacier, go for **Seven**

Lakes Basin-High Divide Loop (18.2 mi/29.2 km rt).

On the west side, the most popular backpacking trips last 3-5 days. The **Hoh River Trail** (34.8 mi/56 km rt) combines a gentle rain forest walk with a climb to Glacier Meadows, where wildflowers intersperse among glacial moraine below Mount Olympus. For long beach treks, aim for **Rialto Beach to Cape Alava** (40 mi/64.4 km rt) or **Third Beach to Hoh River** (30.6 mi/49.3 km rt), but check tide levels before heading out.

Wilderness camping permits are required. Make **reservations** (www.recreation.gov, $6 plus $8 pp/night) up to six months in advance; popular routes book up immediately. The **Wilderness Information Center** (3002 Mount Angeles Rd., 360/565-3100, daily Apr.-Oct.) has a limited number of bear canisters (first come, first served), which are required in some locations.

CLIMBING

The end of the Hoh River Trail launches experienced mountaineers to climb 7,980-foot (2,432-m) **Mount Olympus,** the tallest peak in the park. The climbing season (late June-early Sept.) is

BACKPACKING IS A POPULAR ACTIVITY IN THE PARK.

SPRUCE RAILROAD TRAIL

short, and the route demands technical route-finding, navigating glacial crevasses, and spidering up a rock spire; you'll need ice axes, harnesses, ropes, and crampons. Permits are not required for climbing, but are required for backcountry camping.

Mountain Madness (800/328-5925, www.mountainmadness.com) and **International Mountain Guides** (360/569-2609, www.mountainguides.com) lead climbing trips.

BIKING

The paved **Spruce Railroad Trail** (10 mi/16 km one-way) along Lake Crescent's north shore offers a car-free bike route through forest, two tunnels, and across bridges while intermittent views of the lake and mountains appear. Beginning at the **Lyre River Trailhead** (parking, vault toilet), the trail briefly climbs before easing to a gentle cruise. At the McFee Tunnel, foot trails from both ends lead to a bridge over **Devil's Punchbowl.** From the tunnel, the bike trail passes through another tunnel before working its way above and away from the lakeshore. The trail is part of the 135-mile (215-km) **Olympic Discovery Trail** (https://olympicdiscoverytrail.org) that extends from Port Townsend to La Push. Bike rental shops are in Port Angeles and at Log Cabin Resort at Lake Crescent.

KAYAKING AND RAFTING

Several lakes make for exceptional paddling. Lake Crescent, Lake Ozette, and Lake Quinault have boat launches for watercraft. **Lake Crescent Lodge** and **Log Cabin Resort** rent kayaks, rowboats, canoes, and paddleboards for Lake Crescent. **Adventures Through Kayaking** (2358 US 101, 360/417-3015, www.atkayaking.com) leads kayak or paddleboard tours on Lake Crescent and provide lessons and rentals. For Lake Quinault, **Lake Quinault Lodge** rents kayaks, paddleboards, canoes, and rowboats.

For guided river rafting, **Hoh River Rafters** (360/683-9867, www.hohriver-rafters.com) leads trips down the Hoh River. Owner Pat Neal also guides fishing trips in the area.

FISHING

Lake Crescent contains Beardslee rainbow trout, Crescenti cutthroat trout, and abundant kokanee runs May-October (no license needed). The **Sol Duc River** has steelhead and salmon (Washington Catch Cards required).

WINTER SPORTS

With 400 inches (1,016 cm) of annual snow, **Hurricane Ridge** becomes a winter playground December-March. You can downhill ski, cross-country ski, snowboard, tube, and snowshoe. Hurricane Ridge Road is open to uphill traffic 9am-4pm Friday-Sunday, weather permitting (carry tire chains). Call the **Road and Weather Hotline** (360/565-3131) for conditions.

For downhill skiing and snowboarding, **Hurricane Ridge Ski and Snowboard Area** (848/667-7669, www.hurricaneridge.com, 10am-4pm Sat.-Sun. Dec.-Mar., fee) operates two rope tows and a Poma lift and rents tubes for sliding. A gift shop rents downhill skis, cross-country skis, and snowshoes.

Ranger-led **snowshoe walks** (2pm Sat.-Sun. mid-Dec.-Mar., adults $7,

SNOWSHOEING ON HURRICANE RIDGE

children $3) last 1.5 hours and include snowshoes. Sign up 30 minutes before the start time at the Hurricane Ridge Visitor Center.

WHERE TO STAY

INSIDE THE PARK

For summer stays, make **reservations** (888/896-3818, www.olympicnational-parks.com) one year in advance at four lodges.

Lake Crescent

The historic **Lake Crescent Lodge** (416 Lake Crescent Rd., 360/928-3253, May-Jan., from $158) has cabins with fireplaces, motel rooms, and lodge rooms with shared baths. The lodge **restaurant** (7:30am-10:30am, 11am-2:30pm, and 5pm-9pm daily May-mid-Oct.) overlooks the lake and has a bar and gift shop.

At the north end of Lake Crescent, the **Log Cabin Resort** (3183 E. Beach Rd., 360/928-3325, late May-Sept., from $84) has cabins and a few large chalets. The modest on-site **restaurant** (8am-10am, 11am-1pm, and 5pm-8pm daily) serves breakfast, lunch, and dinner.

Sol Duc

Sol Duc Hot Springs Resort (12076 Sol Duc Hot Springs Rd., 360/327-3583, Apr.-Oct., from $230) consists of 32 no-frills cabins next to the hot springs complex; some rooms have kitchens. The resort's **Springs Restaurant** (7:30am-10am, 11am-2pm, and 5pm-9pm daily) and **Espresso Bar & Lounge** (7:30am-10pm daily) serve cafeteria-style breakfast, lunch, and dinner.

Lake Quinault

Built in 1926, **Lake Quinault Lodge** (345 South Shore Rd., 360/288-2900, year-round, from $265) is a classic national park hotel with rooms in the original lodge, a newer building with larger rooms, or a small annex. The lodge's **Roosevelt Dining Room** (7:30am-11am and 5pm-8pm daily) serves breakfast, lunch, and dinner.

Kalaloch

Kalaloch Lodge (157151 US 101, 866/662-9928, www.thekalalochlodge. com, year-round, from $210) sits on a bluff overlooking the ocean. Accommodations include Bluff Cabins, smaller Kalaloch Cabins, and guest rooms in the main lodge. The lodge's **Creekside**

NAME	LOCATION	PRICE	SEASON	AMENITIES
Heart O' the Hills	Hurricane Ridge	$20	year-round	tent and RV sites
Fairholme	Lake Crescent	$24	Apr.-Sept.	tent and RV sites
Lake Crescent Lodge	Lake Crescent	from $158	May-Jan.	cabins, motel and lodge rooms, dining
Log Cabin Resort	Lake Crescent	from $84	May-Sept.	cabins, chalets, RV sites, dining
Sol Duc	Sol Duc	$29-51	Apr.-Oct.	tent and RV sites
Sol Duc Hot Springs Resort	Sol Duc	from $230	Apr.-Oct.	cabins, RV sites, dining
Ozette	Lake Ozette	$24	year-round	tent and RV sites
Hoh	Hoh Rain Forest	$24	year-round	tent and RV sites
Lake Quinault Lodge	Lake Quinault	from $265	year-round	lodge rooms, dining
Kalaloch Campground	Kalaloch	$24	year-round	tent and RV sites
Kalaloch Lodge	Kalaloch	from $210	year-round	cabins, lodge rooms, dining
Mora	Rialto Beach	$24	year-round	tent and RV sites
Staircase	Staircase	$24	year-round	tent and RV sites

KALALOCH

Restaurant (8am-8pm daily winter, 7am-9pm daily summer) serves breakfast, lunch, and dinner, with reservations essential in summer.

Campgrounds

On Lake Crescent, **Log Cabin Resort** (3183 E. Beach Rd., 360/928-3325 or 888/896-3818, late May-Sept., 38 sites, $25-45) has campsites for tents and full hookups for RVs (35-ft/10.6-m limit, back-in sites). Most other campgrounds inside the park will fit only smaller RVs.

Four campgrounds accept **reservations** (877/444-6777, www.recreation. gov, $24-29 standard sites, $51 electrical hookups) for summer starting six months in advance; they are first come, first served the rest of the year. **Sol Duc Campground** (mid-Apr.-Oct., 82 sites plus 17 RV electric hookups) is at the Sol Duc Hot Springs complex. **Kalaloch Campground** (year-round, 170 sites) is on the ocean, and **Mora Campground** (year-round, 94 sites) is closest to Rialto Beach. In deep rain forest, **Hoh Campground** (year-round, 72 sites) is near the Hoh Rain Forest Visitor Center.

All remaining campgrounds are first come, first served. **Heart O' the Hills Campground** (year-round, 105 sites) is near Hurricane Ridge. **Fairholme Campground** (late Apr.-late Sept., 88 sites) is near a noisy highway and Lake Crescent. **Ozette Campground** (year-round, 15 sites) is on Lake Ozette at the end of a remote road. **Staircase** (year-round, 49 sites) is on the Skokomish River in the southeastern park corner.

Primitive campgrounds ($15) have no drinking water: **Deer Park** (Deer Park Rd., June-mid-Oct., 14 tent-only sites) in the park's northeast corner, **South Beach** (mid May-Sept., 55 sites) on the coast near Kalaloch, **Graves Creek** (year-round, 30 tent-only sites) and **North Fork** (North Shore Rd., year-round, 9 tent-only sites) near Lake Quinault in the park's southwest, and **Queets** (Upper Queets River Rd., year-round, 20 sites) in the westside Queets Valley.

OUTSIDE THE PARK

Port Angeles, Port Townsend, and **Sequim** serve as gateway towns for the north side of Olympic National Park. Tiny **Forks** and **Kalaloch** are bases for exploring the park's coastal side. **Hoodsport** is a small eastside base with minimal services. **Olympic National Forest,** which surrounds the park, is loaded with campgrounds.

GETTING THERE

AIR

The closest international airport is **Seattle-Tacoma International Airport** (SEA, 800/544-1965 or 206/787-5388, www.portseattle.org/sea-tac). Car rentals are at the airport.

BUS

Dungeness Bus Lines (360/417-0700, http://dungeness-line.com) operates the Dungeness Line between Sea-Tac airport and Port Angeles, with three stops in Seattle. The nearly five-hour ride travels twice eastbound and twice westbound per day.

CAR

From Seattle, drive south on I-5 through Tacoma, then turn north on WA 16 to Bremerton. From Bremerton, take WA 3 north to WA 19 where it meets US 101 north to Port Townsend and Port Angeles. Port Angeles and US 101 are 20 miles (32 km) north of the Hurricane Ridge Visitor Center in Olympic National Park. Plan 4-5 hours for the drive of 185 miles (300 km).

▼ HIKIER AT RIALTO BEACH

FERRY

Washington State Ferries (206/464-6400, www.wsdot.wa.gov) cross Puget Sound to the Olympic Peninsula: from Seattle to Bainbridge Island and Bremerton, from Edmonds to Kingston, and from Whidbey Island to Port Townsend. On the Olympic Peninsula, highways connect to US 101.

GETTING AROUND

No public transportation goes into the park, so you will need a car to get around. Driving along US 101 will give you plenty of views of trees with snippets of the beach but not the mountains and rain forests. Lots of driving is required between park regions, and you'll need to take paved spur roads to visit them. Check the park's **Road and Weather Hotline** (360/565-3131) for travel conditions.

From Port Angeles, **Hurricane Ridge** is 20 miles (32 km, 45 min) south of downtown, where Race Street becomes Mount Angeles Road and then Hurricane Ridge Road. West of Port Angeles, US 101 reaches the southern side of **Lake Crescent** in 22 miles (35 km, 30 min) and the **Sol Duc** entrance in 30 miles (48 km, 1 hr) via Sol Duc Road.

To reach **Lake Ozette,** turn off WA 112 just west of Sekiu onto Hoko-Ozette Road and drive 21 miles (34 km) south to the road's end.

To get to the **Hoh Rain Forest,** take US 101 to Upper Hoh Road and drive 18 miles (29 km) to the visitors center. It's about 90 miles (145 km, 2 hrs) from Port Angeles.

Along US 101 on the coast, **Kalaloch** is 91 miles (146 km, 2.5 hrs) south of Port Angeles. **Ruby Beach** is on the northernmost point of the Kalaloch coast, 8 miles (13 km) north of Kalaloch Lodge and 27 miles (43 km) south of Forks.

US 101 skirts the western edge of **Lake Quinault** 32 miles (52 km, 45 min) south of Kalaloch. The Quinault Rain Forest is accessed off the North Shore or South Shore Roads. It's a 120-mile drive (193-km, 3.3 hrs) from Port Angeles.

SIGHTS NEARBY

At the north end of WA 112, **Museum at the Makah Cultural and Research Center** (Makah Reservation, 1880 Bayview Ave., Neah Bay, 360/645-2711, http://makahmuseum.com, 10am-5pm daily, $6) features artifacts from the Lake Ozette archaeological site.

KLAHHANEE RIDGE TRAIL

MOUNT RAINIER NATIONAL PARK

Washington

WEBSITE:
www.nps.gov/mora

PHONE NUMBER:
360/569-2211

VISITATION RANK:
18

WHY GO:
Visit the most glaciated peak in the contiguous United States.

KEEPSAKE STAMPS ▼▼▼

▲ BENCH LAKE AND MOUNT RAINIER

MOUNT RAINIER NATIONAL PARK is named for the most impressive geographical landmark in the Pacific Northwest. At 14,411 feet (4,392 m), this volcano is the tallest peak in the Cascade Mountains, which stretch from Canada to California. Glaciers tumble from its icy cone, the most of any peak in the Lower 48. Towering "Takhoma," as it was called by the six Indigenous groups who lived on its flanks for thousands of years, dominates the horizon, making it an icon of Washington state's identity.

At the two highest car-accessible points—Paradise and Sunrise—the icy summit feels within your grasp, just one flower-filled meadow away. But it looms 8,000-9,000 feet (2,438-2,743 m) higher, where the air thins and even walking takes effort. Its lower elevations cradle nooks of old-growth forests, serene alpine lakes, and plunging waterfalls.

PLANNING YOUR TIME

More than 100 miles (161 km) south of Seattle, Mount Rainier beckons. Visitors come to explore the park's five developed areas and some venture into the wilderness. **Paradise** sits on the south slope of the mountain, while **Sunrise** perches on the northeast. Set at the edge of tree line, both offer elevated locations with big views, visitors centers, and trailheads. Inside the Nisqually Entrance on the southwest side of the park, **Longmire** has a hotel, restaurant, and museum. In the southeast corner, near the Stevens Canyon Entrance, **Ohanapecosh** has a visitors center and a campground. In the northwest corner, **Mowich Lake** gets fewer visitors, mostly hikers and campers, due to its long dirt road access.

The majority of visitors come during the mild **summer** season (June-Sept.) when temperatures hang in the 50s, 60s, and 70s (10-26°C). July and August see long midday lines at the Nisqually and White River Entrances, and parking lots fill at Sunrise, Paradise, and popular trailheads 10am-4pm. Plan to go early in the day. Fall and spring can be rainy and cool or have moderate warm temperatures. Snow remains at Paradise into July and keeps Sunrise closed until July 4. In winter, snow closes park roads, except for Nisqually Entrance Station to Paradise, which remains open year-round; the park service plows snow on the road so vehicles equipped for snow travel may drive up.

ENTRANCES AND FEES

There are three entrance stations: the **Nisqually Entrance** (open year-round) at the southwest corner, the **Stevens Canyon Entrance** (late May-mid-Sept.) at the southeast corner, and the **White River Entrance** (late June-mid-Oct.) in the northeast. For the remote **Mowich Lake** area, pay fees in a drop box just past the park entrance.

The entrance fee is $30 per vehicle ($25 motorcycle, $15 individual) and good for seven days. Purchase a pass in advance online (YourPassNow.com) to go through the entrance station faster.

VISITORS CENTERS

At Paradise, the **Henry M. Jackson Memorial Visitor Center** (360/569-6571, 10am-5pm daily May-mid-June and Oct., 10am-7pm daily mid-June-Sept., shorter hours and days Oct.-mid-June) is a modern take on traditional alpine design. Inside, watch an introductory park film, see exhibits, pick up a map for the Paradise trails, check weather and trail conditions for hiking, and have a bite at the snack bar. The center is the starting point for ranger-led daily nature walks in summer and weekend snowshoe treks in winter.

At Sunrise, the historic log cabin **Sunrise Visitor Center** (360/663-2425,

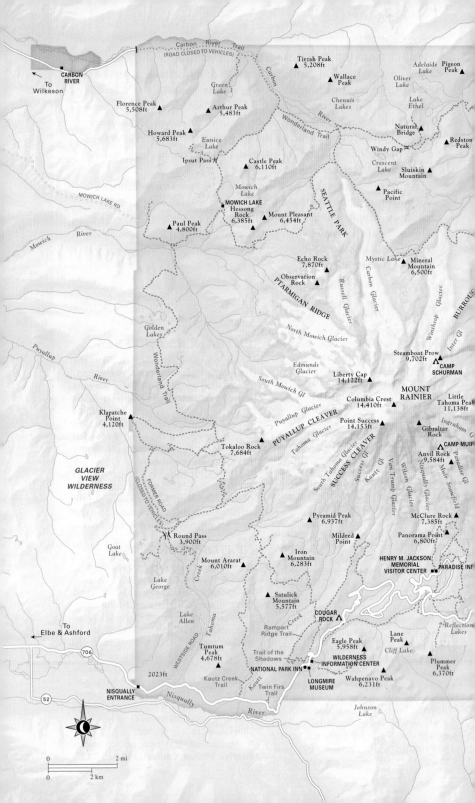

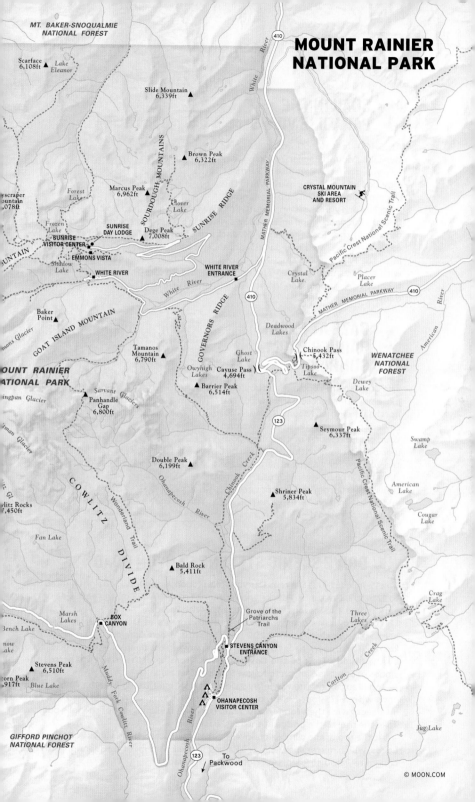

MOUNT RAINIER NATIONAL PARK

MT. BAKER-SNOQUALMIE
NATIONAL FOREST

Scarface
6,108ft ▲   Lake
Eleanor

Slide Mountain
6,339ft ▲

Brown Peak
6,322ft ▲

SOURDOUGH MOUNTAINS

Forest
Lake

Marcus Peak
6,962ft ▲

Clover
Lake

SUNRISE RIDGE

yscraper
ountain
,078ft

Frozen
Lake

SUNRISE
DAY LODGE

Dege Peak
7,008ft ▲

SUNRISE
VISITOR CENTER
EMMONS VISTA

Shadow
Lake

WHITE RIVER

White   River

WHITE RIVER
ENTRANCE

Crystal
Lake

CRYSTAL MOUNTAIN
SKI AREA
AND RESORT

Pacific Crest National Scenic Trail

MATHER MEMORIAL PARKWAY

Placer
Lake

MATHER MEMORIAL PARKWAY   410

410

Baker
Point ▲

GOAT ISLAND MOUNTAIN

mons Glacier

Deadwood
Lakes

American   River

WENATCHEE
NATIONAL
FOREST

OUNT RAINIER
ATIONAL PARK

Tamanos
Mountain
6,790ft ▲

Ghost
Lake

Chinook Pass
5,432ft

Dewey
Lake

ingpan Glacier

Sarvant Glaciers

Owyhigh
Lakes

Cayuse Pass
4,694ft

Tipsoo
Lake

Panhandle
Gap
6,800ft ▲

▲ Barrier Peak
6,514ft

Swamp
Lake

rman Glacier

123

Seymour Peak
6,337ft ▲

COWLITZ

Double Peak
6,199ft ▲

Ohanapecosh   River

Chinook   Creek

American
Lake

itz Rocks
,450ft

DIVIDE

Fan Lake

Shriner Peak
5,834ft ▲

Pacific Crest National Scenic Trail

Cougar
Lake

Wonderland Trail

Bald Rock
5,411ft ▲

Crag
Lake

Marsh
Lakes

BOX
CANYON

Grove of the
Patriarchs Trail

Three
Lakes

Bench Lake

Muddy Fork Cowlitz River

STEVENS CANYON
ENTRANCE

now
ake

Stevens Peak
6,510ft ▲

corn Peak
,917ft   Blue Lake

OHANAPECOSH
VISITOR CENTER

Carlton   Creek

Jug Lake

GIFFORD PINCHOT
NATIONAL FOREST

Ohanapecosh   River

123

To
Packwood

© MOON.COM

Top ❸

NISQUALLY GLACIER FROM PARADISE TRAILS

❶ SOAK IN THE PARADISE VIEWS

At 5,400 feet (1,650 m), with glacier-clad Mount Rainier standing before you, gorgeous **Paradise** is the most crowded place in the park, with the large parking lot filling up in summer. Late July and August is prime time for viewing the peak framed by fields of wildflowers, but year-round access allows visitors to revel in fall colors and snowy winter beauty too. Tour the **Henry M. Jackson Memorial Visitor Center** (360/569-6571, 10am-7pm daily mid-June-Sept., shorter hours and days Oct.-mid-June). Pop in to see **Paradise Inn** (mid-May-Sept.), built in 1916, an imposing wooden lodge with classic "parkitecture." The impressive lobby soars with high ceilings, stone fireplaces, and mountain views. Access Paradise from Longmire or the Stevens Canyon Road.

❷ GAZE AT MOUNT RAINIER FROM SUNRISE

The **Sunrise** area occupies a subalpine plateau with spectacular views of the northeast side of Mount Rainier—the towering summit feels just beyond your grasp. It's one of the most popular destinations within the park, but the window for visiting is narrow (late June or early July-early Sept.). Hiking trails depart from the visitors center, and a walk-in picnic area is the perfect place for alfresco dining with a view.

VIEW OF MOUNT RAINIER FROM SUNRISE

❸ DRIVE SCENIC STEVENS CANYON ROAD

The 19-mile (31-km) **Stevens Canyon Road** (open June-Oct., RV height limited due to 12.5-ft/3.8-m tunnel) packs with scenery. From WA 123 on the east side of the park, it links the Stevens Canyon Entrance with Paradise.

The road starts deep within old-growth forests of Douglas fir and western hemlock at an elevation of 2,200 feet (670 m). At **Box Canyon,** a trail (0.3 mi/0.5 km rt, 20 min, easy) leads to a footbridge spanning the deep, narrow gorge carved by the **Muddy Fork of the Cowlitz River.** From here, the road cuts across the slopes of Stevens Canyon to follow Stevens Creek uphill.

A pullout along the way offers side views of multitiered **Martha Falls,** which ends with a 125-foot (38-m) plunge. For a closer look, pull off the road where it intersects with the **Wonderland Trail,** 0.5 mile (0.8 km) west of the falls pullout. Take the trail to the bridge at the falls' base.

At the top of the climb, a pullover spot lets you absorb the views at **Reflection Lakes,** which mirror snow-capped Rainier in their waters. At the junction with the Longmire-Paradise Road, turn right to reach Paradise.

Best Hike

SKYLINE TRAIL

DISTANCE: 5.5 miles (8.8 km) round-trip
DURATION: 4.5 hours
ELEVATION CHANGE: 1,700 feet (518 m)
EFFORT: strenuous
TRAILHEAD: Jackson Visitor Center at Paradise

For impressive views of Rainier and thick wildflower meadows, the **Skyline Trail** climbs above the timberline for massive views of the mountain's rock clefts and tumbling glaciers. The popular trail begins by ascending stone steps etched with words from John Muir. It climbs steeply and directly to Panorama Point with up-close views of Nisqually Glacier. With some exposure and steep snowfields that linger on the upper part into July, this trail is not for acrophobes (check conditions in the visitors center before hiking). From Panorama Point, continue eastward down the Skyline Trail to loop down into Paradise Valley and climb to **Myrtle Falls** before descending back to the parking lot.

SKYLINE TRAIL LOOP

McClure Rock 7,385 ft

Nisqually Glacier

Panorama Point 6,800 ft

Golden Gate

Skyline Trail

Mount Rainier National Park

Edith Creek

STEVENS-VAN TRUMP HISTORICAL MONUMENT

Sluiskin Falls

Myrtle Falls

Paradise Park

Paradise Valley

PARADISE RD

Paradise Park

HENRY M. JACKSON MEMORIAL VISITOR CENTER

PARADISE INN

PARADISE RANGER STATION

PARADISE RD

0   .5 mi

0   .5 km

© MOON.COM

10am-6pm daily July-early Sept.) houses natural history displays and has telescopes for viewing Mount Rainier's glaciers and spying climbers. Rangers provide maps of Sunrise hiking trails and lead daily nature walks. Across the parking lot, **Sunrise Day Lodge** (July-Sept.)

ONE DAY IN MOUNT RAINIER

Drive the park road to **Paradise** or **Sunrise** and concentrate your time here. Stop at pullouts en route, tour the visitors centers, and hike to soak up the mountain's splendor.

has a gift shop and a cafeteria (expect long lines during meal times).

At the Stevens Canyon Entrance is the tiny **Ohanapecosh Visitor Center** (360/569-6581, hours vary June-Sept.) with trail maps and information. In summer, rangers lead nature walks several times a week.

At **Longmire Wilderness Information Center** (360/569-6650, 7:30am-5pm daily mid-May-mid-Oct.) you can get passes for and information about backcountry hiking and camping.

SCENIC DRIVES
LONGMIRE TO PARADISE

Open year-round as snow conditions permit, the 12-mile (19-km) drive from Longmire to Paradise ascends through evergreen forests where periodic openings provide down-valley and up-mountain vistas. Three miles (4.8 km) before Paradise, stop at the overlook for **Narada Falls,** where a steep trail drops to

PINNACLE PEAK TRAIL

see the water plunging down the sheer cliff. After passing the turnoff to the Stevens Canyon Road, you'll reach the parking lot at Paradise with the visitors center, hiking trails, picnic area, and Paradise Inn, a National Historic Landmark. In summer, take the one-way downhill Paradise Valley Road on your return to Longmire.

The Nisqually Entrance Station west of Longmire sees long lines in summer; plan to arrive before 9am. In winter (chains required, including for 4WD), the gates at Longmire open 9am-4pm, allowing access to Paradise. Check on conditions before driving as the road can have a delayed opening or be closed during storms.

SUNRISE PARK ROAD

A steep and curvy road to 6,400 feet (1,951 m), **Sunrise Park Road** (15 mi/23 km, early July-late Sept.) pops to the highest point in the park reachable by car—and getting there is part of the fun. From the **White River Entrance station** off WA 410, the road climbs on switchbacks through evergreen forests to emerge at Sunrise Point with a small parking lot and big views of Mount Rainier. Continue the final few miles along meadowed slopes with all-encompassing vistas. This subalpine plateau has spectacular views of Rainier's two largest glaciers (Emmons and Winthrop), plus the distinctive Little Tahoma on the east flank. The road terminates at the visitors center, day lodge, trailheads, and picnic area.

The White River Entrance may close when parking lots fill up, allowing one car in when one departs; plan to arrive before 9am to avoid a long wait in line, especially on weekends and holidays. Due to the steepness and sharp curves, RVs and trailers longer than 25 feet (7.6 m) are not recommended beyond White River Campground.

MOWICH LAKE

The remote **Mowich Lake** area tucks into the park's northwest corner and sees fewer visitors. Reach it by taking WA 165 south from Buckley to Carbonado and crossing the Carbon River Gorge Bridge to a junction. Veer right for 17 washboard gravel miles (27 km) on Mowich Lake Road to **Mowich Lake** (open mid-July-mid-Oct.), the largest and deepest body of water in the park. The lake has a picnic area, tent-only campground, and several trails.

SIGHTS

LONGMIRE

Longmire is home to the **Longmire Museum** (360/569-6575, 9am-4:30pm daily June, 9pm-5pm July-Sept., off-season hours vary). The small facility, located in the original park headquarters, contains displays on the park's natural history, along with exhibits of basketry, a small totem pole, and photos from the park's early days. It's 7 miles (11 km) from the Nisqually Entrance in the park's southwest corner.

OHANAPECOSH

The Ohanapecosh area consists of a visitors center, hiking trails, remnants of a hot springs resort, and a campground along the Ohanapecosh River. Old-growth forests provide a thick canopy overhead in this southeast corner of the park.

RECREATION

HIKING

The prime hiking season runs July-September, after most of the snow is gone. Wildflowers usually peak late July-August.

Longmire

Across the road from Longmire National Inn, the **Trail of the Shadows** (0.7 mi/1.1 km rt, 30 min, easy) takes a stroll around the meadow where Longmire's resort once stood. Cutting off from this trail, a longer loop continues up **Rampart Ridge Trail** (4.6 mi/7.4 km rt, 2.5 hrs, moderate) to a majestic view over the Nisqually River far below, then joins the Wonderland Trail. Go clockwise for better views of Mount Rainier.

With a 1,200-foot (366-m) ascent partly on log steps across a rocky face comes the reward of **Comet Falls** (3.8 mi/6.1 km rt, 2 hrs, strenuous), a 301-foot-tall (92-m) ribbon. Locate the trailhead halfway between Longmire and Paradise, west of Christine Falls.

Paradise

For flamboyant florals and subalpine forest, the **Nisqually Vista Trail** (1.2 mi/1.9 km rt, 45 min, moderate) overlooks the Nisqually River and Glacier. The **Alta Vista Trail** (1.5 mi/2.4 km rt, 1 hr, moderate) ascends steps at the north side of the Paradise parking lot to wander through scrubby alpine trees

LUPINE ON SOURDOUGH RIDGE

VIEW OF MOUNT RAINIER FROM SUMMERLAND

and lush meadows. This trail can be combined with others to loop back to Paradise, or roam farther for more floral beauty and overlooks of the Nisqually Glacier at **Glacier Vista** (add 0.9 mi/1.5 km rt). Snow can linger into July.

Between Paradise and Stevens Canyon, the **Pinnacle Peak Trail** (2.5 mi/4 km rt, 2 hrs, strenuous) starts at the Reflection Lakes parking lot to climb to a saddle between Pinnacle and Plummer Peaks. Retaining snow into July, the trail gains 1,050 feet (320 m) to the saddle for huge Rainier views. You can follow a rough trail to the top of Plummer Peak, but Pinnacle is for skilled climbers only. From a trailhead just east of Reflection Lakes, an easier trail filled with bear grass and flowers cruises to **Bench and Snow Lakes** (2.4 mi/3.9 km rt, 1.5 hrs, moderate).

Ohanapecosh

West of the Stevens Canyon Entrance station, the **Grove of the Patriarchs Trail** (1.1 mi/1.8 km rt, 1 hr, easy) crosses the crystalline Ohanapecosh River via a suspension bridge onto an island of virgin old-growth trees. These thousand-year-old Douglas firs, western hemlocks, and western red cedars tower over ferns. Flooding in late 2021 damaged the bridge; check on repair status before starting this hike.

From Ohanapecosh Campground, the **Silver Falls Trail** (2.7 mi/4.3 km rt, 1.5 hrs, easy) follows the river through old-growth forest to the 75-foot (23-m) Silver Falls.

A rigorous grind up a steep, shadeless ridge goes to **Shriner Peak Trail** (8 mi/12.9 km rt, 5 hrs, strenuous). Big 360-degree views from the peak make it worth the elevation gain (3,400 ft/1,036 m). Find the trailhead 3.5 miles (5.6 km) north of the Stevens Canyon Entrance on WA 123.

Sunrise

From the Sunrise Visitor Center parking lot, trails gain views of Mount Rainier's biggest glaciers. The **Sunrise Nature Trail** (1.5 mi/2.4 km rt, 1 hr, easy) follows a self-guided loop. The **Shadow Lake Loop** (3 mi/4.8 km rt, 1.5 hrs, moderate) drops to a rim overlooking the White River valley, follows the ridge to Shadow Lake, and returns via Frozen Lake and Sourdough Ridge. The trail to 7,317-foot (2,230-m) **Mount Fremont Lookout** (5.6 mi/9 km rt, 3 hrs, strenuous) trots up **Sourdough Ridge** to Frozen Lake before branching off north to mountain goat terrain.

The **Burroughs Mountain Trail** ventures the closest of all the Sunrise trails to the mountain and has a moderately strenuous climb (1,000 ft/305 m).

After multiple trail junctions near Frozen Lake, the route ascends a north-facing slope that holds steep snow late into summer. At the top, a panoramic view of Mount Rainier splays out from the windswept and sun-exposed plateau of the **First Burroughs** (4.7 mi/7.5 km, 2.5 hrs). You can extend to **Second Burroughs** (7.4 mi/11.9 km rt, 3.5 hrs) or **Third Burroughs** (10.4 mi/16.7 km, 5.5 hrs). To complete the loop via Shadow Lake, follow the Sunrise Rim Trail from First Burroughs, descending the south-facing slope past **Glacier Overlook.**

From the White River Campground, the **Glacier Basin Trail** (6.5 mi/10.5 km rt, 6 hrs, strenuous) pops out of the forest into an idyllic basin of meadows. Views take in Steamboat Prow and Mount Ruth with Rainier behind. A side spur (1 mi/1.6 km rt) crosses remnants left by the Emmons Glacier, the largest of the mountain's glaciers.

The trail along Fryingpan Creek switchbacks up to **Summerland** (8.5 mi/13.7 km rt, 4.5-5 hrs, strenuous) to reach prolific wildflower meadows and streams below Little Tahoma and Rainier. The trailhead is 3 miles (4.8 km) west of the White River Entrance; arrive by 8am for a spot in the small parking lot.

Mowich Lake

To see the less developed side of Rainier, drive the 17-mile (27-km) rough-graveled Mowich Lake Road (located near Carbonado on WA 165 south of Buckley) to Mowich Lake. Climbing to **Spray Park** (6 mi/9.7 km rt, 4 hrs, moderate) takes in Spray Falls on a short spur trail and vast wildflower meadows with a backdrop of the ice-capped Rainier. The less demanding trail to **Tolmie Peak Lookout** (6.5 mi/10.5 km rt, 4 hrs, moderate) passes Eunice Lake before winding up switchbacks to a big view of Rainier.

BACKPACKING

A 93-mile (150-km) loop circling Mount Rainier, the **Wonderland Trail** traverses passes, deep forests, rivers, and alpine meadows—all with changing views of the glaciated mountain. The strenuous trail has copious ups and downs (22,000 ft/6,705 m of elevation gain). Backpackers need 9-14 days for the entire loop. Starting at multiple trailheads, hikers choose from 18 designated trailside camps and three front-country campgrounds for overnighting. Challenges include crossing rivers where bridges have washed out and traversing Panhandle Gap, which holds snow all year (most of the route is snow-free late July-Sept.)

Wilderness permits are required. Due to high demand, a **lottery** in early March awards the opportunity to submit an early **reservation** ($26) that same month. In late April, all remaining permits are offered online. **Walk-up permits,** subject to availability, are offered in person 24 hours in advance at Wilderness Information Centers at Longmire, White River, Paradise, or Carbon River Ranger Station.

WONDERLAND TRAIL

SKIERS AT MOUNT RAINIER

CLIMBING

For climbers, Mount Rainier is a premier summit and training peak, where raging winds, whiteouts, avalanches, hidden crevasses, rockfall, and altitude increase the hazard. About 10,000 people attempt the summit every year; about 60 percent of guided clients and 45 percent of independent climbers succeed. Independent trips require fluency in rock climbing, navigation, glacier travel, and crevasse rescue. Technical gear (ropes, harnesses, crampons, and ice axes) and the skill to use it is vital. Most climbs launch from Paradise to overnight at Camp Muir before clambering via Disappointment Cleaver and Ingraham Glacier to the highest point at the Columbia Crest. A second common route goes from White River Campground through Glacier Basin onto the Inter and Emmons Glaciers to overnight at Camp Schurman before ascending the Emmons and Winthrop Glaciers.

Climbing the peak usually requires two days. Some parties opt for an extra day to acclimate. Fees include a **climbing cost recovery fee** ($36-52) and a reservation for a **wilderness permit for overnighting** ($26). Once in the park, you must also obtain a **climbing permit** (free) from the Paradise Climbing Information Center or White River Wilderness Information Center within 24 hours of departure.

The main climbing season is May-September, but in 2021, excessive heat exposed significant hazards on the glacier routes, forcing the climbing season, including guided climbs, to end a month early. This is expected to happen more frequently, so consider booking your trip earlier in the season to avoid cancellation.

For guided climbs, contact **Alpine Ascents International** (206/378-1927, www.alpineascents.com), **International Mountain Guides** (360/569-2609, www.mountainguides.com), or **RMI Expeditions** (888/892-5462, www.rmiguides.com).

WINTER SPORTS

In winter, most visitors head to **Paradise** (Dec.-Mar., chains required in vehicle) to play in a supervised **snow-play** area. Bring your own soft sliding toys, such as inner tubes. **Cross-country skiers** and **snowshoers** tour ungroomed roads or trails to Alta Vista or Reflection Lakes.

Rent skis, avalanche beacons, snowshoes, and other winter gear from the **Longmire General Store** (360/569-2275, 9am-8pm daily mid-June-Aug., 10am-5pm Mon.-Fri., 9:30am-6pm Sat.-Sun. Sept.-mid-June). You can also arrange ski lessons and tours.

From Jackson Visitor Center, rangers lead **snowshoe walks** (free) on winter weekends and holidays. Snowshoes are free to use during these walks.

WHERE TO STAY

INSIDE THE PARK

With limited lodging, **reservations** (855/755-2275, www.mtrainierguest-services.com) are mandatory; book one year ahead for summer stays.

In Longmire, the **National Park Inn** (360/569-2411, year-round, from $179, deposit required) has 25 guest rooms; some share baths. The **dining room** (7am-10:30am, 11:30am-3:30pm, and 4pm-7:30pm Sun.-Thurs., 7am-10:30am, 11:30am-3:30pm, and 4pm-8pm Fri.-Sat.) serves three meals daily.

Erected in 1916 at Paradise and renovated in 2019, **Paradise Inn** (360/569-2413, mid-May-Sept., from $200, deposit required), a National Historic Landmark, is an imposing timber lodge with an impressive lobby, high ceilings, hand-painted lampshades, stone fireplaces, and mountain views. Some small guest rooms share bath facilities; others have private baths. The **dining room** (7am-9:30am, noon-2:30pm, and 5:30pm-8pm daily) serves breakfast, lunch, and dinner.

There are small eateries at **Paradise Camp Deli** (Jackson Visitor Center, 10am-6:45pm daily mid-June-mid-Sept., 11am-4pm Sat.-Sun. Oct.-May) and **Sunrise Day Lodge Snack Bar** (10am-7pm daily late June-early Sept., 11am-3pm Sat.-Sun. Sept.). **Longmire General Store** (360/569-2275, 9am-8pm daily mid-June-Aug., 10am-5pm Mon.-Fri., 9:30am-6pm Sat.-Sun. Sept.-mid-June) sells snacks.

Two campgrounds accept **reservations** (877/444-6777, www.recreation.gov) up to six months in advance. **Cougar Rock** (late-May-late-Sept., $20), between Longmire and Paradise, has 173 tent and RV sites. **Ohanapecosh** (late-May-late Sept., $20), south of the Stevens Canyon Entrance, has 188 tent and RV sites. Amenities include drinking water, flush toilets, and dump stations, but no hookups.

Two campgrounds are first come, first served. **White River** (late June-late Sept., $20), along the road to Sunrise, has 112 tent and RV sites. The primitive **Mowich Lake Campground** (early July-early Oct., free) has 13 walk-in tent sites.

OUTSIDE THE PARK

The surrounding towns of **Ashford, Greenwater,** and **Enumclaw** have limited amenities. More options lie farther north in **Seattle** and **Tacoma.**

GETTING THERE

AIR

Seattle-Tacoma International Airport (SEA, 800/544-1965 or 206/787-5388, www.portseattle.org/sea-tac), served by about two dozen airlines, is closest to the park. **Portland International Airport** (PDX, 7000 NE Airport Way, 877/739-4636, www.flypdx.com) is farther from the park, just across the Oregon border. Both airports have car rentals.

CAR

From Seattle (90 mi/145 km, 2 hrs) to the Nisqually Entrance, drive south on I-5 to exit 127. Go east on WA 512. Turn south on WA 7 to Elbe and turn east on WA 706 to Ashford and the **Nisqually Entrance** (open year-round), the busiest entrance of the park. To reach the **White River Entrance** (summer only), the closest entrance to Seattle, drive to Enumclaw and WA 410. **Stevens Canyon** (usually open May-Nov.) is farthest from the Seattle area.

From Portland (139 mi/224 km, 2.5 hrs), drive north on I-5 to exit 68. Go east on US 12 to Morton, then north on WA 7 to Elbe. Go east on WA 706 to Ashford and the **Nisqually Entrance.**

GETTING AROUND

The park has no public transportation and **no gasoline.** You'll need a gassed-up car to get around.

In winter, most of the park roads close due to snow (Oct. or Nov.-May or June). The road from Nisqually Entrance through Longmire to Paradise remains open year-round, conditions permitting. In winter, vehicles are required to carry tire chains, and the road from Longmire to Paradise closes nightly and can remain closed during the day due to storms or poor road conditions.

NORTH CASCADES NATIONAL PARK

Washington

WEBSITE:
www.nps.gov/noca

PHONE NUMBER:
360/854-7200

VISITATION RANK:
60

WHY GO:
Rugged glaciated scenery.

KEEPSAKE STAMPS ▼▼▼

▲ HIDDEN LAKE AND SAHALE PEAK

More than 300 glaciers still cling to the mountains within **NORTH CASCADES NATIONAL PARK,** by far the greatest concentration in the Lower 48. But glacial retreat and more frequent fires are rapidly altering the landscape.

Today, most visitors reach the park by car, driving the North Cascades Highway. But beyond the road is a vast wilderness of ice-chewed peaks, turquoise lakes, and long finger waterways such as Ross Lake and Lake Chelan. Access to these areas is via foot, horse, or boat, just as it was for the Indigenous Lake Chelan and Upper Skagit people who used Cascade Pass as their trade route.

PLANNING YOUR TIME

North Cascades National Park lies north of Seattle and east of Bellingham. Most visitors spend their time at three destinations: the **North Cascades Highway,** which bisects the park; **Ross Lake;** and upper **Lake Chelan.**

Late June-September is the prime time to visit, when North Cascades Highway is open and temperatures are in the 60s-90s (16-32°C). Fall colors arrive in October-early November, sometimes accompanied by early snow. Late November-April, snow pounds the park, closing 44 miles (71 km) of North Cascades Highway.

ENTRANCES AND FEES

Most visitors access the park via WA 20 east from **Marblemount** or west from Winthrop. The park has no official entrance stations and no entrance fee.

VISITORS CENTERS

North Cascades Visitor Center (WA 20, milepost 120, 206/386-4495, 9am-4:30pm daily mid-May-Sept., 9am-4:30pm Sat.-Sun. mid-Apr.-mid-May and Oct.), near the town of Newhalem, contains exhibits, a bookstore, a theater, and wheelchair-accessible trails.

SIGHTS
ROSS LAKE

The 540-foot-high (165-m) **Ross Lake Dam** holds back 23-mile-long (37-km) **Ross Lake.** You can see the lake from **Ross Lake Overlook** (milepost 134) on the North Cascades Highway. The only road to **Ross Lake National Recreation Area** is to the north via Hope, British Columbia, on a 40-mile (64-km) route to **Hozomeen Campground** and **boat launch.**

Near the lake's south end, **Ross Lake Resort** (206/486-3751, www.rosslakeresort.com, mid-June-Oct.) rents canoes, kayaks, motorboats, and fishing gear to day-trippers. It also has lodging and a water taxi service to trailheads and lakeshore campsites. To get to the resort takes about one hour in three stages: Diablo Lake Ferry, a resort land shuttle ($10), and a short boat ride up-lake ($3).

MOUNT SHUKSAN

Mount Shuksan (9,131 ft/2,783 m) is hands-down the most photographed peak in the park due to its rugged rocky summits flanked by glaciers. From Bellingham, drive east 60 miles (97 km) up the Mount Baker Highway (WA 542) to two locales just outside the park. Near Mount Baker Ski Area, take classic reflection photos of the peak from Picture Lake, rimmed by a paved accessible trail (0.5 mi/0.8 km rt, 20 min, easy) and drive to Artist Point (late summer-fall), where the road terminates, to get even closer. Hikers can revel in more intimate views in the meadows and boulder-strewn fields en route to **Lake Ann** (8.2 mi/13 km rt, 4 hours, moderate). A national parks or Northwest Forest Pass is required for parking.

NORTH CASCADES NATIONAL PARK

BRITISH COLUMBIA

WASHINGTON

MANNING PARK HEADQUARTERS, LODGE, AND VISITOR CENTER

MANNING PROVINCIAL PARK

To Hope, B.C.

SILVER-SKAGIT ROAD

SKAGIT VALLEY PROVINCIAL PARK

CHILLIWACK LAKE PROVINCIAL PARK

CANADA
UNITED STATES

Pacific Crest National Scenic Trail

To Mazama

Mount Winthrop 7,850ft ▲

Castle Pass ▲

Hopkins Pass ▲

Woody Pass ▲

Holman Pass ▲

Mount Ballard 8,301ft ▲

Deception Pass ▲

Devils Dome Loop

Devils Pass ▲

Joker Mountain 7,603ft ▲

Skagit Peak 6,800ft ▲

Spratt Mountain 7,258ft ▲

Dry Creek Pass ▲

Jack Mountain 9,066ft ▲

Devils Dome Loop

Beebe Mountain 7,416ft ▲

Devils Creek

Ruby Creek

Hozomeen Mountain 8,066ft ▲

HOZOMEEN ▲

ROSS LAKE

Desolation Peak 6,102ft ▲

Ross Lake

ROSS LAKE OVERLOOKS

Panth...

ROSS DAM ▲

20

Diablo Lake DIABLO LAKE OVERLOOK

ROSS LAKE NATIONAL RECREATION AREA

Mount Prophet 7,640ft ▲

Perry Creek

Little Beaver Trail

Mount Spickard 8,979ft ▲

Silver Lake

Beaver Pass 3,620ft ▲

Luna Peak 8,311ft ▲

Mount Fury 8,291ft ▲

Sourdough Mountain 6,120ft ▲

Diablo DIABLO DAM

Thunder Creek

Mount Redoubt 8,969ft ▲

Beaver Creek

Little Beaver Creek

Challenger Glacier

Elephant Butte 7,380ft ▲

Azure Lake

Gorge Lake

GORGE DAM

Pyramid Peak 7,182ft ▲

Colonial Glacier

Neve Glacier

Snowfield Peak 8,347ft ▲

Copper Mountain 7,142ft ▲

Whatcom Peak 7,574ft ▲

Mount Challenger 8,207ft ▲

Challenger River

Pinnacle Peak 6,819ft ▲

GORGE CREEK FALLS

Newhalem

NORTH CASCADES NATIONAL PARK VISITOR CENTER

Chilliwack Trail

Chilliwack River

Hannegan Trail

Baker River

Mount Terror 8,151ft ▲

NORTH CASCADES NATIONAL PARK

Mount Despair 7,292ft ▲

Mount Triumph 7,271ft ▲

Damnation Peak 5,635ft ▲

Thornton Lakes

Thornton Lakes Trail

Hannegan Pass ▲

Mount Shuksan 9,131ft ▲

Price Lake

Crystal Gl

Mount Blum 7,680ft ▲

Berdeen Lake

Green Lake

Bacon Peak 7,061ft ▲

Diobsud Buttes 5,893ft ▲

Watson Lakes

Baker Lake

Mount Hermann 6,286ft ▲

542

MOUNT SHUKSAN

LAKE CHELAN

Lake Chelan National Recreation Area adjoins the park's south end, which includes the upper 4 miles (6.4 km) of the lake and lower 10 miles (16 km) of Stehekin Valley. Only hikers and boaters can reach the isolated hamlet of **Stehekin** (steh-HEE-kin), 50 miles (81 km) up Lake Chelan. Most Stehekin day visitors arrive on the **Lady of the Lake** or **Lady Express** (509/682-4584, http://ladyofthelake.com, 8:30am-2:45pm or 6pm daily May-mid-Oct., 3-5 days weekly mid-Oct.-Apr., adults $50-98, kids half price) for lunch and to explore the tiny village.

RECREATION

HIKING

From Diablo at the North Cascades Environmental Learning Center, the **Diablo Lake Trail** (7.6 mi/12.2 km rt, 4 hrs, moderate) leads to Ross Dam; you can chop the mileage in half by returning via the Diablo Lake Ferry. Catch the **Sourdough Mountain Trail** (10.4 mi/16.7 km rt, 6 hrs, strenuous) from behind the swimming pool in Diablo to climb 4,870 feet (1,484 m) on a relentless switchback-loaded ascent to the historic Sourdough Lookout. Sumptuous views take in lakes and peaks.

Off the Cascade River Road 10 miles (16 km) east of Marblemount, the **Hidden Lake Trail** (9 mi/14.4 km rt, 5 hrs, moderately strenuous) climbs 2,900 feet (884 m) through a creek and avalanche basin filled with cow parsnip, false hellebore, and fireweed. It ends at a lookout over deep blue Hidden Lake, **Sahale Peak,** and other gems of the North Cascades.

From the North Cascades Highway at milepost 151 (national parks

BACKPACKING IN THE NORTH CASCADES

Top 3

1 CRUISE ON TURQUOISE DIABLO LAKE

DIABLO LAKE

Turquoise **Diablo Lake** glistens behind Diablo Dam on the Skagit River. From the **North Cascades Environmental Learning Center** (1940 Diablo Dam Rd., 360/854-2599, www.ncascades.org) on the lake's north shore, **lake tours** (360/854-2589, www.seattle.gov, July-mid-Sept., adults $42-45, kids half price, reservations required) on a glass-ceilinged boat frequently sell out. The **Diablo Lake Lunch Tour** (10:15am check-in Thurs.-Mon., 4 hrs) and **Diablo Lake Afternoon Cruise** (1pm check-in Fri.-Sun., 2.5 hrs) take in waterfalls, peaks, and two dams.

2 DRIVE SCENIC NORTH CASCADES HIGHWAY

The **North Cascades Highway** (WA 20, early May-late Nov.) slices across the park. Most visitors drive the 21 miles (34 km) from the west entrance to Washington Pass Overlook before turning around. In winter (late Nov.-Apr.), snow and avalanches close the road from Ross Dam to east of Washington Pass (mileposts 134-178).

From Marblemount, go east past **North Cascades Visitor Center** to **Newhalem.** Next to **Skagit General Store** (milepost 120) is **Old Number Six,** a 1928 Baldwin steam locomotive that hauled passengers and supplies to the Skagit River dams in pre-highway days. The **Trail of the Cedars Nature Walk** (0.3 mi/0.5 km rt, 30 min, easy) tours 1,000-year-old trees.

East of Newhalem, the highway climbs along the three dams and reservoirs of Gorge, Diablo, and Ross. Stop at three overlooks: See **Gorge Creek Falls** plunging into the gorge, peer down on the turquoise waters of **Diablo Lake,** and gaze at **Ross Lake,** the centerpiece of **Ross Lake National Recreation Area.**

After the road exits the national park, it climbs through Okanogan National Forest to crest **Rainy Pass** (4,860 ft/1,481 m). A trailhead leads to a paved wheelchair-accessible trail to **Rainy Lake** (2 mi/3.2 km rt, 1 hr, easy, parking $5). Then the road crests the higher **Washington Pass** (5,483 ft/1,671 m), where a short paved trail goes to viewpoints of **Liberty Bell**—the symbol of the North Cascades Highway—and **Early Winter Spires.** From the passes, the highway spins down into the Methow Valley to Winthrop, 30 miles (48 km) eastward.

3 OVERNIGHT AT STEHEKIN

No road nor cell phone service reaches **Stehekin** (steh-HEE-kin), located 50 miles (81 km) up Lake Chelan. This tiny community revels in backcountry assets: breathing room, hiking, kayaking, horseback riding, and biking. Wheelchair-accessible shuttle buses cart visitors along about 15 miles (24 km) of road, which connect the boat dock with lodgings and trailheads. The most popular destination is the 312-foot-high (95-m) Rainbow Falls, reached via an accessible trail (0.3 mi/0.5 km rt, 15 min, easy).

Most Stehekin visitors arrive on the ***Lady of the Lake*** or ***Lady Express*** (509/682-4584, http://ladyofthelake.com, 8:30am-2:45pm or 6pm daily May-mid-Oct., 3-5 days weekly mid-Oct.-Apr., adults $50-98, kids half price). A hearty few come by foot over Cascade Pass, just like Indigenous traders did. Overnighting at Stehekin (three rustic lodges or camping) allows you to soak up the solitude—and the night sky ablaze with stars.

CASCADE PASS

pass or Northwest Forest Pass required for parking, $5), start in Okanagan-Wenatchee National Forest to climb 2,800 feet (853 m) to **Easy Pass** (7 mi/11.2 km rt, 4 hrs, strenuous) in the national park. Expansive fragile wildflower meadows spread out,

DIABLO LAKE TRAIL

backdropped by glaciated peaks, and in fall the larch turn golden. Look for mountain goats. Snow remains on this trail into July.

BACKPACKING

A strenuous two-day trip (11.8 mi/18.9 km rt) climbs to **Cascade Pass** and up **Sahale Arm** to the base of **Sahale Glacier.** A washout closed the road in 2021 at milepost 20, which means fording a stream (tricky in high water) and walking 3 miles (4.8 km) each way to the trailhead.

For a four- to five-day loop (35 mi/56 km rt), tackle a portion of the Pacific Northwest Trail to cross **Hannegan Pass,** traverse **Copper Ridge,** drop to the **Chilliwack River,** and return over the pass; camp at Boundary, Copper Lake, Indian Creek, and Copper Creek. Check on the status, as wildfires closed a portion of this area in 2021.

Permits ($20) are required year-round. Reservations (www.recreation.gov, $6) for peak season trips (late May-Sept.) are via early access lottery (early Mar.) or general application (from late Apr.) Limited walk-up permits are at North Cascades Wilderness Information Center (7280 Ranger Station Rd., Marblemount, 360/854-7245, 7am-6pm daily July-Aug., 8am-5pm daily May-June and Sept.).

Best Hike

CASCADE PASS

DISTANCE: 7.4 miles (11.9 km) round-trip

DURATION: 5 hours

ELEVATION CHANGE: 1,700 feet (518 m)

EFFORT: strenuous

TRAILHEAD: From Marblemount, follow the rugged gravel Cascade River Road (check conditions at the Wilderness Information Center before driving; no RVs) for one hour (23 mi/37 km) to Cascade Pass Trailhead.

More than 30 switchbacks help you gain the elevation to ascend from old-growth forest to **subalpine meadows** at **Cascade Pass.** After the switchbacks, the trail crosses talus slopes, home to marmots and pikas; this steep area can still retain snow into July. Upon reaching the pass, a 360-degree view spreads out with summer wildflower meadows full of glacier lilies or pink mountain heather in the foreground and backdropped by waterfalls, peaks, and glaciers. A washout closed the road in 2021 at milepost 20; until it's repaired, you'll need to ford a stream (difficult crossing in high water) and walk 3 miles (4.8 km) each way to the trailhead.

WHERE TO STAY

INSIDE THE PARK

Spend the night at rustic resorts for a serious dose of peace and quiet. Make reservations a year in advance for these prized getaways that are only accessible by boat or on foot.

Ross Lake Resort (206/386-4437, www.rosslakeresort.com, mid-June-Oct., from $230) has cabins and bunkhouses that float on the water. Cabins

▼ LAKE CHELAN

NORTH CASCADES NATIONAL PARK

have full kitchens with shared barbecue grills. The resort rents motorboats, kayaks, and canoes and has a water taxi service to trailheads and campsites along the lakeshore.

At the head of Lake Chelan, Stehekin has three lodging options. The **North Cascades Lodge at Stehekin** (855/685-4167, https://lodgeatstehekin.com, from $214) has lodge rooms (May-Oct.) and units with kitchens (year-round). Amenities include a convenience store, kayak rentals, and a **restaurant** (mid-May-mid-Oct.) that serves three meals daily. Nine miles (15 km) up the valley, **Stehekin Valley Ranch** (509/682-4677, http://stehekinvalleyranch.com, mid-June-early Oct., adults from $130) operates its cabins, wagons, and tent cabins won solar power with all meals and shuttle transportation included. Two miles (3.2 km) from the boat dock, **Stehekin Pastry Company** (509/682-7742, https://stehekinpastry.com, early May-late Oct.) serves breakfast, lunch, pastries, and pies plus rents two log cabins (from $260, 2-night minimum).

Along North Cascades Highway, the only food is at **Skagit General Store** (milepost 120, Newhalem, 206/386-4489, 7:30am-5pm Mon.-Fri., 10am-5pm Sat.-Sun.).

Several campgrounds line North Cascades Highway. Most have potable water and pit or flush toilets, but no showers or hookups. Make **reservations** (877/444-6777, www.recreation.gov) up to six months in advance. The largest campgrounds open mid-May-mid-September: **Newhalem Creek** (milepost 120, 107 sites, $24) and **Colonial Creek** (milepost 130, 137 sites, $24). Open year-round, the smaller **Goodell Creek** (milepost 119, 19 sites, tents only, $20) and tiny primitive **Gorge Lake** (milepost 126, 8 sites, $20) are reservable for stays late May to mid-September; outside this period, the campgrounds are first come, first served.

Accessible only from British Columbia, Canada, **Hozomeen Campground** (Silver/Skagit Rd., 75 sites, first come, first served, late May-Oct., free) sits at the north end of Ross Lake. The 40-mile (64-km) rough graveled Silver/Skagit Road goes south from Hope, British Columbia, to this remote campground in the United States.

The park has **boat-in backcountry campsites** on Diablo Lake (launch at Colonial Creek), Ross Lake (launch at Hozomeen Campground), and Lake Chelan near Stehekin (launch at Chelan or 25-Mile Creek State Park). Pick up backcountry camping permits (free)

24 hours before departure from the **North Cascades Wilderness Information Center** (7280 Ranger Station Rd., Marblemount, 360/854-7245, 7am-6pm daily July-Aug., 8am-5pm daily May-June and Sept.) or the nearest ranger station. Apply in spring for a **reservation** ($20) for summer and fall.

OUTSIDE THE PARK

Accommodations, food, and services are in **Bellingham, Burlington, Mount Vernon, Sedro-Woolley, Concrete,** and **Marblemount.** To the east, look for services in **Winthrop, Twisp,** and **Chelan.** Campgrounds cluster in Mount Baker-Snoqualmie Nationa! Forest and Okanagan-Wenatchee National Forest, which surround the national park.

GETTING THERE AND AROUND

AIR

The closest international airport is **Seattle-Tacoma International Airport** (SEA, 800/544-1965 or 206/787-5388, www.portseattle.org/sea-tac). The airport has car rentals.

CAR

A car is essential for getting around and across the North Cascades. It's a 126-mile (203 km, 2.5 hrs) drive from Seattle to the North Cascades Visitor Center in Newhalem. From Seattle, drive 65 miles (105 km) north on I-5 to Burlington. Exit onto WA 20 and continue 60 miles (97 km) east to the park entrance.

BOATS

Hikers, backpackers, and campers make use of boats as shuttles on lakes. On Diablo Lake, the **Diablo Lake Ferry** (11:30am and 2:30pm daily, $45) carts hikers and day-trippers up-lake. On Lake Chelan, the **Lady of the Lake** (509/682-4584, http://ladyofthelake.com, 8:30am-2:45pm or 6pm daily May-mid-Oct., 3-5 days weekly mid-Oct.-Apr., adults $50-98, kids half price) goes from Chelan and 25-Mile to Stehekin. On Ross Lake, **Ross Lake Resort** (206/386-4437, www.rosslakeresort.com, mid-June-Oct.) runs a water taxi service to trailheads and lakeshore campsites. Take the Diablo Lake Ferry to connect with the resort's land shuttle ($10), and then shuttles up Ross Lake.

NORTH CASCADES HIGHWAY

SOUTHWEST

Across the Southwest, cliffs and canyons dominate the mysterious landscape. Here, the national parks range from red-rock spires to river-cut canyons, water pockets, and arches. You can even slide down sand dunes and explore underground caves. This land of variety is littered with unique sights: petrified trees in badlands, giant saguaros in desert, and ancient bristlecone pines in mountains.

Three prominent canyons top the parks. Zion tucks a narrow slot into soaring colorful walls. In Bryce Canyon, a geologic fairyland of rock spires rises beneath high cliffs. At the Grand Canyon, layers of geologic history transport visitors back in time millions of years. Through all of them, rich colors vie for your attention, lit up by sunrises and sunsets.

◀ RAFTS ON THE COLORADO RIVER AT THE BOTTOM OF GRAND CANYON

NEVADA

WYOMING

Salt Lake City

Cheyenne

Great Basin NP

UTAH

COLORADO

Denver

Capitol Reef NP

Arches NP

Canyonlands NP

Zion NP

Bryce Canyon NP

Great Sand Dunes NP & PRES

Grand Canyon NP

Mesa Verde NP

Santa Fe

Petrified Forest NP

Albuquerque

ARIZONA

NEW MEXICO

Phoenix

White Sands NP

Saguaro NP

Carlsbad Caverns N

El Paso

Guadalupe Mountains NP

SOUTHWEST

TEXAS

Big Bend NP

0   50 mi

0   50 km

© MOON.COM

The National Parks of
THE SOUTHWEST

GRAND CANYON, AZ

The massive, mile-deep canyon is a wonder. Hike its rim or descend into the inner canyon (page 275).

PETRIFIED FOREST, AZ

A scenic drive tours pastel badlands strewn with petrified wood (page 297).

SAGUARO, AZ

The Sonoran Desert houses unique forests with saguaros that live longer than humans (page 303).

GREAT BASIN, NV

You can hike high among ancient bristlecones on Wheeler Peak or dive underground into the Lehman Caves (page 310).

ZION, UT

Sheer cliffs and monoliths frame large canyons and tighten into narrow slots (page 317).

BRYCE CANYON, UT

Unique red and pink hoodoos shoot up from a steep mountainside (page 334).

CAPITOL REEF, UT

Waterpocket Fold rises from the desert in an enormous wrinkle of rock (page 347).

ARCHES, UT

Delicate rock arches create windows in the scenery (page 360).

CANYONLANDS, UT

Expansive vistas, trails, and scenic back roads take in hundreds of miles of canyon country (page 370).

MESA VERDE, CO

The park's geometric stone-and-mortar cliff dwellings echo the area's long human history (page 384).

GREAT SAND DUNES, CO

This park holds the continent's tallest sand dunes in one immense sandbox (page 393).

WHITE SANDS, NM

White gypsum sand dunes stretch for miles, looking like snow and even requiring plowing for wind-blown drifts on the roads (page 401).

CARLSBAD CAVERNS, NM

Expansive underground caves contain delicate, lacy stalactites (page 409).

GUADALUPE MOUNTAINS, TX

The summit of the highest point in Texas overlooks multihued canyons and desert (page 415).

BIG BEND, TX

This mountain, canyon, and desert park yields colorful cacti, tropical birds, and views into Mexico (page 422).

1: BLUE MESA, PETRIFIED FOREST
2: SAGUARO CACTUS, SAGUARO
3: DUNES, WHITE SANDS

Best OF THE PARKS

Inner Canyon: Descend into the Grand Canyon on foot, by mule, or on a raft to gaze up at the immense colorful walls (page 279).

Desert View Watchtower: See one of architect Mary Colter's finest accomplishments—a rock tower inspired by the structures built by Ancestral Puebloans on the edge of the Grand Canyon (page 279).

The Narrows: Hike the bed of the Virgin River in Zion between high fluted walls—only 20 feet (6 m) apart in some places—where little sunlight penetrates and mysterious side canyons beckon (page 321).

Sunrise and Sunset Points: Walk a stretch of the Rim Trail between these two viewpoints for stunning views of Bryce Canyon (page 338).

Delicate Arch: Admire sunset as it's framed by this fragile, freestanding rock formation, which rises from a slickrock bluff in Arches (page 363).

Grand View Point: Perch yourself on top of 1,000-foot (305-m) cliffs at this dramatic vista, with Canyonlands spread out beneath your feet (page 375).

Cliff Dwelling Tours: Tour North America's largest cliff dwellings at Mesa Verde for a spectacular glimpse into the lives of the Ancestral Puebloans (page 389).

Big Room: Take a self-guided tour through the Big Room at Carlsbad Caverns to experience the intricacies in the largest single-room cave in North America (page 412).

PLANNING YOUR TRIP

Plan at least **one week** to tour a selection of Southwestern parks; to hit all of the parks, you'll need 2-3 weeks. Make advance **reservations** for inside the park: one year for lodging and six months for campgrounds. Summer heat bakes this region into an arid crisp, but the shoulder seasons of **spring** and **fall** offer more pleasant temperatures, along with slightly fewer people. Winter **closes the road** between Zion and Bryce, the East Entrance and North Rim of Grand Canyon, part of Mesa Verde, and higher elevations of Great Basin.

Salt Lake City and Las Vegas provide the best access to many Southwestern national parks.

▲ DESERT VIEW WATCHTOWER

Road Trip

You can visit the major national parks of the Southwest by driving a loop of roughly 1,000 miles (1,610 km). Fly into **Las Vegas, Nevada,** and then rent a car and hit the road! Make reservations well in advance for all park lodges or campgrounds.

BRYCE CANYON FROM THE NAVAJO LOOP TRAIL

Zion and Bryce

255 miles (410 km) / 4.5 hours

From Las Vegas, drive 165 miles (265 km, 3 hrs) northeast on I-15 and cut east on UT 9 to **Zion,** where barren towering rock walls surround a verdant oasis. Explore iconic attractions like **Court of the Patriarchs,** the **Emerald Pools,** and the **Narrows.** Spend the night in the **Zion Lodge.**

For the 87-mile (140 km, 1.5 hrs) drive to **Bryce Canyon,** exit Zion via the Zion-Mount Carmel Highway (UT 9) and turn north onto US 89, east onto UT 12/63, and south onto UT 63 to

reach the canyon of red and pink hoodoos—delicate fingers of stone rising from a steep mountainside. Explore the rim at spots like **Inspiration Point,** take a short hike below the rim on the **Queen's Garden Trail,** and watch the sun set over the canyon. Stay the night at the **Lodge at Bryce Canyon.**

Capitol Reef

133 miles (214 km) / 2.5 hours

Leave Bryce going north on UT 63 by 8am for the drive to **Capitol Reef.** Continue north onto UT 22 and north again onto UT 62. In Koosharem, turn east onto UT 24, which goes south and then east to Capitol Reef, where the Fremont

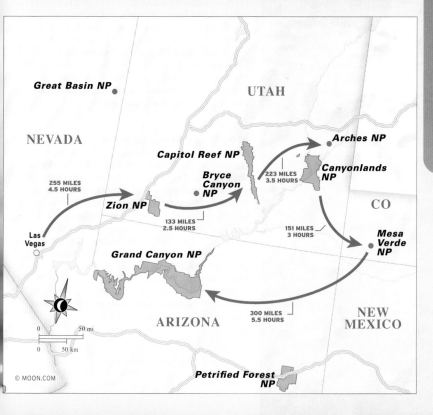

© MOON.COM

River carves a magnificent canyon through **Waterpocket Fold.** Stop at the **Fremont Petroglyphs** and hike to **Hickman Bridge** before finishing the day at **Sunset Point.**

Arches and Canyonlands

223 miles (359 km) / 3.5 hours

From Fruita inside Capitol Reef, continue northeast on UT 24, east on I-70, and south on US 191 for 147 miles (237 km, 2.5 hrs) to **Moab,** gateway to Arches and Canyonlands, where you can stay for two nights. In the afternoon, just north of Moab, turn north into **Arches** (10 mi/16 km rt, 18 min) to drive the park road to see colorful rock walls, arches, and fins. Stop to walk to four arches at **The Windows** and hike to **Delicate Arch.**

The next day, visit the vast **Canyonlands,** where the Colorado River tunnels through an otherworldly landscape of sandstone. Drive north of Moab on US 191 and southwest on UT 313 to the **Island in the Sky District** (66 mi/106 km rt, 90 min). Stop at the visitors center and explore viewpoints like **Shafer Canyon Overlook.** Hike the short **Grand View Trail,** overlooking Monument Basin before returning to Moab.

Mesa Verde

151 miles (243 km) / 3 hours

From Moab, drop south on US 191 and turn east onto US 491 into Colorado. In Cortez, take US 160 east to reach Mesa Verde. Get tickets online in advance for a ranger-led tour of one of the cliff dwellings: **Cliff Palace, Balcony House,** or **Long House.** If time permits, drive to Wetherill Mesa to walk through several archaeological sites or visit **Chapin Mesa Archeological Museum.** Overnight at **Far View Lodge.**

Grand Canyon

300 miles (485 km) / 5.5 hours

From Mesa Verde, head west on US 160 to US 89. Go south on US 89 and west on AZ 64 to reach the South Rim of Grand Canyon. Enter the park at the **East Entrance** to stop at **Desert View Watchtower** and **Grandview Point** for your first views before driving to Grand Canyon Village and the visitors center. Catch the sunset from **Yavapai Point** and overnight at **El Tovar** or **Bright Angel Lodge.** In the morning, take the shuttle to **Hermit's Rest** and walk the rim between two viewpoints on the return before driving from Grand Canyon south on AZ 64 to I-40 west and then US 93 northwest, becoming I-11 to return to Las Vegas (280 mi/450 km, 4.5 hrs).

1: DELICATE ARCH, ARCHES NATIONAL PARK
2: LONG HOUSE ON WETHERILL MESA, MESA VERDE
3: NORTH KAIBAB CANYON, GRAND CANYON NATIONAL PARK

GRAND CANYON NATIONAL PARK

Arizona

KEEPSAKE STAMPS ▼▼▼

WEBSITE:
www.nps.gov/grca

PHONE NUMBER:
928/638-7888

VISITATION RANK:
4

WHY GO:
Enjoy rim-side views, inner canyon trails, and rafting the Colorado.

▲ COLORADO RIVER IN GRAND CANYON NATIONAL PARK

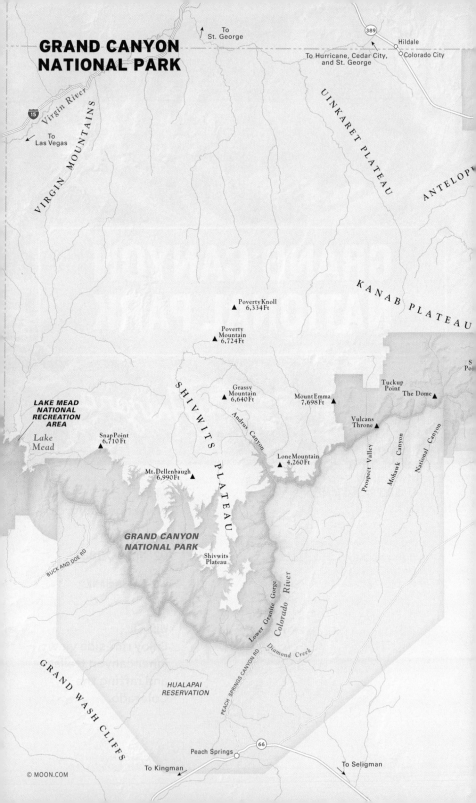

GRAND CANYON NATIONAL PARK

To St. George

389

Hildale
Colorado City

To Hurricane, Cedar City,
and St. George

VIRGIN MOUNTAINS

15 Virgin River

To
Las Vegas

UINKARET PLATEAU

ANTELOPE

KANAB PLATEAU

Poverty Knoll
6,334 Ft

Poverty
Mountain
6,724 Ft

S
Po

SHIVWITS PLATEAU

Grassy
Mountain
6,640 Ft

Andrus Canyon

Mount Emma
7,698 Ft

Tuckup
Point

The Dome

Vulcans
Throne

LAKE MEAD
NATIONAL
RECREATION
AREA

Lake
Mead

Snap Point
6,710 Ft

Lone Mountain
4,260 Ft

Prospect Valley

Mohawk Canyon

National Canyon

Mt. Dellenbaugh
6,990 Ft

GRAND CANYON
NATIONAL PARK

BUCK AND DOE RD

Shivwits
Plateau

Lower Granite Gorge

Colorado River

Diamond Creek

PEACH SPRINGS CANYON RD

HUALAPAI
RESERVATION

GRAND WASH CLIFFS

Peach Springs

66

To Kingman

To Seligman

© MOON.COM

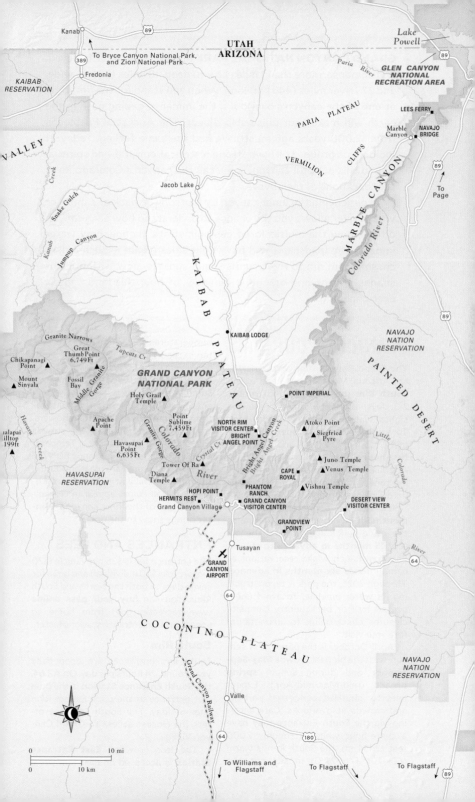

GRAND CANYON NATIONAL PARK must be seen to be believed. It is immense: more than 1 mile (1.6 km) deep, 18 miles (29 km) wide, and 275 river miles (445 km) long. When you stand for the first time at one of the canyon's overlooks, the immense gaping gash in the earth will make your pulse skip a beat. The Ancestral Puebloans from 12,000 years ago must have had the same feeling. Today, 11 Indigenous groups still have strong historical, cultural, and spiritual ties to this colorful canyon. Some call the canyon's Colorado River the "backbone of their lives."

Experiencing the inner canyon by foot, on the back of a mule, or via the river allows you the chance to understand how each canyon differs, how the multicolored geologic strata change, how water impacts the landscape, and how night skies gleam in such a dark chasm. From rim to river, sunrises and sunsets glow with brilliant shades of pink and orange, a reminder of how this landscape is ever-changing.

PLANNING YOUR TIME

The Grand Canyon runs across northern Arizona. Most visitors head to the **South Rim** (open year-round), where 2-3 days is enough time to see the sights, watch a sunset, and day-hike. To visit the **North Rim** (open mid-May-mid-Oct.), add 1-2 days and plan for a **five-hour drive** between the two rims. Arizona does not observe daylight saving time but stays on Mountain Standard Time year-round.

It's vital to book reservations **13 months in advance** to stay at one of the inside-park lodges or enter the lottery **15 months in advance** to stay at Phantom Ranch. Make reservations at campgrounds **six months in advance.** Through 2026, the park is reconstructing its water pipeline. To avoid unexpected trail or backcountry campsite closures, check online for impacts before your visit.

April-October is the park's busy season, with the biggest crowds **May-September** and during school **spring breaks** (mid-Mar.-mid-Apr.). Expect lines for shuttles, congested parking, and crowds at overlooks. Cars entering via the South Entrance may have a three-hour wait. At roughly 7,000 feet (2,134 m), the South Rim is warm (60s-70s F/16-21ºC) in summer, but temperatures in the inner canyon often exceed 110ºF (43ºC). During high-heat events, the NPS issues warnings to avoid activity and exposure 10am-4pm. Summer monsoons bring slightly cooler temperatures, but often with late afternoon lightning and thundershowers.

During **spring** and **fall,** the crowds thin and are more laid-back. Temperatures in the inner canyon range 80-97ºF (27-36ºC); the rims are pleasant during the day, but chilly at night with morning frost. Fall colors appear in November in some of the inner canyons. **Winter** brings snow to the rims.

ENTRANCES AND FEES

The entrance fee is $35 per vehicle ($30 motorcycle, $20 individual) and good for seven days to both the North and South Rims. You can **buy your pass online** (www.recreation.gov) from home to speed through entrance stations faster.

South Rim

South Rim entrances are open daily year-round, 24 hours per day. On AZ 64, the **South Entrance Station** is the busiest entrance in the park. Expect long lines midday. The South Entrance offers the closest access to Grand Canyon Village.

The less crowded **East Entrance Station** is accessed on East Rim Drive

Top ③

MOHAVE POINT ON THE HERMIT ROAD

① TOUR HERMIT ROAD

On the South Rim, the viewpoints on **Hermit Road** (7 mi/11 km) are some of the best in the park, especially for sunsets. Several offer peekaboo views of the Colorado River. When the road is closed to cars (spring-fall), ride the **free shuttle buses** (4:30am-sunset daily Mar.-Nov., 2 hrs rt), walk the Rim Trail, or bike the route from Grand Canyon Village to **Hermit's Rest.** Shuttles stop at eight viewpoints along the way. Catch the shuttle at the **Hermit's Rest Transfer Stop,** west of the Bright Angel Lodge. When Hermit Road opens to cars in winter (Dec.-Feb.), you can drive your vehicle to most viewpoints.

② DESCEND INTO THE INNER CANYON

COLORADO RIVER AT PHANTOM RANCH

The inner canyon offers unparalleled intimacy with changes of color and lighting, a close-up view of rock layers, and rugged terrain. **Day-hike** a few miles below the rim or opt for something grander: Ride a mule; stay overnight at **Phantom Ranch** (enter the lottery 15 months in advance); backpack the canyon by overnighting at **designated backcountry campsites** like Cottonwood, Bright Angel, and Havasupai Garden (apply for permit online during 11-day window 4 months prior to trip month, $8 pp/night, $10 reservation fee); or **float the Colorado River** on a guided raft trip.

Descending to the river and back to the rim in one day is *not advised.* It requires significant fitness, advanced training, and carefully planned water and food supplies.

③ EXPERIENCE INDIGENOUS CULTURE AT DESERT VIEW

Desert View Inter-Tribal Cultural Heritage Site is the first of its kind in the national park system. It celebrates 11 Indigenous groups: the Havasupai, Hopi, Hualapai, Kaibab Band of Pauites, Las Vegas Band of Paiutes, Moapa Band of Paiutes, Navajo Nation, Pauite Tribe of Utah, San Juan Southern Paiute Tribe, Pueblo of Zuni, and Yavapai-Apache Nation. The heritage site is on **Desert View Drive,** 25 miles (40 km) east of Grand Canyon Village.

The site centers on **Desert View Watchtower** (9am-5pm daily, hours vary seasonally). The 1932 structure was designed by Mary Colter, who was inspired by the towers built by Ancestral Puebloans throughout the region. You reach the tower's upper floor by climbing the twisting, steep steps curving around the open middle, past walls painted with visions of Hopi lore and religion by Hopi artist Fred Kabotie. (Pick up *The Watchtower Guide* in the gift shop on the bottom floor for interpretations of the figures and symbols.) From the often windy top of the watchtower, the South Rim's highest viewpoint, the whole arid expanse of the canyon opens up. At the watchtower, Indigenous artisans demonstrate skills in jewelry, weaving, pottery, and crafts throughout the year.

ONE DAY IN GRAND CANYON

One day at Grand Canyon will only taunt you to return for longer. Plan to tour the South Rim by entering through the East Entrance. Check out the **Desert View** sights, then drive to **Grand Canyon Village** and have lunch at **El Tovar.** After lunch, hop the **Hermit Road Shuttle,** getting off to hike a segment of the **South Rim Trail.** If you can, linger until sunset to catch the color from **Hopi Point.**

(AZ 64). The road heads west for 33 miles (53 km) to Grand Canyon Village, providing pullouts and canyon views on the way.

North Rim

The **North Entrance Station** (May 15-Oct. 15) is the sole entrance to the North Rim. Drive AZ 67 south from Jacob Lake 36 miles (58 km) to reach the entrance. It is a five-hour drive (220 mi/355 km) between the South Rim and the North Rim.

VISITORS CENTERS

South Rim

The South Rim has two main visitors centers. Both have bookstores, information, maps, and brochures. Ranger programs change seasonally. Kids can also participate in the educational Junior Ranger Program. **Grand Canyon Visitor Center** (Grand Canyon Village, 8am-6pm daily summer, hours vary seasonally) is the park's main welcome and information center, with a theater showing an orientation film about the canyon. **Desert View Visitor Center** (9am-5pm daily) sits on Desert View Point about 25 miles (40 km) east of Grand Canyon Village. This is the stop

for those entering the park from the East Entrance.

South Rim also has three other information stations. **Verkamp's Visitor Center** (Grand Canyon Village, 9am-5pm daily) has an information desk and park exhibits in addition to crafts and park souvenirs. **Canyon View Information Plaza** (9am-5pm daily), near Mather Point, has outdoor displays on the history of the canyon. For those planning to hike into the canyon, the **South Rim Backcountry Information Center** (8am-noon and 1pm-5pm daily) has maps, permits, and information about water, weather, and trail conditions.

North Rim

The **North Rim Visitor Center** (9am-5pm daily May 15-Oct. 15) is near Grand Canyon Lodge and Bright Angel Point. Stop here for park maps, brochures, and exhibits on North Rim science and history. A bookstore is on-site, and rangers offer a full program of talks and guided hikes. The **North Rim Backcountry Information Center** (8am-noon and 1pm-5pm daily mid-May-Oct.) has maps, permits, and information about water, weather, and trail conditions.

▼ MATHER POINT OVERLOOK

HOPI HOUSE

SIGHTS

SOUTH RIM

The South Rim is the most developed portion of Grand Canyon National Park. It is home to **Grand Canyon Village Historic District,** a small assemblage of hotels, restaurants, gift shops, and lookouts that offer some of the best viewpoints of the canyon. You can also see some of Arizona's most evocative buildings, all of them National Historic Landmarks.

The South Rim's **Desert View Road** has 19 named viewpoints, from the eastern Desert View to the western Hermit's Rest. The best and easiest way to see the canyon viewpoints is to take the park's free shuttle or walk along the **Rim Trail.**

Mather Point

Mather Point is named for the first National Park Service director, Stephen T. Mather. Walking out onto the two railed-off rocks will make you feel like you're hovering on the edge of the canyon's abyss. The point can get crowded. From Mather Point, walk along the **Rim Trail** west to Yavapai Point and Geology Museum.

Yavapai Point and Geology Museum

First opened in 1928, **Yavapai Point and Geology Museum** (9am-5pm daily, free) is a limestone-and-pine museum designed by architect Herbert Maier. The site for the stacked-stone structure was handpicked by canyon geologists as best for viewing the various strata. Inside are displays about canyon geology and a huge topographic relief map of the canyon. Seasonal ranger programs take place outside at the Yavapai Point Amphitheater overlooking the canyon.

Hopi House

Designed by architect Mary Colter and built by the Fred Harvey Company, the 1905 **Hopi House** (928/638-2631, 9am-5pm daily, hours vary seasonally) used Hopi workers and local materials to build this replica of a 10,000-year-old pueblo. To increase tourism dollars, the company then hired the famous Hopi-Tewa potter Nampeyo to live here with her family while demonstrating her artistic talents and Hopi lifeways to tourists. Today, it is an Indigenous arts museum, one of the best places in the region for viewing and buying high-end Hopi, Navajo, and Pueblo art.

El Tovar Hotel

El Tovar was the South Rim's first great hotel. Designed in 1905 by Charles Whittlesey for the Santa Fe Railroad, El Tovar has the look of a Swiss chalet. It has a log-house interior with mounted heads of elk and buffalo. Combining cozy rusticity and elegance, this Harvey Company jewel has hosted dozens

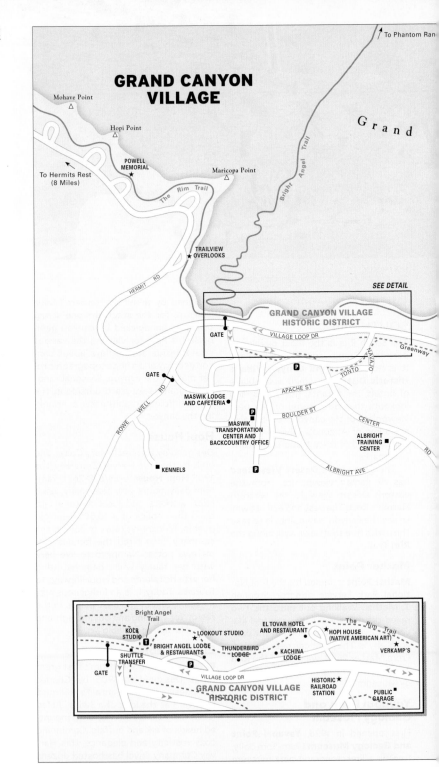

GRAND CANYON VILLAGE

To Phantom Ran[ch]

Mohave Point △

Hopi Point △

POWELL MEMORIAL ★

To Hermits Rest (8 Miles)

Maricopa Point △

Grand

The Rim Trail

Bright Angel Trail

HERMIT RD

TRAILVIEW OVERLOOKS ★

SEE DETAIL

GRAND CANYON VILLAGE HISTORIC DISTRICT

GATE

VILLAGE LOOP DR

Greenway

GATE

ROWE WELL RD

The

MASWIK LODGE AND CAFETERIA ●

MASWIK TRANSPORTATION CENTER AND BACKCOUNTRY OFFICE

APACHE ST

BOULDER ST

NAVAJO

TONTO

CENTER

ALBRIGHT TRAINING CENTER ■

RD

■ KENNELS

ALBRIGHT AVE

Bright Angel Trail

KOLB STUDIO

LOOKOUT STUDIO ★

EL TOVAR HOTEL AND RESTAURANT

★ HOPI HOUSE (NATIVE AMERICAN ART)

The Rim Trail

BRIGHT ANGEL LODGE & RESTAURANTS ★

THUNDERBIRD LODGE

KACHINA LODGE

VERKAMP'S

SHUTTLE TRANSFER

GATE

VILLAGE LOOP DR

GRAND CANYON VILLAGE HISTORIC DISTRICT

HISTORIC RAILROAD STATION ★

PUBLIC GARAGE ■

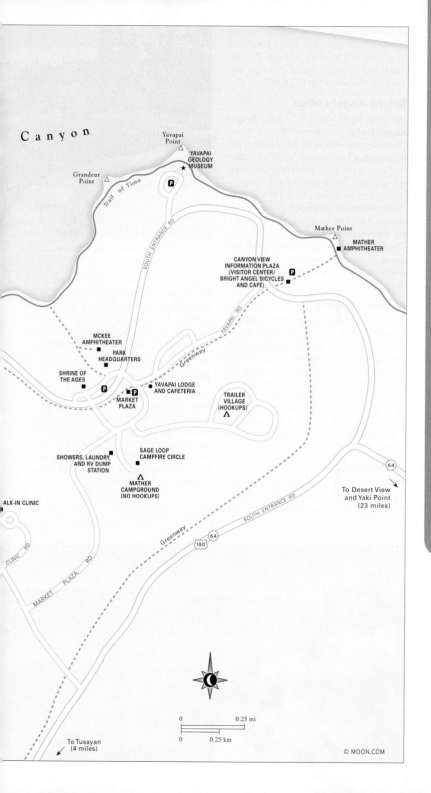

Canyon

Yavapai Point

YAVAPAI GEOLOGY MUSEUM

Grandeur Point

Trail of Time

Mather Point

MATHER AMPHITHEATER

CANYON VIEW INFORMATION PLAZA (VISITOR CENTER/ BRIGHT ANGEL BICYCLES AND CAFE)

SOUTH ENTRANCE RD

YAVAPAI RD

Greenway

MCKEE AMPHITHEATER

PARK HEADQUARTERS

SHRINE OF THE AGES

YAVAPAI LODGE AND CAFETERIA

MARKET PLAZA

TRAILER VILLAGE (HOOKUPS)

SHOWERS, LAUNDRY, AND RV DUMP STATION

SAGE LOOP CAMPFIRE CIRCLE

MATHER CAMPGROUND (NO HOOKUPS)

ALK-IN CLINIC

CLINIC RD

MARKET PLAZA RD

64

To Desert View and Yaki Point (23 miles)

Greenway

SOUTH ENTRANCE RD

180 64

0   0.25 mi

0   0.25 km

To Tusayan (4 miles)

© MOON.COM

of famous visitors, including George Bernard Shaw and presidents Theodore Roosevelt and William Howard Taft. Inside it has two gift shops, a lounge, and the best restaurant in the park.

Bright Angel Lodge

Off the lobby of the rustic **Bright Angel Lodge** is a small History Room (7am-10pm daily) with fascinating exhibits about Fred Harvey, architect Mary Colter, and the early years of southwestern tourism. You'll see Colter's "geologic fireplace," which imitates the canyon's varied strata. A geologist collected the stones from the inner canyon and loaded them on mules for the journey out. The fireplace's strata appear exactly like those stacked throughout the canyon walls, equaling a couple of billion years of earth-building from bottom to rim.

Lookout Studio

Mary Colter designed the **Lookout Studio** (8am-8pm daily summer, hours vary seasonally), a little stacked-stone watchhouse that seems an extension of the rim. The stone patios jutting out over the canyon are popular places for photos and canyon gazing. Built in 1914 to provide a comfortable but natural building that blended with its environment, the lookout now contains a store selling books and souvenirs.

Kolb Studio

Built in 1904 right on the canyon's rim, **Kolb Studio** (8am-7pm daily) was the home and studio of the famous Kolb

EL TOVAR HOTEL OVERLOOKING CANYON

Brothers, pioneer canyon photographers, moviemakers, river rafters, and entrepreneurs. Inside are a gift shop, gallery, and display about the brothers, who in 1912 rode the length of the Colorado in a boat with a movie camera rolling.

Hermit's Rest

Hop on and off the park's free shuttle bus (4:30am-sunset daily Mar.-Nov.) to tour the 7 scenic miles (11 km) along Hermit Road, from Grand Canyon Village to Hermit's Rest. Along the way, epic vistas await. Carry a water bottle or two with you. Some of the viewpoints have restrooms.

▼ LOOKOUT STUDIO

CAPE ROYAL ON THE NORTH RIM

Trailview Overlook is the first stop, with views of Bright Angel Trail as the route follows switchbacks down into the canyon to overlook the Colorado River.

Maricopa Point provides a vast, mostly unobstructed view of the canyon all the way to the river. To the west, look for the rusted remains of the Orphan Mine.

Powell Point holds a memorial to explorer and writer John Wesley Powell, who led the first and second river expeditions through the canyon in 1869 and 1871. It's a good spot for sunset views.

Hopi Point offers sweeping views of the western canyon. It is the most popular viewing point for sunsets. Isis Temple and the Temple of Osiris rock formations dominate the north view across the canyon.

Mohave Point peers down into the Colorado River. Also visible are the red-and-green cliffs named **The Abyss.** Below the viewpoint you can see the red-rock mesa called the Alligator.

Pima Point is the last viewpoint, with wide-open views to the west and the east that plunge to the canyon's bottom with the Colorado River visible.

The final stop on the Hermit Road is the rest house called **Hermit's Rest** (9am-5pm daily, hours vary seasonally). Inside the low-slung stone cabin, a huge yawning fireplace fills the warm rustic front room, outfitted with a few chairs and a Navajo blanket or two splashing color against the gray stone. Outside, the views of the canyon are spectacular. Walk to the Hermit Trailhead to see the cobblestone trail.

Tusayan Museum and Ruin

The **Tusayan Museum** (9am-5pm daily, free) has a small exhibit about the canyon's early human settlers. The museum (3 mi/4.8 km west of Desert View; 22 mi/35 km east of Grand Canyon Village) is near an 800-year-old Ancestral Puebloan ruin with a self-guided trail and regularly scheduled ranger walks.

NORTH RIM

Bright Angel Point looks over Bright Angel Canyon with a view of Roaring Springs, the source of Bright Angel Creek. At 8,803 feet (2,683 m), **Point Imperial** is the highest point on the North Rim with the best all-around view of the canyon. **Cape Royal,** at the end of a 23-mile (37 km) one-way drive, takes in the South Rim and its landmarks.

Grand Canyon Lodge

Perched on the edge of the North Rim, **Grand Canyon Lodge** (www.grand-canyonforever.com) is a rustic log-and-stone structure built in 1927-1928. Its warm Sun Room frames the canyon through huge picture windows.

At sunset, head out to the back patio to watch the sun sink over the canyon. Right near the door leading out to the patio is sculptor Peter Jepsen's life-size bronze of **Brighty,** a famous canyon burro and star of the 1953 children's book *Brighty of the Grand Canyon* by Marguerite Henry.

SCENIC DRIVES

DESERT VIEW DRIVE

The South Rim's **Desert View Drive** (25 mi/40 km) heads east of Grand Canyon Village to exit via the park's East Entrance. Along the way, canyon viewpoints offer scenic vistas with fewer crowds. Take a side road to reach **Grandview Point.** The site where the original canyon lodge once stood takes in a sweeping bend in the Colorado River, a monument called the Sinking Ship to the east, and Horseshoe Mesa to the north.

Moran Point, east of Grandview, offers impressive views of the canyon and the river. (The point is named for the national park painter Thomas Moran.) Directly below, you'll see Hance Rapid, one of the largest on the river. Next you'll come to **Lipan Point,** with its wide-open vistas and the best view of the river from the South Rim. At **Desert View,** climb the namesake watchtower to catch a faraway glimpse of sacred Navajo Mountain near the Utah-Arizona border, the most distant point visible from within the park.

CAPE ROYAL SCENIC DRIVE

On the North Rim, the paved **Cape Royal Scenic Drive** (23 mi/37 km) boasts dramatic views. The route crosses the forested **Walhalla Plateau** between Grand Canyon Lodge and Cape Royal. Plan at least half a day to include short trails to stunning viewpoints of the canyon. Bring water and snacks.

Leave the lodge just before dawn to watch the sun rise from **Point Imperial,** a side road (3 mi/4.8 km) at the beginning of Cape Royal Road. Continue along the drive to **Vista Encantada** (Charming View) as it rises above Nankoweap Creek. Just beyond is **Roosevelt Point,** where you can hike the **Roosevelt Point Trail** (0.4 mi/0.6 km rt, easy) to a view worthy of the man who saved Grand Canyon from development by declaring it a national monument.

The drive terminates at **Cape Royal.** Walk the **Cape Royal Trail** (0.8 mi/1.3 km rt, 30 min) past a rock arch called **Angel's Window.** The trail terminates at an expansive view where clear days let you spot the South Rim's Desert View Watchtower across the gorge and the river far below.

HIKING

This is arid country. Avoid hiking midday (10am-4pm) and carry at least one gallon of water per person per day.

▼ HIKER IN THE CANYON

SOUTH KAIBAB TRAIL

Even for one-hour drops into the canyon, take plenty of water. All canyon trails descend—which means it will take twice as long to climb back up. Hikers are wise to adopt the canyon motto: **Down is optional, up is mandatory.** Hiking to the canyon bottom and back in one day is *not advised*. However, some hikers with significant fitness, advanced training, and carefully planned water and food supplies do it.

SOUTH RIM

South Kaibab Trail

Steep and often shadeless with three day-hike destinations, the **South Kaibab Trail** has fewer crowds. You may also spot bighorn sheep, deer, and California condors. **Ooh Aah Point** (1.8 mi/2.9 km rt, 1-2 hrs, moderate) lets you peer into the canyon from steep switchbacks. **Cedar Ridge** (3 mi/4.8 km rt, 2-4 hrs, strenuous) grabs views of O'Neill Butte and Vishnu Temple. The limit for a one-day hike, **Skeleton Point** (6 mi/9.7 km rt, 4-6 hrs, strenuous) overlooks the Colorado River. The trailhead (no parking for private cars) is near Yaki Point, accessed via the Kaibab/Rim shuttle bus.

Hermit Trail

The **Hermit Trail** (7 mi/11.3 km rt, 3-4 hrs, strenuous) leads to some less visited areas of the canyon, especially secluded **Dripping Springs.** For mid-level to expert hikers, the route plunges down the Hermit Trail's steep, rocky, almost stair-like switchbacks to Dripping Springs Junction. Veer left to traverse along a ridgeline across Hermit Basin with awe-inspiring unobstructed

SKELETON POINT

Best Hike

BRIGHT ANGEL TRAIL

DISTANCE: 3-9.5 miles (4.8-15.3 km) round-trip

DURATION: 2-9 hours

ELEVATION CHANGE: 2,908 feet (886 m)

EFFORT: moderate to strenuous

TRAILHEAD: Grand Canyon Village on the South Rim

The **Bright Angel Trail** is the most popular trail into the Grand Canyon. Many visitors walk a short stretch down Bright Angel just to get a feeling of what it's like below the rim. Hiking down, you quickly leave behind the crowded rim and enter a sharp arid landscape, twisting down switchbacks on a path that is often rocky underfoot. The trail is steep, and it doesn't take long for the rim to look far away and people on the rim to look like scurrying ants.

The hike to **Mile-and-a-Half Resthouse** (3 mi/4.8 km rt, 2-4 hrs) passes through the upper tunnel and begins the steep switchbacks. Farther on is **Three-Mile Resthouse** (6 mi/9.7 km rt, 4-6 hrs). Both rest houses have water (check with rangers about water availability in winter). A rather tough day hike, beautiful **Havasupai Garden** (9 mi/14.5 km rt, 6-9 hrs) is a cool, green oasis in the arid inner canyon. Due to extreme heat, this route is not recommended in the summer.

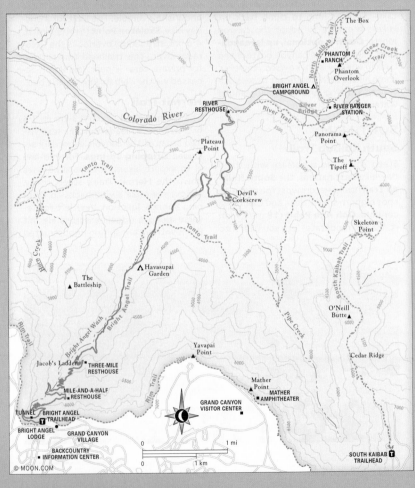

© MOON.COM

TUNNEL ON BRIGHT ANGEL TRAIL

views. At Boucher Trail Junction, continue west on the often narrow and exposed trail up a side canyon to Dripping Springs. A shock of fernlike greenery drapes over a rock overhang with spring water trickling into a small collecting pool. The hike back up is punishing on the waterless trail.

Rim Trail

The **Rim Trail** (12.6 mi/20.3 km one-way, 5-7 hrs, easy-moderate) is the best way to see the South Rim. The mostly paved trail runs from **South Kaibab Trailhead** and through Grand Canyon Village, ending at **Hermit's Rest.** It hits major sights and overlooks along the way.

With 13 **shuttle stops,** you can hop on and off the trail at your pleasure. Past the Bright Angel Trailhead, the path becomes a dirt single-track between Powell Point and Monument Creek Vista. **Yavapai Point** (0.7 mi/1.1 km one-way, 1 hr) has stunning canyon views from the Yavapai Observation Station. Grand Canyon Village to **Hopi Point** (0.8 mi/1.3 km one-way, 1 hr) is best at sunset.

The relatively flat, paved **Trail of Time** (2.3 mi/4.6 km one-way, 1.5 hrs) has markers following two billion years of the canyon's geologic timeline against the canyon vista backdrop. Interpretive signs tell the story, and you can touch large rock samples from layers within the canyon. The segment between Verkamp's Visitor Center and the Yavapai Geology Museum is wheelchair-accessible (1.3 mi/2.1 km).

NORTH RIM

It's cool on the high, forested North Rim, making hiking in summer less of a chore. From Grand Canyon Lodge, **Transept Trail** (4 mi/6.4 km rt, 2 hrs,

NORTH KAIBAB CANYON BELOW SUPAI TUNNEL

BACKPACKER ON THE TONTO PLATEAU

easy) travels through forest to the campground.

Uncle Jim Trail

The **Uncle Jim Trail** (4.7 mi/7.6 km rt, 2.5 hrs, easy) winds through old stands of spruce and fir, sprinkled with quaking aspen, to Uncle Jim Point. Tradition dictates giving your best roar into the canyon known as Roaring Springs.

Widforss Trail

The mostly flat **Widforss Trail** (10 mi/16 km rt, 5 hrs, easy) leads along the Transept Canyon through ponderosa pine, fir, and spruce, with a few stands of aspen mixed in. At Widforss Point, you can stare across the great chasm. For a shorter interpretive hike, follow the first half of the trail using the guide available at the visitors center.

North Kaibab Trail

The **North Kaibab Trail** is the only North Rim route into the inner canyon and the Colorado River. A short walk down to **Coconino Overlook** (1.4 mi/2.3 km rt, 1-2 hrs, moderate) offers views of the San Francisco Peaks and the South Rim. Lower destinations go to **Supai Tunnel** (4 mi/6.4 km rt, 3-4 hrs, strenuous), which was blasted out of rock in the 1930s by the Civilian Conservation Corps, and **Redwall Bridge** (5.2 mi/ 8.4 km rt, 4-6 hrs, strenuous), which was built in 1966 after a flood.

Strong hikers can descend the North Kaibab to **Roaring Springs** (9.4 mi/15 km rt, 6-8 hrs, strenuous). The springs fall headlong out of the cliff to spray mist and rainbows into the hot air. Start your hike early and bring plenty of water. The approximately 3,000-foot (910-m) climb back out of the canyon is grueling. In summer, there is water at the trailhead, Supai Tunnel, and Roaring Springs.

The North Kaibab Trailhead is a few miles north of Grand Canyon Lodge, accessed via the **hiker's shuttle** (twice daily) from the lodge. Purchase tickets 24 hours in advance.

RECREATION
BACKPACKING

The inner canyon beckons backpackers with rugged trails and **designated backcountry campsites** on the rim-to-rim trails and the **Tonto Plateau** between Havasupai Garden and Hermit Trail. **Permits** ($10 plus $12 pp/night) are required; apply for **reservations** during a 10- to 12-day window 4-5 months in advance.

▶ NORTH KAIBAB TRAIL

BACKPACKING RIM-TO-RIM

This classic journey begins on the South Rim at the **Bright Angel** or **South Kaibab Trailhead** to cross the Colorado River and connect with the North Rim via the **North Kaibab Trailhead.** Most backpackers plan 3-4 days for the trip and rely on **Trans-Canyon Shuttle** (928/638-2820, www.trans-canyonshuttle. com, twice daily each direction, May 15-Oct. 15, $90) for the five-hour return drive back to the starting rim. Advanced planning, reservations, and physical preparation are imperative for this trip.

The Bright Angel and North Kaibab Trails have three developed backcountry campgrounds with restrooms, drinking water, and campsites with picnic tables, pack poles, and food storage bins. From the South Rim, the Bright Angel Trail descends 9.5 miles (15 km, 4,380 ft/1,335 m) to **Bright Angel Campground** near the Colorado River and Phantom Ranch. A much steeper plunge, the South Kaibab Trail drops 4,780 feet (1,457 m) in 7 miles (11 km) to the same point.

From the North Rim, the **North Kaibab Trail** travels 14 miles (22.5 km) into the canyon with the greatest elevation change (5,761 ft/1,756 m). The most common rim-to-rim route connects the Bright Angel and North Kaibab Trails, with a two-night stay at Bright Angel Campground to explore and rest.

For hikers climbing out of Bright Angel Campground, a predawn start is a must. Due to the extreme elevation gains, many choose to break the uphill grunt into two days by camping at **Havasupai Garden** on the Bright Angel Trail or at **Cottonwood** on the North Kaibab Trail. (The South Kaibab Trail has no camping. Due to its steep, waterless pitch, it is recommended only for descents.)

A **permit** ($10, plus $12 pp/night) is required, and it's not easy to get. The park receives more than 30,000 requests for backcountry permits annually but issues only 13,000. To apply for a permit, visit the park website for an application, submission dates (usually four months in advance), and regulations. For more information, contact the South Rim Backcountry Information Center (928/638-7875, 8am-noon and 1pm-5pm daily).

BRIGHT ANGEL TRAIL

BIKING

When **Hermit Road** (7 mi/11 km one-way, Mar.-Nov.) closes to cars, it remains open to cyclists who can ride from Grand Canyon Village to Hermit's Rest. To make a loop, opt for the paved **Hermit Road Greenway Trail** (2.8 mi/4.5 km one-way), a portion of the Rim Trail from Monument Creek Vista to Hermit's Rest.

Near Grand Canyon Visitor Center, **Bright Angel Bicycles and Café** (928/679-0992, www.bikegrandcanyon.com, 8am-6pm daily) rents bikes, safety equipment, and trailers. They also guide bike tours of the South Rim.

RIVER TRIPS

River rafters place the trip along the Colorado River through the Grand Canyon at the top of their bucket lists. Huge white-water rapids alternate with placid turquoise pools. At night, star-filled evenings accompany campers as owls hoot deep in the gorge. Rafting season runs **April-October.** Guided river trips range 3-18 days on dories, motorized rafts, oared or paddle rafts, or kayaks. Some trips include a hike down one of the corridor trails to the river. Book a year in advance.

The best place to start is the **Grand Canyon River Outfitters Association** (www.gcroa.org), a nonprofit group of

RAFTING ON THE COLORADO RIVER AT THE BOTTOM OF THE GRAND CANYON

SOUTHWEST ◆ ARIZONA ◆ Grand Canyon National Park

about 16 licensed river outfitters monitored and approved by the National Park Service. Each has a good safety record and similar rates.

For experienced big-water river navigators, **self-guided trips** for 2-25 days require **permits** ($90 pp) that can be acquired through an annual **weighted lottery** ($25) in February. Contact the **River Permit Office** (928/638-7843 or 800/959-9164) for details or look online.

MULE RIDES

Grand Canyon mules have been dexterously picking along the skinny trails, loaded with packs and people, for generations. Weight and age restrictions apply. On the South Rim, **Xanterra** (303/297-2757 or 888/297-2757, www.grandcanyonlodges.com) leads mule rides along the **East Rim** (2 hrs, $156) or down the Bright Angel Trail into the canyon to overnight at **Phantom Ranch** (1-2 nights, $705-1,029 for 1 person, $1,227-1,691 for 2 people, meals included). Make reservations 13 months in advance.

On the North Rim, **Canyon Trail Rides** (435/679-8665, www.canyon-rides.com, May 15-Oct. 15, 3 hrs, $50-

100) go to rim overlooks or down into the canyon to the Supai Tunnel.

WHERE TO STAY

INSIDE THE PARK

South Rim

Xanterra (303/297-2757 or 888/297-2757, www.grandcanyonlodges.com) operates five lodges in Grand Canyon Village. Make reservations 13 months in advance for stays April-October and 6 months in advance in other seasons.

El Tovar (from $278) is a 1905 National Historic Landmark near the rim with 78 rooms and suites. The hotel's **restaurant** (928/638-2631, 7am-10:30am, 11am-3pm, and 4:30pm-9pm daily, reservations recommended) serves some of the best food in Arizona. Off the log-cabin lobby is a cocktail lounge with a window on the canyon, a mezzanine sitting area overlooking the lobby, and a gift shop with Native American art and crafts.

Bright Angel Lodge (from $128) retains a rustic character that fits perfectly with the wild canyon just outside. Most lodge rooms have only one bed and no TVs. Utilitarian "hiker" rooms have refrigerators and share showers.

NAME	LOCATION	PRICE	SEASON	AMENITIES
Mather Campground	South Rim	$18	year-round	tent sites
Trailer Village	South Rim	from $61	year-round	RV sites
Bright Angel Lodge	South Rim	from $128	year-round	hiker rooms, hotel rooms, cabins, dining
Maswik Lodge	South Rim	from $262	year-round	motel rooms, cabins, dining
Yavapai Lodge	South Rim	from $192	year-round	motel rooms, dining
Kachina Lodge	South Rim	from $249	year-round	motel rooms
Thunderbird Lodge	South Rim	from $262	year-round	motel rooms
El Tovar Hotel	South Rim	from $278	year-round	hotel rooms, dining
Desert View Campground	East Rim	$18	May-mid-Oct.	tent sites
North Rim Campground	North Rim	$18-50	May 15-Oct. 31	tent sites
Grand Canyon Lodge	North Rim	from $158	May 15-Oct. 15	cabins, motel rooms, dining
Havasupai Garden	Inner Canyon	permit required	year-round	hike-in tent sites
Bright Angel	Inner Canyon	permit required	year-round	hike-in tent sites
Cottonwood	Inner Canyon	permit required	year-round	hike-in tent sites
Phantom Ranch	Inner Canyon	$62-172	year-round	hike-in or mule-in dorms, cabins, food

The lodge's cabins have private baths, TVs, and sitting rooms. The **Arizona Steakhouse** (928/638-2631, 11am-2:30pm and 5pm-9pm daily Mar.-Dec.) serves Southwestern dishes in a casual atmosphere, and the **Fred Harvey Burger** (928/638-2631, 11am-3:30pm and 4:30pm-9pm daily) plates standard rib-sticking food.

Kachina Lodge and **Thunderbird Lodge** (both from $262) both offer basic rooms with TVs, safes, private baths, and refrigerators.

Maswik Lodge (303/297-2757, www.grandcanyonlodges.com, from $262) has motel-style rooms, the cafeteria-style **Maswik Food Court** (928/638-2631, 6:30am-8pm daily), and a sports bar. The older North rooms are simpler, with stairs only to the second floor. The South rooms, revamped in 2021, have elevator access to the second floor; 30 of the rooms have kitchenettes.

Near Market Plaza, **Yavapai Lodge** (Delaware North, 11 Yavapai Lodge Rd., 877/404-4611, www.visitgrandcanyon.com, from $192) is a basic motel with air-conditioning, refrigerators, and TVs. The west section has no air-conditioning but is pet-friendly. The lodge **restaurant** (7am-9pm daily) has a limited menu of hot and cold sandwiches. The **Canyon Village Market & Deli** (7am-8pm daily, hours vary seasonally) sells groceries, camping supplies, and deli foods.

North Rim

Built in the late 1920s, the remote **Grand Canyon Lodge** (928/638-2611

PHANTOM RANCH

or 877/386-4383, www.grandcanyon-forever.com, mid-May-mid-Oct., from $158) is the only hotel on the North Rim. It has several small, comfy lodge rooms and dozens of cabins with private baths; some have gas fireplaces.

The rustic log-and-stone lodge has a large central lobby, a **dining room** (4:30pm-9:30pm daily mid-May-mid-Oct., dinner reservations required), deli, saloon, gift shop, general store, and gas station.

Inner Canyon

Designed in 1922 by Mary Colter for the Fred Harvey Company, **Phantom Ranch** (888/297-2757, www.grand-canyonlodges.com, dorms $62, cabin $172) has the only accommodations inside the canyon. Reservations are on a **lottery system** beginning 15 months in advance. Located near the mouth of Bright Angel Canyon, the complex is shaded by cottonwoods that were planted in the 1930s by the Civilian Conservation Corps. Phantom Ranch has several rustic, air-conditioned cabins and dormitories, one for men and one for women; both offer restrooms with showers.

The lodge's **Phantom Ranch Canteen** (with air-conditioning!) sells beer and lemonade. The canteen offers two meals daily: breakfast (eggs, pancakes, and bacon) and dinner, with a choice of steak, stew, or vegetarian. It also offers a boxed lunch with a bagel, fruit, and salty snacks. Meal reservations are required.

Camping

For RVers on the South Rim, **Trailer Village** (Delaware North, 877/404-4611, www.visitgrandcanyon.com, from $61) has hookups.

For all other campgrounds in the park, make **reservations** (877/444-6777, www.recreation.gov, $18-25) six months in advance. Due to stiff competition, reserve sites as soon as dates are released.

Two campgrounds are on the South Rim. **Mather Campground** (327 sites, reservations accepted Mar.-Nov., first come, first served Dec.-Feb.) has coin-operated showers and laundry. Grand Canyon Village is a 15-minute walk, and a shuttle stop is nearby. One loop stays open in winter with limited services. Near the park's East Entrance, **Desert View Campground** (mid-Apr.-mid-Oct., 50 sites) is for tents and small RVs, but has no showers.

The **North Rim Campground** (87 sites, mid-May-Oct.) has campsites near the rim, with showers and a coin-operated laundry.

OUTSIDE THE PARK

Plentiful accommodations, restaurants, and services are available in **Tusayan, Williams,** and **Flagstaff.**

GETTING THERE

AIR

Most visitors fly into **Phoenix Sky Harbor International Airport** (PHX, 3400 E. Sky Harbor Blvd., 602/273-3300, www.skyharbor.com), rent a car, and drive about 3.5 hours north to the South Rim. Flying into Las Vegas's **McCarran International Airport** (LAS, 5757 Wayne Newton Blvd., 702/261-5211, www.mccarran.com) places you within five hours' drive of the park. **Flagstaff Pulliam Airport** (FLG, 6200 S. Pulliam Dr., 928/213-2930, www.flag-staff.az.gov) is a 1.5-hour drive from the park. **Grand Canyon Airlines** (www.grandcanyonairlines.com) has flights from Boulder City, Nevada, near Las Vegas, to **Grand Canyon Airport** (GCN) at Tusayan; however, car rentals are not available.

BUS

Groome Shuttles (928/350-8466, www.groometransportation.com) offers service from Flagstaff to the Grand Canyon (daily Mar.-Oct., $80 rt). Connections also go between Phoenix's Sky Harbor Airport and Flagstaff ($49 one-way) several times a day.

From Tusayan, a free **shuttle** (8am-9:30pm daily Mar. 1-Sept. 30) runs from the National Geographic IMAX theater into the park to the Grand Canyon Visitor Center. Purchase your entrance ticket at the IMAX before getting on the shuttle.

TRAIN

From Williams, the **Grand Canyon Railway** (800/843-8724, www.thetrain.com, $67-226 rt) takes about 2.5 hours to reach the South Rim Depot. Fiddlers often stroll through the restored historic cars; some trips stage a mock train robbery with bandits on horseback.

CAR

Most visitors drive to the park's South Rim from **Flagstaff** or **Williams,** entering through the south or east gates. The **South Entrance** is the busiest; traffic backs up during summer. The quickest way to the South Entrance is via AZ 64 from Williams (55 mi/89 km). From Flagstaff, take US 180 through the forest past the San Francisco Peaks to merge with AZ 64 at Valle (80 mi/129 km) to get to the entrance.

To reach the **East Entrance,** take US 89 north from Flagstaff to Cameron, then take AZ 64 west to the entrance. Entering through the East Entrance lands you at Desert View, Desert View Watchtower, and Tusayan Museum and Ruin.

For the **North Entrance** (open mid-Mar.-Nov.), take US 89A between Fredonia and Page to Jacob Lake. Go south on AZ 67 for 36 miles (58 km) to the entrance and 14 miles (22.5 km) farther to the North Rim.

GETTING AROUND
SOUTH RIM

Driving is unnecessary on the South Rim thanks to the park's shuttle service and the Rim Trail, which both link multiple locales. Just park your vehicle early in the day and use the shuttle system to get around. The **Backcountry Information Center** has a large parking lot; the southern portion can accommodate RVs and trailers. The **Market Plaza** and **Visitor Center** have large lots and shuttle stops.

The park operates free **shuttle services** (before sunrise-after sunset, every 10-30 min) on four color-coded routes: Hermit's Rest Road (red, Mar.-Nov.), Tusayan (purple, spring-fall), the Village (blue, year-round), and Kaibab/Rim (orange, year-round). The **Grand Canyon Pocket Map** (online or at entrance stations) shows the routes and stops. There is no shuttle that travels east from Grand Canyon Village to the East Entrance.

Narrated bus tours (888/297-2757, www.grandcanyonlodges, year-round) run on Desert View Drive or Hermits Rest Road. Sunset and sunrise tours are also available.

NORTH RIM

The drive from the South Rim to the North Rim is 215 miles (345 km, 5 hrs). AZ 67 from Jacob Lake to the North Rim typically closes to vehicles from late November until May.

The **Trans-Canyon Shuttle** (928/638-2820, www.trans-canyonshuttle.com, $90 one-way, reservations required) makes a twice-daily round-trip excursion between the North and South Rims.

The **Hikers Shuttle** (departs twice daily in morning, May-15-Oct. 15, $4-7) goes from Grand Canyon Lodge to the North Kaibab Trailhead. Buy tickets the day before at the lodge.

SIGHTS NEARBY

Hualapai Skywalk (888/868-9378 or 928/769-2636, www.grandcanyonwest.com), at Eagle Point on the Hualapai Reservation, extends 4,000 feet (1,219 m) above the Grand Canyon floor on a glass-bottom viewing bridge.

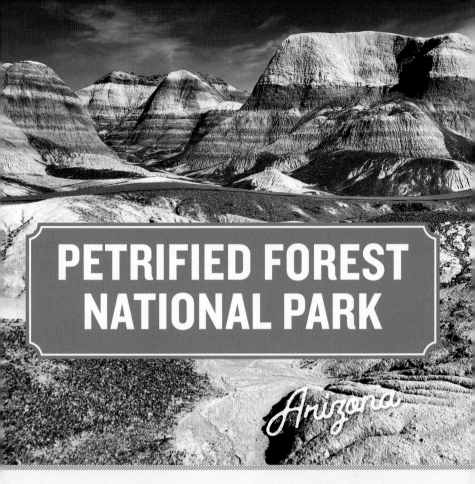

PETRIFIED FOREST
NATIONAL PARK

Arizona

KEEPSAKE STAMPS ▼▼▼

WEBSITE:
www.nps.gov/pefo

PHONE NUMBER:
928/524-6228

VISITATION RANK:
36

WHY GO:
See petrified trees
loaded with colorful
quartz crystal.

▲ BLUE MESA IN PETRIFIED FOREST
NATIONAL PARK

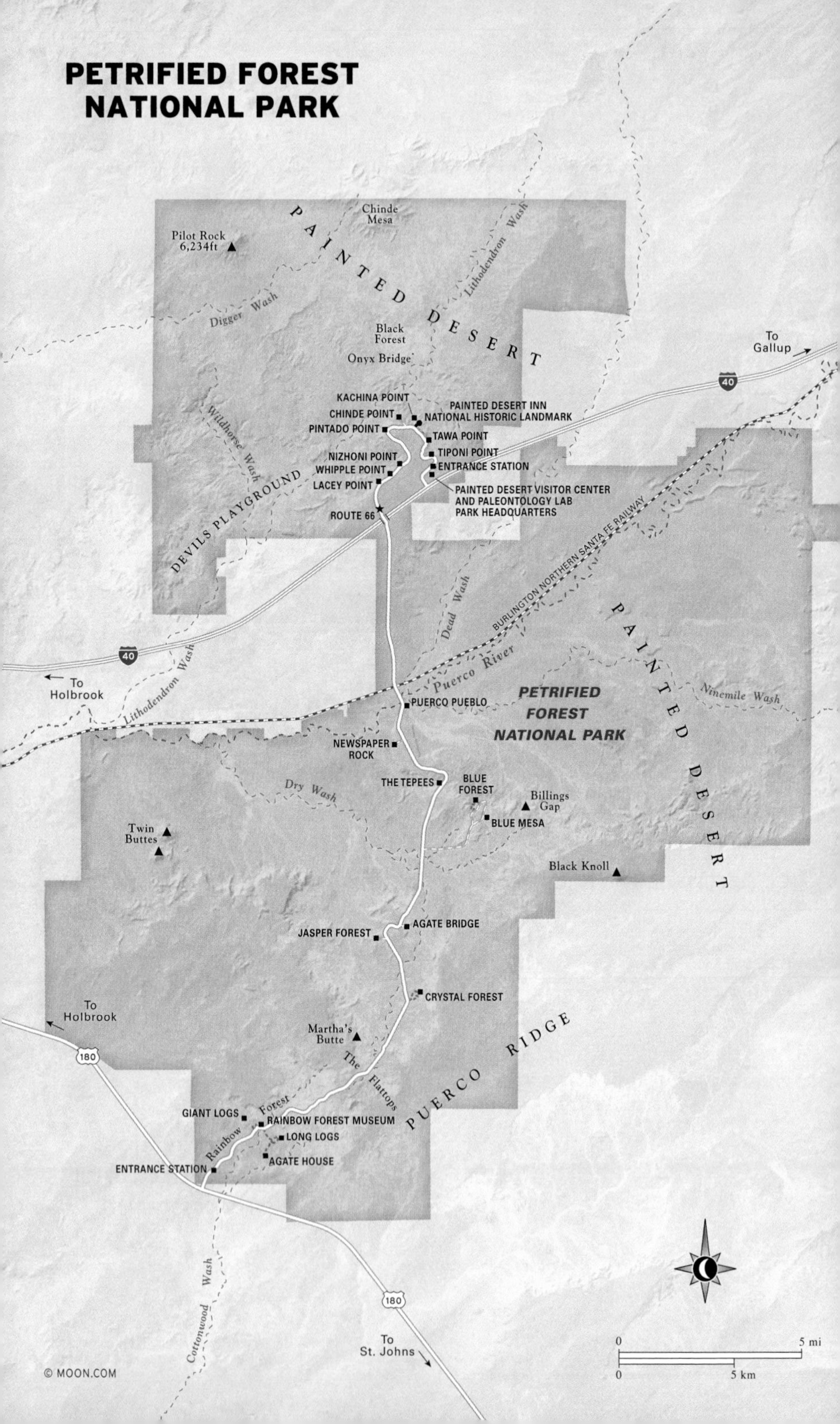

PETRIFIED FOREST NATIONAL PARK

PAINTED DESERT

Chinde Mesa

Pilot Rock 6,234ft ▲

Digger Wash

Wildhorse Wash

DEVILS PLAYGROUND

Black Forest

Onyx Bridge

KACHINA POINT ■
CHINDE POINT ■
PINTADO POINT ■

PAINTED DESERT INN
NATIONAL HISTORIC LANDMARK

TAWA POINT
TIPONI POINT

NIZHONI POINT ■
WHIPPLE POINT ■
LACEY POINT ■

ENTRANCE STATION

ROUTE 66

PAINTED DESERT VISITOR CENTER
AND PALEONTOLOGY LAB
PARK HEADQUARTERS

Lithodendron Wash

To Gallup

40

40

To Holbrook

Lithodendron Wash

Dead Wash

BURLINGTON NORTHERN SANTA FE RAILWAY

Puerco River

PAINTED DESERT

Ninemile Wash

PUERCO PUEBLO ■

PETRIFIED
FOREST
NATIONAL PARK

NEWSPAPER ROCK ■

Dry Wash

THE TEPEES ■

BLUE FOREST ■

Billings Gap ▲

BLUE MESA ■

Twin Buttes ▲
▲

Black Knoll ▲

JASPER FOREST ■

AGATE BRIDGE ■

To Holbrook

CRYSTAL FOREST ■

Martha's Butte ▲

The Flattops

PUERCO RIDGE

180

GIANT LOGS ■
RAINBOW FOREST MUSEUM ■
LONG LOGS ■

Rainbow Forest

AGATE HOUSE ■

ENTRANCE STATION ■

Cottonwood Wash

180

To St. Johns

© MOON.COM

0   5 mi
0   5 km

What was once a swampy forest frequented by ancient oversize reptiles is now **PETRIFIED FOREST NATIONAL PARK,** a blasted scrubland strewn with quartz trees some 225 million years old. Each petrified log reveals a smooth multicolored splotch or swirl on the interior where tree rings would be. The ancient Puebloans used their petrified fragments to build tools and houses.

The landscape fills with pastel-hued badlands shouting color. Orange and rusty hues give way to blue, purple, gray, and white layers. Equally remarkable are the scads of archaeological sites from the Ancestral Puebloans and thousands of fossils from dinosaurs.

PLANNING YOUR TIME

Petrified Forest National Park is in northeast Arizona, approximately 116 miles (187 km) east of Flagstaff. **Spring** (Feb.-May) is the best time to be in Arizona's lowland deserts. The weather hangs in the high 70s and 80s (21-32°C). Typically, triple-digit heat smothers the park June through October, yet crowds visit March-October. By November the weather cools off, and winter settles on the desert with sometimes freezing temperatures and dustings of snow.

The park is bisected by I-40. For a one-day visit, follow the paved 28-mile (45-km) road between the north and south entrances. Open hours for the park road vary through the year: 7am-7pm daily mid-April-August (until 7:30pm mid-May-early Aug.), 7am-6pm daily September 1-14, and 8am-5pm daily mid-September-mid-April. The road is gated at night.

ENTRANCES AND FEES

The entrance fee is $25 per vehicle ($20 motorcycle, $15 individual) and valid for seven days. Two entrances access the park. The **north entrance** is just beyond Painted Desert Visitor Center off I-40 (exit 311). The **south entrance** is off US 180.

VISITORS CENTERS

The park has two visitors centers with maps, park films, restrooms, and bookstores. At the north entrance, **Painted Desert Visitor Center** (8am-6pm daily summer, shorter hours fall-spring) has hands-on exhibits and backcountry permits. The historic **Rainbow Forest Museum** (8am-6pm daily summer, shorter hours fall-spring) is at the south entrance. It contains fossils and displays about the dinosaurs that once ruled this land.

SIGHTS

PAINTED DESERT

The **Painted Desert** sprawls on the north end of the park, lighting up with hues of orange, yellow, and pink. Eight viewpoints on the park road north of the visitors center allow places to stop to absorb the colors. Interpretive signs fill you in on the geology and formations. **Tiponi Point** provides the best orientation to the Painted Desert. **Tawa Point** lets you gaze straight down at formations. **Pintado Point** allows for long views across the Painted Desert wilderness. Use the park map to locate the overlooks.

PUERCO PUEBLO RUIN

In the central area of the park road, **Puerco Pueblo** is a collection of ruins that were occupied 700-800 years ago. You can see the foundations of a kiva and several rooms. A collection of rocks contains petroglyphs, and a modern stone building has interpretive information. From the Puerco Pueblo parking area, take the paved **Puerco Pueblo Loop** (0.3 mi/0.5 km rt, 45 min, easy) to tour the site.

DARK SKY

With little humidity to clog visibility, Petrified Forest National Park is designated an International **Dark Sky Park.** For the best stargazing, go backpacking into the Painted Desert wilderness on a moonless night (free permit required) to sleep under the Milky Way. Rainbow Forest Museum hosts nighttime astronomy programs periodically throughout the year. Petrified Forest Field Institute (www.petrifiedforestfieldinstitute.org) leads full moon and Milky Way photo expeditions.

PALEONTOLOGY LAB

The renowned **Paleontology Lab** has more than 35,000 fossil specimens found in the park, including three new dinosaur species in 2020. At the **Painted Desert Visitor Center** complex, the Paleontology Lab offers a demonstration program (9am-3pm Wed.-Sun.) to see fossils from the Triassic period. Junior Rangers can also do a Junior Paleontologist Program by picking up a book at either visitors center to earn a paleontology badge. **Petrified Forest Field Institute** (www.petrifiedforestfieldinstitute.org) offers hands-on fossil digs for adults and special fossil work for kids.

SCENIC DRIVE

To see this masterpiece of a national park, drive the **28-mile (42-km) park road** (open 7am-7:30pm daily summer, shorter hours fall-spring), stopping at the pullouts. Start at the north entrance and the **Painted Desert Visitor Center,** where the road enters the Painted Desert. You'll pass several viewpoints, including **Tawa Point,** where the views are long, subtle, colorful, and barren.

Two miles (3.2 km) from the north entrance, stop at the **Painted Desert Inn** (Kachina Point, 9am-4pm daily) to see the National Historic Landmark. Past the inn is **Pintado Point,** offering one of the best views of this strange landscape. As the road turns south, look for the rusted husk of a **1932 Studebaker** sitting alone off the side of the road. This artifact marks the line that old Route 66 once took through the park, roughly visible now in the alignment of the power lines stretching west behind the car.

Cross I-40 and continue south to the **Newspaper Rock** petroglyphs; you can view some of the more than 650 petroglyphs through spotting scopes from a spur road to the overlook. Farther on, the **Puerco Pueblo ruin** preserves the cultural legacy of the Ancestral Puebloans that once lived and thrived on this high-desert plain. Continuing south, look out for the hard-to-miss red-and-gray formations aptly named **The Tepees.** Farther south, **Blue Mesa Scenic Road** departs eastward. Then, the **Agate Bridge** pullout features a 110-foot-long (34-m) bridge made of petrified logs. In the next stretch are two fallen

PAINTED CANYON

Top ③

1 VISIT PAINTED DESERT INN

PAINTED DESERT INN

Two miles (3.2 km) north of the north entrance, **Painted Desert Inn** (9am-4pm daily) is a National Historic Landmark perched on Kachina Point. With its original walls built from petrified wood and native stone, the inn launched as a restaurant and hotel for travelers in the 1920s, before the National Park Service purchased the building. Later, it serviced drivers on Route 66. Following World War II, the Fred Harvey Company operated a restaurant and store in the inn redesigned by Mary Colter, the genius of Southwestern style and elegance. Her vision and color scheme turned the inn into a Pueblo Revival-style structure for modern visitors. She commissioned Hopi artist Fred Kabotie to paint murals full of Hopi mythology and symbolism on the inside walls.

Local Indigenous artisans share their heritage and culture through skill demonstrations (10am-3pm Wed.-Mon.); some of their creations are for sale. Docent-led tours are available on request (daily summer). Outside, you can see one of the most dramatic petroglyphs in the state—a large stylized mountain lion etched into a slab of rock.

2 EXPLORE BLUE MESA

About midway on the park road, Blue Mesa rises from the desert floor in layered shades of purple, blue, gray, and white. These badlands of bentonite clay are littered with petrified wood, and paleontologists have unearthed buried fossils here. **Blue Mesa Scenic Road** (5.2 mi/8.4 km rt) loops around the top of Blue Mesa with several stops at overlooks. From the Blue Mesa Sun Shelter, follow the paved and gravel **Blue Mesa Loop** (1 mi/1.6 km rt, 45 min, moderate), also called the Blue Forest Trail, into the bowels of the blue bentonite clay cliffs, worn and sculpted into fantastic shapes. Prepare for a steep descent and a climb on the return hike.

3 WALK THROUGH CRYSTAL FOREST

Crystal Forest is no vertical grove of trees. It's a forest of fallen petrified giants around 225 million years old. Petrification happens when trees are buried and, over time, groundwater replaces their organic matter with inorganic minerals. Here you can see petrified bark on the outside and brilliant crystallized interiors where the logs have split. Walk from the Crystal Forest parking area on the paved **Crystal Forest Loop** (0.75 mi/1.2 km rt, 30 min, easy) to see trees and their shiny rounds of maroon, yellow, and white crystal. Remember: These trees are protected.

CRYSTALIZED PETRIFIED WOOD

petrified forests: Drive through a barren loop to see **Jasper Forest** and stop to walk the paved loop through **Crystal Forest.** The scenic road tour terminates at the **Rainbow Forest Museum.**

RECREATION

HIKING

Accessible from the park's scenic road are several short side hikes that offer a deeper connection with the landscape. Between Tawa Point and Kachina Point, you can walk the unpaved **Painted Desert Rim Trail** (1 mi/1.6 km rt, 30 min, easy) for views of this exotic and colorful landscape.

PETRIFIED LOG WITH VISIBLE BARK

Several short hikes depart from the Rainbow Forest Museum. For a short walk on a paved trail, take the **Giant Logs Trail** (0.4 mi/0.6 km rt, 30 min, easy) to visit the park's largest petrified trees. The partially paved **Long Logs Loop** (1.6 mi/2.6 km rt, 1 hr, easy) heads south of the road to see some of the park's longest and most numerous petrified trees in a logjam. A spur trail goes to **Agate House,** a pueblo built from petrified wood about 700 years ago.

BICYCLING

Cyclists can ride the 28-mile (42 km) park road but must exercise caution—many drivers are staring at the views instead of the road. Mountain bikers can ride a section of sagebrush-covered Old Route 66 that lacks pavement and the first portion of the Long Logs Loop.

WHERE TO STAY

INSIDE THE PARK

There are no campgrounds or lodgings inside the park. Backcountry camping is permitted in the park's wilderness area (free permit required). The only place to get a meal is the south entrance's Fred Harvey Company restaurant, **Painted Desert Diner** (928/524-3756, 9am-5pm daily), which serves fried chicken, Navajo tacos, burgers, and other road-food favorites in a cool Route 66 retro dining room. The south entrance visitors center sells snacks.

OUTSIDE THE PARK

Accommodations and restaurants are available in the nearby towns of **Holbrook** and **Winslow;** however, **Flagstaff** offers the best variety of each and the most services.

GETTING THERE AND AROUND

There is no public transportation to or within the park. Only one road traverses the park, running 28 miles (42 km) between the north and south entrances.

AIR

The closest international airport is **Phoenix Sky Harbor International Airport** (PHX, 3400 E. Sky Harbor Blvd., 602/273-3300, www.skyharbor.com), a four-hour drive to the park entrance. **Flagstaff Pulliam Airport** (FLG, 6200 S. Pulliam Dr., 928/213-2930, www.flagstaff.az.gov) is two hours from either park entrance. Both airports have car rentals.

CAR

To reach the north entrance to Petrified Forest National Park by car, take I-40 to exit 311. From Holbrook, it's about 26 miles (42 km) east; from the New Mexico-Arizona border, it's about 50 miles (80 km) west. To go to the south entrance, exit at Holbrook (exits 285 or 286) and take US 180 for 21 miles (34 km) to the south entrance.

SAGUARO
NATIONAL PARK

Arizona

KEEPSAKE STAMPS ▼▼▼

WEBSITE:
www.nps.gov/sagu

PHONE NUMBER:
520/733-5153

VISITATION RANK:
25

WHY GO:
See stately
saguaros in the
Sonoran Desert.

▲ SAGUARO CACTUS

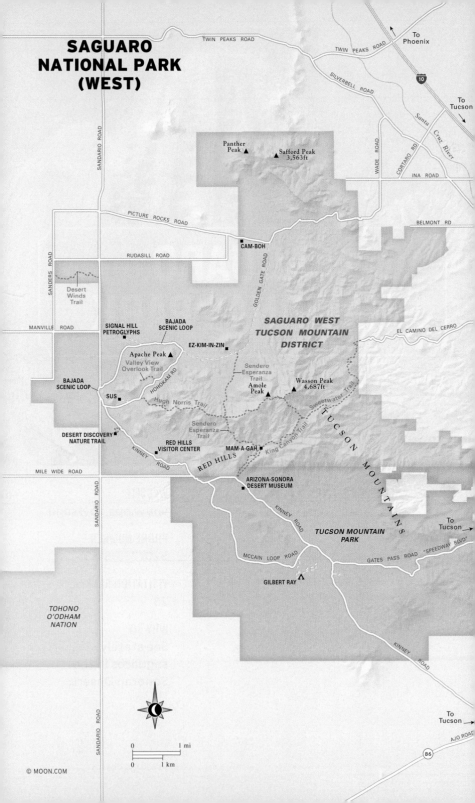

SAGUARO NATIONAL PARK (WEST)

TWIN PEAKS ROAD

TWIN PEAKS ROAD

To Phoenix

SILVERBELL ROAD

10

To Tucson

SANDARIO ROAD

Santa Cruz River

WADE ROAD

CORTARO RD

INA ROAD

Panther Peak ▲

Safford Peak 3,563ft ▲

PICTURE ROCKS ROAD

BELMONT RD

RUDASILL ROAD

CAM-BOH

SANDERS ROAD

EL CAMINO DEL CERRO

Desert Winds Trail

GOLDEN GATE ROAD

SAGUARO WEST TUCSON MOUNTAIN DISTRICT

MANVILLE ROAD

SIGNAL HILL PETROGLYPHS

BAJADA SCENIC LOOP

EZ-KIM-IN-ZIN

Apache Peak ▲

Valley View Overlook Trail

Sendero Esperanza Trail

Wasson Peak 4,687ft ▲

Amole Peak ▲

BAJADA SCENIC LOOP

HOHOKAM RD

Hugh Norris Trail

SUS

Sweetwater Trail

DESERT DISCOVERY NATURE TRAIL

Sendero Esperanza Trail

RED HILLS VISITOR CENTER

KINNEY ROAD

MAM-A-GAH

King Canyon Trail

TUCSON MOUNTAINS

MILE WIDE ROAD

RED HILLS

SANDARIO ROAD

ARIZONA-SONORA DESERT MUSEUM

KINNEY ROAD

To Tucson

TUCSON MOUNTAIN PARK

McCAIN LOOP ROAD

GATES PASS ROAD "SPEEDWAY BLVD"

Gilbert Ray

TOHONO O'ODHAM NATION

KINNEY ROAD

To Tucson

N

0   1 mi
0   1 km

To Tucson

AJO ROAD

86

© MOON.COM

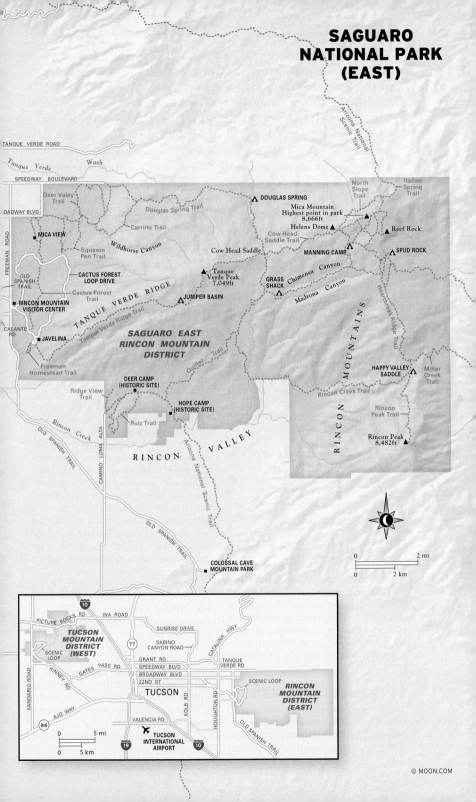

This is where the icon of the Southwest holds court. The country's largest cacti, the saguaro (sa-WAH-ro), grow slowly, achieving arms and full stature at around 125 years old. Some extend to 50 feet (15 m) tall. Their white blossoms in May are fleeting, opening only for one day. **SAGUARO NATIONAL PARK** serves as a sanctuary for these regal cacti that have significance for the Tohono O'odham people, who historically have harvested their fruit in early summer.

The park's two sections, separated by the city of Tucson, protect a magnificent slice of saguaro forest. Numbers of saguaro are dwindling due to prolonged drought, rising temperatures, and wildfires. Saguaro forests have a thick underbrush of ocotillo, prickly pear, cholla, mesquite, and palo verde. Combined, it's the Sonoran Desert at its best.

PLANNING YOUR TIME

Saguaro National Park is split by the city of Tucson in southern Arizona. A one-hour drive apart, both the Saguaro East (Rincon Mountains) and Saguaro West (Tucson Mountains) sections are worth visiting. If you have time only for one, choose Saguaro East, which is older and larger. Despite their proximity to Tucson, you'll need a car to visit either section.

The park has two **peak visitor seasons** (Feb.-Apr. and Nov.-Dec.). If you want to hit the wildflower blooms, plan for late February or March. The best times to visit are March-May and September-November, when moderate temperatures hover around 85-95°F (29-35°C). In summer, the desert is too hot, zooming into triple digits even in the shade. Temperatures are a bit cooler in the mountains. In July and August, count on daily late-afternoon thunderstorms. Though hot and humid during the day, these monsoon months are a wonderful time to see more blooms. In winter, temperatures dip to the mid-50s to mid-70s (13-24°C).

ENTRANCES AND FEES

The entrance fee is $25 per vehicle ($20 motorcycle, $15 individual), valid for seven days at both sections of the park. Park entrances are open sunrise-sunset daily; however, you can bike or walk into the park 24 hours daily.

The entrances to Saguaro East and Saguaro West are split across Tucson, separated by 33 miles (53 km), which can take up to an hour to drive.

VISITORS CENTERS

Each section of the park has a visitors center with exhibits, maps and information, bookstores, and a film that narrates the connection between Indigenous people and the desert. Schedules for ranger-led walks and talks vary year-round, but generally take place November-May. Junior Ranger Programs are available for kids and include earning a badge and checking out a self-guided Discovery Day Pack. The Not So Junior Ranger Program adds a fun element for parents and seniors to collect points while touring the park.

Start your tour of Saguaro West at the large **Red Hills Visitor Center** (2700 N. Kinney Rd., 520/733-5158, 9am-5pm daily), where you can learn about the saguaro.

Backed by the 8,600-foot (2,621-m) Rincon Mountains at Saguaro East, the small **Rincon Visitor Center** (3693 S. Old Spanish Trail, 520/733-5153, 9am-5pm daily) has an outdoor plant exhibit, helpful with identifying the Sonoran flora. Nighttime ranger-led programs include full moon walks and stargazing through telescopes.

Top ③

① PEER AT PETROGLYPHS

In Saguaro West, a walk from the **Signal Hill Picnic Area** on Bajada Loop Drive climbs the **Signal Hill Petroglyphs Trail** (0.5 mi/0.8 km rt, 30 min, easy). Its boulder-topped hill has several petroglyphs—symbols carved in the rock—above the trail on the way up. At the top, some petroglyphs are right next to the trail railing while dozens decorate the sides of rock slabs. These petroglyphs, stories from the Hohokam people, date from 450-1450 CE.

PETROGLYPH ON SIGNAL HILL

② TOUR DESERT DISCOVERY NATURE TRAIL

From a parking area on Kinney Road 1 mile (1.6 km) north of the Red Hills Visitor Center at Saguaro West, the **Desert Discovery Nature Trail** (0.5 mi/0.8 km rt, 20 min, easy) is a wheelchair-accessible paved interpretive pathway that loops through a saguaro forest. Signs identify cacti and plants. Many older saguaros tower high overhead, with barrel cactus and prickly pear at their feet.

③ CYCLE CACTUS FOREST LOOP

Cyclists flock to the paved **Cactus Forest Loop Drive** (8 mi/12.9 km one-way) in Saguaro East below the Rincon Mountains. The road is not family-friendly but an intermediate to expert road cyclist's delight. The rolling route swoops down gullies only to climb up again and has a steep ascent on the east side. Tucson has several rental bike companies; some will deliver to the visitors center.

CYCLISTS ON CACTUS FOREST LOOP

SCENIC DRIVES

TUCSON MOUNTAIN DISTRICT (SAGUARO WEST)

To see the western section of the park, especially in the heat of summer, drive the two-way **Bajada Loop** (6 mi/9.7 km, dawn to dusk daily, RVs and trailers not recommended) through a thick saguaro forest. The route is graded dirt and can get dusty, but you can also walk or bike the loop. This loop accesses several picnic areas, plus short trails to **Valley View Overlook** and the **Signal Hill Petroglyphs.**

RINCON MOUNTAIN DISTRICT (SAGUARO EAST)

To see the eastern section of the park, drive very slowly along the **Cactus Forest Loop Drive** (8 mi/13 km one-way, dawn-dusk daily, no oversize vehicles). The route begins at the visitors center and winds up across the bajada. The desert here is gorgeous, especially after a rainstorm or early in the morning during the wildflower bloom months. On the loop's east side, stop at two overlooks to see the **Sonoran Desert** and the **Cactus Forest.** Circle the wheelchair-accessible paved **Desert Ecology Trail** (0.25 mi/0.4 km rt, 15 min, easy) to learn about life in the desert. As the road climbs below the mountains, stop at the **Rincon Mountain Overlook** to take in the views.

RECREATION

HIKING

Both sections of Saguaro National Park offer superior desert hiking. In Saguaro West, the trail to **Valley View Overlook** (0.8 mi/1.3 km rt, 30 min, easy) offers a big payoff for little effort. A short drop into Bajada Wash leads to a gentle climb across a hillside with a few stone steps to the top, where you can rest on a bench to view saguaros and the Sonoran Desert spreading out across the Avra Valley.

In Saguaro East, the **Freeman Homestead Trail** (1 mi/1.6 km rt, 1 hr, easy) adds interpretive signs for kids on this route that loops past a homestead site, large saguaros, and a desert wash. The **Cactus Forest Trail** (2-2.5 mi/3.2-4 km rt, 1 hr, easy) is a mostly flat trail that goes to two lime kilns. Start at the north or south trailhead to walk among the green-armed giants.

BACKPACKING

Trails go to six primitive backcountry campgrounds in the **Saguaro Wilderness Area** of **Saguaro East.** A permit ($8) is required. **Reservations** (www.recreation.gov) are available six months in advance. Call for

▼ SAGUARO NEW SPINE GROWTH

Best Hike

WASSON PEAK

DISTANCE: 8 miles (12.9 km) round-trip
DURATION: 4-5 hours
ELEVATION CHANGE: 1,800 feet (549 m)
EFFORT: strenuous
TRAILHEAD: Kings Canyon Trailhead in Saguaro West

In Saguaro West, a strenuous hike goes up 4,687-foot (1,428 m) **Wasson Peak,** which is the highest in the Tucson Mountains and yields 360-degree views. Plan to launch from the trailhead just across Kinney Road near the Arizona-Sonora Desert Museum around 6am to beat the heat; take plenty of water too. Start by picking up the **King Canyon Trail** for 3.5 miles (5.6 km) to the top of the peak, hiking on shadeless switchbacks through typical bajada desert. From the summit, make a loop by heading down the **Hugh Norris Trail** to its junction with the **Sendero Esperanza Trail** and taking the **Gold Mine Trail** back to the car.

information about water sources (520/733-5153), which are springs or intermittent streams; you may need to carry one gallon of water per person per day during droughts.

MOUNTAIN BIKING

In Saguaro West, the gravel **Bajada Loop** (6 mi/9.7 km) offers an opportunity to pedal through a forest of saguaros. The only downside is contending with copious dust kicked up from cars. In Saguaro East, mountain bikers can ride the **Cactus Forest Trail** (2.5 mi/4 km), a single-track, two-way path that bisects Cactus Forest Loop Drive.

WHERE TO STAY

There are no developed campgrounds within the park. The closest developed campground is the **Gilbert Ray Campground** (8451 W. McCain Loop, off Kinney Rd., 520/724-5000, $10-20) in Tucson Mountain Park near Saguaro West. The city of **Tucson** is filled with plentiful accommodations, restaurants, and services.

GETTING THERE AND AROUND

AIR

Tucson International Airport (TUS, 7250 S. Tucson Blvd., 520/573-8100, www.flytucson.com) is in between the

two park sections. It is 16 miles (26 km, 25 min) from Saguaro East and 22 miles (35 km, 30 min) from Saguaro West. Rental cars are available.

BUS AND TRAIN

For public transportation to Tucson, **Greyhound** (801 E. 12th St., 520/792-3475, www.greyhound.com) and **Amtrak** (400 N. Toole Ave., 800/872-7245, www.amtrak.com) both have stations downtown. Amtrak lines include the Sunset Limited and the Texas Eagle.

The city of Tucson operates **Sun Tran** (520/792-9222, www.suntran.com, 6am-7pm Mon.-Fri., 8am-5pm Sat.-Sun.), a bus line with stops all over Tucson. Note that routes do not extend to the parks.

No public transportation is available from Tucson to the parks or inside the parks.

CAR

To reach the park's **Saguaro West** from I-10, take Speedway Boulevard west to Kinney Road. Turn right and drive 4 miles (6.4 km). At the junction with Mile Wide Road, veer right 1 mile (1.6 km) to continue on Kinney Road to the Red Hills Visitor Center.

To reach **Saguaro East** from I-10, exit the freeway east onto Houghton Road. Drive 8 miles (13 km) north to Escalante Road and turn right for 2 miles (3.2 km). At Old Spanish Trail, turn left to reach the park entrance road.

GREAT BASIN
NATIONAL PARK

Nevada

WEBSITE:
www.nps.gov/grba

PHONE NUMBER:
775/234-7331

VISITATION RANK:
53

WHY GO:
Explore ancient
bristlecone pines and
limestone caves.

KEEPSAKE STAMPS ▼▼▼

▲ MILKY WAY OVER GREAT BASIN
  NATIONAL PARK

Carved out of Humboldt National Forest, **GREAT BASIN NATIONAL PARK** drapes its mountainous slopes with groves of 4,000-year-old bristlecone pines, one of the oldest living organisms on the planet. Their longevity comes from their ability to survive a harsh arid climate and poor soil. Underground, the quartzite limestone corridors of the Lehman Caves are even older, carved by water over millions of years.

You can drive on the highest road in Nevada to camp near 10,000 feet (3,048 m) on Wheeler Peak. With minimal light pollution, the dark skies ignite with brilliant stars, seen today just as they have been by the five Indigenous groups who have inhabited this land for centuries.

PLANNING YOUR TIME

Great Basin National Park straddles the Nevada-Utah state line near the end of US 50, "The Loneliest Road" in east-central Nevada. It's a remote park far from anywhere else. Many visitors treat the park as a day trip, viewing the caves and driving to the peak before continuing on their way elsewhere. Those who spend a few days here can acclimate for the hike to the 13,063-foot (3,981-m) summit of Wheeler Peak.

The park crowds with visitors on **summer** (June-Sept.) weekends, when the weather is mild, with highs of 85°F (29°C) and lows of 55°F (13°C).

BRISTLECONE PINE

Mosquito season runs June-July. Make reservations for cave tours or risk being turned away. Fall and spring can be cool but pleasant, while winter brings snow to the mountain peaks.

ENTRANCE AND FEES

The entrance to the park is along NV 488 (Lehman Caves Rd.), which ends at the Lehman Caves Visitor Center. The park has no entrance station and no entrance fee.

VISITORS CENTERS

At **Lehman Caves Visitor Center** (5500 W. NV 488, 775/234-7510, 8am-5pm daily summer, 8am-4pm daily fall-spring), you can purchase same-day cave tour tickets, peruse exhibits, watch an orientation film, and pick up park information and maps.

Outside the park, the **Great Basin Visitor Center** (57 N. NV 487, Baker, 775/234-7520, 9am-5pm daily Apr.-Oct.) shows a film, and features exhibits on park flora, fauna, and cave formations.

SIGHTS

NIGHT SKY

Due to little light pollution, Great Basin has stunning night skies. In summer, evening **astronomy programs** (8:30pm Thurs., free) include a ranger presentation at the visitors center followed by telescope viewing of celestial objects. When the full moon brightens the

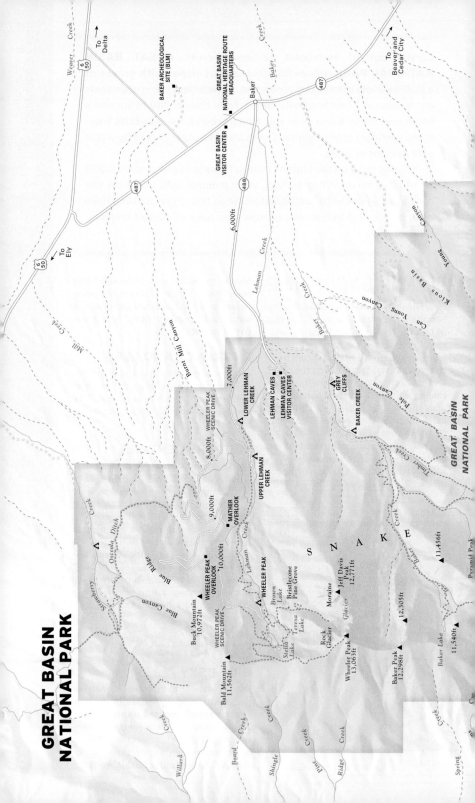

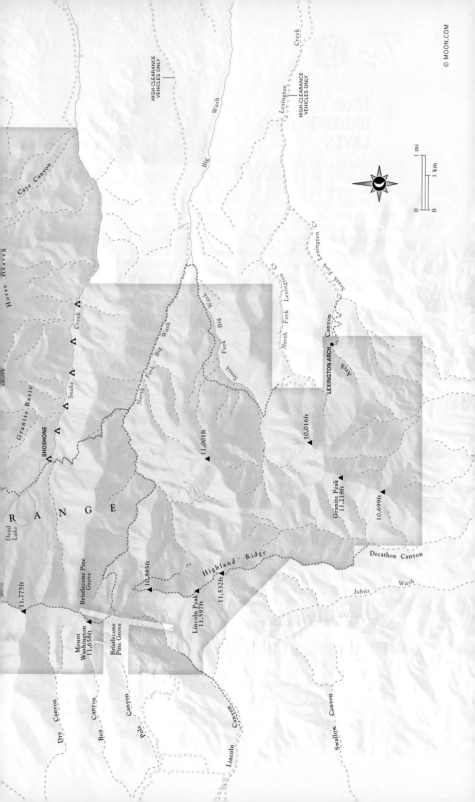

Top ❸

LEHMAN CAVES

① TOUR UNDERGROUND CAVES

Five hundred million years ago, Nevada sat under a shallow sea, teeming with creatures like the ichthyosaur (now Nevada's official state fossil). Eons of pressure changes, incessant heating and cooling cycles, erosion, and calcification acted on that primordial seabed—pushing it into mountain ranges, changing sandstone into marble, and cutting deep gashes in the rock. The result, countless calcite dribbles later, is the **Lehman Caves,** with ornate stalagmites, stalactites, and "soda straws."

Rangers lead two **cave tours** (departing every 2 hours 9am-3pm daily summer, twice daily spring and fall, once daily Fri.-Sun. winter, adults $12-15, ages 5-15 and seniors $6-8, under age 5 free). Make **reservations** (877/444-6777, www.recreation.gov) up to six months in advance. The **Lodge Room Tour** (0.4 mi/0.6 km, 1 hr) is perfect for kids. The tour passes through three main cave rooms—the Gothic Palace, the Music Room, and the Lodge Room. The **Grand Palace Tour** (0.6 mi/1 km, 1.5 hrs) includes the Lodge Room Tour with additional access to the Grand Palace, which holds the Parachute Shield. Kids must be older than five on this tour.

② TAKE A SCENIC SUMMIT DRIVE

Wheeler Peak Scenic Drive (June-Oct., weather permitting, no vehicles or trailer combos over 24 ft/7.3 m permitted) switchbacks 12 miles (19 km) along Lehman Creek toward 13,063-feet (3,981-m) Wheeler Peak. This extraordinary drive curves at 8,500 feet (2,591 m) where Wheeler Peak comes into prime view. Stop at **Mather Overlook,** at 9,000 feet (2,743 m), where the views are even better. The road keeps climbing, with the peak ahead and the vast valley behind, until reaching the parking lot for the Summit Trail. The scenic drive ends 1 mile (1.6 km) later at Wheeler Peak Campground at a breath-sucking 9,886 feet (3,013 m).

WHEELER PEAK SCENIC DRIVE

③ RIDE THE STAR TRAIN

This International Dark Sky Park features a unique ranger-led experience. At sunset, board the **Nevada Northern Railway** (777/289-2085, https://nnry.com, select Fri. nights mid-May-mid-Sept., adults $56, kids $25) in Ely outside the park to ride into the dark night. When the train stops, Great Basin rangers trained in astronomy guide the stargazing through telescopes. Make reservations a year in advance, or check for available cancellations.

Best Hike

WHEELER PEAK SUMMIT

DISTANCE: 8.6 miles (13.8 km) round-trip
DURATION: 5-6 hours
ELEVATION CHANGE: 2,900 feet (853 m)
EFFORT: strenuous
TRAILHEAD: Wheeler Peak Trail Parking Area

Hardy hikers set their sights on Wheeler Peak, though its trails are usually snow-buried until mid-June. From the trailhead near Wheeler Peak Campground, the **Wheeler Peak Summit Trail** climbs to the top of the 13,063-foot (3,981-m) peak. Start by 7am to avoid getting caught in midafternoon thunderstorms, which are common and treacherous on the mountain. The route ascends gently through forest interrupted by periodic wildflower meadows. After 2 miles (3.2 km), it will steepen and exit the forest. Most of the route switchbacks up a windy rock-strewn ridge that yields bigger and bigger views until taking in the full 360-degree panorama at the summit.

sky, rangers guide **moonlight hikes** instead (free, tickets at visitors center). On some summer afternoons, rangers set up **solar telescopes** for viewing the sun at Lehman Caves Visitor Center. The park's sky programs culminate in a three-day **Astronomy Festival** (Sept.).

HIKING

At the visitors center, the **Mountain View Nature Trail** (0.3 mi/0.5 km, 20 min, easy) is a gentle stroll that passes **Rhodes Cabin,** a historical exhibit. Pick up a trail guide at the visitors center to learn about flora and geology.

On **Wheeler Peak,** two trails at higher elevation, best June-September, depart near the campground. The **Bristlecone and Glacier Trail** (4.6 mi/7.4 km rt, 2-3 hrs, strenuous) links an interpretive trail circling a sanctuary of bristlecone pines with Great Basin's only remnant glacier. Past the temple of the pines, the Glacier Trail becomes steep and rocky over the next mile. Soon you enter a cirque, a valley carved by the extant glacier at the head, bookended by sheer cliffs, with the summit of Wheeler Peak in full view. The **Alpine Lakes Loop Trail** (2.7 mi/4.3 km rt, 2 hrs, moderate) passes Teresa and Stella Lakes with easy grades and views of mighty peaks.

At the end of Baker Creek Road is the trailhead for the steep **Baker Lake and Johnson Lake Loop Trail** (13.1 mi/21.1 km rt, 7 hrs, strenuous). Reach scenic Baker Lake in 5 miles (8 km). Continuing to Johnson Lake requires a 1-mile (1.6-km) climb over the 10,800-foot (3,292-m) Johnson Pass below Pyramid Peak. Several points on the trail provide 360-degree vistas, including inspiring looks at Baker Peak and Wheeler Peak. Just before Johnson Lake are the remains of the Johnson Lake Mine, now reduced to a few cabin ruins, discarded mining equipment, and an aerial tramway.

STELLA LAKE BELOW WHEELER PEAK

WHEELER PEAK ON THE SUMMIT TRAIL

WHERE TO STAY

INSIDE THE PARK

Great Basin has no lodges, but it does have five developed **campgrounds** ($20-30) with vault toilets, picnic tables, drinking water (seasonal), and tent pads. No hookups are available.

Four campgrounds accept **reservations** (877/444-6777, www.recreation.gov) up to one month in advance during peak season; off season, they are first come, first served. A paved road goes to scenic **Upper Lehman Campground** (23 sites, May-Oct., reservations accepted late May-Sept.) and **Lower Lehman Campground** (11 sites, year-round, reservations accepted late May-Oct.), favored by trailers and RVs for easier access. The paved road reaches **Wheeler Peak Campground** (37 sites, May-Oct., vehicle length limited to 24 ft/7.3 m); due to the altitude at 9,886 feet (3,013 m), some people have difficulty breathing and sleeping here. **Grey Cliffs Campground** (16 sites, May-Oct., reservations accepted late May-Sept.) is on the gravel Baker Creek Road.

The fifth campground is first come, first served. Accessed via a gravel road, **Baker Creek Campground** (37 sites, May-Oct.) has loops along the creek.

Primitive campsites with fire grates and picnic tables (no water) line the dirt **Snake Creek Road** (year-round, free). The sites are difficult to reach, muddy in spring, and snow-covered in winter.

Inside the visitors center, the **Great Basin Café and Gift Shop** (8am-5pm daily Apr.-Oct., shorter hours spring and fall) serves breakfast and lunch.

OUTSIDE THE PARK

The tiny town of **Baker,** 6 miles (9.7 km) from the park entrance, has a couple of lodging and dining options. **Ely,** 67 miles (108 km) northwest, is the largest nearby town with more services.

GETTING THERE AND AROUND

AIR

The nearest major international airports are **Salt Lake City International Airport** (SLC, 776 N. Terminal Dr., 801/575-2400, www.slcairport.com), 235 miles (380 km) northeast in Salt Lake City, Utah, and **McCarran International Airport** (LAS, 5757 Wayne Newton Blvd., 702/261-5211, www.mccarran.com), 305 miles (490 km) south in Las Vegas, Nevada. Car rentals are available at both airports.

CAR

There is no public transportation into or within the park; a car is necessary. Access is via US 50, also known as "The Loneliest Road." From the junction of US 50, NV 487 heads south for 5 miles (8 km) to the town of Baker. At Baker, take NV 488 (Lehman Caves Rd.) west for 6 miles (9.7 km) into the park.

ZION NATIONAL PARK

Utah

KEEPSAKE STAMPS ▼▼▼

WEBSITE:
www.nps.gov/zion

PHONE NUMBER:
435/772-3256

VISITATION RANK:
2

WHY GO:
Explore one of
the West's most
impressive canyons.

▲ ZION NARROWS AND
THE VIRGIN RIVER

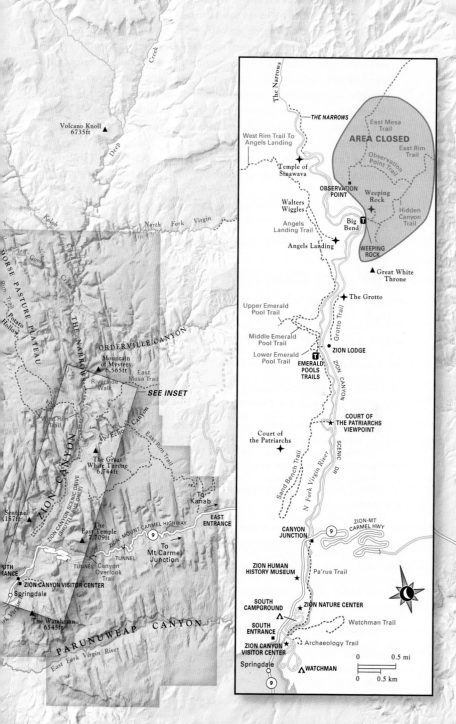

ZION NATIONAL PARK

Volcano Knoll
6735ft

Creek

Deep

Kolob

North Fork Virgin

Goose

Creek

HORSE PASTURE PLATEAU

Rim Trail

Potato
Hollow

THE NARROWS

ORDERVILLE CANYON

Mountain
of Mystery
6,565ft

East
Mesa Trail

Riverside
Walk

SEE INSET

West Rim
Trail

Echo Canyon

East Rim Trail

ZION CANYON

The Great
White Throne
6,744ft

To Kanab

Sentinel
157ft

ZION CANYON SCENIC DRIVE
(SHUTTLE BUS ONLY)

The
East Temple
7,709ft

ZION-MOUNT CARMEL HIGHWAY

9

EAST
ENTRANCE

To
Mt Carmel
Junction

TUNNEL

TUNNEL

Canyon
Overlook
Trail

UTH
ANCE

ZION CANYON VISITOR CENTER

Springdale

The Watchman
6545ft

PARUNUWEAP CANYON

East Fork Virgin River

The Narrows

THE NARROWS

West Rim Trail To
Angels Landing

Temple of
Sinawava

Walters
Wiggles

Angels
Landing Trail

Angels Landing

East Mesa
Trail

AREA CLOSED

East Rim
Trail

Observation
Point Trail

**OBSERVATION
POINT**

Weeping
Rock

Big
Bend

Hidden
Canyon
Trail

**WEEPING
ROCK**

Great White
Throne

The Grotto

Upper Emerald
Pool Trail

Middle Emerald
Pool Trail

Lower Emerald
Pool Trail

**EMERALD
POOLS
TRAILS**

ZION LODGE

Grotto Trail

ZION CANYON

ZION

SCENIC

DR.

Court of
the Patriarchs

**COURT OF
THE PATRIARCHS
VIEWPOINT**

Sand Bench Trail

N Fork Virgin River

**CANYON
JUNCTION**

9

**ZION-MT
CARMEL HWY**

**ZION HUMAN
HISTORY MUSEUM**

Pa'rus Trail

**SOUTH
CAMPGROUND**

ZION NATURE CENTER

Watchman Trail

**SOUTH
ENTRANCE**

Archaeology Trail

**ZION CANYON
VISITOR CENTER**

Springdale

9

WATCHMAN

| 0 | 0.5 mi |

| 0 | 0.5 km |

ZION NATIONAL PARK packs the wonders of the Southwest into a compact area. Color runs rampant: pale yellows, pinks, oranges, reds, and chocolate paint its sandstone landscape.

Here, energetic streams and other forces of erosion have created finely sculptured rock, from slender slot canyons through which you can barely squeeze to the monolith-flanked canyons along the Virgin River. Little trickles of water percolating through massive chunks of sandstone have left behind surprisingly rich habitats, where a variety of plants find niches in lush fern grottos. This land has also been home to the Ancestral Puebloans, the Fremont people, and more recently the Southern Paiute.

The first thing to catch your attention is the sheer 2,000-foot (610-m) cliffs and great monoliths of Zion Canyon. After that, the park's intricacies will tickle your eyes: freestanding arches, the patterned sandstone of Checkerboard Mesa, and a petrified forest. It's a place that enchants.

PLANNING YOUR TIME

Zion National Park is in southwest Utah, 84 miles (135 km) southwest of Bryce Canyon National Park. Visitors usually drop in at the visitors center, travel the Zion Canyon Scenic Drive, and take short walks on the Riverside Walk Trail. A stay of 2-4 days lets you take in more of the grand scenery and hike other inviting trails. Private vehicles are allowed into Zion Canyon only in winter (mid-Nov.-Feb., excluding Dec. holidays); free shuttles get you through the canyon in spring, summer, and fall. Crowds come into Zion Canyon February-late November. Try to avoid holidays and Utah school breaks in October.

Many people check off Zion Canyon as "seeing the park." But as impressive as it is, Zion Canyon is only a small slice of this national park. Roads venturing into other sections—Kolob Canyons and Kolob Terrace Road to Lava Point—see far fewer people, have breathing room, and offer equally enchanting scenery.

Summer (May-Sept.) is the busiest season, with midday lines at the entrance to Zion Canyon, the shuttle stops, and Zion Canyon Visitor Center. Summer temperatures in the canyons can be uncomfortably hot, with highs hovering above 100°F (38°C).

Spring and **autumn** are the choice seasons for the most pleasant temperatures. They are also good for the best chances of seeing wildlife and wildflowers. Mid-October-early November, cottonwoods and other trees blaze with color.

In **winter,** nighttime temperatures drop to near freezing, and weather tends to be unpredictable. Snow may block some of the high-country trails and the road to Lava Point, and some trails close for safety from ice falls.

ENTRANCE AND FEES

From Springdale, the **South Entrance** is on UT 9 near the visitors center and shuttle bus stops. It has a pedestrian entrance. During high season, this entrance backs up with long lines of cars, which must wait for parking spots to open; take the free shuttle from Springdale instead. The **East Entrance** is on the Zion-Mount Carmel Highway near Mount Carmel. The **Northwest Entrance** (off I-15, exit 40) is on the Kolob Canyons Road.

The entrance fee is $35 per vehicle ($30 motorcycle, $20 individual) and valid for seven days.

Top ❸

ZION CANYON

① EXPLORE ZION CANYON

Zion Canyon Scenic Drive winds along the floor of the canyon, cut by the North Fork of the Virgin River. Both canyon walls rise with immense cliffs. The drive terminates at the Temple of Sinawava, where the wheelchair-accessible **Riverside Walk** (2.2 mi/3.5 km rt, 1.5 hrs, easy) follows the river to the Narrows. During spring-fall, a **shuttle bus** ferries visitors along this route to nine stops; you can drive it in winter. Hiking trails branch off to lofty viewpoints and narrow side canyons.

② RIVER-HIKE THE NARROWS

Hike inside the Virgin River, below high fluted walls. You'll be wading much of the time in knee- to chest-deep water. From shuttle stop 9 and the end of **Riverside Walk** (2.2 mi/3.5 km rt, 1 hr, easy), the shortest route follows the Narrows upstream to **Orderville Canyon** (3 mi/4.8 km rt, 3-4 hrs, moderate, no permit needed), then back downstream. To hike the **entire Narrows** (16 mi/26 km one-way, strenuous, 12 hrs-2 days, permit required, https://zionpermits.nps.gov, $15-25, $5 reservation fee), consider going with a guide. Early summer and early fall are the best times to go. Savvy hikers rent canyoneering shoes, walking sticks, neoprene socks, dry bags, and dry suits for cool weather. Before you go, check with the visitors center on water levels, flash flooding forecasts, and the presence of toxic cyanobacteria (blooms come and go).

③ DRIVE ZION-MOUNT CARMEL HIGHWAY

CHECKERBOARD MESA

Built in the late 1920s, the **Zion-Mount Carmel Highway** (UT 9, 10 mi/16 km one-way, 1-2 hrs in summer traffic) features unique road engineering amid geological wonders. It's worth driving both directions between the East Entrance Station and Zion Canyon, but the westbound route yields a spectacular descent via two tunnels and six switchbacks into the canyon. On the eastern plateau, the road tours sandstone slickrock, hoodoos, the White Cliffs, and photo-worthy **Checkerboard Mesa,** a weathered mound riddled with vertical and horizontal fractures.

While the route is open 24 hours daily, RVs can only access the long tunnel when traffic control rangers are present (8am-8pm daily May-Aug., shorter hours the rest of the year, $15, pay at entrance station), closing down travel for one-way driving when necessary to allow RVs, buses, trailers, and some truck-campers to pass.

ONE DAY IN ZION

Park your car at **Zion Canyon Visitor Center.** Enjoy the exhibits, then jump on the **free park shuttle** for sightseeing in Zion Canyon, hopping off whenever you want. Stroll the **Riverside Walk** to see the **Narrows** and **Temple of Sinawava.** Return on the shuttle to Zion Lodge for lunch at the **Red Rock Grill.** Then take a longer hike: **Watchman Trail** for big views or the **Emerald Pools** for an easier stroll.

VISITORS CENTERS

Zion Canyon

Located between the Watchman and South Campgrounds, **Zion Canyon Visitor Center** (8am-6pm daily mid-Apr.-late May and Sept.-early Oct., 8am-7pm daily late May-Aug., 8am-5pm daily early Oct.-mid-Apr.) has information about trails, weather, shuttles, and ranger programs. Junior Rangers can get booklets to earn badges, including one on the night sky. The bookstore sells books and topographic and geologic maps. During summer, the visitors center entrance can have long waiting lines; go early or late for fewer crowds.

The **backcountry desk** (7am-5pm daily late Apr.-late Nov.) issues permits for backpacking and canyoneering. A backcountry shuttle board allows hikers to coordinate transportation between trailheads, and a list of authorized concessionaire shuttles is available to get to and from remote trailheads.

Kolob Canyons

The **Kolob Canyons Visitor Center** (8am-5pm daily mid-Mar.-mid-Oct., 8am-4:30pm daily mid-Oct.-mid-Mar.) has information on exploring the Kolob region. Hikers can learn current trail conditions and obtain the permits required for overnight trips and Zion Narrows day trips. The visitors center is just off I-15 (exit 40) at the start of Kolob Canyons Road.

SIGHTS

ZION NATURE CENTER

Zion Nature Center (shuttle stop 2, 1pm-6pm Sun.-Fri., 10am-6pm Sat. late May-mid-Aug.) hosts natural history programs for kids, including Junior Ranger activities for ages 6-12. It's at the northern end of South Campground, an easy walk along the Pa'rus Trail from the Zion Canyon Visitor Center or the Human History Museum.

ZION HUMAN HISTORY MUSEUM

The **Zion Human History Museum** (shuttle stop 2, 10am-6pm daily mid-Apr.-late May, 9am-6pm daily late May-early Oct., 10am-5pm early Oct.-mid.-Apr.) focuses on southern Utah's cultural history, with a film introducing the park, plus exhibits on Indigenous people and Mormon history. It's the first shuttle stop after the visitors center.

COURT OF THE PATRIARCHS

The **Three Patriarchs** (shuttle stop 4), a trio of peaks to the west, overlook

KOLOB CANYONS

Birch Creek. They are known as (from left to right) Abraham, Isaac, and Jacob. Mount Moroni, the reddish peak on the far right, partly blocks the view of Jacob.

NORTH FORK OF THE VIRGIN RIVER

The North Fork of the **Virgin River** cuts through Zion Canyon. You'll see it from shuttle stops and trails. For strolls along the river, the paved wheelchair-accessible **Pa'rus Trail** (3.5 mi/5.6 km rt, 2 hrs, easy, shuttle stops 1-3) runs from the visitors center and South Campground to the museum and Canyon Junction, crossing the Virgin River several times. It is also open to bicycles and pets.

WEEPING ROCK

Weeping Rock (shuttle stop 7) is home to hanging gardens. The rock "weeps" because this is a junction between porous Navajo sandstone and denser Kayenta shale. The **Weeping Rock Trail** (0.4 mi/0.6 km rt, 20 min, easy), which climbs to this dripping alcove, is closed indefinitely due to a rock slide in 2019.

BIG BEND

Big Bend (shuttle stop 8) is where you'll see rock climbers on the towering walls. Pull out your binoculars to watch their moves on the face of the vertical walls.

TEMPLE OF SINAWAVA

The last shuttle stop is at the **Temple of Sinawava** (shuttle stop 9), where 2,000-foot-tall (610-m) rock walls stretch skyward from the Virgin River. The paved interpretive **Riverside Trail** (2.2 mi/3.5 km rt, 1 hr, easy) winds upstream along the river with the first 0.4 mile (0.6 km) wheelchair-accessible. The trail goes to the Virgin River Narrows, a place where the canyon becomes too skinny for even a sidewalk to squeeze alongside, and hikers wade up the **Narrows.**

SCENIC DRIVES
KOLOB CANYONS ROAD

Kolob Canyons Road (I-15, exit 40, 5 mi/8 km) is in the northwestern corner of the park. From the Kolob Canyons Visitor Center, the paved scenic drive winds past the dramatic Finger Canyons of the Kolob to the terminus at Kolob Canyons Viewpoint. The road has many pullouts where you can stop to admire the scenery as it climbs in elevation. The first part of the drive follows the 155-mile-long (250-km) Hurricane Fault that forms the west edge

ZION-MOUNT CARMEL HIGHWAY

TEMPLE OF SINAWAVA

of the Markagunt Plateau. Look for the tilted rock layers deformed by friction as the plateau rose nearly 1 mile (1.6 km). After crossing Lee Pass, the road ends at a climb to the 6,369-foot (1,949-m) **Timber Creek Overlook** (1 mi/1.6 km rt, moderate), where views take in the Pine Valley Mountains, Zion Canyon, and distant Mount Trumbull.

KOLOB TERRACE ROAD

From the town of Virgin on UT 9, the paved **Kolob Terrace Road** (23 mi/37 km, early June-early Nov.) accesses a high plateau roughly parallel to and west of Zion Canyon. The steep road runs north through ranchland and up a narrow tongue of land, with drop-offs on either side. After reaching a high plateau, the land widens. The Hurricane Cliffs rise from the gorge to the west, and the back side of Zion Canyon's big walls are to the east.

At Lava Point Road, turn right and follow the dirt road 1.8 miles (3 km) east through aspen, ponderosa pine, Gambel oak, and white fir to reach 7,900-foot (2,408-m) **Lava Point** and its tiny primitive campground. A panorama takes in the Cedar Breaks area, Pink Cliffs, Zion Canyon Narrows and tributaries, the monoliths of Zion Canyon, and Mount Trumbull on the Arizona Strip to the south. Lava Point is a good place to cool off in summer—temperatures are about 20 degrees (12°C) cooler than in Zion Canyon. Expect the trip from Virgin to Lava Point to take about one hour.

HIKING

ZION CANYON

Watchman Trail

SHUTTLE STOP: Zion Canyon Visitor Center

From a trailhead north of Watchman Campground, the **Watchman Trail** (3.3 mi/5.3 km rt, 2 hrs, easy) climbs to a bench below Watchman Peak, where views encompass lower Zion Canyon and the town of Springdale.

Sand Bench Trail

SHUTTLE STOPS: Court of the Patriarchs and Zion Lodge

The **Sand Bench Trail** (7.6 mi/12.2 km rt, 4 hrs, moderate) has good views of the Three Patriarchs, the Streaked Wall, and other monuments of lower Zion Canyon. You'll most likely meet horses on this trail (Mar.-Oct.).

Emerald Pools Trails

SHUTTLE STOP: Zion Lodge

Spring-fed pools, small waterfalls, and views of Zion Canyon make this climb to the **Emerald Pools** (1-3 hrs, easy-moderate) worthwhile, but don't expect solitude on these popular trails. From the footbridge at Zion Lodge, three trails diverge. Turn right for the paved, wheelchair-accessible trail to the **Lower Emerald Pool** (1.2 mi/1.9 km rt), a recessed alcove with hanging gardens and misty falls. Turn left at the footbridge to go to the pair of **Middle Emerald Pools** (2.2 mi/3.5 km rt total) at the base of small waterfalls. A trail also connects Lower Pool and Middle Pools to link the two routes. From Middle Pool, a steep up-and-back 0.4-mile (0.6-km) spur trail leads to **Upper Emerald Pool** (2.6 mi/4.2 km rt total), a magical spot with a white-sand beach below towering cliffs.

Observation Point Trail and Hidden Canyon

SHUTTLE STOP: Weeping Rock

The trails to **Observation Point** (8 mi/ 12.9 km rt, 4-6 hrs, strenuous), on the upper edge of Zion Canyon, and narrow **Hidden Canyon** (2.5 mi/4 km rt, 2.5 hrs, strenuous), with its high walls blocking most sunlight, are closed due to a rock slide in 2019. Check with the visitors center or online for status updates.

▾ SUNSET OVER WATCHMAN PEAK

ZION-MOUNT CARMEL HIGHWAY

From the small parking lot east of the tunnel, the **Canyon Overlook Trail** (1 mi/1.6 km rt, 1 hr, moderate) has great views from the heights without the stiff climbs found on most other Zion trails. The trail winds in and out along the ledges (some fenced) of Pine Creek Canyon. Panoramas at trail's end take in lower Zion Canyon, Bridge Mountain, Streaked Wall, and East Temple. The immense Great Arch of Zion—termed a blind arch because it's open on only one side—lies below.

KOLOB CANYONS ROAD

You're likely to have the trails to yourself in this quiet section of the park. Access these hikes from the Kolob Canyons Road, which begins off I-15 (exit 40).

Starting 2 miles (3.2 km) east from the Kolob Canyons Visitor Center, **Taylor Creek Trail** (5 mi/8 km rt, 2.5-4 hrs, moderate) heads upstream into the canyon of the Middle Fork of Taylor Creek to Double Arch Alcove and a dry fall that blocks the way (water flows over it during spring runoff and after rains).

The 287-foot (87-m) span on **Kolob Arch** makes it one of the world's largest arches. From Lee Pass, **La Verkin**

WATERFALL AT UPPER EMERALD POOL

Creek Trail (14 mi/22.5 km rt, 7-8 hrs, strenuous) drops into Timber Creek, then pops over hills to the year-round La Verkin before turning up side canyons to the arch. The return climb back to the trailhead can be hot and tiring.

KOLOB TERRACE ROAD

From the Lava Point Trailhead, the **West Rim Trail** (June-early Nov.) offers two hiking options. You can walk the trail as an out-and-back trek into **Potato Hollow** (13 mi/21 km rt, 6-7 hrs, strenuous) to overlook Wildcat Canyon. Or hike the trail one-way (13.3 mi/21.4 km, 6-8 hrs, strenuous) beyond Potato Hollow southeast into Zion Canyon. Many hikers do this as a point-to-point hike by setting up a shuttle (contact the visitors center backcountry desk). While the total route drops 3,600 feet (1,097 m) in elevation, two-thirds of that plunges in a knee-pounding descent in the last 4.7 miles (7.6 km) to the Grotto.

RECREATION

BACKPACKING, CANYONEERING, AND ROCK CLIMBING

Permits

All overnight backpacking, canyoneering, and rock climbing trips in Zion require permits, as do some single-day canyoneering trips. Obtain **permits** by reservation (https://zionpermits. nps.gov, $15-25, $5 reservation fee) online two months in advance or in person from Zion Canyon Visitor Center one day in advance. Competition for permits is cutthroat: Apply for a reservation at 10am Mountain Time on the fifth day of the month when permits release, as most are gone within minutes. To nab a remaining permit in person, be in line long before the backcountry office opens at 7am the day before your hike.

Guides and Shuttles

Shuttles to backcountry trailheads outside Zion Canyon, equipment rentals, and guide services for hiking, canyoneering, and rock climbing are available from **Zion Rock and Mountain Guides** (435/772-3303, www.

WALTER'S WIGGLES ON WEST RIM TRAIL

zionrockguides.com) and **Zion Adventure Company** (435/772-1001, www.zionadventures.com). Two companies have equipment rentals: **Zion Outfitter** (7 Zion Park Blvd., 435/772-5090, www.zionoutfitter.com) and **Zion Guru** (795 Zion Park Blvd., 435/632-0432, www.zionguru.com).

Backpacking

For two-day backpacking trips, **Kolob Arch** (14 mi/22.5 km) makes a great destination. The **West Rim Trail** offers a point-to-point 13-mile (21-km) trip from Lava Point Trailhead to Zion Canyon.

Canyoneering

Hands down, the best two-day canyoneering trip is on the **Narrows** (16 mi/26 km). The "top down" route starts at Chamberlain's Ranch and hikes downstream to the Riverside Walk. Only one-night stays are allowed. No camping is permitted below Big Springs. From Kolob Terrace Road, two routes go through the **Subway** (Left Fork of North Creek, 9-9.5 mi/14-15.2 km rt, 9-10 hrs, ultra-strenuous, no camping permitted, day permit required) that demands route-finding, scrambling on obstacles, and wading. The hiking route goes bottom-up and back; the technical canyoneering route goes one-way top-down.

For all canyoneering trips, opt to go when water levels are lowest and thunderstorms are fewer, to avoid flash flooding (May-June, Sept.-Oct.). Ask about the presence of toxic cyanobacteria in the water and, if it's present, safety precautions. Outfitters in Springdale rent specially designed river-hiking boots, neoprene socks, walking sticks, and dry suits. They also provide shuttle services to trailheads and

ROCK CLIMBERS ON A ZION WALL

Best Hike

WEST RIM TRAIL TO ANGELS LANDING

DISTANCE: 5.4 miles (8.7 km) round-trip
DURATION: 4-5 hours
ELEVATION CHANGE: 1,488 feet (453 m)
EFFORT: strenuous
TRAILHEAD: The Grotto

Not for acrophobes, the trail up to **Angels Landing** tiptoes along a narrow rib with cliff drop-offs on both sides. But for those up for the challenge, it's a hike full of entertainment with huge rewards. The finale puts you on a high-elevation point in the middle of Zion Canyon with 360-degree views, including the Great White Throne and the Organ.

After crossing the bridge over the North Fork of the Virgin River, the route heads north along 2 miles (3.2 km) of pavement on the **West Rim Trail.** As the hot trail ascends the narrow Refrigerator Canyon between Angels Landing and Cathedral Mountain, the air cools a bit. Then, **Walter's Wiggles,** a feat of trail engineering, zigzags for 21 short switchbacks up to Scout Lookout. From the lookout saddle, turn off the West Rim Trail toward Angels Landing to climb 0.5 mile (0.8 km) along the top of the rib. Along steeper pitches and narrow stairsteps, chains bolted into the rock serve as handholds in sections that are only wide enough for one person, with no passing. The rib plunges vertically off both sides, leading to the last skinny ramps to the summit.

Due to crowds on the chained section, the park requires a **permit** to climb above Scout Lookout. There are two **lotteries for permits** (www.recreation.gov, $6 fee plus $3 pp): one in advance and the other the day before. The advance lottery opens quarterly (1-3 months in advance) for 20 days, with notification coming 5 days later. The day-before lottery opens 12:01am-3pm; you will be notified by email at 4pm if you won a permit for the next day. For either lottery, you will need to choose one of three start times from the Grotto. Print or download your permit ahead of time. Check the park website for current regulations.

CHAINS ON ANGELS LANDING TRAIL

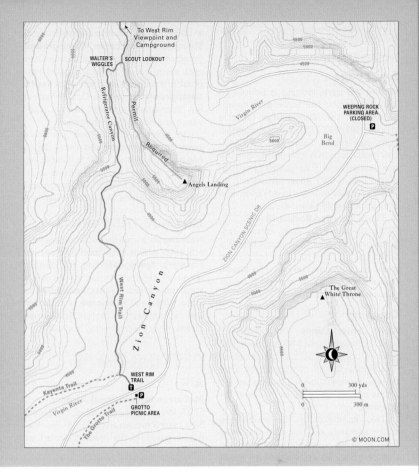

guide services for the Narrows, but not the Subway.

Rock Climbing

Zion's vertical walls attract technical rock climbers to about a dozen sites with various routes. The peak seasons for climbing are March-May and September-early November. Single-day climbs do not require permits, but bivouac climbs do. Check online for current seasonal route closures that protect nesting peregrine falcons and California condors.

BIKING

Between the park entrance and Canyon Junction, the paved **Pa'rus Trail** is open to cyclists for easy family pedaling. Bike parking is plentiful at the visitors center, Zion Lodge, and most trailheads. Outside the Zion Canyon area, **Kolob Terrace Road** is a good place for cyclists to pound down the miles to Kolob Reservoir (44 mi/71 km rt). Bike rentals and maps are available in Springdale at **Zion Outfitter** (7 Zion Park Blvd., 435/772-5090, www.zion-outfitter.com). Bikers can ride park roads, which are best before or after shuttle hours. No bikes are permitted in the Zion-Mount Carmel Tunnel.

HORSEBACK RIDING

Trail rides on horses and mules leave from the corral near **Zion Lodge** (435/679-8665, www.canyonrides.com, mid-Mar.-Oct.) and head down the Virgin River. A one-hour trip goes to the Court of the Patriarchs, and a half-day ride follows the Sand Bench Trail.

WHERE TO STAY
INSIDE THE PARK
Zion Lodge

Within the park, lodging is limited to Zion Lodge and the three park campgrounds. Rustic **Zion Lodge** (shuttle stop 5, 888/297-2757, www.zionlodge.com, year-round, from $220) has accommodations in hotel rooms near the main lodge or in cute cabins (gas fireplaces but no TV). Reservations can be made up to 13 months in advance, and they book fast for April-October.

The lodge's **Red Rock Grill** (435/772-7760, 11:30am-8pm daily, dinner reservations required 5pm-8pm) offers a Southwestern and Mexican-influenced menu for lunch and dinner. The **Castle Dome Café** serves decent fast food, including salads and coffee.

Camping

Make **reservations** (877/444-6777, www.recreation.gov, $20 standard, $30 electric hookup, $50-130 group sites) in advance for all campgrounds. Due to high competition for campsites, be online as soon as sites are released for booking.

Two campgrounds lie inside the south entrance to Zion Canyon. They have drinking water but no showers. Campers have access, via the park's free shuttles, to restaurants and showers in Springdale. **Watchman Campground** (year-round, 203 sites) has some sites with electrical hookups and takes reservations six months in advance. **South Campground** (mid-Mar.-Oct., 117 sites) has reservations available 14 days in advance and no electrical hookups.

Up Kolob Terrace Road, primitive **Lava Point Campground** (May-Sept.) has six sites with a vault toilet but no drinking water. The campground is an 80-minute drive from Zion Canyon and takes reservations 14 days in advance.

OUTSIDE THE PARK

Near the park's south entrance are several small towns with good services for travelers. **Springdale** has the widest range of services, including excellent lodgings and restaurants; **Rockville** has a few B&Bs; and **Hurricane** is a hub for less expensive chain motels. **St. George** offers many places to stay and eat.

GETTING THERE
AIR

McCarran International Airport (LAS, 5757 Wayne Newton Blvd., 702/261-5211, www.mccarran.com) in Las Vegas, Nevada, is the closest airport at

▼ KOLOB ARCH

SUBWAY SLOT CANYON

170 miles (275 km) from the park. Major domestic airlines and smaller no-frills carriers serve McCarran. **Salt Lake City International Airport** (SLC, 776 N. Terminal Dr., 801/575-2400, www.slcairport.com), better for travelers who want to make a road-trip loop through all of Utah's parks, is more than 300 miles (485 km) north of Zion. Both airports have car rentals.

CAR

To get to the south entrance of Zion National Park from Las Vegas, drive 119 miles (192 km) northeast on I-15 to St. George and turn east on UT 9 for 42 miles (68 km), a 2.5-hour route. From Salt Lake City, take I-15 south, UT 17 southeast, and UT 9 east for 310 miles (500 km); the driving time is 4.5 hours.

For Kolob Canyons entrance and Kolob Canyons Road, take I-15 to exit 40. For the Kolob Terrace Road, take UT 9 to Virgin and turn north.

To drive from Bryce Canyon National Park, take US 89 south and UT 9 west on the Zion-Mount Carmel Highway to the east entrance.

GETTING AROUND

DRIVING

Zion Canyon Scenic Drive is only open to private vehicles mid-November to early February, excluding December holidays. The road may close when parking spots fill.

February to mid-November, Zion Canyon Scenic Drive is closed to private vehicles and access is via shuttle bus. In summer, visitors park at Zion Canyon Visitor Center, where the small lot usually fills by 8am. To avoid congestion, park in Springdale and take the free shuttle into the park.

The Kolob Canyons area in the park's northwest corner has its own entrance. Reach this area via **Kolob Canyons Road,** which begins just off I-15 at exit 40.

To visit a less traveled part of the park, take UT 9 north to the tiny town of Virgin on the **Kolob Terrace Road.** The road goes to backcountry sites and Lava Point, but has no entrance station or visitors center.

SHUTTLE BUS

Two separate **free shuttles** (daily mid-Feb.-mid-Nov., 6am-8:15pm late May-late Sept., shorter hours in shoulder seasons, additional service Feb. weekends and Dec. holidays) run throughout Zion, and some are now electric. The **Springdale buses** stop at nine locations outside the park in Springdale and go to the pedestrian entrance station near Zion Canyon Visitor Center. The **Zion Canyon shuttle buses** stop at

CANYONEERS SCALE ZION'S WALLS AND CLIFFS.

eight locations inside the park, including scenic overlooks, trailheads, and Zion Lodge. You can transfer between the two shuttle systems at Zion Canyon Visitor Center. The buses, which run every 7-10 minutes, are wheelchair-accessible. They're equipped with a front bike rack that fits regular bikes but not mountain bikes or e-bikes; pets are not allowed.

ZION-MOUNT CARMEL TUNNEL

On Zion-Mount Carmel Highway, most RVs (including buses, trailers, fifth-wheels, and some truck-campers) will require oncoming traffic to be stopped to allow one-way travel through the 1-mile-long (1.6-km) tunnel. Drivers must time their trips for when traffic control rangers are present (8am-8pm daily late Apr.-late Aug., shorter hours the rest of the year). Traffic is slow on the serpentine road and stops about every 45 minutes for one-way access through the tunnel.

RVs are measured at the entrance stations where, if you are within the vehicle limits (under 13 ft, 1 inch tall), a **permit** ($15) will be issued for travel through the tunnel while rangers manage one-way traffic for your passage. The fee is good for two trips through the tunnel within seven days. Height, width, and length restrictions will ban access for the largest RVs, forcing alternate routes into the park. Bicycles and pedestrians are not allowed in the tunnel.

TOURS

The **Zion Canyon Field Institute** (435/772-3264, www.zionpark.org) runs educational programs ranging from animal tracking to photography to archaeology.

THE NARROWS

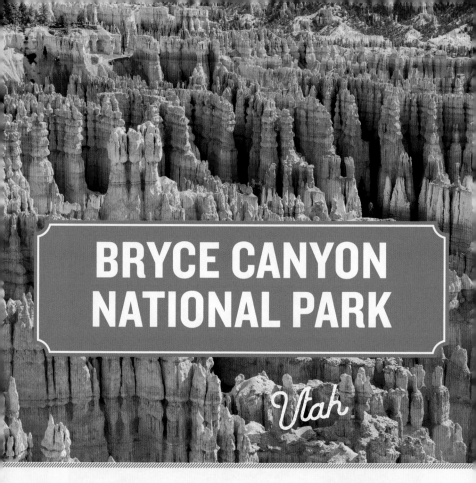

BRYCE CANYON NATIONAL PARK

Utah

WEBSITE:
www.nps.gov/brca

PHONE NUMBER:
435/834-5322

VISITATION RANK:
15

WHY GO:
Spy sculpted hoodoos and colorful hues.

KEEPSAKE STAMPS ▼▼▼

△ BRYCE CANYON FROM
INSPIRATION POINT

In **BRYCE CANYON NATIONAL PARK,** a geologic fairyland of spires rises below the high cliffs of the Paunsaugunt Plateau. In a series of massive amphitheaters, this intricate maze, eroded from a soft limestone, glows with warm shades of reds, oranges, pinks, yellows, and creams. The rocks provide a continuous show of changing color throughout the day as the sun's rays and cloud shadows move across the landscape. The hoodoos seem to form shapes; the Paiute people, who came through on seasonal hunting or gathering expeditions, attributed them to the Legend People transformed by Coyote into rocks. Today's visitors see the natural rock sculptures as Gothic castles, Egyptian temples, subterranean worlds inhabited by dragons, or the vast armies of a lost empire.

You can gaze at the sculpted hoodoos from viewpoints and trails on the plateau rim. But a whole different world awaits when you hike down the steep trails among the magical spires.

PLANNING YOUR TIME

Bryce Canyon is in southern Utah, between Zion National Park and Grand Staircase-Escalante National Monument. Allow a full day to tour the park, stopping at visitors centers, cruising the scenic drive, and taking a few short walks. Sunsets and sunrises reward overnight visitors, while moonlit nights reveal yet another spectacle. Those staying at least three days can hike into the amphitheaters on longer trails. The park's elevation ranges 6,600-9,100 feet (2,012-2,773 m), at which some people may feel the effects of altitude: lightheadedness, headaches, and shortness of breath. Drink lots of water to counter dehydration.

The busy season is **April-October.** Make advance reservations for lodging and camping. **September-October** are choice hiking months—the weather is at its best and the crowds are slightly smaller, although nighttime temperatures in late October can dip well below freezing. The high elevation means it's usually much cooler here than at Utah's other national parks. Expect pleasantly warm days in summer, frosty nights in spring and autumn, and snow at almost any time of year. The visitors center,

▼ SILENT CITY IN WINTER

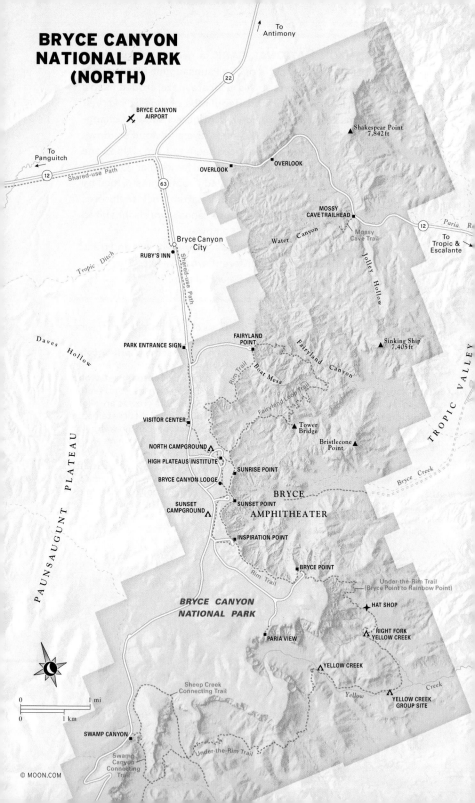

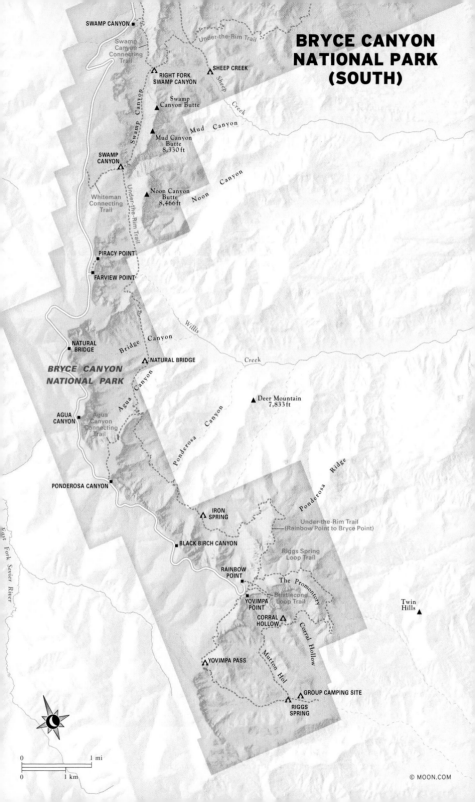

Top ❸

① TAKE IN PANORAMAS FROM SUNRISE AND SUNSET POINTS

VIEW FROM SUNSET POINT

Sunrise and Sunset Points overlook stunning canyon scenery all through the day, but their names indicate when best to visit for photographing the colors below. About 1 mile (1.6 km) south of the visitors center on side spur roads, the points are connected by a wheelchair-accessible paved section of the Rim Trail (1 mi/1.6 km rt, 30 min, easy). Panoramas from each point take in large areas of Bryce Amphitheater and beyond. The lofty Aquarius and Table Cliff Plateaus rise along the skyline to the northeast. At Sunset Point, rangers also give geology talks (30 min, times vary, summer).

② VIEW HOODOOS FROM INSPIRATION POINT

HOODOOS FROM INSPIRATION POINT

Weathering along vertical joints has cut many rows of narrow gullies, some more than 200 feet (61 m) deep. The result is a fantastical maze of hoodoos in the **Silent City.** To overlook this wonder, drive south on the park road (no trailers) about 2 miles (3.2 km), turning left onto Bryce Point Road and then left again to reach **Inspiration Point.** A short but steep walk ascends **Upper Inspiration Point** (0.4 mi/0.6 km rt, 15 min, easy); you can also take in the scenery from two lower points.

③ TOP OUT AT YOVIMPA AND RAINBOW POINTS

VIEW OF THE VALLEY FROM RAINBOW POINT

The land drops away in rugged canyons at the end of the scenic drive (17 mi/27 km south of the visitors center, no trailers). At an elevation of 9,115 feet (2,778 m), this is the highest area of the park; some people may feel light-headed and easily winded at this elevation. **Rainbow Point** is a few footsteps north of the parking lot, where views take in the Pink Cliffs and hoodoos. Walk south of the parking lot to **Yovimpa Point** (0.2 mi/0.3 km rt, 10 min, easy) for a bigger view of the Grand Staircase, descending eastward in multicolored plateaus.

ONE DAY IN BRYCE CANYON

Get up early and catch the free park shuttle so you don't miss the scene at **Sunrise Point.** If you don't want to hike down and climb back up the **Queen's Garden and Navajo Loop Trail,** take a walk along the **Rim Trail.** After lunch, catch the shuttle to **Inspiration Point** for huge views of Bryce Amphitheater and out across layers of plateaus. Hike to **Bryce Point** to catch the return shuttle.

scenic drive, and a campground stay open year-round, but snow can close some trails and the Scenic Drive at 3 miles (4.8 km) past the visitors center.

ENTRANCE AND FEES

The entrance fee is $35 per vehicle ($30 motorcycle, $20 individual) and good for seven days. The park entrance is on UT 63 past Ruby's Inn; fee stations are inside the park adjacent to the visitors center. Buy entrance passes in advance online (www.recreation.gov).

VISITORS CENTERS

At the **visitors center** (435/834-5322, 8am-8pm daily May-Sept., 8am-6pm daily Apr. and Oct., 8am-4:30pm daily Nov.-Mar.), geologic exhibits illustrate how the land was formed and how it has changed. Historical displays interpret the Paiute people, early explorers,

and the first settlers. Rangers guide short hikes (mid-May-early Sept.), give daily geology talks (winter), and lead full moon hikes among the hoodoos (tickets by lottery, dates vary). As an International Dark Sky Park, Bryce hosts an annual Astronomy Festival (4 days, June) and gives summer night sky presentations often with telescope viewing. On UT 63, the visitors center is adjacent to the park entrance fee station.

SCENIC DRIVE

The 19-mile (31 km, one-way, no trailers south of Sunset Point Campground) **park road** is a scenic drive with spurs shooting eastward to impressive overlooks that also serve as trailheads into the canyons. Snow and storms may temporarily close this road in winter at Gate 3 (3 mi/4.8 km past the visitors center). Very little of the canyon is visible from the road, so you'll need

▼ SUNRISE AT BRYCE POINT

to stop at viewpoints, making the adventure 2-3 hours. To contend with crowds, get an early start driving the complete road first; then stop on your return for easier right-turn access into the overlooks. Check the NPS app (download it before leaving home) for the self-guided audio tour.

SIGHTS

FAIRYLAND POINT

From **Fairyland Point,** whimsical forms line Fairyland Canyon a short distance below, beckoning you to descend into the "fairyland." To reach the turnoff, drive north 0.3 mile (0.5 km) inside the park boundary, then turn east and go 1 mile (1.6 km).

BRYCE POINT

A spectacular sunrise location, **Bryce Point** overlooks the south end of Bryce Amphitheater with a full view of its intricate geology. It also yields expansive scenery to the north and east. At **Paria View,** cliffs drop precipitously into the headwaters of Yellow Creek, a tributary of the Paria River. Look for a section of the Under-the-Rim Trail winding up a hillside near the mouth of the amphitheater below. Distant views take in the Paria River Canyon, White Cliffs (Navajo sandstone), and Navajo Mountain. Drive 1.2 miles (1.9 km) south of the visitors center and turn left on Bryce Point Road for 2 miles (3.2 km) to reach Bryce Point. Backtrack 0.5 mile (0.8 km) and turn left for 0.4 mile (0.6 km) for Paria View.

FARVIEW POINT

The sweeping panorama of **Farview Point** takes in levels of the Grand Staircase that include the Aquarius and Table Cliff Plateaus to the northeast, Kaiparowits Plateau to the east, and White Cliffs to the southeast. Look beyond the White Cliffs to see a section of the Kaibab Plateau that forms the North Rim of the Grand Canyon in

▼ NATURAL BRIDGE

CHINESE WALL ON FAIRYLAND LOOP TRAIL

Arizona. The point is over 9 miles (14.5 km) south of the visitors center.

NATURAL BRIDGE

This large **Natural Bridge** spans 54 feet (16.5 m) and is 95 feet (29 m) high. Despite its name, the arch was formed by weathering from rain and freezing water, not by stream erosion like a true natural bridge. Once the opening reached ground level, runoff began to enlarge the hole and dig a gully through it. It is just off the road to the east, 1.9 miles (3.1 km) past Farview Point.

AGUA AND PONDEROSA CANYONS

You can admire sheer cliffs and hoodoos from the **Agua Canyon Overlook** (1.5 mi/2.4 km south of Natural Bridge).

HIKE THE NAVAJO LOOP TRAIL.

Best Hike

QUEEN'S GARDEN AND NAVAJO LOOP TRAIL

DISTANCE: 3.5 miles (5.6 km) round-trip
DURATION: 2.5-3 hours
ELEVATION CHANGE: 600 feet (183 m)
EFFORT: moderate
TRAILHEAD: Sunrise Point

From Sunrise Point, this loop drops into the middle of Bryce Amphitheater, starting with the less steep **Queen's Garden Trail.** Colorful hoodoos line the trail as it descends through switchbacks and tunnels while absorbing views of the greater amphitheater. At the end of a short spur trail stands a hoodoo resembling a portly Queen Victoria. Return back up the trail from here for a shorter hike (1.8 mi/2.9 km rt, 1.5 hrs). Continuing on the main trail, the route drops and climbs to **Navajo Loop,** where the choice of routes begins for the steep climb to the rim. At the signed junction, one trail goes up the deep, dark, and narrow long canyon of Wall Street (closed in winter), and the other (open year-round) passes Two Bridges and Thor's Hammer. Both end with switchbacks climbing to the rim at Sunset Point. Finish the loop with an easy walk east along the **Rim Trail** to Sunrise Point. Other options include reversing the loop, hiking only the **Navajo Loop Trail** (1.3 mi/2.1 km rt, 1.5 hrs, moderate), or connecting with the **Peekaboo Loop Trail.**

SWITCHBACKS ON NAVAJO LOOP TRAIL

With a little imagination, you may be able to pick out the Hunter and the Rabbit below. The **Ponderosa Canyon Overlook** (1 mi/1.6 km south of Agua Canyon Overlook) offers a panorama similar to that at Farview Point.

RECREATION

HIKING

The **Rim Trail** (11 mi/17.7 km rt, 5-6 hrs, easy) follows the edge of Bryce Amphitheater between **Fairyland** and **Bryce Points** (5.5 mi/8.8 km one-way). Most people just walk sections of it on leisurely strolls, use the trail to connect with other routes, or create point-to-point hikes returning via the shuttle, which stops at Sunrise, Sunset, Inspiration, and Bryce Points. Between **Sunrise** and **Sunset Points** (0.5 mi/0.8 km one-way), the trail is paved and nearly level, wheelchair-accessible, and closest to the lodge. Between **Inspiration** and **Bryce Points** (1.5 mi/2.4 km one-way, 1 hr) the route overlooks the Silent City hoodoo maze on a gently rolling trail.

The **Fairyland Loop Trail** (8 mi/12.9 km rt, 4-5 hrs, strenuous) winds in and out of colorful rock spires in the northern part of Bryce Amphitheater and includes views of Tower Bridge. The route gains and loses elevation several times, including the climb to exit to the rim (2,309 ft/704 m), making the trail feel much longer. You can start the loop from Fairyland Point or Sunrise Point, connecting the two via the Rim Trail.

From Bryce Point, the steep **Peekaboo Loop Trail** (5.5 mi/8.8 km rt, 3-4 hrs, strenuous), which requires clockwise travel only around the loop, is loaded thick with hoodoos. The trail tours the southern part of Bryce Amphitheater, which has some of the most striking rock features, including the Cathedral and Wall of Windows. You can also start from Sunset Point (5.5 mi/8.8 km rt via Navajo Loop Trail) or from Sunrise Point (7 mi/11.3 km rt via Queen's Garden Trail).

The **Bristlecone Loop Trail** (1 mi/1.6 km rt, 30 min, easy) begins from either Rainbow or Yovimpa Point and goes to ancient bristlecone pines—some 1,800 years old—along the rim. Viewpoints include the Four Corners.

BACKPACKING

Although backpacking in Bryce is strenuous due to copious ups and downs, fewer people and dark skies for stargazing are the rewards. Novices can do the **Riggs Spring Loop Trail** (8.8 mi/14.2 km), but the rugged **Under-the-Rim Trail** (22.9 mi/36.9 km) requires route-finding skills. Pick up **permits** ($10, plus $5 pp/day) for designated campsites up to 48 hours in advance at the visitors center. Use shuttles for point-to-point hikes. Approved bear canisters are required; the visitors center loans out canisters for free.

HORSEBACK RIDING

Wranglers lead trail rides April-October. **Canyon Trail Rides** (Lodge at Bryce Canyon, 435/679-8665, www.canyonrides.com, Apr.-Oct.) offers guided two- or three-hour rides that descend to the canyon floor; the longer ride follows the Peekaboo Loop Trail.

WHERE TO STAY
INSIDE THE PARK

Advance reservations at lodges and campgrounds are imperative for April-October; make them as soon as reservations are accepted. Due to the high elevation, sleeping may be difficult for some.

TUNNEL ON QUEEN'S GARDEN TRAIL

THE HOODOOS

About 60 million years ago, sediments filtered into a large body of water named Lake Flagstaff. Silt, calcium carbonate, and other minerals settled on the lake bottom. These sediments consolidated and became the Claron Formation, a soft, silty limestone with some shale and sandstone. Lake Flagstaff disappeared long before the land began to rise with the Colorado Plateau uplift about 16 million years ago. Uneven pressures beneath the plateau caused it to break along fault lines into a series of smaller plateaus at different levels, collectively known as the Grand Staircase. Bryce Canyon National Park occupies part of one of these plateaus—the Paunsaugunt.

The spectacular Pink Cliffs on the park's east edge contain the famous erosional features known as hoodoos, carved in the Claron Formation. Variations in hardness of the rock layers result in these strange features. Water flows through cracks, wearing away softer rock around hard erosion-resistant caps. When a cap becomes so undercut that the overhang allows water to drip down, a "neck" of rock is left below the harder cap. Iron and manganese provide the distinctive coloring.

The hoodoos continue to change—new ones form and old ones ebb away. Wind plays little role in creating this landscape; it's the freezing and thawing, snowmelt, and rainwater that dissolve weak layers, pry open cracks, and carve out the forms. The plateau cliffs, meanwhile, recede at a rate of about 1 foot (0.3 m) every 50-65 years; look for trees on the rim that now overhang the abyss. Listen, and you might hear pebbles plinking away down the steep slopes.

The **Lodge at Bryce Canyon** (877/386-4383, http://brycecanyonforever.com, Mar.-Oct., rooms from $135, cabins $231), a National Historic Landmark, is the only lodge inside the park. Accommodations include lodge suites, motel-style guest rooms, and lodgepole pine cabins. Horseback rides and park tours depart from the lodge, which also hosts evening entertainment and ranger talks. Make reservations 13 months in advance. The lodge's **dining room** (7am-10am, 11:30am-3pm, and 5pm-10pm daily Apr.-Oct.) is classy and atmospheric, with a large stone fireplace and white tablecloths. A short walk from the main lodge is **Valhalla Pizzeria and Coffee Shop** (noon-8pm daily mid-May-mid-Sept.).

▲ HOODOOS OF BRYCE CANYON

The park has two campgrounds ($20 tents, $30 RVs). Plan to arrive early to claim first-come, first-served sites at **Sunset Campground** (99 sites, mid-Apr.-Oct.), which is across the road from Sunset Point. The **North Campground** (96 sites, year-round) is near the visitors center. Make **reservations** (877/444-6777, www.recreation.gov) six months in advance for late May-early October; otherwise, sites are first come, first served (early Oct.-late May).

OUTSIDE THE PARK

On UT 63 just north of the park boundary, **Best Western Ruby's Inn** (26 S. Main St., 435/834-5341 or 866/866-6616, www.rubysinn.com, from $80, year-round) has a hotel, dining, and a general store, plus recreational outfitters, entertainment, and shopping.

Tropic has a cache of motels, and **Panguitch** is a stopover on the road between Zion and Bryce Canyon National Parks, with reasonably priced motels and good dining. Dixie

SURROUNDED BY HOODOOS, FAIRYLAND LOOP TRAIL

BRYCE CANYON SHUTTLE BUS

National Forest has three Forest Service campgrounds.

GETTING THERE

AIR

Salt Lake City International Airport (SLC, 776 N. Terminal Dr., 801/575-2400, www.slcairport.com) is a four-hour drive (275 mi/445 km) via I-15 south to the park. **McCarran International Airport** (LAS, 5757 Wayne Newton Blvd., 702/261-5211, www.mccarran.com) in Las Vegas, Nevada, is another option, with a four-hour drive via I-15 north to the park. Both airports have car rentals.

CAR

Two routes go to Bryce, both with captivating scenery. From Bryce Junction (7 mi/11 km south of Panguitch at the intersection of US 89 and UT 12), head 14 miles (23 km) east on UT 12 to the park turnoff on UT 63. From Escalante, it's 46 miles (74 km) west on UT 12 to the turnoff onto UT 63 for Bryce. Once on UT 63, drive the final 4 miles (6.4 km) into the park (winter snows occasionally close this section).

GETTING AROUND

You can drive your own vehicle into Bryce Canyon National Park. However, trailers cannot go past Sunset Campground. For day visitors, trailer parking is available at the visitors center. For free **parking** to catch shuttles, park at the visitors center or near Ruby's Inn, outside the park entrance.

SHUTTLE BUS

During the summer, the National Park Service runs the **Bryce Canyon Shuttle** (every 15-20 min, 8am-8pm daily mid-May-Sept., shorter hours off-season, free) from the shuttle parking and boarding area at the intersection of UT 12 and UT 63 to the visitors center, with stops at Ruby's Inn and Ruby's Campground. From the visitors center, the shuttle travels to the park's developed areas, including all the main viewpoints, Sunset Campground, and Bryce Canyon Lodge.

TOURS

Free **shuttle bus tours** (435/834-5290, 9am and 1:30pm daily mid-Apr.-mid-Oct., reservations required) go all the way to Rainbow Point. Make reservations at Ruby's Inn, Ruby's Campground, or the shuttle parking area.

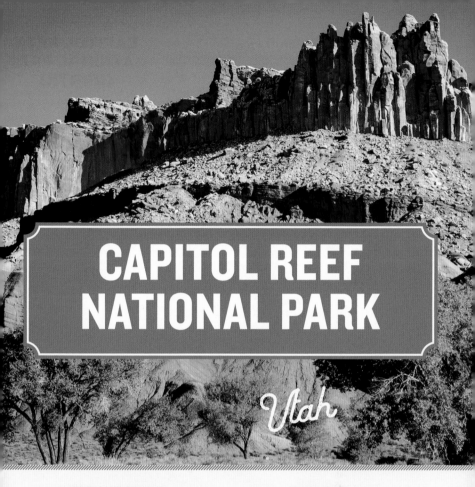

CAPITOL REEF
NATIONAL PARK

Utah

KEEPSAKE STAMPS ▼▼▼

WEBSITE:
www.nps.gov/care

PHONE NUMBER:
435/425-3791

VISITATION RANK:
20

WHY GO:
See spectacular cliffs
and colorful geology.

▲ CAPITOL REEF NATIONAL
PARK'S PAINTED DESERT

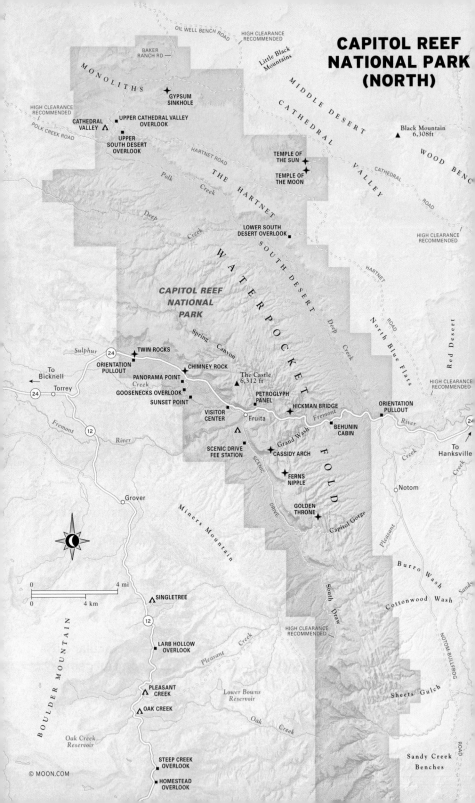

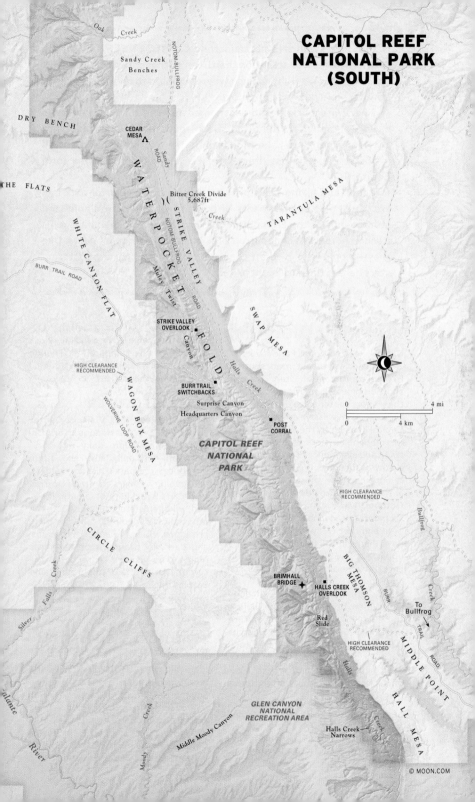

CAPITOL REEF
NATIONAL PARK
(SOUTH)

Oak Creek

Sandy Creek Benches

DRY BENCH

NOTOM-BULLFROG

CEDAR MESA

Sandy Road

THE FLATS

WATERPOCKET FOLD

Bitter Creek Divide 5,687ft

STRIKE VALLEY

NOTOM-BULLFROG ROAD

Creek

TARANTULA MESA

WHITE CANYON FLAT

BURR TRAIL ROAD

Miley Twist

SWAP MESA

STRIKE VALLEY OVERLOOK

Canyon

Halls Creek

HIGH CLEARANCE RECOMMENDED

WAGON BOX MESA

BURR TRAIL SWITCHBACKS

WOLVERINE LOOP ROAD

Surprise Canyon
Headquarters Canyon

POST CORRAL

CAPITOL REEF NATIONAL PARK

HIGH CLEARANCE RECOMMENDED

Bullfrog

CIRCLE CLIFFS

Creek

Falls Creek

Silver

BRIMHALL BRIDGE

HALLS CREEK OVERLOOK

Red Slide

BIG THOMSON MESA

BURR

HIGH CLEARANCE RECOMMENDED

To Bullfrog

TRAIL

MIDDLE POINT

ROAD

Escalante River

Moody Creek

Middle Moody Canyon

GLEN CANYON NATIONAL RECREATION AREA

Halls Creek

Halls Creek Narrows

HALL MESA

0   4 mi
0   4 km

© MOON.COM

Named for its white Navajo sandstone, **CAPITOL REEF NATIONAL PARK** receives less attention than Utah's other parks. However, it is special in its own right, a place where sculpted rock layers in a rainbow of colors put on a fine show.

The Waterpocket Fold—so named for the many small pools of water trapped by the tilted strata—extends 100 miles (161 km) between Thousand Lake Mountain in the north and Lake Powell in the south. Its most dramatic cliffs and rock formations form Capitol Reef.

Roads and hiking trails provide access to the colorful rock layers. You'll also see remnants of human history—petroglyphs and storage bins of the Fremont people and Ancestral Puebloans, plus a schoolhouse and other structures built by Mormon pioneers. Like these people who lived off the land, you can soak up the glittering stars here in the dark night skies.

PLANNING YOUR TIME

Capitol Reef National Park flanks UT 24, a major east-west road south of I-70 in south-central Utah. Travelers short on time will enjoy a quick stop at the visitors center and a drive on UT 24 through an impressive cross section of Capitol Reef cut by the Fremont River.

You can see more of the park, hike trails, and experience the night sky with a stay of 2-4 days. Visiting the park's remote north or south require several more days. Crowds show up **April-October.** Make camping reservations six months in advance.

In **summer** (May-Sept.), expect hot days (highs in the upper 80s-low 90s/ upper 20s-low 30s C) and cool nights. Late afternoon thunderstorms are common in July-August; impending storms are warnings for flash flooding. Winter brings cool days (highs in the 40s/4ºC) and night temperatures in the low 20s and teens (-6ºC and below). Snow accents the colored rocks while rarely hindering traffic on the main highway. But it may halt travel on back roads and trails before the sun quickly melts it.

ENTRANCES AND FEES

The entrance fee is $20 per vehicle ($15 motorcycle, $10 individual). The entrance fee is only collected for vehicles on the Scenic Drive; a self-pay kiosk is just past the campground. Though UT 24 bisects Capitol Reef National Park, driving the road is free.

VISITORS CENTER

At the **Capitol Reef Visitors Center** (Hwy. 24/52 West Headquarters Dr., Torrey, 8am-4:30pm daily mid-May-Oct., 9am-4pm daily Nov.-Feb.), a film introduces the park's history, wildlife, and geology. Hikers can pick up trail maps and checklists of plants, birds, and wildlife. Easter through October, rangers offer geology talks, evening programs, Junior Ranger Programs, and dark sky programs on moonless nights. The visitors center is at the turnoff for Fruita Campground and Scenic Drive.

SIGHTS

TWIN ROCKS, CHIMNEY ROCK, AND THE CASTLE

From the west, **UT 24** drops from the broad mountain valley near Torrey to Sulphur Creek, with dramatic rock formations soaring to the horizon. A huge amphitheater of stone rings the basin, with formations such as **Twin Rocks, Chimney Rock,** and the **Castle** glowing in deep red, blue, and yellow tones.

Top ❸

❶ WATCH THE SUN SET AT SUNSET POINT

Enjoy panoramic views of the Fremont River gorge, the Capitol Reef cliffs, and the distant Henry Mountains at **Sunset Point.** Plan your evening around viewing the sunset; it's worth hanging out for the whole show. From the Goosenecks Overlook parking area, waltz along the slickrock trail to Sunset Point (0.8 mi/1.3 km rt, 20 min, easy). Bring a flashlight and use caution when hiking back in the dark.

SUNSET FROM SUNSET POINT

❷ ADMIRE PETROGLYPHS FROM THE PAST

The Fremont people lived in Capitol Reef from 600 to 1300 CE and left their **petroglyphs** carved and pecked into Wingate sandstone cliffs. A pullout 1.1 miles (1.8 km) east of the visitors center on the north side of UT 24 accesses two short wheelchair-accessible boardwalks. The closest one has a spotting scope for viewing. The Fremont petroglyphs here include several mountain sheep and human figures with headdresses. The east boardwalk includes depictions of a necklace and other animals. Rangers give regular talks about the Fremont people (times vary, May-Oct., free). Photos are best in morning shade before stark sun and tree shadows arrive.

❸ TOUR SCENIC DRIVE

Before departing on the out-and-back **Scenic Drive** (16-21 mi/26-34 km rt, 1.5 hrs), pick up an interpretive brochure at the visitors center. The paved road with gravel spurs takes in 11 geologic stops with spires, escarpments, canyons, buttes, mud cracks, and ripple marks.

From the visitors center, Scenic Drive climbs up a desert slope, with the rock walls of the Waterpocket Fold rising to the east. Turn eastward off the pavement to explore **Grand Wash** (1 mi/1.6 km one-way). The dirt road follows a dry sandy channel through a twisting gulch lined with sheer rock walls and terminates at Cassidy Arch Trailhead.

Back on the paved road, continue south past **Slickrock Divide.** The reef's rock deepens into a ruby red and erosion forms odd columns and spires. Most striking is the white-topped red rock of **Egyptian Temple.** Turn east onto a gravel road to tour the narrow convolutions of **Capitol Gorge** (2.2 mi/3.5 km one-way), the route of the main state highway through the reef for 80 years. Capitol Gorge Trail departs from the terminus.

Before returning on Scenic Drive, high-clearance vehicles can add on the dirt **Pleasant Creek Road** (3 mi/4.8 km one-way). It trots south below the reef to Pleasant Creek, fed by perennial waters from Boulder Mountain that cut a deep canyon.

PANORAMA POINT

Take in the sweeping view from **Panorama Point** (2.6 mi/4.2 km west of the visitors center). To reach the point, follow signs south to Panorama Point. Enjoy views of Capitol Reef, the distant Henry Mountains to the east, and looming Boulder Mountain to the west. It's a great stargazing location on moonless nights.

GOOSENECKS OVERLOOK

The Goosenecks of Sulphur Creek are located on a gravel road 1 mile (1.6 km) south of Panorama Point. A walk (0.2 mi/0.3 km rt, 5 min, easy) leads to the **Goosenecks Overlook** on the rim with dizzying views of the creek below. The overlook at **Sunset Point** (0.8 mi/1.3 km rt, 20 min, easy) views Capitol Reef cliffs and distant Henry Mountains.

FRUITA

The Fruita area contains a breadth of history stretching along the narrow Fremont River canyon. On the north side of UT 24 is the **Fruita Schoolhouse,** a one-room log structure from 1896. Although the schoolhouse is locked, you can peer inside the windows. Farther east is the small **Behunin Cabin.** Around 1883, Elijah Cutler Behunin used blocks of sandstone to build it for his wife and 11 of their 13 children to share (the kids slept outside). Peek through the window to see the dirt-floor structure.

In the **Fruita Rural Historic District,** south of the visitors center on Scenic Drive, you'll pass orchards where you can pick cherries, apricots, apples, pears, or peaches in season. (Call the summer fruit hotline at 435/425-3791 for information.) A **blacksmith shop** displays tools, harnesses, farm

HISTORIC SCHOOLHOUSE IN FRUITA

CAPITOL GORGE TRAIL

machinery, and Fruita's first tractor. **Ripple Rock Nature Center** has activities and exhibits for kids. Typical of rural Utah farmhouses of the early 1900s, the **Gifford Homestead** houses cultural demonstrations and sells handmade baked goods and gifts. Rangers conduct evening Star Talks here (30 min, dates and times vary, free).

CATHEDRAL VALLEY

Only the most adventurous travelers enter the remote canyons of the park's northern district of Cathedral Valley. Four-wheel-drive roads lead through stately sandstone monoliths, volcanic remnants, badlands country, many low mesas, and vast sand flats. The district's two main roads—**Hartnet Road** and **Cathedral Road** (aka Caineville Wash Rd.)—combine with a short stretch of UT 24 to form a loop, with a campground at their junction. Sights include the Temples of the Sun and Moon.

NIGHT SKIES

As an **International Dark Sky Park,** Capitol Reef excels for stargazing. You can attend ranger programs or the annual **Heritage Starfest** (2 days, Sept.), but it's perfect for self-guided stargazing. While remote Cathedral Valley and Cedar Mesa Campgrounds have dark locales, you'll also get away from lights at spots easier to reach: Fruita Campground amphitheater, Panorama Point, and Slickrock Divide on Scenic Drive.

GIFFORD HOMESTEAD

THE WATERPOCKET FOLD

About 65 million years ago, well before the Colorado Plateau uplifted, sedimentary rock layers in south-central Utah buckled, forming a steep-sided monocline, a rock fold in horizontal layers with one very steep side. A monocline is a "step-up" in the rock layers along an underlying fault. On the west side of the Waterpocket Fold, the rock lifted more than 7,000 feet (2,134 m) higher than the layers to the east. The 100-mile-long (161-km) fold eroded over millions of years, which slowly removed the upper layers to reveal the warped sedimentary layers at its base. Continued erosion of the sandstone has left many basins, or "water pockets." Desert animals depend on these seasonal water sources, often called "water tanks," and they were a water source for the Fremont people. Erosion of the tilted rock layers continues today, forming colorful cliffs, massive domes, soaring spires, stark monoliths, twisting canyons, and graceful arches. One of the best viewpoints to get a sense of the Waterpocket Fold is along **Burr Trail Road,** which climbs up the fold between Boulder and Notom-Bullfrog Road.

HICKMAN BRIDGE

SCENIC DRIVE

NOTOM-BULLFROG ROAD

Notom-Bullfrog Road (70 mi/113 km) crosses some of the younger geologic layers of the **Waterpocket Fold.** Half of this road is outside the national park. The northern and southern segments are paved but 35 miles (57 km) in the middle are bumpy dirt, gravel, and washboards. It starts 9 miles (14 km) east of the visitors center outside the park off UT 24. After passing several washes and a private ranch, the dirt road reenters the park between miles 20-37.5 with options to explore **Cedar Mesa Campground** (mile 22.3), **Burr Trail Road** (mile 34.1), and **Surprise Canyon** (mile 36). The road ends at Bullfrog Marina in Glen Canyon National Recreation Area.

HIKING

UT 24

From 3 miles (4.8 km) west of the visitors center, **Chimney Rock Loop Trail** (3.6 mi/5.8 km rt, 2 hrs, moderate) ascends 590 feet (180 m) in elevation to a ridge overlooking Chimney Rock, a fluted spire of dark red rock capped by a block of hard sandstone.

From 2 miles (3.2 km) east of the visitors center, **Hickman Bridge Trail** (1.8 mi/2.9 km rt, 1 hr, moderate) follows the Fremont River's green banks a short distance before climbing a dry

◄ NATURAL WATER TANKS ABOVE CAPITOL GORGE   CHIMNEY ROCK

Best Hike

GRAND WASH TRAIL

DISTANCE: 4.4 miles (7.1 km) round-trip
DURATION: 2-3 hours
ELEVATION CHANGE: 200 feet (61 m)
EFFORT: easy
TRAILHEAD: 4.5 miles (7.2 km) east of the visitors center on UT 24

One of only five canyons cutting completely through the reef, **Grand Wash** offers easy hiking, where the lighting shifts across tall shadowed canyon walls. There's no trail—just follow the dry riverbed. (Flash floods can occur during storms.) A short distance from the trailhead, canyon walls rise 800 feet (244 m) above the floor and narrow to as little as 20 feet (6 m) in width; this stretch of trail is known as the **Narrows.** After the Narrows, the wash widens, and wildflowers grow. You can add on the **Cassidy Arch Trail** (3.4 mi/5.5 km rt, 2-3 hrs, strenuous) that climbs the north wall of Grand Wash near the end of the trail before returning.

ENTERING THE GRAND WASH NARROWS

wash shaded by cottonwood, juniper, and piñon trees. The trail terminates under the 133-foot-long (40-m) natural bridge, eroded from the Kayenta Formation.

For longer options, take the Hickman Bridge Trail for 0.25 mile (0.4 km), then turn right at the signed fork onto the **Rim Overlook Trail** (4.6 mi/7.4 km rt, 3.5 hrs, strenuous). It climbs 1,100 feet (335 m) to an overlook with panoramic views of Fruita and the Fremont River valley below, the great cliffs of Capitol Reef above, and the Henry Mountains to the southeast. Continue ascending another 2.2 miles (3.5 km) to reach **Navajo Knobs** (9.4 mi/15.1 km rt, 4-5 hrs, strenuous) via a series of rock-cairned slickrock benches. The route rims the Waterpocket Fold and finishes with a magnificent panorama at the rocky knobs.

NATURAL ROCK SCULPTURE ON FRYING PAN TRAIL

FRUITA

From the Fruita blacksmith shop, the **Fremont Gorge Overlook trail** (4.6 mi/7.4 km rt, 2.5 hrs, strenuous) crosses a native prairie on Johnson Mesa and steeply climbs 1,090 feet (332 m) to the overlook above the Fremont River. From Fruita Campground amphitheater, the **Fremont River Trail** (2 mi/3.2 km rt, 1 hr, moderate) passes orchards along the Fremont River to climb sloping rock strata to a viewpoint of Fruita, Boulder Mountain, and the reef.

Across the road from Fruita Campground, **Cohab Canyon Trail** (3.4 mi/5.5 km rt, 2 hrs, moderate) follows steep switchbacks, then gentler grades into an upper canyon hiding multiple side slots. On the east side of the canyon, a junction turns off onto the **Frying Pan Trail** (5.8 mi/9.3 km rt, 2 hrs, moderately strenuous) for an up-and-down romp through slickrock, canyons, and piñons among red rock formations as the views get bigger and better. On its east end, it connects with the Cassidy Arch Trail. For those looking for a bigger adventure and who can set up a car shuttle, you can hike Cohab Canyon, Frying Pan, Cassidy Arch, and Grand Wash (10.2 mi/16.4 km, 6 hrs, strenuous) to finish at Grand Wash Trailhead on UT 24.

SCENIC DRIVE

Off Grand Wash Road, the **Cassidy Arch Trail** (3.4 mi/5.5 km rt, 2-3 hrs, strenuous) climbs the north wall of Grand Wash, then winds across slickrock to a vantage point close to the arch.

The **Old Wagon Trail Loop** (3.8 mi/6.1 km rt, 2 hrs, moderate) crosses a wash, then ascends steadily through piñon and juniper woodland via a wagon road on Miners Mountain to a high knoll for the views of Capitol Reef. Find

SCENIC DRIVE THROUGH CAPITOL GORGE

the trailhead on the west side of Scenic Drive 0.7 mile (1.1 km) south of Slickrock Divide.

At the end of Scenic Drive, **Capital Gorge Road** terminates at a trailhead for two routes. On the **Capitol Gorge Trail** (2 mi/3.2 km rt, 1 hr, easy), Fremont petroglyphs appear on the left above the wash after 0.1 mile (0.2 km). The narrows of Capitol Gorge close in at 0.3 mile (0.5 km). In 0.5 mile (0.8 km), look for a pioneer register on the right to see the names and dates of early travelers and ranchers scratched in the canyon wall. At 0.75 mile (1.2 km), a spur trail goes left to climb to natural water tanks typical of those in the Waterpocket Fold. The **Golden Throne Trail** (4 mi/6.4 km rt, 4 hrs, strenuous) climbs 1,100 feet (335 m) in a steady grade to a viewpoint of the Golden Throne, a massive monolith of yellow-hued Navajo sandstone capped by a thin layer of red Carmel Formation.

BACKPACKING

Experienced backpackers can enjoy rugged routes of slickrock, slots, and canyons; most have minimal established trails. Pick up free permits at the visitors center, and consult about water sources, which may guide choices of routes. Camping is undesignated, so use Leave No Trace ethics in selecting a site.

▼ CASSIDY ARCH

A BOARDWALK-LINED TRAIL

WHERE TO STAY

INSIDE THE PARK

There are no accommodations or restaurants inside the park. Campgrounds have picnic tables and fire rings or grates, but no showers or hookups.

Surrounded by orchards and lush grass, **Fruita Campground** (year-round, 71 sites, $25) has drinking water (May-Oct.) and restrooms. Reserve sites (877/444-6777, www.recreation.gov) six months in advance for March-October, but they are first come, first served November to February.

Two year-round primitive campgrounds (free) have first-come, first-served sites, but no water. In the southern district is **Cedar Mesa Campground** (5 sites), 23 miles (37 km) on Notom-Bullfrog Road. In the northern district, **Cathedral Valley Campground** (6 sites, high-clearance vehicles recommended) is near the Hartnet Junction, about 30 miles (48 km) north of UT 24.

OUTSIDE THE PARK

At the junction of UT 12 and UT 24, the town of **Torrey** has several lodging options and a restaurant. Several Forest Service campgrounds are south of Torrey on Boulder Mountain along UT 12.

GETTING THERE AND AROUND

AIR

The closest international airport is **Salt Lake City International Airport** (SLC, 776 N. Terminal Dr., 801/575-2400, www.slcairport.com), 225 miles (360 km) north via I-15 to US 50 and UT 24. Rental cars are available.

CAR

There is no public transportation into or within the park; you'll need a car. Travelers coming from Zion and Bryce should head north on UT 12 from the town of Boulder. Twisty UT 12 will take you over Boulder Mountain to UT 24 at the town of Torrey; Capitol Reef is just 11 miles (18 km) east.

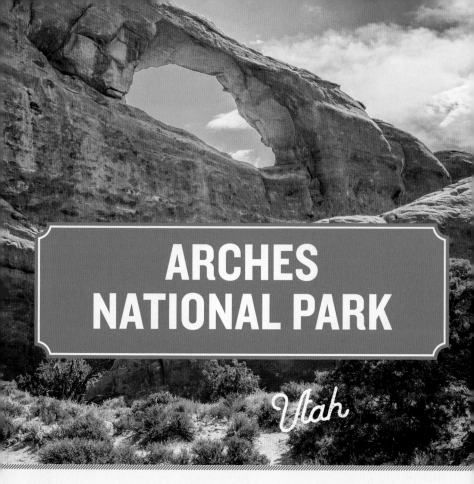

ARCHES NATIONAL PARK

Utah

WEBSITE:
www.nps.gov/arch

PHONE NUMBER:
435/719-2299

VISITATION RANK:
16

WHY GO:
Hike amid natural
sandstone arches.

KEEPSAKE STAMPS ▾▾▾

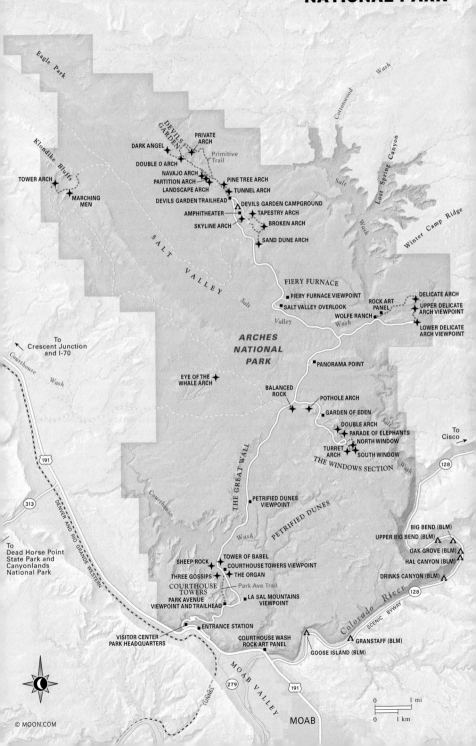

ARCHES
NATIONAL PARK

Eagle Park

Klondike Bluffs

TOWER ARCH

MARCHING MEN

DEVILS GARDEN

DARK ANGEL

PRIVATE ARCH

DOUBLE O ARCH

NAVAJO ARCH

PARTITION ARCH

LANDSCAPE ARCH

PINE TREE ARCH

TUNNEL ARCH

DEVILS GARDEN TRAILHEAD

DEVILS GARDEN CAMPGROUND

AMPHITHEATER

TAPESTRY ARCH

BROKEN ARCH

SKYLINE ARCH

SAND DUNE ARCH

Primitive Trail

SALT VALLEY

Salt Valley

FIERY FURNACE

FIERY FURNACE VIEWPOINT

SALT VALLEY OVERLOOK

ROCK ART PANEL

WOLFE RANCH

DELICATE ARCH

UPPER DELICATE ARCH VIEWPOINT

LOWER DELICATE ARCH VIEWPOINT

Cottonwood Wash

Lost Spring Canyon

Winter Camp Ridge

Salt Wash

ARCHES
NATIONAL
PARK

PANORAMA POINT

EYE OF THE WHALE ARCH

BALANCED ROCK

POTHOLE ARCH

GARDEN OF EDEN

DOUBLE ARCH

PARADE OF ELEPHANTS

NORTH WINDOW

TURRET ARCH

SOUTH WINDOW

THE WINDOWS SECTION

To Cisco

Salt Wash

THE GREAT WALL

Courthouse Wash

PETRIFIED DUNES VIEWPOINT

PETRIFIED DUNES

Salt Wash

128

BIG BEND (BLM)

UPPER BIG BEND (BLM)

OAK GROVE (BLM)

HAL CANYON (BLM)

DRINKS CANYON (BLM)

To Crescent Junction and I-70

191

DENVER AND RIO GRANDE WESTERN

313

To Dead Horse Point State Park and Canyonlands National Park

SHEEP ROCK

TOWER OF BABEL

COURTHOUSE TOWERS VIEWPOINT

THREE GOSSIPS

THE ORGAN

COURTHOUSE TOWERS

PARK AVENUE VIEWPOINT AND TRAILHEAD

Park Ave Trail

LA SAL MOUNTAINS VIEWPOINT

ENTRANCE STATION

VISITOR CENTER PARK HEADQUARTERS

COURTHOUSE WASH ROCK ART PANEL

GRANSTAFF (BLM)

GOOSE ISLAND (BLM)

Colorado River

SCENIC BYWAY

128

TUNNEL

279

MOAB VALLEY

191

MOAB

© MOON.COM

0   1 mi

0   1 km

More than 2,000 rock arches have formed within the maze of red sandstone fins at **ARCHES NATIONAL PARK**. It's the densest concentration of natural arches in the world. Balanced rocks and tall spires add to the splendor. These features formed from sands that bonded into Entrada Sandstone, then bulged upward into domes and cracked in parallel lines. Rain and wind erosion added the final touches of artistry.

While Ancestral Puebloans seasonally farmed the park area thousands of years ago, their descendants—the Acoma, Cochiti, Santa Clara, Taos, and Hopi peoples, among other groups—still find the park's rock art speaking their history. The Ute people also find their past in the large petroglyph panel near Wolfe Ranch, which documents acquisition of horses from the first Spanish in the area.

PLANNING YOUR TIME

Located in southeastern Utah about four hours from Salt Lake City, Arches is easy to reach via US 191. Due to its proximity to Island in the Sky in Canyonlands National Park, most visitors go to both on the same trip. Its position just outside Moab gives it loads of options for lodgings, camping, and dining; make reservations, as the town packs out in spring and fall. With no food services inside the park, bring a lunch and water. To visit all the stops on the park road and hike a few short trails takes all day.

March through October is high season; expect long entrance lines, congestion on the park road, and full parking lots at all sights and trailheads. Be flexible to return to locations later in the day if parking is not available. If possible, avoid the holidays and Utah school breaks (third week of Oct.). Unless you are camping inside the park, RV and trailer drivers are better off leaving rigs at campgrounds in Moab and renting a car if necessary to tour the park as oversize parking options are minimal. Make a **timed-entry reservation** three months in advance; for **camping,** make reservations six months in advance.

Fall and **spring** are the most popular times to visit, as daytime temperatures are moderate. Real desert heat sets in during late May-early June. Temperatures then soar into the 90s and 100s (32-38°C) at midday, although the dry air makes the heat more bearable. Early morning is the choice time for summer travel. Autumn begins after late summer rains end and lasts into November or even December; days are bright and sunny with ideal temperatures, but nights become cold.

ENTRANCES AND FEES

The sole entrance to Arches is 5 miles (8 km) north of downtown Moab on US 191. The entrance fee is $30 per vehicle ($25 motorcycle, $15 individual) and good for seven days.

Due to overcrowding, Arches requires **timed-entry reservations** (www.recreation.gov, $2) for visits from early April to early October (6am-5pm daily). This reservation is in addition to your entry fee but is not required if you have campground, backcountry, or Fiery Furnace reservations.

Reservations are released **three months in advance** for a month's worth of dates and **nightly** at 6pm (Mountain Time) for the next day. It's possible to enter the park before 6am or after 5pm without an entry reservation, but be prepared for long lines. Check online for updates to the reservation system.

VISITORS CENTERS

Past the park entrance, the **visitors center** (7:30am-6pm daily Mar.-Sept., 8am-5:30pm daily Oct., 8am-4:30pm daily Nov., 9am-4pm daily Dec.-Feb.) provides a good introduction to the area. Exhibits and a film cover rock

Top ❸

❶ EXPLORE THE WINDOWS

NORTH WINDOW

The Windows (12 mi/19 km from the entrance) area holds four massive arches. From the Windows parking area, a series of short easy trails lead to the arches. Portions are wheelchair-accessible on packed surfaces, but other sections have steps and uneven surfaces. Take the Windows Trailhead to walk below **North Window, South Window,** and **Turret Arch. Double Arch,** a short walk from the second trailhead, has two arches framing a large opening overhead. On the way back to the main park road, stop at **Garden of Eden Viewpoint** for a panorama of the Salt Valley.

❷ WRIGGLE THROUGH THE FIERY FURNACE

A labyrinth of red sandstone, the **Fiery Furnace** is a series of fins and slots that require using your hands and feet to shimmy over obstacles. There is no trail or route markers through this maze. The route is moderately strenuous with steep ledges, narrow cracks, a couple of jumps, and places where you must hoist yourself up off the ground. There is no turning back once the hike starts, so make sure you're physically prepared and properly equipped. You can join a **ranger-led hike** (twice daily May-Sept., 3 hrs, $16). Experienced hikers skilled with navigation can go self-guided ($10). **Permits** are required for both. **Reservations** (877/444-6777, www.recreation.gov) are released six months in advance for the ranger-led hike and seven days in advanced for self-guided permits; due to high demand, make reservations on the first day possible.

❸ CATCH THE SUNSET AND NIGHT SKY

Arrive an hour before sunset to join the hordes of photography fans waiting to snap photos of the sunset framed through **Delicate Arch.** Other features such as **Balanced Rock** and the reds of **Fiery Furnace** also light up at sunset. Then, after dark, this **International Dark Sky Park** is prime for viewing the Milky Way at the night sky viewing area at **Panorama Point,** a 20-minute drive from the visitors center. Located away from lights and in a wide-sky zone, the viewing area has seats specif-

MILKY WAY AT BALANCED ROCK

ically for stargazing, and on select summer nights, rangers offer telescope viewing. Other outstanding night sky viewing locations include **Balanced Rock Picnic Area** and **The Windows** area. For night sky viewing, use a red flashlight to protect your night vision and allow 30 minutes for your eyes to become accustomed to the dark.

BALANCED ROCK

layers, geology, human history, wildlife, and plants. Staff members can answer questions and issue backcountry permits.

SIGHTS

MOAB FAULT

A pullout for **Moab Fault** offers an amazing view of Moab Canyon and its huge fault. The rock layers on this side of the canyon have slipped down more than 2,600 feet (792 m) in relation to the other side.

PARK AVENUE

Great sandstone slabs form a skyline on each side of **Park Avenue,** a dry wash version of the famed New York City street. The large rock monoliths of **Courthouse Towers** rise on the west, followed by the sandstone towers forming the **Three Gossips.** You can also see these from the road at Courthouse Towers Viewpoint.

BALANCED ROCK

The gravity-defying **Balanced Rock** is a boulder more than 55 feet (17 m) high that rests precariously atop a 73-foot (22-m) pedestal. For a closer look, take the 0.3-mile (0.5-km) trail that encircles it.

FIERY FURNACE

A viewpoint off the park road offers a look into the **Fiery Furnace,** closely packed pink, orange, and red sandstone fins that form a maze of deep slots with many arches and at least one natural bridge. The Fiery Furnace gets its name from sandstone fins that can turn flaming red at sunrise or sunset.

▼ PARK AVENUE

SKYLINE ARCH

SCENIC DRIVE

Arches has one **main park road** (36 mi/58 km rt) that cruises past fantastical monoliths and the artistry of weathered red rocks. From the visitors center, the road begins a long but well-graded climb up the cliffs to the northeast.

After cresting onto the mesa top, you'll gaze out onto a landscape loaded with geological sights thrusting up from the sagebrush desert, including solidified dunes backdropped by the La Sal Mountains. Short, paved spurs turn off to sightseeing features and trailheads. The road terminates at Devils Garden Trailhead and campground.

Between March and October, expect traffic congestion and full parking lots, which may force you to bypass some sights and return later.

RECREATION
HIKING
Park Avenue

Named in a nod to New York City, **Park Avenue** (1 mi/1.6 km one-way, 30 min, moderate) is a dry wash rising on both sides with immense sandstone slabs. From the South Park Avenue Trailhead, the path drops down the wash as the large rock monoliths of **Courthouse Towers** rise on the west, followed by the sandstone towers forming the **Three Gossips.** The trail ends at North Park Avenue Trailhead, where you can start instead for an uphill hike or return up to the south trailhead.

HIKERS AT DELICATE ARCH

ONE DAY IN ARCHES

With the park's scenic drive and short hikes, even those who have only one day can explore its easily accessed arches. Drive the main park road to The Windows area, where you can walk to **North Window** and **South Window.** Stop to walk a little of **Park Avenue** before driving to the trailhead for the iconic freestanding **Delicate Arch.**

Sand Dune and Broken Arches

From the Sand Dune Arch parking area, a walk on red sand leads to the small ground-level **Sand Dune Arch** (0.3 mi/0.5 km rt, 20 min, easy) tucked within fins. The loop trail to **Broken Arch** (2 mi/3.2 km rt, 1 hr, easy), which isn't really broken, also goes through sand dunes, fins, and slickrock.

Skyline Arch

From the Skyline Arch parking area, **Skyline Arch Trail** (0.4 mi/0.6 km rt, 20 min, easy) trots to the base of the arch. In 1940, a giant boulder fell from its opening, doubling the size of the arch in just seconds.

Delicate Arch View

For distant views of the park's iconic arch, drive 1.2 miles (1.9 km) on Wolfe Ranch Road beyond Wolfe Ranch to **Delicate Arch Viewpoints** for a short wheelchair-accessible trail (300 ft/91 m rt, 10 min, easy) and a steeper trail (0.5 mi/0.8 km rt, 30 min, easy).

Devils Garden Loop

A full walk of **Devils Garden** (7.9 mi/12.6 km rt, 4 hrs, moderate) leads to eight arches, but you can also do a short hike with three arches. At Devils Garden Trailhead, you can pick up a trail guide. After the hard-packed trail skitters between huge rocks, a side spur drops to the right to two arches: Partway down, turn right to go to **Tunnel Arch,** with a symmetrical opening, and then return to this spur to descend and climb to **Pine Tree Arch,** named for piñon pine that once grew inside. Back on the main trail, continue north and take a left at the junction to ascend with rougher footing to several viewpoints of the 306-foot (93-m) **Landscape Arch.** It is one of the longest unsupported rock

PINE TREE ARCH

THE FIERY FURNACE

Best Hike

DELICATE ARCH TRAIL

DISTANCE: 3 miles (4.8 km) round-trip
DURATION: 2 hours
ELEVATION CHANGE: 480 feet (146 m)
EFFORT: moderately strenuous
TRAILHEAD: Wolfe Ranch

The freestanding **Delicate Arch** is a backcountry wonder. After a broad path through spring wildflowers hits the slickrock, the trail's angle changes to a steep climb up a huge slab marked by cairns. Then, the route winds through a sand and slickrock wash to cut around a large wall to come at the arch from behind. The final segment of trail follows slickrock ledges up to a small arch and then beyond to the natural amphitheater where Delicate Arch sits in a curved slickrock bowl. Sunset is popular due to the lighting on the arch. A spur trail near the trailhead leads to Ute petroglyphs depicting horses, riders, and a few bighorn sheep.

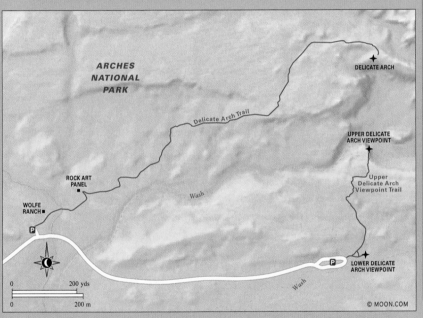

spans in the world. Turn around here for a shorter hike (1.9 mi/3.1 km rt, 1 hr, easy).

Beyond Landscape Arch, the trail narrows to reach the remains of **Wall Arch,** which collapsed in 2008. A short side trail branches off to the left to **Partition Arch** and **Navajo Arch.** The main trail continues to **Double O Arch,** with a large oval-shaped opening and a smaller hole underneath, followed by a cairned spur to **Dark Angel,** a distinctive rock pinnacle. The main trail becomes primitive to loop to a spur to **Private Arch** and then back to Landscape Arch via Fin Canyon.

BIKING

The rolling terrain of the main park road appeals to road cyclists. Relatively fit mountain bikers can go for the 24-mile (39-km) ride to **Tower Arch** and back via a dirt road. From the Devils Garden parking area, take Salt Valley Road for about 7.5 miles (12 km). Turn left onto a jeep road that leads to the "back door" to Tower Arch.

MOAB

The largest town in southeastern Utah, **Moab** makes an excellent base for exploring Arches and Canyonlands National Parks and the surrounding canyon country. Its backcountry mountain biking is world renowned, featuring slickrock, canyon, and technical trails. Rafting trips on the Colorado River are nearly as popular. Also possible are a host of other outdoor recreational diversions, including horseback riding, rock climbing, and off-road driving.

The **Moab Information Center** (25 E. Center St., 435/259-8825, www.discovermoab.com, 8am-7pm Mon.-Sat., 9am-6pm Sun.) is the best source for information about the area's recreational options. **Canyonlands Field Institute** (435/259-7750 or 800/860-5262, http://cfimoab.org) leads weekend day hikes (mid-Apr.-mid-Oct., from $480 per group, including transportation and fees) near Moab with a natural history emphasis.

Mountain Biking

Mountain biking season packs the area **mid-March to late May** and **mid-September to October.** The interconnected **MOAB Brand Trails** are best for beginners or riders who are new to slickrock. The super-technical **Slickrock Bike Trail** appeals to advanced and expert riders. Several shops offer guided mountain bike trips and rentals: **Rim Tours** (1233 S. US 191, 435/259-5223, www.rimtours.com), **Magpie Cycling** (711 N. 500 W., 435/259-4464, www.magpiecycling.com), **Western Spirit Cycling** (478 Mill Creek Dr., 435/259-8732, www.westernspirit.com), and **Escape Adventures** (Moab Cyclery, 391 S. Main St., 800/596-2953, www.escapeadventures.com).

Rafting

Outfitters offer both laid-back and exhilarating trips that range from daylong to multiday. Rafting season runs **April-September.** Most do-it-yourself river-runners obtain their permits by lottery (apply Jan.-Feb., Mar. drawing); the Moab Information Center's BLM ranger can advise on this process. The following outfitters offer guided rafting options:

Adrift Adventures (378 N. Main St., 435/259-8594, www.adrift.net)

Canyonlands Field Institute (800/860-5262, http://cfimoab.org)

Moab Adventure Center (225 S. Main St., 866/904-1163, www.moabadventurecenter.com)

Navtec Expeditions (321 N. Main St., 800/833-1278, www.navtec.com)

Red River Adventures (1140 S. Main St., 877/259-4046, www.redriveradventures.com)

Sheri Griffith Expeditions (2231 S. US 191, 435/259-8229 or 800/332-2439, www.griffithexp.com)

Camping

There are 27 **BLM campgrounds** ($20, first come, first served) in the Moab area. Plan to arrive early to claim a site in spring and fall. The campgrounds are concentrated on the banks of the Colorado River—along UT 128 toward Castle Valley, along UT 279 toward the potash factory, and along Kane Creek Road—and at the Sand Flats Recreation Area near the Slickrock Bike Trail. Only a few of these campgrounds can handle large RVs; none have hookups, and few have piped water. For a full list of BLM campgrounds and facilities, visit www.discovermoab.com.

LANDSCAPE ARCH

ROCK CLIMBING

Rock climbers find plenty of drool-worthy cracks and nubbins in the park. Most go for the sheer stone faces of **Park Avenue** or **Owl Rock,** the small owl-shaped tower on the Windows Road. Stop by the visitors center for a free **permit** (https://archespermits.nps.gov) and to learn of climbing route closures (generally Mar.-mid-Aug.) that protect raptors and bighorn sheep. **Pagan Mountaineering** (59 S. Main St., Moab, 435/259-1117, www.paganclimber.com) rents and sells climbing gear.

WHERE TO STAY

INSIDE THE PARK

Come prepared with a picnic lunch; there are no accommodations or food inside the park. Picnic areas with tables and toilets are at the visitors center, opposite Balanced Rock, Panorama Point, Delicate Arch viewpoint, and Devil's Garden.

Devils Garden Campground (877/444-6777, www.recreation.gov, year-round, $25) tucks some sites under rock formations while others offer great views. Reserve a site six months in advance for March-October as soon as the dates are released; the campground is first come, first served November to February. A camp host is on-site, and firewood is available ($5).

OUTSIDE THE PARK

Moab has copious accommodations, food, and services. Bureau of Land Management (BLM) campsites are on side routes off US 191: UT 313 on the way to Canyonlands National Park's Island in the Sky District and UT 128 along the Colorado River.

GETTING THERE AND AROUND

AIR

Salt Lake City International Airport (SLC, 776 N. Terminal Dr., 801/575-2400, www.slcairport.com) is 235 miles (380 km) north of Moab. The four-hour drive follows I-15, US 6, I-70, and US 191. Rental cars are available.

CAR

Arches National Park is 27 miles (43 km) south of I-70 and 5 miles (8 km) north of Moab, both off US 191. If you're driving from Moab, allow 15 minutes to reach the park; slow-moving RV traffic often crowds the route.

Parking for oversize vehicles inside Arches is limited. If possible, leave the RV or trailer at your campground.

TOURS

Canyonlands Field Institute (800/860-5262 or 435/259-7750, http://cfimoab.org) guides one-day and multiday educational adventures and programs in Arches.

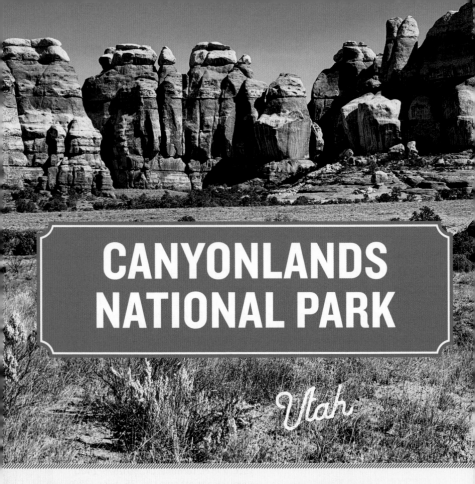

CANYONLANDS NATIONAL PARK

Utah

WEBSITE:
www.nps.gov/cany

PHONE NUMBER:
435/719-2313

VISITATION RANK:
28

WHY GO:
Explore Utah's
canyon country.

KEEPSAKE STAMPS ▼▼▼

▲ CHESLER PARK IN THE
NEEDLES DISTRICT

Utah's canyon country puts on a supreme performance in this vast park. The deeply entrenched Colorado and Green Rivers collide at its heart, then rage south as the mighty Colorado roars through tumultuous Cataract Canyon. The rivers split the park into distinct districts full of serrated cliffs, spires, boulders, and colorful rock that lights up at sunrise and sunset. Desert mesas plunge thousands of feet into canyon webs, some of which have seen little to no human exploration. In places, petroglyphs pay tribute to Ancestral Puebloans and the Fremont people, forebearers of the Ute and Paiute.

You won't find elaborate park facilities—most of **CANYONLANDS NATIONAL PARK** remains a primitive backcountry park prized by hikers, backpackers, mountain bikers, 4WD explorers, and river rafters. In fact, paved roads only reach limited places in two districts. This is a wilderness with breathing space, beauty, and a dark night sky spread with a zillion stars.

PLANNING YOUR TIME

Canyonlands is divided into separate districts. The Colorado and Green Rivers form the **Rivers** district and divide the park into three other regions. **Island in the Sky** lies between the Colorado and Green Rivers; it is the quickest to visit with limited time. To the southwest, **The Maze** is for backcountry travelers on rough roads suitable only for 4WD vehicles. To the southeast, **The Needles** attracts campers, hikers, and backpackers. The small **Horseshoe Canyon Unit,** farther west, preserves astounding petroglyphs and ancient rock paintings.

Due to Canyonlands' proximity to Arches National Park, most visitors combine trips to the two national parks. Make campground reservations six months in advance. No roads directly connect the districts. Visitors must leave the park to drive from one district to another (2-4 hrs).

Most of the park is canyon backcountry best accessed by backpacking, 4WD touring, river rafting, and mountain biking. Some day trips and all overnight trips require permits. Reserve these as soon as possible due to extreme competition.

March-October sees the most visitors; **spring** (Mar.-May) and **fall** (Sept.-Oct.) are the best times to visit. In summer, temperatures can climb to more than 100°F (38°C). Winter days tend to be bright and sunny, with nighttime temperatures in the teens or below zero; snow and ice may close roads and trails.

ENTRANCES AND FEES

Each district has its own entrance. The entrance fee is $30 per vehicle ($25 motorcycle, $15 individual) and good for seven days.

Permits

Permits (877/444-6777, www.recreation.gov) are required for backcountry exploration. If you are going off-pavement on dirt roads, trails, or rivers, you will need a permit for one-day activities (with the exception of day hiking) and all overnights. Activities requiring permits include backpacking, mountain biking, 4WD and motorcycle touring, and river rafting. Advance reservations are extremely competitive in fall and spring; plan to reserve as soon as dates are released.

Day-use permits are required for **4WD vehicles, motorcycles,** and **mountain bikes** on several of the park's dirt and rock roads: White Rim, Elephant Hill, Salt Creek/Horse Canyon, and Lavender Canyon. They are also

CANYONLANDS
NATIONAL PARK

279

Potash

LONG CANYON

POTASH ROAD

ANTICLINE OVERLOOK

River

DEAD HORSE POINT STATE PARK

VISITOR CENTER

Pyramid Butte

LOCKHART CANYON

DEAD HORSE POINT OVERLOOK

GOOSENECK OVERLOOK

Musselman Arch

Little Bridge Canyon

313

To US 191 and Moab

SHAFER TRAIL

SHAFER CANYON OVERLOOK

Colorado

MEANDER CANYON

ISLAND IN THE SKY VISITOR CENTER

Airport Tower

WHITE RIM

Washer Woman

WHITE RIM RD

MONUMENT BASIN

Moses and Zeus

CANYON

MESA ARCH

Aztec Butte

CANDLESTICK TOWER OVERLOOK

BUCK CANYON OVERLOOK

GRAND VIEW POINT OVERLOOK

TAYLOR

TRAIL

The Breach

WHALE ROCK

Upheaval Dome

HOLEMAN SPRING CANYON OVERLOOK

WILLOW FLAT

GREEN RIVER OVERLOOK

ORANGE CLIFFS OVERLOOK

Island In The Sky District

Junction Butte

HORSETHIEF POINT

MINERAL CANYON

MINERAL ROAD

Hardscrabble Bottom

UPHEAVAL DOME

Upheaval Canyon Trail

Candlestick Tower

WHITE

RIM

Green

Upheaval Bottom

Fort Bottom

Potato Bottom

River

Green

Syncline Loop

WHITE RIM RD

Anderson Bottom

Ekker Butte

PANORAMA POINT OVERLOOK

Barrier Creek

HORSESHOE CANYON

Buttes of the Cross

GLEN CANYON NATIONAL RECREATION AREA

Cleopatras Chair

ORANGE CLIFFS

THE SPUR

GREAT GALLERY PICTOGRAPHS

Horseshoe Canyon Unit

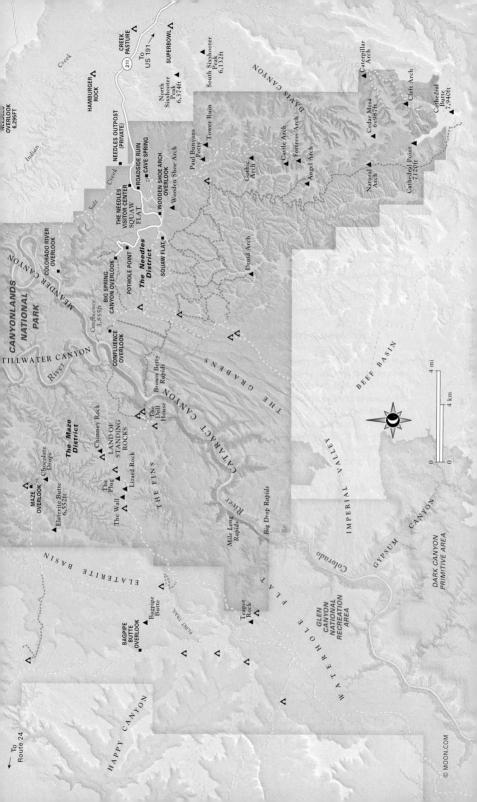

ONE DAY IN CANYONLANDS

Begin your day at the **Island in the Sky Visitor Center,** which overlooks an 800-foot-deep (244-m) natural amphitheater. After a 6-mile (9.7-km) drive south, you'll find the trail for the easy walk to **Mesa Arch,** which rewards you with one of the most dramatic vistas in Utah: an arch on the edge of a giant cliff. For lunch, hit the picnic area at **Grand View Point,** another 6 miles (9.7 km) south, for astonishing views over red-rock canyons. After lunch, hike Grand View Point Trail to a second vista before touring overlooks of **Upheaval Dome.**

required for **river rafting, kayaking,** and **canoeing** the Green and Colorado Rivers upstream from the Confluence (Flatwater) and Cataract Canyon.

Get permits online ($6) one day in advance at 8am Mountain Time. You can also pick up day-of permits (first come, first served, free) in person at park visitors centers. For the White Rim, 25 day-of permits are available.

All **backcountry camping** requires a permit year-round, no matter whether you are on a road, trail, or river. **Backcountry permits** ($36, plus $5 pp/night) for **backpackers, 4WD vehicles, motorcycles,** and **mountain bikes** are released starting at 8am Mountain Time on specific dates during the year: November 10 for **spring** (Mar. 10-June 10), February 10 for **summer** (June 10-Sept. 9), and May 10 for **fall** (Sept. 10-Dec. 9).

For **winter** (Dec. 10-Mar. 9), reservations release August 10 for Island in the Sky and Maze trips; for The Needles, you can only get **walk-up permits** (late Nov.-Mar. 9) at the visitors center. Year-round, **unreserved permits** are available in person (first come, first served) at visitors centers two days in advance.

River permits ($36, plus $25 pp/trip) are required for the Green and Colorado Rivers, including flatwater sections and Cataract Canyon. They are released in two seasons: in **mid-December** for reservations for mid-April through mid-October and in **mid-June** for reservations for mid-October to mid-April. Check online for specific dates.

VISITORS CENTERS

While **Moab Information Center** (25 E. Center St., Moab, 435/259-8825, www.discovermoab.com, 8am-7pm Mon.-Sat., 9am-6pm Sun.) is outside the

▼ COLORADO RIVER AND ISLAND IN THE SKY

Top ❸

MESA ARCH

❶ CATCH THE VIEW BENEATH MESA ARCH

From Mesa Arch Trailhead on Grand View Road at Island in the Sky, the **Mesa Arch Trail** (0.5 mi/0.8 km rt, 30 min, easy) follows a loop to a Navajo sandstone arch perched on the rim of a sheer 800-foot (244-m) cliff. The arch frames views of rock formations below and the La Sal Mountains in the distance. For the best (albeit crowded) photo op, arrive by sunrise to watch the glowing orb peek between the narrow arch's gap—or catch the moonrise.

❷ GAZE OUT FROM GRAND VIEW POINT

GRAND VIEW POINT

Island in the Sky's Grand View Point Road (12 mi/19 km) terminates at the best view: **Grand View Point.** Its perch overlooks Monument Basin, countless canyons, the Colorado River, The Needles, and mountain ranges in the distance. Rangers give periodic geology talks at the wheelchair-accessible viewpoint. It is also the best place for stargazing, on your own or with periodic ranger-led telescope-viewing programs. To absorb more of the immense scenery, walk **Grand View Point Trail** (2 mi/3.2 km rt, 1.5 hrs, easy) on slickrock and rugged rock steps to the actual point where a knob beckons scramblers. Go early in the morning to avoid crowds.

❸ ADMIRE PICTOGRAPHS IN HORSESHOE CANYON

GREAT GALLERY AT HORSESHOE CANYON

An outstanding day trip, **Horseshoe Canyon** contains exceptional prehistoric rock art. Ghostly life-size pictographs in the **Great Gallery** and rock art left by the Fremont people and Ancestral Puebloans provide an intriguing look into the past. The **Horseshoe Canyon Trail** (7 mi/11.3 km rt, 5-6 hrs, strenuous) drops from the canyon rim on a path to a slog through a long, sandy wash to the gallery. Rangers sometimes guide hikes here. From UT 24, a dirt washboarded 2WD road goes east to Horseshoe Canyon (32 mi/52 km). It's 2.5 hours from Moab (do not navigate with GPS).

GREEN RIVER

national park, it's the best place to get oriented due to its central location between Island in the Sky, Needles, and Arches National Park. It has information, brochures, maps, and books.

The **Island in the Sky Visitor Center** (8am-5pm daily late Apr.-mid-Sept., limited hours spring and fall, Thurs.-Mon. Jan.-Feb.) is located just before the neck crosses to Island in the Sky. It has maps, a bookstore, exhibits, a short park film, and permits. Rangers offer programs spring-fall with intermittent stargazing events.

Stop at the **Needles Visitor Center** (west end of UT 211, 8am-5pm daily summer, hours vary spring and fall) for information on hiking, back roads, permits, maps, brochures, books, and a film.

The Maze is served by the tiny **Hans Flat Ranger Station** (8am-4:30pm daily year-round).

ISLAND IN THE SKY

Island in the Sky is a triangle of mesas and canyons between the Green and Colorado Rivers. Paved roads lead to impressive overlooks along the upper mesa rim, while trails access geologic features. Below the rim, the White Rim Road (4WD) makes a loop above the rivers on a route favored by mountain bikers. To reach Island in the Sky from Moab (40 min), drive 32 miles (51 km)

north on UT 191 and southwest on UT 313 to the visitors center.

SCENIC DRIVES
Grand View Point Road

From the visitors center, **Grand View Point Road** (12 mi/19 km one-way) tours overlooks. First, turn into **Shafer Canyon Overlook** to look down on the twisting Shafer Trail Road that goes to the White Rim Road 1,200 feet (366 m) below. Then, pull over at viewpoints for **Candlestick Tower, Buck Canyon,** and **Orange Cliffs.** The road's terminus holds the best view at **Grand View Point,** stretching to The Needles and distant mountain ranges.

Upheaval Dome Road

From the main park road, turn north on **Upheaval Dome Road** (10 mi/16 km rt). The best viewpoint is on the dirt spur road that goes 1.5 miles (2.4 km) to **Green River Overlook.** Views plunge thousands of feet to the river oxbows below. The road also goes to two hikes: Whale Rock and Upheaval Dome.

HIKING
Grand View Point Road

From White Rim Overlook Picnic Area, the **White Rim Overlook Trail** (1.8 mi/2.9 km rt, 1 hr, easy) trots east along a peninsula to an overlook of canyons and the La Sal Mountains.

Best Hike

CHESLER PARK AND THE JOINT

DISTANCE: 6-11 miles (9.7-17.7 km) round-trip
DURATION: 3-7 hours
ELEVATION CHANGE: 1,780 feet (543 m)
EFFORT: moderately strenuous
TRAILHEAD: Elephant Hill Trailhead

In The Needles district, the broad sage-brush and desert wildflower-filled Chesler Park is rimmed with red and white spires. From the trailhead, the well-signed **Chesler Park Viewpoint Trail** (6 mi/9.7 km rt, 3-4 hrs, moderately strenuous) climbs and drops several times through sand, slickrock, and narrow fissures while taking in spectacular geologic formations. Portions are steep, rocky, and sometimes on narrow ledges. After passing through Elephant Canyon, the trail ascends a small pass through spires to overlook Chesler Park. For a longer adventure, continue through **Chesler Park to The Joint** (11 mi/17.7 km rt, 5-7 hrs, strenuous). The trail circles the park before dropping on steps into **The Joint,** a long narrow crack barely wide enough for a person. Return the way you came for both trails.

Upheaval Dome Road

From the Aztec Butte Trailhead, **Aztec Butte Trail** (2 mi/3.2 km rt, 1 hr, moderate) climbs a dome that contains ruins of Ancestral Puebloan granaries. From the Whale Rock Trailhead, **Whale Rock Trail** (1 mi/1.6 km rt, 45 min, moderate) skitters along to a sandstone formation that resembles a whale. You can follow slickrock from the tail to the whale's back.

At the road's terminus, trails go to views of Upheaval Dome, a geological curiosity of a rocky crater about 3 miles (4.8 km) across and 1,200 feet (366 m) deep. The **Crater View Trail** (1.8 mi/2.9

VIEWS FROM THE WHITE RIM ROAD

BIKERS ON THE WHITE RIM ROAD

km rt, 1 hr, easy) leads to two overlooks on the rim while the **Syncline Loop Trail** (8.3 mi/13.3 km rt, 5-7 hrs, strenuous) circles up and down completely around the dome. Halfway around, the **Upheaval Dome Canyon Trail** (add 3 mi/4.8 km rt, 2 hrs) goes into the crater itself.

MOUNTAIN BIKING AND 4WD ROADS

The **White Rim Road** (100 mi/161 km, 2-4 days) lies below the sheer cliffs of Island in the Sky. Travel along the winding road presents a constantly changing panorama of rock, canyons, river, and sky. You'll see all three levels of Island in the Sky: high plateaus, the White Rim, and the rivers. From the visitors center on UT 313, the east entrance is Shafer Trail Road, 1 mile (1.6 km) north, and the west entrance is Mineral Bottom Road, aka Horsethief Trail, 9 miles (14.5 km) north.

The route is open for mountain bikes, e-bikes, motorcycles, and high-clearance 4WD vehicles. **Permits are required** for day use and overnighting at designated campsites. The road has no services or developed water sources; take plenty of water and tools to fix flats.

This is an epic adventure. The slow winding route has a few steep, single-lane, rocky, or sandy sections that make for white-knuckle driving or riding. It's a bucket-list trip for mountain bikers. Endurance riders do the loop in one monster day, but most prefer to take up to four days (self-supported or with vehicle support to haul water and gear). Bike shops, rentals, and guides are based in Moab.

THE NEEDLES

The Needles district showcases some of the finest rock sculptures in Canyonlands National Park. Spires, arches, and monoliths appear in almost any direction you look. Prehistoric ruins and rock art exist in a greater variety and quantity than anywhere else in the park. A paved road, several 4WD roads, and many hiking trails offer a variety of ways to explore the Needles. From Moab, reach the Needles (2 hrs) by traveling south on US 191 for 40 miles (64 km) and then turning right on UT 211 and going 34 miles (55 km) to the visitors center.

POTHOLE POINT

SCENIC DRIVES

From the visitors center, the paved park road threads into the Needles (6.4 mi/10.3 km one-way) where you can take short walks to sights. **Roadside Ruin** (0.3 mi/0.5 km rt, 10 min, easy) has a well-preserved granary left by the Ancestral Puebloans. The clockwise interpretive loop of **Cave Spring Trail** (0.6 mi/1 km rt, 20 min, easy) provides an introduction to the park's geology. **Pothole Point Trail** (0.6 mi/1 km rt, 20 min, easy) features dissolved sandstone holes. The road terminates at **Big Spring Canyon Overlook**.

HIKING

The Needles has outstanding day hiking and backpacking (overnight trips require permits for preassigned campsites; ask about water sources). Interconnected trails loop through several canyons with routes that include sandy washes, slickrock passes

LADDER ON BIG SPRINGS-ELEPHANT CANYON LOOP

and ramps, cairned routes, exposed ledges, rock-hewn foot holes, and steel ladders. The best routes make loops, which you can do in either direction.

Squaw Flat Trailhead

From the Squaw Flat Trailhead, the **Squaw Canyon-Lost Canyon Loop** (8.7 mi/14 km rt, 4-6 hrs, moderate) climbs over a slickrock pass. Most of the trail goes through vegetated washes, where you may need to wade. You can also loop the other direction to connect **Squaw Canyon to Big Spring Canyon** (7.5 mi/12.1 km rt, 3-4 hrs, moderate) via a steep slickrock climb over red and white sandstone.

With many climbs and drops, the **Big Springs-Elephant Canyon Loop** (10.8 mi/17.3 km, 6-7 hrs, strenuous) offers long segments of slickrock walking, plus squeezing through narrow joints and climbing over passes.

THE JOINT IN THE NEEDLES

COLORADO RIVER

Elephant Hill Trailhead

Druid Arch Trail (11 mi/17.7 km rt, 6-7 hrs, strenuous) climbs into Elephant Canyon flanked with large white-domed red rocks and ascends to a viewpoint of the freestanding arch.

MOUNTAIN BIKING AND 4WD ROADS

Mountain bikes, e-bikes, motorcycles, and 4WD vehicles with high clearance and low gears can explore the Needles backcountry on rugged roads of sand, mud, and slickrock. **Permits are required** for both day trips and overnight trips. Camping is in designated sites with toilets. Bring your own water.

Salt Creek Canyon and Horse Canyon Roads

The **Salt Creek Canyon Road** (26 mi/42 km rt) begins near Cave Spring Trail, crosses sage flats, and then heads deep into a spectacular canyon with a side trip to 150-foot-high (46-m) Angel Arch. Salt Canyon is frequently closed due to quicksand after flash floods in summer and shelf ice in winter. **Horse Canyon Road** (13 mi/21 km rt) turns left shortly before the mouth of Salt Canyon for a trip to Tower Ruin.

Elephant Hill

The **Elephant Hill Roads** (distances vary, no rigs or combos over 21 ft/6.4 m) are technically challenging loops through canyons. The narrow steep roads have loose rock, stairstep drops, and sharp turns. Some parts are one-way. One route goes to the Confluence Overlook Trail, another to the Joint Trail.

THE MAZE

The maze is rugged wilderness. Due to the difficulty of travel, most visitors come for three days minimum, camping in primitive sites. **Backcountry permits are required.** This district has no cell service, no reliable GPS, **no developed water sources,** and no services. All travelers must be able to handle emergencies (flat tires, medical, and equipment malfunctions) and must be self-sufficient (carry water, read topographical maps, and be proficient with navigation). **Gas up** before reaching the Maze.

Getting here from Moab (3.5 hrs) involves 134 miles (216 km) of driving via I-70, UT 24, and a 46-mile (74 km) 2WD dirt road to **Hans Flat Ranger Station** (435/259-2652, 8am-4:30pm daily) before driving 2-6 hours to your destination.

SCENIC DRIVES

Only 4WD high-clearance rigs should tackle the slow rough roads of the Maze. Check road conditions first at the ranger station. Avoid travel during or after rains due to slippery rocks and clay. Nine primitive campsites are available.

Fourteen miles (23 km) south of the ranger station, the narrow single-lane **Flint Trail Road** (2.8 mi/4.5 km one-way) descends switchbacks, but stop first at the signed overlook to scout for vehicles headed up. A rough, rocky trek with switchbacks, drop-offs, and steep pitches leads to the **Maze Overlook** (60 mi/97 km rt, 6 hrs, 2 campsites) for canyon views. A second route goes to the **Land of Standing Rocks** (74 mi/119 km rt, 10 hrs, 3 campsites) to see the Wall, Standing Rock, and Chimney Rock or farther to the tall rounded spires of **The Doll House** (add 10 mi/16 km rt, 2 hrs, 3 campsites). Be prepared for extremely rough road after Teapot Rock Camp; carry extra gas and vehicle repair gear.

HIKING

Experienced self-sufficient hikers can explore the Maze on unmarked strenuous routes of cairned paths from the mesa to canyon bottoms and slogs through sandy washes. A few places require using hands and feet to climb or descend boulders; bring a 25-foot (7.6-m) rope to haul packs up or down. Most hikers camp in designated zones for several days, taking day hikes to explore. Consult with rangers about potential water sources.

From the Maze Overlook, the **Maze Overlook Trail** (2 mi/3.2 km rt, 2 hrs) drops over a Class IV boulder into the South Fork of Horse Canyon, where a sandy wash goes to the prehistoric Harvest Scene pictographs (add 3 mi/4.8 km rt, 2 hrs). Two miles (3.2 km) east of the bottom of the Flint Trail Road, the steep **Golden Stairs** (4 mi/6.4 km rt, 3-4 hrs) descends to the Land of Standing Rocks Road for views of Ernies Country and the Fins. From the Doll House, the **Spanish Bottom Trail** (2.4 mi/3.9 km rt, 2-3 hrs) plunges 1,260 vertical feet (384 m) to Spanish Bottom beside the Colorado River.

THE RIVERS

The Rivers district includes long stretches of the **Green** and **Colorado Rivers.** River-floating provides one of the best ways to experience the inner depths of the park. Above the confluence, the rivers have flat water for paddlers in canoes, sea kayaks, and rafts. Below the confluence, the volume of water squeezes through 14-mile (22-km) **Cataract Canyon** with Class III-V white water. Self-guided boaters need **river permits** for day trips and overnights.

RAFTING CATARACT CANYON

To make it easy, commercial trips take care of everything. The following outfitters in Moab are authorized by the National Park Service. Most offer single-day and multiday trips.

Adrift Adventures (378 N. Main St., 435/259-8594 or 800/874-4483, www.adrift.net)

Sheri Griffith Expeditions (2231 S. UT 191, 435/259-8229 or 800/332-2439, www.griffithexp.com)

Western River Expeditions (225 S. Main St., 801/942-6669 or 866/904-1160, www.westernriver.com)

WHERE TO STAY

INSIDE THE PARK

Developed park campgrounds have picnic tables, toilets, and fire rings, but no RV hookups.

Island in the Sky

On Murphy Point Road, the **Willow Flat Campground** (year-round, 12 sites, $15) is available first come, first served. Sites fill up early in all seasons except winter. Get drinking water at the visitors center.

The Needles

Located 3 miles (4.8 km) south of the visitors center, **The Needles Campground** (year-round, 26 sites, $20) snuggles under slickrock. Rangers present evening programs at the amphitheater spring-autumn. Make reservations six months in advance (877/444-6777, www.recreation.gov). Potable water is available spring-fall.

OUTSIDE THE PARK

With scads of lodging, restaurants, and services, **Moab** is a tourist town. Book reservations for spring and fall six months in advance.

Near the Island in the Sky District, the year-round campground at **Dead Horse Point State Park** (800/456-2267, www.reserveamerica.com, book four months in advance) fills daily February-November. Primitive Bureau of Land Management (BLM) campsites flank UT 313.

Just outside the Needles district, **Needles Outpost** (435/459-0777, www.needlesoutpost.com, mid-Mar.-

late Oct.) has campsites without hookups. Nearby BLM land also offers a number of places to camp, including two first-come, first-served campgrounds in the Canyon Rims Special Recreation Management Area.

GETTING THERE AND AROUND

The closest airport is **Salt Lake City International Airport** (SLC, 776 N. Terminal Dr., 801/575-2400, www.slcairport.com), 235 miles (380 km) north of Moab. The four-hour drive follows I-15, US 6, I-70, and US 191. Rental cars are available; however, 4WD vehicles with high clearance are preferred.

CAR

Island in the Sky

From Moab, drive 11 miles (18 km) north on US 191 and turn left (west) onto UT 313. If you are coming in from I-70, drive 20 miles (32 km) south on US 191 from exit 182 to reach the junction. Continue on this paved road for 22 miles (35 km) west, and then south, to reach the park entrance. From Moab, allow 45 minutes to reach the park.

The Needles

To reach the Needles district, drive 40 miles (64 km) south from Moab (or 14 mi/23 km north from Monticello) on US 191, and then turn west onto UT 211 for 38 miles (61 km).

The Maze and Horseshoe Canyon

South of I-70, UT 24 and UT 95 access dirt roads to the western canyons. The easiest way in is the dirt washboarded 2WD road from UT 24 to Hans Flat Ranger Station (46 mi/74 km). Beyond the ranger station, a 2WD dirt road goes north to Horseshoe Canyon (32 mi/52 km), and extremely rugged 4WD high-clearance roads go to Maze destinations (30-47 mi/48-76 km).

TOURS

Canyonlands Field Institute (800/860-5262 or 435/259-7750, http://cfimoab.org) guides one-day and multiday educational adventures and programs.

MESA VERDE NATIONAL PARK

Colorado

WEBSITE:
www.nps.gov/meve

PHONE NUMBER:
970/529-4465

VISITATION RANK:
39

WHY GO:
Marvel at ancient
cliff dwellings.

KEEPSAKE STAMPS ▼▼▼

▲ CLIFF DWELLING AT MESA VERDE
NATIONAL PARK

Nearly 5,000 archaeological sites spread across **MESA VERDE NATIONAL PARK.** They contain relics of the Ancestral Puebloan people who once farmed the mesa tops and lived in tiny mud-brick rooms. After living on the mesa for nearly 600 years, they began building pueblos beneath the impressive overhanging cliffs. Some 600 intricate multistory cliff dwellings, ranging from one-room storage areas to entire villages, are tucked into enormous sandstone alcoves. Petroglyphs offer further hints of their culture, which lasted about 700 years until they vacated the sites within a generation or so.

The land making up the national park was taken from the treaty lands of the Ute people. Today, 26 Indigenous groups maintain special connections with Mesa Verde. In the late 1800s a researcher unearthed the remains of 20 Ancestral Puebloans along with burial artifacts and sent them to Europe to be studied. In 2020, the Hopi Tribe, Pueblo of Acoma, Pueblo of Zia, and Pueblo of Zuni successfully repatriated the remains for reburial in Mesa Verde National Park.

PLANNING YOUR TIME

Mesa Verde National Park is in southwestern Colorado, near the Four Corners of Colorado, Utah, Arizona, and New Mexico. It's easy to link a visit to Mesa Verde with several nearby national monuments. The region boasts impressive ruins and acre upon acre of gorgeous slickrock scenery, where crimson and white sandstone monoliths tower above vegetation and secluded archaeological sites.

The park's main draw is its remarkable cliff dwellings. **Balcony House, Cliff Palace,** and **Long House** can only be visited on ranger-guided tours. In summer, it's not always possible to visit both Balcony House and Cliff Palace on the same day due to high demand for tours. Consider staying 2-3 days or visit **Long House** (road open May-mid-Oct.), the park's second-largest dwelling, instead.

Tour season runs from May to mid-October (no tours in winter), although most crowds arrive **May-September.** Book tickets for tours 14 days in advance online. Take a screenshot of your receipt or print it before leaving home.

Hot summer temperatures climb into the 90s (32°C and above), and summer afternoon thunderstorms dole out lightning. Spring and fall, when 60-75°F (16-24°C) is the norm, are ideal times to visit. In spring the cottonwoods along the sparse creeks leaf out, and in autumn they turn gold, backdropped by distant mountaintops dusted with fresh snow. Winter nights are chilly, but the daytime temperatures are usually pleasantly cool. Expect snowstorms November-April.

ENTRANCE AND FEES

The park entrance is accessed via one clearly signed road that branches south from US 160. Upon turning onto the park entrance road, the visitors center appears on the left; this is where you'll pay the entrance fee January-March. The actual park entrance station is 0.5 mile (0.8 km) farther down the park road; pay the entrance fee here late March-December.

The entrance fee is $20 per vehicle January-April and November-December and $30 per vehicle May-October ($15-25 motorcycle, $10-15 individual). All entrance fees are valid for seven days.

VISITORS CENTER

The **Mesa Verde Visitor and Research Center** (7:30am-7pm daily late May-early Sept., shorter hours in winter) is housed in a scenic building. View

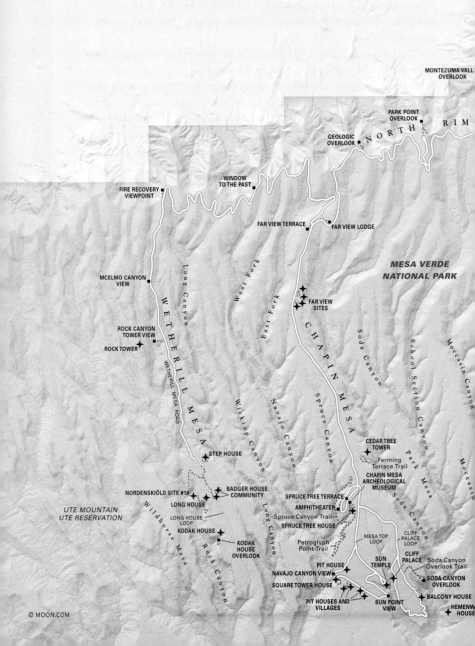

MESA VERDE NATIONAL PARK

491
To Dove Creek
Cortez
160
To Shiprock

MONTEZUMA VALL OVERLOOK

PARK POINT OVERLOOK

GEOLOGIC OVERLOOK

NORTH RIM

WINDOW TO THE PAST

FIRE RECOVERY VIEWPOINT

FAR VIEW TERRACE

FAR VIEW LODGE

MESA VERDE NATIONAL PARK

MCELMO CANYON VIEW

Long Canyon

West Fork

East Fork

FAR VIEW SITES

ROCK CANYON TOWER VIEW

ROCK TOWER

WETHERILL MESA

WETHERILL MESA ROAD

CHAPIN MESA

Soda Canyon

School Section Canyon

Moccasin Canyon

Wickiup Canyon

Navajo Canyon

Spruce Canyon

CEDAR TREE TOWER

Park Mesa

Moccasin

Farming Terrace Trail

STEP HOUSE

CHAPIN MESA ARCHEOLOGICAL MUSEUM

NORDENSKIÖLD SITE #16

BADGER HOUSE COMMUNITY

LONG HOUSE

SPRUCE TREE TERRACE

AMPHITHEATER

Soda Canyon

UTE MOUNTAIN UTE RESERVATION

Wildhorse Mesa

LONG HOUSE LOOP

Long Canyon

Spruce Canyon Trail

SPRUCE TREE HOUSE

KODAK HOUSE

Rock Canyon

KODAK HOUSE OVERLOOK

Petroglyph Point Trail

MESA TOP LOOP

CLIFF PALACE LOOP

CLIFF PALACE

Soda Canyon Overlook Trail

PIT HOUSE

SUN TEMPLE

SODA CANYON OVERLOOK

NAVAJO CANYON VIEW

SQUARE TOWER HOUSE

PIT HOUSES AND VILLAGES

SUN POINT VIEW

BALCONY HOUSE

HEMENW HOUSE

© MOON.COM

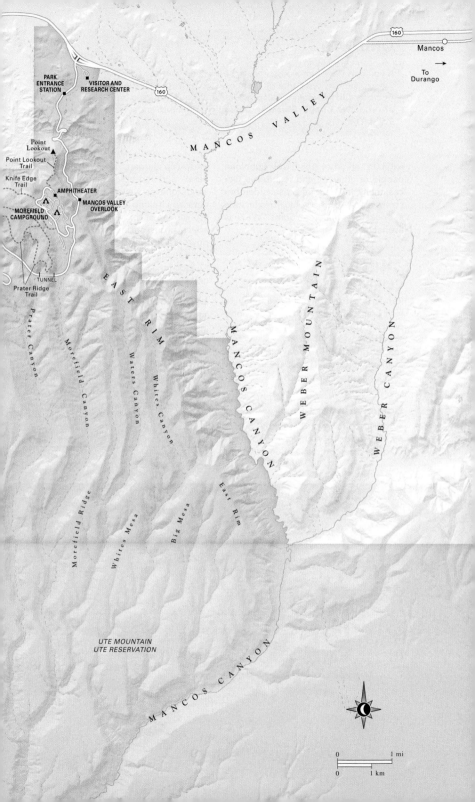

ONE DAY IN MESA VERDE

If you only have half a day, drive the park road south to the Chapin Mesa area, where you can see some of the mesa-top sites at **Far View** and take a tour of either **Cliff Palace** or **Balcony House**. If you can spend a full day, add in an afternoon at **Chapin Mesa Archeological Museum** and walk the **Petroglyph Point Trail.**

exhibits on the Ancestral Puebloan people, original art, and sculptures. Occasionally, Indigenous artisans demonstrate arts and crafts. Facilities include a bookstore and restrooms. Wi-Fi is available.

SIGHTS

CLIFF DWELLING TOURS

Ranger-led tours are the only way to visit some of the cliff dwellings. Competition for tickets is high; book **reservations** (877/444-6777, www.recreation.gov, $8-45) 14 days in advance at 8am Mountain Time. Save a screenshot or print your receipt before leaving home.

Balcony House Tour

With just 38 rooms, nearby **Balcony House** (daily May-Oct.) is an intermediate-size complex. To access their mesa-top gardens, the villagers used hand- and footholds carved into the sandstone, as well as tall wooden ladders. You'll climb a 32-foot (10-m) modern version of this during the tour. This adventurous outing involves climbing down a 100-foot (30-m) staircase into the canyon and clambering through a 12-foot-long (3-m), 18-inch-wide (46-cm) tunnel.

Long House Tour

The park's second-largest cliff dwelling is **Long House** (daily May-mid-Oct., weather permitting). Excavated between 1959 and 1961, the Long House includes about 150 rooms and 21 kivas whose beams date to 1145 CE. Archaeologists believe that 150-175 people once lived beneath the shadow of its 300-foot-long (91-m) alcove. Of special note is a well-preserved triangular

▽ BALCONY HOUSE

Top ❸

1 TOUR CLIFF PALACE

The largest of the under-the-rim dwellings, **Cliff Palace** (daily late June–mid-Oct., $8) has more than 150 rooms and 23 circular kivas—distinctive circular pits used for performing cultural rituals. Considering that three-quarters of the park's 600 cliff dwellings contain just 1-5 rooms, Cliff Palace is exceptionally big, a neighborhood where an estimated 100 people once lived. You'll notice how small and cramped the rooms feel. At that time, the average man

CLIFF PALACE

stood 5 feet, 4 inches (1.6 m) tall and the average woman was about 5 feet (1.5 m) tall. To tour Cliff Palace, you must be able to climb several ladders, the highest of which is 15 feet tall (4.6 m). Visits are only possible on ranger-led tours, which include the **Twilight Tour.** Book reservations (877/444-6777, www.recreation.gov, $8-45) 14 days in advance right at 8am Mountain Time, as tickets go fast. Bring a screenshot or printed copy of your ticket with you. You can also look down at Cliff Palace from a Mesa Top Loop Road overlook.

2 EXPLORE CHAPIN MESA ARCHEOLOGICAL MUSEUM

A National Historic Landmark, the **Chapin Mesa Archeological Museum** (roughly 9am-5pm daily, limited hours in winter, free) contains artifacts from the Ancestral Puebloan people who used to inhabit Mesa Verde. It shows a 25-minute orientation film and has educational exhibits that include dioramas and other cultural items. Nearby, rangers give daily talks at overlooks of **Spruce Tree House.** The museum is located on Chapin Mesa, 21 miles (34 km) south of park entrance.

3 DRIVE NORTH RIM ROAD

SPRUCE TREE HOUSE

The curvy **North Rim Road** (12 mi/19 km one-way) skims along canyon rims between Morefield Campground and Far View Lodge. It goes through a tunnel and passes three overlooks: Montezuma Valley, Park Point, and Geologic Overlook, each offering a different take on the rugged mesa-and-canyon scenery. Of the three, **Park Point** at 8,572 feet (2,613 m) is the highest point in the park, with a 360-degree view where you can see the four states of the Four Corners. This road accesses Chapin Mesa and Mesa Top Loop Roads plus Wetherill Mesa Road.

Best Hike

PETROGLYPH POINT

DISTANCE: 2.4 miles (3.9 km) round-trip
DURATION: 1.5 hours
ELEVATION CHANGE: 300 feet (91 m)
EFFORT: moderate
TRAILHEAD: Gated trailhead near Chapin Mesa Archeological Museum

The crowded **Petroglyph Point Loop** accesses close-up views of ancient rock art, including hunting scenes, spirals, and dainty handprints. The rocky, narrow path follows a canyon wall with steep drop-offs, and you may need to use your hands to help climb a steep stone stairway. The last portion of the loop is a flat forest walk. Entrance to the trail is through a gated trailhead (check with a ranger for current open hours). Register to hike at the trailhead or Chapin Mesa Archeological Museum, where an interpretive brochure is also available.

tower rising four stories from floor to ceiling at the western end of the alcove. Visiting the site requires walking 2.25 miles (3.6 km) round-trip from Wetherill Mesa Kiosk, and you'll climb two 15-foot (4.6-m) ladders as part of the tour.

Other Cliff Dwelling Tours

You can also reserve a spot on the **Twilight Tour of Cliff Palace** or the **Sunrise Tour of Balcony House** to experience the cliff dwelling under unique lighting conditions. Other tours (by reservation) go through **Oak Tree House, Yucca House,** and **Mug House.**

FAR VIEW

A self-guided stroll to **Far View House** (8am-sunset daily, 1.5 mi/2.4 km rt, 1-2 hrs, easy) visits several pueblo villages, including eye-catching spiral petroglyphs at the **Pipe Shrine House.** Far View is 5 miles (8 km) north of the Chapin Mesa Archeological Museum.

NIGHT SKIES

As an **International Dark Sky Park,** Mesa Verde celebrates the night sky that was important for the Ancestral Puebloans spiritually and practically. Ranger-led programs are offered through the year. An annual star party with telescope viewing is held in early October at Morefield Campground Amphitheater. Check online for current schedules. For self-guided night sky viewing, go to Geologic Overlook, Mancos Overlook, or Montezuma Valley Overlook on the park road for broad skies.

SCENIC DRIVES

MESA TOP LOOP ROAD

Mesa Top Loop Road (6 mi/10 km, 8am-sunset daily) tours several overlooks, including **Navajo Canyon View** and **Sun Point View,** which offer plunging views down adjacent canyons. Twelve self-guided stops include several pit houses, an overlook of **Cliff Palace,** and the ceremonial **Sun Temple,** which may have been an astronomical observatory. Mesa Top Loop Road is 23 miles (37 km) south of the park entrance, beyond the Chapin Mesa Archeological Museum.

WETHERILL MESA

Wetherill Mesa Road (8am-6pm daily May-Oct. weather permitting) tours a long protruding peninsula of land bordered by impressive canyons whose sandstone cliffs host many natural alcoves. Ancestral Puebloans took advantage of many of these landmarks to build storage buildings and homes in their protective shadows. Stop at overlooks to take in **McElmo Canyon** and **Rock Canyon Tower.** At the road's terminus at Wetherill Mesa Kiosk, you can hike to Step House or Badger House. The road is on the west side of

PETROGLYPH POINT TRAIL

the park, 27 miles (43 km) from the visitors center.

RECREATION
HIKING

From Morefield Campground, the **Knife Edge Trail** (2 mi/3.2 km rt, 1 hr, moderate) follows a steep bluff along the original entrance road built in 1914 to an overlook of Montezuma Valley.

On Chapin Mesa, **Spruce Canyon Trail** (2.4 mi/3.9 km rt, 1.5 hrs, strenuous) descends into the canyon to cross a seasonal trickle of a stream on small bridges before climbing about 500 feet (152 m) back up. Registration to hike is required at the Chapin Mesa Archeological Museum or the nearby gated trailhead; check with the museum for current hours. On Cliff Palace Loop Road, the **Soda Canyon Overlook Trail** (1.2 mi/1.9 km rt, 45 min, easy) descends to the canyon rim for views of archaeological sites, including Balcony House, in the canyon below. Find the trailhead 1 mile (1.6 km) north of the Balcony House parking area.

From the Wetherill Mesa Kiosk at the terminus of Wetherill Mesa Road (daily May-Oct., weather permitting), two trails go to archaeological sites

that you can explore via self-guided tours. A winding trail descends to **Step House** (hours and days vary, 1 mi/1.6 km rt, 1 hr, moderate), where you can walk around a cliff dwelling and see a pit house and petroglyphs before climbing back up. The **Badger House Trail** (2.25 mi/3.6 km rt, 1.5-2 hrs, easy) visits four mesa-top archaeological sites on a graveled and paved trail.

BICYCLING

Cyclists enjoy the thrill of the park's curvy roads and their steep climbs and descents, but they come with challenges: narrow roadways, no shoulders, broken pavement, and congested traffic. Riding early or late in the day is a more pleasant experience. All roads in the park permit bicycles, with the exception of Wetherill Mesa Road.

WHERE TO STAY
INSIDE THE PARK

Located 15 miles (24 km) south of the park entrance, **Far View Lodge** (970/529-4422 or 800/449-2288, www.visitmesaverde.com, May-Sept., from $140) is the only lodging option in the park. It has 150 Southwestern-styled rooms that lack TVs but have sweeping views and free Wi-Fi. Rates include a full breakfast; dinner is available at the **Metate Room Restaurant** (5pm-9:30pm daily in season); reservations are strongly recommended.

Morefield Campground (970/529-4422 or 800/449-2288, www.visitmesaverde.com, mid-Apr.-mid-Oct., 267 sites, from $36) is 4 miles (6.4 km) south of the park entrance. Some sites can be reserved in advance. Amenities include flush toilets, showers, a camp store, laundry, and a dump station.

The casual, self-service **Far View Terrace Café** (0.25 mi/0.4 km south of Far View Lodge, 7am-10am and 11am-2pm daily May-Sept.) has Navajo tacos. Farther up the road, near the Chapin Mesa Archeological Museum, the **Spruce Tree Terrace Café** (11am-3pm daily Mar.-Apr., limited hours other seasons) serves barbecue. The **Knife Edge Café** (7am-10am daily May-Sept., 11am-6pm daily June-Aug., 11am-2pm daily Aug.-Sept.) is near the campground.

OUTSIDE THE PARK

Located 10 miles (16 km) from the park entrance, the small town of **Cortez** offers basic services in between the area's many monuments.

GETTING THERE

AIR

The closest international airport is **Denver International Airport** (DEN, 8500 Peña Blvd., Denver, 303/342-2000, www.flydenver.com). **Durango-La Plata County Airport** (DRO, 1000 Airport Rd., Durango, 970/382-6050, www.flydurango.com) offers daily service by United and American, including nonstop service to Denver. Car rentals are available.

Animas Transportation (2023 Main Ave., Durango, 970/259-1315, www.animastransportation.com) will shuttle a carload to the park on a per-mile basis, which works out to about $150 one-way.

CAR

East-west US 160 connects Mesa Verde National Park with Durango, 35 miles (56 km) east of the park entrance, and Cortez, 10 miles (16 km) west.

GETTING AROUND

There is no public transportation within the park. You'll need a car to get around, and the roads are steep, extremely curvy, and narrow, with no shoulders. **Gas** is available at the campground. Inside the park (about 15 mi/24 km south of US 160), the road splits: one branch turns west toward Wetherill Mesa (May-Oct. only), while the main road continues south to Chapin Mesa, the location of Balcony House and Cliff Palace.

Guided bus tours (Aramark, 800/449-2288, www.visitmesaverde.com, twice daily May-Sept., $68-88) are an option for touring the park. The 700 Years Tour (4 hrs) takes in the Cliff Palace and other sites. The Introduction to Mesa Verde Tour (3 hrs) stops at Far View Terrace and Spruce Tree Overlook. Purchasing tickets in advance is recommended. You can also buy them in person at Morefield Campground, Far View Lodge, or Far View Terrace.

SIGHTS NEARBY

Canyons of the Ancients Visitor Center and Museum (27501 Hwy. 184, Dolores, 970/882-5600, www.blm.gov, 9am-5pm Thurs.-Sat. Mar.-Oct., shorter hours Nov.-Feb.), 10 miles north of Cortez, serves as an introduction to the region's archaeological attractions and an information center for Canyons of the Ancients National Monument.

Canyons of the Ancients National Monument (27501 Hwy. 184, Dolores, 970/882-5600, www.blm.gov, 9am-5pm Thurs.-Sat. Mar.-Oct., shorter hours Nov.-Feb., free), southwest of Cortez, is a relatively untouched wilderness of flat-topped mesas and twisting canyons whose sandstone walls harbor the largest concentration of archaeological sites in the country.

Four Corners Monument (U.S. 160, 38 mi/61 km south of Cortez, 928/206-2540, www.navajonationparks.org, 8am-8pm daily late May-mid-Aug.) marks the only spot in the United States where four states—Colorado, New Mexico, Arizona, and Utah—meet.

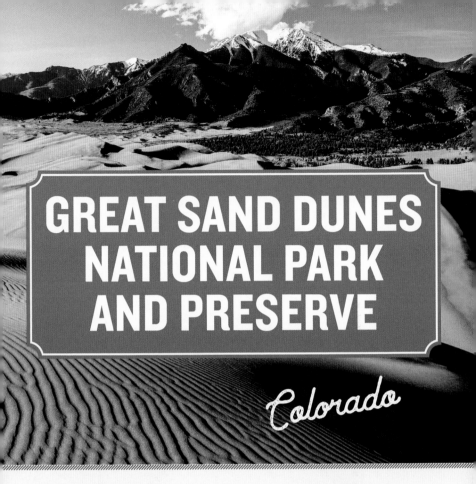

GREAT SAND DUNES NATIONAL PARK AND PRESERVE

Colorado

WEBSITE:
www.nps.gov/grsa

PHONE NUMBER:
719/378-6395

VISITATION RANK:
35

WHY GO:
Slide down the tallest sand dunes in North America.

▲ GREAT SAND DUNES
NATIONAL PARK

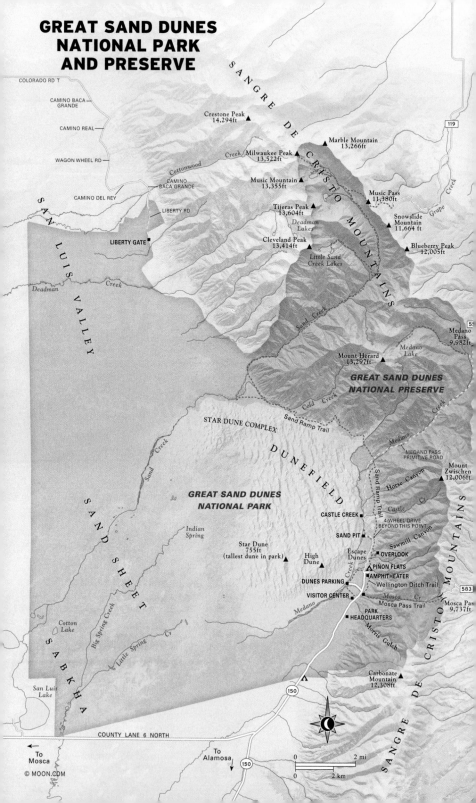

Along the eastern edge of Colorado's San Luis Valley is a vast, high-elevation basin almost as large as the state of New Jersey. Tucked into this valley, **GREAT SAND DUNES NATIONAL PARK AND PRESERVE** holds a remarkable dune field with mounds of sand up to 750 feet (228 m) high. While these are the tallest dunes in North America, their height fades with the incredible backdrop—the long line of the jagged Sangre de Cristo Mountains. Water flowing from the mountains surrounds the dunes with braided streams. Contrary to other geological formations that alter more slowly with time, the dunes change daily. Shifting sands move with wind, water, and gravity, creating a fluid landscape that always seems to be in motion.

PLANNING YOUR TIME

Great Sand Dunes National Park is in southern Colorado, less than 65 miles (105 km) north of the state line with New Mexico and about four hours south of Denver. This is the arid Southwest, although the Sangre de Cristos form a reminder of Colorado's northern high mountains.

Elevations span 7,520-13,604 feet (2,292-4,146 m), which keep temperatures in the 50-80°F (10-27°C) range during the day May-September; this is the crowded season. Winter temperatures range 30-45°F (-1-7°C), sometimes with a few inches of snowfall. Year-round, the arid desert weather often has blue skies, but nighttime temperatures can plunge to cool and even frigid zones. Summer can produce afternoon lightning storms.

Despite the temperature, the surface of the sand heats up in summer; during midday, the sand can exceed 140°F (60°C). Plan for early morning or evening excursions on foot. During windstorms, which are frequent in spring, wear protective glasses.

ENTRANCE AND FEES

The entrance fee is $25 per vehicle ($20 motorcycle and bicycle, $15 individual) and good for seven days. The entrance station is on CO 150 at the park headquarters.

VISITORS CENTER

Located 0.7 mile (1.1 km) beyond the entrance station, the **Great Sand Dunes Visitor Center** (11999 CO 150, Mosca, 8:30am-5pm daily summer, 9am-4:30pm daily fall-spring) has interactive exhibits, park information, a bookstore, and a Junior Ranger Program. View the dunes through spotting scopes on the back porch. Ranger-led talks and walks (May-fall, schedules vary weekly) are held at the visitors center or campground amphitheater. Visitors with disabilities can use sand-friendly wheelchairs.

SIGHTS

NIGHT SKIES

This **International Dark Sky Park** is an outstanding place to spot the Milky

---

ONE DAY IN GREAT SAND DUNES

A visit to Great Sand Dunes is all about the dunes. If you only have one day to explore its wonders, choose from a quick cruise to **scenic viewpoints,** a longer **hike** to the tip of the dunes themselves, or rent a **sandboard** and ride down the slopes for a speedy rush.

Top ❸

❶ DRIVE TO SCENIC VIEWPOINTS

Bordered on the north by Sand Creek and to the east and south by Medano Creek, the **dune field** resembles a sea of sand waves. The tallest dune is 755-foot (230-m) **Star Dune;** the second tallest is 699-foot (213-m) **High Dune.** For the closest views, drive to the Dunes Parking Lot at the end of a spur

STAR DUNE

road just past the visitors center. The shifting back and forth of the wind keeps the dunes relatively in place. Though the dune field covers 30 square miles (78 sq km)—an area estimated to contain five billion cubic meters of sand—it is only 10 percent of the total sand in the area.

❷ GO SAND SLEDDING AND BOARDING

Specifically designed gear is used for sledding or boarding on the sand dunes. Near the park entrance, the **Great Sand Dunes Oasis** (7800 CO 150 N., Mosca, 719/378-2222, www.greatdunes.com, May-mid-Oct., $20) rents sandboards and sand sleds. From the Dunes Parking Lot, wade Medano Creek to access the closest slopes with a good pitch for sliding.

❸ SPLASH IN MEDANO CREEK

The shallow and wide Medano Creek provides a short seasonal family splash and float place. Bring the inflatable float toys for kids to enjoy the small surge waves that come a couple times each minute downstream. Water flow reaches its peak late May-early June, when weekends pack out beaches with families playing in the sand near Dunes Parking Lot, Sand Pit Picnic Area, and Castle Creek Picnic Area. The creek usually dries up August-March.

ENJOYING THE DUNES

Best Hike

HIGH DUNE

DISTANCE: 2.5 miles (4 km) round-trip
DURATION: 2-3 hours
ELEVATION CHANGE: 699 feet (213 m)
EFFORT: strenuous
TRAILHEAD: Dunes Parking Lot

Hiking the **High Dune on First Ridge** is a grunt: each footstep sinks into the sand as you make slow headway up. Start by crossing Medano Creek, and then follow the ridge up. Sometimes zigzagging up the ridge helps. Footsteps from previous hikers may disappear as winds shift sands, so stick to the ridge. The view from the top of the dune spreads across the entire dune field with the Sangre de Cristo Mountains rising above.

Way, especially in late summer and fall. You can also catch the Perseid meteor shower in August. On moonless nights, use a red flashlight to go out stargazing to let your eyes adjust to the dark, and go to a less-crowded viewing spot north of the campground. On full-moon nights, you can walk on the dunes without a flashlight due to the brightness. The park has several ranger-led nighttime programs (May-Sept., free), including full moon dune walks, stargazing, and viewing nocturnal migrations of salamanders and frogs. Current schedules are online and at the visitors center.

into Great Sand Dunes National Preserve in the **Sangre de Cristo Mountains.** Check road conditions first at the visitors center before driving north beyond the campground to ascend to 10,040 feet (3,060 m) at Medano Pass. You may need to deflate tire pressure to handle the sand, rocks, and stream crossings on this rugged unpaved road, but you can refill on your return at the air station at the amphitheater parking lot. Fall is best for leaf color. Jeep rentals and tours are available through **Pathfinders 4X4** (719/496-6288, http://pathfinders4x4.com).

SCENIC DRIVE

For high-clearance 4WD vehicles only, **Medano Pass Primitive Road** (22.4 mi/36 km rt, closed in winter) climbs

HIKING

From Loop 2 in Piñon Flats Campground, a trail goes to **Dunes Overlook** (2.3 mi/3.7 km rt, 1.5-2.5 hrs, moderate)

TUBING MEDANO CREEK

COTTONWOODS ALONG MEDANO CREEK

HOW THE SAND DUNES FORM

The formula for creating sand dunes is simple: Wind and water deposit the sand in piles. This ongoing process forms and reshapes the dunes; some shift several feet in a week. The sand comes from the San Juan Mountains to the west via prevailing winds and the Sangre de Cristo Mountains to the east by washing down creeks.

The dunes' midsection contains 90 percent of the sand. But two other sections are different. The **sabkha,** wetlands of dried white mineral beds, flank the western portion of the dunes. Along the park's south boundary, the large **sand sheet** is mostly covered by grassland swept over by prevailing winds. Fields of yellow sunflowers show up in August. You can view both of these features at several pullouts on the park entrance road and on County Lane 6 North, between CO 150 and Mosca.

with a 450-foot (137-m) ascent occurring in switchbacks. The overlook takes in the dune field across Medano Creek drainage.

The Montville-Mosca Pass Trailhead launches two hikes. The easier **Montville Nature Trail** (0.5 mi/0.8 km rt, 30 min, easy) goes through a forest with views of the first dune ridge. The tougher **Mosca Pass Trail** (7 mi/11.3 km rt, 3.5-4 hrs, strenuous) climbs more than 1,400 feet (427 m) along trickling Mosca Creek through the forest to 9,737-foot (2,968-m) Mosca Pass in the Sangre de Cristo Mountains.

From the Point of No Return parking area, a trail reaches to two picnic areas on Medano Creek on the edge of the dunes. These are prime destinations for families, where kids can frolic in the creek and play on the sand. The

Sand Pit (1.5 mi/2.4 km rt, 1 hr, easy) has gentle sand slopes, while **Castle Creek** (3 mi/4.8 km rt, 1.5-2 hrs, moderate) has a 400-foot (122-m) dune that you can slide down and into a creek.

RECREATION
FAT TIRE BIKING

Bring your own fat tire bikes (not mountain bikes) to handle the sand, rocks, and creeks on the challenging Medano Pass Primitive Road (22.4 mi/36 km rt, closed in winter). The route, lined with primitive campsites, climbs to 10,040 feet (3,060 m) at **Medano Pass** in the Sangre de Cristo Mountains.

▼ ASPEN ABOVE THE DUNES

SUNSET OVER THE DUNES

HIKER ON TOP OF HIGH DUNE

WHERE TO STAY

INSIDE THE PARK

Some of the 88 sites at the park's **Piñon Flats Campground** (877/444-6777, www.recreation.gov, Apr.-Oct., $20) can be reserved up to six months in advance. The remaining 44 sites are first come, first served. Amenities include flush toilets and drinking water. On **Medano Pass Primitive Road** (4WD only), primitive campsites (21 sites, first come, first served, free) have bear boxes and fire rings.

OUTSIDE THE PARK

The **Great Sand Dunes Oasis** (7800 CO 150 N., Mosca, 719/378-2222, www.greatdunes.com, May-mid-Oct.) has a restaurant, convenience store, motel, campground, and gas station just outside the park entrance. The town of **Alamosa,** 34 miles (55 km) south, has limited services. Nearby lodging options include the primitive **Zapata Falls Campground** (BLM San Luis Valley Field Office, 719/852-7074) and motel rooms at **Great Sand Dunes Lodge** (719/378-2900, www.gsdlodge.com, Mar.-Oct.). Located 7.8 miles (15 min) from the park entrance, **Zapata Ranch**

(5305 CO 150, Mosca, 719/257-3043, www.ranchlands.com, $1,125-2,725 for 3-7 nights) is a working cattle ranch with horseback riding, educational programs, and all-inclusive accommodations. It's the only licensed provider of horseback rides into the park.

GETTING THERE AND AROUND

AIR

The closest airports are **Denver International Airport** (DEN, 8500 Peña Blvd., 303/342-2000, www.flydenver.com) and the smaller **Colorado Springs Airport** (COS, 7770 Milton E. Proby Pkwy., 719/550-1900, https://coloradosprings.gov/flycos). Car rentals are available at both.

CAR

Great Sand Dunes National Park is 255 miles (410 km) south of Denver and 170 miles (275 km) south of Colorado Springs via I-25 South and US 160 West. From US 160 near Alamosa, take CO 150 north for 20 miles (32 km) to the visitors center. There is no public transportation to or within the park.

WHITE SANDS NATIONAL PARK

New Mexico

KEEPSAKE STAMPS ▼▼▼

WEBSITE:
www.nps.gov/whsa

PHONE NUMBER:
575/479-6124

VISITATION RANK:
31

WHY GO:
Walk in the world's largest gypsum dune field.

▲ GYPSUM SAND DUNES

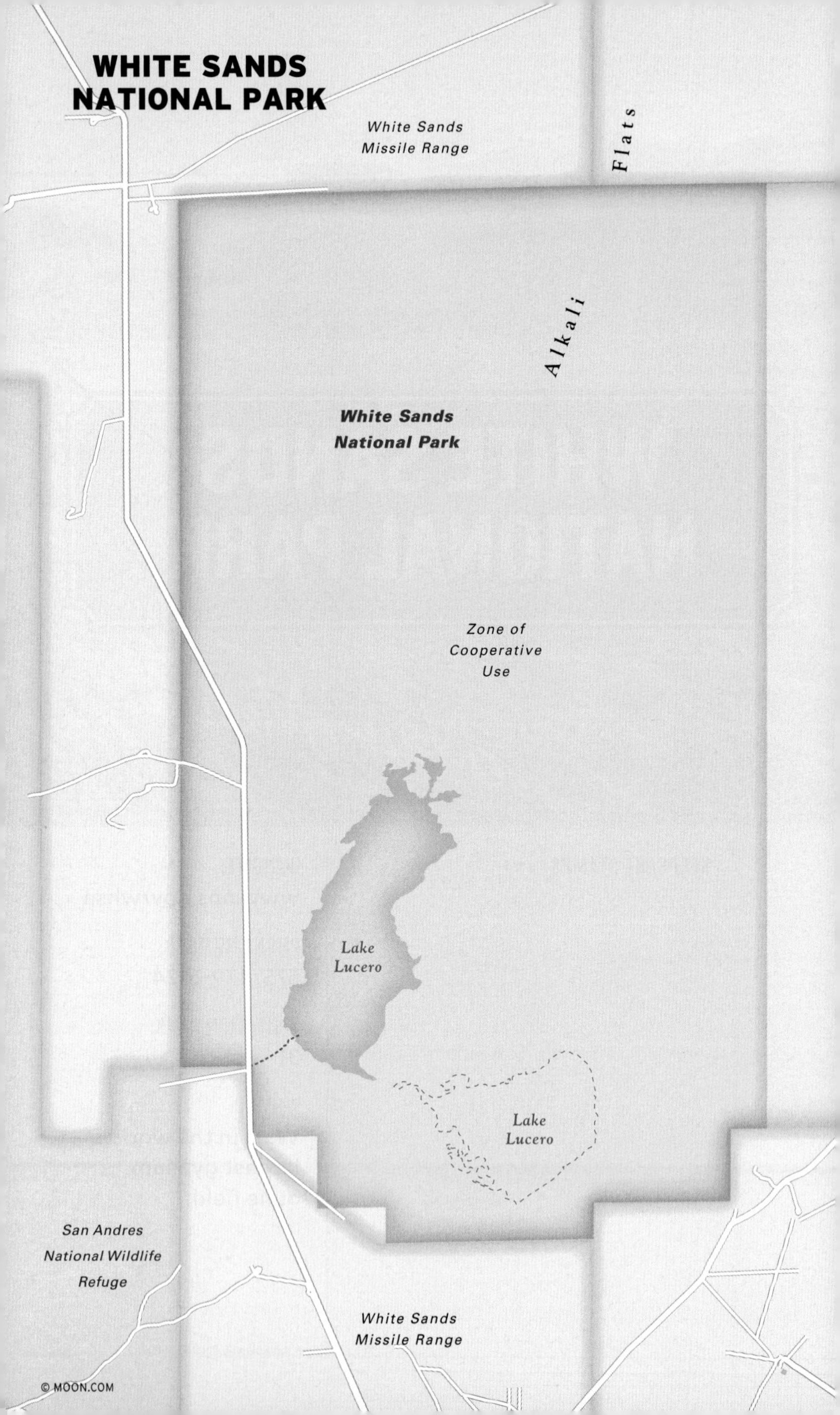

WHITE SANDS
NATIONAL PARK

*White Sands
Missile Range*

Flats

Alkali

**White Sands
National Park**

*Zone of
Cooperative
Use*

*Lake
Lucero*

*Lake
Lucero*

*San Andres
National Wildlife
Refuge*

*White Sands
Missile Range*

© MOON.COM

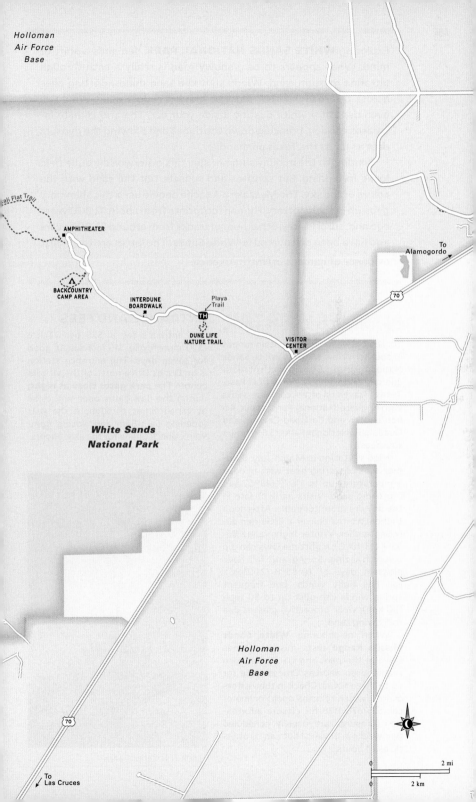

Holloman
Air Force
Base

Alkali Flat Trail

AMPHITHEATER

BACKCOUNTRY
CAMP AREA

INTERDUNE
BOARDWALK

Playa
Trail

TH

DUNE LIFE
NATURE TRAIL

VISITOR
CENTER

To
Alamogordo

70

White Sands
National Park

Holloman
Air Force
Base

70

To
Las Cruces

0   2 mi

0   2 km

Exploring **WHITE SANDS NATIONAL PARK** demands a shift of mind. What appears to be a snowy road is really a path through ultrafine gypsum sand. Winds shift the sand dunes, drifting piles across the roadway that must be plowed almost daily. Wind will even deposit a white dusting inside your car. The arid climate increases erosion, breaking down the dunes and blowing the gypsum dust as far as the Texas panhandle.

Blinding in the midday summer sun, this otherworldly dune field looks forbidding. But sunrises and sunsets tint the sand with the colors of the sky. The Mescalero Apache people used this shimmery gypsum in their pottery. Human footprints from about 12,000 years ago and, surprisingly, other human tracks from around 22,000 years ago have been discovered in White Sands. The latter are the oldest evidence of humans in North America.

PLANNING YOUR TIME

Tucked between high mountain ranges in southern New Mexico, White Sands National Park is 3.5 hours south of Albuquerque and 1.5 hours north of El Paso, Texas. Travelers often combine visits with Saguaro National Park, about 4.5 hours west, and Carlsbad Caverns and Guadalupe National Parks, 3.5-4 hours southeast.

High visitation is March-July. **Summer** sees blistering heat with midday temperatures up to 110°F (43°C) and scorching sand. Visits early or late in the day are more tolerable. Afternoon thunderstorms deliver a little rain July-September. Winter highs range 55-65°F (13-18°C); nighttime lows can dip below freezing. Spring and fall have pleasant days of 70-85°F (21-29°C). Fall has light winds, but frequent spring winds can gust up to 50 mph (80 kph); wear protective glasses due to blowing sand.

When neighboring **White Sands Missile Range** tests missiles, Dunes Drive in the park and US 70 between Alamogordo and Las Cruces close for up to three hours. Check in the visitors center (which remains open) online or call 575/678-1178 for closure information. Closures are usually scheduled two weeks in advance but can be as little as 24 hours.

ENTRANCE AND FEES

The entrance fee is $25 per vehicle ($20 motorcycle, $15 individual), good for seven days. The entrance station is on Dunes Drive north of the visitors center. The **park gates close at night;** during the day, gates open and close at varied times throughout the year (opening 5am-8am and closing 6pm-9pm). Check online for the exact hours.

YUCCA IN INTERDUNE AREA

Top ❸

❶ TOUR DUNES DRIVE

Dunes Drive (16 mi/26 km rt, 45 min) goes north from the visitors center on pavement surrounded by thick desert scrub. But soon the vegetation thins and white dunes become more prominent with yuccas anchored into the sand. Wind blows sand drifts over the road margins. At 5 miles (8 km), the pavement is replaced by packed sand that is plowed daily with berms on the side that look like snow. Be ready to encounter washboards, potholes, and

DUNE RIPE FOR SLIDING

larger drifts of sand along the curves amid dunes of brilliant white gypsum. Pull-outs have exhibits, picnic areas have vault toilets, and parking areas allow you to walk amid the dunes. Don't stray out of visual distance from the road unless you are on a marked trail.

❷ REVEL IN THE FULL MOON

Visit at night to delight in the moonlight glinting off gypsum dunes. Rangers lead **Full Moon Hikes** (877/444-6777, www.recreation.gov, 1.5 hrs, Apr.-Oct., $8 adults, $4 kids) on the Dune Life Nature Trail once a month on the night before the full moon. Reservations, which can be made up to 30 days in advance, are required. **Full Moon Nights** (1-2 hrs, May-Oct., free) take place at the natural dune amphitheater near the end of Dunes Drive once a month with live music, ranger talks, or artists. Bring a camp chair or blanket for sitting.

❸ PLAY IN THE WHITE SAND

The park's huge dune field is unique due to its fine white gypsum sand. To play in the mesmerizing sand, drive to the loop at the end of Dunes Drive where you can slog up a dune, check how fast the wind and dust erase your tracks, and winnow the sand through your fingers. You can walk anywhere on the sand, but to be safe, stay in sight of the roadway. If you bring a waxed plastic snow saucer or buy one at the gift shop at the visitors center, you can even slide down a dune. It's best when the sand is packed following a rain; choose one with a safe run-out away from plants and the road.

FOOTPRINTS IN THE SAND

Best Hike

ALKALI FLATS

DISTANCE: 5 miles (8 km) round-trip
DURATION: 3 hours
ELEVATION CHANGE: 94 feet (29 m)
EFFORT: strenuous
TRAILHEAD: Alkali Flats
Trailhead at the end of
Dunes Drive

Don't be fooled by the "flats" in the name. **Alkali Flat Trail** vaults up and down over the shadeless gypsum dunes in the heart of the park. Each step sinks into the sand on this loop. With one white dune looking like the next and wind filling in footprints, it's easy to get lost. Follow the orange markers; if you can't see the next trail marker, turn around. The trail looks over the dry bed that once housed ice-age Lake Otero.

TRAILHEAD FOR ALKALI FLATS

VISITORS CENTER

At the junction of US 70 and Dunes Drive, **White Sands Visitor Center** (9am-6pm daily late May-early Sept., 9am-5pm daily early Sept.-late May) is a historic pueblo-style building constructed in the 1930s. It offers park information, interactive exhibits, a film, and a bookstore. Outside is a native plant garden. A gift shop sits behind the visitors center.

HIKING

SELF-GUIDED HIKES

Since shifting sands erase footprints, routes in the sand are lined with trail markers, each within spotting distance of the last one. If you can't see the next marker, turn around, as it's unsafe to continue. Spring winds often reduce visibility. In the shifting sands, even a short walk will feel like a slog.

In the vegetated gypsum dunes, follow green markers and interpretive signs on the **Playa Trail** (Dunes Dr., 0.5 mi/0.8 km rt, 30 min, easy) to a depression that collects rainfall into a temporary lake.

Dune Life Nature Trail (Dunes Dr., 1 mi/1.6 km rt, 45 min, moderate), with blue trail markers, climbs to the top of a partially vegetated dune to make a loop in soft sand, passing 14 interpretive signs.

The **Interdune Boardwalk** (Dunes Dr., 0.4 mi/0.6 km rt, 20 min, easy) is an

ONE DAY IN WHITE SANDS

For a one-day trip, tour **Dunes Drive.** Follow the easy, accessible **Interdune Boardwalk** to learn about this unique desert. For a real adventure, hike out on the dunes to experience the feel of the fine gypsum sand beneath your feet.

elevated interpretive trail. The wheelchair-accessible route takes in a variety of desert vegetation.

RANGER-LED HIKES

The ranger-led **Sunset Stroll** (1 mi/1.6 km, 45-60 min, departs daily one hour before sunset, easy-moderate, free) walks up loose sand dunes and stops for interpretive talks. Meet at the signed Sunset Stroll Parking Area, 5 miles (8 km) down Dunes Drive. Ask at the visitors center for the current meeting time; the stroll is designed to finish with sunset.

A steep gully descends to **Lake Lucero** (1.5 mi/2.4 km, 3 hrs, moderate) on this ranger-led trip (once monthly Nov.-Apr., reservations required). The dry lake bed is filled with selenite crystals, some up to 2 feet (0.6 m) long and the source of the gypsum feeding the dunes. You'll caravan in your own car across the neighboring missile range to the trailhead. Make reservations (877/444-6777, www.recreation. gov, $8 adults, $4 kids) up to 30 days in advance.

BACKPACKING

The only way to stay in the park overnight is if you're backpacking and camping in the backcountry. You can watch the sunrise and sunset smear color across the sparkling sand. With orange trail markers, the **Backcountry Camping Trail** (2 mi/3.2 km rt, 2 hrs, moderate) climbs several steep dunes to reach the 10 primitive campsites among the white gypsum with no shade, toilets, or water. Though the trail

PICNIC TABLE WITH WINDSCREEN

GYPSUM DUNES

White Sands is estimated to contain 4.5 billion tons of gypsum. Similar to salt, gypsum dissolves in water but recrystallizes when dry. This mineral, which is used in toothpaste, makes up 98 percent of the dunes in White Sands. About 12,000 years ago, after the last ice age, rain and melting snow washed the dissolved gypsum down from the surrounding mountains into the large Lake Otero, which eventually dried up to form dunes. Today, the mineral still washes down from the mountains to pool seasonally at Lake Lucero. When the water evaporates, it leaves fragile selenite crystals to be broken down by wind and water blowing across the dunes.

is short, it will take more time to hike due to the loose sand. Plan to bring a tent, 1 gallon (3.8 l) of water per person per day, and a landfill-safe toilet bag. Pick up first-come, first-served **permits** ($10) at the visitors center. The trailhead is 6 miles (9.7 km) north on Dunes Drive and has a vault toilet.

RECREATION
MOUNTAIN BIKING

Bring your own fat tire or mountain bikes to handle the sand on Dunes Drive. Drifting sand and washboards add to the challenge of this unique ride.

WHERE TO STAY
INSIDE THE PARK

No lodgings or camping is available inside the park. Plows create several large sandy parking-lot picnic areas on Dunes Drive. They have tables with

▼ INTERDUNE BOARDWALK TRAIL

wind screens, raised grills, and vault toilets. The gift shop behind the visitors center carries convenience foods.

OUTSIDE THE PARK

The closest lodgings, dining, and services are in **Alamogordo,** 15 miles (24 km) from the park, but there are more plentiful options in **Las Cruces,** which is roughly a one-hour drive. The nearest campgrounds are 30-45 minutes away.

GETTING THERE AND AROUND
AIR

The closest airport is **El Paso International Airport** (ELP, 6701 Convair Rd., 915/212-0330, www.elpasointernationalairport.com). Car rentals are available.

CAR

You'll need a car to get to and explore White Sands. The nearest gas station is in Alamogordo, 15 miles (24 km) east of the park.

From El Paso, Texas, drive north on I-10, then take I-25 to US 70 east to reach the park (95 mi/153 km, 1.5 hrs).

From Albuquerque, drive south on I-25, east on US 380, and south on US 54 to Alamogordo and then east on US 70 to the park (225 mi/360 km, 3.5 hrs).

From Carlsbad Caverns National Park, drive north on US 285 and west on US 82 to Alamogordo to catch US 70 west to reach the park (190 mi/305 km, 3.5 hrs).

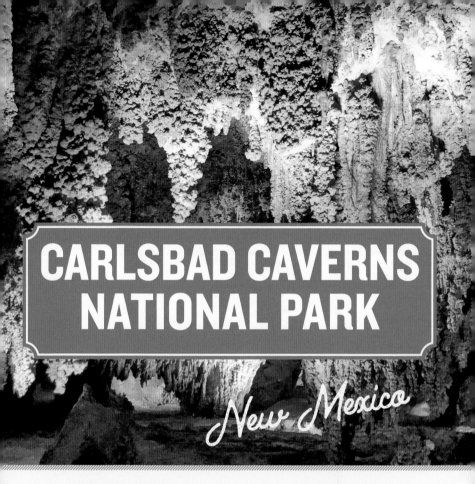

CARLSBAD CAVERNS NATIONAL PARK

New Mexico

KEEPSAKE STAMPS ▼▼▼

WEBSITE:
www.nps.gov/cave

PHONE NUMBER:
575/785-2232

VISITATION RANK:
44

WHY GO:
Tour underground
limestone caves.

▲ BIG ROOM, CARLSBAD CAVERNS

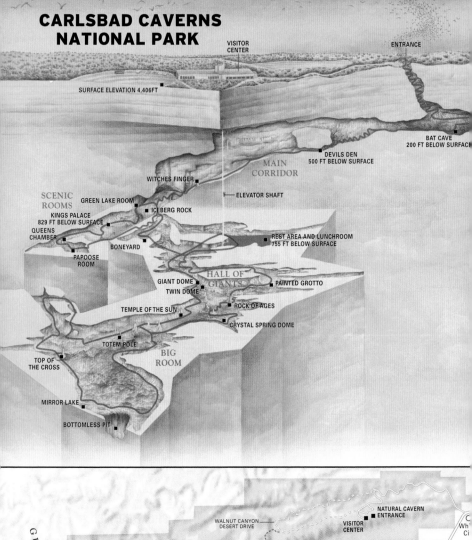

CARLSBAD CAVERNS NATIONAL PARK

VISITOR CENTER

ENTRANCE

SURFACE ELEVATION 4,406FT

BAT CAVE
200 FT BELOW SURFACE

DEVILS DEN
500 FT BELOW SURFACE

MAIN CORRIDOR

WITCHES FINGER

ELEVATOR SHAFT

SCENIC ROOMS

GREEN LAKE ROOM

ICEBERG ROCK

KINGS PALACE
829 FT BELOW SURFACE

QUEENS CHAMBER

REST AREA AND LUNCHROOM
755 FT BELOW SURFACE

BONEYARD

PAPOOSE ROOM

HALL OF GIANTS

GIANT DOME

TWIN DOME

PAINTED GROTTO

TEMPLE OF THE SUN

ROCK OF AGES

CRYSTAL SPRING DOME

TOTEM POLE

BIG ROOM

TOP OF THE CROSS

MIRROR LAKE

BOTTOMLESS PIT

GUADALUPE MOUNTAINS

CARLSBAD CAVERNS NATIONAL PARK

WALNUT CANYON DESERT DRIVE

NATURAL CAVERN ENTRANCE

VISITOR CENTER

Rattlesnake Canyon Trail

North Slaughter Canyon Trail

SLAUGHTER CANYON CAVE

RATTLESNAKE SPRINGS

418

Yucca Canyon Trail

62 180

To Carlsbad

To Guadalupe Mountains National Park and El Paso

0   5 r
0   5 km

© MOON.

CARLSBAD CAVERNS NATIONAL PARK is mesmerizing. Scientists theorize that these natural caves under the Guadalupe Mountains began to form several million years ago. As petroleum deposits reacted with groundwater, they turned into sulfuric acid, which ate through the stone, leaving vast hollow caverns. The caves started to fill with stalagmites and stalactites about 500,000 years ago. These still-growing features vary from hulking towers that ripple like clay to delicate needles that look more like icicles than stone.

Belowground, everyone visits the Big Room, a giant cathedral dripping with stalactites, one of the 119 known caves in the cavern system. At 145 known miles (233 km), Lechuguilla is the longest cave, loaded with rare gypsum and sulfur formations. Aboveground, the Chihuahuan Desert is studded with flowering cacti that feed a colony of Brazilian free-tailed bats, whose flight at dusk wows visitors.

PLANNING YOUR TIME

Reaching Carlsbad Caverns requires a long drive to southern New Mexico near the border with Texas. Plan at least one day to explore the caverns, though the more adventurous group tours are worth a second day. **May-September** is high season, with a full tour schedule and long lines inside and outside the cave. For greater solitude, visit in **December** (before the holidays) or **January-February.**

Though not all tours operate in winter, you'll have the place to yourself, in near silence. Book guided cave tours up to six months in advance. To prevent transmitting white-nose syndrome to the bat population, do not wear any clothing or shoes you have worn in other caves.

While temperatures may soar aboveground in summer, the caves hover at 56°F (13°C) year-round. Bring a sweater or warm coat and pack a lunch, as the park cafeteria is pretty institutional.

THE NATURAL ENTRANCE AT CARLSBAD CAVERNS

Top ❸

FLOWSTONE TOWER IN THE BIG ROOM

① ZOOM DOWN INTO THE BIG ROOM

The **Big Room** (elevator entry/exit 8:30am-6:45pm daily late May-early Sept., 8:30am-4:45pm daily early Sept.-late May) is the largest cave by volume in the caverns. An elevator whisks you 754 feet (229 m) down to the cavern floor. Lit with soft white lights, the Big Room glows like a natural cathedral: The ceiling soars into darkness within the immense chamber. Along the 1.25-mile (2-km) path, you'll pass the **Hall of Giants** and the **Bottomless Pit.** Plan 1.5 hours to complete the **Big Room Self-Guided Trail.** Expect crowds May-September.

② HIKE DOWN THE NATURAL ENTRANCE

Descend into the cavern on foot via the **Natural Entrance** (entry/exit 8:30am-4:30pm daily late May-early Sept., 8:30am-3:30pm daily Sept.-late May), which drops about 750 feet (228 m) through the **Main Corridor** along a strenuous 1.25-mile (2 km, one-way) trail dense with switchbacks. Walking down the Natural Entrance conveys the scale of this underground cave system: You have to hike for about 30 minutes around **Iceberg Rock,** a 200,000-ton (181,437-metric ton) boulder. The paved route has several steep sections with handrails, and the path may be slippery. Plan one hour to complete the **Natural Entrance Self-Guided Trail.** The path ends at the entrance to the Big Room and the elevators, which you can take back up.

③ MARVEL AT BATS IN FLIGHT

Late May-mid-October, hundreds of thousands of bats rush out from the depths of the caverns and into the bug-filled twilight. Half an hour before sunset at the amphitheater at the top of the Natural Entrance Trail, rangers give a short talk about the bats (ask at the visitors center for times). When the **Bat Flight** begins, you hear the soft flapping of their wings and feel the rush of air as they pass overhead.

AN OUTDOOR AMPHITHEATER PROVIDES SEATING FOR THE BAT FLIGHT.

Hiking boots are the best footwear for slick trails and rocky surfaces.

Due to the park's proximity to **Guadalupe Mountains National Park** (about 40 min), many visitors link visits to the two parks.

ENTRANCE AND FEES

Go to the visitors center to pay entrance fees or show your park pass. In the summer, allow for an extra hour's wait in lines at the visitors center. The entrance ticket is $15 per adult (age 16 and older) and good for three days. Entry fees and passes get you into the self-guided Big Room and down the Natural Entrance Trail, but additional fees are required for guided tours.

VISITORS CENTER

The **visitors center** (727 Carlsbad Caverns Hwy., 8am-7pm daily late May-early Sept., 8am-5pm daily early Sept.-late May) is at the end of the park entrance road. Pick up cave tour tickets and park information here. It also has a gift shop. For self-guided trails, you can rent an **audio tour** ($5). At the bottom of the elevators and Natural Cave Entrance Trail, the cave floor has a snack bar and restrooms hidden behind rock formations.

RANGER-GUIDED TOURS

A group tour offers an alternative to the crowds in the Big Room: It's quieter and you'll see a lot more of the caverns. **Reservations** (877/444-6777, www.recreation.gov) are required and can be booked between 48 hours and six months in advance. If available, remaining tickets are sold on the day of tours at the visitors center. Be sure to ask what time to arrive; some tours require hour-long hikes to the departure point. Children can get half-price tickets.

KING'S PALACE

King's Palace (daily year-round, 1 mi/1.6 km, 1.5 hrs, $8, minimum age 4) is the deepest part of the caves open to the public. The tour passes giant formations as well as tiny details such as a bat's skeleton grown into a stalagmite.

Best of all, it includes a few minutes with the lights turned off, when you get to stand in the cool, smothering black. Unlike the other ranger-led tours, the paved trail is only steep at the entrance and exit.

LEFT HAND TUNNEL

Left Hand Tunnel (daily year-round, 0.5 mi/0.8 km, 2 hrs, $7, minimum age 6) is best for a sheer sense of discovery. A small group of visitors carries flickering lanterns through fantastic rock formations—made all the more bizarre as they loom out of the darkness.

LOWER CAVE

Lower Cave (four times a week year-round, 1 mi/1.6 km, 3 hrs, $20, minimum age 12) requires some exertion, as the path starts with a clamber down 60 feet (18 m) of rope and narrow ladders. Formations include toothpick-like stalactites and the perfectly round and white formations called "cave pearls."

SLAUGHTER CANYON CAVE

Slaughter Canyon Cave (once weekly year-round, 1 mi/1.6 km, 5.5 hrs, $15,

THE BIG ROOM

minimum age 8) is 5 miles (8 km) south of Whites City off a well-signed county road. After a steep 0.5-mile (0.8-km) hike to the cave entrance, the walk takes you by formations like the glittering crystal-covered column dubbed the Christmas Tree.

HALL OF THE WHITE GIANT AND SPIDER CAVE

For those who aren't afraid of tight spaces, the **Hall of the White Giant** and **Spider Cave** (once weekly in summer, 1 mi/1.6 km, 4 hrs, $20, minimum age 12) are strenuous but rewarding trips. Expect to wiggle through some very narrow tunnels and to get muddy in the process. Gloves, knee and elbow pads, and helmets are provided.

NIGHT SKY PROGRAMS

Nighttime aboveground is magical. These June-October free ranger-led nocturnal adventures take place on select dates following the bat flight program. Register on the morning of the program to be one of the 25 people on a **Star Walk** (0.5 mi/0.8 km rt) or **Full Moon Hike** (1.5 mi/2.4 km rt). **Star Parties** (no registration needed) take place on moonless nights.

WHERE TO STAY

INSIDE THE PARK

There are no accommodations or campgrounds inside the park. **Primitive backcountry camping** is allowed with a permit (free) available at the visitors center. Inside the visitors center, the **Carlsbad Caverns Trading Company** sells a limited menu of to-go snacks and drinks.

OUTSIDE THE PARK

Guadalupe Mountains National Park (915/828-3251, www.nps.gov/gumo) is where people usually camp when visiting Carlsbad Caverns. It's 35 miles (56 km) south of Whites City on US 62/180. **Carlsbad,** 27 miles (43 km) north of the park on US 62/180, has accommodations, and **Roswell** has national chain hotels.

GETTING THERE AND AROUND

AIR

The closest airport is **El Paso International Airport** (ELP, 6701 Convair Rd., 915/212-0330, www.elpasointernationalairport.com) in Texas. It has rental cars. From here, drive east on US 62/180 to Whites City, New Mexico (138 mi/222 km, 2.5 hrs).

CAR

From Carlsbad, New Mexico, drive 20 miles (32 km, 30 min) south on US 62/180 to reach Whites City. Fill your gas tank in Carlsbad to avoid being at the mercy of the one pricey station in Whites City.

From Whites City, drive 7 miles (11 km) west on winding Carlsbad Caverns Highway. Plan 30 minutes to reach the visitors center due to the curvy road and slow vehicles. Watch for wildlife darting onto the road.

POOL OF WATER IN BIG ROOM

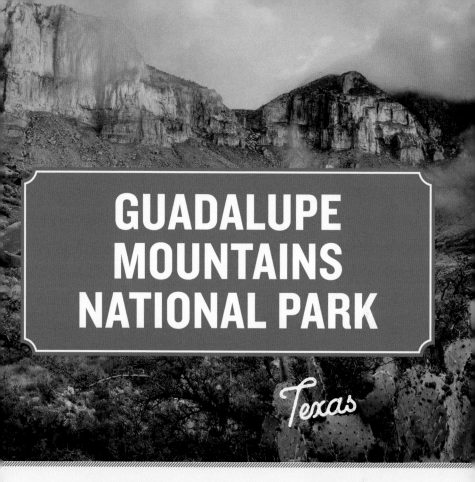

GUADALUPE MOUNTAINS NATIONAL PARK

Texas

KEEPSAKE STAMPS ▼▼▼

WEBSITE:
www.nps.gov/gumo

PHONE NUMBER:
915/828-3251

VISITATION RANK:
49

WHY GO:
Hike ancient
fossil reefs.

▲ EL CAPITAN, GUADALUPE
MOUNTAINS NATIONAL PARK

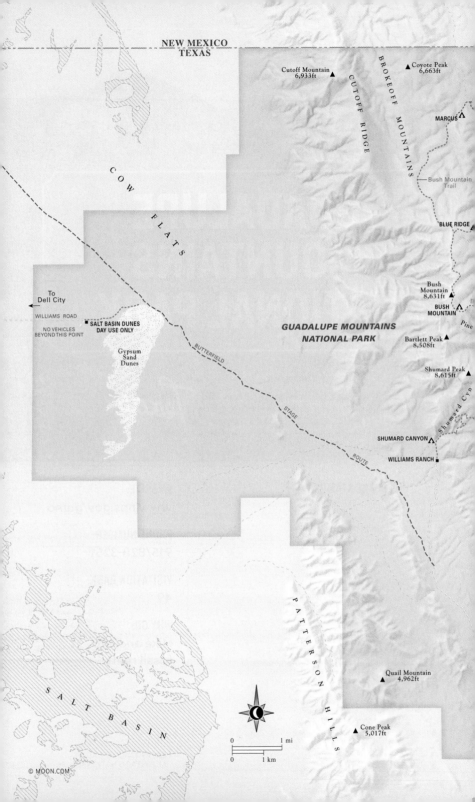

NEW MEXICO
TEXAS

Cutoff Mountain
6,933ft

▲ Coyote Peak
6,663ft

BROKEOFF MOUNTAINS

CUTOFF RIDGE

MARCUS

Bush Mountain
Trail

COW FLATS

BLUE RIDGE

To
Dell City

Bush
Mountain
8,631ft

WILLIAMS ROAD

NO VEHICLES
BEYOND THIS POINT

■ SALT BASIN DUNES
DAY USE ONLY

BUSH
MOUNTAIN

B

Pine

GUADALUPE MOUNTAINS
NATIONAL PARK

Bartlett Peak
8,508ft ▲

Gypsum
Sand
Dunes

BUTTERFIELD

Shumard Peak
8,615ft ▲

Shumard Cyn

STAGE

SHUMARD CANYON

ROUTE

WILLIAMS RANCH ■

PATTERSON HILLS

Quail Mountain
4,962ft
▲

SALT BASIN

Cone Peak
5,017ft
▲

0   1 mi

0   1 km

© MOON.COM

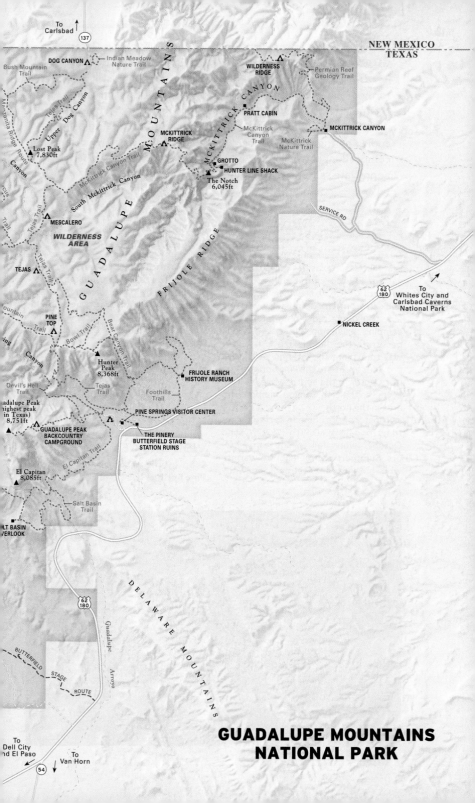

To Carlsbad

137

NEW MEXICO
TEXAS

DOG CANYON

Bush Mountain
Trail

Indian Meadow
Nature Trail

WILDERNESS
RIDGE

Permian Reef
Geology Trail

Tejas Trail

Upper Dog Canyon

Manzanita Ridge Route

Lost Peak
7,830ft

McKittrick Canyon Trail

McKITTRICK
RIDGE

PRATT CABIN

McKittrick
Canyon
Trail

McKITTRICK CANYON

McKittrick
Nature Trail

GUADALUPE MOUNTAINS

McKITTRICK CANYON

South Mckittrick Canyon

GROTTO
HUNTER LINE SHACK

The Notch
6,045ft

MESCALERO

WILDERNESS
AREA

FRIJOLE RIDGE

SERVICE RD

Tejas Trail

TEJAS

62
180

To
Whites City and
Carlsbad Caverns
National Park

Bear Canyon Trail

PINE
TOP

Bowl Trail

NICKEL CREEK

Hunter
Peak
8,368ft

FRIJOLE RANCH
HISTORY MUSEUM

Canyon

Devil's Hell
Trail

Tejas
Trail

Foothills
Trail

uadalupe Peak
(highest peak
in Texas)
8,751ft

PINE SPRINGS VISITOR CENTER

GUADALUPE PEAK
BACKCOUNTRY
CAMPGROUND

THE PINERY
BUTTERFIELD STAGE
STATION RUINS

El Capitan Trail

El Capitan
8,085ft

Salt Basin
Trail

LT BASIN
ERLOOK

62
180

Guadalupe

DELAWARE MOUNTAINS

Arroyo

BUTTERFIELD

STAGE

ROUTE

To
Dell City
nd El Paso

To
Van Horn

54

GUADALUPE MOUNTAINS
NATIONAL PARK

Beckoning high in the distance from the Chihuahuan Desert, the **GUADALUPE MOUNTAINS** are a natural wonder straddling the Texas-New Mexico border. Built from a marine fossil reef that formed under tropical waters more than 260 million years ago, the mountains extend from desert floor to craggy summits. They include Guadalupe Peak, the highest point in Texas. Originally occupied by the Nde (Mescalero Apache) people, this landscape is a compelling destination for hikers, backpackers, and campers who appreciate solitude and rugged desert.

PLANNING YOUR TIME

Guadalupe Mountains National Park is in far West Texas, 114 miles (183 km) east of El Paso and 55 miles (89 km) south of Carlsbad, New Mexico. While you can drop in for a single day, you'll be able to explore more on a multi-night camping excursion. No paved roads penetrate the park; hiking is the only way to explore the interior. US 62/180 provides access to the Pine Springs Visitor Center in the south, while NM 137 accesses the Dog Canyon campground area in the north.

Most visitors come in **spring** (Mar.-May) for days of 60-90°F (16-27°C) and October when fall foliage turns colors. **Summers** can be slightly warmer while fall and winter see cool and windy conditions. The park, visitors center, and campground are open year-round, but some higher elevations can see snow on the trails (Dec.-Jan.) and winds can howl up to 70 mph (112 kph).

Due to the park's proximity (a 40-min drive) to **Carlsbad Caverns National Park** in New Mexico, many visitors combine a tour of this park with a trip to the caverns.

ENTRANCE AND FEES

The entrance fee is $10 per person and valid for seven days. There are no entrance stations; pay the fee at trailhead kiosks or in the visitors center.

VISITORS CENTER

Drop by the park's visitors center at **Pine Springs** (US 62/180, 915/828-3251,

OVERLOOKING PINE SPRINGS

Top ❸

EL CAPITAN

① SPY EL CAPITAN

Approaching the park from the west or south, **El Capitan** (8,085 ft/2,464 m) is the most prominent peak in view. While not the highest peak in the park, its limestone vertical cliffs, reminiscent of a far more popular peak in Yosemite by the same name, mark the southern end of the exposed marine fossil reef. You can best see it from US 62/180 between the two picnic areas outside the park, south of Pine Springs Visitor Center. For up-close views, the **El Capitan Trail** (11.3 mi/18.2 km rt, 6-8 hrs) tours below the cliffs.

② HIKE THE PINERY NATURE TRAIL

From the visitors center, tour the wheelchair-accessible paved **Pinery Trail** (0.75 mi/1.2 km rt, 20 min, easy) to the fragile rock-walled ruins of a stagecoach station that once served the Butterfield Mail Coach and mule trains. The limestone structure was the place to get fresh horses and repair wagons. Interpretive signs on the path introduce you to the flora that thrives in the arid Chihuahuan Desert.

③ VISIT A HISTORIC RANCH

At an oasis 1.5 miles (2.4 km) northeast of the visitors center, the **Frijole Ranch Museum** (usually 8am-4:30pm daily) contains exhibits about the Mescalero Apache people and early ranchers who eked out livings here in the Chihuahuan Desert. Adjacent to the museum is a one-room schoolhouse and a springhouse. A paved wheelchair-accessible trail goes to **Manzanita Spring** (0.4 mi/0.6 km rt, 15 min, easy), a haven for birds.

ROCK WALL RUINS ON THE PINERY NATURE TRAIL

Best Hike

DEVIL'S HALL

DISTANCE: 4.2 miles (6.7 km) round-trip
DURATION: 3 hours
ELEVATION CHANGE: 550 feet (168 m)
EFFORT: strenuous
TRAILHEAD: Pine Springs Campground

Beginning at Pine Springs Campground, the **Devil's Hall Trail** follows a maintained path for 1 mile (1.6 km) before the fun begins. Hikers must navigate the route through a wash filled with gravel, loose rock, and debris by scrambling over boulders to reach a pour-over known as Hiker's Staircase. After climbing the natural staircase, the route squeezes into a narrow steep-walled canyon where the sides look like layers of pancaked rock. This route can be dangerous when wet; avoid hiking during rain.

DEVIL'S HALL

8am-6pm daily Apr.-Oct., 8am-4:30pm daily Nov.-Mar.) to pick up maps and brochures, find out the current weather forecast, view interpretive exhibits, browse the bookstore, and talk to the knowledgeable park staff.

RECREATION

HIKING

Hikers are required to pack out all toilet paper and menstrual products, and use landfill-safe toilet bags. For self-guided interpretive trails, walk **McKittrick Canyon Nature Trail** (0.9 mi/1.4 km rt, moderate) or the **Indian Meadow Nature Trail** (0.6 mi/1 km rt, easy) at Dog Canyon.

From the Frijole Ranch Trailhead, a loop trail goes to the oasis of **Smith Spring** (2.3 mi/3.7 km rt, 1-2 hrs, moderate). Wildlife, birds, and the shady oasis indicate the importance of water in the Chihuahuan Desert environment.

To experience the majesty of McKittrick Canyon, allow most of the day to reach the high ridges. Start at the McKittrick Canyon contact station to descend the **McKittrick Canyon Trail** (2.4-7.6 mi/3.9-12.2 km one-way) before reaching the first milestone—Pratt

Cabin, the 1929 structure of geologist and land donator Wallace Pratt. Another 1.1 miles (1.8 km) leads to Grotto Picnic Area, one of the canyon's most scenic areas. With enough time and stamina, continue 4.1 more miles (6.6 km) to McKittrick Ridge for views of colorful canyon walls and rugged outcroppings. McKittrick Canyon is known for fall color.

From Pine Springs Campground, the **Guadalupe Peak Trail** (8.4 mi/13.5 km rt, 6-8 hrs) leads to stunning views atop the highest point in Texas. With a 2,906-foot (886-m) ascent, the trek climbs at a moderate clip to 8,751 feet (2,667 m), where huge views take in the expansive desert and mountain surroundings. The summit contains a large obelisk installed by American Airlines. At 1 mile (1.6 km) before the summit is a backcountry campsite.

BACKPACKING

There are 59 wilderness camping sites; all require a **permit** ($6 pp/night). Due to the isolated nature of these sites, it's essential to bring at least 1 gallon (3.8 l) of water per person per day, ample food (open fires are prohibited), and emergency gear. Camping in the designated wilderness requires using landfill-safe toilet bags. **Reservations** (www.recreation.gov, $6) are available four months in advance. First-come, first-served permits are issued at Pine Springs Visitor Center.

WHERE TO STAY

The park's two campgrounds ($20) are available by reservation (www.recreation.gov) six months in advance. Both have drinking water and flush toilets (no showers). No hookups are available.

Near the park's headquarters and visitors center, **Pine Springs Campground** (20 tent sites, 19 RV sites) sprinkles graveled tent sites among junipers and RV sites in a paved parking lot. The nearby trailhead goes to Guadalupe Peak and Devil's Hall.

Sitting at 6,280 feet (1,914 m), **Dog Canyon Campground** (9 tent sites, 4 RV sites) is tucked in a secluded tree-filled and steep-walled canyon on the north side of the park. Its higher elevation and sheltered location result in

TRAIL UP GUADALUPE PEAK

cooler temperatures than Pine Springs. The canyon also protects the area from strong winds that blast through in winter and spring. Cooking grills are available for charcoal fires.

GETTING THERE AND AROUND

The nearest international airport is in **El Paso** (ELP, 6701 Convair Rd., 915/212-0330, www.elpasointernationalairport.com), 114 miles (184 km) west of the Guadalupe Mountains via US 62/180. Rental cars are available.

Arriving from the east, take either I-20 or I-10 to Van Horn. Then head north for about an hour on TX 54, one of the most scenic drives in the state, to reach the park.

There is no public transportation into or within the park. The nearest gas station is 44 miles (71 km) away in Dell City, so gas up before you arrive.

BIG BEND
NATIONAL PARK

Texas

WEBSITE:
www.nps.gov/bibe

PHONE NUMBER:
432/477-2251

VISITATION RANK:
37

WHY GO:
Experience the
Rio Grande.

KEEPSAKE STAMPS ▼▼▼

▲ SANTA ELENA CANYON, BIG BEND
NATIONAL PARK

This park's namesake bend in the Rio Grande isn't the only enormous feature here. **BIG BEND NATIONAL PARK** encompasses spectacular canyons, mesmerizing desert, awe-inspiring mountains, and unexpected temperate woodlands teeming with birdsong. High mountain cliffs house peregrine falcons; colorful tropical birds nest here in spring; and birds from the north migrate here in winter to enjoy the warm climate.

Ancient limestone cliffs flank steep-walled Santa Elena Canyon, formations that lend a sacred aura to the slot where the Rio Grande slices its way toward the Gulf of Mexico. Downstream, the Chisos Mountains rise with views extending across the river into Mexico. This landscape of canyons, river, mountains, and desert has been home to Indigenous people for 10,000 years, most recently the Chisos, Mescalero Apache, and Comanche. They saw the dark skies above yielding a brilliant Milky Way. Today, you can too.

PLANNING YOUR TIME

Big Bend National Park sits in an isolated pocket of southwest Texas. With driving times and distances considerable, a car is the only means of access. Advanced planning is required: make reservations for lodging and camping six months in advance for visits in peak season—**February-May** and **October-December.**

PRICKLY PEAR CACTUS

Plan to spend 2-5 days in Big Bend National Park. Some visitors never leave the scenic drives, but hiking or camping is the best way to soak up its variety.

Big Bend's weather is only comfortable October-April. Summer is ridiculously hot—this *is* the Chihuahuan Desert—and despite the increased elevation and low humidity, triple-digit temperatures are brutal. May and June are the hottest months. Later in summer, periodic rainstorms along with occasional heavy thunderstorms and flash flooding help ease the intensity of the heat. Winter is the most volatile season in Big Bend; mild temperatures through extremes are possible, from 85°F (29°C) to periods of light snow.

ENTRANCES AND FEES

The park has two entrance stations: The **North Entrance Station** (via US 385 from Marathon) and the western gate at **Maverick Junction Entrance Station** (TX 118). The entrance fee is $30 per vehicle ($25 motorcycle, $15 individual) and good for seven days.

VISITORS CENTERS

The main visitors center is the park headquarters at **Panther Junction** (8:30am-5pm daily), 26 miles (42 km) from the North Entrance Station and 25 miles (40 km) from the Maverick

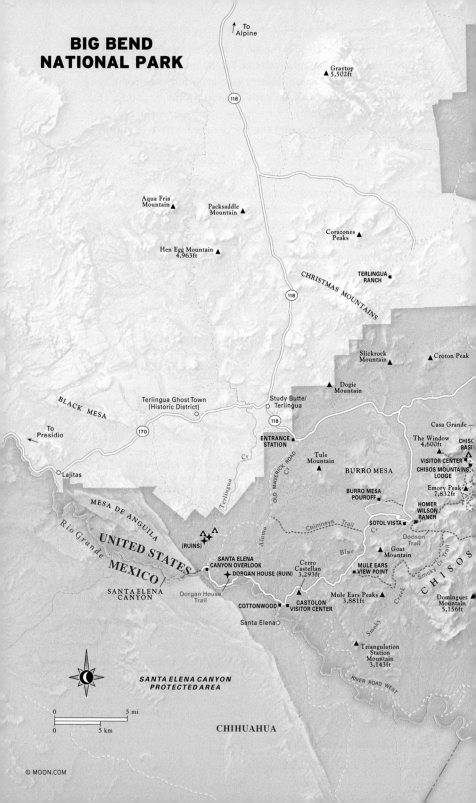

BIG BEND
NATIONAL PARK

To Alpine

▲ Graytop
5,502ft

118

Aqua Fria ▲
Mountain

Packsaddle ▲
Mountain

Corazones ▲
Peaks

Hen Egg Mountain ▲
4,963ft

TERLINGUA ■
RANCH

CHRISTMAS MOUNTAINS

118

Slickrock ▲
Mountain

▲ Croton Peak

BLACK MESA

Terlingua Ghost Town
(Historic District)

Study Butte/
Terlingua

Dogie ▲
Mountain

Casa Grande

To
Presidio

170

118

ENTRANCE
STATION

Tule ▲
Mountain

BURRO MESA

The Window
4,600ft

CHISC
BASI

VISITOR CENTER
CHISOS MOUNTAINS
LODGE

Lajitas

Cr

Terlingua

OLD MAVERICK ROAD

Cr

BURRO MESA ■
POUROFF

Emory Peak ▲
7,832ft

HOMER
WILSON
RANCH

MESA DE ANGUILA

Alamo

Chimneys Trail

SOTOL VISTA ■

Cr

Dodson
Trail

Rio Grande

UNITED STATES
MEXICO

(RUINS)

Blue

Goat ▲
Mountain

Smoky & Trail

CHISOS

SANTA ELENA
CANYON OVERLOOK

SANTA ELENA
CANYON

DORGAN HOUSE (RUIN)

Dorgan House
Trail

COTTONWOOD

Cerro
Castellan
3,293ft

MULE EARS ■
VIEW POINT

Mule Ears Peaks ▲
3,881ft

Creek

Dominguez ▲
Mountain
5,156ft

CASTOLON
VISITOR CENTER

Santa Elena

Smoky

Triangulation ▲
Station
Mountain
3,143ft

RIVER ROAD WEST

SANTA ELENA CANYON
PROTECTED AREA

CHIHUAHUA

0   5 mi

0   5 km

© MOON.COM

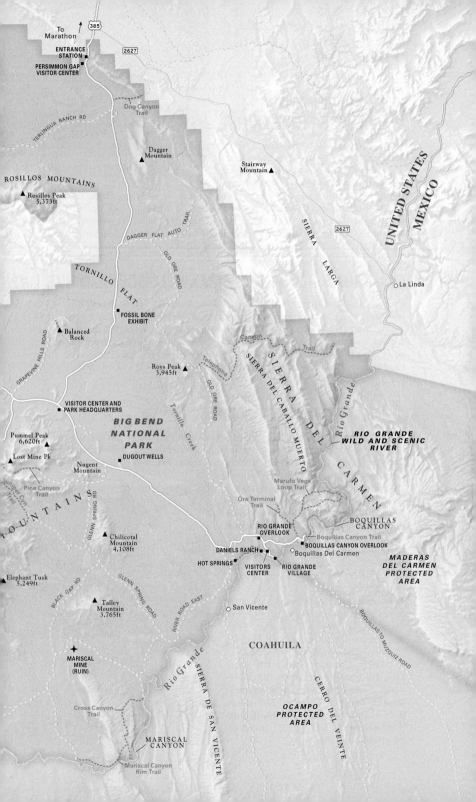

Top **3**

CHISOS VILLAGE IN THE CHISOS MOUNTAINS

① EXPLORE THE CHISOS MOUNTAINS

From Panther Junction, the Chisos Mountains rise like a forested island above the arid Chihuahuan Desert. This unique mixed forest fills with a cacophony of birdsong in spring. The mountains are topped by **Emory Peak.** To see them up close, drive steep **Chisos Basin Road** (6 mi/9.7 km one-way, RV limit 24 ft/7.3 m, trailer limit 20 ft/6.1 m), up dramatic hairpin turns (10 mph/16 kph limit) to **Chisos Mountains Lodge** and **Chisos Basin Visitor Center.** From Chisos Basin, trails depart for hikers and backpackers to explore the forest, cliffs, and vistas into Mexico.

② CRUISE ALONG ROSS MAXWELL SCENIC DRIVE

Crossing the western portion of the park, **Ross Maxwell Scenic Drive** (30 mi/48 km one-way) tours through the vast desert slowly shifting into volcanic rock formations. Stop at **Mule Ears Overlook** to see the striking peaks before driving through the volcanic ash of Tuff Canyon. Drop by the historic village of **Castolon** for an hour to explore the exhibits in the century-old structures. Then, continue west to the road terminus at **Santa Elena Canyon Overlook,** where immense cliffs pinch the Rio Grande.

③ RAFT THE RIO GRANDE

Famed as the international boundary between the United States and Mexico, the Rio Grande provides rafting opportunities amid the steep walls of **Santa Elena Canyon.** Expect 13 miles (21 km) of easy desert paddling and 7 miles (11 km) of huge Class IV rapids, where the river funnels through the towering cliffs overhead.

Downstream, the designated **Rio Grande Wild and Scenic River** flows past giant limestone cliffs of **Mariscal Canyon** (10 mi/16 km) and froths with Class II-III rapids. For a multiday float for canoes or rafts, **Boquillas Canyon** (33 mi/53 km) is tamer, with Class I-II rapids.

Permits (www.recreation.gov, $10) are required for overnight rafting trips, available six months in advance. Print out the permit two weeks in advance to bring with you. To book guided river trips, rent gear, or hire shuttles, contact **Big Bend River Tours** (800/545-4240, www.bigbendrivertours.com), **Desert Sports** (432/371-2727, www.desertsportstx.com), or **Far Flung Outdoor Center** (432/371-2633, www.bigbendfarflung.com).

RIVER RAFTING ON THE RIO GRANDE

ONE DAY IN BIG BEND

If you only have one day to spend in the park, stop at **Panther Junction Visitor Center** before taking a scenic drive into the **Chisos Mountains** to **Chisos Basin Visitor Center.** Follow that with the **Ross Maxwell Scenic Drive** out to **Santa Elena Canyon Overlook** to see the **Rio Grande** spilling from the huge slot. If you have time, hike the short trail into the canyon.

Junction Entrance Station. This visitors center offers interpretive exhibits and scores of books, brochures, and maps. You can also get schedules for **free ranger-led programs** (varies weekly) that include guided walks and evening amphitheater programs. If you can catch a night sky telescope program, you'll be treated to brilliant sights unseen around city lights, an attribute that makes Big Bend an **International Dark Sky Park.** On full moon nights, rangers guide moonlight walks.

Entering from the North Entrance Station, you will first pass through the seasonal visitors center at **Persimmon Gap** (10am-12:30pm and 1pm-4pm daily Nov.-Apr.). The park's smaller visitors centers include **Chisos Basin** (8:30am-noon and 1pm-4pm daily year-round), **Castolon** (10am-4pm daily Nov.-Apr.) in the Castolon Historic District, and **Rio Grande Village** (9am-4pm daily Nov.-Apr.).

SCENIC DRIVES

OLD MAVERICK ROAD

High-clearance vehicles can tackle the dirt-and-gravel **Old Maverick Road** (14 mi/23 km one-way). The road completes the loop between Ross Maxwell Scenic Drive, Santa Elena Canyon Overlook, and Maverick Junction. Speckled with historical sites, such as the **Terlingua Abaja** ruins, it slices across the Terlingua Creek Badlands. Plan one hour for the washboarded drive.

SIGHTS

FOSSIL DISCOVERY EXHIBIT

Off the Persimmon Gap Entrance Road (US 385, 8 mi/13 km north of Panther Jct.), the roadside **Fossil Discovery Exhibit** (http://fossildiscoveryexhibit.com, dawn-dusk daily, not

RUINS OFF OLD MAVERICK ROAD

THE RIO GRANDE THROUGH SANTA ELENA CANYON

Best Hike
LOST MINE TRAIL

DISTANCE: 4.8 miles (7.7 km) round-trip
DURATION: 3-4 hours
ELEVATION CHANGE: 1,045 feet (319 m)
EFFORT: moderate
TRAILHEAD: Chisos Basin Road, mile 5.1

The **Lost Mine Trail** offers an ideal combination of moderate grades, varied vegetation, multiple vantage points, and an interpretive brochure at the trailhead. Views take in nearby Casa Grande and Juniper Canyon at a saddle about 20 minutes up the trail. Then, after ascending through the oak and pine forest, the trail tops out with a panoramic view of the Sierra del Carmen in Mexico.

recommended for RVs or trailers, free) is the best place to learn about the dinosaurs that inhabited Big Bend up to 130 million years ago and some of the 1,200 species of fossils unearthed in the park. The accessible site contains large murals, tactile displays, dinosaur bones, a shaded picnic area, a fossil playground for kids, and an interpretive trail (0.2 mi/0.3 km rt, 10 min, moderate) to see geologic points.

CASTOLON HISTORIC DISTRICT

The history of isolated life on the border is preserved at **Castolon Historic District,** a collection of buildings from the 20th century. Castolon Visitors Center (10am-4pm daily Nov.-Apr.) is housed in the historic Officer's Quarters building. **Magdalena House** has exhibits of early-20th-century life in this two-nation bicultural community.

RECREATION
HIKING

In the Chisos Mountains, two trails depart from Chisos Basin Trailhead. The **Window Trail** (5.6 mi/9 km rt, 3-4 hrs, moderate) goes downhill to the top of an often dry pour-over (no railings) through a slot with a western vantage of the desert; the return is uphill. To climb the highest peak, take the **Emory Peak Trail** (10.5 mi/16.9 km rt, 5-6 hrs, strenuous), which starts on the Pinnacles Trail before turning off on the steep spur to the summit for those 360-degree views.

Find short trails at Rio Grande Village. From the campground at site 18, **Rio Grande Village Nature Trail** (0.75 mi/1.2 km rt, 30 min, easy) starts with a boardwalk across a natural spring wetland followed by a climb to the top of a cactus and scrub hill with sweeping vistas of the Rio Grande and Mexico. From the Hot Springs Parking Lot, where you can pick up an interpretive brochure, **Hot Springs Historic Trail** (1 mi/1.6 km rt, 45 min, easy) takes in old resort and homestead ruins, pictographs, and a historic hot springs pool (105°F/41°C).

RIO GRANDE RUNNING INTO BOQUILLAS CANYON

Check conditions first before planning to soak.

Two river trails on opposite sides of the park take in mighty canyon walls. From the end of Ross Maxwell Scenic Drive, the **Santa Elena Canyon Trail** (1.7 mi/2.7 km rt, 1-2 hrs, moderate) climbs switchbacks, concrete steps, and a rocky path before descending into the canyon below sheer cliffs 1,500 feet (457 m) high on each side of the narrow gap forged by the Rio Grande. From the Boquillas Canyon Spur Road, **Boquillas Canyon Trail** (1.4 mi/2.3 km rt, 1 hr, moderate) ascends to overlook the Rio Grande before dropping to the sandy shore as the canyon walls squeeze in.

Two desert hikes lead to geologic features. From Grapevine Hills Road, the **Grapevine Hills Trail** (2.2 mi/3.5 km rt, 1.5 hrs, easy) trots through a gravel wash before finishing with a steep climb to see Balanced Rock, a large boulder wedged between two towering rocks. To stand below a 100-foot-tall (30-m) water-smoothed pour-over, walk to **Lower Burro Mesa Pour-Off** (1 mi/1.6 km rt, 30 min, easy) on a spur off Ross Maxwell Scenic Drive.

BACKPACKING

Almost 20 miles (32.2 km) of prime backpacking trails loop through the **Chisos Mountains.** Forested canyons with colorful birds warbling in song lead to high scenic rim walks overlooking the Rio Grande thousands of feet below. Spread throughout the loops are 41 designated campsites with food storage lockers; four junctions include composting toilets. A 2021 wildfire burned the South Rim and southeast section; consult the visitors center for trail status.

Most hikers limit trips to 2-3 days due to unreliable water sources. **Permits** (www.recreation.gov, $10) are required; you can reserve six months in advance but will need to print your permit two weeks in advance. Remaining permits are available 24 hours in advance from Panther Junction Visitor Center.

▼ BALANCED ROCK ON THE GRAPEVINE HILLS TRAIL

WHERE TO STAY

INSIDE THE PARK

The only accommodations in the park are at **Chisos Mountains Lodge** (432/477-2291 or 877/386-4383, www.chisosmountainslodge.com, from $145). Situated nearly 1 mile (1.6 km) high in a basin surrounded by mountains, the complex offers a no-frills experience of hotel, motel, lodge rooms, and five coveted historic Roosevelt Stone Cottages. Book one year in advance for November-April visits. The **Chisos Mountains Lodge Restaurant** (7am-10am, 11am-4pm, and 5pm-8pm daily, $8-20) serves Tex-Mex fare, standard dishes, hearty breakfasts, and to-go hiker lunches.

Three **campgrounds** are available by **reservation only** (877/444-6777, www.recreation.gov, $16) up to six months in advance. They have drinking water, picnic tables, grills, and flush toilets, but no hookups. Located in the mountains, **Chisos Basin** (60 sites, year-round) is best for tents and small RVs (RV limit 24 ft/7.3 m, trailer limit 20 ft/6.1 m). **Rio Grande Village** (100 sites, year-round) is on the Rio Grande on the eastern edge of the park. Set in a cottonwood oasis between Castolon and Santa Elena

Canyon, **Cottonwood** (22 sites, Nov.-Apr.) has pit toilets instead of flush.

Forever Resorts operates **Rio Grande Village RV Campground** (432/477-2293, 25 sites, year-round, from $37) with full hookups for RVs in back-in sites as well as showers. Reservations are required.

Permits are required for the dozens of primitive drive-up **backcountry campsites** (www.recreation.gov, $10, available 6 months in advance), typically consisting of only a flat gravel pad (no toilets). Most require high-clearance or 4WD vehicles. You'll need to bring water, landfill-safe toilet bags, and pack out all of your trash.

OUTSIDE THE PARK

A few motels and campgrounds are in **Terlingua/Study Butte.** For more choices, stay in **Marathon.**

GETTING THERE AND AROUND

AIR

The closest airport is **Midland International Air & Space Port** (MAF, 9506 Laforce Blvd., 432/560-2200, www.fly-maf.com), four hours from Big Bend. An alternative is **El Paso International Airport** (ELP, 6701 Convair Rd., 915/212-0330, www.elpasointernationalairport.com), which offers a few more flights but is five hours from the park. Both have rental cars.

CAR

From Midland, drive south on US 385 for 230 miles (370 km, 3.5 hours) to the park visitors center. There is no public transportation available to Big Bend or inside the national park.

Big Bend has three types of roads (all marked on the park map you can pick up at the entrance station): paved, graveled dirt, and primitive. Paved roads are mostly narrow with skimpy shoulders and some curvy parts; watch your speed as javelina, deer, and jackrabbits can run out in front of vehicles. Most high-clearance vehicles can handle the graveled dirt roads, which may have potholes and washboards. The rough primitive roads are only for high-clearance 4WD rigs.

ROAD TO RIO GRANDE VILLAGE

ROCKY MOUNTAINS

The Rocky Mountains climb along the backbone of the Continental Divide. In Rocky Mountain National Park, the hairpin bends of Trail Ridge Road reveal snowcapped peaks and alpine tundra. Farther south, the Black Canyon of the Gunnison squeezes through a narrow fissure.

Anchoring the middle are a pair of parks in a landscape rife with bison. Yellowstone sputters with geysers, mud pots, and hot springs while Grand Teton struts a line of sawtooth peaks.

In the north, Glacier rises with jagged arêtes and glacier-carved basins, sliced through by Going-to-the-Sun Road.

To the east are the prairies of the Great Plains. Colorful Badlands and Theodore Roosevelt National Parks break up grasslands, while Wind Cave hides underground.

◄ EMERALD LAKE, ROCKY MOUNTAIN NATIONAL PARK

ROCKY MOUNTAINS

Glacier NP

MONTANA

Helena

Billings

Theodore Roosevelt NP

NORTH DAKOTA

SOUTH DAKOTA

IDAHO

Yellowstone NP

Grand Teton NP

WYOMING

Wind Cave NP

Badlands NP

NEBRASKA

Salt Lake City

Cheyenne

UTAH

Rocky Mountain NP

Denver

COLORADO

Black Canyon of the Gunnison NP

0   100 mi
0   100 km

© MOON.COM

The National Parks of
THE ROCKY MOUNTAINS

ROCKY MOUNTAIN, CO

Alpine lakes, lush meadows teeming with elk, and a glaciated landscape of deep valleys beneath soaring summits create awe-inspiring splendor (page 439).

BLACK CANYON OF THE GUNNISON, CO

This narrow, deep chasm cuts through black volcanic rock to create one of the country's most dramatic canyons (page 456).

YELLOWSTONE, WY

The first national park remains one of the finest, with gushing geysers, thundering waterfalls, and epic wildlife (page 463).

GRAND TETON, WY

A craggy spine of peaks laced with hiking trails spills into glacial lakes and historic Jackson Hole ranches (page 487).

GLACIER, MT

Captivating scenery, wondrous trails, huge lakes, and scenic drives fill this park that shares a border with Canada (page 505).

BADLANDS, SD

A wall of tall spires, grassy buttes, and colorful eroding cliffs present an otherworldly landscape (page 528).

WIND CAVE, SD

Beneath the ground's surface is the seventh-longest cave in the world; above ground, elk and bison herds roam (page 536).

THEODORE ROOSEVELT, ND

This badland and grassland landscape projects a raw beauty favored by Theodore Roosevelt (page 545).

1: MORMON ROW, GRAND TETON
2: SCENIC DRIVE, BADLANDS
3: BISON, THEODORE ROOSEVELT

Best OF THE PARKS

Wildlife-Watching: Pull out binoculars in Rocky Mountain, Yellowstone, and Theodore Roosevelt to search for elk, bighorn sheep, bears, wolves, and wild horses (pages 443, 469, and 549).

Trail Ridge Road: Drive the winding hairpin curves on this scenic traverse across the Continental Divide in Rocky Mountain (page 443).

Old Faithful Geyser: Watch one of the most regular geysers erupt (page 469).

Going-to-the-Sun Road: Drive the only road bisecting Glacier on a skinny cliff shimmy to Logan Pass (page 509).

Badlands Loop Road: Tour this road through South Dakota's Badlands, dotted with scenic turnouts and dramatic vistas (page 532).

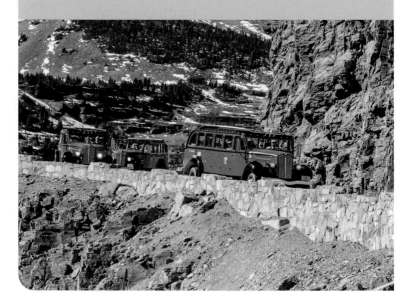

PLANNING YOUR TRIP

Plan at least **two weeks** to tour the national parks of the Rockies. Make advance **reservations** for inside Glacier, Yellowstone, Grand Teton, and Rocky Mountain: 12-18 months for lodging and 6-12 months for camping. Winter buries these parks in snow, so first-timers prefer **summer** when visitors centers and services are open and the weather is pleasantly warm.

High Season

Summer (May-October) is high season in the Rockies, when the parks see the most visitors. July and August see the huge crowds and the best weather.

Summer heralds the opening of the high-elevation scenic drives—pending weather conditions and snow removal—such as Trail Ridge Road in Rocky Mountain and Going-to-the-Sun Road in Glacier.

Low Season

In **winter** (Nov.-Apr.), deep snows bury the parks, and many park roads close for the season. Even though winter sees fewer people, it's the time for snow sports. In Yellowstone, visitors go to Old Faithful on snowcoaches or snowmobiles, while roads in Glacier and Grand Teton become snowshoeing and cross-country skiing paths.

▲ GOING-TO-THE-SUN ROAD, GLACIER

Road Trip

GRAND TETON, YELLOWSTONE, AND GLACIER

String together these three iconic parks in a **one-week** road trip. Fly into **Jackson Hole Airport, Wyoming,** rent a car, and enjoy the park on the same day. Make reservations for historic in-park lodges up to 13 months in advance. Fly out of **Glacier International Airport** in Kalispell, Montana

JENNY LAKE, GRAND TETON

Grand Teton

5 miles (8 km) / 10 minutes

Drive north on US 26/89/191 to Moose. Turn left onto Teton Park Road, stopping to tour the **Craig Thomas Discovery and Visitor Center.** Farther north, enjoy views of the Tetons from **Jenny Lake,** with a walk along the lakeshore overlooks. If time permits, hop the boat shuttle to hike to **Hidden Falls** and **Inspiration Point.** Continue north on Teton Park Road and US 89/191/287 to

Jackson Lake Lodge. Spend the night, dine in the **Mural Room,** and go **horseback riding** the next morning. Then, drive north along Jackson Lake on US 89/191/287 and pass through **John D. Rockefeller, Jr. Memorial Parkway.**

Yellowstone

45 miles (72 km) / 1 hour

Drive the South Entrance Road to **West Thumb Geyser Basin** and walk the boardwalk to see **Yellowstone Lake.**

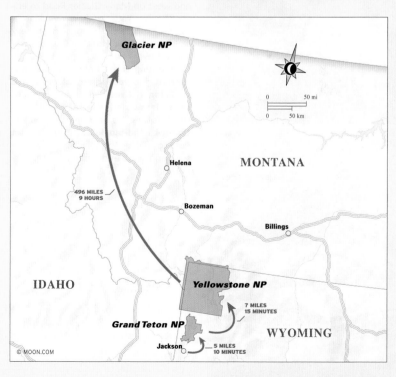

Glacier NP

496 MILES 9 HOURS

Helena

MONTANA

Bozeman

Billings

0   50 mi
0   50 km

IDAHO

Yellowstone NP

7 MILES 15 MINUTES

Grand Teton NP

WYOMING

Jackson   5 MILES 10 MINUTES

© MOON.COM

Then, head west on Grand Loop Road (US 89) to pop over the Continental Divide to watch **Old Faithful Geyser** and tour the Upper Geyser Basin. Spend the night at historic **Old Faithful Inn.** In the morning, continue north on Grand Loop Road (US 89) through Madison Junction to Norris Junction to walk through **Norris Geyser Basin.** Then, go east on Norris-Canyon Road and head south on Grand Loop Road to explore several overlooks on the North Rim of **Grand Canyon of the Yellowstone.** Go north on Grand Loop Road to Tower Junction, where the Northeast Entrance Road (US 212) goes to **Lamar Valley** for wildlife-watching. Return to Grand Loop Road heading west to end your day at **Mammoth Hot Springs** and overnight at **Mammoth Hot Springs Hotel.**

Glacier

500 miles (805 km) / 10 hours

Hit the road by 7am for this long haul up the Rocky Mountains. Take US 89 north, I-90 west, US 12/287 north, and I-15 north. Exit onto US 287 northward, followed by US 89 and US 2 along the Rocky Mountain Front to Browning. Head north on MT 464 and US 89, and west on Many Glacier Road to enter Glacier. You should arrive just in time to dine amid mountain scenery at **Many Glacier Hotel** and watch the sun set over the Continental Divide. In the morning, take a boat ride on **Swiftcurrent** and **Josephine Lakes** to hike to **Grinnell Lake.** The following day, drive Many Glacier Road east and US 89 south for a cliffside drive west on the **Going-to-the-Sun Road.** Stop at **Logan Pass** to soak up the splendor before descending west and aiming for the airport on US 2.

1: PORCELAIN BASIN AT NORRIS GEYSER BASIN
2: LOWER FALL, GRAND CANYON OF THE YELLOWSTONE
3: MANY GLACIER HOTEL

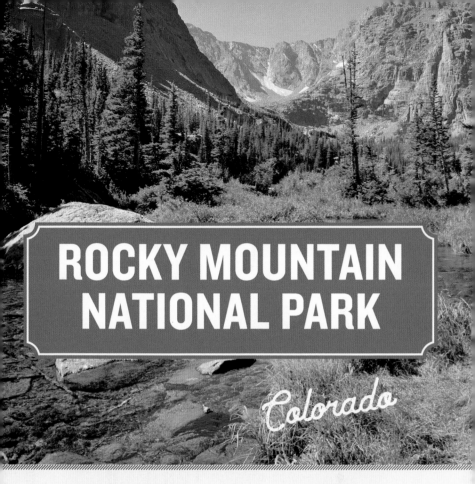

ROCKY MOUNTAIN NATIONAL PARK

Colorado

KEEPSAKE STAMPS ▼▼▼

WEBSITE:
www.nps.gov/romo

PHONE NUMBER:
970/586-1206

VISITATION RANK:
5

WHY GO:
Explore high peaks
and watch wildlife.

▲ DREAM LAKE

ROCKY MOUNTAIN NATIONAL PARK

▲ Signal Mountain 11,262ft

▲ Comanche Peak 12,702ft

The Needles ▲

LUMPY RIDGE

LUMPY RIDGE TRAILHEAD ▪

Lake Estes

Estes Park

36

Prospect Mtn ▲

BEAVER MEADOWS VISITOR CENTER ▪

FALL RIVER VISTOR CENTER ▪

ASPENGLEN △

34

DEER MOUNTAIN TRAILHEAD ▪

Deer Mountain 10,013ft ▲

MORAINE PARK ▪

Moraine Park

▲ Mummy Mtn

▲ Hagues Peak

Lawn Lake

Bighorn Mtn ▲

Mount Tileston ▲

SHEEP LAKES ▪

LAWN LAKE TRAILHEAD ▪

BEAVER MEADOWS ENTRANCE STATION ▪

MANY PARTS CURVE ▪

Crystal Lake

Fairchild Mtn ▲

M U M M Y   R A N G E

Ypsilon Lake

Spectacle Lakes

ALLUVIAL FAN ▪

34

ENDOVALLEY ▪

★ TRAIL RIDGE ROAD

Rocky Mountain National Park

▲ Flatiron Mtn 12,333ft

▲ Desolation Peaks 12,949ft

MEDICINE BOW CURVE ▪

ALPINE RIDGE TRAILHEAD ▪

ALPINE VISITOR CENTER ▪

LAVA CLIFFS ▪

FOREST CANYON ▪

F O R E S T   C A N Y O N

R   O   C   K   Y   M   O   U   N   T   A   I   N   S

CORRAL CREEK TRAILHEAD ▪

Long Draw Reservoir

TUNDRA COMMUNITIES TRAILHEAD ▪

CONTINENTAL DIVIDE

Mount Julian 12,928ft ▲

Mount Ida 12,880ft ▲

▲ Mount Neota

Specimen Mtn 12,489ft ▲

Shipler Mtn ▲

COLORADO RIVER TRAILHEAD ▪

34

▲ Thunder Mtn

▲ Lulu Mtn

S H I P L E R ' S   P A R K

TIMBER LAKE △

▲ Mount Richthofen 12,940ft

Lead Mtn 12,537ft ▲

Howard Mtn 12,810ft ▲

Mount Cumulus 12,725ft ▲

Mount Nimbus 12,706ft ▲

Mount Stratus ▲

Baker Mtn ▲

N E V E R   S U M M E R   M O U N T A I N S

At **ROCKY MOUNTAIN NATIONAL PARK,** rugged scenery is guaranteed. Meadows, forests, and lakes butt up against a backdrop of sheer cliffs and soaring peaks that dominate the Continental Divide. You'll find some of the highest summits in the Lower 48 and the highest paved road in the United States.

From low valleys to 14,259-foot-high (4,346-m) Longs Peak, the enormous changes in elevation create a mosaic of ecosystems that top out in alpine tundra. A thick blanket of snow drapes the mountains in winter, but summer heralds the opening of Trail Ridge Road, the signature scenic drive, a winding ribbon of hairpin bends. Its corridor follows a Ute seasonal hunting path to travel across the mountains. When aspens change to bright gold in fall, the air resounds with elk bugles and bighorn rams banging horns. This park captivates all the senses.

PLANNING YOUR TIME

Rocky Mountain National Park is separated by the Continental Divide into east and west sides. These two sides only connect when **Trail Ridge Road** (US 34, Memorial Day-mid-Oct.) is open. When the road is closed (mid-Oct.-Memorial Day), **Estes Park** offers the main driving access into the park.

Rocky Mountain is one of the country's busiest national parks. **Summer** (May-Sept.) booms with visitors; July sees the biggest crowds. Due to extreme elevation differences, the weather is changeable and unpredictable—even in summer. You might leave Denver's lowland heat to arrive in chilling winds at 12,000 feet (3,658 m). Summer afternoons frequently bring thunderstorm deluges. Spring and fall offer a mix of warm sun, rain, or snow; fall tends toward blue skies. For elk calving season, visit late May-early June. To listen to bugling bull elk, go in fall. Winter (Dec.-Mar.) pummels the mountains with snow.

In addition to regular park entry fees, **timed-entry reservations** are required late May to mid-October to enter the park. Get these 1-2 months in advance or at 5pm the day prior.

Rocky Mountain has no park lodges. Make **lodging reservations** 9-12 months in advance in Estes Park or Grand Lake. Make **camping reservations** six months in advance for park campgrounds.

ENTRANCES AND FEES

From the gateway town of **Estes Park,** the bustling east side has two entrances open year-round: **Fall River Entrance Station** (US 34) and **Beaver Meadows Entrance St ation** (US 36). Access the west side through the **Grand Lake Entrance Station** (US 34, year-round), north of the town of Grand Lake. Secondary entrances are at **Longs Peak Road** and **Wild Basin Road.**

The **one-day entrance fee** is $30 per vehicle ($25 motorcycle, $15 individual). The seven-day **entrance fee** is $35 per vehicle ($30 motorcycle, $20 individual). In addition to the entry fee, you'll need a **timed-entry reservation** (www.recreation.gov, $2) late May to mid-October for all entrances.

TRAIL RIDGE ROAD

Top ❸

1 WATCH ELK AND BIGHORN SHEEP

Hearing the eerie sounds of a 700-pound (318-kg) **bull elk** echoing

YOUNG BULL ELK

through the autumn air is a quintessential Rocky Mountain experience. During **fall breeding season** (mid-Sept.-mid-Oct.), anxious males round up their harems and bugle a loud noise that begins with a deep resonance, then rises to a high-pitched squeal, before ending in grunts. Catch this rutting ritual at dusk and dawn, on roads around **Moraine** and **Horseshoe Parks** and **Upper Beaver Meadows.** Meadow closures (5pm-10am daily Sept.-Oct.) protect the wildlife.

Sheep Lakes (US 34) are the best place to look for **bighorn sheep,** often seen in late spring between 9am and 3pm. At the **Bighorn Crossing Zone** in Horseshoe Park, rangers toting stop signs control traffic to allow sheep to move in and out of the meadow, while also providing great photo ops for visitors.

2 DRIVE TRAIL RIDGE ROAD

The 48-mile (77-km) paved **Trail Ridge Road** (US 34, late May-mid-Oct.) is the only road crossing the park between Estes Park and Grand Lake. Topping out at 12,183 feet (3,713 m), it is the country's highest paved road. From lush montane forests in deep valleys, the road quickly climbs above the tree line into a harsh windswept tundra, home to tiny wildflowers and wildlife. Because the road is open 24 hours daily, it offers high-elevation night sky viewing for stars.

Pullouts along the way offer safe places to stop for photos and enjoy the forever views. On the east side, top viewpoints include **Hidden Valley, Many Parks Curve,** and **Rainbow Curve.** Farther west, walk the interpretive **Tundra Communities Nature Trail** (1.1 mi/1.8 km rt, 30 min, easy) before crossing the road's unmarked high point to the **Alpine Visitor Center,** where steps climb the **Alpine Ridge Trail** (0.6 mi/1 km rt, 30 min, moderate), nicknamed "Huffer's Hill."

On the west side, Trail Ridge Road crosses the **Continental Divide** at **Milner Pass.** Below that, **Farview Curve** overlooks the Colorado River and Kawuneeche Valley.

3 CLIMB LONGS PEAK

The 14,259-foot (4,356-m) **Longs Peak** is the highest peak in Rocky Mountain National Park with a distinct flat-topped summit and east face (the Diamond). About 30,000 mountaineers and technical rock climbers attempt to summit its difficult and challenging routes each summer.

The **Keyhole Route** (15 mi/24 km rt, 10-15 hrs, strenuous) ascends nearly 5,000 vertical feet (1,524 m) of scrambling, steep drop-offs, extreme exposure, and sometimes-icy rocks—all amid fast-changing alpine weather. The climb requires a predawn start from the Longs Peak Trailhead and campground, located south of Estes Park via CO 7. Alternately, many climbers overnight (permit required) partway up in the Boulder Field.

Fortunately, you don't *have* to climb Longs Peak to admire it. See it from the easily accessible northern shore of **Bear Lake.**

THE KEYHOLE ON LONGS PEAK

VISITORS CENTERS

Beaver Meadows Visitor Center

The **Beaver Meadows Visitor Center** (US 36, 8am-6pm daily summer, 8am-4:30pm daily winter) is the park's primary access point. It has an information desk, bookstore, nature exhibits, and public Wi-Fi. Beginning in mid-April, rangers also offer a variety of programs. The **Backcountry Permit Office** (970/586-1242), where you can obtain backcountry permits on a space-available basis, is below the center.

Fall River Visitor Center

Just east of the Fall River Entrance Station is the **Fall River Visitor Center** (US 34, 9am-5pm daily late May-mid-Oct.), with brochures, maps, and a bookstore.

Alpine Visitor Center

The **Alpine Visitor Center** (Trail Ridge Rd., 970/586-1222, 9am-4:30pm daily late May-mid-Oct.) has one of the best views in Colorado, a panorama looking down Fall River Canyon toward Estes Park far below. The center has exhibits, restrooms, and the **Trail Ridge Store,** the only place in the park where you can grab food or snacks.

Kawuneeche Visitor Center

The west side of Rocky Mountain National Park has just one entrance that leads to **Kawuneeche Visitor Center** (16018 US 34, Grand Lake, 970/627-3471, 9am-5pm Wed.-Sun. summer, reduced hours fall-spring), where you can pick up maps, peruse exhibits, hop on public Wi-Fi, and reserve backcountry campsites.

SIGHTS

MORAINE PARK

The large meadow west of the Beaver Meadows Entrance Station is **Moraine Park** (US 36), one of the best places to spot wildlife, especially **elk.** Moraine Park stretches from **Bear Lake Road** to **Deer Ridge Junction** (US 36/34). You can obtain great views of the meadow from both roads, as well as from the two side roads that pierce the meadow's eastern side to access several trailheads, picnic areas, and the Moraine Park Stables.

Housed in a historic log-and-stone building, the seasonal **Moraine Park Discovery Center** (Bear Lake Rd., 970/586-1363, 9am-4:30pm daily late May-

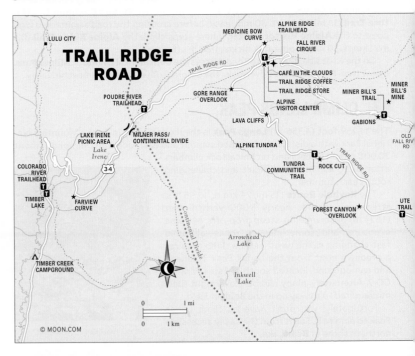

AVOID THE CROWDS

Crowds fill parking lots, visitors centers, roads, and trailheads in summer 9am-3pm. The Bear Lake Road corridor parking lots fill 5am-6pm. Timed-entry reservations are required late May to mid-October. Here are some tips avoid the crowds:

Hit the trails close to **sunrise** or later in the **evening.**

Ride the earliest **hiker shuttles** from Estes Park to the Park & Ride on Bear Lake Road.

Visit the **west side** midday, when crowds clog the east side.

Take the free **shuttle buses** whenever possible to avoid traffic.

mid-Oct.) has a natural history exhibit describing how the park's distinctive landscape formed, a 0.5-mile (0.8-km) nature trail, and a gift shop and bookstore.

BEAR LAKE

The shimmering, cobalt-blue waters of **Bear Lake** (shuttle 6:30am-7:30pm daily late May-mid-Oct., free) are nestled beneath the soaring summit of Hallett Peak, with many impressive mountains, including Longs Peak, rising to the south and east. The best way to experience its beauty is by strolling the interpretive **Bear Lake Nature Trail**

(0.8 mi/1.3 km rt, 30 min, easy). From the shore, you'll enjoy great views of Longs Peak and other towering peaks while walking through spruce, lodgepole pine, and fir trees. Bear Lake also launches extended hikes and offers picnicking with stunning views.

ALLUVIAL FAN

The prominent, treeless scar on the northern flank of **Horseshoe Park** was created in just a few hours when, on July 15, 1982, the Lawn Lake Dam collapsed, sending 129 million gallons (488 million liters) of water racing down

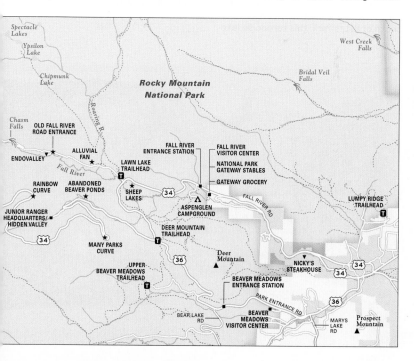

ONE DAY IN ROCKY MOUNTAIN

Start with a morning visit to **Bear Lake** for a stroll around its turquoise waters. Then drive up **Trail Ridge Road,** stopping at pullovers to enjoy the views. Picnic up on Trail Ridge with a sack lunch at an overlook of your choice. Walk the Alpine Communities Trail, visit the **Alpine Visitor Center,** and climb the Alpine Ridge Trail (known as Huffer's Hill) for 360-degree views and a selfie with the elevation sign that says "12,005 feet."

Roaring River and knocking down trees in its path. When the water reached flat Horseshoe Park, it slowed and dropped the debris it was carrying, creating a distinct cone of sand, gravel, and boulders called an alluvial fan. In 2013, another flood swept down. From the west or east **Alluvial Fan Parking Areas** (Endovalley Rd. off Fall River Rd.), walk the **Alluvial Fan Trail** (0.4 mi/0.6 km rt, 20 min, easy) over the debris. The wide trail, rebuilt in 2020, has removed architectural barriers for wheelchairs; the west side has inclines of under 8 percent with flat areas for resting.

LILY LAKE

At the toe of the Twin Sisters Peaks, **Lily Lake** is one of Rocky Mountain's most accessible alpine lakes. Lying just feet from CO 7 about 7 miles (11 km) south of Estes Park, this turquoise lake is a popular place to picnic and stroll along the shoreline. The flat **wheelchair-accessible trail** (0.8 mi/1.3 km rt, 30 min, easy) makes a great walk for families and visitors not yet acclimated to the elevation.

ENOS MILLS CABIN MUSEUM

Housed in a wooden cabin built in 1885, the small **Enos Mills Cabin Museum** (6760 Hwy. 7, 970/586-4706, tour reservations required) has old photographs, letters, and other artifacts that help visitors appreciate the achievements of the "Father of Rocky Mountain National Park." The highlights are the gorgeous scenery and the opportunity to learn about the family's history from one of Mills's relatives.

▼ BEAR LAKE

LILY LAKE

WILD BASIN

Tucked into the park's southeastern corner on a narrow gravel road, beautiful **Wild Basin** (parking lot fills by 9am in summer) is home to a series of waterfalls and gorgeous wildflowers, including clusters of Colorado blue columbine, the state flower. Crowds are often smaller in this outlying park zone that is primarily a hiking destination. But **Lower Copeland Falls** (0.6 mi/1 km rt, 20 min, easy) spills over a ledge for those wanting a short destination.

MILNER PASS

Contrary to what one would expect, **Trail Ridge Road** (late May-mid-Oct.) crosses the Continental Divide at Milner Pass, at 10,759 feet (3,279 m) several thousand feet lower than Alpine Visitor Center. Small **Poudre Lake** tucks into the meadow, and you can walk five minutes or so on the **Ute Trail** along the lake before it climbs into the forest.

KAWUNEECHE VALLEY

The main entrance to the park's west side is on **Trail Ridge Road** (US 36). While the full road only opens summer and fall (late May-mid-Oct.), a seasonal gate closure below Farview Curve allows for year-round visits to the lower elevations of Kawuneeche Valley.

Descending the western side of Trail Ridge Road, you're treated to spectacular views of the craggy peaks of the Never Summer Range, the upper Colorado River valley, lush meadows in Kawuneeche Valley, dense pine forests, and glimpses of the shimmering blue waters of Grand Lake. **Farview Curve,** a large pullout, takes in the best views.

On the valley floor, the **Holzwarth Historic Site** is the site homesteaded by German immigrant John Holzwarth Sr. From the parking area, walk the smooth **trail** (1.3 mi/2.1 km rt, 45 min, easy) that crosses the Colorado River before looping through the historic hand-hewn wooden cabins. Although visitors can only go inside the buildings in summer (mid-June-Labor Day), you can walk around the site year-round.

Harbison Meadows is the former site of two more homesteads belonging to sisters Annie and Kitty Harbison, who along with their family migrated here from Kansas in the late 1800s. Today, the empty grass meadows are a beautiful spot to enjoy a picnic lunch and watch for wildlife.

SCENIC DRIVES

OLD FALL RIVER ROAD

Built between 1913 and 1920, **Old Fall River Road** (open July-Sept.) is one of the park's signature scenic drives. From US 34, at the bend between Sheep Lakes and Horseshoe Park, the road heads northwest from the Endovalley Road to the Alpine Visitor Center on Trail Ridge Road. After leaving the valley, the rugged road climbs steadily through thick evergreen forest. About 1 mile (1.6 km) from its start, a five-minute walk drops from a small pullout on the left side down a stone pathway to **Chasm Falls.** From this stop, the road continues beneath the looming hulk of 12,454-foot (3,796-m) Mount Chapin. After passing **Willow Park,** where you can often spot elk, Old Fall River Road crosses into the treeless alpine tundra. Near the crest at **Fall River Pass,** the road contours around the **Fall River Cirque,** a giant cookie bite that a glacier sculpted out of the hard rock, before joining Trail Ridge Road at the Alpine Visitor Center.

Although the dirt surface is frequently graded and accessible to regular passenger vehicles, it's intended as a leisurely scenic drive, with a **15 mph (24 kph)** speed limit, no guardrails, and 16 tight switchbacks. Because it's too narrow and winding for cars to safely pass, the **11-mile (18-km) route** is a **one-way drive.**

HIKING

Trailhead parking lots fill early—many between 5am and 7am. Frequent afternoon thunderstorms make hiking

HOLZWARTH HISTORIC SITE

DREAM LAKE

early in the morning best, especially for trails that are above the tree line. Use the park shuttle bus (7:30am-8pm daily late May-mid-Oct.) to avoid the anxiety of parking.

Many trails have reopened from the 2020 Cameron Peak and East Troublesome Fires that burned about 10 percent of the park. Consult visitors centers for current conditions, as trails through fire scars can see ongoing damage from flash flooding, mudslides, falling trees, and unstable ground. Most of the trails are in designated wilderness where hikers must be self-reliant and responsible for their own safety.

From Estes Park, you can hike with a licensed guide through **Scot's Sporting Goods** (970/586-2877, www.scotssportinggoods.com) or **Kep Expeditions** (970/214-5255, www.kepexpeditions.com).

EAST SIDE

Lawn Lake

To explore the Mummy Range in the park's northeastern corner, **Lawn Lake Trail** (Lawn Lake Trailhead, Endovalley Rd., 12.4 mi/20 km rt, 6-7 hrs, strenuous) follows the path of the Roaring River up to Lawn Lake, surrounded by wildflower meadows and glaciated rock. Crystal Lake sits 1.5 miles (2.4 km) beyond Lawn Lake.

Deer Mountain

At the start of Trail Ridge Road, **Deer Mountain** (Deer Ridge Junction, US 34/36, 6 mi/9.7 km rt, 3-4 hrs, strenuous) makes a good first summit at 10,013 feet (3,052 m). It is usually accessible by late spring.

BEAR LAKE ROAD

Fern Lake

The **Fern Lake Trail** (Fern Lake Rd., near Moraine Park Campground, 7.6 mi/12.2 km rt, 4-5 hrs, easy, shuttle stop) follows a creek through a deep and shady valley past several pretty waterfalls to narrow Fern Lake, rimmed with lily pads.

Bear Lake

Bear Lake Trailhead (end of Bear Lake Rd., parking lot fills by 8:30am in summer, shuttle stop) is the start of many hikes. The **Bear Lake shoreline stroll** (0.5 mi/0.8 km rt, 20 min, easy) suits most visitors. On the northeast side of the lake, strong hikers take off at a junction to reach the historic **Flattop Mountain Trail** (8.8 mi/14.2 km rt, 5 hrs, strenuous). After turning left at two more junctions, the trail climbs to the summit of 12,324-foot (3,756-m)

Best Hike

LUMPY RIDGE AND GEM LAKE

DISTANCE: 5.2 miles (8.4 km) round-trip
DURATION: 2.5 hours
ELEVATION CHANGE: 1,000 feet (305 m)
DIFFICULTY: moderate
TRAILHEAD: Lumpy Ridge/ Gem Lake

The climb up Lumpy Ridge goes through ever-green forest and ancient granite, which ice, wind, and rain have sculpted over millions of years into the ridge's distinctive knobs. From the trailhead, go left to ascend below the captivating **Twin Owls** rock out-crop. At the main trail, a right turn marches below the owls and past the next junction through aspen trees that turn brilliant golds in early autumn. After ascending several small switchbacks, you'll reach a distinctive rock formation called **Paul Bunyan's Boot** (note the hole in the "sole"). From here, the final climb is steep, but distant views take in Longs Peak, Mount Meeker, and Estes Park. At **Gem Lake,** several rocky outcrops and a small sandy beach make ideal lunch spots. On the return, turn left at the first junction to reach the trailhead more directly.

Flattop Mountain, located on the Continental Divide. En route, the trail passes overlooks of Dream and Emerald Lakes, plus views of Longs and Hallett Peaks.

A few feet up the Bear Lake Trail is the **Emerald Lake Trailhead,** which goes south and west to a string of deep-blue lakes. The shortest destination is spritely **Nymph Lake** (1 mi/1.6 km rt, 30 min, easy), after which the trail climbs steeply to celestial **Dream Lake** (2.2 mi/3.5 km rt, 1.5 hrs, moderate). Just before Dream Lake, the trail forks at a junction to go on either side of Hallett Peak. Turn left to ascend to sparkling **Lake Haiyaha** (4.2 mi/6.8 km rt, 2.5 hrs, moderate) with views up Chaos

Canyon. The right fork goes to **Emerald Lake** (3.6 mi/5.8 km rt, 2 hrs, moderate) at the base of Tyndall Gorge.

Glacier Gorge

The **Glacier Gorge Trailhead** (Bear Lake Rd., parking lot fills by 6am in summer, shuttle stop) is the starting point for several destinations. The first is the three-story **Alberta Falls** (1.6 mi/2.6 km rt, 1 hr, easy) before the climb ramps up through two signed junctions. At the second junction, turn south for **Mills Lake** (5.6 mi/9 km rt, 3 hrs, moderate) and **Black Lake** (10 mi/16.1 km rt, 5-6 hrs, strenuous) tucked into Glacier Gorge. Continue straight instead to switchback up to **Loch Vale** (6 mi/9.6

▼ LUMPY RIDGE

CHASM LAKE

km rt, 3 hrs, moderate) and on to Timberline Falls, where some scrambling using hands is required to reach **Sky Pond** (9.8 mi/15.8 km rt, 5-6 hrs, strenuous), with its stunning backdrop and crystal-clear waters.

SOUTH OF ESTES PARK

South of Estes Park, CO 7 leads to spur roads to access trailheads. No shuttles access these.

Twin Sisters Peaks

From the top of **Twin Sisters Peaks** (gravel road opposite Lily Lake, 7.4 mi/11.9 km rt, 4 hrs, strenuous), the 360-degree views take in Estes Park, the national park, and the Great Plains. The trail leads through the forest, past a landslide, and up switchbacks. A long straight slope through granite slabs reaches the saddle between the two peaks, the higher of which is the 11,428-foot (3,483-m) eastern peak.

Longs Peak Road

Tucked at the base of Longs Peak, **Chasm Lake** (end of Longs Peak Rd., 8.4 mi/13.5 km rt, 4.5 hrs, strenuous) sits in a rocky basin at 11,823 feet (3,604 m). From the Longs Peak Trailhead, the path switchbacks up through the forest to reach the rocky tundra. It sweeps over a ridge and traverses a cliff walk to enter a hanging basin where a scramble with some use of hands goes up a boulder moraine to the lake.

Wild Basin Road

In the southeastern corner of the park, the **Wild Basin Trailhead** (end of Wild Basin Rd., parking lot fills by 9:30am in summer) accesses several waterfalls, beginning with **Copeland Falls** (0.6 mi/0.9 km rt, 30 min, easy). A bridge crosses the long **Calypso Cascades** (3.6 mi/5.8 km rt, 2 hrs, moderate) where it spills through the forest. **Ouzel Falls** (5.4 mi/8.7 km rt, 3 hrs, moderate) spits down a rock face.

WEST SIDE

Colorado River to Lulu City

The **Colorado River Trail** (Colorado River Trailhead, Trail Ridge Rd., 6.2 mi/10 km rt, 3 hrs, easy) wanders through Shipler Park at the base of the Never Summer Range to **Lulu City,** a mining town built in 1879 that, at its peak, had about 200 residents. Only the foundations from a couple of cabins remain.

North Inlet Trail

North of Grand Lake, the **North Inlet Trail** (County Rd. 663) goes to the gushing **Cascade Falls** (7 mi/11.3 km rt, 3.5 hrs, moderate) and the Big Pool

ALBERTA FALLS

SKY POND TRAIL

(9.6 mi/15.4 km rt, 5 hrs, moderate), a swimming hole.

East Inlet Trail

On Grand Lake's east side, the **East Inlet Trail** leads to **Adams Falls** (West Portal Rd., 0.6 mi/1 km rt, 20 min, easy), a short stroll that showcases a pretty cascade of water tumbling down the final steep pitch before mixing with the smooth waters of Grand Lake.

RECREATION

BACKPACKING

Many of the day hikes in Rocky Mountain can be extended to two days, such as the hike to **Lawn Lake** (12.4 mi/20 km rt) in the Mummy Range on the east side. On the west side, the **East Inlet Trail** leads to **Lone Pine Lake** (11 mi/17.7 km rt).

By setting up shuttles, you can tackle point-to-point trails. Hike a portion of the 3,100-mile (4,988-km) **Continental Divide Scenic Trail** (30 mi/48.3 km one-way, 2-3 days) by starting in Arapaho National Forest on the Bowen Pass Spur Trail and hiking through the Never Summer Wilderness before entering the park to loop with the Tonahutu Creek Trail and finish at North Inlet Trailhead. From the North Inlet Trailhead, you can hike over the Continental Divide to Flattop Mountain (12 mi/19.3 km one-way) and Bear Lake (17 mi/27.4 km one-way).

Permits (www.recreation.gov, $30 plus $6 fee, nonrefundable) for designated campsites are required. Reservations open in early March. Visit the wilderness office at Beaver Meadows or Kawuneeche Visitor Centers to pick up your permit by noon the day before departure. Approved bear canisters are required (Apr.-Oct.).

ROCK CLIMBING

The park is well known for its world-class technical rock climbing and mountaineering. **Lumpy Ridge's** granite walls feature almost 400 trad routes; many of these climbing routes are closed March-July to protect nesting birds of prey. The most famous route ascends the Diamond, the sheer diamond-shaped alpine wall on **Longs Peak's** upper east face. The **Colorado Mountain School** (341 Moraine Ave., Estes Park, 855/929-6733, http://coloradomountainschool.com) offers classes and guided climbing trips.

HORSEBACK RIDING

Two stables within the park offer more than a dozen rides daily: **Sombrero**

TIMED-ENTRY RESERVATIONS

In addition to paying the entrance fee, you'll need a **timed-entry reservation** (www.recreation.gov, $2) to enter Rocky Mountain National Park.

Every day from **late May to mid-October,** timed entries are required for travel anywhere in the park: **9am-3pm** for all entrances and roads in the park excluding Bear Lake corridor, and **5am-6pm** for everywhere including Bear Lake corridor. (You do not need a reservation to enter the park or Bear Lake corridor before or after hours, nor in spring before late May and fall after mid-October.)

Make reservations **online** as soon as tickets are released, **1-2 months** in advance. About 75 percent of tickets are released at this point; the other 25 percent become available at 5pm the day before.

Tickets are for **one day.** If you plan multiple days in the park, you will need one ticket for each day.

Tickets allow you to enter the park during an allotted **two-hour window.** They do not guarantee parking at trailheads or popular sights.

If you have advance reservations for **camping, backpacking,** or **horseback riding** in the park, you will not need a timed-entry reservation; your service reservation will gain you entry. Likewise, you will not need a timed-entry reservation with **licensed outfitters or tours.**

Stables (970/533-8155, www.sombrero.com) and **Glacier Creek Stable** (970/444-2716, www.www.rockymountainhorserides.com).

FISHING

The park's lakes and streams delight anglers. Two great locations for catch-and-release fishing are **Fern Lake** and **Lawn Lake,** both of which host native greenback cutthroat trout. To fly-fish for brown and cutthroat trout, go for the clear, rushing **Colorado River.** Lower Trail Ridge Road offers several access points, including the Holzwarth Historic Site.

WHERE TO STAY

INSIDE THE PARK

There are no lodgings available within Rocky Mountain National Park; camping is the only overnight option and it's very popular, with only a small number of sites available. All campgrounds include drinking water, picnic tables, fire grates, food storage lockers, and vault or flush toilets. No hookups are available for RVs.

Make **reservations** (877/444-6777, www.recreation.gov) six months in advance for tent and RV camping. Sites go fast, so book promptly after dates are released.

- **Moraine Park Campground** (year-round, 244 sites, $35) sits about 2.5 miles (4 km) south of the Beaver Meadows Entrance Station. Facilities include a dump station and shuttle stops. In winter, toilets and drinking water are not available; sites are first come, first served.

- **Glacier Basin Campground** (June-Sept., 150 sites, $35) is about 6 miles (9.7 km) south of the Beaver Meadows Entrance Station. A park shuttle stop is nearby.

- **Aspenglen Campground** (late May-late Sept., 52 sites, $35) is on a hillside near the Fall River Visitor Center.

- **Longs Peak Campground** (June-Sept., 26 sites, $30) is the best place to stay if you're planning on an early start to climb Longs Peak. The sites are for tents only.

- **Timber Creek Campground** (late May-early Nov., 98 sites, $35) is on Trail Creek Road adjacent to the Colorado River. It's the only campground on the west side.

MOOSE IN SHEEP LAKES

OUTSIDE THE PARK

Estes Park serves as the gateway to the park's east side, providing easy access to Bear Lake and Moraine Park. Most restaurants and accommodations surround the junction of US 34 and US 36. **Grand Lake** is the west side's tourist hub, but accommodations are limited. Book ahead for May-September, the busiest season.

GETTING AROUND

DRIVING

From Beaver Meadows, US 36 continues west and then north, passing Bear Lake Road which heads south to connect Moraine Park and Bear Lake. At the Deer Ridge Junction, the road splits: Trail Ridge Road climbs west, while US 34 drops north to meet Old Fall River Road before veering west to the Fall River Visitor Center.

Trail Ridge Road

The Fall River Visitor Center on US 34 offers convenient access to both Trail Ridge and Fall River Roads (open seasonally). In summer, Trail Ridge Road is accessible from the east side at the junction of US 34 and US 36. Trail Ridge Road (US 34, open May-mid-Oct.) is the only road into the park's west side. In winter, the road closes and the west side must be accessed through the Grand Lake Entrance Station.

SHUTTLES

From Estes Park Visitor Center (500 Big Thompson Ave.), the **Hiker Shuttle** (www.recreation.gov, 9am-2:15pm daily late May-early Oct., $2) runs to the Park & Ride (Bear Lake Rd.). Return shuttles run until 5:15pm. Two other shuttles (6:30am-7pm daily late May-mid-Oct.) are the orange **Bear Lake Route** that runs every 10-15 minutes to Glacier Gorge and Bear Lake Trails and the green **Moraine Park Route** that runs every 30 minutes to spots including Sprague Lake, Fern Lake, and Moraine Park Campground.

There is no public transport or shuttle service to the west side of Rocky Mountain National Park, on Trail Ridge Road, or in the Fall River area.

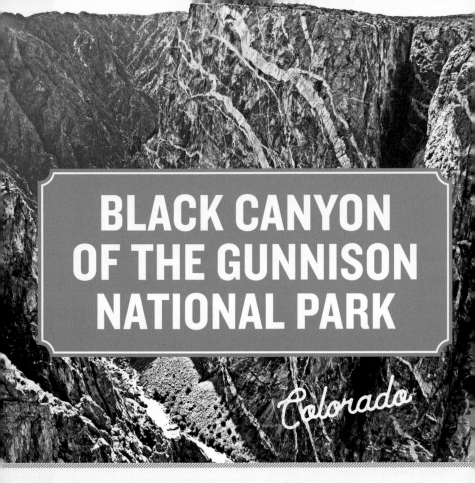

BLACK CANYON OF THE GUNNISON NATIONAL PARK

Colorado

WEBSITE:
www.nps.gov/blca

PHONE NUMBER:
970/641-2337, ext. 205

VISITATION RANK:
48

WHY GO:
Peer down into the thin slice of this deep, dark, steep-walled gorge.

KEEPSAKE STAMPS ▼▼▼

Millions of years ago, the powerful Gunnison River first chewed through soft volcanic rock like a saw blade, creating the slot for the **BLACK CANYON OF THE GUNNISON.** Once the river had carved this initial channel, it remained there, chipping away at the hard metamorphic rock below. The vertical canyon walls are so tough that they barely retreated. Archaeological evidence of the early Ute people only appears high above, on the rims.

While the canyon isn't the longest or deepest in the country, it is narrow, deep, and dark. The canyon's sheer walls are higher than Chicago's Willis Tower, and its inner gorge is so narrow—only 1,100 feet (335 m) across at its thinnest—that it receives only minutes of sunlight each day. Below the Chasm View overlook at the Gunnison River, the canyon shrinks to a narrow slot, forcing the river to gush with monster rapids.

PLANNING YOUR TIME

In western Colorado, the Black Canyon of the Gunnison sits southeast of Grand Junction between Montrose and Gunnison. The park's North and South Rims are only 0.25 mile (0.4 km) apart in places; however, to get from one rim to the other takes 2-3 hours of driving. The park is open year-round, with all roads open mid-April to mid-November. In winter, roads close, with the exception of the South Rim Road to Gunnison Point. Due to more difficult accesses for the North Rim and East Portal Roads, most visitors only go to the **South Rim.**

Peak visitation is in **summer** (May-Sept.) when days range 55-90°F (13-32°C) and frequent afternoon thunderstorms appear. Winter days see 15-40°F (-9-5°C) as the norm, with varied snow depths on the ground. Temperatures can fluctuate radically in one day; bring layers of clothing.

ENTRANCES AND FEES

The main entrance to the park is through the South Rim via **CO 347.** The North Rim entrance is south of Crawford, where you can pay fees at the ranger station or a self-pay kiosk. The entrance fee is $30 per vehicle ($25 motorcycle, $15 individual) and valid for seven days.

VISITORS CENTER

Located at Gunnison Point, the **South Rim Visitor Center** (CO 347, 8am-6pm daily late May-early Sept., reduced hours off-season) has exhibits, a film, maps, a bookstore, backcountry permits, and Junior Ranger Programs. Rangers lead geology walks, Chasm View talks, night sky talks, constellation tours, and telescope viewing.

SCENIC DRIVES
NORTH RIM ROAD

From the park entrance for the North Rim, take the gravel **North Rim Road** (14 mi/23 km rt, mid-Apr.-mid-Nov.) to six viewpoints, including **The Narrows View,** which overlooks the canyon's narrowest point (40 ft/12 m wide at river level).

EAST PORTAL ROAD

Between the South Rim entrance and campground, the **East Portal Road** (14 mi/23 km rt, mid-Apr.-mid-Nov.) begins a steep descent to the river. It plunges with a 16 percent grade and tight, sharp switchbacks to the bottom of the Black Canyon of the Gunnison in Curecanti National Recreation Area at **Crystal Dam.** (No vehicles longer than 22 ft/6.7 m permitted, including trailer combos.)

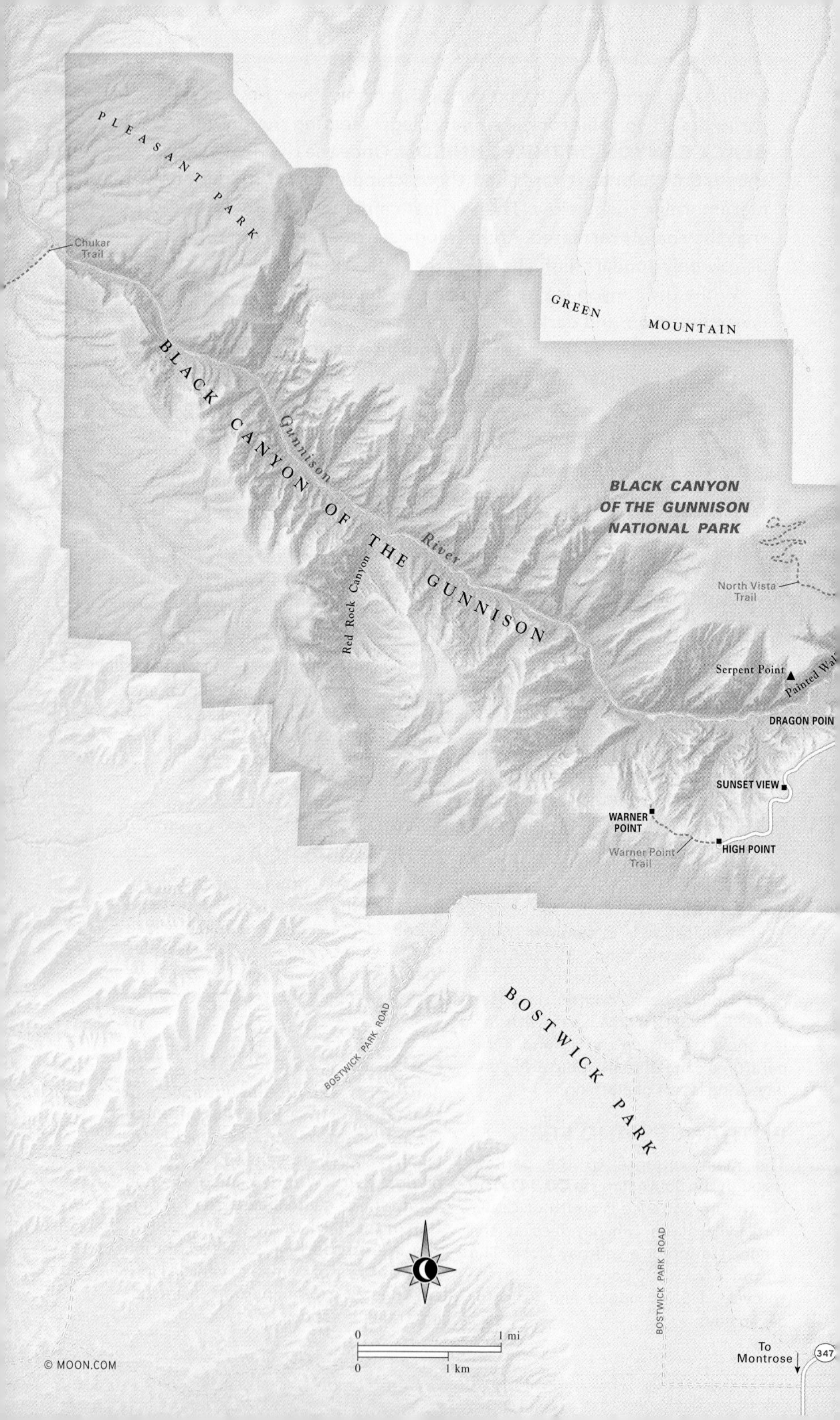

PLEASANT PARK

Chukar
Trail

GREEN MOUNTAIN

BLACK CANYON OF THE GUNNISON

Gunnison River

**BLACK CANYON
OF THE GUNNISON
NATIONAL PARK**

Red Rock Canyon

North Vista
Trail

Serpent Point ▲ Painted Wal

DRAGON POIN

SUNSET VIEW

**WARNER
POINT**

Warner Point
Trail

HIGH POINT

BOSTWICK PARK

BOSTWICK PARK ROAD

BOSTWICK PARK ROAD

0 _____ 1 mi

0 _____ 1 km

To
Montrose   347

© MOON.COM

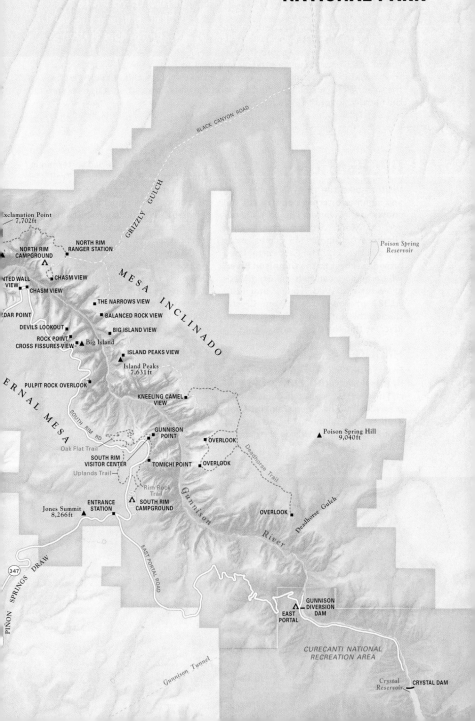

BLACK CANYON
OF THE GUNNISON
NATIONAL PARK

BLACK CANYON ROAD

GRIZZLY GULCH

Poison Spring
Reservoir

Exclamation Point
7,702ft

NORTH RIM
CAMPGROUND

NORTH RIM
RANGER STATION

NTED WALL
VIEW

CHASM VIEW

CHASM VIEW

MESA INCLINADO

THE NARROWS VIEW

CEDAR POINT

BALANCED ROCK VIEW

DEVILS LOOKOUT

BIG ISLAND VIEW

ROCK POINT

Big Island

CROSS FISSURES VIEW

ISLAND PEAKS VIEW

Island Peaks
7,631ft

PULPIT ROCK OVERLOOK

RNAL MESA

KNEELING CAMEL
VIEW

Poison Spring Hill
9,040ft

SOUTH RIM RD.

GUNNISON
POINT

OVERLOOK

Oak Flat Trail

SOUTH RIM
VISITOR CENTER

TOMICHI POINT

OVERLOOK

Deadhorse Trail

Uplands Trail

Rim Rock
Trail

Gunnison

OVERLOOK

Deadhorse Gulch

Jones Summit
8,266ft

ENTRANCE
STATION

SOUTH RIM
CAMPGROUND

OVERLOOK

River

347

EAST PORTAL ROAD

PINON SPRINGS DRAW

GUNNISON
DIVERSION
DAM

EAST
PORTAL

CURECANTI NATIONAL
RECREATION AREA

Gunnison Tunnel

Crystal
Reservoir

CRYSTAL DAM

Best Hike

NORTH VISTA TRAIL

DISTANCE: 3 miles (4.8 km) round-trip
DURATION: 1.5 hours
ELEVATION CHANGE: 370 feet (113 m)
DIFFICULTY: moderate
TRAILHEAD: near the North Rim Ranger Station

On the North Rim, saunter the flat and gently rolling **North Vista Trail.** The trail picks up several stunning views into the Black Canyon of the Gunnison, but nothing compared to the view at Exclamation Point Overlook. From the point, cliffs plunge vertically to the river below (watch your footing), and the view looks straight upriver through the narrow slot of the inner canyon.

RECREATION

Visitors bike the rim roads in spring and summer or **cross-country ski** and **snowshoe** in winter. The park's sheer vertical walls attract expert **rock climbers** for about 145 climbs, most rated above 5.10. The East Portal Road provides access to the **Gunnison River,** where anglers can **fish** the Gold Medal Water and Wild Trout Water (200 yd/183 m downstream from Crystal Dam to the North Fork of the Gunnison River) within the steep canyon walls.

HIKING

From South Rim Visitor Center, the sunny **Rim Rock Nature Trail** (2 mi/3.2 km rt, 1 hr, easy) is a level, self-guided interpretive path. The steep **Oak Flat Loop Trail** (2 mi/3.2 km rt, 1 hr, strenuous) drops below the rim inside the canyon, but not to the river.

At South Rim Road's terminus, the **Warner Point Nature Trail** (1.5 mi/2.4 km rt, 45 min, moderate) wanders through piñon-juniper forest with views of the San Juan Mountains. Pick up a guide to the trail's flora at the visitors center.

On the North Rim from the campground loop, **Chasm View Nature Trail** (0.3 mi/0.5 km rt, 15 min, easy) starts in a piñon-juniper forest to wander near the rim for a look across the canyon at Chasm View on the South Rim. A second overlook takes in Painted Wall and Serpent Point. Watch for peregrine falcons.

Green Mountain Trail (7 mi/11.3 km rt, 3.5 hrs, strenuous) begins on the North Vista Trail and can be combined with hiking to Exclamation Point. But the route continues on farther for

▼ GUNNISON RIVER

Top ❸

❶ DRIVE SOUTH RIM ROAD

VIEW INTO THE CANYON

The paved **South Rim Road** (14 mi/23 km rt, Apr.-mid-Nov.) has a dozen over-looks between Tomichi Point and **High Point,** the road's end. The following four overlooks are the best: From two viewpoints at **Gunnison Point,** orange lichen cliffs plunge down to the Gunnison River while vertical light-colored dikes slice the broken North Rim wall. At **Chasm View,** the depth drops by 1,820 feet (556 m) to the river in one of the narrowest sections, making ultrasteep walls where you might spot expert rock climbers. You can walk from Chasm View to **Painted Wall View,** which gets its name from layers of lighter rock amid the black across Colorado's highest cliff. With picnic tables, **Sunset View** is the best place to eat while soaking up the immense canyon.

❷ CATCH THE SUN, MOON, AND STARS

North Rim overlooks are prime for **sunrise,** but on the South Rim, from Cedar Point you can catch first light on the Painted Wall. Farther on the South Rim, the west-facing **Sunset View** is best for watching the sun drop over the canyon. At night, pull out your astrophotography skills for shooting the Milky Way in this certified **International Dark Sky Park.** In summer, the Milky Way moves directly overhead late at night, but earlier in fall. Due to minimal light interference, the best South Rim viewpoints for stargazing are Chasm View, Dragon Point, and Sunset View. On the North Rim, try Chasm View Nature Trail or Kneeling Camel View. Use red lights (not white) for walking, and give your eyes 30 minutes to adjust to the darkness.

❸ SCRAMBLE INTO THE INNER CANYON

With no trails from rim to river, six scrambling routes dive into the inner canyon. Only for strong and fit hikers, they require using hands and feet on boulders, exposed roots, steep ledges, and loose rock in ultrasteep ravines. At the visitors center, consult a ranger about your route (six are available) and get a free wilderness permit for day or overnight hiking. Most first-timers do the **Gunnison Route** (3 mi/4.8 km rt, 4-5 hrs, strenuous), a Class III gully with 1,800 feet (549 m) elevation drop and a grueling crawl straight back up. Be cautious of poison ivy and rockfall.

SUNSET OVER THE CANYON

ONE DAY IN BLACK CANYON OF THE GUNNISON

Stop at the **South Rim Visitor Center** and stretch your legs on the **Rim Rock Nature Trail** to gaze into the canyon's abyss. Then, spend your day cruising the paved **South Rim Road,** stopping at the overlooks between the visitors center and High Point, the road's end.

360-degree views of Grand Mesa, the Uncompahgre Plateau, and a different perspective peering down into the canyon.

WHERE TO STAY

INSIDE THE PARK

With no lodging inside the park, camping is the only option. Drinking water is trucked in during summer; off-season, campers should bring their own. On South Rim Road, **reservations** (877/444-6777, www.recreation.gov) are accepted in summer at the **South Rim Campground** (year-round, 88 sites, $16-22). Sites are first come, first served outside the summer season, and 23 have electrical hookups. Nearby is the Night Sky Viewing and Telescope Site.

Two other campgrounds are first come, first served. The smaller **North Rim Campground** (Apr.-mid-Nov., 13 sites, $16) is on the North Rim Road. Bordering the park in Curecanti National Recreation Area, the **East Portal Campground** (May-mid.-Oct., 15 sites, $16) is 5 miles (8 km) down the steep and hairpin East Portal Road (no vehicles over 22 ft/6.7 m, including trailer combos).

OUTSIDE THE PARK

Accommodations and food are available in the towns of **Gunnison, Grand Junction,** and **Montrose.**

GETTING THERE AND AROUND

AIR

The closest international airport is **Denver International Airport** (DEN, 8500 Peña Blvd., 303/342-2000, www.flydenver.com). Small regional airports include the **Gunnison-Crested Butte Airport** (GUC, 519 Rio Grande Ave.,

Gunnison, 970/641-2304, www.flygunnisonairport.com), the **Montrose Regional Airport** (MTJ, 2100 Airport Rd., 970/249-3203, www.flymontrose.com), and the **Grand Junction Regional Airport** (GJT, 2828 Walker Field Dr., 970/244-9100, www.gjairport.com). All airports have rental cars.

CAR

From **Denver,** the Black Canyon of the Gunnison is 5-6 hours' drive via I-70, US 285, and US 50.

To reach the **South Rim,** take US 50 west from Gunnison for about 62 miles (100 km) or east from Montrose for 14 miles (23 km). Turn onto CO 347, which becomes the paved South Rim Road.

To access the **North Rim,** follow US 50 east. Turn left onto CO 92 and drive west and then north to Black Canyon Road, just before the Crawford State Park entrance. Turn left onto Black Canyon Road and follow signs for the next 12 miles (19 km) to reach the park's North Rim. The paved road becomes gravel for 7 miles (11 km) in the park. Plan at least 2-3 hours to drive from rim to rim.

In winter (mid-Nov.-mid-Apr.), park roads close, except for South Rim Road from the visitors center to Gunnison Point.

There is no public transit in the park.

SIGHTS NEARBY

Bordering Black Canyon of the Gunnison National Park, **Curecanti National Recreation Area** (www.nps.gov/cure) is also an International Dark Sky Park. It has three reservoirs (Blue Mesa, Morrow Point, and Crystal Reservoir) with campgrounds, boating, and fishing. A ranger-led **boat tour** (970/641-2337, ext. 205, www.recreation.gov, 10am and 1pm Wed.-Mon. mid-June-early Sept., 1.5 hrs) requires reservations (www.recreation.gov).

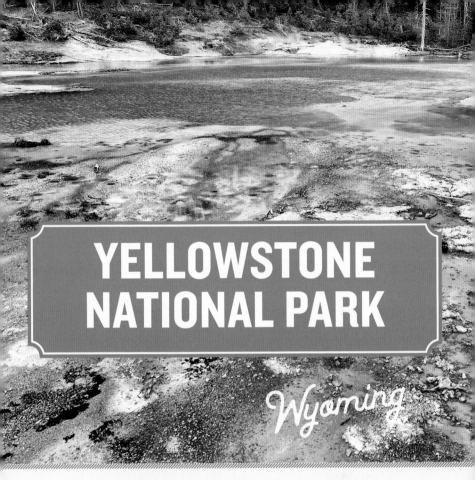

YELLOWSTONE NATIONAL PARK

Wyoming

KEEPSAKE STAMPS ▼▼▼

WEBSITE:
www.nps.gov/yell

PHONE NUMBER:
307/344-7381

VISITATION RANK:
3

WHY GO:
Watch wildlife, geysers, and volcanic wonders.

▲ PALETTE SPRING, MAMMOTH HOT SPRINGS

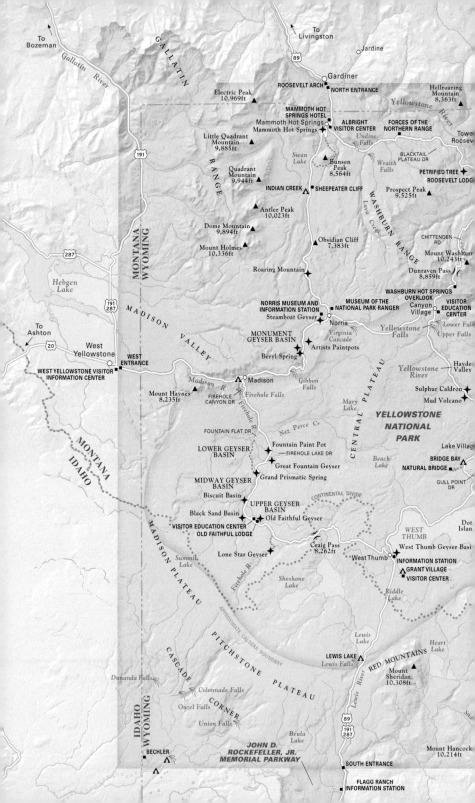

YELLOWSTONE
NATIONAL PARK

BUFFALO PLATEAU

MONTANA
WYOMING

Cooke City

Silver Gate

Colter Pass
8,048ft

NORTHEAST ENTRANCE

To Red Lodge

Barronette Peak
10,404ft

Abiathar Peak
10,928ft

212

△ SLOUGH CREEK

PEBBLE CREEK

Druid Peak
9,583ft

The Thunderer
10,554ft

YELLOWSTONE FOREVER INSTITUTE

Tower Fall
ower Fall

Mount Norris
9,936ft

Cache Mountain
9,596ft

296

LAMAR VALLEY

Soda Butte Creek

GRAND CANYON
OF THE YELLOWSTONE

APPROXIMATE CALDERA BOUNDARY

Lamar River

Parker Peak
10,203ft

Saddle Mountain
10,670ft

White Lake

Pelican Cone
9,643ft

Castor Peak
10,854ft

Pollux Peak
11,067ft

ABSAROKA RANGE

FISHING BRIDGE

LeHardys Rapids

Pyramid Peak
10,497ft

MUSEUM AND
VISITOR CENTER

Steamboat Point

Stevenson Island

LAKE BUTTE
OVERLOOK

Cody Peak
10,267ft

Avalanche Peak
10,566ft

EAST ENTRANCE

To Cody

LLOWSTONE
LAKE
rface elevation
7,733ft

Grizzly Peak
9,948ft

Top Notch Peak
10,238ft

Sylvan Pass
8,530ft

20   14
16

Frank Island

Mount Doane
10,656ft

Reservation Peak
10,629ft

Mount Stevenson
10,352ft

Mount Langford
10,774ft

SOUTHEAST ARM

The Promontory

Mount Schurz
11,139ft

SOUTH ARM

Colter Peak
10,683ft

Eagle Peak
11,358ft
(highest point
in the park)

Overlook Mountain
9,321ft

Trail Lake

Yellowstone River

Table Mountain
11,063ft

TWO OCEAN PLATEAU

Turret Mountain
10,995ft

Mountain   Creek

ABSAROKA RANGE

CONTINENTAL DIVIDE

THOROFARE

0   5 mi

0   5 km

© MOON.COM

In **YELLOWSTONE NATIONAL PARK,** rumblings of a supervolcano boil to the surface—spewing, spitting, oozing, and bubbling. Steam rolls from vividly colored pools, muddy cauldrons burp sulfurous gases, and blasts of hot water shoot high into the air. This cantankerous landscape contains some of the world's most active hydrothermal features, gushing from spouters like iconic Old Faithful, while minerals create artful travertine terraces at Mammoth Hot Springs.

Yellowstone is also home to the biggest remaining wild herds of bison in the country. Several Indigenous groups partner with the park to manage the bison's numbers and preserve them. Bison jams are common on park roads. Bears, elk, pronghorn, wolves, and bighorn sheep also wander the landscape. So many wild animals cluster in Lamar Valley that it has gained fame as "America's Serengeti." Yellowstone itself has become famous as the country's first national park.

PLANNING YOUR TIME

Yellowstone National Park tucks into the northwest corner of Wyoming, its north and west borders spilling over into Montana and Idaho.

Summer (May-Sept.) sees the most visitors, with July and August luring the biggest crowds. All park lodges, campgrounds, and visitors centers are open, as are most park roads. Temperatures range 60-80°F (16-27°C), depending on elevation, and afternoon thundershowers are common.

In **winter,** deep snows blanket the park. Park roads close (early Nov.-late Apr.), except for the road between Yellowstone's North and Northeast Entrances. Tours are via guided snowcoaches or snowmobiles (mid-Dec.-early Mar.). Lodgings are available at Mammoth Hot Springs and Old Faithful.

Spring (Mar.-May) offers car-free bicycling on park roads that won't open to vehicles until late April or May. By May, most visitor services return. Weather bounces between blue skies, rain, and snow. Come in May for bison-calving season, or in June to spot bighorn sheep ewes with newborn lambs and grizzly bears foraging along Yellowstone Lake.

In **fall** (Sept.-Nov.), cooler days yield pleasant hiking with fewer crowds and dwindling services. Sporadic snowstorms can temporarily close park roads until winter descends in early November.

To guarantee lodging, camping, tour, or dinner reservations any time of year, make reservations **13 months in advance.** Some campgrounds take reservations six months in advance. You can also try for camping reservations **two weeks** ahead.

ENTRANCES AND FEES

The entrance fee is $35 per vehicle ($30 motorcycle, $20 individual) and good for seven days. You can **buy your pass online** (www.recreation.gov) from home to speed through entrance stations faster. Yellowstone has five entrance stations; several are closed in winter. Drive times between entrances can take several hours.

- **North Entrance** (US 89, near Gardiner, MT) is open year-round and provides the closest access to Mammoth Hot Springs.

- **Northeast Entrance** (US 212, west of Silver Gate, MT) is open year-round and links the Beartooth Highway with the Lamar Valley. Winter snow shuts

ONE DAY IN YELLOWSTONE

Drive Lower Grand Loop Road to walk the boardwalks in **Midway Geyser Basin** and **Upper Geyser Basin** before catching **Old Faithful** as it erupts. Then cruise across the Continental Divide to drive along **Yellowstone Lake** into **Hayden Valley** to see bison and elk. Finish by gazing from **Artist Point** into the **Grand Canyon of the Yellowstone.**

the roads east of Cooke City, but access remains open between the park entrance and Cooke City.

- **West Entrance** (US 20, West Yellowstone, MT), the busiest entrance in the park, is open mid-April to early November. In winter, it admits only snowcoaches and snowmobiles.

- **East Entrance** (US 20), between Fishing Bridge and Cody, Wyoming, is open mid-May to early November.

- **South Entrance** (US 89/191/287), on the border between Yellowstone and Grand Teton, is open mid-May to early November. In winter, it admits only snowcoaches and snowmobiles.

VISITORS CENTERS

Inside the park, visitors centers offer exhibits, park maps, bookstores, road conditions, trail information, Junior Ranger Program booklets, and naturalist talks and walks.

Old Faithful Visitor Education Center (307/344-2751, 8am-8pm daily June-Sept., 9am-5pm daily Oct.-Mar., seasonal closures occur) has exhibits on geysers, hot springs, mud pots, and fumaroles. Geyser eruption predictions are available, and the theater rotates park films.

Albright (Mammoth) Visitor Center (Mammoth Hot Springs, 307/344-2263, 8am-6pm daily June-Sept., 9am-5pm daily Oct.-May) has exhibits on the cultural and natural history of the Northern Range. The **backcountry office** (8am-4pm daily June-Aug.) issues permits for backcountry camping, boating, and fishing.

Canyon Visitor Education Center (Canyon Village, 307/344-2550, 8am-6pm daily May-mid-Sept., hours vary other seasons) features films, murals,

OLD FAITHFUL VISITOR EDUCATION CENTER

AVOID THE CROWDS

Avoid July, which sees the heaviest visitation.

Visit in **June** or **September** when crowds thin in comparison to midsummer, in **May** for newborn bison and elk calves, or in **October** for fall colors, bear activity, and elk bugling.

Go in **winter** for the beauty of the icy landscape and prolific steam in geyser basins.

Avoid popular spots midday (10am-4pm) such at the North and South Rim Drives at Grand Canyon of the Yellowstone, when most of the crowds swell. Utilize the **early morning** and **late afternoon-evening** hours instead.

Hit the super-crowded **Midway** and **Norris Geyser Basins** in early morning **by 9am** or evening **after 5pm.**

Visit the **Upper Geyser Basin** (Old Faithful, Black Sands, Biscuit) at **sunset** (8pm-9:30pm in summer) or **sunrise** (5am-6:30am in summer).

Go wildlife-watching in the **morning** and **evening,** when animals are more active.

Park early. Plan to be at your trailhead parking lot by **8am-9am** or earlier.

Stop at picnic areas for restroom breaks; geyser basins and canyon-area restrooms usually have lengthy lines.

Enter via the **East, Northeast, or North Entrance** if you're visiting July-August rather than waiting in the long lines at the West and South Entrances.

and geology exhibits and contains a **backcountry office** (8am-4pm daily June-Aug.).

Fishing Bridge Visitor Center (Yellowstone Lake, 307/344-2450, 8am-7pm daily late May-early Sept., hours vary other seasons) showcases bird and waterfowl specimens and has an outdoor amphitheater for naturalist presentations.

Grant Visitor Center (Grant Village, 307/344-2650, 8am-7pm daily late May-early Oct., hours vary other seasons) has exhibits on fire and a park film.

In West Yellowstone, **West Yellowstone Visitor Information Center** (30 Yellowstone Ave., 307/344-2876, 8am-8pm daily late May-early Sept., shorter hours fall-spring) has information and **backcountry permits** (8am-4pm daily June-Aug.).

SIGHTS

MAMMOTH HOT SPRINGS

Raised boardwalks and stairways loop through the Mammoth Hot Springs,

where sulfur fills the air and limestone creates travertine terraces and calcium carbonate sculptures.

Explore the **Lower Terraces,** where colors change depending on water flow. Stroll the boardwalk to **Liberty Cap,** a 37-foot-tall (11-m) dormant hot springs cone, then visit **Palette Spring,**

FISHING BRIDGE

Top **3**

1 MARVEL AT OLD FAITHFUL

When **Old Faithful Geyser** erupts, it shoots up to 8,400 gallons (31,797 l) of hot water as high as 185 feet (56 m). It's one of the most regular geysers in the park, erupting every 60-90 minutes. Often it sputters for 20 minutes before an eruption, which lasts a few minutes. In summer, massive crowds fill the benches surrounding the geyser 30 minutes in advance.

Old Faithful is behind the Old Faithful Visitor Education Center, which has exhibits that explain the geyser's inner workings. Eruption times are posted at the visitors center or on the NPS app.

OLD FAITHFUL GEYSER

2 WATCH WILDLIFE

Wildlife captivates in Yellowstone. The massive **Lamar Valley** is America's Serengeti thanks to its hefty numbers of abundant wildlife. The Lamar River flows through the sagebrush valley where immense herds of **bison** feed. Between herds, look for **pronghorn, bighorn sheep, elk, bears, coyotes,** and **wolves.** In late fall, listen for bighorn sheep butting heads or elk bugling.

Sliced by the Yellowstone River, the bucolic **Hayden Valley** contains prime wildlife-watching with frequent bison jams. Watch for **coyotes, moose, elk, raptors, grizzly bears, trumpeter swans, wolves,** and hordes of **Canada geese.**

Along the **Madison River,** pullouts aid viewing of **bison, elk, deer,** and **raptors.** In fall, bull elk often round up harems, with the bulls' bugling echoing across the valley.

3 GAZE INTO THE GRAND CANYON OF THE YELLOWSTONE

The Yellowstone River cuts a colorful deep and narrow swath through the **Grand Canyon of the Yellowstone.** The river crashes over the **Upper Falls** before thundering down the **Lower Falls,** the park's tallest and most famous waterfall. Three roads access overlooks surrounding the 20-mile-long (32-km) canyon. Trails trot along the rim, while switchbacks and stairways plunge into the canyon for closer views (but require strenuous return climbs).

LOWER FALL, GRAND CANYON OF THE YELLOWSTONE

where orange and brown thermophiles color the sinter. The main boardwalk circles the striking travertine sculptures of **Minerva Terrace. Cleopatra, Mound,** and **Jupiter Terraces** flank the stairs to an overlook. At the top, a boardwalk leads to brilliant orange and white **Canary Spring.** Three parking lots access the lower terraces south of Mammoth Village.

The one-way **Upper Terrace Drive** (1.5 mi/2.4 km, mid-May-early Nov.) tours a paved loop of older formations such as **Orange Spring Mound.** The entrance is 2 miles (3.2 km) south of Mammoth Village on the road toward Norris.

Fort Yellowstone

In the pre-National Park Service decades, the village of Mammoth was **Fort Yellowstone,** which housed the U.S. Army unit that managed the park 1891-1916. A self-guided walking tour sees the **Bachelor Officers' Quarters** (Albright Visitor Center), **parade ground,** red-roofed **officers quarters,** and other buildings.

Roosevelt Arch

In Gardiner, the original park entrance road crosses under the 1903 stone-and-mortar **Roosevelt Arch,** dedicated to

LIBERTY CAP

President Theodore Roosevelt. Passenger vehicles can drive through the narrow entrance, or you can park on Park Street to walk through the arch and **Arch Park.**

▼ MAMMOTH TERRACES

ROOSEVELT ARCH

TOWER FALL

Tower Fall (2.3 mi/3.7 km south of Tower Jct.) plunges from its brink between rhyolite spires, dropping from a hanging valley into a ribbon that spews in a long freefall. An overlook near the Tower Fall parking lot offers the best view.

TOWER FALL

NORRIS GEYSER BASIN

Interpretive boardwalks and paths loop through two hydrothermal basins at **Norris Geyser Basin.** At 459°F (237°C) below the surface, it is the hottest and oldest geyser basin. **Norris Geyser Basin Museum & Information Station** (307/344-2812, 9am-5pm daily late May-mid-Oct.) has exhibits and ranger-led walks into the basin.

Back Basin

Back Basin (1.5 mi/2.4 km rt, 1 hr, easy) houses the blue **Emerald Spring** and **Steamboat Geyser,** the world's tallest geyser. The route loops past blue-green **Cistern Spring** and the red-or-ange-rimmed pool of **Echinus Geyser,** the world's largest acidic geyser. A collection of fumaroles, hot springs, mud pots, roiling **Porkchop Geyser,** and spitting **Minute Geyser** finish the loop.

Porcelain Basin

The acidic **Porcelain Basin** (0.75 mi/1.2 km rt, 30 min, easy), which contains the park's highest concentration of silica, has **Crackling Lake** bubbling along its edges. While **Pinwheel Geyser** is defunct, active **Whirligig Geyser** spills into a stream of orange iron oxide and green thermophiles. **Hurricane Vent** roars steam, and **Porcelain Springs** contains blue pools.

LOWER GEYSER BASIN

Between Madison Junction and Old Faithful, the Lower Geyser Basin houses **Fountain Paint Pot** (8 mi/13 km south of Madison Jct.) and **Firehole Lake Drive** (9.3 mi/15 km south of Madison Jct.).

An interpretive boardwalk loops around **Fountain Paint Pot** (0.5 mi/0.8 km, 30 min, easy) that includes all four hydrothermal features: geysers, mud pots, hot springs, and fumaroles.

The one-way **Firehole Lake Drive** (3 mi/4.8 km) passes eight thermal features. Brown **Firehole Lake** is the road's largest hot spring. **Great Fountain Geyser** shoots a high spray every 10-14 hours for up to an hour.

MIDWAY GEYSER BASIN

About 10 miles (16 km) south of Madison Junction, **Midway Geyser Basin** (0.7 mi/1.1 km, 30 min, easy) loops a boardwalk across the Firehole River. The dormant crater of **Excelsior Geyser** contains a steaming turquoise pool spilling into the river. **Grand Prismatic Spring,** the third-largest hot spring in the world, radiates fiery arms of orange, gold, and brown thermophiles from the yellow-rimmed, blue hot pool.

OLD FAITHFUL AREA
Old Faithful Inn

Built in 1903-1904, **Old Faithful Inn** epitomizes "parkitecture." With a steep-pitched roof and gabled dormers, the lobby vaults five stories high. It centers on a giant stone fireplace and hand-crafted clock built from wood, copper, and iron. Daily **tours** (hours vary, daily early May-early Oct., free) are available.

Upper Geyser Basin

Maps at the visitors center aid in navigating interconnected loops of **Upper Geyser Basin** (4.5 mi/7.2 km, 3 hrs, easy). Walk as many or as few loops in this largest of the geyser basins. The visitors center and the NPS app let you know predictions for notable geyser eruptions.

From the Old Faithful viewing area behind the visitors center, cross the Firehole River to reach **Geyser Hill,** where **Beehive Geyser** is the largest geyser. The smaller **Anemone Geyser**

PORCELAIN SPRINGS, NORRIS GEYSER BASIN

GRAND PRISMATIC SPRING

erupts every 10 minutes while **Plume Geyser** spouts a few times an hour. Clear-blue **Heart Spring** sits near the **Lion Geyser Group,** a family of sputtering geysers.

At **Castle Geyser,** a cone geyser built into the largest sinter formation in the world, the **Firehole River Loop** crosses two bridges to reach **Grand Geyser,** a fountain geyser. Just north are a pair of colorful hot springs, **Beauty Pool** and **Chromatic Pool.**

At the west end of the basin, **Grotto Geyser** squirts water from its odd-shaped cone. **Riverside Geyser** shoots an arc of water over the river at six-hour intervals. The striking green, orange, and yellow **Morning Glory Pool** marks the turnaround point.

A spur loop to the south, **Daisy Geyser Basin** arcs past **Daisy Geyser,** which erupts every 2-3 hours. Turn around at **Punch Bowl,** which boils in its raised sinter bowl.

Biscuit Basin

Located 3.5 miles (5.6 km) north of Old Faithful, a bridge crosses the Firehole River to reach **Biscuit Basin** (0.7 mi/1.1 km rt, 30 min, easy). Three hot springs

bring on color: **Black Opal Pool, Wall Pool,** and **Sapphire Pool,** with crystal blue water. The upper loop passes yellow **Mustard Spring** and **Jewel Geyser,** which spits every 10 minutes.

Black Sand Basin

Two miles (3.2 km) northwest of Old Faithful, **Black Sand Basin** (0.6 mi/1 km, 20 min, easy) takes in **Cliff Geyser** and two boardwalk spurs. One goes to **Sunset Lake,** named for its yellow-orange rim, and the other to see **Emerald Pool,** colored from algae.

GRAND CANYON OF THE YELLOWSTONE

North Rim

The one-way **North Rim Drive** (1.2 mi/1.9 km south of Canyon Jct.) visits overlooks of the canyon and the Lower Falls. **Brink of the Lower Falls** has a paved walkway to an upper overlook and a trail (1 mi/1.6 km, 30 min, moderate) that switchbacks to a platform at the lip of the Lower Falls. **Lookout Point** has an upper overlook facing the falls and a stairway that plunges to **Red Rock Point** (0.6 mi/1 km, 20 min,

MORNING GLORY POOL, UPPER GEYSER BASIN

moderate) for a closer perch. **Grand View Overlook** takes in the canyon and Lower Falls. At the end of North Rim Drive, turn right onto the two-lane road to reach **Inspiration Point** for four platforms (several are wheelchair-accessible) overlooking the colorful canyon and river below.

From the **Brink of the Upper Falls Road** (0.4 mi/0.6 km south of North Rim Dr.), a short paved walk follows the river upstream to a viewing platform at the Brink of the Upper Falls (0.4 mi/0.6 km, 20 min, easy), which mesmerizes with a powerful hurtle downstream.

South Rim

From **South Rim Drive** (2.2 mi/3.5 km south of Canyon Jct.), cross the Chittenden Bridge to two parking areas.

Uncle Tom's Point has a paved walkway to a view of the **Upper Falls.** The plunging **Uncle Tom's Trail** (0.7 mi/1.1 km, 30 min, strenuous) drops on switchbacks and 328 steel stairs for the closest view of the **Lower Falls. Artist Point** has the classic view of the canyon and Lower Falls.

YELLOWSTONE LAKE

Yellowstone Lake is the largest high-elevation freshwater lake in North America. Roads tour two shores, with multiple picnic areas for access. On the northern shore, historic **Fishing Bridge** crosses the lake's outlet, the beginning of the Yellowstone River, and farther east **Steamboat Springs** puffs. On the

▼ PUNCH BOWL, UPPER GEYSER BASIN

BISCUIT BASIN

western shore, boat tours go out from **Bridge Bay** daily in summer.

West Thumb Geyser Basin

Northeast of West Thumb Junction, **West Thumb Geyser Basin** (0.6 mi/0.9 km, 30 min, easy) offers loops past three geysers and 11 hot springs, plus fumaroles and mud pots. The lower loop goes to Yellowstone Lake, where visitors once cooked fish in **Fishing Cone. Black Pool** spills with colorful thermophiles and **Abyss Pool** may be one of the deepest in the park.

SCENIC DRIVE

GRAND LOOP ROAD

Most drivers split the 142-mile (229-km) **Grand Loop Road** into 2-3 days, as a one-day push (5-8 hrs) limits the amount of time to stop at sights. Different segments open annually late April through late May.

At **Mammoth Hot Springs,** join the Grand Loop Road (US 89) heading south toward **Norris, Madison Junction,** and **Old Faithful** (52 mi/84 km, 2 hrs, late Apr.-early Nov.). The road climbs south through hoodoos and crawls along the cliffs of **Golden Gate** before topping out at **Swan Lake Flat.** It passes **Obsidian Cliff,** a site of geological and Native American significance, and hissing **Roaring Mountain,** pumping out steam. After **Norris Geyser Basin,** a hotbed of geothermal activity, the road drops into the supervolcano caldera, passing blue **Beryl Springs** and **Gibbon Falls** to reach Madison Junction. From this low point in the caldera, begin climbing along the **Firehole River** toward the geyser basins: **Lower, Midway,** and **Upper;** the Upper Geyser Basin is home to **Old Faithful Geyser.**

From the geyser basins, the road bounces eastward twice over the Continental Divide to **West Thumb Junction** (17 mi/27 km, 45 min, mid-May-early Nov.). Turn left to stop at **West Thumb Geyser Basin.**

Aim north toward **Canyon Village** (36 mi/58 km, 1.5 hrs, mid-May-early Nov.) along **Yellowstone Lake,** passing **Bridge Bay** and **Lake Village,** which houses the historic **Lake Yellowstone Hotel.** After the junction at **Fishing Bridge,** the road hugs the **Yellowstone River,** flowing north to sulfur-smelling **Mud Volcano** and wildlife-rich **Hayden Valley,** where you may get caught in a bison jam. At **Grand Canyon of the Yellowstone,** turn off on one of the three short drives to visit overlooks.

▼ BRINK OF THE LOWER FALL

WEST THUMB GEYSER BASIN

At Canyon Junction, climb north over **Dunraven Pass** and drop through curves down to **Tower Fall** and **Tower Junction** (19 mi/31 km, 45 min, late May-early Nov.). Then, continue west, passing **Petrified Tree** and **Undine Falls** before closing the loop at **Mammoth Hot Springs** (18 mi/29 km, 45 min, year-round).

HIKING

MAMMOTH HOT SPRINGS AREA

Bunsen Peak

From the Old Bunsen Peak Road Trailhead south of Mammoth, the trail to **Bunsen Peak** (4.6 mi/7.4 km rt, 3 hrs, strenuous) winds back and forth up the mountain, passing Cathedral Rock en route. Steep switchbacks lead across talus slopes to the summit for unobstructed views of Swan Lake and many of Yellowstone's peaks.

Wraith Falls

The trail to **Wraith Falls** (1 mi/1.6 km rt, 1 hr, easy) travels through a sagebrush-scented meadow to the falls as it cascades down a wide-angled rock face squeezed into a canyon.

NORTHEAST AREA

Lost Lake Loop

Hikers have plenty of things to see on the **Lost Lake Loop** (4 mi/6.4 km rt, 2.5 hrs, moderate): a waterfall, the small lake, and Petrified Tree. From Roosevelt Lodge, take the left spur to the **Lost Creek Falls Trail** to climb a pine-shaded ravine to the falls before continuing on **Lost Lake Trail** to the lake. The trail heads west to **Petrified Tree,** where it mounts a hill to the east before dropping behind Tower Ranger Station and back to Roosevelt Lodge.

Trout Lake

Trout Lake (1.2 mi/1.9 km rt, 1.5 hrs, strenuous) is an idyllic little lake sitting at about 7,000 feet (2,134 m) in elevation in the Absaroka Mountains. From the trailhead (Northeast Entrance Rd.) the path catapults vertically through a Douglas fir forest to circle the lake.

OLD FAITHFUL AREA

Observation Point

For a different vantage point of Old Faithful while it is erupting, climb to **Observation Point** (1.6 mi/2.6 km rt).

Lone Star Geyser

From the Lone Star Geyser Trailhead east of Old Faithful, the **Lone Star Geyser Trail** (4.8 mi/7.7 km rt, 2-3 hrs, easy, bikes permitted) goes along the Firehole River on an old service road to a huge pink and gray sinter cone. The geyser erupts about every three hours with spurts lasting 30 minutes.

Mystic Falls

From Biscuit Basin parking lot, the boardwalk loop provides access to the trailhead for **Mystic Falls** (2.4 mi/3.9 km rt, 1.5 hrs, moderate). Turn right and hike to a junction. Take the left fork and ascend along the creek to Mystic Falls, a waterfall that feeds a series of cascades.

CANYON AREA

Mount Washburn Lookout

At 10,243 feet (3,107 m), the **Mount Washburn Lookout** yields 360-degree views from the highest peak in Yellowstone. Two strenuous trails climb to the summit. From Dunraven Pass on Grand Loop Road, the **Dunraven Pass Trail** (6 mi/9.7 km rt, 4 hrs) follows an old road up to crest a ridge and finish by circling to Mount Washburn Lookout. From the end of Chittenden Road, north of Dunraven Pass, the steeper **Chittenden Trail** (5.8 mi/9.3 km rt, 4 hrs, bikes permitted) packs more elevation gain in its meadowed switchbacks up to the summit.

Cascade Lake

From Cascade Picnic Area north of Canyon Junction, the trail cuts through forest, wildflower meadows, and marshes to reach the idyllic **Cascade Lake** (4.4 mi/7 km rt, 2.5 hrs, easy). Cradled in a basin surrounded by meadows, the lily-padded lake can house trumpeter swans.

Point Sublime

From Artist Point parking lot on South Rim Road, the rolling trail to **Point Sublime** (3 mi/2.4 km rt, 1.5 hrs, easy) leaves crowds behind to peer into Grand Canyon of the Yellowstone. Exposed overlooks (no railings) take in the depths, blue river, red and pink walls, and hoodoos before the forest claims the canyon.

Clear Lake and Ribbon Lake

From the Wapiti Picnic Area on South Rim Drive, the **Clear Lake-Ribbon Lake Trail** (7.3 mi/11.8 km, rt, moderate) makes a lollipop loop. It passes the shallow, hot spring-fed **Clear Lake,** a side spur to **Lily Pad Lake,** and **Ribbon Lake.** The loop goes through thermal areas (stay on the path for safety).

WRAITH FALLS

Best Hike

GRAND PRISMATIC OVERLOOK AND FAIRY FALLS

DISTANCE: 1.2-6.7 miles (1.9-10.7 km) round-trip

DURATION: 1-3 hours

ELEVATION CHANGE: 52-129 feet (16-39 m)

EFFORT: easy

TRAILHEAD: Fairy Falls parking area

At 200 feet (61 m), Fairy Falls is the park's fourth-highest waterfall, and it provides a scenic year-round destination for hikers, bikers, and skiers. A spur trail adds an overlook of Grand Prismatic Spring to see the cobalt hot spring and the fiery arms of thermophiles. The trail is closed in spring until late May because of bear activity.

From **Fairy Falls Trailhead,** cross the Firehole River and hike the abandoned road. To climb to the overlook of **Grand Prismatic Spring** (1.2 mi/1.9 km rt), take the signed 0.5-mile (0.8-km) spur to ascend steeply in elevation to the platform. From there, continue onward to drop to the old roadway and turn westward to reach the junction with the **Fairy Falls Trail** at 1.1 miles (1.8 km). Turning west, hike 1.5 miles (2.4 km) through a young lodgepole forest to the base of the falls. In summer, the falls plunge ribbonlike into a pool; in winter, it's an ice sculpture. With the spur to Grand Prismatic Overlook, the round-trip distance is 6.7 miles (10.7 km) to the falls.

FAIRY FALLS

LAKE YELLOWSTONE AREA

Storm Point Loop

From the pullout at **Indian Pond** on the East Entrance Road, the **Storm Point Loop** (2.3 mi/3.7 km rt, 1.5 hr, easy) launches from where the Nez Perce (Nimiipuu) people camped while fleeing the U.S. Army in 1877 to avoid being forced onto a reservation. At a junction, go left to reach the rocky **Storm Point** on Lake Yellowstone. The trail continues west along windblown sandy bluffs before entering the forest to return.

Elephant Back Mountain

From Grand Loop Road south of Fishing Bridge, the trail up **Elephant Back Mountain** (3.6 mi/5.8 km rt, 2.5 hrs, moderate) climbs steadily to a loop to the summit. Take in Lake Yellowstone and its namesake hotel as well as Stevenson Island.

Natural Bridge

From Bridge Bay Marina, the **Natural Bridge Trail** (2.6 mi/4.2 km rt, 1.5 hrs, easy, closed late spring-early summer for grizzlies) goes to a rhyolite rock that Bridge Creek eroded through. The route follows an old road to the

TROUT LAKE TRAIL

interpretive exhibit and a loop that goes up behind the bridge.

RECREATION

BACKPACKING

Point-to-point backpacking trips in the **Black Canyon of the Yellowstone** (16.5 mi/26.5 km, 3 days) go from **Hellroaring Creek Trailhead** to **Blacktail Creek Trailhead.** Choose from 19 campsites, with the best flanking the Yellowstone River.

From the Lone Star Geyser Trailhead, the **Bechler River Trail** (30 mi/48.3 km, 3-5 days) descends into the land of waterfalls with the best campsites at Ouzel, Colonnade, and Albright Falls. Due to annual flooding, permit reservations are only available starting July 15.

Permits (www.recreation.gov, $5 pp/night plus $10 fee) are required. For peak season, obtain one via **early access lottery** (Mar. 1-20, $10) or **general application** (from late Apr.). Limited **walk-up permits** are available two days ahead. Off-season, permits are available 14 days ahead. Permit competition is stiffest for lake destinations for 2-3 days.

BIKING

In spring (late Mar.-mid-Apr.), roads between Mammoth and West Yellowstone open to bicyclists but remain closed to vehicles. Bring your own bike, as rentals are only available in West Yellowstone.

Several side roads permit bikes in both directions while cars are limited to one-way travel. The **Old Gardiner Road** (10 mi/16.1 km rt) connects Gardiner with Mammoth Hot Springs. **Blacktail Plateau Drive** (12 mi/19.3 km rt) rolls through higher-elevation terrain with wildlife.

Only a handful of trails allow bikes, including Lone Star Geyser, Fountain Freight Road, and Old Faithful to Morning Glory Pool. More challenging, the

MYSTIC FALLS

LONE STAR GEYSER

BIKING GRAND LOOP ROAD

Chittenden Trail (5.8 mi/9.3 km rt) climbs to Mount Washburn Lookout.

HORSEBACK RIDING

Wranglers lead one-hour and two-hour **Saddle Up** (Xanterra, 307/344-7311, www.yellowstonenationalparklodges. com, daily June-early Sept.) horseback tours from the corrals at Roosevelt and Canyon.

BOATING AND FISHING

Yellowstone Lake attracts boaters for sightseeing, cruising, angling, sailing, and paddling permits and inspections required, from $20/week nonmotorized, $40/week motorized). **Bridge Bay Marina** (Xanterra, 307/344-7311, www.yellowstonenationalparklodges. com, late May-Oct., daily mid-June-early Sept.) has a boat launch, marina services, and rentals. On the West Thumb, **Grant Village Marina** (mid-June-Oct.) has a boat launch but no services.

For **fishing** (late May-early Nov., permit required, from $40/3 days), the **Firehole, Madison,** and lower **Gibbon Rivers** offer prime fly-fishing for rainbow and brown trout. Portions of the

Yellowstone River offer an outstanding trout fly-fishery too. **Yellowstone Lake** and **Lewis Lake** work for shoreline fishing, float-tube fishing, spin-casting, fly-fishing, and fishing from motorboats or rowboats.

WINTER SPORTS

In winter (mid-Dec.-early Mar.), visitors can explore groomed trails on snowshoes or cross-country skis and tour the snow-buried roads of Yellowstone in heated snowcoaches. Led by interpretive guides, snowcoaches stop at sights for photos and wildlife. Tours depart from **Mammoth Hot Springs** and **Old Faithful Snow Lodge** (reservations 307/344-7311, www.yellowstonenationalparklodges.com) and from companies in West Yellowstone, Gardiner, and Flagg Ranch. Reservations are required. Guided snowmobile tours are also available.

WHERE TO STAY

INSIDE THE PARK

Make **reservations** (307/344-7311, www.yellowstonenationalparklodges.com) for lodges, restaurants, and campgrounds **13 months in advance.** In winter, **dinner reservations** are required at Mammoth Hotel Dining Room and Snow Lodge.

In summer, reservations are mandatory for the Old West Dinner Cookout and are strongly recommended for Old Faithful Inn, M66 Grill at Canyon Village, Grant Village Dining Room, and Lake Hotel Dining Room. Restaurant hours shorten fall-spring.

Mammoth Hot Springs

Mammoth Hot Springs Hotel (2 Mammoth Hotel Ave., late Apr.-Oct. and mid-Dec.-early Mar., from $197) has hotel rooms and cabins. It is the only winter hotel accessible by private vehicle. Eateries include **Mammoth Hotel Dining Room** (11:30am-2:30pm and 5pm-10pm daily summer, limited hours fall-spring) and **Mammoth Terrace Grill** (7am-9pm daily).

Tower Junction

Roosevelt Lodge and Cabins (Roosevelt Lodge Rd., early June-early Sept., from $114) has cabins with wood-burning stoves and private or shared baths. The 1920s lodge has a **dining room** (11:30am-7pm daily). For the **Old West Dinner Cookout** (reservations required), guests saddle up or ride a wagon from the corrals to the cookout.

Old Faithful

The most requested lodge in the park, **Old Faithful Inn** (May-Oct., from $208) is a National Historic Landmark with 10 room styles and a five-story log lobby. It has a **dining room** (6:30am-10am, 11:30am-2:30pm, and 4:30pm-10pm daily) and a deli.

Old Faithful Lodge (mid-May-early Oct., from $116) has small motel-style rooms in duplex or fourplex cabins with private baths or a communal bath and shower cabin. The lodge has a **cafeteria** (6:30am-10am and 11am-8pm daily) and bake shop.

Snow Lodge (late Apr.-mid-Oct. from $189, mid-Dec.-Feb. from $180) has modern lodge rooms and cabins located a short walk from the lodge. Restaurants include the **Obsidian Dining Room** (6:30am-10:30am and 5pm-10:30pm daily) and the **Geyser Grill** (11am-8pm daily).

Canyon Village

Canyon Lodge and Cabins (May-Sept., from $264) has the newest lodgings. Hotel rooms are in multi-story lodges and motel-style rooms in cabins. The complex includes the **Canyon Lodge M66 Bar and Grill** (6:30am-10:30am and 5pm-10pm daily mid-May-early Sept.) and **Canyon Lodge Eatery** (6:30am-10am, 11:30am-3pm, and 4:30pm-9:30pm daily mid-May-mid-Oct.).

Yellowstone Lake

A National Historic Landmark, **Lake Yellowstone Hotel and Cabins** (mid-May-early Oct., from $285) is a striking colonial-style structure with renovated hotel rooms and suites, motel rooms in an older lodge, and cabins. Restaurants include a **dining room** (6:30am-10am and 5pm-10pm daily), a bar, and a deli.

Set back from the shore of Yellowstone Lake, **Lake Lodge Cabins** (early June-late Sept., from $179) has rustic

▼ WINTER SUNSET IN YELLOWSTONE

LAKE YELLOWSTONE HOTEL

cabins with private baths. The lodge has a **cafeteria** (6:30am-9:30pm daily) and a bar.

On West Thumb Bay, **Grant Village Lodge** (Grant Village, June-Oct., from $306) has hotel rooms with private baths. Restaurants include the **dining room** (6:30am-10am, 11:30am-2:30pm, and 5pm-10pm daily) and **Grant Village Lake House Restaurant** (5pm-9pm daily).

Camping

The park has more than 2,000 campsites in 12 campgrounds. The largest five accept **reservations** (307/344-7311, www.yellowstonenationalpark-lodges.com) 13 months in advance. **Madison** (May-mid-Oct., $29), **Canyon** (late May-late Sept., showers, $34), **Bridge Bay** (mid-May-early Sept., $29), and **Grant Village** (early June-mid-Sept., showers, $34) do not have hookups. **Fishing Bridge RV Park** (May-Sept., $83) has full hookups and showers.

The park's smaller campgrounds ($20-25) are **Mammoth** (year-round), **Indian Creek** (mid-June-mid-Sept.), Norris (mid-May-Sept.), **Slough Creek** (mid-June-mid-Oct.), **Pebble Creek** (mid-June-Sept.), **Tower Fall** (early June-early Sept.), and **Lewis Lake** (mid-June-mid-Oct.). **Reservations** (www.recreation.gov) are available six months ahead for most of the sites; the remaining reservations are available two weeks ahead. These campgrounds do not have hookups or showers.

OUTSIDE THE PARK

Find lodging, restaurants, and services in **West Yellowstone, Gardiner,** and **Silver Gate-Cooke City.**

GETTING THERE

AIR

Bozeman Yellowstone International Airport (BZN, 406/388-8321, 850 Gallatin Field Rd., Belgrade, MT, www.bozemanairport.com) is closest to the park entrances at West Yellowstone and Gardiner, about 1.5 hours. **Jackson Hole Airport** (JAC, 1250 E. Airport Rd., Jackson, WY, 307/733-7682, www.jacksonholeairport.com) is closest to the south entrance, about an hour's drive. **Billings Logan International Airport** (BIL, 1901 Terminal Circle, Billings, MT, 406/247-8609, www.flybillings.com) works for summer access (late May-mid-Oct.) to the park's north and east roads. All airports have rental cars.

CAR

I-90 crosses east-west through Montana north of Yellowstone. Between Billings and Butte, multiple routes drop south to reach the park's **West, North,** and **Northeast Entrances.** East of Bozeman, drivers can take US 89 south through Gardiner to the North

Entrance. West of Bozeman, US 191 drops south to the park entrance at West Yellowstone.

The most scenic approach is the **Beartooth Highway** (US 212, late May-mid-Oct., weather permitting), which runs 68 miles (109 km) from Red Lodge, Montana, to the Northeast Entrance. Plan three hours for the drive, and check road and weather conditions.

From the west, US 14 enters the park's East Entrance via **Cody, Wyoming.** Yellowstone's **South Entrance** straddles the border with Grand Teton National Park on US 89/191/287.

GETTING AROUND

There is no park shuttle. In summer, you'll need a vehicle to get around. In winter, visitors can ride snowcoaches or snowmobiles from West Yellowstone, Mammoth, or Flagg Ranch to Old Faithful or the Grand Canyon of the Yellowstone.

DRIVING

Two-lane roads are the standard in Yellowstone. Curves, wildlife, and scenery complicate driving. Watch out for crowds and wildlife jams.

Use pullouts for sightseeing and wildlife-watching.

The Grand Loop Road from Mammoth Village east to Tower Junction and the Northeast Entrance Road are the only roads that are open year-round. All other roads close in winter.

PARKING

Parking lots in the park fill 10am-5pm (and restroom lines are long too). RVs will find limited parking. At trailheads, claim a parking spot before 9am.

Two giant parking lots are available at Old Faithful, and they pack out in summer. The smaller parking lot is between Snow Lodge and Old Faithful Inn. The larger parking lot is southwest of Old Faithful Lodge.

TOURS

Xanterra (307/344-7311, www.yellowstonenationalparklodges.com) operates wildlife-watching, geyser basin, and winter snowcoach tours. Reservations are required. **Yellowstone Forever Institute** (406/848-2400, www.yellowstone.org) offers expert-led educational tours year-round. Multiple companies in West Yellowstone, Gardiner, and Jackson also run full-day sightseeing tours.

OLD FAITHFUL INN

WHERE TO STAY IN YELLOWSTONE

NAME	LOCATION	PRICE	SEASON	AMENITIES
Mammoth Campground	Mammoth Hot Springs	$25	year-round	campsites
Mammoth Hot Springs Hotel	Mammoth Hot Springs	from $197	Apr.-Oct., Dec.-Mar.	hotel rooms, cabins, dining
Tower Fall Campground	Tower-Roosevelt	$20	early June-early Sept.	campsites
Roosevelt Lodge and Cabins	Tower-Roosevelt	from $104	early June-early Sept.	cabins, dining
Slough Creek Campground	Northeast Entrance	$20	mid-June-mid-Oct.	campsites
Pebble Creek Campground	Northeast Entrance	$20	mid-June-Sept.	campsites
Madison Campground	Madison	$29	May-mid-Oct.	campsites
Indian Creek Campground	Mammoth/Norris	$20	June-Sept.	campsites
Norris Campground	Norris	$25	May-Sept.	campsites
Old Faithful Lodge	Old Faithful	from $116	May-Oct.	cabins, dining
Snow Lodge	Old Faithful	from $180	Apr.-Oct., Dec.-Feb.	hotel rooms, cabins, dining
Old Faithful Inn	Old Faithful	from $208	May-Oct.	hotel rooms, dining
Canyon Campground	Canyon Village	$34	late May-late Sept.	campsites, showers
Canyon Lodge and Cabins	Canyon Village	from $264	May-Sept.	hotel rooms, cabins, dining
Fishing Bridge RV Park	Fishing Bridge	$83	May-Sept.	RV hookups
Bridge Bay Campground	Lake Village	$29	mid-May-early Sept.	campsites, marina
Lake Lodge Cabins	Lake Village	from $179	June-Sept.	motel rooms, cabins, dining
Lake Yellowstone Hotel and Cabins	Lake Village	from $285	May-Oct.	hotel rooms, cabins, dining
Grant Village Campground	Grant Village	$34	June-Sept.	campsites
Grant Village Lodge	Grant Village	from $306	June-Oct.	hotel rooms, dining
Lewis Lake Campground	South Entrance Road	$20	June-Oct.	campsites

GRAND TETON
NATIONAL PARK

Wyoming

KEEPSAKE STAMPS ▼▼▼

WEBSITE:
www.nps.gov/grte

PHONE NUMBER:
307/739-3399

VISITATION RANK:
7

WHY GO:
Bask in the beauty
of the Tetons.

▲ BRADLEY LAKE TRAIL

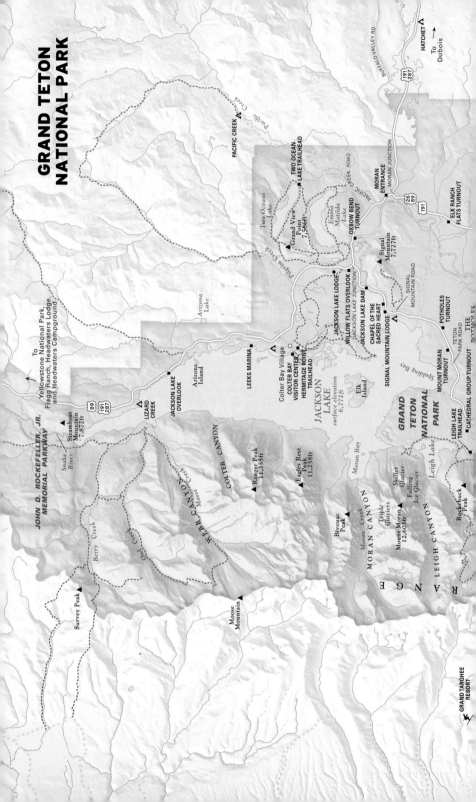

GRAND TETON
NATIONAL PARK

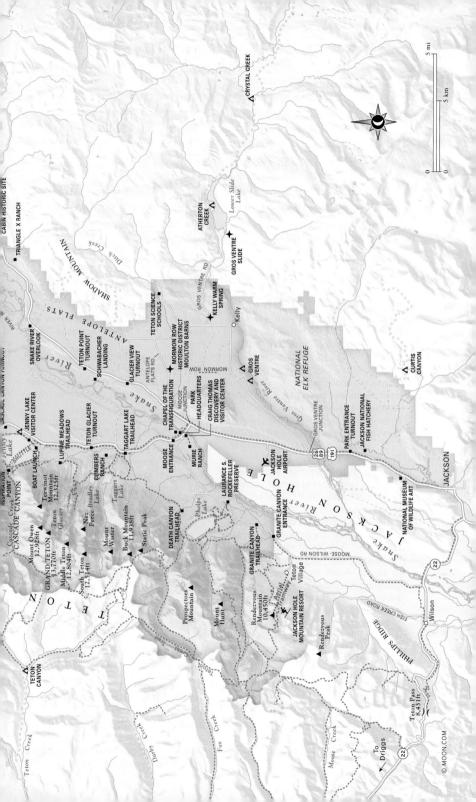

In **GRAND TETON NATIONAL PARK,** sawtooth spires claw the sky in one of the youngest mountain ranges in the Rockies. Towering thousands of feet culminating in the Grand Teton itself, these mountains dwarf the wildlife that roams across the floor of Jackson Hole. These peaks were likely first summited by Native Americans, who gave them spiritual value. The Snake River people—Northern Paiute, Bannock, and Shoshone—named the trio of Grand, Middle, and South Tetons the "Hoary-Headed Fathers."

Snuggled at the base of the peaks, glacial lakes string along the valley floor, offering picturesque places to hike, paddle, and fish. Boating on Jackson Lake, floating the Wild and Scenic Snake River, pedaling paved pathways, and skiing winter slopes are all enjoyed beneath the skyscraping grandeur of the Tetons.

PLANNING YOUR TIME

Grand Teton National Park is in Wyoming, sandwiched between the town of Jackson and Yellowstone National Park. **Summer** (May-Sept.) is high season, when visitors centers, campgrounds, lodges, marinas, and services are open; most **roads are open May to mid-November.** Lower-elevation trails are snow-free in June, while higher-elevation trails don't melt out until mid-July.

In summer, warm days in the 70s-80s (21-31ºC) can evolve into afternoon thunderstorms, especially in the mountains. Spring and fall yo-yo between sunny days and rain or high-elevation snow. Winter snows blanket the ground late November through April.

Most visitor services **close in winter.** Teton Park Road closes **November-April,** from Taggart Lake Trailhead to Signal Mountain Lodge, when it is groomed for cross-country skiing and snowshoeing. **US 26/89/191** provides year-round access to the park.

To guarantee lodgings, tours, and dining, make reservations at least **one year in advance.** Camping reservations should be made six months in advance.

ENTRANCES AND FEES

Grand Teton has three entrance stations that are open year-round. The **Moran Entrance** (US 26/89/191 and US 26/287) accesses the north half of the park from Jackson and the east. The **Granite Canyon Entrance** is the south entrance to the Moose-Wilson Road, north of Teton Village. The **Moose Entrance** (Teton Park Rd.) accesses Teton Park Road.

The entrance fee is $35 per vehicle ($30 motorcycle, $20 individual) and valid for seven days. Buy passes in advance (www.recreation.gov) to save time.

VISITORS CENTERS

All visitors centers have information on ranger programs and guided hikes, maps, current weather, trail conditions, and permits for backcountry camping and boating. Bookstores carry field guides and books on wildlife, human history, and geology.

Craig Thomas Discovery and Visitor Center

Craig Thomas Discovery and Visitor Center (Moose, 307/739-3399, 8am-7pm daily May-Oct., shorter hours spring and fall) has natural history exhibits, wildlife sculptures, a 30-foot (9-m) climbing wall, kids' exhibits, a park film, and a topographic map that shows wildlife migration and glacier progression.

Jenny Lake Visitor Center

At South Jenny Lake, the cramped **Jenny Lake Visitor Center** (Moose, 307/739-3392, 8am-7pm daily June-early Sept., 8am-5pm daily mid-May-early June and Sept.) has an art exhibit.

Top ❸

① GAZE AT GRAND TETON

The Teton Mountains are dominated by their highest peak—the 13,775-foot (4,198-km) **Grand Teton.** Carved by erosion from ice, water, and wind, the Grand Teton spirals into a pinnacle. A lure for climbers, the Grand serves as a notch in the belts of mountaineers who summit its vertical cliffs. The best way

GRAND TETON AND TETON GLACIER

to enjoy the peak is by hiking to **Bradley Lake, Amphitheater Lake, Hurricane Pass,** or **Lake Solitude.** For the best car-accessible views of the peak, eyeball its crags through binoculars at the **Teton Glacier Turnout** on Teton Park Road. For photo ops, head to the **Chapel of the Transfiguration** or **Mormon Row.**

② CRUISE TETON PARK ROAD

Teton Park Road (20 mi/32 km, May-Oct.) is all about getting views of the Tetons. From Craig Thomas Discovery and Visitor Center in Moose, drive north through the Moose Entrance Station and turn right to see the **Menor's Ferry Historic District** and the small log **Chapel of the Transfiguration.** Continue north to **Teton Glacier Turnout,** where you can spot small **Teton Glacier** and towering **Grand Teton.** Stop at **South Jenny Lake** to walk from the visitors center to overlooks of the idyllic waters.

From North Jenny Lake, turn left for a detour on **Jenny Lake Road** (4 mi/6.4 km one-way). Stop at the **Cathedral Group Pullout** for views of three prominent peaks. Continue north on Teton Park Road, stopping at the **Mount Moran turnout** to examine the black dike and small glaciers in the mountain's upper cliffs. Next, **Signal Mountain Summit Road** (10 mi/16 km rt) climbs to Jackson Overlook for sweeping Teton views. At Jackson Lake Dam, walk the paved path to the shore of **Jackson Lake.**

③ ENJOY JENNY LAKE

Tucked below the Grand Teton, **Jenny Lake** beckons photographers to capture its grandeur. Early morning often offers reflections in smooth water. To see the lake, stroll the new wheelchair-accessible **Discovery Loop** (0.5 mi/0.8 km rt, 30 min, easy) from the interpretive plaza to several lake overlooks and benches for soaking up scenery. You can also explore the small visitors center, ranger station, and store, take scenic boat tours, and paddle, hike, or camp.

JENNY LAKE

ONE DAY IN GRAND TETON

Pair up two activities for a taste of the Tetons. In the morning, explore **Jenny Lake** by sauntering the interpretive plaza and lake overlooks, hopping the boat shuttle across the lake, and hiking to **Hidden Falls** and **Lower Inspiration Point**. In the afternoon, relax on a float trip down the **Snake River** as the twisting waterway shifts your viewpoint of the skyscraping **Teton Mountains**.

Jenny Lake Ranger Station (307/739-3343, 8am-5pm daily early June-early Sept.) has information on trail conditions, mountain climbing, and permits.

Colter Bay Visitor Center

Colter Bay Visitor Center (Colter Bay Village, Moran, 307/739-3594, 8am-7pm daily June-early Sept., 8am-5pm daily May-early June and Sept.-Oct.) has craft demonstrations, a small exhibit on Indigenous art, and a park film.

North of Colter Bay, tiny **Flagg Ranch Information Station** (John D. Rockefeller, Jr. Memorial Parkway, US 89/191/287, 307/543-2372, 9am-4pm daily early June-early Sept.) has information on road conditions and activities on John D. Rockefeller, Jr. Memorial Parkway.

SIGHTS

MORMON ROW

Mormon Row is a treat for history buffs, photographers, and wildlife lovers. Originally a Mormon ranch

settlement that started in the 1890s, the tract grew to 27 homesteads. Today, its six clusters of buildings are on the National Register of Historic Places, including the famous **Moulton Barn** that appears in the foreground of so many photos of Grand Teton. Mormon Row is in the southeast corner of the park, off Antelope Flats Road.

LAURANCE S. ROCKEFELLER PRESERVE CENTER

The **Laurance S. Rockefeller Preserve Center** (Moose-Wilson Rd., 307/739-3654, 9am-5pm daily early June-late Sept.) sits in a 1,000-acre (405-ha) preserve that was once a Rockefeller family ranch. The preserve's center contains sensory exhibits, nature videos, and natural soundscapes. Rangers lead daily programs, talks, hikes, sunrise strolls, and evening walks. Trails tour the preserve. The parking lot usually fills 9am-4pm; visit early in the morning or late in the afternoon. Portions of the Moose-Wilson Road will close for construction through 2025; check online or at visitors centers for details and access information.

MENOR'S FERRY HISTORIC DISTRICT

North of the Moose Entrance, **Menor's Ferry Historic District** (Teton Park Rd., Moose) preserves buildings from the 1890s. In summer, rangers guide afternoon walks, or you can take a self-guided tour of the site's cabins, barns, smokehouse, farm implements, wagons, replica ferry, and **general store** (9am-4:30pm daily late May-late Sept.). The **Chapel of the Transfiguration** holds the famous clear window over the altar that frames Grand Teton.

MORMON ROW

THE MURIE RANCH

At the north end of Moose-Wilson Road, the **Murie Center** (Teton Science School, 1 Murie Ranch Rd., Moose, 307/732-7752, www.tetonscience.org, 9am-5pm daily mid-May-mid-Oct., free) is a National Historic Landmark. Pick up a self-guided walking tour guide on the Muries' front porch or take a docent-led **tour** (Mon.-Fri. in summer) inside one of the ranch cabins.

SIGNAL MOUNTAIN

At 7,720 feet (2,353 m) high, **Signal Mountain** (Signal Mountain Summit Rd., 10 mi/16 km rt, May-Oct., no trailers or large RVs) cowers below the massive Tetons. Two forested routes climb steeply to reach the summit: drive or bike the paved road or hike the trail (6.8 mi/10.9 km rt, 4 hrs, moderate). The summit has two overlooks: **Jackson Point Overlook** on the south with majestic Teton Mountain views and **Emma Matilda Overlook** on the north facing the Absarokas.

JACKSON LAKE LODGE

With views of Mount Moran and Jackson Lake, **Jackson Lake Lodge** (307/543-3100, www.gtlc.com, mid-May-early Oct.) is a National Historic Landmark. Windows frame the Teton Mountains, which compete for attention with the 10 "Rendezvous Murals" by Carl Roters, a late-20th-century American artist. John D. Rockefeller Jr. hand-selected the location on **Lunch Tree Hill** for its unobstructed mountain views. Commissioned by Rockefeller and built in 1955, the three-story lodge blends modern international architecture with artful takes on Western and Native American elements. It also houses a small selection of Indigenous artifacts.

COLTER BAY

Colter Bay (US 89/191/287) is one of those do-everything places with sights galore. To see the offshore islands, take a scenic cruise or rent a boat, canoe, or kayak. A maze of hiking trails loops the peninsulas, passing tiny lakes. Around Colter Bay, Jackson Lake often reflects Mount Moran and the Teton Mountains at sunrise or sunset.

WILDLIFE-WATCHING

Moose-Wilson Road

Moose-Wilson Road (16 mi/26 km, mid-May-Oct., portions closed through 2025 for construction), a shortcut between Teton Village and Moose, weaves through beaver, porcupine, bear, and moose habitat, especially at **Sawmill Ponds** and the **Laurance S. Rockefeller Preserve.**

Antelope Flats Road

Antelope Flats Road (US 89/191/287, 1.1 mi/1.8 km north of Moose Junction) is a habitat for bison, pronghorn, moose, coyotes, and raptors such as northern harriers and American kestrels. In spring, look for migrating elk and newborns of bison and pronghorn.

Blacktail Ponds Overlook

Active beavers maintain the dams that keep water in **Blacktail Ponds** (US 89/191/287, 1.3 mi/2.1 km north of Moose Junction). Stop at the overlook to see moose, ospreys, waterfowl, and songbirds.

Oxbow Bend

With slow-moving convolutions of water, **Oxbow Bend** (US 89/191/287, 1 mi/1.6 km east of Jackson Lake

MENOR'S FERRY HISTORIC DISTRICT

AVOID THE CROWDS

To avoid the crowds of summer, visit in the quieter **spring** and **fall,** although weather can be erratic. If lower-elevation hiking and sightseeing are on your agenda, the shoulder seasons are the perfect time, with snow-clad peaks standing out against a blue sky. Most roads are open, and wildlife is active. **Spring** brings the chance to see bison and pronghorn newborns, and during fall, the air fills with the sound of elk bugling. **Fall** also brings outstanding hiking, with warm bug-free days and cool nights. During early spring or late fall, you may need to stay in Jackson or Teton Village when in-park facilities are closed.

Junction) has river otters, beavers, and muskrats. Moose forage on willows. Squawking American pelicans add to the cacophony from songbirds, and ospreys and bald eagles hunt for fish.

HIKING

MOOSE-WILSON ROAD

Through 2025, portions of the Moose-Wilson Road and the Death Canyon Trailhead will be closed for paving and reconstruction. Check the status online or at visitors centers. Trailheads should be accessible via one direction on the road or alternate trailheads.

Phelps Lake

At the Laurance S. Rockefeller Preserve (park by 9am), the **Lake Creek-Woodland Trail Loop** (3 mi/4.8 km rt, 1.5 hrs, moderate) is the most direct route through moose country to Phelps Lake. **Phelps Lake Loop** (6.3 mi/10.1 km rt, 3.5 hrs, moderate) climbs via Lake Creek to circle the lake for a changing perspective on the Teton Mountains.

Phelps Lake Overlook and Static Peak Divide

From the Death Canyon Trailhead, the trail ascends to a saddle overlooking **Phelps Lake** (2 mi/3.2 km rt, 1.5 hrs, moderate). Strong hikers up for 5,100 feet (1,554 m) of a grueling climb go farther into Death Canyon before shooting up a rocky scree and cliff ridge to **Static Peak Divide** (16.3 mi/26.2 km rt, 9-12 hrs, strenuous), where a short path zips up to the summit for a view of Grand Teton.

TETON PARK ROAD

Taggart and Bradley Lakes

Get an early start in order to claim a parking spot at the popular Taggart Lake Trailhead to hike to this pair of idyllic lakes. **Taggart Lake** (3 mi/4.8 km rt, 1.5 hrs, moderate) is perfect for families and wading. Make the full loop that includes **Bradley Lake** (5.9 mi/9.5 km rt, 3-4 hrs), which sits below Grand Teton.

Surprise and Amphitheater Lakes

From the Lupine Meadows Trailhead, the trail to **Surprise and Amphitheater Lakes** (10.1 mi/16.3 km rt, 6 hrs, strenuous) climbs to a junction with the Taggart Lake Trail before piling on the switchbacks to reach a small hanging valley cradling Surprise Lake. The trail ascends about 10 more minutes into a second basin housing Amphitheater Lake, tucked below Disappointment Peak.

Lake Solitude

Ride the Jenny Lake shuttle boat (fee) to the west shore boat dock and trailhead for **Lake Solitude** (14.2 mi/22.8 km rt, 8 hrs, strenuous). Follow the trail to Hidden Falls and Inspiration Point before joining Cascade Canyon Trail. At the Forks of Cascade Canyon, turn right to climb out of the forest into vast wildflower meadows surrounding blue Lake Solitude.

Holly Lake and Paintbrush Divide

Holly Lake (13 mi/20.9 km rt, 7 hrs, strenuous) sits in an alpine cirque populated by pikas. From String Lake Trailhead, cross the outlet and hike north along the base of Rockchuck Peak to

JACKSON POINT OVERLOOK ON SIGNAL MOUNTAIN

reach Paintbrush Canyon. Climb west through forest, avalanche slopes, and huge boulders into a hanging basin to reach the lake. Strong hikers grunt up farther through scree and across steep snowfields to top 10,720-foot (3,267-m) **Paintbrush Divide** and a 4,100-foot (1,250-m) elevation gain. But once here, most descend via **Paintbrush-Cascade Loop** (19 mi/30.6 km rt, 10-13 hrs, strenuous), a bucket-list route to Lake Solitude and Cascade Canyon to connect with the Jenny Lake Trail back to the trailhead.

Leigh Lake–Rockchuck Loop

Walk the **Leigh Lake-Rockchuck Loop** (3.7 mi/6 km rt, 2 hrs, moderate) counterclockwise for big views of Jenny Lake and the Tetons. From the Leigh Lake Trailhead, hike along String Lake and the creek to a junction near Leigh Lake. Cross a bridge and climb to a second junction, where a left turn breaks onto the open slopes of Rockchuck Peak to descend to the foot of String Lake to catch the Jenny Lake Trail that finishes at the String Lake Trailhead.

JACKSON LAKE

Heron Pond and Hermitage Point

From the Hermitage Point Trailhead at Colter Bay Village, **Heron Pond Trail** (3 mi/4.8 km rt, 2 hrs, moderate) takes in a variety of views on a gently rolling path. At each junction, turn right to reach Jackson Lake Overlook and lily-padded **Heron Pond** with the Tetons reflected in the water. After Heron Pond, turn left to loop to Swan Lake for the return to the trailhead.

To continue on to **Hermitage Point** (9.7 mi/15.6 km rt, 5 hrs, moderate) after Heron Pond, turn right at all junctions along the peninsula's west side, where views span Jackson Lake and Mount Moran. At the point, curve along the east side of the peninsula. At the next junction, turn left to return to the trailhead via Swan Lake.

Emma Matilda and Two Ocean Lakes

Two glacially carved lakes are located 1 mile (1.6 km) apart in a maze of forest

MOOSE COW AND CALF

and meadow trails. From the trailhead at Two Ocean Lake, hike a counterclockwise loop around **Two Ocean Lake** and **Emma Matilda Lake** (6.4-10.7 mi/10.3-17.2 km rt, 4-6 hrs, moderate). The loop takes in the higher **Grand View Point** for outstanding views of the Tetons and the lakes. To just hike up to **Grand View Point** (6 mi/9.7 km rt, 3 hrs, moderate), start at Jackson Lake Lodge.

RECREATION

BACKPACKING

The king of backpacking trips is the **Teton Crest Trail** (38-58 mi/61-93 km), a high-elevation romp with major elevation gains and descents. The route crosses Fox Creek Pass, Death Canyon Shelf, Mount Meek Pass, Alaska Basin, Hurricane Pass, and Paintbrush Divide at 10,400-10,720 feet (3,169-3,267 m). The **38-mile (61-km) point-to-point** route requires a shuttle between trailheads, or you can complete the loop by adding 20 miles (32.2 km) on the Valley Trail **(58-mi/93-km loop).** Many hikers gain elevation by starting at Jackson Hole Mountain Resort's aerial tram (fee), reducing the total distance to 34 miles (55 km). Along the Teton Crest,

you can camp at Marian Lake, Death Canyon Shelf, South Fork Cascade, and Upper Paintbrush. Shorter routes go up Paintbrush, Cascade, Death, and Granite Canyons to the crest.

Backcountry permits (www.recreation.gov, early Jan.-mid-May, $45) are required. Limited **walk-up permits** ($35) are available 24 hours ahead from Jenny Lake Ranger Station (307/739-3343, 8am-5pm daily early June-early Sept.), Colter Bay Visitor Center, or Craig Thomas Discovery and Visitor Center. Approved bear canisters are required. You may need an ice ax into August for snowfields on the Teton Crest.

BIKING

The **Multi-Use Pathway** (29 mi/47 km dawn-dusk) is a mostly level, paved cycling and walking path that parallels the roads between Jenny Lake, Moose, Antelope Flats Road, and Jackson. For the most scenic ride, the Moose-Jenny Lake segment (7.7 mi/12.4 km) skims just below the Tetons. The section from Jackson to Gros Ventre Junction closes November-April for migrating elk. Rent bikes from Dornan's **Adventure Sports** (12170 Dornan Rd., Moose, 307/733-2415, http://dornans.com, 10am-5pm daily early May-late Sept.).

DEATH CANYON SHELF ON TETON CREST TRAIL

ROCK CLIMBING

To reach Teton summits demands technical climbing skills and the gear for rock or ice routes. Climbing the **Grand Teton** involves 14 miles (22.5 km) of hiking and 6,545 feet (1,995 m) of ascent and descent. More than 35 climbing routes lead to its summit, with countless variations. The most popular and famous route for climbing the Grand is the exposed Upper Exum Ridge. Mid-July-August offers the best weather.

Exum Mountain Guides (South Jenny Lake, 307/733-2297, http://exumguides.com) leads individual and group climbs, plus offers climbing instruction and camps. **Jenny Lake Ranger Station** (307/739-3343, 8am-5pm daily early June-early Sept.) has current climbing conditions, route information, and backcountry camping **permits.**

HORSEBACK RIDING

Grand Teton Lodging Company (reservations 307/543-3100, www.gtlc.com, daily June-early Sept., $50-80) offers one- and two-hour horseback rides from corrals at Colter Bay Village, Jackson Lake Lodge, and Flagg Ranch.

BOATING AND FISHING

Clean, drain, and dry boats before bringing them to the park. Boating permits and AIS inspections are required. Buy **permits** online (www.recreation.gov, $17 nonmotorized including all paddle craft, $56 motorized) or at visitors centers in Moose and Colter Bay. You can

AMPHITHEATER LAKE

LAKE SOLITUDE

also get fishing permits at the visitors centers. Dornan's **Adventure Sports** (12170 Dornan Rd., Moose, 307/733-2415, http://dornans.com, 10am-5pm daily early May-late Sept.) rents canoes, kayaks, and paddleboards.

Jenny Lake

Boating on **Jenny Lake** (boat launch on Lupine Meadows Rd.) is a quiet, idyllic experience; only hand-propelled boats or motorboats with 10 horsepower or less are permitted. **Jenny Lake Boating** (Jenny Lake boathouse, 307/734-9227, www.jennylakeboating.com, 7am-7pm daily mid-June-early-Sept., shorter hours in fall) rents kayaks and canoes. North of Jenny Lake, **String Lake** has a canoe and kayak launch site (North Jenny Lake Rd.). The lake connects via a portage to **Leigh Lake,** where paddlers can overnight in solitude at eight prime backcountry campsites (permit required).

Jackson Lake

Fifteen islands inhabit **Jackson Lake,** and their boat-accessible backcountry campsites (permit required) are perfect destinations for boaters and paddlers. Three marinas offer launch sites late May-late September: **Leek's Marina** and **Signal Mountain Lodge** (both 307/543-2831, www.signalmountainlodge.com), and **Colter Bay Marina** (307/543-3100, www.gtlc.com). Rent motorboats, canoes, and kayaks from Colter Bay Marina and Signal Mountain Lodge.

Rafting the Snake River

Rafts, kayaks, and canoes can float the **Wild and Scenic Snake River** below Jackson Lake Dam. Start at Jackson Lake Dam or Cattleman's Bridge Site to take out at Pacific Creek. Only experienced paddlers should put in at Deadman's Bar and take out at Moose Landing (10 mi/16 km, 2 hrs), an advanced section with strong currents, waves, logjams, and a maze of braided streams.

Guided scenic float trips (mid-May-Sept.) on the Snake River depart from **Jackson Lake Lodge** (Grand Teton Lodging Company, 307/543-3100, www.gtlc.com), **Signal Mountain Lodge** (307/543-2831, www.signalmountainlodge.com), and from

Best Hike

HIDDEN FALLS AND INSPIRATION POINT

DISTANCE: 1.9-5.5 miles (3-8.8 km) round-trip
DURATION: 1.5-3 hours
ELEVATION CHANGE: 428 feet (130 m)
EFFORT: moderately strenuous
TRAILHEAD: Jenny Lake Visitor Center

Hidden Falls is a tall tumbler in Cascade Canyon, and Lower Inspiration Point, a rocky knoll squeezed between Mount Teewinot and Mount St. John. Hordes of hikers clog this trail. The boat shuttle (fee) reduces this hike to 1.9 miles (3.5 km) from the west boat dock.

From the visitors center, head west toward the east boat dock and cross the bridge at the outlet of Jenny Lake at Cottonwood Creek. Arc west along the south shore of Jenny Lake, passing the boat launch and two junctions for Moose Pond Loop to take the scenic lakeshore to the lake's west side. Ascending Cascade Creek, follow the well-signed junctions to **Hidden Falls.** Continue upwards by crossing two bridges below the falls to climb the south-facing engineered stairstep ledge to **Lower Inspiration Point.**

Moose through **Barker-Ewing Scenic Float Trips** (307/733-1800 or 800/365-1800, www.barkerewing.com) or **National Park Float Trips** (307/733-5500, http://nationalparkfloattrips.com). Guided Snake River fishing trips are offered through **Snake River Angler** (10 Moose St., Moose, 307/733-3699, www.snakeriverangler.com) and **Triangle X** (307/733-2183, www.trianglex.com).

WHERE TO STAY
INSIDE THE PARK
Moose

On the Snake River, **Dornan's Spur Ranch Cabins** (307/733-2415, www.dornans.com, May-Oct. and Dec.-Mar., from $175) have full kitchens. Their eateries include **Pizza Pasta Company** (11:30am-8:30pm daily, shorter hours in winter), the **Chuckwagon** (307/733-2415, hours and days vary, mid-June-early Sept.) in a covered outdoor pavilion with picnic tables, and **Moose Trading Post & Deli** (9am-5pm daily winter, 8am-7pm daily summer).

Jenny Lake

Built in 1920, **Jenny Lake Lodge** (400 Jenny Lake Loop, 307/543-3100, www.gtlc.com, June-early Oct., from $776) offers rustic luxury in 37 log cabins.

Reserve a year in advance. **Reservations** (307/543-3100) are recommended for breakfast and lunch and required for dinner, along with a dress code.

The **Grand Teton Climber's Ranch** (Teton Park Rd., 307/733-7271 summer, 303/384-0110 fall-spring, http://americanalpineclub.org, early June-mid-Sept., $17-27) offers small, hostel-style coed log cabins with wooden bunks. Facilities include sex-separated restrooms and shower houses and an outdoor cook shelter. Bring your own sleeping bag, pad, cooking gear, food, and towels.

Jackson Lake

Jackson Lake Lodge (307/543-3100, www.gtlc.com, mid-May-early Oct., from $356) is a National Historic Landmark built in 1955 with a commanding Teton panoramic view, an outdoor swimming pool, and horseback riding. Guest rooms are in the main lodge, separate two-story lodges, or in cabins. Reserve a year in advance. The complex includes four restaurants: the upscale **Mural Room** (7am-9:30am, 11:30am-1:30pm, and 5:30pm-9pm daily), the café-style **Pioneer Grill** (6am-10pm daily), the **Blue Heron Lounge** (11am-11pm daily) with back patio service, and the **Pool Cantina and BBQ** (11am-4pm and 5:30pm-8pm daily mid-June-mid-Aug.).

LOWER INSPIRATION POINT

Reservations (307/543-3463) for the Mural Room and Pool Cantina are accepted starting in late May.

Signal Mountain Lodge (1 Inner Park Rd., 307/543-2831, www.signal-mountainlodge.com, mid-May-mid-Oct., from $288) sits on Jackson Lake with stunning Teton views. The lodge has a variety of different room options and is so popular that it takes **reservations 16 months out.** The complex has two restaurants: **Peaks Restaurant** (5:30pm-10pm daily) and **Trapper Grill** (7am-10pm daily). Up the road at Leek's Marina, **Leek's Pizzeria** (307/543-2494, noon-8pm daily late May-mid-Sept.) serves pizza and pasta.

At Colter Bay, where water and hiking activities abound, **Colter Bay Cabins** (Colter Bay Village, 307/543-3100, www.gtlc.com, late May-early Oct., from $210) come in three sizes. Reserve a year in advance. Eateries include **Café Court Pizzeria** (11am-10pm daily late May-early Sept.) and the **Ranch House** (6:30am-11am and 11:30am-9:30pm daily late May-Sept.). **Colter Bay Cookouts** (reservations required) offer outdoor dining around a western-style campfire via **Cookout boat cruises** (307/543-3100, June-mid-Sept.) and **Cookout horseback** or **wagon rides**

(307/543-3100, Sun.-Fri. early June-early Sept.).

Flagg Ranch

Closest to Yellowstone, **Headwaters Lodge & Cabins at Flagg Ranch** (John D. Rockefeller, Jr. Memorial Parkway, 307/543-3100, www.gtlc.com, June-Sept., from $251) has three room types. Reserve a year in advance. **Sheffields Restaurant & Bar** (7am-10am, 11:30am-2pm, and 5pm-9:30pm daily June-Sept.) has the only dining. In the adjacent campground, tiny **camper cabins** ($81) serve those on a budget.

Triangle X Ranch

Triangle X Ranch (2 Triangle X Ranch Rd., 307/733-2183, http://trianglex.com, mid-May-mid-Oct. and late Dec.-mid-Mar.) is a dude ranch with lodgings in cabins. Early June-late August is peak season (from $2,057 pp/week), with shorter stays in the off-season (mid-May-early June and Sept.-Oct., from $294 pp/day).

Camping

All campgrounds in Grand Teton can be reserved **six months** in advance (www.recreation.gov). Competition is keen;

▼ BIKING MULTI-USE PATHWAY

RAFTING THE SNAKE RIVER

make reservation as soon the booking window opens. **Gros Ventre Campground** (May-mid-Oct., 279 sites, 39 electrical hookups, $42-71) is nearest to Jackson. Popular **Jenny Lake Campground** (May-Sept., 61 sites, $42) is for tents only.

Five campgrounds flank Jackson Lake: **Signal Mountain** (early May-mid-Oct., 81 sites, 24 electrical hookups, $45-90), **Colter Bay** (late May-Sept., 324 sites, 13 ADA electrical hookups, $38-60), **Colter Bay RV Park** (early May-early Oct., 112 sites with full hookups, $92-102), **Colter Bay Tent Village** (late May-early Sept., 66 tent cabins with communal baths, from $85), and **Lizard Creek** (June-Sept., 60 sites, $41).

Closest to Yellowstone, **Headwaters Campground & RV Park** (Flagg Ranch, mid-May-Sept., 141 sites, $47-95) has tent sites, RV hookups, and camper cabins.

OUTSIDE THE PARK

Jackson and **Teton Village** offer lodgings, restaurants, and amenities.

GETTING THERE

AIR

Jackson Hole Airport (JAC, 1250 E. Airport Rd., Jackson, 307/733-7682, www.

jacksonholeairport.com) is actually inside Grand Teton National Park, just north of Jackson. It's a 15-minute drive north to the park's main visitors center and the Moose Entrance. **Idaho Falls Regional Airport** (IDA, 2140 N. Skyline Dr., 208/612-8221, www.idahofallsidaho.gov) may have cheaper flights, but it's more than a two-hour drive to the park. Both airports have rental cars.

CAR

US 89/191/287 (open year-round) exits Yellowstone south to immediately enter John D. Rockefeller, Jr. Memorial Parkway and Grand Teton National Park. The road stretches south to Moran Junction, the park's east entrance, and links with the Outside Road (US 26/89/191) and Inside Road (Teton Park Rd.).

From the south, **US 26/89/191** leads north from the town of Jackson to the park's Moose and Moran Entrances.

From Idaho, **ID 33/WY 22** crosses over Teton Pass to Jackson, Wyoming, connecting with US 89/191/287 north into the park.

From eastern Wyoming, drivers from I-80 can take **US 189 or US 191** toward Jackson. From I-25 East, the route goes over Togwotee Pass (US 26) for a stunning descent to Moran Junction.

Winter weather can make for white-outs and icy roads. Check conditions for park roads by calling 307/739-3682.

GETTING AROUND

DRIVING

US 26/89/191 (Outside Road) is open year-round from Moran to Moose and Jackson. **US 89/191/287** opens year-round from Moran to Flagg Ranch and Yellowstone's South Entrance.

Teton Park Road (Inside Road) is fully open May-November. The segment from Taggart Lake Trailhead to Signal Mountain Lodge closes in winter. **Moose-Wilson Road** is a narrow paved and seasonal dirt road that closes in winter; portions will be closed for reconstruction through 2025.

During July and August, **parking** lots at trailheads pack out. Plan to arrive before 8am to claim a spot.

SHUTTLES

On Jenny Lake, **Jenny Lake Boating** (307/734-9227, www.jennylakeboating.com, daily mid-May-late Sept., 7am-7pm early June-early Sept., shorter hours early and late season, $8-18)

runs shuttles from the boat dock near the visitors center across the lake to trailheads.

TOURS

From Jackson Lake Lodge, scenic **bus tours** (Grand Teton Lodging Company, 307/543-3100, www.gtlc.com, 8:30am Mon., Wed., and Fri. late May-early Oct., 4 hrs, $52-92) offer guided narration and travel to Jenny Lake Overlook, the Chapel of the Transfiguration, and Oxbow Bend.

From Colter Bay Marina, **Jackson Lake boat tours** (Grand Teton Lodging Company, 307/543-3100, www.gtlc.com, daily mid-June-Sept., $21-76) soaks up the lustrous views of Mount Moran on daytime and campfire meal cruises. Reservations are required; hours and times vary.

On Jenny Lake, **Jenny Lake Boating** (South Jenny Lake, 307/734-9227, www.jennylakeboating.com, daily mid-May-late Sept., $15-25) guides one-hour interpretive tours. Reservations by credit card are strongly recommended.

The **Teton Science School** (700 Coyote Canyon Rd., Jackson, 307/733-1313, www.tetonscience.org, daily year-round) leads educational wildlife-watching expeditions.

COLTER BAY MARINA BOAT RENTAL AND TOURS

NAME	LOCATION	PRICE	SEASON	AMENITIES
Grassy Lake Road	John D. Rockefeller, Jr. Memorial Parkway	free	June-Sept.	tent sites
Lizard Creek	Jackson Lake	$41	June-Sept.	tent sites
Headwaters Campground & RV	John D. Rockefeller, Jr. Memorial Parkway	$47-95	mid-May-Sept.	tent and RV sites, camping cabins
Headwaters Lodge & Cabins at Flagg Ranch	John D. Rockefeller, Jr. Memorial Parkway	from $251	June-Sept.	motel rooms, cabins, camper cabins, dining
Colter Bay Campground	Colter Bay	$38-60	late May-Sept.	tent and RV sites, ADA sites
Colter Bay RV Park	Colter Bay	$92-102	May-Oct.	RV sites
Colter Bay Tent Village	Colter Bay	from $85	May-Sept.	tent cabins
Colter Bay Cabins	Colter Bay	from $210	May-Oct.	cabins
Jackson Lake Lodge	Jackson Lake	from $356	May-Oct.	hotel rooms, cottages, dining
Signal Mountain Campground	Signal Mountain	$45-90	May-Oct.	tent and small RV sites
Signal Mountain Lodge	Signal Mountain	from $288	May-Oct.	motel rooms, cabins, dining
Jenny Lake Campground	Jenny Lake	$42	May-Sept.	tent sites
Jenny Lake Lodge	Jenny Lake	from $776	June-Oct.	cabins, dining
Grand Teton Climber's Ranch	Teton Park Road	$17-27	early June-mid-Sept.	dorm bunks
Gros Ventre Campground	Moose	$42-71	May-Oct.	tent and RV sites
Dornan's Spur Ranch Cabins	Moose	from $175	May-Oct., Dec.-Mar.	cabins, dining
Triangle X Ranch	Moose/Moran	rates vary	May-Oct., Dec.-Mar.	dude ranch

SIGHTS NEARBY

At the southern edge of the park, **Jackson Hole Mountain Resort** (3395 Cody Ln., Teton Village, 307/733-2292 or 888/333-7766, www.jacksonhole. com, daily late May-early Oct. and late Nov.-early Apr.) has summer activities, including an ultrascenic ride to the 10,450-foot (3,185-m) summit of Rendezvous Mountain in the Tetons via their aerial tram, and skiing and snowboarding in winter.

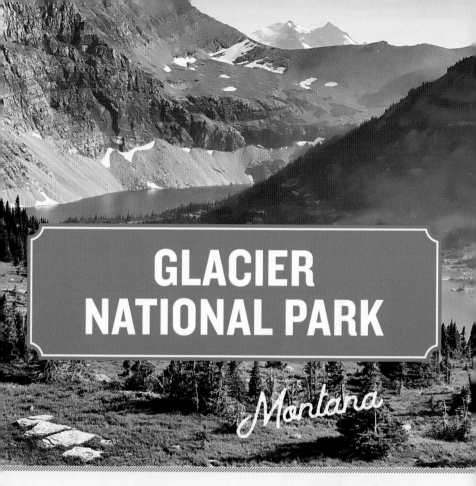

GLACIER
NATIONAL PARK

Montana

KEEPSAKE STAMPS ▼▼▼

WEBSITE:
www.nps.gov/glac

PHONE NUMBER:
406/888-7800

VISITATION RANK:
10

WHY GO:
See glaciers and
wildlife along
scenic drives.

▲ HIDDEN LAKE OVERLOOK

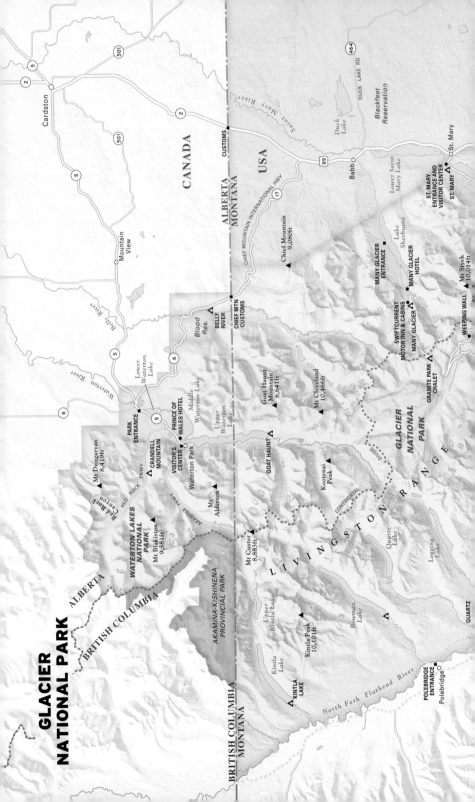

GLACIER NATIONAL PARK

Known as the Crown of the Continent, **GLACIER NATIONAL PARK** is a place where earth's forces have left their imprints on the landscape with jagged arêtes, red pinnacles, and glacier-carved basins. The Blackfeet called these sacred mountains the "Backbone of the World." It's home to grizzly bears, wolves, mountain goats, wolverines, and bighorn sheep, animals once hunted by the Blackfeet and Kootenai peoples. Amid some of the oldest rock in North America, a handful of glaciers cling to high elevations, struggling to survive in their last years of life.

The Continental Divide splits Glacier into west and east sides. Slicing through the park's heart, the historic Going-to-the-Sun Road twists and turns on a narrow cliff climb. Tunnels, arches, and bridges lead sightseers over precipices where seemingly no road could go. Glacier preserves one of the nation's most amazing historic and natural landscapes, a place to visit before the warming climate further alters the landscape forever.

PLANNING YOUR TIME

In northwest Montana on the Canadian border, Glacier is a remote location, but popular enough to clog during its short summer season. Make **reservations 13 months in advance** for in-park lodgings and **6 months** for camping. You will also need reservations to drive **Going-to-the-Sun Road** and Polebridge entrances in summer (available 120 days or 24 hours in advance). Download or print your tickets before arriving. RVs and car-trailer combos over 21 feet (6.4 m) are not permitted to drive on Going-to-the-Sun Road.

Summer (June-Sept.) attracts crowds when lodges, campgrounds, and trails are open. Barring deep snows, Going-to-the-Sun Road is open **mid-June to mid-October,** with peak visitation and the best weather in July-August. Snow buries some trails into July.

Although saddled with unpredictable weather, the off-season, **October through May,** offers less hectic visits. Keep in mind that **commercial services are closed** and **Going-to-the-Sun Road closes to vehicles.** Low-elevation trails are usually snow-free in mid-May and October while snow buries higher-elevation trails. In winter, snow closes most park roads, which become quiet snowshoeing and cross-country ski trails.

ENTRANCES AND FEES

The entrance fee is $35 per vehicle ($30 motorcycle, $20 individual; winter $25 per vehicle, $20 motorcycle, $15 individual) and good for seven days. You can **buy your pass online** (www.recreation.gov) from home to speed through entrance stations faster.

You will also need **vehicle reservations** (www.recreation.gov, daily late May-mid-Sept., $2) for certain parts of the park. Make reservations as soon as they're released 120 days in advance.

BIGHORN SHEEP

Top ❸

① TOUR GOING-TO-THE-SUN ROAD

Going-to-the-Sun Road (mid-June–mid-Oct.) stands in a class by itself. The 50-mile (81-km) historic transmountain

GOING-TO-THE-SUN ROAD

highway bisects Glacier's heart, with tight curves that hug cliff walls producing scary white-knuckle driving. Yet its beauty, diversity, color, flora, fauna, and raw wildness will leave an impression like no other. Although you can drive its length in less than 2 hours, most visitors take 4-8 hours, driving over and back for different views and stopping for hikes. You can avoid driving by taking **shuttles** (stop at lodges, campgrounds, and trailheads) or **tour buses** (stop at sights). **Reservations** (www.recreation.gov) are required to drive the road 6am-5pm daily late May-early September.

② GAZE AT GLACIERS

Glacier National Park's glaciers are melting rapidly. So where can you see them while they still exist? On Going-to-the-Sun Road, **Jackson Glacier Overlook** offers the best views of Jackson and Blackfoot Glaciers. In Many Glacier, hike to **Grinnell Glacier,** the most accessible glacier. On the jagged wall above the lake perch the tiny **Salamander Glacier** and **Gem Glacier,** both shrunken to static snowfields. From Si-

SPERRY GLACIER

yeh Bend on Going-to-the-Sun Road, hike Siyeh Pass Trail to see **Piegan Glacier** while climbing to the pass and **Sexton Glacier** while descending to Sunrift Gorge. A hefty climb to Comeau Pass accesses the scoured basin that cradles **Sperry Glacier.**

③ EXPLORE MANY GLACIER

Jagged parapets rim **Many Glacier,** where you can park the car and hike for days. Five valleys loaded with hiking trails and scenic lakes radiate from the core, which holds a campground, a picnic area, cabins, and **Many Glacier Hotel,** a National Historic Landmark. Tour the restored hotel and sit on the deck to watch bears and bighorn sheep through binoculars.

An easy walking trail circles **Swiftcurrent Lake,** a mountain-rimmed pool preferred by moose. Paddlers can rent kayaks and rowboats or ride a **tour boat** on Swiftcurrent and Josephine Lakes, which shortens the walk to milky turquoise **Grinnell Lake.** At the end of the day, take in the sunset over the Continental Divide and watch on moonless nights for a sky full of stars and the northern lights.

MANY GLACIER HOTEL AND SWIFTCURRENT LAKE

ONE DAY IN GLACIER

Glacier's biggest attraction is the 50-mile (81-km) **Going-to-the-Sun Road.** A tour of the road over Logan Pass yields a small taste of the park's grandeur, with waterfalls, immense glacier-carved valleys, and serrated peaks. Drive the road to **Logan Pass** and stop to hike to **Hidden Lake Overlook, Avalanche Lake,** or **St. Mary Falls.** If you can, squeeze in a **boat tour** on St. Mary Lake.

(A percentage of the tickets are held back, then released 24 hours in advance.) Tickets must be printed out or on your smartphone.

A **Going-to-the-Sun Road reservation** (good for 3 days, 6am-4pm) is required for entering the **St. Mary, West Glacier,** or **Camas entrances,** but does not guarantee parking at trailheads or Logan Pass.

A **Polebridge reservation** (good for 1 day, 6am-6pm) is required for the Polebridge entrance in the North Fork to reach Bowman or Kintla Lakes; campers will need entrance tickets to claim first-come, first-served campsites.

You will not need an entrance reservation if you have service reservations on the Sun Road corridor; your shuttle, bus or boat tour, horseback riding, lodging, or camping reservation will gain you entry.

It's possible to enter before and after reservation hours without a reservation, but be prepared for long lines of cars at the entrances.

Glacier National Park is split along the Continental Divide, with several entrances on each side.

East Entrances

- **St. Mary** (off US 89, open May-Oct.) is the east portal for Going-to-the-Sun Road. Entrance reservations aren't required from mid-June to mid-July, before the Sun Road is fully open for the season.

- **Two Medicine** (Two Medicine Rd., off MT 49, open late May-Oct.) leads to Two Medicine Lake. This entrance may close when parking fills, usually 10am-2pm from June to early September.

- **Many Glacier** (Many Glacier Rd., off US 89, open mid-May-early Nov.) leads to Many Glacier and Swiftcurrent. This entrance may close when parking fills, generally 10am-2pm from June to early September.

▼ ST. MARY LAKE

BOWMAN LAKE

- **Cut Bank** (off US 89, open June-Sept.) has a dirt road that leads to Cut Bank Campground and a trailhead.

West Entrances

- **West Glacier** (off US 2, open year-round) is the west portal for Going-to-the-Sun Road and Lake McDonald. Expect long lines in peak season before 6am and after 5pm.
- **Camas** (east end of Camas Rd., from Outside North Fork Rd., open mid-May-Oct.) connects to Apgar, Lake McDonald, and Going-to-the-Sun Road.
- **Polebridge** (Outside North Fork Rd., open late May-Oct.) accesses Bowman and Kintla Lakes as well as the Inside North Fork Road.

VISITORS CENTERS

Glacier National Park has three small visitors centers lining Going-to-the-Sun Road. They have maps, information, bookstores, backcountry desks for permits, and shuttle stops. Because the park is an International Dark Sky Park, the centers offer night astronomy programs.

Two ranger stations can also provide trail information and backcountry permits: **Many Glacier Ranger Station** (milepost 12.4, Many Glacier Rd., 406/888-7800, 8am-5pm daily late May-mid-Sept.) and **Two**

Medicine Ranger Station (Two Medicine Rd., 406/888-7800, 7am-5pm daily summer).

Apgar Visitor Center

Apgar Visitor Center (406/888-7800, daily mid-May-mid-Oct., Sat.-Sun. fall-spring) anchors the west entrance of Going-to-the-Sun Road. It has a shuttle stop and large parking lot for leaving your car all day. A five-minute walk goes to the **Apgar Backcountry Permit Office** (Apgar, 406/888-7859 May-Oct., 406/888-7800 Nov.-Apr., 8am-4pm daily May-Oct.), the main office for overnight backpacking permits. Rush hour is the first 2-3 hours of each morning in July and August; lines begin forming long before 6am.

Logan Pass Visitor Center

Logan Pass Visitor Center (406/888-7800, daily mid-June-Sept.) perches at the apex of Going-to-the-Sun Road. It's a seasonal outpost with a few displays. It has a shuttle stop.

St. Mary Visitor Center

St. Mary Visitor Center (406/888-7800, daily late May-early Oct.), at the East Entrance Station, has the most exhibits, shows films, and offers Native American programs. A night-sky observatory containing a powerful telescope projects live images of celestial objects on large screens in the parking lot.

AVOID THE CROWDS

Glacier sees crowds in summer. So what can you do to have a more enjoyable trip?

Get status updates. The **Glacier Information Display** (www.nps.gov/applications/glac/dashboard) shows fill status for parking lots and campgrounds and roads that have been closed due to crowds. The park also posts updates on Twitter (@GlacierNPS).

Visit in June or September. June still has high-elevation snow, which may preclude access to some trails and Logan Pass except by bicycle; plan for limitations pending road plowing and weather. September allows more access to Logan Pass, but weather can bounce between warm temperatures and snow.

Drive Going-to-the-Sun Road at sunset. You can drive Going-to-the-Sun Road 24 hours daily during the months it's open. Catch the sunset (time varies 8pm-9:45pm) to encounter fewer people. Plus, evening yields better lighting for photography. Hang out at Logan Pass to soak up the Milky Way after dark.

Camp and stay put. Rather than fighting for a first-come, first-served spot in a new campground every morning, select a campground to use as home base. Then, drive to other locations as day trips.

SIGHTS

NORTH FORK

Just before reaching the entrance at Polebridge in the North Fork, you'll breeze through the same-named junction of **Polebridge**. It's a remote place lacking electricity, flush toilets, and cell service but includes an historic mercantile and a restaurant.

From Polebridge, potholed dirt roads launch bouncing rides into the park to two remote lakes with campgrounds and trails. **Bowman Lake** sits in a narrow, glacier-scoured trough. Secluded **Kintla Lake** tucks deep in the trees. Drop in a canoe, kayak, or paddleboard to tour the quiet shorelines.

The roads to both lakes can close when parking fills up. Before driving up the North Fork, check at the Apgar Visitor Center or the Glacier Information Display online (www.nps.gov/applications/glac/dashboard) for the status of the roads.

LAKE MCDONALD

Catching water from Glacier's longest river, **Lake McDonald** stretches 10 miles (16 km) long, 1.5 miles (2.4 km) wide, and 472 feet (144 m) deep to be the park's largest and deepest lake.

Visitors fish, boat, paddle, and swim in its cold blue water. Access the lakeshore via three picnic areas, many pull-outs along Going-to-the-Sun Road, or historic **Lake McDonald Lodge,** where scenic **boat tours** launch daily. At the lake's foot, **Apgar** crowds in summer due to its restaurant, camp store, two inns, a boat ramp, swimming beach, paddling and boat rentals, campground, and picnic area.

GOING-TO-THE-SUN ROAD

Going-to-the-Sun Road sees rush hours 5am-7am and 5pm-7pm daily in summer, as visitors access the road outside the hours that tickets are needed for entry. If you want to avoid the lines and crowds, get reservations in advance to drive the road. Tickets are required 6am-5pm daily late May to early September.

Ticketed drivers can often enjoy crowd-free drives in the afternoon. Some trailhead parking areas (Avalanche, The Loop, Logan Pass, St. Mary Falls, and Sun Point) are notoriously crowded all day, with parking lots filling often by 7am. You may have to forego a sight or hike for later in the day. Often you can snag a parking spot at

Logan Pass 3pm-5pm. To avoid traffic and parking hassles, let someone else do the driving: Shuttles go to trailheads, and interpretive bus tours stop at sights. RVs and car-trailer combos over 21 feet (6.4 m) are not allowed to cross over Logan Pass on this road.

West Side

From Apgar, the Going-to-the-Sun Road cruises along **Lake McDonald,** the largest lake in the park, which has the historic **Lake McDonald Lodge** at its upper end and boat tours. The road follows **McDonald Creek,** the longest river in the park, with stops to see its tumbling rapids and waterfalls before reaching Avalanche, where the **Trail of the Cedars** runs through a rainforest, the easternmost in the continental United States.

When the road swings north, its path climbs through engineering feats that garnered the road's designation as a National Civil Engineering Landmark. Its **West Tunnel** has two stunning alcoves framing Heaven's Peak, and **The Loop** is the only hairpin.

Above the Loop, the road cuts through cliffs with views of the ribbonlike **Bird Woman Falls** and stairstep **Haystack Falls.** The **Weeping Wall** wails profusely in June, enough to douse cars driving the inside lane, but in August, drips slow to a trickle.

After **Big Bend,** drive slowly uphill to see **Triple Arches** (no pullout) at the very narrow S-turns. As the road arcs up the final mile to the pass, a wheelchair-accessible path goes to **Oberlin**

HAYSTACK FALLS

Bend Overlook, the best spot for photographing the road's west side and the knifelike **Garden Wall** on the Continental Divide.

Logan Pass

Sitting atop the Continental Divide at 6,646 feet (2,026 m), **Logan Pass** rules an alpine wonderland of wildflower meadows, snowfields, and mountain goats. In June, high walls of snow rim the parking lot; July brings on wildflowers, and late summer turns meadows

▼ A VIEW FROM GOING-TO-THE-SUN ROAD AT SUNSET

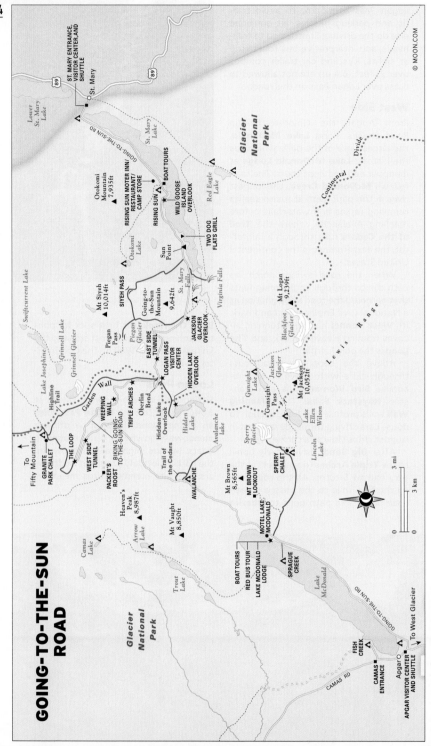

GOING-TO-THE-SUN ROAD

© MOON.COM

golden. Explore the small **visitors center** and scan surrounding slopes for goats, bighorn sheep, and bears. A paved, wheelchair-accessible interpretive trail loops above the visitors center, and a boardwalk trail climbs to **Hidden Lake Overlook.** Moonless nighttime visits to the pass yield ultra-clear skies full of stars.

East Side

From Logan Pass, the road drops by the cascades of **Lunch Creek,** a good place to sit on the rock wall to look up at **Piegan Mountain.** Below, the **East Side Tunnel,** dug out entirely by hand, pops

MOUNTAIN GOAT

WATERTON LAKES NATIONAL PARK

Bordering Glacier in Canada, Waterton Lakes National Park serves as the entrance to Glacier's remote north country. Together, the two national parks are the world's first **International Peace Park.** They are also an **International Dark Sky Park,** a **Biosphere Reserve,** and a **World Heritage Site.** Waterton has trails, campgrounds, backcountry campsites, picnic areas, and two scenic roads. Motels, restaurants, a campground, boat tours, and visitor services cluster in Waterton Townsite.

The **Waterton Lakes Visitor Information Centre** (403/859-5133, www.pc.gc.ca) provides information, maps, permits, and licenses. The entrance gate is open 24 hours daily year-round (staffed early May-early Oct.). To enter, purchase a **Parks Canada day pass** (C$8-20, May-Oct.).

Sights and Activities

Chief Mountain International Highway: This two-nation scenic road arcs past Chief Mountain, sacred to the Blackfeet, and crosses through Glacier and Waterton.

Boat Tour: Hop aboard the historic MV International for a ride on the deepest lake in the Canadian Rockies. You'll float across the international boundary to Goat Haunt, USA, in Glacier.

Goat Haunt, USA: Accessible only by boat or on foot, Goat Haunt is a launchpad onto Glacier's remote northern trails.

Bison Paddock: In a tribute to the great wild herds that once roamed the prairies, Parks Canada maintains a small herd of bison.

Crypt Lake: A boat ride leads to the trailhead, where switchbacks ascend to what looks like impassable cliffs. A hidden tunnel curls into a hanging valley holding an alpine lake cowering below peaks in Glacier.

Getting There

North of Babb, Montana, **Chief Mountain International Highway** (30 mi/48 km) connects Glacier with Waterton. Its season and hours are linked to the Canadian and U.S. immigration and customs stations at the border (open daily mid-May-Sept., 7am-10pm June-Labor Day, 9am-6pm May and Sept.). At the north terminus, turn west onto Highway 5 and south into Waterton.

with a downhill view of **Going-to-the-Sun Mountain.**

After **Siyeh Bend,** the route drops into the trees for a peekaboo look through binoculars at **Jackson Glacier.**

Along **St. Mary Lake,** a short uphill stroll goes to **Sunrift Gorge,** a narrow canyon cut by Baring Creek. **Sun Point** (5-min walk) marks the site of the park's Going-to-the-Sun Chalets atop the rock promontory jutting into the lake. Midway down the lake, the road arrives at one of the most photographed spots, where sharp peaks dwarf tiny **Wild Goose Island.**

Around a bluff, **Rising Sun** has visitor services, including a boat tour, while **Two Dog Flats** lures elk, coyotes, and bears to grassland meadows bordered by aspen groves. The Going-to-the-Sun Road terminates in the town of **St. Mary.**

ST. MARY

The turquoise and often windy **St. Mary Lake,** at nearly 10 miles (16 km) long the second-largest lake in the park, flanks the east side of Going-to-the-Sun Road. Peaks pinch its upper end, while the small seasonal town of **St. Mary** anchors its east end with visitor services. Midway, **Rising Sun** has a campground, motel, picnic area, boat launch, and scenic **boat tours.** To overlook the lake, hike from **Sun Point to Baring Falls** (1.6 mi/2.6 km rt, 1 hr, easy). To skip rocks, enjoy a **lakeshore stroll at Rising Sun** from the picnic area to the boat launch (0.4 mi/0.7 km one-way, 15 min, easy).

TWO MEDICINE

Two Medicine Lake is the highest road-accessible lake in Glacier at almost 1 mile elevation (1.6 km). Peaks rich in Blackfeet history flank the lake. En route, a trail goes to **Running Eagle Falls** (0.6 mi/1 km rt, 20 min, easy), where part of the falls runs underground and spits out through a cavern halfway down the cliff face. At the lake, jump on the historic **Sinopah tour boat** or rent a kayak or small motorboat to go fishing. The National Historic Landmark dining hall now operates as the **Two Medicine Camp Store.** Two Medicine has trails to lakes, passes, and scenic overlooks.

RUNNING EAGLE FALLS

HIKING

Ranger-led hikes go to multiple destinations; check at visitors centers or online for schedules. **Glacier Guides** (11970 US 2 E., West Glacier, 406/387-5555, www.glacierguides.com, mid-May-Sept.) leads day hikes and backpacking trips.

GOING-TO-THE-SUN ROAD

Sperry Chalet and Sperry Glacier

From the trailhead at Lake McDonald Lodge, the **Sperry Trail** (12.4 mi/20 km rt, 6-7 hrs, strenuous) climbs to historic **Sperry Chalet** (Belton Chalets, 406/387-5654 or 888/345-2649, www.sperrychalet.com, July-early Sept.) for lodging and meals. Make reservations in early January; they go fast. With an overnight stay, you can add on the trail up to **Sperry Glacier** (6.6 mi/10.6 km rt, 4 hrs, strenuous).

Trail of the Cedars and Avalanche Lake

Adjacent to Avalanche Campground, a boardwalk loops through a lush rainforest of cedars, hemlocks, and cottonwoods on the **Trail of the Cedars** (0.7 mi/1.1 km rt, 30 min, easy). Departing from the loop's southeast end, the trail to **Avalanche Lake** (4.6 mi/7.4 km rt,

TRAIL OF THE CEDARS

2.5 hrs, moderate) turns uphill along Avalanche Gorge before climbing steadily through woods littered with glacial erratics into a cliff-rimmed cirque with waterfalls.

Hidden Lake Overlook

From Logan Pass, the trail to **Hidden Lake Overlook** (2.7 mi/4.3 km rt, 1.5 hrs, moderate) climbs a boardwalk through alpine meadows with mountain goats and bighorn sheep. Then the path cuts around a moraine to reach the Continental Divide overlooking blue Hidden Lake.

Piegan and Siyeh Passes

From Siyeh Bend on Going-to-the-Sun Road, a trail climbs to the wildflower meadows of **Preston Park,** where a junction separates into two trails. Go left for **Piegan Pass** (9 mi/14.5 km rt, 4-5 hrs, moderate); the route with views of Piegan Glacier swings around a basin to the pass and returns on the same trail. Go right for **Siyeh Pass** (10 mi/16.1 km one-way, 6 hrs, strenuous) to switchback up to the pass and down Baring Creek to Sunrift Gorge. Use the shuttle to return to your vehicle.

St. Mary and Virginia Falls

The trail to **St. Mary Falls** (1.6 mi/2.6 km rt, 1 hr, easy) and **Virginia Falls** (3.2 mi/5.2 km rt, 2 hrs, moderate) sees a constant stream of people. The west trailhead descends from the shuttle stop while the east trailhead launches from the vehicle parking lot; both spurs connect to the main trail. At gushing St. Mary Falls, a wooden bridge crosses blue-green pools. Then, the trail switchbacks up to Virginia Falls, a broad waterfall spewing mist.

HIDDEN LAKE OVERLOOK TRAIL

Best Hike

HIGHLINE TRAIL AND GRANITE PARK CHALET

DISTANCE: 11.4 miles (18.3 km) point-to-point

DURATION: 5-6 hours

ELEVATION CHANGE: 1,300 feet (396 m) up; 3,700 feet (1,128 m) down

EFFORT: strenuous

TRAILHEADS: Logan Pass and the Loop

Beginning at **Logan Pass,** this point-to-point walk along the **Highline Trail** (mid-July-mid-Oct.) tiptoes along the Continental Divide to historic **Granite Park Chalet** before dropping to the **Loop.** Wildflowers peak mid-July-early August. Use park shuttles to get to and from trailheads.

The trail starts with a cliff walk above the Going-to-the-Sun Road before crossing a flowering land that gave the Garden Wall arête its name. Starting at the 3-mile (5-km) point, more than half the total elevation gain is packed into one climb interrupted with a break at the saddle below Haystack Butte. After the high point, the trail drops and swings through several large bowls before passing Bear Valley to reach Granite Park Chalet atop a knoll with panoramic views before descending to The Loop.

You can overnight at the rustic stone-and-log **Granite Park Chalet** (Belton Chalets, 406/387-5654 or 888/345-2649, www.graniteparkchalet.com, July-early Sept., from $85 pp). Reservations are required. **Online bookings for the upcoming summer go fast, starting in early January.**

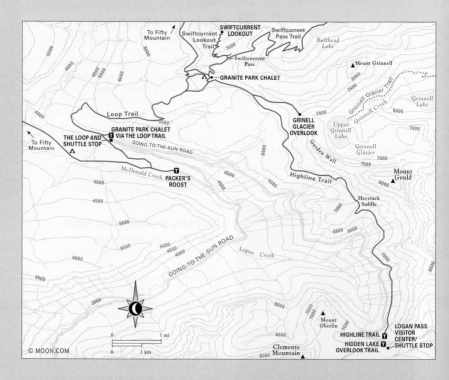

HIGHLINE TRAIL

MANY GLACIER

Grinnell Lake and Grinnell Glacier

From Swiftcurrent Picnic Area or Many Glacier Hotel, circle Swiftcurrent Lake to reach Josephine Lake and walk the trail along the lake's north shore to signed junctions on the west end. Taking the boat shuttle (fee) to the west end of Josephine Lake shortens both routes. For **Grinnell Lake** (2.2 mi/3.5 km rt, 1.5 hrs plus boat shuttle; full trail 6.8 mi/10.9 km rt, 4 hrs, easy), head west from Josephine to cross a river on a swinging bridge to reach the turquoise lake backed by a large waterfall. For **Grinnell Glacier** (7.2 mi/11.6 km, 4 hrs plus boat shuttle; full trail 10.6 mi/17.1 km rt, 6 hrs, strenuous), climb uphill from Josephine's northwest inlet through wildflowers, waterfalls, cliffs, and moraine to reach the shrinking glacier with a large lake at its snout.

Iceberg Lake and Ptarmigan Tunnel

From behind Swiftcurrent Motel, the trail to **Iceberg Lake** (9.6 mi/15.4 km rt, 5 hrs, moderate) shoots up a short, steep jaunt, then maintains an easy railroad grade to the lake that retains icebergs until late summer. At the signed junction after Ptarmigan Falls, a turnoff for the **Ptarmigan Tunnel Trail** (10.6 mi/17.1 km rt, 6 hrs, strenuous) ascends above the tree line, passing Ptarmigan Lake and switchbacking up to the historic tunnel. The doors to the tunnel are open mid-July to late September.

TWO MEDICINE

Scenic Point

From Two Medicine Road, **Scenic Point** (7.8 mi/12.6 km rt, 4-5 hrs, strenuous)

GRINNELL GLACIER

ICEBERG LAKE

is a short climb up switchbacks with big scenery. Above the tree line, the trail traverses a talus slope before descending to Scenic Point and views of the plains.

Twin Falls and Upper Two Medicine Lake

Hop the tour boat (fee) to hike to **Twin Falls** (1.8 mi/2.9 km rt, 1 hr, easy), a double waterfall. Continuing farther climbs to **Upper Two Medicine Lake** (4.4 mi/7 km rt, 3 hrs, moderate), a subalpine lake tucked below Lone Walker Peak.

RECREATION
BACKPACKING

Glacier National Park's backpacking is unrivaled, with miles of well-marked scenic trails. Sixty-six designated backcountry campgrounds spread campers out to avoid crowds, and **permits** ($7 pp per night) guarantee solitude. Pick up permits 24 hours in advance at Apgar Backcountry Office or other permit locations; submit advance reservations online starting mid-March ($40). Go for popular trails such as **Gunsight Pass** (28 mi/45.1 km, including Sperry

▼ SCENIC POINT OVERLOOKING TWO MEDICINE LAKE

BACKPACKERS ON GUNSIGHT PASS TRAIL

Glacier), or head for something remote like **Boulder Pass** (33 mi/53.1 km). Bring rope for hanging food.

BIKING

Going-to-the-Sun Road is an unforgettable bicycle trip. While the 3,500-foot (1,067-m) climb up the west side seems intimidating, it's not steep . . . just a constant uphill grind amid stunning scenery. Cycling begins in early April as snowplows free the pavement. Without cars on the road, riders climb from Lake McDonald Lodge or Avalanche as far as plowed roads permit. By May, free bicycle-carrying shuttles run from Lake McDonald Lodge to Avalanche. After the road opens to cars, cyclists may continue to ride, but due to heavy traffic, the west side closes to bikes 11am-4pm.

HORSEBACK RIDING

Swan Mountain Outfitter (406/387-4405, www.swanmountainglacier.com, early June-early Sept.) guides horseback trail rides from corrals at Apgar, Lake McDonald Lodge, and Many Glacier.

BOATING AND PADDLING

Aquatic Invasive Species (AIS) have forced the park to adopt stringent boating guidelines to protect the pristine waters. Clean, drain, and dry all boats before arriving. You'll need permits (free) and AIS inspections; check online for where to get these depending on timing and lake location. Boating is allowed generally on west side lakes early May-October and east side lakes late May-late September.

Paddlers can ply the waters of Lake McDonald, Bowman Lake, Kintla Lake, Two Medicine Lake, St. Mary Lake, and Swiftcurrent Lake. Motorized boats

GOING-TO-THE-SUN ROAD

TWO MEDICINE LAKE

are allowed on Lake McDonald and Bowman Lake (under 10 hp); check on the status for St. Mary Lake. All have boat launches. Lake McDonald also permits launching from pullouts along Going-to-the-Sun Road. Use caution on St. Mary Lake, as winds here kick up fast.

Glacier Park Boat Company (406/257-2426, www.glacierparkboats. com, daily mid-June-mid-Sept.) rents canoes, kayaks, small motorboats, and rowboats at Apgar, Lake McDonald Lodge, Many Glacier, and Two Medicine. **Polebridge Outfitters** (265 Polebridge Loop, Polebridge, 406/888-5229, www.polebridgemerc.com) rents paddleboards, kayaks, and canoes.

FISHING

Glacier is a trout fishery. To fish the large lakes like **Lake McDonald** and **Two Medicine Lake,** anglers have more success tossing in a line from a boat rather than fishing from shore. **Many Glacier Valley** has lots of fishing holes: Grinnell, Josephine, Swiftcurrent, Red Rock, and Bullhead Lakes support trout populations.

Pick up free fishing permits and regulations at visitors centers or ranger stations. Rent fishing gear at **Glacier Outfitters** (196 Apgar Loop Rd., Apgar, 406/219-7466, www.goglacieroutfitters.com, 8am-8pm daily mid-May-

late Sept., shorter hours in shoulder seasons).

RAFTING

Glacier has two boundary rivers for rafting—the Wild and Scenic **Middle Fork** and **North Fork of the Flathead River.** The rafting season runs May-September, with water levels usually peaking in late May. By late August, both rivers are at their lowest levels.

West Glacier houses four rafting companies that offer scenic floats and white-water thrills. Contact **Glacier Raft Company** (106 Going-to-the-Sun Rd., 406/888-5454, www.glacierraftco.com), **Great Northern Whitewater** (12127 US 2 E., 406/387-5340 or 800/735-7897, www.greatnorthernresort.com), **Montana Raft Company** (11970 US 2 E., 406/387-5555, www.glacierguides.com), or **Wild River Adventures** (11900 US 2 E., 406/387-9453 or 800/700-7056, www.riverwild.com).

Glacier Outdoor Center (406/888-5454, www.glacierraftco.com) rents rafts and inflatable kayaks.

WHERE TO STAY

INSIDE THE PARK

Advance **reservations** for all in-park lodgings are imperative. Book **13 months in advance** (Xanterra,

LAKE MCDONALD

855/733-4522, www.glaciernational-parklodges.com) for Many Glacier Hotel, Lake McDonald Lodge, Rising Sun Motor Inn, Swiftcurrent Motor Inn, and Village Inn Motel.

For Apgar Village Lodge and Motel Lake McDonald, make **reservations** (Pursuit Glacier Park Collection, 844/868-7474, www.glacierparkcollection.com) **one year in advance.**

Lake McDonald

In Apgar, **Apgar Village Lodge** (33 Apgar Loop Rd., late May-early Oct., from $150) clusters small motel rooms and rustic cabins within a few steps of Lake McDonald. On Lake McDonald's beach, every one of the 36 guest rooms in the **Village Inn Motel** (62 Apgar Loop Rd., mid-May-Sept., from $183) wakes up to an unobstructed million-dollar view.

Near the upper end of Lake McDonald, historic **Lake McDonald Lodge** (288 Lake McDonald Lodge Loop, late May-late Sept., from $121) has four types of accommodations: main lodge rooms, cabin rooms, suites, and budget rooms with shared baths. **Russell's Fireside Dining Room** (6:30am-10am, 11:30am-2pm, and 5pm-9:30pm daily) serves breakfast, lunch, and dinner with no reservations. The cozy **Lucke's Lounge** (11:30am-10pm daily) has a limited menu. **Jammer Joe's Grill and Pizzeria** (11am-9pm daily) serves cafeteria style.

At the Lake McDonald Lodge complex, **Motel Lake McDonald** (3 Lake McDonald Lodge Loop, mid-June-mid-Sept., from $165) is an old 1950s-style two-story motel.

St. Mary Lake

On the east side of Going-to-the-Sun Road, **Rising Sun Motor Inn** (2 Going-to-the-Sun Rd., mid-June-mid-Sept., from $181) has cabin rooms and motel units, the **Two Dog Flats Grill** (6:30am-10pm daily), and a store.

Many Glacier

On Swiftcurrent Lake, **Many Glacier Hotel** (milepost 11.5, Many Glacier Rd., mid-June-mid-Sept., from $225) is the largest and most popular of the park's historic lodges. Rooms and suites facing the lake have outstanding views. **Ptarmigan Dining Room** (6:30am-10am, 11:30am-2:30pm, and 5pm-9:30pm daily) serves breakfast, lunch, and dinner. The adjacent **Swiss Lounge** (11:30am-10pm daily) offers small bites.

At Many Glacier Road's terminus, **Swiftcurrent Motor Inn** (2 Many Glacier Rd., mid-June-mid-Sept., from $122) has cabins with or without baths, motel rooms, and **Nell's at Swiftcurrent Restaurant** (6:30am-10am and 11am-10pm daily).

NAME	LOCATION	PRICE	SEASON	AMENITIES
Apgar Campground	Apgar	$20	Apr.-Oct.	tent and RV sites
Fish Creek	Apgar	$23	late May-Sept.	tent and RV sites
Apgar Village Lodge	Apgar	from $150	May-early Oct.	motel rooms, cabins
Village Inn Motel	Apgar	from $183	May-Sept.	motel rooms
Logging Creek	North Fork	$10	July-Aug.	tent sites
Quartz Creek	North Fork	$10	July-Aug.	tent sites
Bowman Lake	North Fork	$15	May-Sept.	tent sites
Kintla Lake	North Fork	$15	June-Sept.	tent sites
Avalanche Campground	Going-to-the-Sun Road	$20	June-Sept.	tent and RV sites
Rising Sun	Going-to-the-Sun Road	$20	May-Sept.	tent and RV sites
Sprague Creek	Going-to-the-Sun Road	$20	May-Sept.	tent and RV sites
Lake McDonald Lodge	Going-to-the-Sun Road	from $121	May-Sept.	hostel, lodge, cottage rooms, dining
Motel Lake McDonald	Going-to-the-Sun Road	from $165	June-Sept.	motel rooms
Rising Sun Motor Inn	Going-to-the-Sun Road	from $181	June-Sept.	cabins, motel rooms, dining
Granite Park Chalet	Going-to-the-Sun Road	$82-117 pp	July-Sept.	backcountry hostel
St. Mary Campground	St. Mary	$23	May-Sept.	tent and RV sites
Many Glacier Campground	Many Glacier	$23	May-Sept.	tent and RV sites
Swiftcurrent Motor Inn	Many Glacier	from $122	June-Sept.	cabins, motel rooms, dining
Many Glacier Hotel	Many Glacier	from $225	June-Sept.	hotel rooms, dining
Cut Bank	Two Medicine	$10	June-Sept.	tent and RV sites
Two Medicine Campground	Two Medicine	$20	June-Sept.	tent and RV sites

Camping

Most of Glacier's 13 campgrounds are first come, first served. **Make reservations six months in advance** (877/444-6777, www.recreation.gov) for Fish Creek, St. Mary, Many Glacier, Sprague Creek, and Apgar as soon as they are released.

Apgar (194 sites, Apgar Loop Rd., Apr.-Oct., $20), **Fish Creek** (178 sites, Fish Creek Rd., late May-early Sept., $23), and **Sprague Creek** (25 sites, Going-to-the-Sun Rd., mid-May-mid-Sept., $20) flank Lake McDonald. **Avalanche Creek** (87 sites, Going-to-the-Sun Rd., mid-June-early Sept., $20) is the closest west-side campground to Logan Pass.

Near St. Mary Lake, **Rising Sun** (84 sites, Going-to-the-Sun Rd., late May-mid-Sept., $20) and **St. Mary** (148 sites,

Going-to-the-Sun Rd., mid-May-mid-Sept., $23) anchor the east side.

On the park's east side, three roads terminate at **Two Medicine** (100 sites, June-late Sept., $20), **Cut Bank** (off MT 49 and US 89, 14 sites, early June-early Sept., $10), and the coveted **Many Glacier** (109 sites, Many Glacier Rd., late May-mid-Sept., $23).

In the remote North Fork, small campgrounds are accessible via rough dirt roads: **Kintla Lake** (13 sites, June-mid-Sept., $15), **Bowman Lake** (46 sites, late May-early Sept., $15), **Quartz Creek** (7 sites, July-Aug., $10), and **Logging Creek** (7 sites, July-Aug., $10). Registration is first come, first served at the Polebridge entrance.

OUTSIDE THE PARK

On the west side of Glacier, lodging, camping, and services are in **West Glacier, Coram, Hungry Horse,** and the **Flathead Valley** (Columbia Falls, Whitefish, Kalispell). On the east side, **St. Mary** and **East Glacier** have visitor services.

GETTING THERE

AIR

The closest airport to the park is **Glacier Park International Airport** (FCA,

BLACK BEAR CUB

4170 US 2, Kalispell, 406/257-5960, www.iflyglacier.com). It's a short drive of 30 minutes via US 2 to the park. The airport has car rentals.

TRAIN

Amtrak's daily **Empire Builder** (800/872-7245, www.amtrak.com) stops at several park perimeter locations: East Glacier, Essex, and West Glacier. High summer travel volumes make reservations imperative, and riders may need to contend with delays.

CAR

From I-90 west of Missoula, Montana, take exit 96 onto US 93 north, which leads to the West Entrance of the park (140 mi/225 km, 2.5 hrs).

GETTING AROUND

DRIVING

Driving in Glacier National Park is not easy. Narrow roads built for cars in the 1930s barely fit today's SUVs, much less RVs and trailers. With no shoulders and sharp curves, roads require reduced speeds and shifting into second gear on extended descents to avoid burning brakes.

Two roads cross the Continental Divide: **Going-to-the-Sun Road** (mid-June-mid-Oct., no RVs or car-trailer combos over 21 ft/6.4 m) bisects the park, while **US 2** (open year-round) hugs Glacier's southern border. Both are two-lane roads. The Going-to-the-Sun Road is the more difficult drive, climbing 1,500 feet (457 m) higher on a skinnier, snakier road than US 2.

BUS SHUTTLES

The **Going-to-the-Sun Road shuttles** (7am-8pm daily July-Labor Day, free) connect Apgar, Logan Pass, and St. Mary, with additional stops at lodges, campgrounds, and trailheads. They depart every 15-30 minutes from signed shuttle stops.

Xanterra (855/733-4522, www.glaciernationalparklodges.com, July-Labor Day, $14 each way) operates shuttles from Many Glacier and Swiftcurrent Motor Inn to St. Mary.

THE EXTINCTION OF GLACIERS

Glacier National Park is named for glaciers that shaped the landscape. Ancient sheets of ice several thousand feet thick advanced and retreated on the landscape 2 million years ago. When they melted, they left behind deep river and lake valleys. More recently, a mini ice age created smaller alpine glaciers about 7,000 years ago before waning. These left behind high mountain cirques, moraines, and strewn boulders.

What is a glacier?

Glaciers are moving ice. As snow piles on a glacier's upper end, it compresses into ice that moves. In order to have the mass to move, a glacier must be about 100 feet (30 m) deep and 25 acres (10 ha) large. Glacier's small glaciers move only inches per year.

What has happened to the glaciers?

Less than two dozen tiny glaciers remain from the 150 that glittered on peaks in 1850. Since then, the glaciers have thinned, split, shrunk, broken into pieces, formed lakes that sped up melting, or melted entirely. Due to less snow and warmer temperatures, some glaciers have lost 80 percent of their size in the past 50 years; the ones left will see extinction in only a handful of years. Scientists from the U.S. Geological Survey (USGS, www.usgs.gov) monitor the glaciers. You can see USGS photos online and at Many Glacier Hotel that compare glacier appearances from the early 1900s to now.

Where can I see a glacier?

With binoculars, you can see Jackson and Blackfoot Glaciers from Going-to-the-Sun Road's east side. Hiking trails pass glaciers: Piegan and Sexton Glacier on the Siyeh Pass Trail and Grinnell Glacier on the Grinnell Glacier Trail.

HISTORIC RED BUS ON GOING-TO-THE-SUN ROAD

BUS TOURS

Departing from all park lodges for Going-to-the-Sun Road, historic **red jammer buses** with rollback canvas tops are operated by **Xanterra** (855/733-4522, www.glaciernationalparklodges.com, late June-Sept.).

Launching from East Glacier, St. Mary, and West Glacier, **Sun Tours** (406/732-9220 or 800/786-9220, www.glaciersuntours.com, daily mid-June-Sept.) leads four- and seven-hour tours over Going-to-the-Sun Road with an emphasis on Blackfeet cultural history.

BOAT TOURS

Glacier Park Boat Company (406/257-2426, www.glacierparkboats.com) runs tours from four locations on historic wooden boats. Buy tickets at the boat docks or make advance reservations by phone, especially for July-August. Tours depart from **Lake McDonald Lodge** (late May-late Sept), **Rising Sun** (mid-June-early Sept.) on St. Mary Lake, **Two Medicine Lake** (early June-mid-Sept.), and **Many Glacier Hotel** (mid-June-mid-Sept.) for a two-boat

tour on Swiftcurrent Lake and Josephine Lake.

TOUR BOAT

◄ JACKSON GLACIER

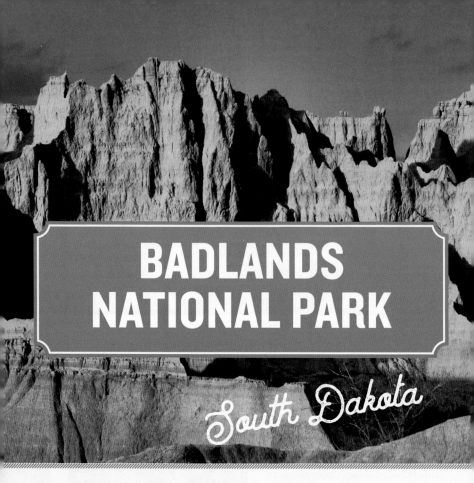

BADLANDS NATIONAL PARK

South Dakota

WEBSITE:
www.nps.gov/badl

PHONE NUMBER:
605/433-5361

VISITATION RANK:
22

WHY GO:
Experience the
prairie badlands.

KEEPSAKE STAMPS ▼▼▼

▲ BADLANDS PEAKS

THE BADLANDS are a wondrous place. In daylight, the twisted spires and pinnacles look gray and faded, but at dawn or dusk, pale yellow, deep burgundy, and light pinks emerge. A visit here is like a visit to another planet, one that is starkly forbidding and strikingly beautiful. No wonder the Lakota people called it *"mako sica,"* which literally means "bad land."

Part of its geology includes an ancient seabed where the Lakota first discovered fossils of marine reptiles, turtle shells, fish bones, and seashells. More recent layers buried early mammals, including horses, camels, and birds. Today, Badlands is a wildlife wonderland, filled with everything from the rare black-footed ferret to bison.

PLANNING YOUR TIME

Once you get to South Dakota, Badlands is an easy park to access, due to its location just south of I-90. Many visitors combine Badlands with a visit to Wind Cave National Park, two hours west. If you are not staying overnight, try to spend at least **3-4 hours** in the park. Overnight visitors, especially photographers, should plan to catch a **sunset** or **sunrise** due to the impressive lighting on the craggy peaks.

While **May-September** is high season, **April-June** is the best time to visit. The grasses are still a luscious green early in the year and the daytime temperatures are mild. June is the wettest month. July and August have very hot days, sometime in the triple digits. Occasional storms bring lightning, hail, or even tornadoes. By fall, brown grasses remove color from the view, but the spires, buttes, and tables of the area are no less beautiful. While the park is open year-round, winter is less hospitable, with strong winds and cold temperatures below freezing. While December and January see the least amount of precipitation, intermittent snow can temporarily close roads and trails.

ENTRANCES AND FEES

Badlands National Park is divided into two units. The **North Unit** is an easy day trip from Rapid City and has three year-round entrances: **Pinnacles Entrance** (SD 240, south of Wall), **Interior Entrance** (SD 44/377, north of Interior), and **Northeast Entrance** (SD 240,

south of I-90). The remoter **South Unit,** or the Stronghold District, is within the Pine Ridge Reservation of the Oglala Lakota, with one road and no hiking trails.

The entrance fee is $30 per vehicle ($25 motorcycle, $15 individual) and good for seven days.

VISITORS CENTERS

The **Ben Reifel Visitor Center** (25216 Ben Reifel Rd., SD 240, 605/433-5361, 9am-4pm daily mid-Apr.-May and Sept.-late Oct., 7am-7pm daily June-mid-Aug., 9am-4pm daily Nov.-mid-Apr.) is at Park Headquarters on the south edge of the Badlands Loop Road. Paleontologists are on-site June-September working to uncover additional fossils. Visitors can tour the **Fossil Preparation Lab** (9am-4:30pm daily mid-June-mid-Sept.), which readies fossils for display.

At the remote South Unit, the **White River Visitor Center** (SD 27, Porcupine, 605/455-2878, 8am-5pm daily June-mid-Oct.) has exhibits, information on backcountry camping and hiking, and impromptu talks on the culture and history of the Oglala Lakota people. It is 20 miles (32 km) south of the town of Scenic, off Bombing Range Road (SD 27) on the Pine Ridge Reservation.

SCENIC DRIVE

South of the Pinnacles Entrance, the gravel **Sage Creek Rim Road** (23 mi/37 km) travels north and west to circle the Badlands Wilderness Area. Look for the **Hay Butte Overlook** and the **Badlands**

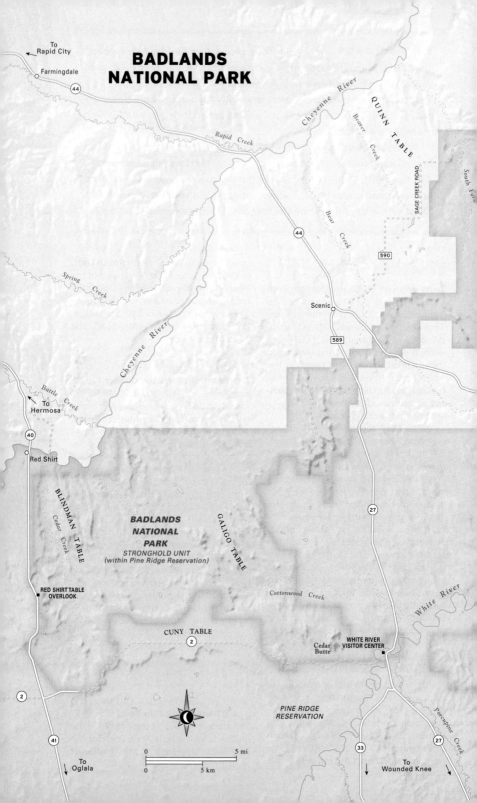

BADLANDS NATIONAL PARK

To Rapid City

Farmingdale

44

Cheyenne River

QUINN TABLE

Beaver Creek

Rapid Creek

SAGE CREEK ROAD

South Fork

44

Bear Creek

590

Spring Creek

Scenic

Cheyenne River

589

Battle Creek

To Hermosa

40

Red Shirt

27

BLINDMAN TABLE

Cedar Creek

BADLANDS
NATIONAL
PARK
STRONGHOLD UNIT
(within Pine Ridge Reservation)

GALIGO TABLE

Cottonwood Creek

White River

RED SHIRT TABLE
OVERLOOK

CUNY TABLE

2

Cedar
Butte

WHITE RIVER
VISITOR CENTER

2

PINE RIDGE
RESERVATION

Porcupine Creek

41

33

27

To Oglala

0   5 mi

0   5 km

To Wounded Knee

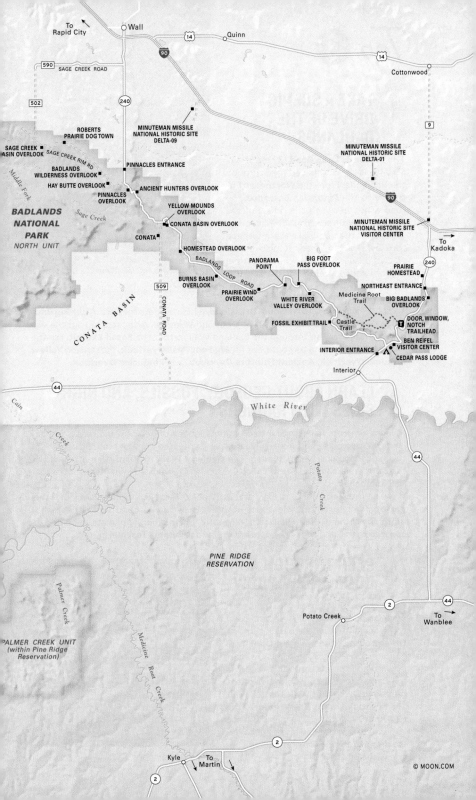

Top ❸

❶ TAKE A SCENIC DRIVE OF THE BADLANDS

The **Badlands Loop Road** (39 mi/63 km, SD 240) is the only paved road through the Badlands. From the **Northeast Entrance** to the **Pinnacles Entrance,** the road winds between the ridges of the **Badlands Wall,** a serrated split in the grasslands that looks like the landscape tore away from itself. It also crosses two passes: Cedar and Dillon. Amid bighorn sheep, prairie dogs, and bison, a dozen scenic turnouts along the road provide dramatic vistas of the Badlands

BADLANDS SCENIC DRIVE

and of the **Buffalo Gap National Grassland,** which borders the park. After **Big Badlands Overlook,** stop to walk to the **Door** and **Window.** After scoping out the visitors center, drive up through the Badland Wall to tour the **Fossil Exhibit.** For the best of the remaining turnouts, opt for **Big Foot Pass Overlook,** the striking **Yellow Mounds Overlook, Ancient Hunters Overlook,** and **Pinnacles Overlook.**

❷ LEARN ABOUT GEOLOGY, FOSSILS, AND NIGHT SKIES WITH RANGERS

Millions of years have gone into creating a legacy of geology and fossils in Badlands. With walks and talks (daily late May-Sept., free), rangers tell the secrets of this landscape and what's hidden. The **Geology Walk** (8:30am, 45 min) meets at the Door Trailhead. The **Fossil Talk** (10:30am and 1:30pm, 30 min) meets at the Fossil Exhibit shelter.

As an International Dark Sky Park, Badlands offers exceptional clarity for **stargazing.** Rangers set up telescopes at Cedar Pass Campground Amphitheater for **night sky tours** (9:30pm daily late May-early Aug., 45 min) of planets, nebulae, and constellations, and the park hosts a two-day **astronomy festival** in July.

❸ PEER THROUGH A DOOR AND WINDOW

Two short scenic boardwalk trails with wheelchair accessibility depart from the Door and Window parking lot. At the end of the boardwalk, the **Door Trail** (0.75 mi/1.2 km rt, 30 min, easy) slopes upward and travels through a "door" in the Badlands Wall to yield views of the grasslands, the outer Badlands Wall, and an eroded maze. The **Window Trail** (0.25 mi/0.4 km rt, 20 min, easy) leads to a window in the Badlands Wall overlooking a dramatic erosion-carved canyon with spires.

OVERLOOK ON DOOR TRAIL

Best Hike

THE NOTCH

The **Notch Trail** ramps up the fun with two challenges. The route starts up a dead-end canyon that requires climbing a wiggly cable-and-log ladder. Then, it tiptoes along a narrow ledge. After regaining more solid footing, it follows a draw up to the "notch," through which a sweeping view of the White River valley is revealed. Avoid hiking this trail in rain due to the treacherous conditions.

DISTANCE: 1.5 miles (2.4 km) round-trip
DURATION: 2 hours
ELEVATION CHANGE: 126 feet (38 m)
EFFORT: moderately strenuous
TRAILHEAD: south end of Door, Window, Notch parking lot

LADDER ON THE NOTCH TRAIL ▶

Wilderness Overlook. The formations here are a little softer and less craggy than the spires along the Badlands Loop Road, but wildlife is more abundant. The park's bison herd is usually seen in this area. Look for the **Roberts Prairie Dog Town,** where a large colony of black-tailed prairie dogs entertain with barking and social antics. At dusk, keep an eye out for the rare black-footed ferret. Just past Roberts Prairie Dog Town is the **Sage Creek Basin Overlook.** Head south and cross a bridge over Sage Creek where you can examine the riverbank to see the Pierre Shale—the oldest visible sedimentary layer in the park, dating back more than 70 million years. Eight miles (12.8 km) past Roberts Prairie Dog Town, a left-hand turn on a gravel road brings you to **Sage Creek Campground.**

SIGHTS

BADLANDS WALL

An escarpment of spindly spires, pinnacles, and severe gullies, the **Badlands Wall** once was the northern bank of the White River. Today, the 60-mile-long

SAGE CREEK RIM ROAD

(97-km) Wall, which looks as if it should wash away in the next rain, exposes the handiwork of erosion. Drive below it, above it, and through it on Badlands Loop Road. All hiking trails in the park explore its bowels or high points.

WILDLIFE-WATCHING

Badlands is full of wildlife that is easy to spot due to very few trees. So where can you see some of the animals? For one, look on the grasslands and prairies, where food is more abundant rather than in the eroded features. Drive Sage Creek Rim Road to see **bison herds.** On the same road, stop at **Roberts Prairie Dog Town** to watch prairie dogs skitter around, chattering at each other.

Look around the higher Cedar Pass and Dillon Pass (Pinnacles area) to find **bighorn sheep.** Along the Badlands Loop Road, watch for foxes, deer, coyotes, pronghorn, burrowing owls, and the black-footed ferret, a rare sight.

FOSSIL EXHIBIT

The **Fossil Exhibit** (0.25 mi/0.4 km rt, 30 min, easy) tours a wheelchair-accessible **boardwalk** between interpretive displays that tell a 75-million-year-old story of the fossils found in Badlands. No real fossils are here, but you can touch the fossil replicas of an early dog, horse, and alligator or bronze casts of larger fossils of titanothere teeth and oreodont bones.

RECREATION

HIKING

From the trailhead 0.5 mile (0.8 km) east of the visitors center, **Cliff Shelf** (0.5 mi/0.8 km rt, 20 min, moderate) loops below the Badlands Wall. Stairs and boardwalk climb and descend through the juniper forest and take in the prairie views.

A steep ascent juts up through colorful rock formations to the natural flat platform of **Saddle Pass** (0.25 mi/0.4 km rt, 30 min, strenuous) in the Badlands Wall. Find the trailhead on Badlands Loop Road about 2 miles (3.2 km) northwest of the visitors center.

The mostly level **Castle Trail** (10 mi/16.1 km rt, 5 hrs, moderate) winds through spires and mounds. Portions cross grasslands with views of Badlands formations to the west and south; watch for cacti and rattlesnakes. Trailheads are on both ends: across from the Door and Window parking lot and across from the Fossil Exhibit Trail.

BIKING

Badlands Loop Road (39 mi/63 km) can be an exhilarating downhill ride from Pinnacles Overlook to the visitors center. But be ready for narrow curvy roads with cars and RVs zipping past.

Mountain bikers prefer the gravel **Sage Creek Rim Road** (23 mi/37 km) but may eat dust from cars. The dead-end dirt **Sheep Mountain Table Road** (14 mi/23 km rt) about 4 miles (6.4 km) south of the town of Scenic off BIA 27/County Road 589 has spectacular views of the South Unit of the park.

Bring your own bicycles; rentals are not available. The visitors center has a brochure detailing loop routes on combined park and county roads and a bike pump and repair station outside.

WHERE TO STAY

INSIDE THE PARK

If you're looking to experience a park sunrise or sunset, you have two

CEDAR PASS CAMPGROUND

ONE DAY IN THE BADLANDS

Spend your one day in the park by entering through the **Northeast Entrance.** Stop to walk the **Door** and **Window Trails** before crossing Cedar Pass to the visitors center to get oriented. Drive north along the **Badlands Loop Road** and tour the **Fossil Exhibit.** Finish your day trip by exiting via the **Pinnacles Entrance** on the north side of the park.

options. **Cedar Pass Lodge** (20681 SD 240, 605/433-5460 or 877/386-4383, www.cedarpasslodge.com, mid-Apr.-mid-Oct., from $182) has cabins with air-conditioning, modern amenities, small decks, and lodgepole pine furnishings. The **lodge restaurant** (8am-6:30pm daily May-Sept., 8am-4:30pm daily Apr. and Oct.) has some vegetarian selections and a limited dinner menu.

The lodge also operates and takes reservations for **Cedar Pass Campground** (96 sites, $23-40 Apr.-Oct., $15 winter with no services) next door. In summer, the campground has cold running water, flush toilets, and pay showers.

The **Sage Creek Wilderness Campground** (Sage Creek Rim Rd., North Unit, year-round, free) offers primitive camping with pit toilets (but no water) and equestrian facilities.

OUTSIDE THE PARK

The town of **Interior,** located at the southern edge of the North Unit of the park, has limited accommodations. The town of **Wall,** 8 miles (13 km) north of the Pinnacles Entrance on the north side of the park, has several accommodations and restaurants.

GETTING THERE AND AROUND

Badlands has no park shuttles or public transportation. You'll need to take a tour, drive, hike, or bicycle to see the park. In winter, check road conditions because severe snowstorms may close roads.

AIR

The nearest airport is **Rapid City Regional Airport** (RAP, 4550 Terminal Rd.,

605/394-4195, www.rapairport.com), 11 miles (18 km) from downtown Rapid City off SD 44. Shuttle service between the airport and downtown is provided by **Airport Express Shuttle** (605/399-9999 or 800/357-9998). Car rental companies are at the airport.

CAR

From Rapid City, two routes go to Badlands National Park. SD 44 skirts the southern edge of the North Unit, entering through the **Interior Entrance.** It's about a 75-mile (121-km) drive (1.5 hrs).

The second route to the park is I-90. It is the fastest route between Rapid City and the park: just 80 miles (128 km) of 80 mph (128 kph) driving. If you are planning on spending the night in or near the park, this is the best route. Travelers headed west on I-90 can take exit 131 at Cactus Flat and go south on SD 240 to the **Northeast Entrance.** It is about 10 miles (16 km) from the Northeast Entrance to the Ben Reifel Visitor Center. Traveling east on I-90, take exit 110 for Wall and drive 7 miles (11 km) south to the **Pinnacles Entrance.**

TOURS

Several tour companies make day trips to Badlands from Rapid City. **Affordable Adventures** (5542 Meteor St., Rapid City, 605/342-7691, www.affordableadventuresbh.com) provides narrated seven-hour tours.

Black Hills Adventure Tours (550 Berry Blvd., Rapid City, 605/209-7817, www.blackhillsadventuretours.com) has narrated driving tours and hiking tours in the park.

GeoFunTrek (605/430-1531, www.geofuntrek.com) has two tours to the Badlands: one classic and one that includes a daylight, sunset, or stargazing tour.

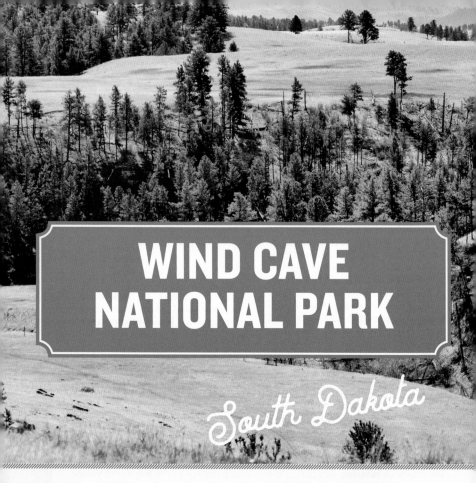

WIND CAVE
NATIONAL PARK

South Dakota

WEBSITE:
www.nps.gov/wica

PHONE NUMBER:
605/745-4600

VISITATION RANK:
32

WHY GO:
Explore underground caves.

KEEPSAKE STAMPS ▼▼▼

▲ WIND CAVE NATIONAL PARK

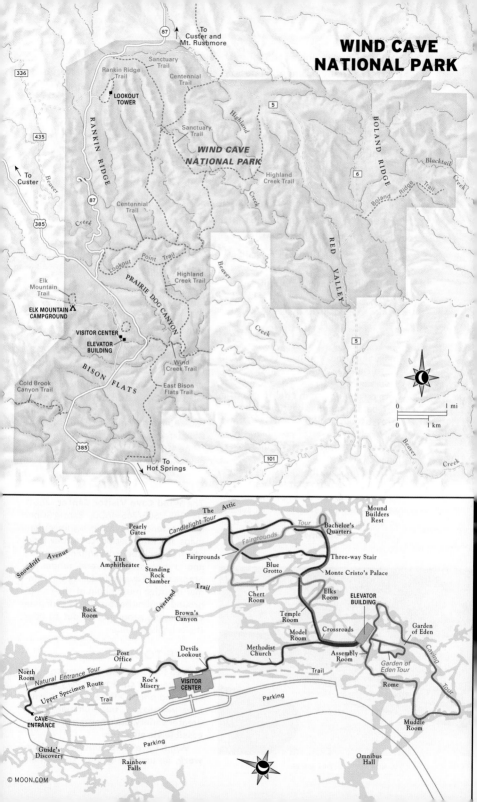

Wind Cave is one of the longest caves in the world. Considered sacred to many Indigenous people, the cave is woven into the stories of the Oglala Lakota people. This park spans two worlds, below the earth's surface and above.

The cave was "discovered" by Europeans in 1881 when two brothers heard a loud whistling noise that came from a small hole in the ground. This natural entrance is the only one ever found. Below one square mile (2.6 sq km) of parkland is a maze of 150 miles (241 km) of explored cave passages.

On the surface, **WIND CAVE NATIONAL PARK** is where East meets West—where the Great Plains prairie meets the ponderosa pine forest. Its mixed-grass prairie supports abundant bison, deer, prairie dogs, pronghorn, wild turkeys, and elk. These animals provided sustenance for the 26 Indigenous groups that used this area, hunting over rounded hills with views as far as the eye can see.

PLANNING YOUR TIME

Tucked in the southwest corner of South Dakota, Wind Cave lies west of Badlands National Park, and many visitors combine both in one trip. On the surface, summer has daytime temperatures usually 80-90°F (27-32°C) and can bring thunderstorms, while winter temperatures are often around freezing with snow.

Underground, the caves maintain a stable temperature that hovers around 53°F (12°C) regardless of the surface weather. Bring a sweatshirt or sweater. While rangers guide one cave tour year-round, **summer** (May-Sept.) is high season, with the most cave tour choices and the most visitors.

ENTRANCES AND FEES

Wind Cave has three entrances: **north** (SD 87 from Custer State Park), **south** (US 385 from Hot Springs), and **west** (US 385 from Pringle). There is no entrance fee; however, guided cave tours range $10-30 per person. These are the only way to enter the cave.

VISITORS CENTER

The **Wind Cave Visitor Center** (26611 US 385, 605/745-4600, 8am-4:30pm daily, extended hours in summer) has maps and information, **cave tour tickets,** free backcountry camping permits, and a bookstore. Several ranger-led programs are available during the summer months; most begin at the campground amphitheater. In fall, unique elk-listening programs go out to hear the animals bugling.

CAVE TOURS

Guided tours are the only way to enter the cave. **Five cave tours** vary in difficulty and price. One cave tour is available year-round, but summer has a greater variety. **Cave tours are only accessible via elevator.**

Wind Cave is famous for its **boxwork,** an unusual type of speleothem

WIND CAVE VISITOR CENTER

Top ③

1 TAKE IT EASY WITH THE GARDEN OF EDEN TOUR

The **Garden of Eden Tour** (3-4 tours daily year-round, adults $14) goes by intricate formations of cave popcorn, boxwork, and flowstone (a calcite formation that looks as if it is flowing over the rocks). Of all the cave tours, this one is the shortest and least strenuous (0.3 mi/0.5 km, 150 stairs, 1 hr). Children under 6 can go for free. Entry and exit to the cave is by elevator.

BOXWORK FORMATIONS

2 PICK UP THE PACE WITH THE NATURAL ENTRANCE TOUR

The **Natural Entrance Tour** (6-12 tours daily Apr.-Oct., adults $16) starts at the only natural entrance to the cave to discover why the cave got its name. However, entry is via an artificially constructed entrance that descends to the middle level of the cave, famous for its extensive boxwork formations. This tour is moderately strenuous (0.6 mi/1 km, 300 stairs mostly downhill, 1.25 hrs). Exit from the cave is via elevator.

3 WORK UP A SWEAT WITH THE FAIRGROUNDS TOUR

The **Fairgrounds Tour** (3-8 tours daily Memorial Day-Labor Day, adults $16) visits the upper and middle levels of the cave. Boxwork is abundant in the middle section, and the upper level of the cave features large rooms decorated with popcorn and frostwork. This tour is the most strenuous of the walking tours (0.6 mi/1 km, 450 total stairs climbing up, 1.5 hrs) with a single staircase of more than 90 stairs.

NATURAL CAVE ENTRANCE

Best Hike

LOOKOUT POINT-CENTENNIAL LOOP

DISTANCE: 4.5 miles (7.2 km) round-trip
DURATION: 2.5-3 hours
ELEVATION CHANGE: 240 feet (73 m)
EFFORT: moderate
TRAILHEAD: Centennial Trailhead

The **Lookout Point-Centennial Trail Loop** combines all of the diversity of the park: a stream ecosystem, prairie grasslands, pine forests, and rolling hills. The hike begins in a stand of ridgetop pines before descending to meander along Beaver Creek between low hills. When the Centennial Trail takes a sharp left, continue straight for a short stretch on the Highland Creek Trail. Where the Highland Creek Trail veers south, head west along the Lookout Point Trail to return to the Centennial Trailhead.

From the visitors center, head north on US 385 and take an immediate right on SD 87. Go 0.7 mile (1.1 km) to the trailhead on the east side.

(cave formation). Boxwork is made of thin slices of calcite that project from the cave walls and intersect with each other in a honeycomb-like fashion.

For tours, make **reservations** (877/444-6777, www.recreation.gov, Mar.-Oct.) up to 120 days in advance. Some first-come, first-served tickets are available at the visitors center 1-2 hours before tours. **Seniors** age 62 and older and **youths** ages 6-15 can get half-price rates on some tours. Some tours have minimum ages for participating, but **children** under six years old can go free on the Garden of Eden, Natural Entrance, and Fairgrounds Tours. Parents or guardians should assess the number of stairs to determine capability.

SPECIALTY CAVE TOURS

ACCESSIBILITY TOUR

The **Accessibility Tour** (30 min, $6) includes seeing the famous boxwork. An elevator takes you in and out of the cave, and accessible parking is near the elevator entrance. Call 605/745-4600 to schedule.

HISTORIC CANDLELIGHT TOUR

The **Candlelight Tour** (1-2 tours daily Memorial Day-Labor Day, adults $16, minimum age 8, advanced reservations recommended) takes place in a less developed area of the cave along a rugged trail. It explores Wind Cave like early cavers did, by carrying a candle bucket, which is the only lighting for the tour. Cave walls loom and shadows dance along the walls, heightening the otherworldly sensation. This strenuous tour

COLORFUL CAVE ROCKS

BRIDGE IN WIND CAVE NATIONAL PARK

MOUNT RUSHMORE

Four hundred people toiled for 14 years to create Mount Rushmore National Memorial, a mountainside carved with the faces of four presidents: Washington, Jefferson, Roosevelt, and Lincoln. But decades earlier, the U.S. government had promised the sacred mountain to the Lakota people. When gold was discovered here, the government broke the treaty and took the Lakota's lands. The fact that this sacred land now sports the faces of European settlers whose policies killed many Indigenous people is viewed by many as desecration.

The Mount Rushmore grounds are open year-round (5am-11pm daily mid-Mar.-Oct., 5am-9pm daily Nov.-mid-Mar.). In summer, the main park buildings are open 8am-10pm daily, with shorter hours or closures in winter. The presidents' faces are illuminated nightly from sunset until closing; during summer, the illumination is preceded by the evening lighting ceremony. A café near the monument entrance is the only dining facility.

Entrance and Visitors Center

This memorial has no entrance fee, but a parking fee is required. At the **Information Center,** find maps to the grounds, schedules for ranger-guided programs, and a park newspaper. The Mount Rushmore Audio Tour: Living Memorial (2 hrs, $6) is available at the **Audio Tour Building.**

The **Lincoln Borglum Visitor Center & Museum** (Grand View Terrace lower level) has interactive exhibits, a timeline of history, and two small theaters showing films. This is where you'll learn about the sculptor and construction.

Sights

The **Avenue of Flags** lines the pedestrian walkway, framing the presidential faces. It ends at **Grand View Terrace,** one of the best viewpoints for photographs. The

(0.6 mi/1 km, 2 hrs) is limited to 10 people. Participants are required to wear shoes with nonslip soles (no sandals).

WILD CAVE TOUR

For the adventurous, the **Wild Cave Tour** (1 tour daily Memorial Day-Labor Day, $45 adults, advance reservations required) demands crawling through some narrow spaces while learning the basics of safe caving. Be prepared to get dirty. The tour is ultra-strenuous (0.5 mi/0.8 km, 4 hrs), much of it spent crawling, and not for the claustrophobic! The park provides kneepads, hard hats, and lights; participants should wear long pants, long sleeves, and sturdy lace-up boots or shoes with nonslip soles. The minimum age is 16, and ages 16-17 must have a signed parental consent form.

HIKING

On the surface, hiking trails range from easy to strenuous. For a short hike, **nature trails** offer interpretive signage and displays. The **Elk Mountain Trail** (1 mi/1.6 km rt, 30 min, easy) begins at the end of the Elk Mountain Campground road and circles up through the forest near the park's boundary. From the visitors center or nearby picnic area,

BISON AT WIND CAVE NATIONAL PARK

mountainside sculpture is huge. George Washington's head is 60 feet (18 m) tall. His eye alone is 11 feet (3 m) wide, and his mouth is 18 feet (5 m) wide.

From Grand View Terrace, a concrete pathway goes to the **Borglum Viewing Terrace,** the site of the artist's first temporary studio. Below, rangers host 15-minute talks at the **Sculptor's Studio** (summer only) which contains the working model for Rushmore, tools, and photographs.

The Presidential Loop (0.6 mi/0.9 km rt, 20 min, easy) brings visitors to the closest viewpoints under the monument. The paved trail is wheelchair-accessible from the Washington side of Grand View Terrace to the base of the mountain. From here, 422 wooden stairs climb up and then down to the Sculptor's Studio.

The **Lakota, Nakota, and Dakota Heritage Village** (summer only) has a collection of tepees, where interpreters talk about traditional Indigenous lifestyles and customs.

Getting There and Around

Mount Rushmore National Memorial (13000 Hwy. 244, 605/574-2523, www. nps.gov/moru, parking $10) is north of Wind Cave National Park (40 mi/64 km, 1 hr) and west of Badlands National Park (83 mi/134 km, 1.5 hrs).

From Rapid City Airport, the fastest road to Mount Rushmore (32 mi/52 km) is US 16, also called Mount Rushmore Road. Once at Rushmore, moving from site to site is all by foot. No shuttles are available.

Several companies lead tours: **Mount Rushmore Tours** (2255 Fort Hayes Dr., Rapid City, 605/343-3113, www.mountrushmoretours.com), **ABS Travel Group** (945 Enchantment Rd., Rapid City, 888/788-6777, www.abstravelgroup.com), and **Golden Circle Tours** (12021 US 16, 605/673-4349, www.goldencircletours.com).

the **Prairie Vista Trail** (1 mi/1.6 km rt, 30 min, easy) focuses on information about the prairie grasses.

RANKIN RIDGE

A bit of uphill climbing yields large landscape views from the park's highest point. The **Rankin Ridge Trail** (1 mi/1.6 km rt, 45 min, moderate) begins and ends at the parking lot of the Rankin Ridge Lookout Tower off SD 87 in the northwest corner of the park. Pick up an interpretive trail guide at the trailhead, hike uphill on the dirt road to the lookout tower, and loop back on a single-track through pine forest.

WIND CAVE CANYON

Wind Cave Canyon (3.6 mi/5.8 km rt, 2 hrs, easy) follows a former service road into Wind Cave Canyon at the park's boundary. This is one of the best places in the park for bird-watching; look along limestone walls to spot cliff swallows and great horned owls. Stands of dead trees make great nesting places for several varieties of woodpeckers.

The trailhead is on the east side of the road, 1 mile (1.6 km) north of the junction of the south entrance and US 385.

WHERE TO STAY
INSIDE THE PARK

The only accommodation is **Elk Mountain Campground** (62 sites, $24 summer, $12 winter), 1 mile (1.6 km) north of the visitors center. Facilities include restrooms with flush toilets and cold running water (late May-early Sept.) but no hookups. Make **reservations** (www.recreation.gov) six months in advance for summer. The rest of the year, the campground is first come, first served.

Backcountry camping is allowed in the northwestern part of the park. Campers must have a **permit,** which is free from the visitors center.

PRARIE DOGS

OUTSIDE THE PARK

Located 7 miles (11 km) south of the park, the city of **Hot Springs** has accommodations for park visitors.

GETTING THERE AND AROUND

AIR

The **Rapid City Regional Airport** (RAP, 4550 Terminal Rd., 605/394-4194, www.rapairport.com) is about 11 miles (18 km) from downtown Rapid City, off SD 44 east. The airport has car rentals.

CAR

For the most direct route (57 mi/92 km, 1.25 hrs) from I-90 and Rapid City, take SD 79 south to US 385, turning right to Hot Springs. The park entrance is 7 miles (11 km) north on US 385. To reach Wind Cave from the south, aim for Hot Springs on US 385.

For drivers coming from Mount Rushmore, drive 4.6 miles (7.4 km) west to US 385 to go south through Hill City, Custer, and Pringle to reach the west entrance of the park (57 mi/92 km, 1.25 hrs).

Inside the park, the visitors center is on a signed side road about 0.5 mile (0.8 km) off US 385. From the south entrance, go 4.5 miles (7.2 km) to the turnoff on the left. From the north and west entrance roads, the visitors center turnoff is on the right just south of the junction of US 385 and SD 87.

There is no public transit within the park. Driving or bicycling is the only way to travel the main paved road. Two dirt roads (NP 5 and NP 6) tour the eastern portion of the badlands.

SIGHTS NEARBY

Crazy Horse Memorial (12151 Ave. of the Chiefs, Crazy Horse, 605/673-4681, www.crazyhorsememorial.org, 8am until after the laser light show daily summer, until 5pm daily winter) is a mountainside sculpture of the Oglala Lakota warrior Crazy Horse that's been under construction since 1948. It's 26 miles (42 km) north of Wind Cave on US 385.

Jewel Cave National Monument (13 mi/18 km west of Custer via US 16, 605/673-8300, www.nps.gov/jeca, 8am-6pm daily summer, shorter hours fall-spring) has ranger-led tours through the third-longest cave in the world.

Custer State Park (13329 US 16A, 605/255-4515, https://gfp.sd.gov), north of Wind Cave via SD 87, is home to 1,300 free-roaming bison and other wildlife best seen from Wildlife Loop Road. Campgrounds are available. The scenic Needles Highway (SD 87), speckled with rock spires and single-lane tunnels, goes through the park along with a portion of Iron Mountain Road (US 16A), with tunnels framing Mount Rushmore and pig-tail curves.

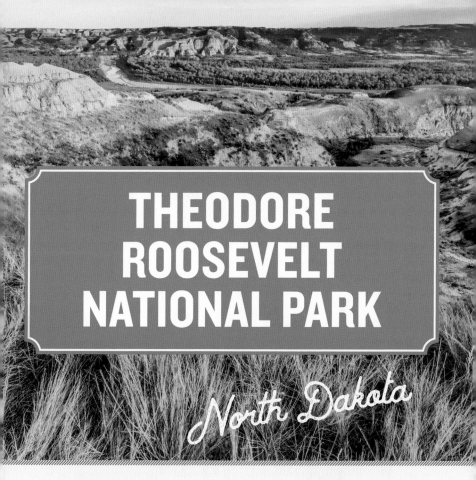

THEODORE ROOSEVELT NATIONAL PARK

North Dakota

KEEPSAKE STAMPS ▼▼▼

WEBSITE:
www.nps.gov/thro

PHONE NUMBER:
701/623-4466

VISITATION RANK:
30

WHY GO:
See wild horses,
bison, and badlands.

▲ THEODORE ROOSEVELT
NATIONAL PARK

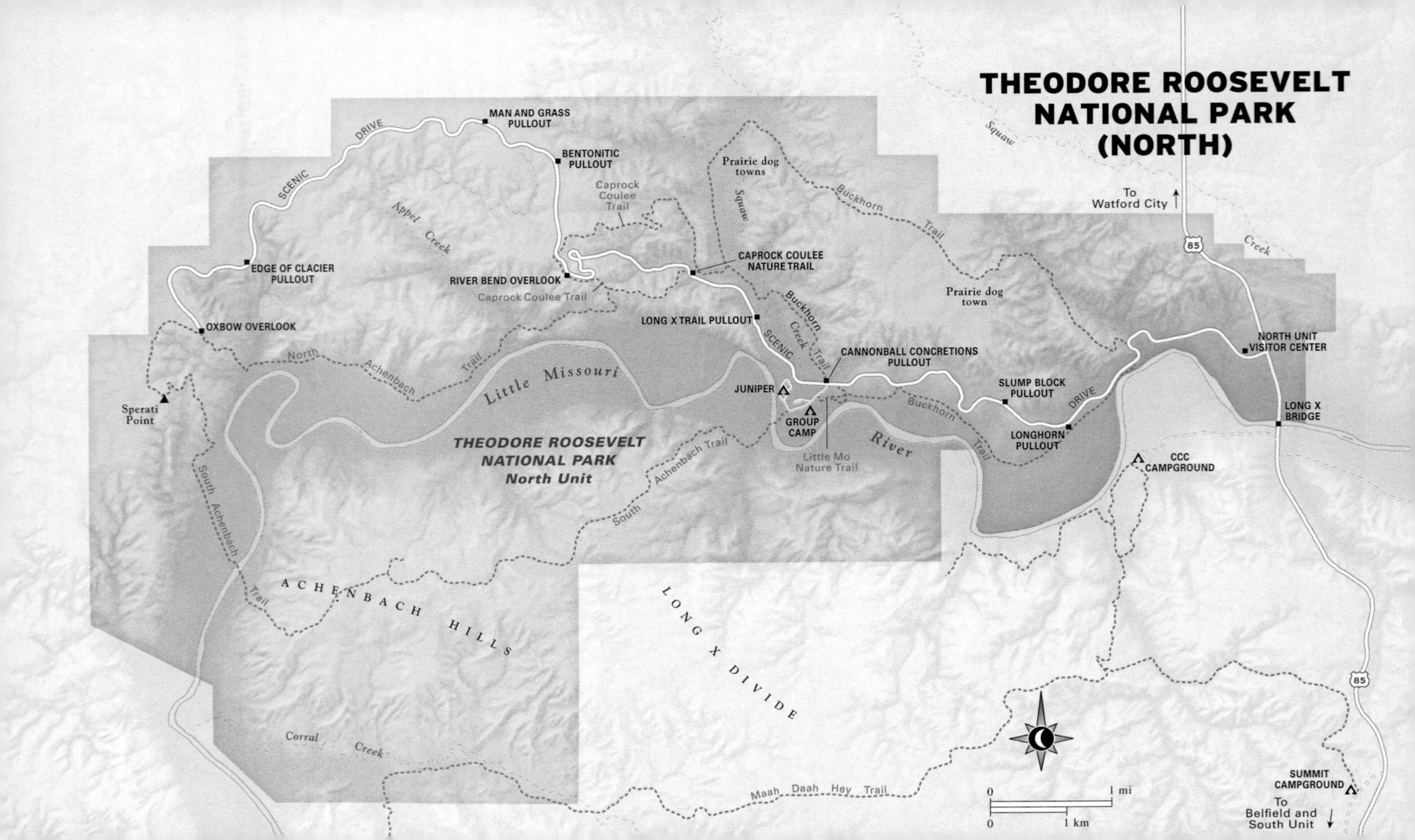

THEODORE ROOSEVELT NATIONAL PARK (NORTH)

Squaw

Creek

To Watford City

85

NORTH UNIT VISITOR CENTER

LONG X BRIDGE

85

SUMMIT CAMPGROUND

To Belfield and South Unit

CCC CAMPGROUND

Prairie dog town

SCENIC DRIVE

SLUMP BLOCK PULLOUT

LONGHORN PULLOUT

CANNONBALL CONCRETIONS PULLOUT

Buckhorn Trail

River

Buckhorn

Trail

Little Mo Nature Trail

Prairie dog towns

Squaw

CAPROCK COULEE NATURE TRAIL

Buckhorn

Creek Trail

SCENIC

GROUP CAMP

JUNIPER

Caprock Coulee Trail

Caprock Coulee Trail

BENTONITIC PULLOUT

MAN AND GRASS PULLOUT

RIVER BEND OVERLOOK

Little Missouri

THEODORE ROOSEVELT NATIONAL PARK North Unit

South Achenbach Trail

Achenbach Trail

LONG X DIVIDE

Maah Daah Hey Trail

ACHENBACH HILLS

Appel Creek

EDGE OF GLACIER PULLOUT

OXBOW OVERLOOK

SCENIC DRIVE

Achenbach

Trail

North

South Achenbach

Trail

Corral Creek

Sperati Point

1 mi

1 km

0

0

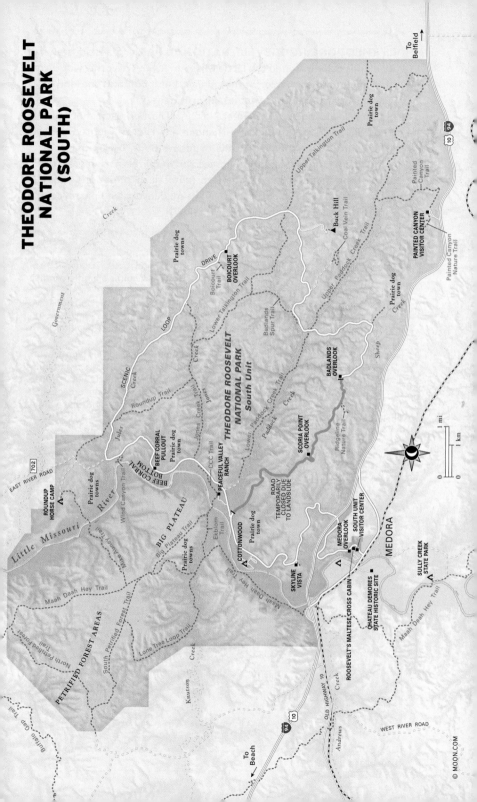

In **THEODORE ROOSEVELT NATIONAL PARK,** grasslands and badlands collide around the Little Missouri River. This otherworldly park might appear barren at first glance, but it contains the kind of raw beauty favored by its namesake president.

These wild lands of the Great Plains still harbor bison, much like they did in the days when the Mandan and Hidatsa hunted here. The wind carries the alarm calls of prairie dogs, broken patches of junipers hide elk, and feral horses thrive on the native grasses. Sandstone and soft clay erode into fantastical formations—hoodoos and pillars with capstones—while mud layers lend pastel colors to bluffs rising from the river.

PLANNING YOUR TIME

Theodore Roosevelt National Park is part of the North Dakota badlands. Three separate parcels make up the park and are linked by the Little Missouri River and the Maah Daah Hey Trail.

The **South Unit** is the most visited and easily accessible, located adjacent to I-94 near the town of Medora. The **North Unit** is 70 miles (113 km) north. The **Elkhorn Ranch Unit** sits between the North and South Units; its remote access requires a high-clearance vehicle.

The North and South Units observe different time zones: the South Unit observes Mountain Time, while the North Unit is in Central Time.

Summer (May-Sept.) is high season, when park services are open and temperatures are warm, though sudden thunderstorms can bring downpours. Winters are bitingly cold and windy. Snow can close park roads.

THEODORE ROOSEVELT'S MALTESE CROSS CABIN

Top ③

1 SEE PAINTED CANYON

PAINTED CANYON

A colorful canyon full of badland erosion is the centerpiece of the South Unit. At Painted Canyon Visitor Center, a paved wheelchair-accessible sidewalk arcs around the rim, garnering panoramic views into the canyon. Lighting for the colors is best in early morning or evening. The **Painted Canyon Nature Trail** (0.9 mi/1.4 km rt, 45 min, moderate) drops into the canyon to see the colorful layers up close. The gated road is open May through October, but you can walk in even when the road is gated.

2 WATCH WILDLIFE

COYOTE

Wildlife-watching in Theodore Roosevelt National Park can rival some of the best parks, with bison, pronghorn, deer, and elk. Prairie dog towns provide places to see the burrowing rodents socialize, scurry for grasses, and chase each other. Since they are the bottom of the food chain, you may also see coyotes or foxes hunting them. Feral or wild horses are one of the biggest attractions, especially in May when you can look at young foals. The North Unit has a herd of longhorn steers as a reminder of the cattle drives that passed through the area in Roosevelt's day. Driving the park roads is the best way to see wildlife; use pullouts for watching rather than stopping in the middle of the road.

3 TOUR THE SOUTH UNIT SCENIC DRIVE

For the best way to see the dramatic badlands, tour the paved South Unit Scenic Drive. Watch for pronghorn, wild horses, and bison on the narrow road with steep, sharp curves and stop at the several **prairie dog towns** that can be noisy with the animals' alarm call barks. Due to a landslide in 2019, the route is an out-and-back tour (30 mi/48 km rt, 2 hrs) rather than a loop. But repairs are underway, with plans to reopen the full loop in late 2024. The route passes multiple interpretive stops.

Views from the **Skyline Vista,** an accessible walkway, take in the Little Missouri River. The renovated **Peaceful Valley Ranch** is the only original remaining ranch house in the South Unit. At **Boicourt Overlook,** another accessible walkway, peer down on rugged eroded waterways that feed the Little Missouri. A spur road goes to the steep trail up **Buck Hill** (0.2 mi/0.3 km rt, 15 min, moderate) to stand at the top of the South Unit.

Best Hike

PETRIFIED FOREST LOOP

DISTANCE: 10.4 miles (16.7 km) round-trip
DURATION: 5-6 hours
ELEVATION CHANGE: 600 feet (183 m)
EFFORT: moderate
TRAILHEAD: Petrified Forest Trailhead

A romp through a badlands wilderness of flat prairie grasslands visits an ancient petrified forest by incorporating several trails in the remote northwest corner of the South Unit. Start the loop on the **North Petrified Forest Trail** to get the tough drops and climbs done early. This trail also has the larger collection of petrified stumps and log chunks on the route. When you meet up with the **Maah Daah Hey Trail** (144 mi/232 km, www.mdhta.com), turn right to traverse grasslands on a short section of this lengthy National Recreation Trail that connects all three units of the park. At the **South Forest Trail,** turn right to see more petrified trees and return to the trailhead. Check with the visitors center for road conditions, drive west on I-94 to exit 23, and follow the signs to Petrified Forest.

Make reservations six months in advance for camping in the South Unit.

ENTRANCES AND FEES

The **South Unit** has two entrances: the main entrance next to the town of Medora and Painted Canyon. The **North Unit** has its own entrance. The **Elkhorn Ranch Unit** has no entrance station.

The entrance fee is $30 per vehicle ($25 motorcycle, $15 individual) and good for seven days. You can **buy your pass online** (www.recreation.gov) from home to speed through entrance stations faster. You can also pay fees at entrance stations during summer or at visitors centers in fall, winter, and spring.

▼ WILD HORSES IN THEODORE ROOSEVELT NATIONAL PARK

THEODORE ROOSEVELT

Theodore Roosevelt traveled to the Dakota Territory in 1883 to hunt bison for two weeks. These rugged badlands took root in his mind, and the landscape captivated him. Before returning to New York, he bought a ranch and a herd of cattle. His ponderosa-pine Maltese Cross Cabin (reconstructed near the South Unit Visitor Center) was part of the ranch and Roosevelt's part-time home as he bounced between New York and the Dakotas. After the deaths of his wife and mother, followed by a heavy political loss, he returned to the ranch intending to quit politics in favor of cattle ranching.

Roosevelt then purchased Elkhorn Ranch to expand his cattle business. In 1884-1885, he hired two men to build the house, barn, and outbuildings. Within two years, a drought coupled with a wickedly cold winter nearly killed off his herd, prompting him to abandon the ranch and return to New York and politics.

Eleven years later, Roosevelt became the 26th president of the United States, attributing his election win to his experiences in North Dakota. He wrote three books on his cowboy life, which formed the backbone for his push for conservation. Roosevelt's legacy includes both good and bad: While he espoused racist values in his policies, he's also known for the establishment of the U.S. Forest Service, the creation of five national parks, and numerous proclamations preserving wildlife reserves, national forests, national monuments, and antiquities.

VISITORS CENTERS

The **South Unit Visitor Center** (8am-5pm daily summer, 8:30am-4pm Fri.-Mon. fall-spring) has a museum with exhibits on geology and history, a bookstore, and restrooms. Ranger-led talks, walks, hikes, and campfire programs are scheduled in June-mid-September. Rangers lead tours of Theodore Roosevelt's **Maltese Cross Cabin** (daily summer) a restored icon from his years in the badlands that was moved here. The **Dakota Nights Astronomy Festival** takes place in early September and offers stargazing with astronomers and rangers.

Farther east in the South Unit is the **Painted Canyon Visitor Center** (8:30am-5pm daily May-Oct.), which has indoor exhibits, a bookstore, hiking trails, and an outdoor overlook with panoramic views of the badlands. Bison frequent the area. The center is off exit 32 of I-94.

The **North Unit Visitor Center** (9am-5pm daily summer, 8:30am-4pm Fri.-Mon. Nov.-Mar.) is housed in temporary trailers at the North Unit entrance. The information desk can advise on current trail conditions. Restrooms and a gift shop are available.

SCENIC DRIVES
ELKHORN RANCH

Theodore Roosevelt had the **Elkhorn Ranch** built in 1884-1885 on land sliced by the Little Missouri River. He abandoned the dwelling two years after losing nearly all his livestock to brutal weather. Today, only stones marking the foundations remain, yet you can still get a sense of the quietude the president enjoyed while ranching in the Dakota Territory.

The Elkhorn Ranch Unit sits north of the South Unit. To get there, take exit 23 off I-94 and drive 35 miles (56 km, 90 min) along the rough gravel road. A high-clearance 4WD vehicle is required. Check first with the visitors center for road conditions and detailed directions.

NORTH UNIT

From the North Unit entrance station, cruise along the 28-mile (45-km) paved and scenic drive with interpretive stops at several overlooks of the Little Missouri. **River Bend,** at the halfway point, and **Oxbow Overlook,** at the road's terminus, are the best places to soak in the views. En route, watch for the herd of **longhorn steers,** maintained by the park, and other wildlife. For a geologic oddity, stop at **Cannonball Concretions Pullout,** where large round rocks are exposed by erosion.

HIKING
SOUTH UNIT

Three trails take off from the South Unit Scenic Drive. The **Wind Canyon Trail** (0.4 mi/0.6 km rt, 20 min, easy) ascends on an uneven trail with steps past a wind-sculpted canyon for views of the Little Missouri, a perfect sunset spot.

The **Coal Vein Trail** (0.8 mi/1.3 km rt, 30-45 min, moderate) is the best way to learn the geology of the badlands—you'll see clay layers, caprocks, slumping, and chimneys. Pick up an interpretive brochure at the trailhead.

Short but steep, the **Ridgeline Trail** (0.6 mi/1 km rt, 30 min, moderate) takes in colorful badlands, grasslands, and bison, with birds and wildflowers in spring. Pick up a nature guide at the trailhead.

NORTH UNIT

Little Mo Trail (0.7-1.1 mi/1.1-1.8 km, 30-45 min, easy) explores the river habitat along the Little Missouri River.

The **Caprock Coulee Nature Trail** (1.5 mi/2.4 km rt, 1 hr, moderate) explores badlands features such as coulees, erosions, and petrified wood. Pick up an interpretive brochure at the trailhead. From the same trailhead, follow a portion of the **Buckhorn Trail** (1.5 mi/2.4 km rt, 1 hr, moderate) to a prairie dog town where you can watch the antics of these furry ground dwellers.

WHERE TO STAY
INSIDE THE PARK

There are no accommodations or restaurants in the park. Camping is the only overnight option.

Two **campgrounds** (year-round, $14) flanking the Little Missouri River have drinking water and flush toilets in summer with reduced services and fees in winter. Campsites are mostly first come, first served; however,

▼ CANNONBALL CONCRETIONS

OXBOW OVERLOOK

reservations (877/444-6777, www.recreation.gov) are available in summer at Cottonwood Campground (6 months in advance for May-Sept) and group campsites at Juniper Campground (12 months in advance year-round). The South Unit's **Cottonwood Campground** has 76 sites. The North Unit's **Juniper Campground** has 50 sites.

Backcountry camping is allowed with a free **permit** available from the visitors centers. There are no established backcountry campsites.

OUTSIDE THE PARK

The closest accommodations and services are located near the South Unit in **Medora.**

GETTING THERE AND AROUND

AIR

The nearest airport is in **Bismarck** (BIS, 2301 University Dr., 701/355-1808, www.bismarckairport.com), 134 miles (216 km) east of the South Unit via I-94. The airport has rental cars.

CAR

There is no public transportation to or within the park. Visiting the park will require a car with long drives between the three units.

To reach the **South Unit,** take I-94 (exit 24 or 27) to the town of Medora and the South Unit Visitor Center. Use exit 32 (7 mi/11 km east of Medora) to reach the Painted Canyon Visitor Center.

From Medora, it's a 70-mile (113-km) drive to the **North Unit.** From I-94 at Belfield, take exit 27 to ND 85.

To reach the **Elkhorn Ranch Unit,** you'll need a high-clearance, 4WD vehicle for the rough gravel road. Obtain road conditions and directions from the visitors centers. From Medora, the drive takes 1.5 hours.

SIGHTS NEARBY

Knife River Indian Villages National Historic Site (564 County Rd. 37, Stanton, 701/745-3300, www.nps.gov/knri, 9am-5pm daily late May-early Sept., 8am-4:30pm daily mid-Sept.-mid-May) is home to a reconstructed earthen lodge, with trails through the Mandan and Hidatsa village site.

GREAT LAKES
AND
NORTHEAST

Along the boulder-strewn shores of Maine lies the only national park in the northeastern United States: Acadia National Park. Watch the sun rise from Cadillac Mountain, stroll the Park Loop Road, and ride the carriage roads at this East Coast gem.

The Great Lakes region is home to three national parks. In Ohio, Cuyahoga Valley contains river canals of historic import. In Indiana, the southern shore of Lake Michigan is home to Indiana Dunes National Park. In Michigan, a cluster of islands in Lake Superior forms Isle Royale National Park. Tucked into a corner of Minnesota is the remote Voyageurs, a haven for boaters.

◄ SUNRISE FROM CADILLAC MOUNTAIN, ACADIA NATIONAL PARK

The National Parks of
THE GREAT LAKES AND NORTHEAST

ACADIA, ME

Drama comes from mountains tumbling to the sea and ocean waves crashing upon granite ledges, while serene lakes provide pastoral alternatives (page 560).

CUYAHOGA VALLEY, OH

Canals and a scenic railway cut through a lush countryside of forests, wetlands, and prairies (page 576).

INDIANA DUNES, IN

Sand dunes flanking the southern beaches of Lake Michigan collide with forest, prairie, and marsh habitats for huge diversity (page 585).

ISLE ROYALE, MI

Seasonal boat tours guide visitors to this isolated archipelago in Lake Superior, prime habitat for wolves and moose (page 593).

VOYAGEURS, MN

Remote forests, 660 miles (1,060 km) of wild shoreline, and more than 500 islands are found in this water-filled park (page 600).

1: JORDAN POND, ACADIA NATIONAL PARK
2: DUELING BULL MOOSE, ISLE ROYALE NATIONAL PARK
3: LEDGES LOOP TRAIL, CUYAHOGA VALLEY

Best OF THE PARKS

Jordan Pond House: Sip afternoon tea at this rustic 19th-century teahouse (page 565).

Kettle Falls Hotel: Grab a meal or a drink at this historic lodge that's only accessible by water (page 604).

Canoeing and Kayaking: Paddle miles of shoreline waters at Isle Royale (page 597).

Ohio and Erie Canal Towpath Trail: Bike along the Cuyahoga River on this historic path (page 579).

Cuyahoga Valley Scenic Railroad: Take a scenic train ride that runs through Ohio's only national park (page 579).

▲ PADDLE VOYAGEURS' WATERS.

PLANNING YOUR TRIP

Plan at least **one weekend** in Acadia and **another week or two** to tour the national parks of the Great Lakes. Make lodging and campground **reservations** up to one year in advance.

September-mid-October is the best time to travel in Maine. Days are warm and mostly dry, nights are cool, fog is rare, bugs are gone, and crowds are few. Foliage turns by early October, usually reaching peak colors mid-month.

Summer (May-Oct.) is the most popular time to visit the Great Lakes, for beach fun, kayaking, and boating. The weather is temperate with long, lingering evenings. July is typically the warmest month, but it's also the buggiest. Time a camping trip in mid-June or after mid-August, when the mosquitoes and blackflies are less bothersome.

Fall is the best time to visit Cuyahoga, when one can savor the vibrant fall foliage and crisp dry air. Hiking and biking trails are available spring through fall.

Touring the Great Lakes

VOYAGEURS AND ISLE ROYALE

You can hit these two remote national parks in **one week.** Fly into **Minneapolis-St. Paul International Airport** and then rent a car for the drive to the parks. You will also need to travel by boat to explore these parks, which are prime destinations for paddlers.

Voyageurs

310 miles (500 km) / 5 hours
From Minneapolis-St. Paul, drive north on I-35 to reach the **Rainy Lake Visitor Center.** Spend three days in **Voyageurs National Park.** Take a boat tour to either **Little American Island** or **Kettle Falls,** then get out on the water yourself in a canoe or kayak.

VOYAGEURS NATIONAL PARK

Isle Royale

275 miles (445 km) / 5 hours
From Voyageurs, drive southeast on US 53 to **Grand Portage** on Lake Superior, the back door to **Isle Royale.** Catch the passenger ferry to **Rock Harbor** and rent a kayak to spend three days paddling the waters around Isle Royale.

From Grand Portage, paddlers can extend their adventures with a side trip to tour the remote **Boundary Waters Canoe Area Wilderness.** This paddling paradise is 66 miles (106 km, 1.75 hrs) southwest from Grand Portage. Take I-35 south to head back to Minneapolis-St. Paul.

0   50 mi
0   50 km

Voyageurs NP

310 MILES
5 HOURS

275 MILES
5 HOURS

Isle Royale NP

Lake Superior

MINNESOTA

MICHIGAN

WISCONSIN

Lake Michigan

St Paul
Minneapolis

© MOON.COM

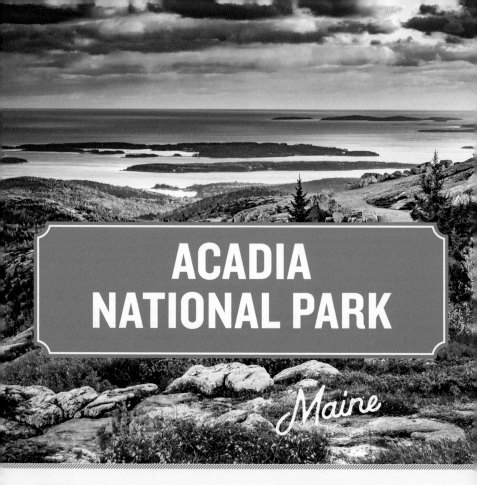

ACADIA
NATIONAL PARK

Maine

WEBSITE:
www.nps.gov/acad

PHONE NUMBER:
207/288-3338

VISITATION RANK:
6

WHY GO:
Travel the rugged
northeast island
seacoast.

KEEPSAKE STAMPS ▼▼▼

▲ CADILLAC MOUNTAIN, ACADIA
NATIONAL PARK

ACADIA NATIONAL PARK extends its reach here and there, like an octopus, sprawling over half of Mount Desert Island. The first national park east of the Mississippi River and the only national park in the northeastern United States, it was created from donated parcels—a big chunk here, a tiny piece there—and slowly fused into its present-day shape.

The park tops out at the pink granite of Cadillac Mountain, the highest point on the East Coast, which is sacred to the Wabanaki peoples who have called this region home for thousands of years—as are the park's mountains, lakes, ponds, and tide pools. Today, even at the height of summer, when the whole world seems to have arrived, it's possible to find peaceful niches and less trodden paths.

PLANNING YOUR TIME

Acadia National Park sits on the Maine coast south of Bangor. Mount Desert Island is the most accessible of the park's watery isles; the Schoodic Peninsula and Isle au Haut require time to explore and are best reached via boat or ferry.

You can circumnavigate Mount Desert Island in one day, hitting the highlights along the Park Loop Road with just enough time to ooh and aah at each. But to truly appreciate Acadia, you must hike the trails, ride the carriage roads, get afloat on a whale-watching cruise or a sea kayak, visit museums, and explore an offshore island or two. A week or longer is best, but you can get a taste of Acadia in 3-4 days.

The region is very seasonal, with most restaurants, accommodations, and shops open **May-October.** Get advance reservations to drive up Cadillac Mountain for sunrise or daytime. May and June bring spring, but also mosquitoes, blackflies, and temperamental weather—sunny and hot one day, damp and cold the next. July and August are summer at its best, but also bring the biggest crowds. September is a gem of a time to visit: few bugs, fewer people, less fog, and autumn's golden light.

Foliage usually begins turning in **early October,** making it an especially beautiful time to visit (weekends spike with visitors). Winter is Acadia's silent season, with several roads closed due to snow.

ENTRANCES AND FEES

The main park entrance is **ME 3** through Ellsworth to Mount Desert Island. ME 3 continues southeast, passing through the **Hulls Cove Entrance** to the gateway town of Bar Harbor and the **Cadillac Mountain Entrance.**

The entrance fee is $30 per vehicle ($25 motorcycle, $15 individual) and good for seven days. You can **buy your pass online** (www.recreation.gov) from home. During peak season, **timed reservations** (www.recreation.gov, late May-late Oct., $6/vehicle) are required to drive **Cadillac Mountain Road.** Reservations are released 90 days and 2 days in advance.

VISITORS CENTERS
Hulls Cove Visitor Center

Reached by climbing 52 steps (and with accessible access too), the modern **Hulls Cove Visitor Center** (25 Visitor Center Rd., Bar Harbor, 8:30am-4:30pm daily May-late June and Sept.-mid-Oct., 8am-6pm daily late June-mid-Oct.) has digital information kiosks, a large relief map of the park, and a bookstore. Pick up schedules for ranger programs and the Island Explorer shuttle bus.

In winter, when the Hulls Cove Visitor Center is closed, National Park Service rangers move visitor information

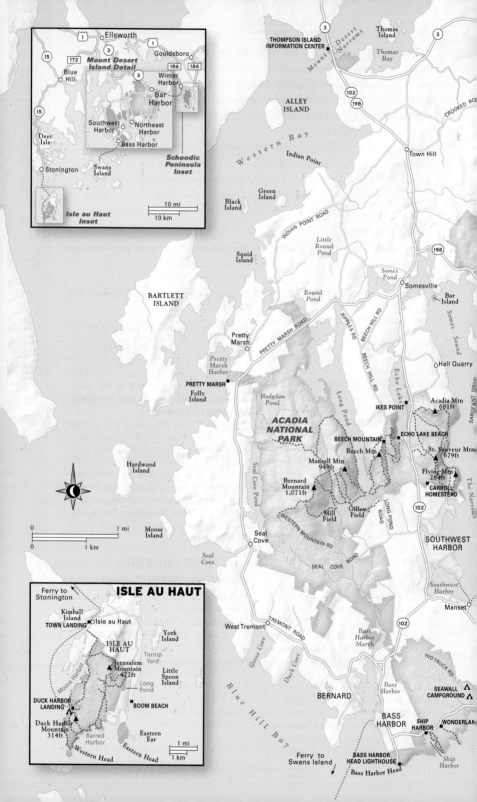

Inset: Mount Desert Island Detail

Ellsworth
Gouldsboro
Blue Hill
Winter Harbor
Mount Desert Island Detail
Bar Harbor
Southwest Harbor
Northeast Harbor
Bass Harbor
Schoodic Peninsula Inset
Deer Isle
Stonington
Swans Island
Isle au Haut Inset

10 mi
10 km

Main map labels

THOMPSON ISLAND INFORMATION CENTER
Thomas Island
Thomas Bay
Mount Desert Narrows
CROOKED RO
ALLEY ISLAND
Town Hill
Indian Point
Western Bay
INDIAN POINT ROAD
Little Round Pond
Somes Pond
Somesville
Bar Island
Black Island
Green Island
Squid Island
Round Pond
Hall Quarry
BARTLETT ISLAND
Pretty Marsh
Pretty Marsh Harbor
PRETTY MARSH ROAD
RUPLES RD
BEECH HILL RD
Echo Lake
SARGENT Drive
PRETTY MARSH
Folly Island
Hodgdon Pond
IKES POINT
Acadia Mtn 681ft
Hardwood Island
Pretty Marsh Harbor
Long Pond
BEECH MOUNTAIN
Beech Mtn
ECHO LAKE BEACH
St. Sauveur Mtn 679ft
Mansell Mtn 949ft
Flying Mtn 284ft
CARROLL HOMESTEAD
Bernard Mountain 1,071ft
Seal Cove Pond
The Narrows
Mill Field
Gilley Field
LONG POND ROAD
102
Moose Island
WESTERN MOUNTAIN RD
SOUTHWEST HARBOR
Seal Cove
Seal Cove
Southwest Harbor
Manset
SEAL COVE ROAD
West Tremont
TREMONT ROAD
Bass Harbor Marsh
102
HIO TRUCK RD
Goose Cove
Duck Cove
BERNARD
Bass Harbor
Blue Hill Bay
SEAWALL CAMPGROUND
BASS HARBOR
SHIP HARBOR
WONDERLAN
Ferry to Swans Island
BASS HARBOR HEAD LIGHTHOUSE
Bass Harbor Head
Ship Harbor

ISLE AU HAUT Inset

Ferry to Stonington
Kimball Island
TOWN LANDING
Isle au Haut
York Island
ISLE AU HAUT
Turnip Yard
Little Spoon Island
Moore Harbor
Jerusalem Mountain 472ft
Long Pond
DUCK HARBOR LANDING
BOOM BEACH
Duck Harbor Mountain 314ft
Barred Harbor
Eastern Ear
Western Head
Eastern Head

1 mi
1 km

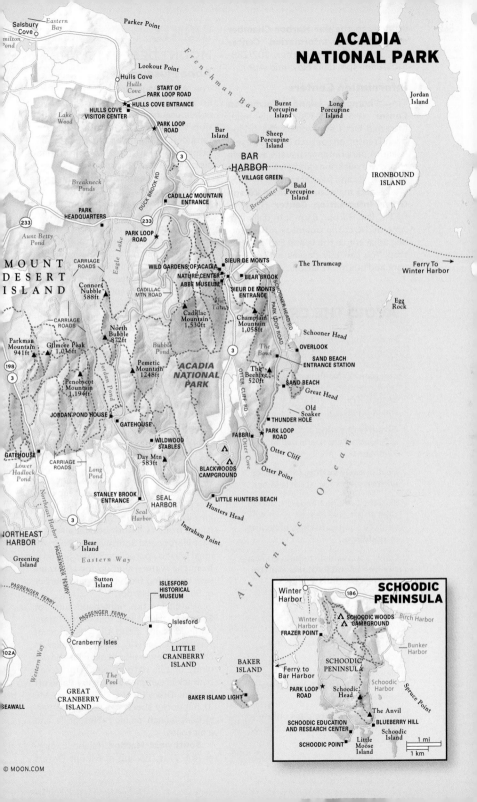

ACADIA NATIONAL PARK

Salsbury Cove
Eastern Bay
milton Pond
Parker Point
Lookout Point
Hulls Cove
Frenchman Bay
START OF PARK LOOP ROAD
HULLS COVE ENTRANCE
HULLS COVE VISITOR CENTER
PARK LOOP ROAD
Lake Wood
Breakneck Ponds
Bar Island
Burnt Porcupine Island
Long Porcupine Island
Jordan Island
3
Sheep Porcupine Island
BAR HARBOR
VILLAGE GREEN
IRONBOUND ISLAND
PARK HEADQUARTERS
233
233
DUCK BROOK RD
CADILLAC MOUNTAIN ENTRANCE
Bald Porcupine Island
Breakwater
Aunt Betty Pond
PARK LOOP ROAD
The Thrumcap
Ferry To Winter Harbor

MOUNT DESERT ISLAND
CARRIAGE ROADS
Eagle Lake
WILD GARDENS OF ACADIA
NATURE CENTER
ABBE MUSEUM
SIEUR DE MONTS
BEAR BROOK
SIEUR DE MONTS ENTRANCE
Egg Rock
Connors Nubble 588ft
CADILLAC MTN ROAD
The Tarn
CARRIAGE ROADS
North Bubble 872ft
Cadillac Mountain 1,530ft
Champlain Mountain 1,058ft
Schooner Head
OVERLOOK
SCHOONER HEAD RD
PARK LOOP ROAD
Parkman Mountain 941ft
Gilmore Peak 1,036ft
Bubble Pond
198
3
Penobscot Mountain 1,194ft
Jordan Pond
Pemetic Mountain 1248ft
ACADIA NATIONAL PARK
3
The Bowl
The Beehive 520ft
SAND BEACH ENTRANCE STATION
SAND BEACH
Great Head
JORDAN POND HOUSE
GATEHOUSE
WILDWOOD STABLES
Old Soaker
THUNDER HOLE
OTTER CLIFF RD
GATEHOUSE
Lower Hadlock Pond
CARRIAGE ROADS
Long Pond
Day Mtn 583ft
FABBRI
PARK LOOP ROAD
Otter Cliff
BLACKWOODS CAMPGROUND
Otter Cove
Otter Point
102A
STANLEY BROOK ENTRANCE
SEAL HARBOR
LITTLE HUNTERS BEACH
Seal Harbor
Hunters Head
3
NORTHEAST HARBOR
PASSENGER FERRY
Bear Island
Eastern Way
Ingraham Point
Greening Island
Sutton Island
ISLESFORD HISTORICAL MUSEUM
PASSENGER FERRY
Islesford
Cranberry Isles
LITTLE CRANBERRY ISLAND
BAKER ISLAND
Western Way
The Pool
GREAT CRANBERRY ISLAND
BAKER ISLAND LIGHT
SEAWALL

SCHOODIC PENINSULA

Winter Harbor
186
Winter Harbor
SCHOODIC WOODS CAMPGROUND
Birch Harbor
FRAZER POINT
Bunker Harbor
SCHOODIC PENINSULA
Ferry to Bar Harbor
PARK LOOP ROAD
Schoodic Head
Schoodic Harbor
Spruce Point
The Anvil
BLUEBERRY HILL
SCHOODIC EDUCATION AND RESEARCH CENTER
Little Moose Island
Schoodic Island
SCHOODIC POINT
1 mi
1 km

© MOON.COM

services to the **Bar Harbor Chamber of Commerce Information Center** (2 Cottage St., Bar Harbor, 207/288-5103, 8am-4pm daily Nov.-mid-Apr.).

Information Centers

Tiny **Thompson Island Information Center** (8:30am-5:30pm daily mid-May-mid-Oct.) sits across the bridge from Trenton en route to Mount Desert Island. A park ranger is usually available to answer questions and give advice on hiking trails and park activities.

The park maintains the small **Village Green Information Center** (19 Firefly Ln., Bar Harbor, 8am-5pm daily late June-mid-Oct.) in downtown Bar Harbor, adjacent to the Island Explorer bus stop. You can buy passes and pick up park and bus information.

AVOID THE CROWDS

From May to October, Acadia seems to be loved to death. Long lines of cars clog the entrances, and parking lots overflow. At peak times, rangers temporarily restrict access. Try these tactics to avoid the congestion:

Go early morning or late in the afternoon. Park roads usually fill 9am-4pm.

Visit in **early spring, late fall,** or **winter,** when visitation is lower.

Skip the parking headache and take an off-the-beaten-path adventure such as **hiking, bicycling,** or **paddling.**

Leave your vehicle behind and take the free **Island Explorer shuttle bus** into the park.

Bicycle or hike the carriage roads, where cars are not permitted.

Go after dark for **stargazing.**

Instead of heading to Cadillac Mountain for sunrise or sunset, catch **sunrise on Ocean Drive** or sunset from a boat.

Buy your **entrance pass online** to get through the entrance station quickly.

SIGHTS

MOUNT DESERT ISLAND

Abbe Museum

The **Abbe Museum** (26 Mount Desert St., Bar Harbor, 207/288-3519, www.abbemuseum.org) is a superb introduction to prehistoric, historic, and contemporary Indigenous tools, crafts, and other cultural artifacts, with an emphasis on Maine's Wabanaki peoples.

The **main campus** (26 Mount Desert St., Bar Harbor, 207/288-3519, www.abbemuseum.org, 10am-5pm daily May-Oct., 10am-4pm Thurs.-Sat. Nov.-Apr., $10 adults, $5 ages 11-17) is home to a collection spanning nearly 12,000 years. Admission to the main campus also includes admission to the **museum's original site** (Sieur de Monts Spring, 2.5 mi/4 km south of Bar Harbor, 9am-5pm daily May-Oct., closed winter, $3 adults, $1 children), a small but handsome building that displays a 50,000-item collection.

Take the time to wander the paths in the adjacent **Wild Gardens of Acadia,** a 0.75-acre (0.3-ha) microcosm of more than 300 plant species native to Mount Desert Island.

Somes Sound

From the northern end of Mount Desert Island heading south toward Northeast Harbor on ME 198, cliff-lined Somes Sound appears to the right. The glacier-sculpted fjard (not as deep or as steeply walled as a fjord) juts 5 miles (8 km) into the interior of Mount Desert Island from its mouth between Northeast Harbor and Southwest Harbor. An ideal way to appreciate Somes Sound is from the water—sign up for an excursion departing from Northeast Harbor or Southwest Harbor.

Watch for the right-hand turn for **Sargent Drive,** and follow the granite-lined route along the east side of the sound. Halfway along, a marker at one of the few pullouts explains the geology of this natural inlet. Traffic can be thick in summer. **Suminsby Park,** off Sargent Drive (400 ft/122 m from ME 3), has rocky shore access, a hand-carry boat launch, picnic tables, grills, and a pit toilet.

Southwest Harbor (Island Explorer Rte. 7) is the hub of Mount Desert

Top ③

① DRIVE THE PARK LOOP ROAD

ACADIA'S PARK LOOP ROAD

On Desert Island, the 27-mile (43-km) **Park Loop Road** (mid-Apr.-Nov., Island Explorer Rte. 3 and Rte. 4) takes in most of the big-ticket sights. Part of the route is one-way, so you'll drive the loop clockwise. From the **Hulls Cove Visitor Center,** the road winds past several of the park's scenic highlights, ascending to the summit of **Cadillac Mountain** with overlooks to magnificent vistas. Along the way are trailheads and overlooks: **Sieur de Monts Spring, Sand Beach, Thunder Hole, Otter Cliff, Fabbri Picnic Area, Jordan Pond House, Bubble Pond,** and **Eagle Lake.**

② SIP AFTERNOON TEA AT JORDAN POND HOUSE

The **Jordan Pond House** (Island Explorer Rte. 5, 2928 Park Loop Rd., 207/276-3316, www.jordanpondhouse.com, 11am-9pm daily) is a modern facility in an idyllic waterside setting. Jordan Pond House began life as a rustic 19th-century teahouse; old photos still line the walls of the current incarnation, which was built after a disastrous fire in 1979. Afternoon tea is still a tradition, with tea, popovers, and strawberry jam served on the lawn until 5pm daily in summer, weather permitting. Expect to wait for seats at the height of summer.

③ TOUR THE CARRIAGE ROADS ON MOUNT DESERT ISLAND

RIDE A HORSE-DRAWN CARRIAGE ON ACADIA'S CARRIAGE ROADS.

In 1913, John D. Rockefeller Jr. began laying out what eventually became a 57-mile (92-km) carriage road system. Motorized vehicles have never been allowed on these lovely graded byways, making them real escapes from the auto world. Devoted now to multiple uses, the "Rockefeller roads" see hikers, bikers, baby strollers, wheelchairs, and even horse-drawn carriages. Rangers guide summer biking and walking tours on the carriage roads, which you can reach via the Island Explorer Routes 5 and 6.

To recapture the early carriage roads era, take one of the horse-drawn open-carriage tours from **Carriages of Acadia** (Wildwood Stables, Park Loop Rd., Seal Harbor, 877/276-3622, www.acadiahorses.com), south of Jordan Pond House. One- and two-hour tours run multiple times daily (mid-June-mid-Oct.). Make reservations, especially in summer.

ONE DAY IN ACADIA

Drive or take the Island Explorer Rt. 4 to tour the **Park Loop Road.** To get a broad view of the mountain-and-island environment, stop at the summit of **Cadillac Mountain.** Stroll the nature trail at **Jordan Pond,** and enjoy afternoon tea at **Jordan Pond House.** Then, tour the museum and paths at **Sieur de Monts Spring.**

With more time, you can hike the Beehive Trail or Precipice Trail, take a boat tour, bike the carriage roads, and explore remote Schoodic Point.

Island's "quiet side." In summer, its tiny downtown district is the island's busiest spot west of Somes Sound.

Bass Harbor Head Lighthouse

At the southern end of Mount Desert, follow ME 102A to the turnoff toward Bass Harbor Head. Drive or bike to the end of Lighthouse Road, walk down a steep wooden stairway, and look up and to the right. **Bass Harbor Head Lighthouse**—its red glow automated since 1974—stands sentinel at the eastern entrance to Blue Hill Bay. Built in 1858, the 26-foot (8-m) tower and lightkeeper's house are privately owned, but the dramatic setting captivates photographers.

Cadillac Mountain

The sunrise awaits those who can drive predawn to the summit of **Cadillac Mountain.** It's a tradition to catch the first rays to hit the eastern United States from Acadia's highest point. (You can also watch the sunrise from Ocean Drive.) Sunset fans also admire the colors across the western horizon.

The **Cadillac Summit Road** (3 mi/4.8 km) does not allow RVs or trailers. All vehicles must have a **reservation** (www.recreation.gov, mid-May-mid-Oct., $6) for either **sunrise** (good for 7 days) or **daytime** (good for one day, through sunset). Reservations launch in two waves: 90 days in advance and 2 days in advance of each date.

Cadillac Mountain also hosts the annual **Acadia Night Sky Festival** (late Sept.) for telescope-viewing of stars and celestial wonders.

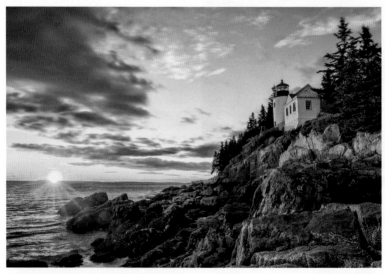

BASS HARBOR HEAD LIGHTHOUSE

SCHOODIC PENINSULA

SCHOODIC PENINSULA

On the mainland, the **Schoodic Peninsula** (Island Explorer Rte. 8) is separated from Mount Desert Island by a two-hour drive. The lack of congestion, even at the height of summer, is the main appeal for a visit to the eastern side of Frenchman Bay. The Schoodic Peninsula also has abundant opportunities for outdoor recreation, two scenic byways, and dozens of artist and artisan studios in unchanged villages. But the biggest attractions are the spectacular vistas of offshore lighthouses, distant mountains, and close-in islands.

To reach the park boundary from ME 1 in Gouldsboro, take ME 186 south to Winter Harbor. Continue through town, heading east, and then turn right and continue to the park.

Winter Harbor

Winter Harbor, known as the gateway to Schoodic, is home to an old-money, low-profile, Philadelphia-linked summer colony on exclusive Grindstone Neck. The landscape of the smaller and far less touristed Schoodic isn't as awe-inspiring as that on Mount Desert, but it has a remoter, rawer edge. Too-frequent fog rolls in to shroud the stunted, scraggly spruce clinging to its pink granite shores. There's a campground and visitors center, along with **carriage roads** for foot or bicycle exploration.

Scenic Drive

The **Schoodic Peninsula Loop** (6 mi/10 km one-way) meanders counterclockwise around the tip of the Schoodic Peninsula. You'll discover picnic areas, trailheads, offshore lighthouses, a welcome center with exhibits, and small turnouts with scenic vistas. Do this loop early in the morning or later in the afternoon. The gorgeous late September-early October foliage increases traffic. If you see a viewpoint you like with room to pull off, stop; it's a long way around to return.

Near the southern end of the loop, a short two-way road goes to **Schoodic Point,** the highlight of the drive, where surf crashes onto big slabs of pink granite. The campus of the **Schoodic Institute** (207/288-1310, www.schoodicinstitute.org), on the site of a former top-secret U.S. Navy base, is housed in the restored **Rockefeller Hall** (9 Atterbury Circle, 10am-5pm daily June-mid-Oct., 10am-5pm Mon.-Fri. winter). It has a small info center staffed by volunteers and park rangers. Exhibits highlight Schoodic's ecology and history, the former Navy base's radio and cryptologic operations, and current research programs. The institute offers ranger-led activities, lectures, and other programs and events.

On the south end of the loop, you'll spot **Little Moose Island,** accessible at low tide. At **Blueberry Hill,** a moor-like setting with low growth allows almost 180-degree views of the bay and islands.

ISLE AU HAUT

The Isle au Haut section of the park sees only 5,000-7,500 visitors annually, with a daily cap of 128. The limited boat service, remoteness of the island, and scarcity of campsites contribute to the low count, leaving the trails and views for only a few hardy souls. The **ranger station** (207/288-3338) has trail maps, information, and the only public facilities.

HIKING
MOUNT DESERT ISLAND
Jordan Pond

The **Jordan Pond Path** (3.3 mi/5.3 km rt, 1.5 hrs, easy) starts from the Jordan Pond parking area and leads through woods and down to the pond to follow the shore before looping back.

Champlain Mountain

Near Sieur de Monts Spring, the **Champlain North Ridge Trail** (Bear Brook Trail, 1.9 mi/3.1 km rt, 2-3 hrs, strenuous) bolts up a steep ascent through pines and granite to Champlain Mountain. The summit yields views of the ocean, islands, Schoodic Peninsula, and Bar Harbor. (Combine this trail with the Precipice and Beechcroft Trails for more distance.)

From the Park Loop Road, the **Precipice Trail** (3.2-mi/5.2-km loop, 3 hrs, strenuous, closed mid-Apr.-mid-Aug.) lures hordes of wannabe climbers to its steep but nontechnical 1,072-foot (327-m) ascent of switchbacks, ladders, and exposed ledges to reach the summit. Return via the Champlain North Ridge Trail and Orange and Black Path.

The **Beachcroft Trail** (2 mi/3.2 km rt, 2-3 hrs, moderately strenuous) is known for its 1,500 beautifully

▾ VIEW OVER JORDAN POND

Best Hike

BEEHIVE LOOP

DISTANCE: 3.2 miles (5.2 km) round-trip
DURATION: 1-2 hours
ELEVATION CHANGE: 450 feet (137 m)
EFFORT: moderately strenuous
TRAILHEAD: Bowl Trailhead on Park Loop Road across from Sand Beach

The sometimes crowded **Beehive Trail** starts and ends on the **Bowl Trail,** which those needing less of a challenge can use to reach the bee-hive-shaped summit, minus the climbing option. Not for acrophobes or tiny kids, the climbing option is a fun scramble (no technical rock-climbing skills needed) with switchbacks, stone steps, handrails, and iron ladders. Ascending the Beehive's southern face, the steep exposed route picks its way up smoothed granite to Beehive summit for views of beaches and bays. When the route crowds with hikers, you may have to wait at the obstacles. From the summit, return via the Bowl Trail, which descends past Bowl Lake.

engineered granite steps. The route gains 1,100 feet (335 m) over Huguenot Head to the summit of Champlain Mountain.

Sand Beach

From the east end of Sand Beach, the **Great Head Trail** (1.9-mi/3-km loop, 1 hr, moderate) circles a headland with views of the ocean, tide pools, and the Beehive.

Gorham Mountain

From Gorham Mountain parking lot, the **Gorham Mountain Trail** (3.5 mi/5.6 km rt, 2 hrs, moderate) shoots up a mountainside to follow cairns across rock ledges to the summit of Acadia's third-highest mountain, with big terrestrial and ocean views.

For an added challenge, detour via **Cadillac Cliffs,** an alternate route paralleling a portion of the Gorham Mountain Trail. Climb the granite stairs and walk under two rock slab tunnels before linking up with the main trail again. For a longer hike, combine this trail with the Bowl Trail and Ocean Path to return to your car.

Bass Harbor

From the Ship Harbor Trailhead, a figure-eight loop makes up the **Ship Harbor Trail** (1.8 mi/2.9 km rt, 45 min, easy). The trail tours the forest to the ocean, where low tides beg for exploring tide pools.

From a mile west of Seawall Campground, the **Wonderland Trail** (1.4 mi/2.3 km rt, 45 min, easy) follows a fire road through a forest of mossy, wind-gnarled trees to a small cobble beach.

Beech Mountain

From the end of Beech Hill Road, climb **Beech Mountain** (1.2 mi/1.9 km rt, 1 hr, moderate) to a fire tower overlooking Echo Lake and the Blue Hill Peninsula.

SCHOODIC PENINSULA

From Blueberry Hill parking lot, trails go to the open ledges on 440-foot-high (134-m) **Schoodic Head** (2.4 mi/3.9 km rt, 1 hr, moderate). Start on the easy Alder Trail to climb through a forest with outstanding bird habitat to reach the Schoodic Trailhead. Turn right to hike the rocky trail to the summit. An alternate route to Schoodic Head goes up the steep and rocky Alder Trail to make a loop (2.3 mi/3.7 km rt, 1 hr, moderate).

ISLE AU HAUT

The most-used park trail is **Duck Harbor Trail** (7.6 mi/12.2 km rt, 4 hrs, moderate), which connects the town landing with Duck Harbor. Though the summit is low, **Duck Harbor Mountain** (2.4 mi/3.9 km rt, 3-4 hrs, strenuous) is the island's toughest trail, loaded with rocks and roots, but rewards with a 360-degree view.

RECREATION

BICYCLING

The best choices for cycling on pavement are the 27-mile (43-km) **Park Loop Road** on Mount Desert Island and the 6-mile (9.7-km) **Schoodic Loop.** Go early or late in the day to avoid the heaviest traffic.

For car-free riding on crushed-rock roads, nearly 45 miles (72 km) of **carriage roads** await on Mount Desert Island and 8.3 miles (13.4 km) on Schoodic Peninsula. Some prohibit bikes, but most are multiuse, with hikers, horses, carriages, and bicycles. Only Class I e-bikes are permitted on them. Find several bike rental shops in Bar Harbor. On Schoodic Peninsula, **Sea Schoodic Kayak and Bike** (8 Duck Pond Rd., Winter Harbor, 833/727-6634, www.seaschoodic.com) rents bicycles. For riding the Mount Desert Island carriage roads, the **Bicycle Express** (late June-Sept., free) runs a bike shuttle between Bar Harbor Village Green and Eagle Lake, and rangers lead frequent summer bike tours.

SWIMMING

Mount Desert Island

Sand Beach (Island Explorer Rte. 3) is Mount Desert Island's biggest sandy beach. Lifeguards are on duty during the summer. The biggest threat can be hypothermia as the saltwater is terminally glacial—in mid-July it still might not reach 60°F (15°C). Avoid the parking lot scramble by taking the shuttle.

The park's most popular freshwater swimming site is **Echo Lake** (Island Explorer Rte. 7), south of Somesville on ME 102. The site is staffed with a lifeguard and can be crowded on hot days.

The eastern shore of **Hodgdon Pond** (also on the western side of the island)

▼ SAND BEACH

EXPLORE LONG POND BY CANOE OR KAYAK.

is accessible by car via Hodgdon Road and Long Pond Fire Road. **Lake Wood,** at the northern end of Mount Desert, has a tiny beach and restrooms. To get to Lake Wood from ME 3, head west on Crooked Road to the unpaved Park Road. Turn left and continue to the parking area. Arrive early on hot days.

Schoodic Peninsula

The best freshwater swimming on the Schoodic Peninsula is at **Jones Beach** (sunrise-sunset daily), a community-owned recreation area on Jones Pond in West Gouldsboro. It has restrooms, a playground, picnic facilities, a boat launch, a swim area with a float, and a small beach. The beach is located at the end of Recreation Road, off ME 195, which is 0.3 mile (0.5 km) south of ME 1.

Isle au Haut

For freshwater swimming on Isle au Haut, head for **Long Pond,** a skinny, 1.5-mile-long (2.4-km) swimming hole on the east side of the island, abutting national parkland. There's a minuscule beach-like area on the southern end with a picnic table and a float.

CANOEING AND KAYAKING

Long Pond (Pretty Marsh Rd.) is the largest lake on Mount Desert Island.

Bring a canoe or kayak to launch at **Pond's End,** to paddle 4 miles (6.4 km) to the southern end of the lake. Another option is to launch your canoe on the quieter, cliff-lined southern end of the lake. To find the put-in, take Seal Cove Road (on the east end of downtown Southwest Harbor) to Long Cove Road. Turn right to enter the small parking area near the pumping station. Almost the entire west side of Long Pond is in Acadia National Park.

If you have a canoe, kayak, or rowboat, you can reach swimming holes in **Seal Cove Pond** and **Round Pond,** both on the western side of Mount Desert. **National Park Canoe & Kayak Rental** (145 Pretty Marsh Rd./Rte. 102, Mount Desert, 207/244-5854, www.nationalparkcanoerental.com, mid-May-mid-Oct.) rents boats; just carry them across the road to Pond's End for launching. Reservations are essential July-August.

Experienced sea kayakers can explore the coastline throughout the **Schoodic Peninsula,** while canoeists can paddle the placid waters of **Jones Pond. Sea Schoodic Kayak and Bike** (8 Duck Pond Rd., Winter Harbor, 833/724-6634, www.seaschoodic.com) has freshwater rental kayaks on Jones Pond.

CLIMBERS PREPARE TO SCALE ACADIA'S GRANITE CLIFFS.

ROCK CLIMBING

Acadia has splendid sites prized by rock climbers: the sea cliffs at Otter Cliff and Great Head, South Bubble Mountain, Canada Cliff (on the island's western side), and the South Wall and the Central Slabs on Champlain Mountain. These are technical climbs requiring ropes, harnesses, protection, and skills. **Acadia Mountain Guides Climbing School** (228 Main St., Bar Harbor, 207/288-8186, www.acadiamountainguides.com) and **Atlantic Climbing School** (67 Main St., 2nd fl., Bar Harbor, 207/288-2521, www.climbacadia.com) both provide instruction and guided climbs.

WHERE TO STAY

INSIDE THE PARK

Mount Desert Island has at least a dozen commercial campgrounds, but only two are within park boundaries. There are no other accommodations inside the park. Make **reservations** (877/444-6777, www.recreation.gov) two months in advance for all park campgrounds. For first-come, first-served campsites, arrive by 8:30am.

Mount Desert Island

Blackwoods Campground (early May-mid-Oct., 281 sites, $30) is popular due to its location on the east side of the island. It has drive-in tent and RV sites (no hookups). A trail connects the campground to the Ocean Drive trail system. The campground is 5 miles (8 km) south of Bar Harbor, off ME 3.

Seawall Campground (late May-mid-Oct., 202 sites, $22-30) has walk-in tent sites and drive-in sites for tents and RVs (no hookups). On ME 102A, the campground is 4 miles (6.4 km) south of Southwest Harbor.

Schoodic Peninsula

Schoodic Woods Campground (late May-mid-Oct., 89 sites, $22-40) has walk-in or drive-in tent sites and RV sites with electricity and water, a welcome center, and an amphitheater. Hiking trails connect to Schoodic Head; nonmotorized paths link the east and west sides of the peninsula. The campground is off Park Loop Road 3 miles (4.8 km) south of Winter Harbor.

Isle au Haut

On Isle au Haut, reservations are mandatory for one of the lean-tos at **Duck**

Harbor Campground (mid-May-mid-Oct., 5 sites, $20). The three-sided lean-tos (8 by 12 ft/2.4 by 3.7 m, 8 ft/2.4 m high) must fit all tents or tarps for up to six people. Call the **Isle au Haut Boat Company** (207/367-5193) for the current ferry schedule before choosing reservation dates.

OUTSIDE THE PARK

Bar Harbor is the largest and best known of the park's communities. It offers lodgings, restaurants, campgrounds, and services. **Ellsworth** and **Trenton** have inexpensive lodgings.

GETTING THERE

AIR

Bangor International Airport (BGR, 287 Godfrey Blvd., 207/992-4600, www.flybangor.com) is served by major U.S. carriers and is located one hour north of the park. Flying into **Boston Logan International Airport** (BOS, Boston, 800/235-6426, www.massport.com) puts you within a five-hour drive of the park going north via I-95. Both airports have rental cars.

   Cape Air (800/227-3247, www.capeair.com) flies from Boston to **Hancock County-Bar Harbor Airport** (BHB, 207/667-7329, www.bhbairport.com), 10 miles (16 km) from the park. The free Island Explorer Route 1 bus connects the Hancock County-Bar Harbor Airport in Trenton with downtown Bar Harbor.

CAR

You can't get to Acadia without going through Ellsworth and Trenton: The only way onto Mount Desert Island is **ME 3** (expect traffic 8am-9am and 3pm-4pm weekdays). **Bar Harbor** is about 20 miles (32 km, 35-45 min) via ME 3 from Ellsworth; about 48 miles (77 km, 75 min) via US 1A and ME 3 from Bangor; and about 280 miles (450 km, 5 hrs) via I-95 and ME 3 from Boston. It's about 12 miles (19 km, 20 min) via ME 233 and ME 198 or 20 miles (32 km, 35 min) via ME 3 to Northeast Harbor.

BUS

Concord Coach (800/639-3317, https://concordcoachlines.com) runs from Boston to Bangor. The **Bar Harbor-Bangor shuttle** (207/479-5911, https://barharborshuttle.net) connects Bangor with Bar Harbor by advance reservation only.

   If you're day-tripping to Mount Desert Island, you can leave your car in Trenton and hop aboard the free **Island Explorer** (www.exploreacadia.com) bus. Once on the island, continue to use the Island Explorer bus system to avoid parking hassles.

▼ VIEW FROM CADILLAC MOUNTAIN

WAVES ON OTTER CLIFF

GETTING AROUND

DRIVING

Traffic gets heavy at midday in summer, so aim for an early morning start. The maximum speed limit on the Park Loop Road is 35 mph (56 kph); be alert for gawkers and photographers stopping without warning, and pedestrians dashing across the road from stopped cars or tour buses. Some roads and parking areas are closed to RVs and trailers; take the Island Explorer shuttle.

Be aware that Acadia has implemented a long-term transportation plan, starting with timed entry reservations for Cadillac Summit. Check online ahead of your visit; reservations may be required for Ocean Drive corridor and Jordan Pond House North.

SHUTTLE BUS

On Mount Desert Island, use the **Island Explorer** (207/667-5796, www.exploreacadia.com, daily late June-mid-Oct., free) bus system to avoid parking hassles. The shuttle bus has 10 routes that link multiple destinations within the park. Although the buses reach a number of key park sights, they are not tour buses. There is no narration, the bus cuts off the Park Loop Road at Otter Cliff, and it excludes the summit of Cadillac Mountain.

GETTING TO SCHOODIC PENINSULA

Winter Harbor is about 25 miles (40 km) via US 1 and ME 186 from Ellsworth. Although Winter Harbor is roughly 41 miles (66 km, 1 hr) from Bar Harbor by car, it's only 7 miles (11 km) by water. You can get here by passenger ferry via **Downeast Windjammer Cruise Lines** (207/288-4585, Bar Harbor, www.downeastwindjammer.com, daily mid-June-late Sept.) or the bus from Ellsworth, but you'll need a vehicle or bicycle to explore beyond the part of the Schoodic Peninsula that's served by the Island Explorer bus.

GETTING TO ISLE AU HAUT

The **Isle au Haut Boat Company** (Seabreeze Ave., Stonington, 207/367-5193, www.isleauhautferry.com) runs a passenger ferry daily year-round with twice daily service in peak season. It

DAY TRIP TO FRENCHBORO, LONG ISLAND

The island officially known as Long Island, but more commonly known as Frenchboro, makes for a delightful day trip. One of only 15 Maine coastal islands that still support a year-round population, Frenchboro is a quiet place where islanders live as they always have—making a living from the sea. You can take the **passenger ferry *R. L. Gott*** (Fri. early Apr.-late Oct.) during its weekly run for the Maine State Ferry Service. The ferry departs Bass Harbor at 8am, arriving in Frenchboro at 9am. You'll have nine hours on the island before the return trip to Bass Harbor departs at 6pm. **Island Cruises** (12 Little Island Way, Bass Harbor, 207/244-5785, www.bassharborcruises.com) offers custom trips to Frenchboro.

The **Frenchboro Historical Society Museum** (207/334-2924, www.frenchboro.lib.me.us, afternoons Memorial Day-Labor Day, free), just up from the dock, has old tools, local artifacts, and a small gift shop. The island has a network of easy and not-so-easy maintained trails through the woods and along the shore. The trails are rustic, and most are unmarked, so proceed carefully. In the center of the island is a beaver pond.

Lunt's Dockside Deli (207/334-2902, https://luntlobsters.typepad.com, 11am-7:30pm Mon.-Sat. mid-June-early Sept.) serves up lobster rolls, steamed clams, and fish chowder. You might even get to watch lobsters being unloaded from a boat.

goes to the town landing in Duck Harbor near the campground and trailheads. Kayaks, canoes, and bicycles can go for an extra fee.

TOURS

Bus Tours

Scenic **bus tours** (207/288-0300, www.acadiatours.com, daily early May-Oct., 2.5-4 hrs) soak up the sights of Park Loop Road while someone else does the driving. From Bar Harbor, these narrated tours stop at Cadillac Mountain, Thunder Hole, and either Sieur de Monts Spring or Jordan Pond House

TAKE A BOAT TOUR TO BAKER ISLAND.

for 20 minutes at each. **Oli's Trolley** (207/288-9899, http://olistrolley.com, daily late Apr.-Oct., 1-4 hrs) guides tours to various locations, including Cadillac Mountain and downtown Bar Harbor.

Boat Cruises

Rangers join boat cruises offering interpretive details on the park sights. The **Baker Island Tour** is booked through **Bar Harbor Whale Watch Co.** (1 West St., Bar Harbor, 207/288-2386 or 888/942-5374, www.barharborwhales.com, mid-June-mid-Sept., 5 hrs) and visits history-rich Baker Island. The tour includes skiff access to the island's farmstead, lighthouse, and intriguing rock formations. The return trip provides a view from the water of Otter Cliff (bring binoculars), Thunder Hole, Sand Beach, and Great Head. Make reservations to guarantee a space.

Other tours include the **Frenchman Bay Cruise** (207/288-4585, www.downeastwindjammer.com, daily mid-May-early Oct., 2 hrs), on a 151-foot (46-m) four-mast schooner, and the **Islesford Historical Cruise** (207/276-5352, www.cruiseacadia.com, daily mid-May-early Oct., 2.5 hrs), which visits Little Cranberry Island to see the Islesford Historical Museum and Somes Sound.

CUYAHOGA VALLEY
NATIONAL PARK

Ohio

WEBSITE:
www.nps.gov/cuva

PHONE NUMBER:
440/717-3890

VISITATION RANK:
13

WHY GO:
Absorb nature
with a slice of
Midwest history.

KEEPSAKE STAMPS ▼▼▼

▲ TOWPATH TRAIL, CUYAHOGA
VALLEY NATIONAL PARK

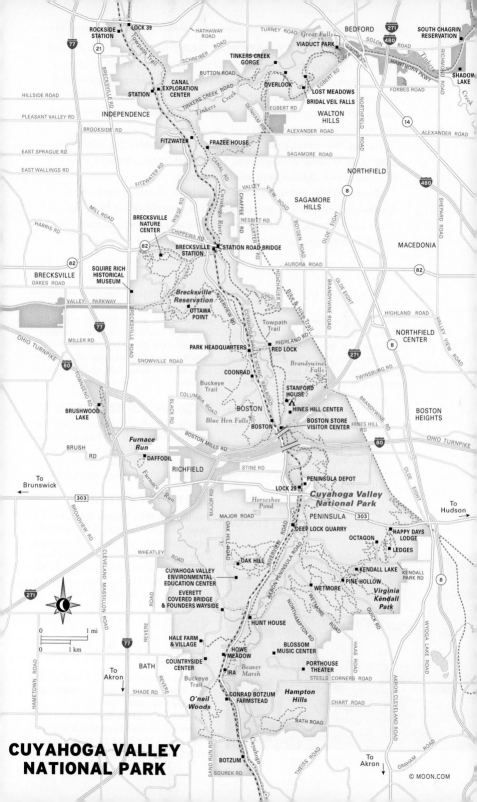

CUYAHOGA VALLEY
NATIONAL PARK

© MOON.COM

CUYAHOGA VALLEY NATIONAL PARK follows the twists and turns of the Cuyahoga River for 22 miles (35 km). In what remains of the Ohio and Erie Canal, the river provided a transportation route through the wilderness in the early 1800s. Its 15 locks aided boats going upstream and downstream, with an adjacent towpath giving the means to haul the boats.

Before the canal system, this parkland housed the Whittlesey people, who never encountered Europeans. Later, this was the land of the Ottawa, Ojibwe, and Mingo peoples.

Deer, coyote, and fish find habitats here—deep ravines and wetlands, open prairie and grasslands. Birds abound: great blue herons, short-eared owls, bobolinks, and bald eagles. Spring peepers provide the evening soundtrack.

PLANNING YOUR TIME

Tucked as a greenbelt in eastern Ohio, Cuyahoga Valley National Park is an easy day trip from either Cleveland or Akron. From north to south, Canal Road (north end) and Riverview Road (south end) cut down the middle of the park along the rivers; meanwhile, I-271 and I-80 cross east-west, along with OH 303 and OH 82, plus a host of smaller roads.

While the park is open daily year-round, May through November draw the most visitors. **Spring** (Mar.-May) is wildflower season, while the reds, golds, and oranges of fall usually hit their peak in **mid-October.** Temperatures for those seasons can hit the low 70s (21-23°C) with very cool nights. In **summer,** the humidity and heat ramp up, with the thermometer often hitting 95°F (35°C). In **winter,** temperatures plunge, yo-yoing from 35°F (1°C) to below freezing, as lake-effect snow rolls in from Lake Erie, to the delight of skiers.

ENTRANCES AND FEES

Cuyahoga Valley National Park has multiple entrances. Start your exploration at the Boston Mills Visitor Center, accessed via I-271 and I-80 on Boston Mills Road. There is no entrance fee.

VISITORS CENTER

The **Boston Mills Visitor Center** (6947 Riverview Rd., Peninsula, 440/717-3890, 8am-6pm daily June-Aug., 9:30am-5pm daily Sept.-May) has information, ranger program schedules, brochures, exhibits, a short park video, bookstore, and a deck overlooking the river.

SIGHTS

CANAL EXPLORATION CENTER

At the intersection of Canal and Hillside Roads, the two-story **Canal Exploration Center** (7104 Canal Rd., Valley View, 216/524-3537, 10am-4pm daily June-Aug., limited days May and Sept.-Oct.) once served as a tavern and a general store. Today, the historic building

EVERETT ROAD COVERED BRIDGE

Top ③

① RIDE THE SCENIC RAILROAD

One of the longest scenic railroads in the nation, the **Cuyahoga Valley Scenic Railroad** (7900 Old Rockside Rd., 330/439-5708, www.cvsr.com, Wed.-Sun. Apr.-Oct., fee) stretches a full 51 miles (82 km) from just south of Cleveland all the way down to Canton—and "scenic" is the operative word. For much of the journey, the tracks bisect

CUYAHOGA VALLEY SCENIC RAILROAD

Cuyahoga Valley National Park while hugging the Cuyahoga River and paralleling the Towpath Trail. Passengers ride in authentic climate-controlled coaches built in the 1950s. More than just a tour train, the railroad is a key resource for visitors to the valley. A round-trip takes about three hours. First-class seats on the second level have more legroom and bigger windows.

② DRIVE THE NATIONAL SCENIC BYWAY

Paralleling the Cuyahoga River, the **Ohio and Erie Canalway National Scenic Byway** (www.ohioanderiecanalway.com) bisects Cuyahoga Valley National Park from the north end of the park at Rockside Road to the south. The route travels Canal Road, Chaffee Road, Chippewa Road, and Riverview Road until it becomes Merriman Road after exiting the park's south boundary. The park's 20-mile (32-km) segment of the byway is part of a larger 110-mile (177-km) route that extends from Cleveland to Schoenbrunn Village, New Philadelphia. Inside the park, the road follows the same route as the Towpath Trail and Cuyahoga Valley Scenic Railroad. Stop to take a hike or visit the restored buildings and living museums that celebrate the canal era and its impact on Ohio's economy.

③ BIKE THE TOWPATH TRAIL

The **Towpath Trail** follows the Cuyahoga River, soaking up historic sites and exhibits. You can bicycle a total of 20 miles (32 km) through the park from north to south; seven access points allow you to shorten the distance. For one-way biking on the towpath, you and your bike can hop on the **Cuyahoga Valley Scenic Railroad** (7900 Old Rockside Rd., 330/439-5708, www.cvsr.com, Wed.-Sun. Apr.-Oct., fee) and then cycle back to your starting point. In addition to regular depot stops, the train has several bike-aboard pickup/drop-off flag stops. Simply flag down the train by waving both hands over your head (a one-hand wave just salutes the engineer). Pay the fare when you board.

TOWPATH TRAIL

Best Hike

BRANDYWINE FALLS

DISTANCE: 1.5 miles (2.4 km) round-trip
DURATION: 1 hour
ELEVATION CHANGE: 180 feet (54 m)
EFFORT: easy
TRAILHEAD: 8176 Brandywine Rd., Sagamore Hills

The trail to **Brandywine Falls** follows a boardwalk through a mossy hemlock forest and gorge to reach a viewing platform facing the falls. The 60-foot (18-m) falls fans out across rock ledges, creating a misty veil. Fall colors come on strong in the gorge in mid-October. Plan to go early or late in the day, as parking can fill 10am-6pm.

hosts exhibits on the canal era with interactive displays that appeal to kids and adults.

HUNT HOUSE

Kids will love the children's nature exhibits at the **Hunt House** (2054 Bolanz Rd., Peninsula, 10am-4pm daily June-Aug., 10am-4pm Sat.-Sun. Apr.-May and Sept.-Oct.). Find it between Riverview Road and Akron Peninsula Road or via the Towpath Trail.

LEDGES LOOP TRAIL

OHIO AND ERIE CANAL TOWPATH TRAIL

The crushed-limestone **Towpath Trail** attracts hikers, runners, bicycles, strollers, and wheelchairs on the 20-mile (32 km) section in the park. The park segment is only a portion of the historic **Ohio and Erie Canal Towpath Trail,** more than 90 miles (129 km) long from Cleveland to Zoar. The path hugs and at times crosses the Cuyahoga River and passes old canal locks, mile markers, wayside exhibits, dense forests, fertile wetlands, and wildlife. Stop off at numerous visitors centers and historic sites along the way. With seven access points, you can go as little or as far as you want.

BLOSSOM MUSIC CENTER

The Cleveland Orchestra's outdoor **Blossom Music Center** (1145 W. Steels Corners Rd., Cuyahoga Falls, 800/686-1141, www.clevelandorchestra.com, spring-fall) is set among dense forests, leafy hillsides, and wide-open skies. Live music includes the orchestra and favorite bands. Seating is on the lawn, but be prepared with rain gear in case of rain. Or spring for seats in the covered pavilion as insurance. Traffic in and out of the park can be brutal, so leave plenty of extra travel time.

HALE FARM & VILLAGE

Want to show your children what life was like before cell phones, computers, and refrigerators? **Hale Farm & Village** (2686 Oak Hill Rd., Bath, 330/666-3711, www.wrhs.org, 10am-4pm Wed.-Sun.

ONE DAY IN THE PARK

Start your visit by driving along the Ohio and Erie Canalway National Scenic Byway. Stop at the **Canal Exploration Center,** then continue south on Riverview Road to the **Boston Mills Visitor Center.** Stretch your legs by walking a little of the **Towpath Trail** south to Lock 29. Continue south on Riverview Road to see the **Everett Road Covered Bridge** and sink into history at the **Hale Farm & Village.**

June-Aug., 10am-4pm Sat.-Sun. Sept.-Oct.) is a town trapped in the mid-1800s, when things like electricity, automobiles, and iPhones were still a few years down the road. This living-history museum employs historic interpreters dressed in period costumes to recount the story of the Western Reserve, the Civil War years, and life in the middle of the 19th century.

EVERETT ROAD COVERED BRIDGE

The striking red **Everett Road Covered Bridge** (2370 Everett Rd., Peninsula) spans Furnace Run, which looks like a placid rock-strewn stream much

of the year. But in 1975, a torrent of water gushed through the ravine and destroyed the original bridge. Located 0.5 mile (0.8 km) west of Riverview Road, the reconstructed one-lane bridge is one of the most photographed locations in Cuyahoga and a tribute to Ohio's legacy of 19th-century covered bridges. Cars can no longer drive on the bridge, but you can walk through it.

RECREATION
HIKING

Twenty miles (32 km) of the **Towpath Trail** are inside the park, with seven

BRANDYWINE FALLS IN CUYAHOGA VALLEY NATIONAL PARK

BRIDAL VEIL FALLS

access points. From the Ira Trailhead, take the Towpath Trail to the **Beaver Marsh** (3801 Riverview Rd., Cuyahoga Falls, 0.8 mi/1.3 km rt, 30 min, easy), which the National Audubon Society has designated an Important Bird Area. For point-to-point hiking on the towpath, hop on the **Cuyahoga Valley Scenic Railroad** (7900 Old Rockside Rd., 303/439-5708, www.cvsr.com, Wed.-Sun. Apr.-Oct., fee) and hike back to your starting point.

The **Blue Hen Falls Trail** (2001 Boston Mills Rd., Peninsula, 0.5 mi/0.8 km rt, 30 min, easy) crosses Spring Creek on a wooden bridge. At the junction, turn right to reach the 15-foot (4.6-m) Blue Hen Falls. Plan to go early or late in the day, as parking can pack out 10am-4pm.

Bridal Veil Falls (Gorge Pkwy., Walton Hills, 0.5 mi/0.8 km rt, 30 min, easy) is accessed by a short boardwalk that leads to a viewing platform.

The **Ledges Loop** (701 Truxell Rd., Peninsula, 2.2 mi/3.5 km rt, 1.5 hrs, moderate) starts on a spur; at the loop, head in either direction. On the east side, Ice Box Cave is closed to protect bats; the west side includes an overlook of the area. Many hikers park at **Kendall Lake** instead of the Ledges Trailhead to add on a 1-mile (1.6-km) loop around the lake. After hiking around Kendall Lake, connect to the Ledges by crossing Kendall Park Road to the Pine Grove Trail and then heading west, after which you will link up with the Ledges Loop. Adding on the lake and connection via Pine Grove ups the distance to 4.8 miles (7.7 km) round-trip.

PADDLING

With the removal of the Brecksville Dam in 2020, the Cuyahoga River became free-flowing inside the park. Bring your own canoe or kayak, and check river gauges and Cuyahoga River Water Trail maps (https://cuyahogariverwatertrail.org) for permanent hazards. **Cuyahoga Valley Scenic Railroad** (330/439-5708, www.cvsr.com, Wed.-Sun. Apr.-Oct., fee) allows kayaks (no canoes) aboard with advance ticket purchase, so you can catch a ride upriver to paddle downstream. Four river accesses are near stations or flag stops.

LEDGES LOOP

WINTER RECREATION

To snowshoe and cross-country ski park trails, including the Towpath, rent gear at the **Winter Sports Center at M.D. Garage** (1550 Boston Mills Rd., 440/717-3890, 10am-4pm Sat.-Sun. late Dec.-Feb., free). Bring your own sled or toboggan to slide down **Kendall Hills** (3 parking lots on Quick Rd., Peninsula). For downhill skiing and snowboarding, **Peak Resorts** (800/875-4241, www.bmbw.com) operates two lifts on weekends and holidays located five minutes apart: **Brandywine Ski Resort** (1146 West Highland Rd., Sagamore Hills) and **Mills Ski Resort** (7100 Riverview Rd., Peninsula). Brandywine also has a tubing hill.

WHERE TO STAY

INSIDE THE PARK

The nearly 175-year-old **Inn at Brandywine Falls** (8230 Brandywine Rd., Sagamore Hills, 330/467-1812, www.innatbrandywinefalls.com, year-round, from $158) is a bed-and-breakfast tucked into the park, literally steps from scenic Brandywine Falls. The inn has six bedrooms furnished with antiques, plus a living room, dining room, and porches. The gourmet breakfast is a candlelit affair.

The historic **Stanford House** (6093 Stanford Rd., Peninsula, 330/657-2909, www.conservancyforcvnp.org, year-round, entire house from $600, 2-night minimum, rooms from $50) has nine bedrooms, plus a dining room, living room, commercial kitchen, outdoor fire circle, and beautiful grounds. The entire house is available for rent.

OUTSIDE THE PARK

Lodging options are plentiful in the surrounding area, which includes **Independence, Akron,** and **Cleveland.** For camping, several Ohio state parks are nearby.

CYCLISTS RIDE ALONG THE TOWPATH TRAIL.

GETTING THERE

AIR

Cleveland Hopkins International Airport (CLE, 5300 Riverside Dr., 216/265-6000, www.clevelandairport.com) is 25 miles (40 km) northwest of the national park, a quick drive via I-480 and I-77. It has car rentals.

TRAIN AND BUS

Amtrak (www.amtrak.com) trains and **Greyhound** (www.greyhound.com) buses stop in Cleveland. **Greater Cleveland Transit** (www.riderta.com) runs a rapid transit system and buses around the Cleveland area.

CAR

From Cleveland, take I-77 south for 16 miles (26 km) to exit 147 and turn left onto Miller Road. Drive 0.6 mile (1 km) and turn right onto OH 21 (Brecksville Rd.) for 0.4 mile (0.6 km). Turn left onto Snowville Road and continue 2.8 miles (4.5 km). Turn right onto Riverview Road and drive 1.7 miles (2.7 km) to reach the visitors center on the left. The drive should take about 30 minutes.

From Akron, drive north on OH 18 (Market St.) for 1.1 miles (1.7 km) and veer right onto Merriman Road for 4.1 miles (6.6 km) to a traffic circle. Take the first exit onto Riverview Road for 4.3 miles (6.9 km) to the visitors center, on the right. The drive should take about 20 minutes.

GETTING AROUND

The **Cuyahoga Valley Scenic Railroad** (7900 Old Rockside Rd., 303/439-5708, www.cvsr.com, Wed.-Sun. Apr.-Oct.) stops at two stations inside the park: Rockside and Peninsula. The train makes 2-3 round-trip journeys through the park with five flag stops where you can board or debark.

During weekends and in summer, **parking** can be difficult. The parking lots at popular trailheads fill 10am-4pm. To access the Towpath Trail, park at Canal Exploration Center, Station Road, or Rockside Rock rather than the busy locations of Boston Store, Hunt House, Ira Trailhead, and Lock 29 in Peninsula.

SIGHTS NEARBY

First Ladies National Historic Site (205 S. Market Ave., Canton, 330/452-0876, www.nps.gov/fila) celebrates U.S. first ladies with tours of the restored 1841 Victorian mansion of Ida Saxton, wife of William McKinley, 25th president of the United States. It's a 40-minute drive south of the park via I-77.

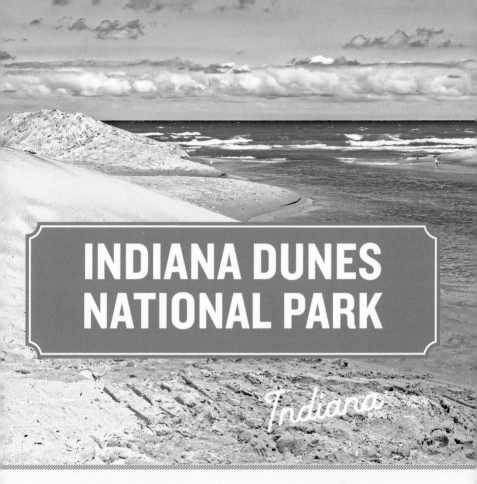

INDIANA DUNES
NATIONAL PARK

Indiana

KEEPSAKE STAMPS ▼▼▼

WEBSITE:
www.nps.gov/indu

PHONE NUMBER:
219/395-1882

VISITATION RANK:
9

WHY GO:
Explore miles of sand dunes.

▲ DUNES ON LAKE MICHIGAN

INDIANA DUNES
NATIONAL PARK

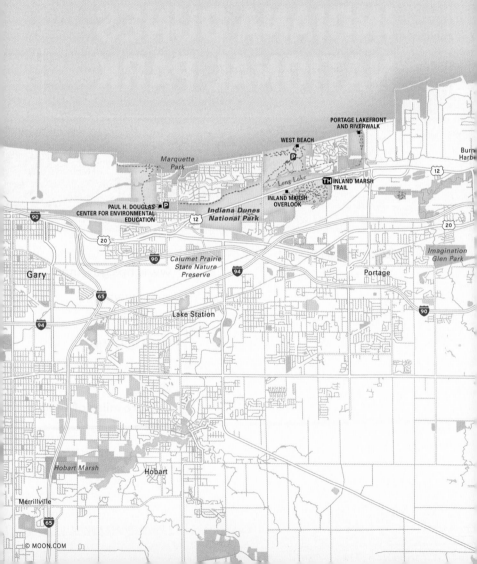

Lake

PORTAGE LAKEFRONT
AND RIVERWALK

WEST BEACH

Marquette
Park

Burn
Harb

12

Long Lake

INLAND MARSH
TRAIL

TH

INLAND MARSH
OVERLOOK

PAUL H. DOUGLAS
CENTER FOR ENVIRONMENTAL
EDUCATION

P

90

Indiana Dunes
National Park

20

12

20

Gary

90

Imagination
Glen Park

Calumet Prairie
State Nature
Preserve

94

Portage

65

Lake Station

94

90

Hobart Marsh

Hobart

Merrillville

65

© MOON.COM

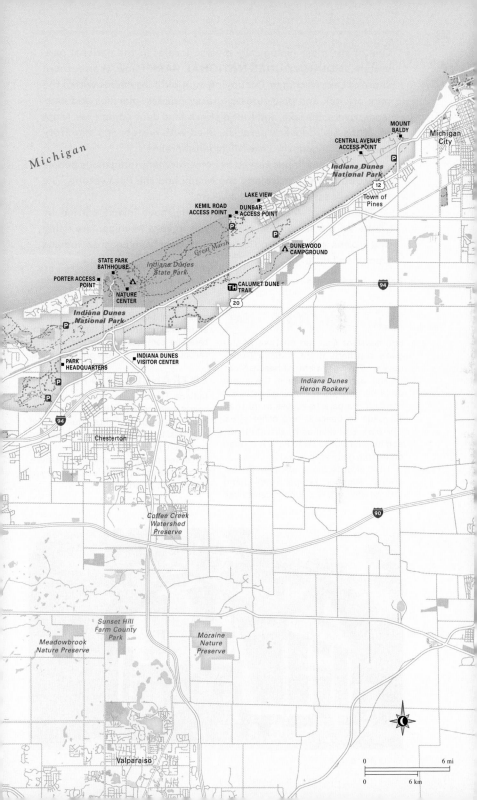

Michigan

MOUNT
BALDY

CENTRAL AVENUE
ACCESS POINT

Michigan
City

**Indiana Dunes
National Park**

12

LAKE VIEW

Town of
Pines

KEMIL ROAD
ACCESS POINT

DUNBAR
ACCESS POINT

Great Marsh

DUNEWOOD
CAMPGROUND

STATE PARK
BATHHOUSE

**Indiana Dunes
State Park**

PORTER ACCESS
POINT

94

CALUMET DUNE
TRAIL

NATURE
CENTER

20

**Indiana Dunes
National Park**

INDIANA DUNES
VISITOR CENTER

PARK
HEADQUARTERS

Indiana Dunes
Heron Rookery

94

90

Chesterton

Coffee Creek
Watershed
Preserve

Sunset Hill
Farm County
Park

Meadowbrook
Nature
Preserve

Moraine
Nature
Preserve

Valparaiso

0   6 mi

0   6 km

One of the most biologically diverse locales in the national park system, **INDIANA DUNES NATIONAL PARK** flanks the southern shore of Lake Michigan. Occupying multiple ecosystems within the park are oak and pine forests, grassy prairies, marshes and wetlands, rivers, the lake, and four distinct sand dune complexes. Most of all, it's a bird-lover's paradise, filled with nesters and migratory fowl that frequent the Lake Michigan shoreline.

These diverse lands served as home for many Indigenous people for 9,000 years, particularly the Miami and the Potawatomi. The Miami called the dunes "Neekawikam."

The dune of Mount Baldy is on the move inland, carried by winds. At the same time, water levels in Lake Michigan are rising and storms are increasing, eroding the sand from beaches. Indiana Dunes is a land of change.

PLANNING YOUR TIME

Southeast of Chicago on Lake Michigan's southern shore, Indiana Dunes covers 15 miles (24 km) of beach. Most of the park sits between the shore and I-94, with US 12 running east-west through the park to access more than 12 roads to beaches and other sites. The park is broken up by private lands and Indiana Dunes State Park. It is open 6am-11pm daily year-round.

Lake effects cause weather fluctuations. Summer temperatures hang around 85°F (29°C). June receives the most rain, but there are often sunny summer skies amid high humidity. Winters see temperatures in the mid-30s (around 1.5°C) and snow on the ground.

ENTRANCES AND FEES

Indiana Dunes has multiple entrance roads that access trailheads, the campground, historic sights, dunes, and beaches. Entrance fees are $25 per vehicle ($20 motorcycle); the pass is good for seven days. For individuals (hikers, bikers, boaters), the fee is $15 per day or $25 per family group.

BAILLY HOMESTEAD

Top ❸

① SWIM AT WEST BEACH

Cool off, sunbathe, or play in the sand. Water temperatures usually reach 65-68°F (18-20°C) in July and August. Bring beach toys and floaties to amp up the fun, but beware of big waves and rip currents. Eight beaches have parking lots (6am-11pm) with restrooms and drinking water; **West Beach** and Lake View have accessible parking lots. All have free entrance except for West Beach (fee station 7am-9pm daily, $6

WEST BEACH

per car Memorial Day-Labor Day), which has summer lifeguards, lockers, showers, and covered picnic shelters (reservations 877/444-6777, www.recreation.gov, $25). To get a parking spot, arrive at Lake View, Dunbar, Kemil, Porter, or Portage Lakefront and Riverwalk beaches by midmorning. West Beach fills on holidays.

② CATCH THE SUNSET

When the sun sets over Lake Michigan, the glow spreads across the water. All of the park beaches provide good locations for enjoying the view. Join a ranger for **Sunset around the Fire** (Portage Lakefront and Riverwalk pavilion, 100 Riverwalk Rd., Portage, Wed., 8pm early summer, 7:30pm midsummer, 7pm late summer, 1 hr, free) and marshmallow roasting in the pavilion fireplace. Rangers also lead a **sunset hike on the Dunes Succession Trail** (Ranger Contact Station at West Beach Parking Lot, 376 N. County Line Rd., Gary, 7pm Sat., 1 hr, $6/car), up the 250 stairs to the top of the dune to watch the setting sun reflecting on the Chicago skyline.

③ GO BIRDING

Impressive migrations in spring and fall pack the dunes with waterfowl, songbirds, and raptors. Particularly during the fall migration, birds fly south along Lake Michigan's shorelines, which converge at the park. Go to the **Great Marsh** to see egrets, green herons, red-winged blackbirds, and kingfishers. Climb a dune to watch hawks. Go to the shore of the lake to see waterfowl. Expert guides are available for birding expeditions during the annual **Indiana Dunes Birding Festival** over the third weekend in May.

HERON

Best Hike

WEST BEACH TRAIL

DISTANCE: 0.9-3.4 miles (1.4-5.4 km) round-trip
DURATION: 0.5-3 hours
ELEVATION CHANGE: 114 feet (34 m)
EFFORT: moderate
TRAILHEAD: West Beach Road parking lot ($6 fee)

The West Beach Trail can be a quick one-loop hike or a longer two- or three-loop route.

Start by walking the paved trail to the beach, across the sand, and up the boardwalk of the **Dune Succession Trail.** It climbs 250 stairs up a high dune for expansive views. Continue south along the stairs to loop back to the parking lot or connect with the flat **West Beach Trail** that tours past prickly pear cactus in an oak and prairie ecosystem. From that loop, return to the south end of the parking lot or intersect with the **Long Lake Loop** to explore wetlands and enjoy platforms for bird-watching. Use caution when trails cross the road.

West Beach (7am-9pm daily late May-early Sept.) charges $6 per vehicle or motorcycle per day.

VISITORS CENTERS

Located south and outside the park, **Indiana Dunes Visitor Center** (1215 N. IN 49, Porter, 219/395-1882, 8am-6pm daily summer, 8:30am-4:30pm daily winter) has information, short videos, exhibits, and a bookstore.

The **Paul H. Douglas Center for Environmental Education** (100 N. Lake St., Gary, 219/395-1824, 9am-5pm daily summer, 9am-4pm daily winter) has a Nature Play Zone for families and interactive exhibits.

▼ CHELLBERG FARM

SIGHTS

FALL COLOR

Hardwood trees turn brilliant colors in fall. Leaf-peeping starts in late September, with colors usually hitting their prime in mid-October and fading through the end of the month. Catch the color in the maple and oak forests on the Calumet Dunes Trail and Dune Ridge Trail. The Glenwood Dunes also yields outstanding fall colors.

BAILLY HOMESTEAD AND CHELLBERG FARM

A National Historic Landmark, the **Bailly Homestead** is a survivor that got its start as a fur trading post in 1822.

The main house has detailing from 19th-century architecture, while the interior has been restored to its 1917 appearance. The 20th-century **Chellberg Farm** was home to three generations of immigrants. A trail (1.1 mi/1.7 km rt, 45 min, easy) goes out and back to both historic locations. Rangers guide a **history hike** (1pm Sun. June-Aug., 2 hrs, free) from the Chellberg-Bailly Parking Lot (Mineral Springs Rd. between US 20 and IN 12, Porter).

RECREATION

HIKING

Rangers lead several guided walks in summer, including up the loose sand of the **Mount Baldy Summit Trail** (0.75 mi/1.2 km, 1 hr, strenuous), which is closed except when going with a ranger. Consult the visitors center for the current schedule.

The accessible paved **Calumet Dunes Trail** (1596 N. Kemil Rd., 0.5 mi/0.8 km, 20 min, easy) explores a forested dune ridge that remains from the shoreline of Lake Chicago, an ancient ancestor that was larger than Lake Michigan 12,000 years ago.

Tucked south of a giant forested dune, the **Dune Ridge Trail** (Kemil

STAIRS ON THE DUNE SUCCESSION TRAIL

Beach Parking Lot, E. State Park Rd., Beverly Shores, 0.7 mi/1.1 km, 30 min, moderate) tours wetlands and hardwood forest with views of Great Marsh and Kemil Beach.

Pick up a map at the trailhead kiosk to navigate the 13 junctions in loops on the **Glenwood Dunes Trail** (1475 N. Brummitt Rd., Chesterton, 1-15 mi/1.6-24 km, 0.5-8 hrs, moderate). Spurs also connect with Dunewood Trace Campground, Dune Park South Shore Railroad Station, and Calumet Dunes Trail.

The **Great Marsh** (South Trailhead Parking Lot on Broadway, Beverly Shores, 1.3 mi/2.1 km rt, 1 hr, easy) tours the largest wetland in the park, the best place to see waterfowl, songbirds, and beavers. The trail trots north and loops around the east side of the wetland, and a spur paved trail goes west to the observation deck. The North Trailhead Parking Lot has accessible parking for wheelchairs to use the paved trail (0.4 mi/0.6 km, 30 min, easy) to the observation deck.

The **Heron Rookery** (1336 600 E., Michigan City, 3.3 mi/5.3 km rt, 2 hrs, easy) follows the Little Calumet River ablaze with wildflowers in spring and a birding paradise. The 100 great blue heron nests are now abandoned.

A National Natural Landmark, the **Cowles Bog** (1450 N. Mineral Springs Rd., Dune Acres, 4.7 mi/7.6 km rt, 4 hrs, moderate) is known for its plant diversity with black oak savannas, swamps, marshes, and beaches.

The **Portage Lakefront and River** (100 Riverwalk Rd., Portage, 0.9 mi/1.4 km rt, 30 min, easy) is a paved, accessible walk along Lake Michigan, good for watching lake storms, migrating birds in spring, and winter lake ice.

BICYCLING

The park contains 37 miles (60 km) of bicycle trails. Most are open year-round and allow e-bikes. Between the town of Pine and Dune Acres, the **Calumet Trail** (19 mi/31 km rt) is a gravel road. The paved **Porter Brickyard Trail** (7 mi/11.3 km rt) has a few hills between Dune Acres and Chesterton. The paved **Prairie Duneland** (22 mi/35 km rt) is a flat rail trail between Chesterton and Hobart. Bike rentals are available near the visitors center from **Pedal Power**

(1215 IN 49, Porter, 219/921-3085, https://pedalpowerrentals.com).

PADDLING

Waves, big winds, and fast-changing conditions make paddling on Lake Michigan a challenge. It's best to take your kayaks, canoes, or paddleboards to the sheltered Little Calumet River and Burns Waterway. To try the lake when it is calm, you can launch from any beach except the swimming area at West Beach.

CROSS-COUNTRY SKIING AND SNOWSHOEING

In winter, many trails become cross-country skiing and snowshoeing routes. The Glenwood Dunes trail system is the best for ungroomed conditions. Bring your own gear.

WHERE TO STAY

INSIDE THE PARK

The park has no lodges and only one campground. **Dunewood Campground** (645 Broadway, Beverly Shores, Apr.-Oct., 66 sites, $25) has tent, RV, and accessible campsites. Amenities include showers, restrooms, and drinking water. Make reservations (877/444-6777, www.recreation.gov) six months in advance.

Grassy walk-in tent sites ($25) are near the Central Avenue Beach parking lot. The walk is about 5-10 minutes. Bring your own water.

OUTSIDE THE PARK

Accommodations, campgrounds, and dining options can be found in **Porter, Portage, Chesterton,** and a campground at **Indiana Dunes State Park.**

GETTING THERE

AIR

Chicago Midway International Airport (MDW, 5700 S. Cicero Ave., 773/838-0600, www.flychicago.com) to the west and **South Bend International Airport** (SBN, 4477 Progress Dr., 574/282-4590, https://flysbn.com) to the east are equidistant from Indiana

Dunes (48 mi/77 km, 1.25 hrs). Both have car rentals.

CAR

Just south of Indiana Dunes, I-94 crosses east-west across Indiana. From South Bend, drive IN 20 to I-94 west. From Chicago, follow I-94 east. From both directions, take IN 49 (exit 26) north to the park or to intersect with US 12, which accesses all roads into the park. From Valparaiso, drive IN 49 north.

TRAIN

The electric South Shore Line runs almost hourly every day between Chicago and South Bend with four stops inside the park. The **Beverly Shores Station** (US 12 and Broadway) is 0.5 mile (0.8 km) north of the park campground. From the west end of **Dune Park Station,** you can walk or bike to Indiana Dunes Visitor Center on the **Dunes Kankakee Trail** (1.3 mi/2.1 km, 30 min, easy). Select weekend trains allow bikes to Dunes Park Station.

BUS

From Gary, Indiana, you can catch the Oak/County Line bus run by **Gary Public Transportation Corp** (219/885-7555, www.gptcbus.com), which goes near the entrance of West Beach but no farther east into the park.

GETTING AROUND

CAR

US 12 goes east-west through the inside of the park to access more than 12 roads to beaches and other sites.

SHUTTLES

A free accessible **shuttle** (10am-6pm Sat.-Sun. Memorial Day weekend-Labor Day) cruises two routes. The Western Park Shuttle (check schedule for times) connects Miller Train Station, Marquette Park, Douglas Center, 5th Avenue and Lake Street, and Lake Street Bridge. The **Eastern Park Shuttle** (every 20-30 min) runs between Dunewood Campground, USGS Great Lakes Research Center, and Kemil Beach Parking Lot.

ISLE ROYALE NATIONAL PARK

Michigan

KEEPSAKE STAMPS ▼▼▼

WEBSITE:
www.nps.gov/isro

PHONE NUMBER:
906/482-0984

VISITATION RANK:
57

WHY GO:
Explore a unique freshwater island.

▲ ISLE ROYALE NATIONAL PARK

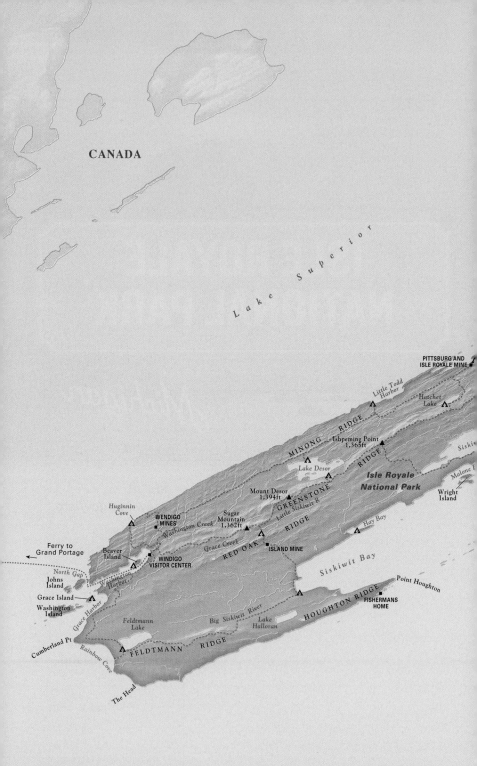

CANADA

Lake Superior

PITTSBURG AND
ISLE ROYALE MINE

Little Todd
Harbor

Hatchet
Lake

MINONG RIDGE

Ishpeming Point
1,365ft

Lake Desor

RIDGE

Siski

Isle Royale
National Park

Malone L

Mount Desor
1,394ft

GREENSTONE

Wright
Island

Huginnin
Cove

Little Siskiwit R

WENDIGO
MINES

Sugar
Mountain
1,362ft

RIDGE

Hay Bay

Washington Creek

Ferry to
Grand Portage

Beaver
Island

WINDIGO
VISITOR CENTER

Grace Creek

RED OAK

ISLAND MINE

Siskiwit Bay

Point Houghton

North Gap
Johns
Island

Washington Harbor

HOUGHTON RIDGE

FISHERMANS
HOME

Grace Island

Washington
Island

Grace Harbor

Feldtmann
Lake

Big Siskiwit River

Lake
Halloran

Cumberland Pt

Rainbow Cove

FELDTMANN   RIDGE

The Head

© MOON.COM

ISLE ROYALE
NATIONAL PARK

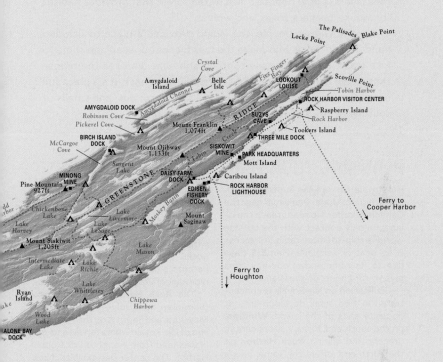

PASSAGE ISLAND
LIGHTHOUSE

The Palisades   Blake Point

Locke Point

Crystal
Cove

Amygdaloid
Island

Belle
Isle

Five Finger
Bay

LOOKOUT
LOUISE

Scoville Point

Tobin Harbor

ROCK HARBOR VISITOR CENTER

AMYGDALOID DOCK

Robinson Cove

Pickerel Cove

Mount Franklin
1,074ft

RIDGE

SUZYS
CAVE

Raspberry Island

Rock Harbor

BIRCH ISLAND
DOCK

McCargoe
Cove

Mount Ojibway
1,133ft

SISKOWIT
MINE

Tookers Island

THREE MILE DOCK

Sargent
Lake

Creek

PARK HEADQUARTERS

Amygdaloid Channel

MINONG
MINE

Pine Mountain
927ft

GREENSTONE

DAISY FARM
DOCK

Tobin

Mott Island

Caribou Island

ROCK HARBOR
LIGHTHOUSE

Chickenbone
Lake

EDISEN
FISHERY
DOCK

Lake
Harvey

Lake
Livermore

Lake
LeSage

Moskey Basin

Mount
Saginaw

Mount Siskiwit
1,205ft

Intermediate
Lake

Lake
Richie

Lake
Mason

Ferry to
Cooper Harbor

Ryan
Island

Lake
Whittlesey

Chippewa
Harbor

Ferry to
Houghton

Wood
Lake

ALONE BAY
DOCK

ISLE ROYALE LIGHTHOUSE

Menagerie
Island

Long
Island

Lake   Superior

0   5 mi
0   5 km

Remote **ISLE ROYALE NATIONAL PARK** is the largest island in frigid Lake Superior, located near the border with Canada. This wilderness park encompasses an archipelago of the 45-mile-long (72-km) Isle Royale and about 400 tiny islands. More than 80 percent of the park is underwater. This upthrust of land consisting of folded rock layers is now host to a rich mixed forest that provides habitat for moose, beavers, foxes, and wolves.

For the Ojibwe people, the island provided a place to fish and hunt. Today, those who make the trek by boat or seaplane come to hike trails, paddle the saw-toothed shoreline, and see the moose that swam here from Ontario several decades back. It's a place full of wilderness and water. Soak up the sights, sounds, and smells of solitude below a starlit sky or the northern lights.

PLANNING YOUR TIME

Isle Royale sits in Lake Superior, north of Michigan's Upper Peninsula near the Canadian border. No roads reach the island; its only contact with the outside world is ship-to-shore radio. All access is by boat or seaplane. Plan **3-5 days** due to its remoteness; one-day trips give you 3-4 hours on the island.

Civilization on Isle Royale is concentrated in two small developments at opposite ends of the island. **Windigo,** on the south end, has a visitors center, grocery, and marina. **Rock Harbor,** on the north end, offers the same, plus a lodge, restaurant, and cabins. The rest of the island is wilderness accessed only by trail, boat, or paddling.

Isle Royale is open daily **mid-April to October** and closed November to mid-April. June-September is the warmest time with the highest visitation, but plan for bugs June-July. The island bans dogs and wheeled vehicles (mountain bikes and canoe carts), except for wheelchairs.

ENTRANCES AND FEES

Most boats and seaplanes land in **Rock Harbor** at the northeast tip of the island. Boats from Minnesota dock in **Windigo,** at the southern tip. The entrance fee is $7 per person per day, or $60 per season, which is collected by ferry or seaplane concessionaires. Private boaters can pay at the visitors centers.

VISITORS CENTERS

Houghton Visitor Center (800 E. Lakeshore Dr., 906/482-0984, 8am-6pm Mon.-Fri., 10am-6pm Sat. June-mid-Sept., 10am-4pm Mon.-Fri. mid-Sept.-May) is on the mainland in Houghton, where the *Ranger III* passenger ferry docks. The visitors center has boating permits, a park orientation video, a Junior Ranger Program, and a park store.

The **Rock Harbor Visitor Center** (8am-6pm daily July-Aug., hours vary May-June and Sept.) is on the northeast end of Isle Royale where ferries and seaplanes land from Houghton or Copper Harbor. The center has exhibits, backcountry permits, ranger-led programs, field guides, and maps.

The **Windigo Visitor Center** (8am-6pm daily July-Aug., hours vary May-June and Sept.-Oct.) is on the southwest end of the island where ferries arrive from Grand Portage, Minnesota. The center has exhibits, backcountry permits, and ranger programs, plus maps and field guides.

RECREATION

HIKING

The islands' wildlife, especially the **moose** and **wolf** populations, is a draw. Hikers have a decent chance of spotting moose in ponds, lowlands, inland lakes, and especially the mineral licks at **Hidden Lake.**

Top **3**

1 HIKE TO SCOVILLE POINT

East of Rock Harbor, the **Scoville Point Trail** (4.2 mi/6.8 km rt, 2 hrs, moderate) traces a rocky finger of forested land in a figure-eight loop to a point surrounded by Lake Superior. The route begins on the Stoll Memorial Loop, which links to the smaller Scoville Point Loop. Go either way around both loops. The bluffs of the rocky point yield outstanding views of the rugged Isle Royale shoreline and islands.

HIKING TRAIL ON ISLE ROYALE

2 PADDLE THE ISLAND WATERS

For paddlers, Isle Royale is a dream destination, a nook-and-cranny wilderness of rocky islands, secluded coves, and quiet bays interrupted only by the low call of a loon. Rental kayaks and canoes are available in Windigo and Rock Harbor.

First-time visitors should aim for the **Five Fingers,** the collection of fjord-like harbors and rocky promontories on the northeast end of the island. The area is well protected (except from northeasterly winds) and offers some of the finest scenery and solitude. Isle Royale is generally better suited to **kayaks,** though canoes can handle these waters in calm weather.

A paddle-hike destination, **Lookout Louise** (2 mi/3.2 km rt, 1 hr, moderate) has spectacular views of the island's ragged northeastern shoreline. To get there from Rock Harbor, paddle for 20 minutes to the trailhead in Tobin Harbor and then hike to the overlook.

3 CAMP IN THE BACKCOUNTRY

Isle Royale has 36 **wilderness campsites** that offer a chance for solitude, wildlife-watching, and soaking up the stars. They are accessible on foot or by boat and some only by canoe or kayak. These first-come, first-served sites include drinking water and vault toilets. A free camping permit, available from visitors centers, is required for all overnight stays. Group sites (7-10 people) require advance reservations ($25).

For backpackers in particular, the **Greenstone Ridge Trail** (42 mi/68 km, 4 days) runs the length of the island through the highest points along the spine of Greenstone Ridge. The route, dotted with wilderness campsites, goes between Rock Harbor and Windigo. Use the boat to return to your starting point.

ONE DAY IN ISLE ROYALE

If you only have one day, take the ferry from Copper Harbor to Rock Harbor, which gives you about three hours to explore. Hike to **Scoville Point** or rent a canoe from **Rock Harbor Lodge** to explore the bay.

Near Rock Harbor Visitor Center, interpretive signs on the Rock Harbor Trail lead to **Suzy's Cave** (3.8 mi/6.1 km rt, 2 hrs, moderate), formed by wave action of a once-deeper Lake Superior. Follow the Lake Superior shoreline to Daisy Farm campground and the **Ojibway Trail** to go to the **Ojibway Fire Tower** (3.4 mi/5.5 km rt, 2 hrs, moderate) for an unmatched view of the island's interior lakes and bays.

From Windigo Visitor Center, head uphill on the **Windigo Nature Trail** (1 mi/1.6 km rt, 40 min, easy) as it rolls through forests of cedar, maple, and birch. From the Feldtmann Lake Trailhead, **Grace Creek Overlook** (3.6 mi/5.8 km rt, 2 hrs, moderate) climbs to a rocky outcrop for views of the island.

BOATING AND FISHING

Isle Royale's scenic waterways beckon private boaters. Boats that dock overnight need a backcountry **permit** (even for anchoring). Pick up free backcountry permits at the island visitors centers or on board the *Ranger III*. The docks in **Rock Harbor** and **Windigo** have pump-out services, fuel, and potable water. Rock Harbor has seasonal dockage with power and water.

A **Michigan fishing license** (24-hour cash-only, available in island stores, longer licenses on mainland) is required to fish Lake Superior. No license is needed to fish the island's inland lakes.

WHERE TO STAY

INSIDE THE PARK

Rock Harbor Lodge (800 E. Lakeshore Dr., 906/337-4993, http://rockharborlodge.com, from $227) has 60 basic motel-style lodge rooms with glorious views of nearby islands and Lake Superior. Nearby, 20 housekeeping cottages include small kitchens, one double bed, and one bunk bed. Reservations are a must.

Rock Harbor has the **Lighthouse Restaurant** and **Greenstone Grill** (7am-10am, noon-1:30pm, and 5:30pm-7:30pm daily late May-early Sept.). The

ROCK HARBOR

Dockside Store (8am-6pm daily) carries food and camping supplies.

Two rustic, one-room **Windigo Camper Cabins** (906/337-4993, http://rockharborlodge.com, from $52) are located in Washington Harbor, 45 miles (72 km) from Rock Harbor.

OUTSIDE THE PARK

On the mainland, **Houghton** and **Hancock** are the gateways to Isle Royale, with lodgings and restaurants.

GETTING THERE

AIR

Two airports are near Grand Portage, Minnesota, the gateway to the park's southwest at Windigo. Both have rental cars. **Thunder Bay International Airport** (YQT, 100 Princess St., Thunder Bay, ON, Canada, 807/473-2600, www.tbairport.on.ca) is 42 miles (68 km) northeast of Grand Portage, less than an hour's drive via MN 61. **Duluth International Airport** (DLH, 4701 Grinden Dr., Duluth, MN, 218/727-2968, http://duluthairport.com) is 150 miles (240 km) south of Grand Portage, a three-hour drive via MN 61.

To go from Houghton, Michigan, to Rock Harbor, the closest airport is **Green Bay-Austin Straubel International Airport** (GRB, 2077 Airport Dr., Green Bay, WI, 920/498-4800, www.flygrb.com). It is 230 miles (370 km) south of Houghton, a four-hour drive.

A pricey charter service, **Isle Royale Seaplanes** (21125 Royce Rd., Hancock, 906/483-4991, https://isleroyaleseaplanes.com, mid-May-mid-Sept., 35 min), fly from Hancock Portage Canal, Michigan, or Grand Marais, Minnesota, to Windigo and Rock Harbor. Reservations are required.

BOAT AND FERRY

Boats and ferries are for passengers only; cars are not permitted. Make reservations for all ferries at least three months in advance, although last-minute spots can be available. Canoes and kayaks are allowed for a fee.

From Houghton, Michigan: The National Park Service operates the 165-foot (50-m) **MV Ranger III** (800 E. Lakeshore Dr., 906/482-0984, May-Sept.,

ISLE ROYALE COVE

6 hrs, from $55 adults) for the 73-mile (117-km) passage to Rock Harbor. Departures go from Houghton (9am Tues. and Fri.) and Rock Harbor (9am Wed. and Sat.). Online reservations open in early January.

From Copper Harbor, Michigan: The **MV Isle Royale Queen IV** (14 Waterfront Landing, 906/289-4437, www.isleroyale.com, daily early May-Sept., 3 hrs, $150) passenger ferry departs at 8am for Rock Harbor; the return trip departs Rock Harbor at 2:45pm.

From Grand Portage, Minnesota: Two ferries run, operated by **Isle Royale Boats** (218/600-0765, www.isleroyaleboats.com, schedule varies, from $87 adults). **MV Voyageur II** (May-early Oct.) travels to Windigo (2 hrs) and Rock Harbor (8.5 hrs) every other day and returns on opposite days. Other drop-off and pickup locations are available. Best for one-day trips, **MV Sea Hunter II** (mid-June-early Sept.) goes to Windigo for a four-hour stop and returns to Grand Portage.

BUS

Indian Trails (800/292-3831, www.indiantrails.com) operates bus service from Green Bay, Wisconsin, to Houghton, Michigan.

GETTING AROUND

The **MV Voyageur II** (218/600-0765, www.isleroyaleboats.com, May-early Oct., schedule varies, from $87 adults, 4.5-5 hrs) circles each half of the island on different days with additional stops. From Rock Harbor, park rangers lead boat tours on the 25-passenger **MV Sandy** (906/482-0984, June-early Sept., times and rates vary) to several destinations.

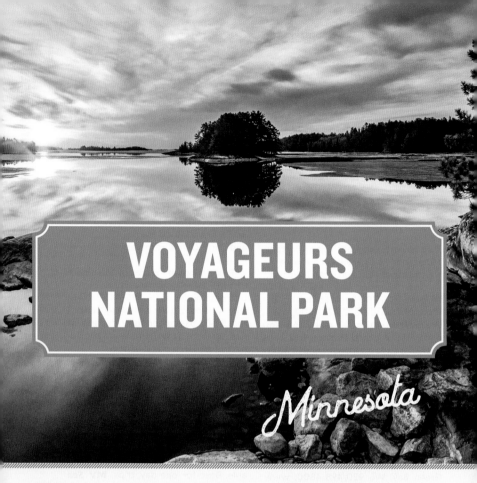

VOYAGEURS NATIONAL PARK

Minnesota

WEBSITE:
www.nps.gov/voya

PHONE NUMBER:
218/283-6600

VISITATION RANK:
50

WHY GO:
Soak up a watery
wilderness.

KEEPSAKE STAMPS ▼▼▼

Befitting the Land of 10,000 Lakes, **VOYAGEURS NATIONAL PARK** is defined by water. The park is centered on four large lakes—Rainy, Kabetogama, Namakan, and Sand Point. Hundreds of lopsided islands, peninsulas, and slender bays make up this wilderness park, formed in the footprint of an ancient glacial lake. Water, which covers more than 40 percent of the park, isn't just part of the scenery; it's the primary means of transportation. Most people see the park from a tour boat, fishing boat, houseboat, kayak, or pontoon.

This is Ojibwe country, but the park was named for early French Canadian fur traders called *voyageurs*. It shares its waters with Canada. Its remote northern location makes it one of the least visited national parks. You'll find space for solitude and to commune with nature, especially on the Kabetogama Peninsula, where night skies light up with brilliant stars or the northern lights.

PLANNING YOUR TIME

Voyageurs National Park follows the northern Minnesota-Ontario border for 55 meandering miles (89 km). Access for most visitors is through one of the four resort areas on the park's periphery. **Rainy Lake** is at the northwest corner, not far from International Falls, while **Crane Lake** is outside the park on the far southeast end. **Kabetogama** and **Ash River** sit in between. Each gateway offers lodgings, food, fishing guides, and water taxis.

Most visitors arrive in **summer** (May-Sept.) for the warmest weather. Mosquitoes are present June-July. Snow covers the park November-early April, creating a playground for snowmobiling, cross-country skiing, and snowshoeing. Lake ice usually lasts until early May.

ENTRANCES AND FEES

The park has three main entrances. East of International Falls, access **Rainy Lake** off MN 11. **Kabetogama** is north of US 53. To reach **Ash River,** drive 12 miles (19 km) northeast of US 53 on the Ash River Trail to Mead Wood Road. Except for roads leading to these entry points, there are no roads inside the park.

There is no entrance fee; however, all overnight visitors must have a **free permit,** available from the park visitors centers or self-registration stations at most boat launches.

VISITORS CENTERS

Roads go to three visitors centers that have exhibits, films, bookstores, and backcountry permits. **Rainy Lake Visitor Center** (1797 Town Rd. 342, 218/286-5258, 9am-5pm daily late May-Sept., 10am-4:30pm Thurs.-Sun. Jan.-late May) offers boat tours and ranger-led programs and has a fishing pier. **Ash River Visitor Center** (9899 Mead Wood Rd., 218/374-3221, 9am-5pm Wed.-Sun. late May-Sept.) is housed in the historic Meadwood Lodge, a 1935 log building. **Kabetogama Lake Visitor Center** (9940 Cedar Ln., 218/875-2111, 9am-5pm daily late May-Sept.) has boat tours and ranger-led programs. **Crane Lake** has a ranger station, which may be unstaffed.

SIGHTS

NIGHT SKIES

Voyageurs is certified as an International Dark Sky Park. When the weather is clear, its skies light up at night with brilliant stars and the Milky Way. In August, shooting stars streak across the sky in the **Perseid meteor shower** (50-75 meteors per hour). Stargazing is best 1am-3am from lakeside camps.

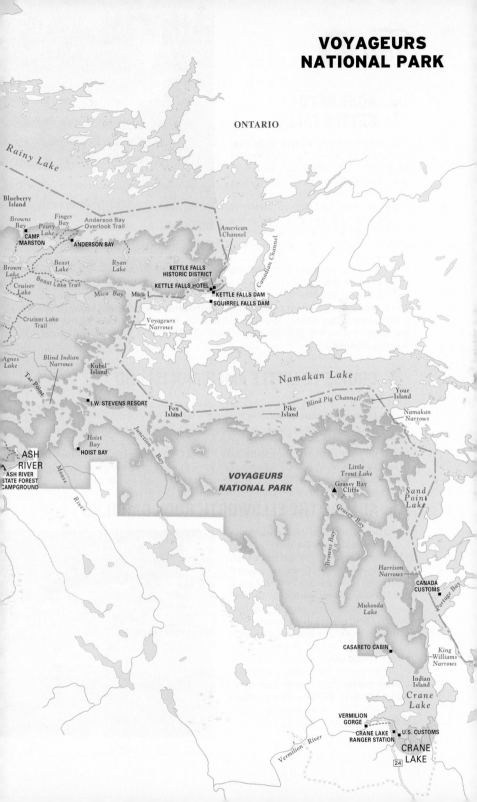

VOYAGEURS NATIONAL PARK

ONTARIO

Rainy Lake

Blueberry
Island

Browns
Bay

Finger
Bay

Peary
Lake

Anderson Bay
Overlook Trail

American
Channel

CAMP
MARSTON

ANDERSON BAY

Canadian Channel

Brown
Lake

Beast
Lake

Ryan
Lake

KETTLE FALLS
HISTORIC DISTRICT

KETTLE FALLS HOTEL

Cruiser
Lake

Beast Lake Trail

Mica Bay

Mica I

KETTLE FALLS DAM

SQUIRREL FALLS DAM

Cruiser Lake
Trail

Voyageurs
Narrows

Agnes
Lake

Blind Indian
Narrows

Kubel
Island

Namakan Lake

Your
Island

Tar Point

I.W. STEVENS RESORT

Fox
Island

Pike
Island

Blind Pig Channel

Namakan
Narrows

Hoist
Bay

HOIST BAY

ASH
RIVER

Junction Bay

VOYAGEURS
NATIONAL PARK

Little
Trout Lake

Grassy Bay
Cliffs

Sand
Point
Lake

ASH RIVER
STATE FOREST
CAMPGROUND

Moose

River

Browns Bay

Grassy Bay

Harrison
Narrows

CANADA
CUSTOMS

Portage Bay

Mukooda
Lake

CASARETO CABIN

King
Williams
Narrows

Indian
Island

Crane
Lake

VERMILION
GORGE

CRANE LAKE
RANGER STATION

U.S. CUSTOMS

CRANE
LAKE

Vermilion River

[24]

Top ③

KETTLE FALLS HOTEL

① BOAT IN TO KETTLE FALLS

The red-and-white **Kettle Falls Hotel** (12977 Chippewa Tr., 218/240-1724 May-Sept., 218/875-2070 Oct.-Apr., www.kettlefallshotel.com) is 16 miles (26 km) from the nearest public road. Visitors arrive by boat to stroll its grounds, enjoy a meal or a drink in the Lumberjack Saloon, or just relax on the endless veranda. The antiques-filled lodge is rumored to have started as a brothel around 1910 and did a thriving business during Prohibition, but then became a fashionable getaway for the rich and famous such as Charles Lindbergh and John D. Rockefeller. Nearby is the **Dam Tender's Cabin,** a restored 1912 log home. To visit the site, catch boat cruises from **Kabetogama Lake Visitor Center** (10am-3:30pm Mon.-Tues. and Fri. July-Aug., 5.5 hrs, $20-40) or **Rainy Lake Visitor Center** (days vary, 6.5 hrs, $23-45). Reservations (877/444-6777, www.recreation.gov) are recommended.

② CRUISE TO LITTLE AMERICAN ISLAND

Gold fever struck Rainy Lake in July 1893 when prospector George Davis hit pay dirt on **Little American Island.** You'll learn the whole story of the Rainy Lake Gold Rush along a short wheelchair-accessible **trail** (0.25 mi/0.4 km rt, 20 min, easy) past a mineshaft, tailings piles, and other remnants from the only area mine that produced significant ore. From Rainy Lake Visitor Center, take the **Little American Island Tour** (1pm Wed. and Fri. July-Aug., 1.5 hrs, $10-20) to visit Little American Island. Reservations (877/444-6777, www.recreation.gov) are recommended.

③ ADMIRE THE ELLSWORTH ROCK GARDENS

On the north shore of Kabetogama Lake, **Ellsworth Rock Gardens** features 62 terraced flower beds and more than 200 geometric and animal-themed sculptures assembled out of local granite. The sculptures were built by Chicago contractor and regular summer visitor Jack Ellsworth between 1944 and 1965 and make this singular spot an ideal picnic ground. A ranger leads a tour of the gardens (0.25 mi/0.4 km rt, 20 min, easy). Reach the gardens on a **boat cruise** (1pm Thurs. late June-Aug., 1.5 hrs, $13-25). Reservations (877/444-6777, www.recreation.gov) are recommended.

ELLSWORTH ROCK GARDENS

ONE DAY IN VOYAGEURS

If you only have one day in the park, take a narrated **boat tour** from Rainy Lake to **Little American Island** or **Kettle Falls.**

At visitors centers, pick up the Junior Ranger Night Explorer booklet for kids.

Due to its northern latitude, Voyageurs also sees the **northern lights,** most often on moonless nights in spring and fall. Look at them from lakeside camps, Rainy Lake Visitor Center, and Ash River Visitor Center.

RECREATION
HIKING

Voyageurs may be all about the water, but hikers will not be disappointed. These trails do not require boat access.

Rainy Lake's **Oberholtzer Trail** (1.9 mi/3 km rt, 1 hr, easy) loops through a cattail marsh, boreal forest, and scenic views of Black Bay. The first half of the trail is wheelchair-accessible.

The hilly path of Ash River's **Blind Ash Bay Trail** (2.5 mi/4 km rt, 1.5 hrs, moderate) follows a rocky ridge to great views of Kabetogama Lake and the narrow namesake bay.

A few miles northwest of the Kabetogama Lake Visitor Center, the slightly hilly **Echo Bay Trail** (2.5 mi/4 km rt, 1.5 hrs, moderate) loops through aspen and conifer stands. The trail passes beaver ponds, and you may spot wolf tracks.

The **Kab-Ash Trail** (27.9 mi/44.9 km one-way, strenuous) links the Kabetogama Lake and Ash River gateways. The path travels through a variety of forest types and over wetland boardwalks for wildlife-viewing.

CANOEING AND KAYAKING

Canoes and kayaks can navigate to 33 day-use sites. Most paddlers start at **Ash River** because it has the easiest access to quiet back bays, though the north end of **Kabetogama Lake** (accessible from the private Woodenfrog Campground) has loads of small islands with few boaters. From Ash River, paddle along the waterway to view wildlife.

SERENE LAKES AWAIT EXPLORATION.

KAYAK ON LAKE KABETOGAMA

Rentals are available at each of the four gateway towns.

Ranger-led canoe tours (1.5-2 hrs, summer only, reservations required, free) launch from **Rainy Lake** (218/286-5258) and **Kabetogama Lake Visitor Centers** (218/875-2111). The historic North Canoe Tours are aboard 26-foot (7.9-m) canoes that you help paddle. Rainy Lake also guides the Beaver Lodge Tour through Black Bay. Make reservations by calling the visitors centers.

BOATING AND FISHING

Boaters can launch from all visitors centers and the Crane Lake Ranger Station. **Permits** (877/444-6777, www.recreation.gov) are required to overnight on houseboats (May-Oct., $10 per night) or camp (May-Sept., $12-35 per night). Reservations for permits open mid-November for the following summer. You'll need a Minnesota fishing license (available in gateway towns) for angling. The gateway towns have marinas, rentals, and free public boat ramps. Boaters should understand the U.S. Coast Guard buoy system and be able to read navigation maps, which are available at visitors centers. To protect the water from aquatic invasive species like zebra mussels, it's important to clean, drain, and dry all watercraft and trailers before arrival.

WINTER RECREATION

Snow blankets Voyageurs in winter, and the lakes freeze. Groomed park trails call to snowmobilers, cross-country skiers, and snowshoers. Winter ice roads are maintained on frozen **Rainy Lake,** around the Kabetogama Peninsula's north end, and on **Kabetogama Lake.** It's the one season when you can drive a (snow) vehicle into the park! Accessed via an ice road, a sledding hill is on **Sphunge Island.**

WHERE TO STAY

INSIDE THE PARK

A night in the historic **Kettle Falls Hotel** (12977 Chippewa Tr., Kabetogama, 218/240-1724 May-Sept., 218/875-2070 Oct.-Apr., www.kettlefallshotel.com, May-Sept., from $90) is a highlight for many visitors. The 12 antiques-filled rooms in the main lodge share three baths; more modern cabins sleep up to six. The hotel rents canoes, kayaks, and boats and provides a shuttle service (fee) from the mainland.

There are more than 270 **boat-in campsites** ($12-35). Sites have fire rings, picnic tables, privies, tent pads, and bear-proof food lockers, and some have canoe rentals. Advance reservations (877/444-6777, www.recreation.gov) for a permit are required.

VIEW OF THE NORTHERN LIGHTS FROM THE ASH RIVER VISITOR CENTER

HOUSEBOATS

A houseboat is a popular means for exploring Voyageurs—it lets you enjoy the wilderness with all the comforts of home. No experience (or license) is needed; rental companies set you up with everything from food to maps. The National Park Service maintains designated mooring sites with fire rings throughout the park, or you can overnight at one of the resort areas. Overnight stays on a houseboat require a **permit reservation** (877/444-6777, www.recreation.gov, available Nov. 15 for following year, $10 per night). Park-authorized rentals include **Northernaire Houseboats** (2690 County Rd. 94, 218/286-5221, www.northernairehouseboats.com) and **Rainy Lake Houseboats** (800/554-9188, www.rainylakehouseboats.com) in the Rainy Lake area and **Ebel's Voyageur Houseboats** (888/883-2357, www.ebels.com) in Ash River.

OUTSIDE THE PARK

Dozens of lodging and campground options sit on the periphery of the park in **International Falls, Rainy Lake, Ranier, Kabetogama Lake, Crane Lake, Ash River,** and **Orr.**

GETTING THERE AND AROUND

The park has no public transit. Most visitors get around in a motorboat, sailboat, canoe, or kayak.

AIR

The nearest airport is **Falls International Airport** (INL, 3214 2nd Ave. E., 218/373-1073, www.internationalfallsairport.com), which has car rentals. The Rainy Lake Visitor Center is 14 miles (23 km) east along MN 11; the Kabetogama Lake Visitor Center is 26 miles (42 km) southeast on US 53.

BOAT

Narrated **boat tours** (June-Sept., 1.5-6.5 hrs, $25-45) go out on national park vessels from visitors centers at Rainy Lake, Kabetogama Lake, and Ash River. Starting in mid-April, make advanced **reservations** (877/444-6777, www.recreation.gov) until midnight prior to the tour. If available, you can also buy walk-in tickets (credit card only) at Rainy Lake or Kabetogama Lake Visitor Centers.

THE SOUTH

The national parks of the South contain multitudes, ranging from Appalachian mountaintops to sandy beaches. The forests in this region are renowned leaf-peeping destinations, with brilliant reds, golds, and oranges in autumn.

As the most visited park in the country, Great Smoky Mountains contains a breadth of experiences to wow hikers and road-trippers alike. Other mountain parks include Shenandoah and New River Gorge.

See for yourself these parks with their celebrated natural attributes: immense caverns at Mammoth Cave, an ancient river at New River Gorge, and old-growth cypress in Congaree. The water parks of Biscayne, Dry Tortugas, and Everglades yield rare wildlife and unique environmental niches. Top off a romp through the South with the historic Gateway Arch and Hot Springs.

◄ AUTUMN COLOR IN GREAT SMOKY MOUNTAINS

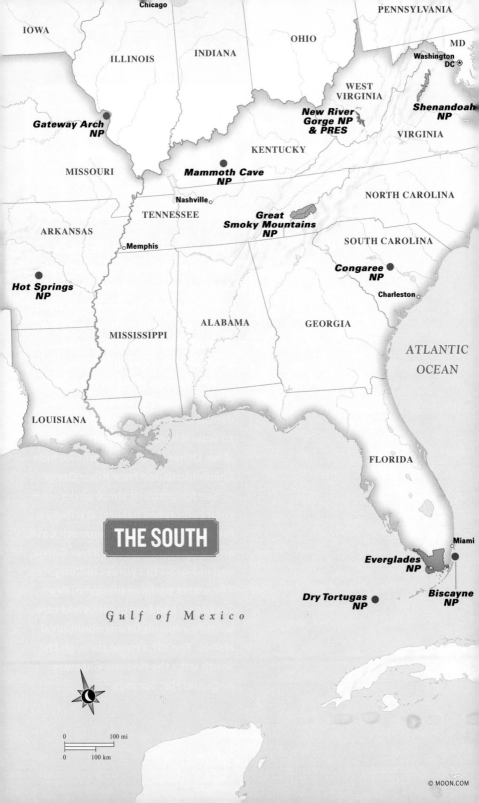

The National Parks of THE SOUTH

GREAT SMOKY MOUNTAINS, NC/TN

The most visited national park has big reason for its popularity: scenic drives, historic early settlements, hikes to high viewpoints, and evening firefly shows (page 615).

SHENANDOAH, VA

This long, narrow park is home to Skyline Drive, hiking trails, and a hardwood forest that blazes with fall colors (page 632).

MAMMOTH CAVE, KY

The world's longest cave system features flowstones, columns, stalactites, and bottomless pits (page 642).

NEW RIVER GORGE, WV

One of the oldest rivers in the country carved a deep path through New River Gorge (page 650).

GATEWAY ARCH, MO

The world's biggest freestanding arch pays tribute to the westward expansion of the United States (page 660).

HOT SPRINGS, AR

This historic landmark houses one of the most sumptuous clusters of natural hot spring bathhouses in North America (page 666).

CONGAREE, SC

The ancient cypress swamp contains what may be the tallest old-growth canopy remaining on earth (page 675).

EVERGLADES, FL

Guided trams, bike routes, and water trails offer access to this fragile swampy ecosystem where alligators and crocodiles coexist (page 680).

BISCAYNE, FL

This largely underwater park features coral reefs, shipwrecks, and mangrove forests on islands (page 694).

DRY TORTUGAS, FL

Reached by boat or seaplane, the park's seven islands combine diverse wildlife, remarkable coral reefs, shipwrecks, pirate legends, and a military fort (page 700).

1: ROARING FORK MOTOR NATURE TRAIL, GREAT SMOKY MOUNTAINS
2: BOARDWALK IN CONGAREE NATIONAL PARK
3: SUNSET OVER THE EVERGLADES

Best OF THE PARKS

Newfound Gap Road: Drive this scenic road through multiple types of forests and over the lowest pass in the Smokies (page 619).

Skyline Drive: Cruise the curves on Shenandoah's scenic ridgetop road with nearly 70 overlooks (page 637).

Mammoth Cave: Explore the most extensive cave system in the world (page 647).

New River: Raft through a deep gorge on one of the oldest rivers in the country (page 653).

Bathhouse Row: Soak in historic hot springs (page 670).

Everglades Wildlife: See alligators, crocodiles, manatees, and flamingos (page 685).

Coral reefs: Snorkel underwater gardens in Dry Tortugas (page 703).

PLANNING YOUR TRIP

Plan at least **two weeks** to tour the national parks of the South. Make lodging and campground **reservations** for Great Smoky Mountains, Shenandoah, and Everglades in advance. Tickets for tours of Mammoth Cave frequently sell out; make advance reservations to guarantee slots. Snow sometimes closes Newfound Gap Road in the Great Smoky Mountains in winter.

May-October is high season in most of the southern U.S. parks, with July and August the busiest months. Expect peak-season rates, congested roads, and difficulty getting reservations. Although summer is the prime tourist season, unless your plans involve some beach time or a stay in a mountain retreat, the humidity in the southern parks can be oppressive.

Accompanied by pleasant weather and fewer tourists, late spring **(May-June)** and fall **(September-October)** are the best times to explore the parks of Virginia, West Virginia, and Tennessee. Fall foliage in the region is some of the most spectacular in the country. South Carolina is best in spring, **mid-March to mid-May,** when natural beauty hits its apex and lodging is at a premium.

Late December-April is high season in Florida, when lodging rates are usually higher. Accommodations often cost less midseason (May-July, late Oct.-mid-Dec.). Summer is the least crowded time to visit Florida: temperatures and humidity are fairly high, and the Atlantic **hurricane season** (June-September) can bring storms.

▲ RAFTING THROUGH NEW RIVER GORGE

Road Trip

GREAT SMOKY MOUNTAINS, SHENANDOAH, NEW RIVER GORGE, AND MAMMOTH CAVE

Connecting three Appalachian national parks, this route links Shenandoah, New River Gorge, and Great Smoky Mountains with an underground finale at Mammoth Cave. Fly into Dulles International Airport outside **Washington DC** and rent a car to start your journey.

Shenandoah

165 miles (260 km) / 4 hours
From Dulles, drive 56 miles (90 km, 1 hr) on I-66 to **Front Royal,** the north entrance to **Shenandoah National Park.** Follow **Skyline Drive** at a leisurely pace to enjoy the scenery, multiple overlooks, and spectacular fall colors.

SKYLINE DRIVE, SHENANDOAH

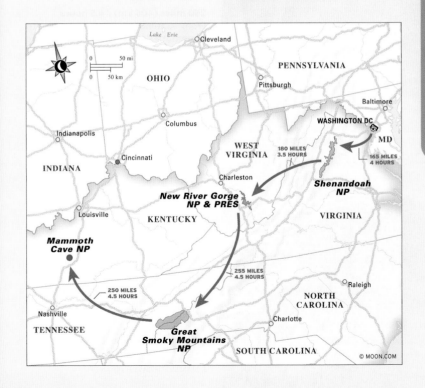

© MOON.COM

Plan for two days in the park on Skyline Drive to exit at Rockfish Gap near **Waynesboro.**

New River Gorge

180 miles (290 km) / 3.5 hours
From Skyline Drive, head west on US 250 to reach I-64. Leave the interstate at exit 156 onto US 60 west. Turn south onto US 19 toward Lansing to reach Canyon Rim Visitor Center and **New River Gorge National Park.** After two days in the park, end your adventures at **Hinton.**

Great Smoky Mountains

255 miles (410 km) / 4.5 hours
From Hinton, take WV 20 south to get onto I-77 south to I-81 south. Continue on I-81, then connect onto I-40 west onto the Winfield Dunn Parkway and US 441 south to **Gatlinburg** and **Great Smoky Mountains National Park.** Your journey crossing the Smokies and looping around back to Gatlinburg begins here on **Newfound Gap Road.** Plan for 2-3 days to explore the park's scenic roads and trails.

Mammoth Cave

250 miles (405 km) / 4.5 hours
From Gatlinburg, go northwest to **Mammoth Cave National Park,** where you can spend the night in the **Lodge at Mammoth Cave.** The following day, go underground with a ranger-led tour, with options ranging from 1.25 to 6 hours.

1: NEW RIVER GORGE BRIDGE
2: CADES COVE ROAD, GREAT SMOKY MOUNTAINS
3: MAMMOTH CAVE ENTRANCE

GREAT SMOKY MOUNTAINS NATIONAL PARK

Tennessee and North Carolina

KEEPSAKE STAMPS ▼▼▼

WEBSITE:
www.nps.gov/grsm

PHONE NUMBER:
865/436-1200

VISITATION RANK:
1

WHY GO:
See the country's
oldest mountains.

▲ GREAT SMOKY MOUNTAINS
NATIONAL PARK

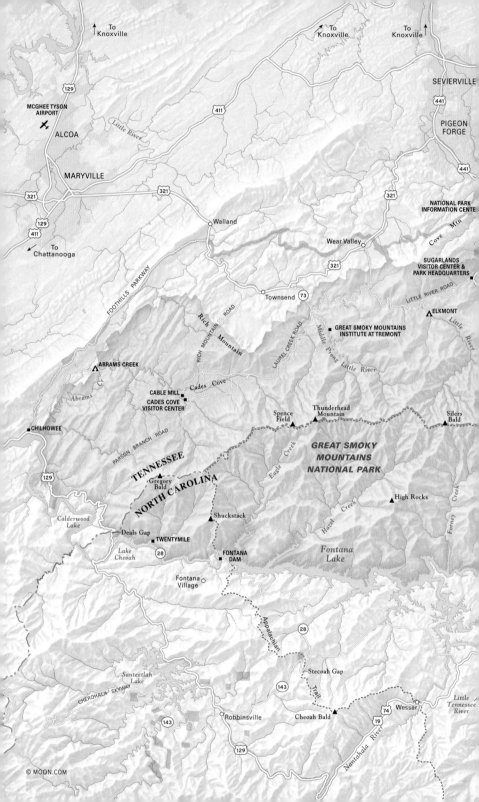

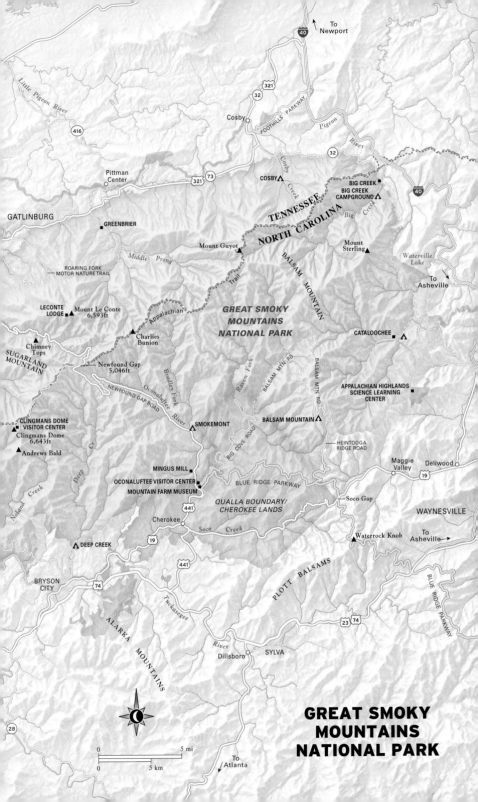

GREAT SMOKY
MOUNTAINS
NATIONAL PARK

GREAT SMOKY MOUNTAINS NATIONAL PARK is the most visited national park in the country, with visitor numbers topping 12 million annually. With a mix of natural wonders and historic charm, the park straddles the North Carolina-Tennessee state line.

On the wild, sparsely populated North Carolina side, the mountains pile up against one another with tall peaks, steep slopes, and deep coves. These places that once were the land of the Cherokee people feel remote and isolated. On the more developed Tennessee side, Cades Cove is a sightseer's delight, with wildlife wandering amid its preserved historic churches, schools, and homesteads.

In autumn, hardwood trees splash color across mountainsides and valleys. Gold, red, and orange hues lure hikers and drivers for one of the most impressive displays in the eastern United States.

PLANNING YOUR TIME

Great Smoky Mountains National Park straddles the border between Tennessee and North Carolina. Most visitors devote a single day to the park, driving **Newfound Gap Road** from Gatlinburg, Tennessee, south to the North Carolina town of Cherokee. But spend at least **three days** here to hike, watch wildlife, and soak up history.

High season is **May-October.** Spring wildflower blooms come on in May. **Summer** (mid-June-mid-Aug.) offers cool mountain air, and October attracts leaf-peepers gawking at blazing reds, yellows, and burgundies.

Due to a vast difference in elevation (5,700 ft/1,737 m) between the park's lowest and highest point, weather can vary wildly. Clingmans Dome, the highest point in the park, has an average high temperature of only 65°F (18°C) in July and can see snow flurries September to June. In Cades Cove, July can swelter in the low 90s (32°C) with humidity.

Winter (Nov.-Apr.) finds the snowy park less crowded but still beautiful. Many **park roads close in winter,** though dates vary. **Newfound Gap Road** remains open except for temporary closures for winter storms. Check current conditions (865/436-1200) before visiting.

Within the park, make **camping reservations** six months in advance and reservations at LeConte Lodge **one year in advance.** Advance reservations for **parking** may be needed at Laurel Falls Trailhead.

ENTRANCES AND FEES

The park has three main entrances. **From Gatlinburg, Tennessee,** at the north end of Newfound Gap Road, US 441 leads south 2 miles (3.2 km) into the park. The southern entrance of Newfound Gap Road is 2 miles (3.2 km) north of **Cherokee, North Carolina,** along US 441. From **Townsend, Tennessee,** TN 73 heads 3 miles (4.8 km) east into the park at Cades Cove.

There's no entrance fee, but you may need a parking tag (from $5).

VISITORS CENTERS

Sugarlands Visitor Center

From Tennessee, **Sugarlands Visitor Center and Park Headquarters** (1420 Fighting Creek Gap Rd., 865/436-1291, 8am-7pm daily June-Aug., 8am-6pm daily Apr.-May and Sept.-Oct., 8am-5pm daily Mar. and Nov., 8am-4:30pm daily Dec.-Feb.) is just inside the park about 2 miles (3.2 km) from Gatlinburg. The center has natural history exhibits, a bookstore, a backcountry office, and a 20-minute film introducing the park.

Oconaluftee Visitor Center

From North Carolina, **Oconaluftee Visitor Center** (1194 Newfound Gap Rd.,

Top **3**

1 DRIVE NEWFOUND GAP ROAD

Easily the most heavily traveled route in the Smokies, **Newfound Gap Road** (US 441, 32 mi/50 km, 1-1.5 hrs) connects Cherokee with Gatlinburg. Newfound Gap Road is the perfect introduction to Great Smoky Mountains National Park: Contour-hugging curves, overlooks with million-dollar views, easy hikes right off the roadway, and a 3,000-foot (914 m) elevation change give you a great overview of these mountains and this spectacular park. During peak times in the summer and fall, you'll encounter traffic jams along this scenic route.

COLORFUL FALL VISTAS ALONG CADES COVE LOOP

2 TOUR CADES COVE

Fields, forests, high peaks, wildlife, and historic structures are just some of the highlights of the **Cades Cove Loop** (11 mi/18 km, 2 hrs, open to bicycles but closed to vehicles Wed. May-early Sept.). This one-way paved road circles the valley floor. Wildlife is especially active in the hours around dawn and dusk. Due to its popularity, expect crowds, especially in the fall. Two shortcuts cross the valley to shorten the drive or circle back for one more look.

In 1850, nearly 700 people called this valley home. Today, a number of historic structures remain: churches, a few barns, log houses, and smaller buildings. Among them is the most photographed structure in the park, the **Methodist Church.** From time to time a wedding is held here, though it's more common for visitors to leave handwritten prayers on scraps of paper at the altar. The **Cable Mill Historic Area** is the busiest section of the loop, where an actual mill still operates, and you can even buy cornmeal or flour ground on-site. Hikes include gentle strolls to homesteads, cabins, and churches, or longer walks to **Abrams Falls.**

3 LOOK OVER THE MOUNTAINS FROM CLINGMANS DOME

At 6,643 feet (2,025 m), **Clingmans Dome** is the third-highest mountain in the eastern United States, and the highest in the Great Smoky Mountains. A flying saucer-like observation tower at the end of a long steep walkway gives 360-degree views of the surrounding mountains. To get to Clingmans Dome, turn off Newfound Gap Road 0.1 mile (0.2 km) south of Newfound Gap, and then take Clingmans Dome Road (closed Dec.-Mar.), which leads 7 miles (11 km) to the parking lot. The peak is near the center of the park, due north from Bryson City, North Carolina. In winter, when the road is closed, the observation tower remains open for those willing to hike.

ONE DAY IN GREAT SMOKY MOUNTAINS

From either entrance, drive the **Newfound Gap Road,** stopping at sights along the way. En route from Clingmans Dome, hike **Andrews Bald** to take in the 360-degree view of the Great Smokies. Finish by circling **Cades Cove** to soak up the pastoral countryside.

828/497-1904, 8am-7pm daily June-Aug., 8am-6pm daily Apr.-May and Sept.-Oct., 8am-5pm daily Mar. and Nov., 8am-4:30pm daily Dec.-Feb.) is 2 miles (3.2 km) north of Cherokee on US 441 (Newfound Gap Rd.). It has history exhibits, ranger programs, a bookstore, and the Mountain Farm Museum outside.

Clingmans Dome Visitor Contact Station

Along Newfound Gap Road is the turnoff to Clingmans Dome and the **Clingmans Dome Visitor Contact Station** (Clingmans Dome Rd., 865/436-1200, 10am-6:30pm daily June-Aug., 10am-6pm daily Apr.-June and Sept.-Oct., 9:30am-5pm daily Nov.). It has park information and a bookstore.

Cades Cove Visitor Center

In Cades Cove, the **Cades Cove Visitor Center** (Cades Cove Loop Rd., 865/436-1200, 9am-4:30pm daily Dec., except Dec. 25, 9am-5pm daily Jan.-June, 9am-7pm daily July-Aug., 9am-6:30pm Sept.-Oct., 9am-5:30pm daily Nov.). It has ranger programs and a bookstore plus indoor and outdoor exhibits, including historic structures illustrating mountain life and culture.

SIGHTS

NEWFOUND GAP ROAD

Mountain Farm Museum

The **Mountain Farm Museum** (Oconaluftee Visitor Center, sunrise-sunset daily year-round, free) showcases some of the finest farm buildings of the park. Most date to the early 1900s. Among them are a barn, an apple house, and the Davis House, a log home built from chestnut wood and constructed before the American chestnut blight decimated the species. During peak times, costumed living-history interpreters demonstrate the day-to-day chores that would've occurred.

Mingus Mill

North of the Oconaluftee Visitor Center you'll find **Mingus Mill** (9am-5pm daily mid-Mar.-mid-Nov., 9am-5pm

▼ CLINGMANS DOME

AVOID THE CROWDS

The most crowded months are July-August and October. In summer, road congestion peaks 10am-5pm on **Newfound Gap Road** and **Cades Cove Loop;** early morning and evening drives will have less traffic. For October leaf-peeping, roads tend to clog in late afternoon and evening; take your driving tour earlier in the day for more breathing room.

Fri.-Sun. Nov.). This historic gristmill was built in 1886; rather than use a waterwheel to power the machinery and the mill in the building, it uses a water-powered turbine to generate mechanical power. The cast-iron turbine still works!

Deep Creek Valley Overlook

The **Deep Creek Valley Overlook** (14 mi/23 km north of Oconaluftee Visitor Center and 16 mi/26 km south of Sugarlands Visitor Center) yields a long view of the mountains, which roll away to the horizon.

Oconaluftee River Valley Overlook

Midway along Newfound Gap Road is the **Oconaluftee River Valley Overlook,** where you can spy the deep cut of the valley formed by the Oconaluftee River.

Newfound Gap

At 5,046 feet (1,538 m), **Newfound Gap** is the highest elevation on Newfound Gap Road with impressive views. The Rockefeller Memorial, a simple stone terrace that straddles the Tennessee-North Carolina state line, commemorates a $5 million gift made by the Rockefeller Foundation to acquire land for the park. To avoid the crowds, go early in the morning or near sunset.

Campbell Overlook

Named after one of the founding members of the Smoky Mountains Hiking Club, the **Carlos Campbell Overlook** (2 mi/3.2 km south of Sugarlands Visitor Center) is home to one of the best views of Mount LeConte. At 6,593 feet (2,009 m), LeConte is the third-highest peak in the Smokies.

GREENBRIER COVE

Greenbrier Cove was once home to a mountain community. This area was settled in the early 1800s, and families farmed, trapped, and hunted the land until the establishment of the national park. This cove has an interesting footnote: Dolly Parton's ancestors, Benjamin C. and Margaret Parton, moved here in the 1850s, and their descendants left when the park was formed. Greenbrier is stunning in all seasons but especially in the spring, when it becomes a wildflower hot spot.

COSBY

For the first half of the 20th century, **Cosby** was known as the moonshine

MINGUS MILL

capital of the world. Today, it is a friendly town with a few restaurants and a handful of cabin rentals at one of the lesser-used park entrances. The real attraction is spring wildflowers and hiking trails such as Hen Wallow Falls.

CATALOOCHEE VALLEY

This isolated valley on the northeastern edge of the park was home in 1910 to more than 1,200 people in the communities of Big and Little Cataloochee. By the 1940s most were gone. Today, only a few **historic structures** remain of the communities that thrived here.

The most prominent building is the **Palmer Chapel.** Built in 1898, it still sees sporadic use. Across the road is the **Beech Grove School,** the last of three schools to serve the children of the valley. Just up the road is the **Caldwell House,** a frame-built home with paneling on the interior walls. The final structure is the **Palmer House** (off Big Creek Rd.), an 1800s log home with a 20th-century addition. Surrounding the historic structures are good locations for wildlife-watching, especially for elk. Pick up a self-guided tour booklet at the valley entrance.

ELKMONT

Listed on the National Register of Historic Places, **Elkmont Historic District** started as a small logging town in 1908. Later, the Wonderland Park Hotel and cottages were added. Once the park was established, cottage owners were granted lifetime leases for their property, and family members continued to renew leases every 20 years until the early 1990s. The hotel collapsed in 2005. Several of the cottages have been restored; you can walk through four of them. The Spence and Appalachian Club cabins take reservations one year in advance for day-use (www.recreation.gov, $150-250).

Fireflies

The **synchronous fireflies** may have been one of the reasons the Wonderland Park Hotel was built in Elkmont. For a two-week window in early summer (late May-early June), their nightly light show delights crowds as drifts of male fireflies rise from the grass to flash their mating signal—blinking in coordination.

Viewing the synchronous fireflies has become so popular that a **lottery** (877/444-6777, www.recreation.gov) controls access to limit traffic congestion. The lottery opens for three days in late April with applicants choosing two dates; results become available by mid-May. Winners receive a parking pass for Sugarlands Visitor Center, where they board a shuttle to Elkmont and back for the firefly show.

FONTANA LAKE

At the southern edge of Great Smoky Mountains National Park lies Fontana Lake, a long reservoir created in the 1940s by **Fontana Dam,** the tallest dam in the eastern United States. It provided much-needed electricity to the factories churning out materials for World War II, including Oak Ridge, Tennessee, where research leading to the atomic bomb was conducted.

The exhibits at the **Fontana Dam Visitor Center** (Fontana Dam Rd., www.tva.gov, 9am-7pm daily Apr.-Aug., 9am-6pm daily Sept.-Oct., free) tell the story of the region and the construction of the dam. There's also a small gift shop and a viewing platform overlooking the dam.

DEEP CREEK

Just south of Cherokee and north of Bryson City, **Deep Creek** is a spot more popular with locals than tourists, but it's worth a stop. Deep Creek is relatively placid, aside from a couple of waterfalls upstream. It's a good place for wading, tubing, picnicking, and hiking.

SCENIC DRIVES
ROARING FORK

The **Roaring Fork Motor Nature Trail** (5.5 mi/8.8 km, 2 hrs, open Mar.-Nov., no RVs or trailers over 25 ft/7.6 m) used to be one of the most beautiful drives in Great Smoky Mountains National Park. This narrow **one-way loop,** which follows the old curvy roadbed of the Roaring Fork Community, passes through what were lush rhododendron thickets and dense hardwood forests. A 2016

ROARING FORK CREEK

wildfire left a landscape of charred tree stands and fewer rhodies and laurel, but the greenery will flourish again in time.

To start, turn onto Historic Nature Trail (Old Airport Rd.) at traffic light 8 in Gatlinburg and follow the signs. Drive a short distance on Cherokee Orchard Road, which runs through what was an 800-acre (324 ha) commercial orchard in the 1920s and 1930s. Shortly after the orchard, you'll be at the head of the trail.

RICH MOUNTAIN ROAD

Rich Mountain Road (7 mi/11 km, 30 min, open mid-Apr.-mid-Nov., no RVs or trailers) is a photographer's dream. Running north from Cades Cove over Rich Mountain to **Tuckaleechee Cove** and **Townsend,** this primitive **one-way gravel road** provides stunning views of Cades and Tuckaleechee Coves. Bear, deer, and turkeys make frequent appearances. The narrow, twisting, and steep road is typically in good condition. It's best for trucks or SUVs (no 4WD needed) but not low-clearance vehicles.

BALSAM MOUNTAIN ROAD

Balsam Mountain Road (14 mi/23 km, 1.5 hrs, open mid-May-Oct., no RVs or trailers) is a secluded drive. Accessible only from the Blue Ridge Parkway near Soco Gap, the curvy narrow road traverses a ridgeline. To reach Balsam Mountain Road, turn off the Parkway (milepost 458) and follow Heintooga Ridge Road to the Heintooga Overlook and Picnic Area; here the road changes names to Balsam Mountain Road and turns to gravel. As soon as it turns into Balsam Mountain Road, it becomes **one-way,** so you're committed to follow it to its end.

FOOTHILLS PARKWAY

Separated from the main body of the national park, the paved **Foothills Parkway** (open year-round, weather permitting) delivers vibrant fall foliage in October. It is in two segments in Tennessee. **Foothills Parkway West** (33 mi/53 km, 1 hr) goes from US 129 at Chilhowee, crosses US 321 near Walland, and ends at US 321 at Wears Valley. From Chilhowee to Walland, the

Best Hike

ANDREWS BALD

DISTANCE: 3.6 miles (5.8 km) round-trip
DURATION: 3 hours
ELEVATION CHANGE: 1,200 feet (366 m)
DIFFICULTY: moderate
TRAILHEAD: Clingmans Dome parking area at the end of Clingmans Dome Road (closed in winter)

The highest grassy bald (a high mountain-top meadow) in Great Smoky Mountains National Park is Andrews Bald. It is a beautiful sight, especially in summer when it's blooming with wildflowers, flame azalea, and rhododendron.

The **Forney Ridge Trail** starts in a spruce-fir forest that was once thick but is now dead or dying due to a tiny bug—the balsam woolly adelgid—that devours Fraser firs. However, the white bones of the tree trunks jutting up from the land are striking. The views get considerably better where the forest opens up at the edge of **Andrews Bald,** yielding a broad panorama.

route hugs the spine of Chilhowee Mountain with more than 15 overlooks, including an observation tower at Look Rock. From Walland to Wears Valley, the curvy route has about 10 overlooks and spans multiple bridges as it arcs past Rocky Mountain. **Foothills Parkway East** (6 mi/10 km, 20 min) goes from I-40, exit 443, over Green Mountain to Cosby with three scenic pullouts.

HIKING
NEWFOUND GAP ROAD
Kephart Prong Trail

After crossing a footbridge over the Oconaluftee River, follow the wide, nearly flat **Kephart Prong Trail** (4 mi/6.4 km rt, 2 hrs, easy) to Kephart Shelter. The route passes the ruins of a 1930s Civilian Conservation Corps camp: foundations, chimneys, a fish hatchery, and narrow-gauge logging railroad tracks.

Charlies Bunion

From the Newfound Gap parking lot, the **Charlies Bunion Trail** (8 mi/12.9 km rt, 7-8 hrs, strenuous) follows the Appalachian Trail and the Boulevard to Mount LeConte. After an hour, the Boulevard forks off to the left; go straight to the Icewater Spring Shelter. From the spring, continue to a short spur trail on the left that leads to the rock outcrop known as Charlies Bunion for the views.

Alum Cave Bluffs to Mount LeConte

Arrive early to get a parking spot for the popular **Alum Cave Bluffs to Mount LeConte Trail** (10 mi/16.1 km rt, 5 hrs, moderate). From Alum Cave Trailhead, it starts off gently climbing alongside Alum Cave Creek amid rhododendrons. After reaching Arch Rock, a natural tunnel at Alum Cave Bluffs, climb stone steps to Inspiration Point for a territorial view; this is the halfway point where many hikers turn around. Then, the path steepens and narrows

VIEWS FROM CHARLES BUNION TRAIL

onto precipitous rock ledges with steel cables bolted into the mountain for handholds. Soon, the trail intersects with Rainbow Falls Trail, leading to the summit of Mount LeConte. This is the shortest trail to LeConte Lodge.

Chimney Tops

Chimney Tops (4 mi/6.4 km rt, 3.5 hrs, strenuous) leads to an outstanding view from its namesake pinnacles. The route climbs along picturesque cascades, pools, and boulders on **Walker Camp Prong** before crossing **Road Prong** twice. At a fork, the right trail steepens and narrows on the ridge and up a steep rock scramble to summit the first of the Chimney Tops.

CADES COVE

John Oliver Cabin Accessible Trail

The **John Oliver Cabin Accessible Trail** (0.6 mi/1 km rt, 20 min, easy) tours fields frequented by deer, bears, and turkeys. The wide paved trail with enough room for wheelchairs to pass each other goes to the historic **John Oliver Cabin.**

Abrams Falls Trail

Abrams Falls Trail (5 mi/8 km rt, 3 hrs, moderate) follows **Abrams Creek** to the waterfall. The trail leaves the creek

three times to climb up and around a ridge to drop to the falls.

Rich Mountain Loop

At the beginning of Cades Cove Loop Road, **Rich Mountain Loop** (8.5 mi/13.7 km rt, 4.5 hrs, moderate) circles around Rich Mountain via several trails: Rich Mountain Loop, Indian Grave Gap, and Crooked Arm Ridge. The trail links up a classic meadow with overlooks of Cades Cove. On the Indian Gap Trail, take the side spur to Cerulean Knob, the highest point on Rich Mountain.

CATALOOCHEE VALLEY

Boogerman Trail

From Cataloochee Campground, the **Boogerman Loop** (7.4 mi/11.9 km rt, 3.5-4 hrs, moderate) starts on the Boogerman Trail to climb, drop, and climb again. It reaches **stone walls** and a **cabin** before turning right onto the **Caldwell Fork Trail.** Cross Caldwell Fork several times before connecting back to the trailhead.

Laurel Falls Trail

As the shortest waterfall hike in the park, **Laurel Falls** (2.6 mi/4.2 km rt, 1.5-2 hrs, moderate) lures excessive crowds of hikers. From Little River Road, a short, steep start on broken pavement

A SMALL WATERFALL IN THE SMOKIES

assumes a gentle grade to the scenic fall. In 2021, a pilot program began issuing advanced **timed-entry reservations** for parking (www.recreation.gov, $14 per vehicle) to alleviate crowding; check online for reservation dates and windows.

ROARING FORK
Rainbow Falls

On Cherokee Orchard Loop Road, **Rainbow Falls Trail** (5.4 mi/8.7 km rt, 3-4 hrs, moderate) is the most popular waterfall hike. The route climbs alongside LeConte Creek via switchbacks and across the creek on a **log bridge.** At another crossing, you can see 80-foot-high (24-m) **Rainbow Falls** above but continue to a spot just below the falls.

GREENBRIER COVE AND COSBY
Ramsey Cascades Trail

Ramsey Cascades (8 mi/12.9 km rt, 5.5 hrs, strenuous) is the park's tallest waterfall, spilling 100 feet (30 m) in a series of steps before collecting in a pool at the base. From Greenbrier Road, the route starts on an easy jeep trail prolific with wildflowers in early summer. Then it steepens and crosses **Ramsey Prong.** When you hear the waterfall, be cautious on the final rocky and slick approach.

BLACK BEAR IN CADES COVE

Porters Creek Trail

On Greenbrier Road, **Porters Creek Trail** (4 mi/6.4 km rt, 2 hrs, moderate) goes to **Fern Branch Falls** at 60 feet (18 m) high. In spring, the path is thick with moss and wildflowers.

Hen Wallow Falls Trail

From the Gabes Mountain Trailhead, take the steady climb up the sometimes rugged **Gabes Mountain Trail** to a signed steep side spur. This side trail goes to **Hen Wallow Falls** (4.4 mi/7.1 km rt, 2-3.5 hrs, moderate) which tumbles 90 feet (27 m) in a fan into a small pool that is full of salamanders. During dry months, the falls are still pretty, but less wow-inducing.

RECREATION
BACKPACKING

Backpacking in the Smokies requires **permits** ($4-8 pp/night) with options to stay in tent sites or backcountry shelters, both with bear cable systems for hanging food. Reservations open 30 days in advance; you can get them at the **Backcountry Information Office** (Sugarlands Visitor Center, 865/436-1297) or **online** (https://smokiespermits.nps.gov). The best two-night trip goes from **Grotto Falls** to **Mount LeConte** (13.9 mi/22.4 km rt, 2 days, strenuous) with the option to overnight in LeConte Shelter. The most coveted trip for 7-8 days is the **Appalachian Trail** (71.6 mi/115.2 km).

BIKING

Bicyclists can ride the one-way **Cades Cove Loop Road** (11 mi/18 km, 1-2 hrs without stops). Cycling is best on Wednesdays (May-early Sept.) when the road closes to motor vehicles; ride in afternoons or evenings for fewer cyclists. The **Cades Cove Store** (near Cades Cove Campground, 865/448-9034) rents bicycles in summer and fall.

FISHING

Smallmouth bass and rock bass are fairly abundant in streams. Anglers go to **Cosby Creek** year-round, fishing along the creek in spring and headwaters in summer. Other top fishing creeks include **Cataloochee Creek, Little**

Pigeon River, and **Little River.** For boat fishing, **Fontana Lake** contains large-mouth, smallmouth, and rock bass plus deeper water has walleye and muskies. You'll need a license from Tennessee or North Carolina, depending on the fishing locale.

HORSEBACK RIDING

Three commercial stables offer guided horseback riding mid-March-mid-November. **Smokemont** (near Cherokee, NC, 828/497-2373, www.smokemontridingstable.com) has rides for 1, 2.5, or 4 hours. **Smoky Mountain** (Gatlinburg, TN, 865/436-5634, www.smokymountainridingstables.com) leads 45-minute rides. **Cades Cove** (10018 Campground Dr., Townsend, TN, 865/448-9009, www.cadescovestables.com) guides one-hour rides.

WHERE TO STAY

INSIDE THE PARK

LeConte Lodge (865/429-5704, www.lecontelodge.com, late Mar.-mid-Nov., from $159) offers the only true lodgings in the park, accessible via a 5.5- to 8-mile (8.8-12.9 km) hike on the easier Trillium Gap Trail, shorter Alum Cave Trail, or more difficult Boulevard Trail. Meals and bedding are included. Even though there is no running water or electricity, the lodge books quickly. Reservations are via lottery **one year in advance.**

The park has 10 campgrounds (plus group and horse camps), equipped with flush toilets, fire rings, and picnic tables. **Reservations** (877/444-6777, www.recreation.gov, $18-36) are accepted up to six months in advance for part or all of the campgrounds.

Three campgrounds offer reservations and first-come, first-served tent and RV sites. **Smokemont** (Cherokee, NC, 142 sites, year-round) is the only campground on Newfound Gap Road. **Elkmont** (Gatlinburg, TN, 220 sites, year-round) and **Cosby** (Cosby, TN, 157 sites, Apr.-Oct.) are on the park's north side.

Reservations are required for seven campgrounds: **Balsam Mountain** (Cherokee, NC, 42 tent and RV sites, mid-May-early Oct.) and **Deep Creek Campground** (Bryson City, NC, 92 tent and RV sites, Apr.-Oct.) are in the south. **Cataloochee** (Waynesville, NC, 27 tent and RV sites, Apr.-Oct.) and **Big Creek** (Newport, NC, 12 walk-in tents sites, Apr.-Oct.) are on the east side. **Abrams**

▼ RAMSEY CASCADES

MIDDLE PRONG OF THE LITTLE RIVER

Creek (Walland, TN, 16 tent and small RV sites, late Apr.-mid-Oct.) and **Look Rock** (Walland, TN, 68 tent and RV sites, electrical sites available, late Apr.-mid-Oct.) are on the west side. **Cades Cove** (Townsend, TN, 159 sites, year-round) is on the north side.

OUTSIDE THE PARK

Most accommodations, dining options, and services are found in **Gatlinburg, Tennessee,** or **Cherokee, North Carolina.** **Cosby, Tennessee,** has a limited selection of accommodations and dining options. For spring, summer, and fall, make reservations at least six months in advance.

GETTING THERE

AIR

Asheville Regional Airport (AVL, 61 Terminal Dr., Asheville, NC, 828/684-2226, www.flyavl.com) is about one hour east of Cherokee. **McGhee Tyson Airport** (TYS, 2055 Alcoa Hwy., Alcoa, TN, 865/342-3000, www.flyknoxville.com) is about one hour west of Gatlinburg. Both airports have car rentals.

CAR

There are three main entrances to Great Smoky Mountains National Park. From **Cherokee, North Carolina,** drive 2 miles (3.2 km) north along US 441 into the park on Newfound Gap Road.

From **Gatlinburg, Tennessee,** follow US 441 south 2 miles (3.2 km) into the park along Newfound Gap Road.

Townsend, Tennessee, provides access to Cades Cove via TN 73, 3 miles (4.8 km) east.

There are 17 additional points of entry into the park via automobile. The majority are gravel roads in varying states of maintenance that require different degrees of driving confidence and skill. If you're up for an adventure, these roads can lead to some beautiful corners of the park.

GETTING AROUND

The park has no shuttles or public transportation—you will need **your own vehicle.** It also has **no gas stations;** fill up in Cherokee, North Carolina, or in Tennessee at Gatlinburg or Townsend. You may need a **parking tag** (from $5) for designated areas inside the park.

APPALACHIAN TRAIL

Cutting through the heart of Great Smoky Mountains National Park, the **Appalachian Trail** runs along the high ridgeline that forms the border between North Carolina and Tennessee. Inside the park, the trail traverses 71.6 miles (115.2 km). It's a highlight for thru-hikers (those hiking the whole 2,190-mi/3,524-km trail between Georgia and Maine), segment hikers (those hiking the whole thing one piece at a time), and day hikers (those just out for a taste). For the lowdown on the Appalachian Trail, contact the **Appalachian Trail Conservancy** (www.appalachiantrail.org) or visit the **National Park Service** (www.nps.gov/appa), where you'll find trip-planning information, maps, trail reports, and more.

Permits

Though there are no fees required to hike the Appalachian Trail outside the national parks, hiking the trail **overnight** in Great Smoky Mountains National Park requires a permit (https://smokiespermits.nps.gov), available 30 days in advance. **Thru-hikers** ($20-40 permit) begin and end their hike at least 50 miles (81 km) from the border of the park and only travel on the Appalachian Trail while in the park. **Segment hikers and backpackers** ($4-8 pp/night permit) are those who hike all or a portion of the Appalachian Trail inside the park. Contact the **Backcountry Information Office** (Sugarlands Visitor Center, 865/436-1297) with questions.

Trail Shelters and Campsites

Great Smoky Mountains National Park has about a dozen **Appalachian Trail shelters,** each of which sleeps 12 people. Numerous backcountry campsites are also along and near the trail. Segment hikers and backpackers can reserve spots in shelters or campsites on their permits. Thru-hikers do not need to reserve specific shelters or campsites on their permits; four first-come, first-served spots are reserved in each shelter for thru-hikers, but you can also sleep in tents outside. For a complete list of shelters and backcountry campsites, consult a park trail map.

Day Hikes

Day hikers are drawn to the Appalachian Trail's fantastic balds (high meadows), like Andrews Bald; knobs like Charlies Bunion; peaks like Mount Cammerer and Rocky Top (yes, the one from the song); and just to say they've hiked part of the Appalachian Trail. The route through the park is always high and at times rocky, steep, or both, but the views are worth it.

THE APPALACHIAN TRAIL

Day hikers who want to log a few miles of the Appalachian Trail will find a few opportunities to get their boots muddy. Notable day hikes include:

Mount Cammerer (11.1 mi/17.9 km rt, 6 hrs, strenuous): Take the Low Gap Trail at the Cosby Campground to the Appalachian Trail, then proceed to the summit and a stone fire tower. Note: Only 4.2 miles (6.8 km) are on the Appalachian Trail.

Rocky Top (13.9 mi/22.4 km rt, 7 hrs, strenuous): Follow the Anthony Creek Trailhead from the Cades Cove picnic area to Bote Mountain Trail. At Spence Field, you'll meet up with the Appalachian Trail; follow it to Rocky Top and spectacular views.

NAME	LOCATION	PRICE	SEASON	SITES	AMENITIES
Abrams Creek	Foothills Pkwy.	$17.50	Apr.-Oct.	16	tent and RV sites
Balsam Mountain	Balsam Mountain Rd.	$17.50	May-Oct.	42	tent sites
Big Creek	off Hwy. 284	$17.50	Apr.-Oct.	12	tent, RV, group, and horse sites
Cades Cove	Cades Cove	$25	year-round	159	tent and RV sites; camp store
Cataloochee	Cataloochee	$25	Apr.-Oct.	27	tent and RV sites
Cosby	Cosby	$17.50	Apr.-Oct.	157	tent and RV sites
Deep Creek	north of Bryson City	$25	Apr.-Oct.	92	tent and RV sites; dump station
Elkmont	Sugarlands Visitor Center	$25-27	year-round	220	tents and RV sites; dump station
Smokemont	Newfound Gap Road	$25	year-round	142	tent and RV sites; dump station

DRIVING

Newfound Gap Road (US 441, 33 mi/53 km) bisects the park from north to south. It's the most heavily traveled route in the park and provides a good introduction for first-time visitors. But the full length of Newfound Gap Road (70 mi/113 km) starts at the southern terminus of the Blue Ridge Parkway, just outside Cherokee, North Carolina, and ends in Knoxville, Tennessee, 32 miles (52 km) northwest of the park. It's easy to make the trip from one end to the other in an afternoon, though it may take a little longer in peak seasons.

To reach **Cataloochee Valley** from I-40, take exit 20 onto US 276. Take an immediate right onto Cove Creek Road. Zigzag up the gravel and paved road following the narrow, winding route for about 12 miles (19 km). It will suddenly open up into the wide, grassy expanse that is Cataloochee Valley. The valley is open to vehicle traffic 8am-sunset.

HISTORIC CABIN AT LECONTE LODGE

SHENANDOAH NATIONAL PARK

Virginia

WEBSITE:
www.nps.gov/shen

PHONE NUMBER:
540/999-3500

VISITATION RANK:
19

WHY GO:
Tour the Blue Ridge
Mountains.

KEEPSAKE STAMPS ▼▼▼

▲ DARK HOLLOW TRAIL

In **SHENANDOAH NATIONAL PARK,** both rare and common animals thrive: big brown bats and black bears, white-tailed deer and bald eagles, and the endangered Shenandoah salamander. But the park's beauty comes from its vast forests. Trees cover about 95 percent of the park, changing color with the season: flowering in spring, greening in summer, and turning gold and red in fall. They emit organic compounds into the air that give the Blue Ridge Mountains their name.

This ridgetop land has hollows long used by Indigenous people for hunting and foraging as far back as 8,000-9,000 years ago. Former homesites of European settlers are visible in crumbling walls and chimneys while mossy cemeteries hide in the underbrush. Skyline Drive winds through lush forests with trails departing to a dozen waterfalls and scads of summits. Paralleling the road, a 101-mile (163-km) segment of the Appalachian Trail traverses the length of the park.

PLANNING YOUR TIME

Only 70 miles (113 km) west of Washington DC, Shenandoah National Park follows the ridge of Virginia's Blue Ridge Mountains for 105 miles (169 km). It is divided into three sections, designated by roads bisecting Skyline Drive.

- The **Northern District** stretches from Front Royal (US 340, MP 0) to Thornton Gap (US 211, MP 31.5).

- From Thornton Gap, the **Central District** continues south to Swift Run Gap (US 33, MP 62.7).

- The **Southern District** goes from Swift Run Gap to Rockfish Gap (I-64, US 250, MP 104.6).

May-October is peak season, especially in **autumn** (Sept.-Oct.) when the leaves turn in a riot of color along Skyline Drive. Expect long lines at entrance stations and slow traffic.

The park and Skyline Drive are open year-round; however, inclement weather can close the road, and fog can impair driving. Winter snowfall can outpace the park's ability to maintain roadways, forcing temporary closures, and some sections may close for the season. Be ready for spring and summer storms to deliver heavy rain, lightning, and hail. During deer-hunting season (mid-Nov.-early Jan.), Skyline closes at night to give the deer a break.

Reservations are imperative. Book park lodges and cabins up to 13 months in advance and campgrounds 6 months in advance. You may also need reservations to hike Old Rag.

ENTRANCES AND FEES

There are entrance stations at four points along Skyline Drive:

- **Front Royal** (MP 0) off US 340 near Front Royal

- **Thornton Gap** (MP 31.5) off US 211 east of Luray

- **Swift Run Gap** (MP 62.7) off US 33 east of Elkton

- **Rockfish Gap** (MP 104.6) off US 250 east of Waynesboro

The entrance fee is $30 per vehicle ($25 motorcycle, $15 individual) and good for seven days.

VISITORS CENTERS

Shenandoah National Park has two visitors centers. The historic, stone **Dickey Ridge Visitor Center** (MP 4.6, 9am-6pm daily Mar.-Nov.) is the first stop when traveling southbound along Skyline Drive. It has restrooms, brochures, backcountry permits, and a gift shop.

The **Harry F. Byrd Sr. Visitor Center** (MP 51, 8:30am-6pm daily Mar.-Nov., 9:30am-4pm Fri.-Sun. Dec.-early Jan., hours vary mid-Jan.-late Mar.)

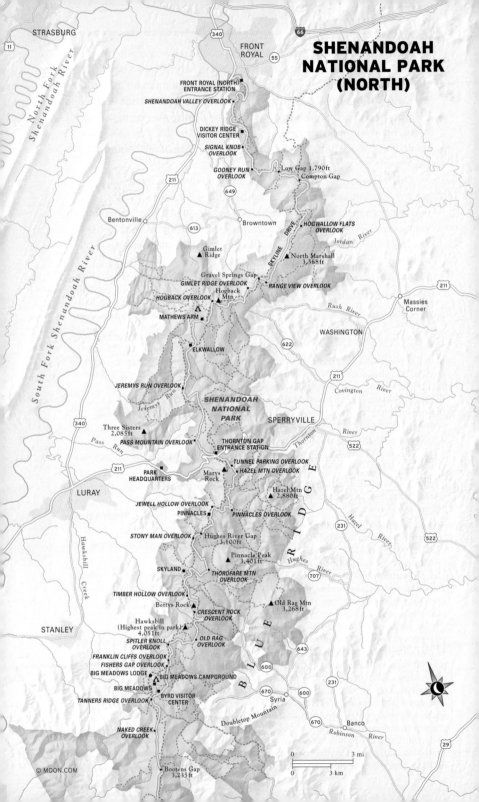

SHENANDOAH NATIONAL PARK (SOUTH)

SHENANDOAH

▲ Grindstone Mountain 2,850ft

THE POINT OVERLOOK

▲ Bush Mountain 3,527ft
▲ Bearfence Mountain
▲ Bluff Mountain

■ Green Mountain 2,149ft

■ LEWIS MOUNTAIN

▲ Piney Mountain 1,975ft

THE OAKS OVERLOOK

▲ Kirtley Mountain 2,593ft

340

Dry Run

▲ Huckleberry Mountain 2,158ft

SOUTH RIVER OVERLOOK

ELKTON

Elk Run

■ SOUTH RIVER

▲ Saddleback Mountain 3,375ft

33

SWIFT RUN GAP ENTRANCE STATION

230

SWIFT RUN OVERLOOK

33

STANARDSVILLE

McGaheysville

649

Smith Roach Gap

BACON HOLLOW OVERLOOK

810

EATON HOLLOW OVERLOOK

■ Powell Gap 2,295ft

Rocky Mount 2,740ft

Simmons Gap 2255ft

TWO MILE RUN OVERLOOK

340

BROWN MTN OVERLOOK

Pinefield Gap 2,530ft

Roach River

ROCKYTOP OVERLOOK

IVY CREEK OVERLOOK

▲ Loft Mountain

Brokenback Mtn 1,750ft

Lynch River

Rivanna River

Port Republic

SHENANDOAH NATIONAL PARK

BIG RUN OVERLOOK

Madison Run

659

LOFT MOUNTAIN

DOYLES RIVER OVERLOOK

GROTTOES

663

■ DUNDO

664

▲ Trayfoot Mtn 3,374ft

Blackrock Gap

TRAYFOOT MTN OVERLOOK

810

▲ Pasture Fence Mtn 2,880ft

Doyles River

RIPRAP OVERLOOK

SKYLINE DRIVE

MOORMANS RIVER OVERLOOK

Moormans River

614

CRIMORA LAKE OVERLOOK

▲ Bucks Elbow Mtn 2,787ft

Mechums River

Turk Mountain 2,981ft

340

SAWMILL RUN OVERLOOK

■ Jarman Gap 2,175ft

810

250

CROZET

64

Sawmill Run

CALF MTN OVERLOOK

■ Beagle Gap 2,532ft

29

250

MCCORMICK GAP OVERLOOK

■ McCormick Gap 2,434ft

64

WAYNESBORO

250

64

250

ROCKFISH GAP (SOUTH) ENTRANCE STATION

South Fork Shenandoah River

Blue Ridge Parkway National Park

0   3 mi
0   3 km

BLUE RIDGE

MOON.COM

ONE DAY IN SHENANDOAH

Skyline Drive traverses the entire length of the park from north to south. A scenic drive along its twisting corridor should be on your one-day agenda. If you have time, add a short day hike along the way.

has restrooms, an information desk, a bookstore, ranger programs, and exhibits, including ones on the park's controversial history of obtaining privately owned lands and of promoting segregated facilities in its early days.

SIGHTS

Sights are listed north to south on **Skyline Drive.** Stops along Skyline Drive are referred to by milepost (MP), and milepost markers appear along the road. Milepost 0 is at Front Royal, at the northern end of Skyline Drive. Milepost 104.6 is at Rockfish Gap at the southern end.

- **(MP 4.6) Dickey Ridge Visitor Center:** Check out the view and get oriented.
- **(MP 6.8) Gooney Run Overlook:** You can see Gooney Run, the stream that drains Browntown Valley. Several turns of the Shenandoah River are

visible here as well, as are Signal Knob and Dickey Ridge.
- **(MP 10.4) Fort Windham Rocks and Compton Gap:** Carson Mountain is unremarkable except for its summit, a geologic feature known as the Fort Windham Rocks, 600- to 800-million-year-old Catoctin lava formations.
- **(MP 20.8) Hogback Mountain Overlook:** The largest overlook area in the park.
- **(MP 22.1) Mathews Arm Campground:** Matthews Arm is near Overall Run Falls, which has the highest drop of all the falls in the park.
- **(MP 24) Elkwallow Wayside:** Stop for food or services.
- **(MP 32.2) Mary's Rock Tunnel:** This 670-foot-long (204-m) tunnel was cut through Mary's Rock in 1932. Narrow in width, Mary's Rock Tunnel is tight for RVs or trailers.

▼ MARY'S ROCK TUNNEL

Top ③

① TOUR SKYLINE DRIVE

Skyline Drive (105 mi/169 km, 3 hrs) curves through Shenandoah National Park from Front Royal to Rockfish Gap, just outside of Waynesboro. Along the narrow ridgetop route, nearly 70 overlooks offer views of the Shenandoah Valley to the west and the piedmont of Virginia to the east. The changing colors of the trees are the attraction: Pink buds bloom in spring, summer brings on jewel-green tones, and fall blazes with reds, golds, and oranges. Constructed in the 1930s by the Civilian Conservation Corps, this touring road was designed for scenic driving and bicycling.

SKYLINE DRIVE IN SPRING

② EXPLORE DARK HOLLOW FALLS

One of the most popular waterfall hikes in Shenandoah, **Dark Hollow Falls** (MP 50.7, 1.4 mi/2.3 km rt, 2 hrs, strenuous) descends and follows Hogcamp Branch. As the trail works downhill, you'll get your first overlook of the 70-foot (21-m) falls before it breaks into several shorter drops. Continue on the trail to the base of the falls at a bridge over the creek before climbing back up.

DARK HOLLOW FALLS

③ CLIMB HAWKSBILL MOUNTAIN

The highest peak in the park, 4,051-foot (1,235 m) **Hawksbill Mountain** tops with a stone-and-mortar platform that contains peak identifiers along the walls. Just to its south is a stone trail shelter. While you can hike from several trailheads, the two shortest routes reach the summit the fastest. Be sure to return down your same trail.

Upper Hawksbill Parking (MP 46.5, 2.1 mi/3.4 km rt, 1.5 hrs, moderate) has a pleasant, less steep ascent with less elevation gain because it starts from a higher trailhead. **Hawksbill Gap Parking** (MP 45.5, 1.7 mi/2.7 km rt, 1.25 hrs, moderate) is a rockier, steeper trail, although it is shorter.

HAWKSBILL SUMMIT OVERLOOK

Best Hike

OLD RAG

DISTANCE: 9.4 miles (15.1 km) round-trip
DURATION: 6-7 hours
ELEVATION CHANGE: 2,378 feet (715 m)
DIFFICULTY: strenuous
TRAILHEAD: Exit east from Thornton Gap (MP 31.5) to Sperryville, then take US 522, VA 321, VA 707 and VA 600 (Nether Rd.) to the Old Rag parking area.

Hiking **Old Rag Mountain** is a rite of passage for many visitors. It's harsh, rocky, and exposed near the summit, so if there's the chance of bad weather (especially lightning), keep an eye on the sky. From the parking lot, walk up Nethers Road about 0.8 mile (1.3 km) to the trailhead. The blue-blazed trail climbs steadily, canting steeper toward the ridge. At the ridgetop, you'll emerge onto the outcrop with a sweeping view. This is where the fun scramble begins, climbing over granite boulders and down cracks, using your hands and feet. After several false summits, the real summit is marked with a concrete post.

To complete the loop, descend via the Saddle Trail (blue blazes) switchbacks, which widen into a fire road after Old Rag Shelter. At a large intersection of fire roads, turn right onto Weakley Hollow Fire Road (yellow blazes) for a forested saunter along creeks to return to the trailhead.

The park launched a program in 2022 requiring **advance reservations** (www.recreation.gov, $1) for day hiking Old Rag March-November. Check ahead for current requirements and fees.

- **(MP 35.1) Pinnacles Overlook:** Look eastward for Old Rag Mountain.

- **(MP 41.7) Skyland Resort:** At the northern entrance to Skyland Resort, the road reaches 3,680 feet (1,122 m) in elevation, Skyline Drive's highest point.

- **(MP 51) Big Meadows:** Big Meadows is home to the largest open meadow in the park, the Harry F. Byrd Sr. Visitor Center, and Big Meadows Wayside for snacks.

- **(MP 77) Brown Mountain Overlook:** Ridges descend to the valley floor in stacked waves; at their head is a mountain with rocky protrusions that in autumn is ablaze with color.

- **(MP 79.5) Loft Mountain:** Grab a bite to eat from Loft Mountain Wayside.

- **(MP 84.8) Blackrock Summit:** This is a beautiful spot to stop and take in the scenery.

- **(MP 92.6) Crimora Lake Overlook:** This is one of the top vistas primarily because of Crimora Lake forming the centerpiece.

- **(MP 98.9) Calf Mountain Overlook:** This viewpoint provides some dizzying scenery. As you round the bend, the road seems to continue right out into the air (but it really just makes a tight turn). The long overlook has near-360-degree views.

- **(MP 105) Rockfish Gap:** The south entrance station marks the end of Skyline Drive and the beginning of the Blue Ridge Parkway.

RECREATION

HIKING

The second-highest peak in the park, **Stony Man** (MP 41.7, 1.6 mi/2.6 km rt, 1 hr, moderate) overlooks Shenandoah Valley from a rocky promontory. From

HISTORIC ROCK WALL ALONG SKYLINE DRIVE

Skyland's Stony Man Parking, go north on the Appalachian Trail to the blue-blazed Stony Man loops. Circle the overlook and return via the Appalachian Trail.

Whiteoak Canyon-Cedar Run Loop (8.2 mi/13.2 km rt, 6.5 hrs, strenuous) features eight waterfalls and a few pools to soak your feet. From Hawksbill Gap Parking (MP 45.5), make a loop by descending Cedar Run Trail, taking the Link Trail, climbing Whiteoak Canyon Trail, and returning to the start via the Whiteoak Canyon Fire Road.

From Big Meadows amphitheater, the **Lewis Falls Trail** (MP 51, 3.3 mi/5.3 km rt, 2.5 hrs, moderate) descends a rocky trail to an observation point of the 81-foot (25-m) falls before circling

back to the trailhead via the Appalachian Trail.

The **Bearfence Mountain Trail** (MP 56.5, 1.4 mi/2.3 km rt, 1 hr, moderate) offers a rocky hand-and-foot scramble to a summit with 360-degree views, a rarity with most of Shenandoah's vegetated mountains. Cross the Appalachian Trail to climb to the top. Continue south, taking two right turns to walk the Appalachian Trail north to your starting point.

The blue-blazed trail to **South River Falls** (MP 62.8, 3.3 mi/5.3 km rt, 3 hrs, strenuous) descends several switchbacks to reach an overlook where the river plunges into the falls and a deep grotto. Then, the route joins an old road, which connects with a short spur trail to the base of the falls and its large pool.

In the Southern District, **Riprap Hollow Trail** (MP 90, 9.8 mi/15.8 km rt, 7-8 hrs, strenuous) makes a loop via the Appalachian Trail north, Riprap Hollow Trail southwest, Wildcat Ridge Trail east, and the Appalachian Trail north. On Riprap Hollow Trail, vistas including Chimney Rock appear descending into Cold Springs Hollow, where a stream cuts through a small gorge to a waterfall and a large swimming hole.

BACKPACKING

The **Appalachian Trail** passes through Shenandoah for 101 miles (163 km),

CLIMBING OLD RAG

BICYCLING SKYLINE DRIVE

mostly paralleling Skyline Drive. Contrary to other wilderness sections of the trail outside the park, this portion of the trail crosses the road many times. The route has minimal water and a couple of shelters.

Backcountry camping **permits** ($20-30) are required. For advance reservations, book permits online (www.recreation.gov). **Appalachian Trail permits** (for long-distance AT hikers) are available by self-registration on the AT near trail entry points.

BICYCLING

Skyline Drive is favored by road cyclists for its ups, downs, and curves. But it has minimal shoulders. Ride single file and wear bright colors. If possible, avoid weekends and fall, when traffic is heavy.

WHERE TO STAY

INSIDE THE PARK

Make **reservations** (DNC Parks & Resorts, 877/847-1919, www.goshenandoah.com) for park lodges and cabins up to 13 months in advance.

Skyland Resort (MP 41.7 and 42.5, early Apr.-late Nov., from $124) has traditional motel-style rooms overlooking the valley, older cabins, and a full-service dining room (7:30am-10am, noon-3pm, and 5pm-9pm daily), adjoining taproom, and grab-and-go items in the lobby.

Big Meadows Lodge (MP 51.2, early May-Oct., from $118) accommodations range from lodge rooms to small rustic cabins. It also has a dining room (7:30am-10am, noon-3pm, and 5pm-9pm daily) with indoor or terrace seating and a taproom.

Lewis Mountain Cabins (MP 57.5, late Mar.-Nov., from $145) are cozy and rustic, with no phone or internet. Each cabin has electricity, a private bath, linens, and an outdoor grill.

For a quick bite, stop by one of three Wayside Food Stops: the **Elkwallow Wayside** (MP 24.1), **Big Meadows Wayside** (MP 51.2), and **Loft Mountain Wayside** (MP 79.5). Camping supplies are also available.

Shenandoah also has four **campgrounds** (early spring-late fall, $30) on Skyline Drive. Make **reservations** (877/444-6777, www.recreation.gov)

SKYLAND RESORT

six months in advance. Campgrounds have picnic tables, fire rings, restrooms, and potable water, but no hookups.

- **Mathews Arm Campground** (MP 22.1, 166 sites) is nearest the north entrance.
- **Big Meadows Campground** (MP 51.2, 221 sites) has showers, walk-in tent sites, and back-in and pull-through RV sites.
- **Loft Mountain Campground** (MP 79.5, 207 sites) has showers, a dump station, a camp store, walk-in tent sites, pull-through RV sites, and views.
- **Lewis Mountain Campground** (MP 57.5, 30 sites) is first come, first served and has showers.

OUTSIDE THE PARK

The northern gateway of **Front Royal** has accommodations and restaurants. The town of **Luray** is the western gateway to Shenandoah National Park and has rental cabins, a few inns and motels, and eateries. For the greatest variety and choices, stay in **Washington DC.**

GETTING THERE AND AROUND

Skyline Drive is the main access through the park. There is no public transit. Inside the park, **gasoline** is only available at the **Big Meadows Wayside** (MP 51.2).

AIR

Several major regional airports serve the region, but **Dulles International Airport** (IAD, 1 Saarinen Circle, Dulles, VA, 703/572-2700, www.flydulles. com) has the most flights. Car rentals are available at the Washington DC airports.

CAR

Front Royal, Virginia, and the entrance to Shenandoah National Park is just a few miles east of where I-66 meets I-81 (18 mi/29 km west). US 340 and US 522 also go through Front Royal. On Skyline Drive, there are only two points where roads intersect the route. US 211 crosses Skyline Drive at Thornton Gap (MP 31.5); from here, the town of **Luray** is 10 miles (16 km) west. Farther south, US 33 intersects Skyline at Swift Run Gap (MP 62.7); the town of **Elkton** is 7 miles (11 km) west. There are entrance stations to Shenandoah National Park at both Thornton Gap and Swift Run Gap.

TOURS

Advance reservations are required for the ranger-led tour to **Rapidan Camp** (877/444-6777, www.recreation.gov, Thurs.-Sun. May-Oct., 2.5 hrs, $10), the former summer camp of President Herbert Hoover and a National Historic Landmark. Two restored cabins—the President's Cabin and the Prime Minister's Cabin—are included on the tour. Tours depart on national park vans from Harry F. Byrd Sr. Visitor Center.

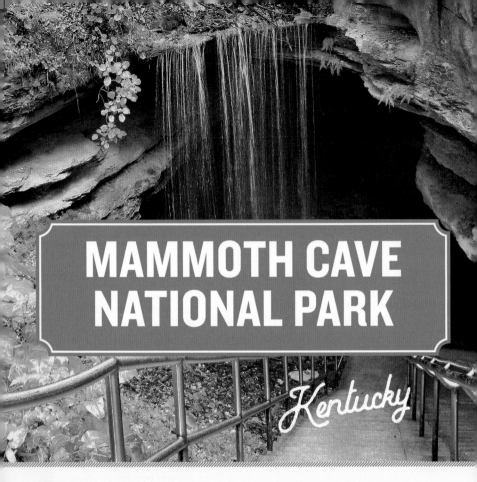

MAMMOTH CAVE NATIONAL PARK

Kentucky

WEBSITE:
www.nps.gov/maca

PHONE NUMBER:
270/758-2180

VISITATION RANK:
40

WHY GO:
Explore the world's
longest cave system.

KEEPSAKE STAMPS ▼▼▼

▲ MAMMOTH CAVE NATIONAL
PARK

Upon entering **MAMMOTH CAVE NATIONAL PARK,** visitors first see dense stands of eastern hardwood forest that are home to large populations of deer and wild turkeys. But beneath this forest lies the park's main attraction: the most extensive cave system in the world. Mammoth Cave is massive, with 420 miles (675 km) of mapped passageways through limestone caverns; new areas are mapped every few years. No known cave in the world is even half as long. It's also a surprisingly diverse ecosystem, supporting approximately 130 life-forms. Indigenous people explored Mammoth Cave 4,000 years ago, although it wasn't until 1798 that the cave was "rediscovered." It became a tourist attraction as early as 1816, making it the second-oldest tourist site in the United States after Niagara Falls.

PLANNING YOUR TIME

Mammoth Cave is 90 miles (145 km) south of Louisville, near the border with Tennessee. The national park is split into two regions: "aboveground" and "belowground." Above the ground you'll find hiking trails, cabins, campgrounds, and rivers for fishing, floating, and paddling. Belowground are the cave tours, most of which are guided. Make reservations six months in advance.

The park is open year-round, with peak visits April-August. Underground, the cave stays a cool 54°F (12°C) year-round. Aboveground, **summer** (May-Sept.) temperatures warm into the 80s (27-32°C) and above, while winters keep it cool in the 40s (4-9°C), with possible snow and ice. Cave tours are limited in winter.

ENTRANCES AND FEES

The park has multiple entrances; most visitors will enter via **Cave City** or **Park City** to reach the Historic Entrance and visitors center. There is no entrance fee to the park, but underground tours require fees.

VISITORS CENTER

Mammoth Cave National Park Visitor Center (8:30am-5:30pm daily Mar.-late Apr., 8am-6:30pm daily late Apr.-Oct., 8:30am-4:30pm daily Nov.-Feb.) is where to go for all tour schedules, tickets, and departures. The center has exhibits, permits, and information on ranger-led walks, evening presentations, and the Junior Ranger Program.

CAVE TOURS

More than a dozen **cave tours** (adults $14-66) are offered daily. Tours range in distance (0.25-5.5 mi/0.4-8.8 km) and time (1.25-6.5 hrs). Introductory and general tours give an overview of the cave, its history, and its formation. Specialty tours include lantern-lit and photography- or geology-focused tours. Review tour details (distance, length, difficulty, and number of stairs) carefully—some tours depart multiple times daily, while others enter the cave elsewhere than the visitors center. **Tour reservations** (877/444-6777, www.recreation.gov) are strongly recommended. In addition to the tours mentioned in *Top 3,* these are some of the options:

To be wowed by large cave rooms like the Rotunda, take the **Historic Tour** (2 mi/3.2 km, 440 stairs, 2 hrs, moderate). First, though, you'll need to enter Fat Man's Misery, a serpentine slot that requires squeezing through sideways. You may need to stoop or squat to avoid bonking your head on Tall Man's Misery. An extended version of this tour is also available.

To dip into the more challenging aspects of caving, join a ranger for

CAVE TOUR

Introduction to Caving (1 mi/1.6 km, 300 stairs, 3.5 hrs, strenuous). You'll be supplied with caving gear but will need to wear sturdy shoes. The adventure demands crawling through tight spaces, climbing, and working around obstacles.

Only offered when other tours sell out, the **Discovery Tour** (10am-2pm daily, 0.75 mi/1.2 km, 160 stairs, 30 min, easy) is the only option for touring the cave self-guided. Stop at the visitors center for tickets the day of the tour (no reservations). Then explore the cave at your own pace, starting with the descent down a trail to the historic entrance. Rangers are staged along the passageway to share interpretive tidbits.

For those needing a wheelchair-accessible tour with their companions, the **Mammoth Cave Accessible Tour** (0.5 mi/0.8 km, no stairs, 2 hrs, easy) uses an elevator entrance into the cave. The tour passes through the Snowball Room and part of Cleaveland Avenue.

RECREATION

HIKING AND BIKING

From the visitors center, short trails loop to the surface of cave features and overlooks of the Green River. The **Sinkhole Trail** (2 mi/3.2 km rt, 1 hr, easy) starts from the paved Heritage Trail and descends to the Echo River Springs Trail. Along the way, the trail passes Mammoth Dome Sink, a huge sinkhole that created Mammoth Dome in the cave.

Starting at Engine No. 4 outside the visitors center, the gravel **Mammoth Cave Railroad Bike and Hike Trail** (18 mi/29 km rt, easy) follows parts of the original train route that once connected Park City with Mammoth Cave Visitor Center.

For spring bird-watching and fall color, hikers and bikers can head north of Green River on the **Maple Springs Trail** (2 mi/3.2 km rt, 1 hr, easy), **White Oak Trail** (5 mi/8 km rt, 2.5 hrs, easy), and **Big Hollow Trail North and South Loops** (9.1 mi/14.6 km rt, 5 hrs, moderate).

CANOEING AND KAYAKING

In 2021, the **Green and Nolin Rivers Blueway** (36 mi/60 km) was designated a National Recreation Trail. **Green River Canoeing** (3057 Mammoth Cave Rd., Cave City, 270/773-5712, www.mammothcavecanoe.com) can outfit you for paddling in a canoe or kayak. Beginners should go from Dennison Ferry to Green River Ferry (7.6 mi/12 km, 3-4 hrs). Skilled paddlers can descend from Green River Ferry to Houchin Ferry (12.4 mi/20 km, 5-6 hrs). Overnight trips require **permits** (www.recreation.gov, $10/trip) for primitive campsites; book a week in advance.

Top ③

① ADMIRE FROZEN NIAGARA

Frozen Niagara Falls is one of the most artistic collections of dripstones and the most famous feature in Mammoth Cave. The **Frozen Niagara Tour** (0.25 mi/0.4 km, 12 stairs, 90 min, easy, $8-16) is best for families with kids. Frozen Niagara is also included on four longer and more difficult tours: Domes and Dripstones, Grand Avenue, Introduction to Caving, and Wild Cave. Make advance **reservations** (877/444-6777, www.recreation.gov).

FROZEN NIAGARA

② GAZE AT DOMES AND DRIPSTONES

Beginning at a sinkhole, the **Domes and Dripstones Tour** (0.75 mi/1.2 km, 500 stairs, 2 hrs, moderate, $11-21) shows off dramatic cave features: large-domed rooms, stalactites, stalagmites, and Frozen Niagara. It is more of a workout with several steep sections. Rangers share the science of cave formations. Make advance **reservations** (877/444-6777, www.recreation.gov).

③ WRIGGLE THROUGH CRAWL SPACES

For a real spelunking adventure, you can crawl, slither, and duckwalk the less accessible cave features. Spring through fall, the **Wild Cave Tour** (5 mi/8 km, 500 steps, 6 hrs, strenuous, $66) is not for claustrophobes or acrophobes. Hiking boots with ankle support are required, but you'll be provided with coveralls, kneepads, gloves, and lamp helmets. Participants must be age 16 or older; make advance **reservations** (877/444-6777, www.recreation.gov).

CRAWL THROUGH ONE OF MAMMOTH'S SMALLER CAVES.

STALACTITES

COTTAGES AT THE LODGE AT MAMMOTH CAVE

WHERE TO STAY

INSIDE THE PARK

Rooms at the **Lodge at Mammoth Cave** (171 Hotel Rd., 844/760-2283, https://mammothcavelodge.com, from $71) may be small and a bit dated, but they have a central location near the visitors center. Request a room on the ravine side to enjoy a view from your balcony. Quaint cottages and cabins offer a more private retreat. Make reservations a year in advance. The lodge has two eateries: **Green River Grill** (7am-10am, 11am-3pm, and 5pm-8pm daily summer, shorter hours winter) for dining and **Spelunkers Café** (8am-5pm daily, closed winter) for light meals, ice cream, and to-go fare.

Three campgrounds are available by reservation (877/444-6777, www.recreation.gov) six months in advance. **Mammoth Cave Campground** (Mar.-Nov., 111 sites, $25-50), a five-minute walk from the visitors center, has flush toilets, hot showers, and two first-come, first-served campsites. **Houchin Ferry Campground** (year-round, $20) has 12 primitive sites on the south bank of the Green River. North of the river, **Maple Springs Group Campground** (Mar.-Nov., $50) has six standard group sites and two group sites with water and electrical hookups for RVs.

OUTSIDE THE PARK

Cave City is the gateway to Mammoth Cave National Park and provides accommodations, dining, and services.

GETTING THERE AND AROUND

The park has no shuttle system or public transportation. Driving is the only way to get around. Do not rely on GPS navigation systems—use a map instead.

AIR

Two international airports are within 100 miles (161 km) of Mammoth Cave. To the north is **Louisville Muhammad Ali International Airport** (SDF, 600 Terminal Dr., Louisville, KY, www.flylouisville.com, 502/368-6524), a 90-minute drive via I-65. To the south is **Nashville International Airport** (BNA, 1 Terminal Dr., Nashville, TN, 615/275-1675, www.flynashville.com), two hours' drive via I-65. Both airports have car rentals.

CAR

Mammoth Cave National Park is west of I-65, between Elizabethtown and Bowling Green. From the north, take exit 53 for Cave City and turn right onto KY 70 to reach the park entrance. From the south, take exit 48 to Park City. Turn left onto KY 255 to the park entrance.

FERRY

The park is divided into north and south sections by the Green River. To go between the sections without driving outside of the park, a tiny **ferry** (270/758-2166, 6am-10pm daily year-round) crosses the river. Vehicles are limited to 12 tons and 16 feet in length. High and low water may close the ferry. For road and ferry updates, check the Twitter page for **Mammoth Cave Roads and Ferry** (@MCNProadsferry).

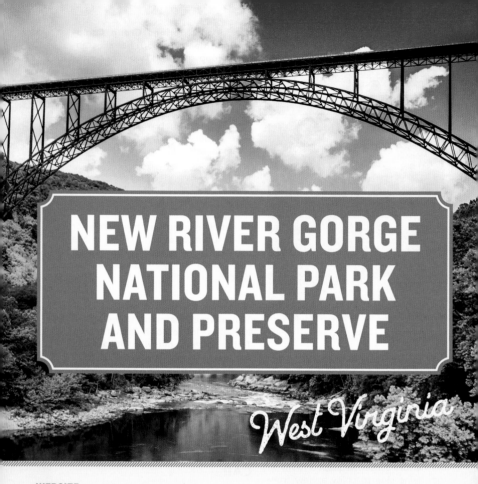

NEW RIVER GORGE NATIONAL PARK AND PRESERVE

West Virginia

WEBSITE:
www.nps.gov/neri

PHONE NUMBER:
303/465-0508

VISITATION RANK:
17

WHY GO:
Raft one of the oldest rivers in North America.

KEEPSAKE STAMPS ▼▼▼

▲ NEW RIVER GORGE BRIDGE

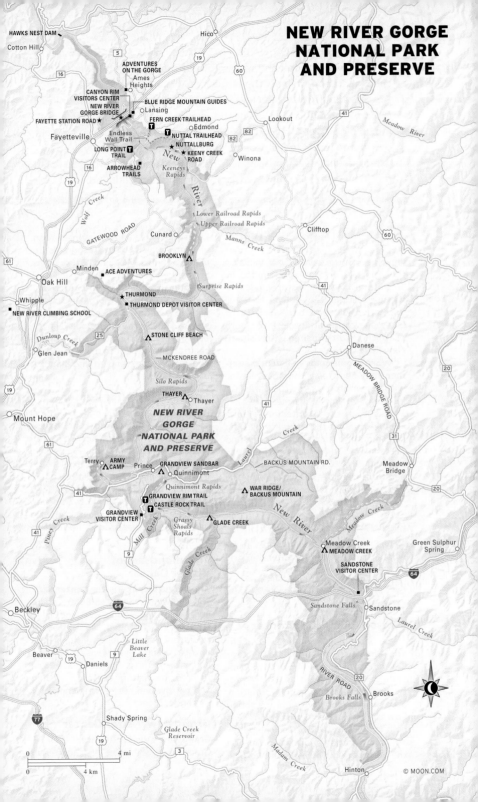

NEW RIVER GORGE
NATIONAL PARK
AND PRESERVE

HAWKS NEST DAM
Cotton Hill

Hico

16
5

19

60

ADVENTURES
ON THE GORGE
Ames
Heights

CANYON RIM
VISITORS CENTER
NEW RIVER
GORGE BRIDGE
FAYETTE STATION ROAD

BLUE RIDGE MOUNTAIN GUIDES
Lansing

FERN CREEK TRAILHEAD
Edmond

NUTTAL TRAILHEAD
NUTTALLBURG

KEENY CREEK
ROAD

Winona

Lookout

41

Meadow River

Fayetteville

Endless
Wall Trail

LONG POINT
TRAIL

ARROWHEAD
TRAILS

16

19

New River

Keeneys
Rapids

Wolf Creek

GATEWOOD ROAD

Lower Railroad Rapids
Upper Railroad Rapids

Manns Creek

Clifftop

60

Cunard

BROOKLYN

61

Minden

ACE ADVENTURES

Surprise Rapids

41

Oak Hill

THURMOND
THURMOND DEPOT VISITOR CENTER

Whipple
NEW RIVER CLIMBING SCHOOL

Dunloup Creek

25

STONE CLIFF BEACH

Danese

20

Glen Jean

MCKENDREE ROAD

MEADOW
BRIDGE
ROAD

19

Silo Rapids

THAYER
Thayer

Mount Hope

NEW RIVER
GORGE
NATIONAL PARK
AND PRESERVE

41

Creek

Laurel

31

Meadow
Bridge

61

Terry
ARMY
CAMP
Prince

GRANDVIEW SANDBAR
Quinnimont

BACKUS MOUNTAIN RD.

20

41

Quinnimont Rapids

WAR RIDGE/
BACKUS MOUNTAIN

New River

Meadow Creek

Green Sulphur
Spring

GRANDVIEW RIM TRAIL
CASTLE ROCK TRAIL

GRANDVIEW
VISITOR CENTER

Piney Creek

41

9

Mill Creek

Grassy
Shoals
Rapids

GLADE CREEK

Glade Creek

Meadow Creek
MEADOW CREEK

SANDSTONE
VISITOR CENTER

64

Beckley

64

Little
Beaver
Lake

Sandstone Falls

Sandstone

Laurel Creek

Beaver

19

9

Daniels

77

Shady Spring

19

Glade Creek
Reservoir

3

RIVER ROAD

20

Brooks Falls

Brooks

0   4 mi
0   4 km

Madam Creek

Hinton

© MOON.COM

NEW RIVER GORGE NATIONAL PARK AND PRESERVE contains hillsides of oak and maple forests interrupted by sandstone cliffs and deep ravines, the largest of which is the V-shaped water-carved gorge of the New River. This waterway flows 53 miles (85 km) through the park, meandering in calm stretches and kicking up big waves and froth in white-water segments. Once a travel corridor for Indigenous peoples, the river was subsequently used by explorers and coal miners before its main attraction turned to recreation. Today it is renowned for rafting and rock climbing.

PLANNING YOUR TIME

New River Gorge is in West Virginia on the Appalachian Plateau, bounded by small rural towns and state parks. To the north is the Gauley River National Recreation Area and to the south is the Bluestone National Scenic River, both of which are often paired with visits to New River Gorge.

While people come year-round, **summer** (May-Sept.) sees the most visitors, with temperatures in the 70s (21-26°C). Ironically, when the warmest weather arrives in July, the favorite time for rafting and floating the river, it's also the peak month for rain squalls. Spring and fall temperatures range from the 50s to the 60s (10-20°C) and winter sees temperatures from the 30s to the 50s (-1 to 15°C). Typically, fall colors in the park peak in late October.

ENTRANCES AND FEES

New River Gorge has multiple highway and rural roads that enter the park. There are no entrance stations, and the park has no entrance fee.

VISITORS CENTERS

Canyon Rim Visitor Center

In the park's north end on US 19, **Canyon Rim Visitor Center** (162 Visitor Center Rd., Lansing, 304/574-2115, 9am-5pm daily year-round) has interpretive exhibits, maps and information, a bookstore, and two films depicting how the New River Gorge Bridge was built and how water formed the gorge. You can also get information here on the neighboring Gauley River National Recreation Area and Bluestone National Scenic River. Ranger programs, including guided hikes and nature walks, are offered year-round. The back deck has immense views of the gorge, and you can drop into the gorge on a boardwalk to two observation platforms for views of the gorge and bridge. The upper observation platform is wheelchair-accessible, but to reach the lower one requires descending and climbing back up 178 steps.

Sandstone Visitor Center

In the south end of the park, just north of exit 139 on I-64, **Sandstone Visitor Center** (330 Meadow Creek Rd., Sandstone, 304/466-0417, 9am-5pm daily June-Oct.) has interactive exhibits on the river's watershed and the cultural history of the park. You can also get maps, brochures, and information on ranger-led programs. The center also has a bookstore and video program on the river.

Thurmond Depot Visitor Center

Thurmond Depot Visitor Center (WV 25, Thurmond, 304/465-8550, 10am-5pm daily June-Aug., RVs and trailers not recommended) is in a historic two-story railroad depot with exhibits on railroading days. Maps, brochures, and information are also available. The road to the visitors center is winding and narrow and not recommended for RVs and trailers.

Grandview Visitor Center

Grandview Visitor Center (WV 9, Grandview, 304/763-3715, noon-5pm

Top 3

RAFTING NEW RIVER

1 FLOAT THE RIVER

The **New River** cuts 53 miles (85 km) through the park to spill into Hawks Nest Lake. The southern half fills with languid pools interrupted by Class II-III water, the most family-friendly section. The northern gorge sports monster waves with Class IV-V rapids and requires maneuvering between boulders in fast-moving water. Trips can last several hours—or several days if you camp along the river. The main paddling season is April-October.

Commercially guided trips go out for half days, full days, and overnights, with transportation included. Provided gear usually includes life jackets and helmets, with overnight trips adding tents, sleeping bags, and meals. Half-day trips start at $80 per person; full-day trips, which include lunch, start around $120 per person. Regional outfitters include **ACE Adventure Resort** (1 Concho Rd., Oak Hill, 800/787-3982, www.aceraft.com), **Adventures on the Gorge** (219 Chestnutburg Rd., Lansing, 855/379-8738, www.adventuresonthegorge.com), **Cantrell Ultimate Rafting** (49 Cantrell Dr., Fayetteville, 304/877-8235, www.cantrellultimaterafting.com), **New and Gauley River Adventures** (115 Oscar White Rd., Lansing, 800/759-7238, www.gauley.com), **River Expeditions** (900 Broadway Ave., Oak Hill, 800/463-9873, www.raftinginfo.com), and **West Virginia Adventures** (231 Wood Mountain Rd., Glen Jean, 800/292-0880, www.trywva.com).

For DIY trips, check the park's Private Boater Information page (www.nps.gov/neri/planyourvisit/whitewater_private.htm) for tips, alerts, and river levels. Canyon Rim Visitor Center posts updated river levels every morning at 9:30am. Permits are not required.

2 ADMIRE SANDSTONE FALLS

The largest waterfall on the New River is **Sandstone Falls.** It's not a huge drop, only 25 feet (7.6 m) at its tallest point, but it spans the entire river. It stretches 1,500 feet (457 m) across, with falls that are broken up by rocky and brushy islands.

To see the falls up close, a **wheelchair-accessible boardwalk** (0.5 mi/0.8 km rt) crosses portions of the river on two bridges that connect with islands and observation platforms. The waterfall is in the south end of the park; drive the partly single-lane River Road (WV 26) up the west side of the river from Hinton to reach the unpaved parking lot.

You can also enjoy the falls from above at **Sandstone Falls Overlook.** A graveled **walkway** (0.2 mi/0.3 km rt)

SANDSTONE FALLS

drops to the overlook where the view plunges 600 feet (183 m) to the river. On WV 20, pullout parking is 3 miles (4.8 km) south of the Sandstone Visitor Center or 8.5 miles (13.7 km) north of Hinton.

3 TOUR THE NEW RIVER GORGE BRIDGE

NEW RIVER GORGE BRIDGE

A tribute to human ingenuity and engineering, the **New River Gorge Bridge** is the longest steel span in the western hemisphere at 3,000 feet (914 m). With its height of 876 feet (267 m), it also lays claim to fame as the third-tallest bridge in the United States.

The bridge is easy to drive, but it's hard to get the full scope of it from above. To photograph the bridge, you'll want to go to other vantage points. Canyon Rim Visitor Center has a **wheelchair-accessible boardwalk** to an upper observation platform with views of the bridge; a lower platform also has views, but you'll need to climb down and back up 178 steps. You can also get a good vantage point from under the bridge by driving **Fayette Station Road.**

Bridge Walk (57 Fayette Mine Rd., Lansing, 304/574-1300, https://bridgewalk. com, 3 hrs, from $72) leads you on a thrilling tour of the 2-foot-wide (0.6-m) catwalk beneath the bridge span. Participants wear harnesses and are fastened to safety cables.

Bridge Day (https://officialbridgeday.com), a festival on the third Saturday in October, attracts up to 100,000 people to walk across the span and take in the views from the top. It's the only day the bridge opens to pedestrians. BASE jumpers leap from the bridge into the gorge, rappelers drop and ascend from the catwalk, and you can zip-line from the catwalk to the gorge or take a catwalk tour.

daily Memorial Day-Labor Day) offers superb views from the rim to the river. Inside, you can pick up maps, brochures, and information. Rangers guide walks and conduct talks.

THURMOND COAL BUILDING

SIGHTS

THURMOND

Remnants of a railroad boomtown are all that remain of Thurmond. At its peak, from the late 1800s to 1930, it had hotels, stores, banks, and eventually a movie theater. The town's train depot has been restored into a visitors center; remaining buildings are listed on the National Register of Historic Places. Access is via the narrow curvy County Road 25 (RVs and trailers are not recommended).

NUTTALLBURG

From 1873 to 1958, Nuttallburg thrived as a coal mining town on New River and its rail line. This historic site preserves one of West Virginia's most intact coal mining towns. You'll see mining equipment, coke ovens, buildings, and coal rail cars. Nuttallburg is located at the end of the narrow, gravel, steep, and curvy Keeney Creek Road (Country Rd. 82/2, RVs and trailers not recommended). As of early 2022 the road was

VIEW FROM MAIN OVERLOOK

closed due to a washout; call ahead to check on its status.

GRANDVIEW

Boasting one of the most famous overlooks of New River Gorge, the part of the park known as Grandview offers views of a horseshoe bend from **Main Overlook.** Visit in mid-May to see purple rhododendrons in bloom or late October for fall colors. Stop in the visitors center, join a ranger-led walk, or enjoy a theatrical production from **Theater West Virginia** (4700 Grandview Rd., 304/256-6800, https://theatrewestvirginia.org, 7:30pm daily June-Aug., $10-20) in the outdoor amphitheater.

AFRICAN AMERICAN HERITAGE TOUR

The self-guided **African American Heritage Tour** visits three park locales and several surrounding communities, stopping at places that tell the story of Black coal miners, rail workers, and others who lived and worked in the local communities. Before departing, download the tour from the NPS app onto your smartphone or pick up a free CD and brochure at Canyon Rim Visitor Center.

The route visits 17 historic sites, such as churches, parks, schools, and memorials, to tell the stories of Black people who mined coal, worked on the railroad, and contributed to communities. Stops 1 (Quinnimont Missionary Baptist Church), 4 (Nuttallburg), and 10 (Thurmond Depot) are inside the park; you can tour the trio in three hours.

SCENIC DRIVE
FAYETTE STATION ROAD

The historic one-way **Fayette Station Road** (7.5 mi/12 km loop, 40 min) links Lansing and Fayetteville by crossing New River on the route used before the construction of the New River Gorge Bridge. Download an audio tour from the park's website for history and sightseeing en route.

Fayette Station Road drops from Lansing on the east side of the river to the bottom of the gorge via three sharp switchbacks and several curves. At the bottom, a narrow reconstructed bridge crosses the river, linking the remains of two small coal mining communities. You can park in the Fayette Station parking lot to enjoy views of the river. The road climbs back up the west

Best Hike

ENDLESS WALL

DISTANCE: 2.4 miles (3.8 km) one-way
DURATION: 1.5 hours
ELEVATION CHANGE: 300 feet (91 m)
DIFFICULTY: easy-moderate
TRAILHEAD: Fern Creek or Nuttall

Used by rock climbers to reach cliff routes, the relatively flat **Endless Wall Trail** trots along the rim of New River Gorge with plenty of viewpoints for peering down to the river. Two trailheads, Fern Creek and Nuttall, are 0.5 mile (0.8 km) apart on the Lansing-Edmond Road.

From the **Fern Creek Trailhead,** the route goes through thick forest to cross Fern Creek. Then, it shimmies along the Endless Wall, the edge of the cliff. No barriers line the precipices here, so use caution and watch young kids. You'll also pass steel ladders that allow rock climbers to descend to pitches in the gorge. Midway, the trail reaches **Diamond Point Overlook.** While the full hike goes between the two trailheads, Diamond Point can also serve as a turnaround point (2 mi/3.2 km rt) if you don't want to hike the entire way. Upon reaching **Nuttall Trailhead** on the opposite end, you can retrace your steps or walk back on the road between the two trailheads (add 0.5 mi/0.8 km).

ENDLESS WALL

side to Fayetteville on several sharp turns (including two hairpin turns). On each side of the river, the road passes beneath the New River Gorge Bridge. You'll also get views of the gorge and lush maple and oak forests. Interpretive exhibits dot the route.

From the Canyon Rim Visitor Center, go north on US 19 and turn right onto County Road 5/82 (Lansing-Edmond Rd.). Turn right again onto the signed Fayette Station Road and then veer left at the fork to begin the tour.

RECREATION

HIKING

At Main Overlook, the **Castle Rock Trail** (0.6 mi/1 km one-way, 30 min,

FAYETTE STATION BRIDGE

ROCK CLIMBING

New River Gorge is world-renowned for sandstone outcrops and cliffs that attract trad and sport climbers year-round (Apr.-June and Sept.-Oct. have the best weather). Inside the park, more than 1,500 routes rated class 5.9-5.12 appeal mostly to experts. Some routes have preset bolts courtesy of the New River Alliance of Climbers (www.newriverclimbing.net). Beginner routes are also available. Pitches range 30-120 feet (9-36 m). Guides often take new climbers to **Bridge Buttress,** and the Endless Wall Trail accesses climbing routes via steel ladders that descend into the gorge.

Beginners can hire guides and get instruction through PCGI-certified **New River Climbing School** (304/308-1400, www.newriverclimbingschool.com) or AMGA-certified **Blue Ridge Mountain Guides** (434/298-4646, www.blueridgemtnguides.com). You can also arrange guided rock-climbing through **Adventures on the Gorge** (219 Chestnutburg Rd., Lansing, 855/379-8738, https://adventuresonthegorge.com).

MOUNTAIN BIKING

Maps for many of the park's mountain biking trails are online. Be aware that these trails permit mountain bikes but not e-bikes.

Keeney's Creek Rail Trail (6 mi/9.6 km rt, easy) tours an old rail bed with a 4 percent grade. It connects several mines and crosses under trestles. Find the trailhead 2 miles (3.2 km) up the curvy, often single-track Keeneys Creek Road (County Rd. 85/2) in the Nuttallburg area.

In the Craig's Branch area, from the Arrowhead Trailhead, the single-track **Arrowhead Trails** (12.8 mi/20.5 km total, easy-moderate) contain four loops built by the Boy Scouts of America. Use the online map to navigate successive loops that increase in skill level and distance farther out from the trailhead.

Bike rentals are available in many of the local bike shops. **Adventures on the Gorge** (219 Chestnutburg Rd., Lansing, 855/379-8738, https://adventuresonthegorge.com) and **ACE Adventures** (1 Concho Rd., Oak Hill, 877/787-3982, https://aceraft.com) offer guided mountain bike tours.

strenuous) trots between visible coal seams along what feels like a castle wall with steep cliffs plunging downslope and overhanging rock walls towering above. The footing is rough and there are no guardrails at the drop-offs. When Castle Rock Trail ends at an intersection, the shortest route to loop back to the trailhead is via a portion of the Grandview Rim Trail (0.5 mi/0.9 km one-way, 15 min, easy). For hikers looking for big views into the gorge without the thrills of Castle Rock, the **Grandview Rim Trail** (3.2 mi/5.1 km rt, 1.5 hrs, moderate) goes from Main Overlook to Turkey Spur Overlook.

The often-crowded **Long Point Trail** (3 mi/4.8 km rt, 1.5 hrs, easy) wanders through a forest of hemlock, pine, and hardwoods in its gentle descent to the gorge rim. After the path goes through a tunnel of rhododendrons, it reaches a rock bluff with a view of New River and the New River Gorge Bridge. In October, the forested hillsides are flanked with autumnal color. The Long Point Trailhead is on Gatewood Road, east of Fayetteville.

ONE DAY IN NEW RIVER GORGE

The best way to spend one day is floating **New River**. But if you'd rather keep your feet on dry land, go to **Canyon Rim Visitor Center** to get oriented and visit the observation platforms to admire the gorge and **New River Gorge Bridge**. Hike **Grandview Rim Trail** or **Endless Wall Trail**. Afterward, from Lansing, drive the curvy **Fayette Station Road** down, across the river, and back up to Fayetteville. Then head to the south end of the park to walk the boardwalk to **Sandstone Falls**.

WHERE TO STAY

INSIDE THE PARK

Campgrounds (first come, first served, free) are the only accommodations in the park. They have minimal facilities: no water, no hookups, and limited restrooms. Most are near the New River: **Stone Cliff Beach** (6 walk-in tent sites, 1 drive-in site), **Army Camp** (11 drive-in tent or RV sites), **Grandview Sandbar** (10 tent or small-medium RV sites, 6 walk-in tent sites, 2 accessible sites), **Glade Creek** (6 walk-in tent sites, 5 drive-in tent or small-medium RV sites, 1 accessible site), **Thayer** (4 walk-in tent sites), **Brooklyn** (4 walk-in tent sites, 1 drive-in tent site), and **Meadow Creek** (11 walk-in tent sites, 28 drive-in tent or small-medium RV sites). **War**

Ridge/Backus Mountain (8 tent or small RV sites) is above the river.

OUTSIDE THE PARK

One resort perches adjacent to the park right on the rim of the gorge. **Adventures on the Gorge** (219 Chestnutburg Rd., Lansing, 855/379-8738, https://adventuresonthegorge.com) has cabins, glamping, RV sites, tent campsites, several dining options, and a swimming pool. The resort also offers rafting, rock climbing, mountain biking, and guided trips.

Hinton, Fayetteville, and **Beckley** have plenty of options for dining, lodging, and camping. Nearby **West**

▼ ROCK CLIMBING IN NEW RIVER GORGE

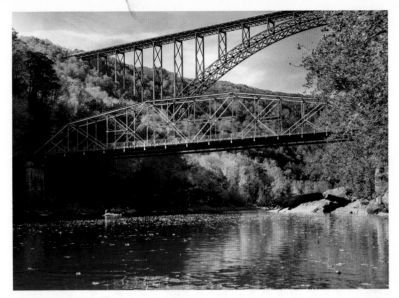

NEW RIVER WITH BRIDGES

Virginia State Parks (https://wvstateparks.com) of Pipestem Resort, Babcock, and Bluestone also have lodges, cabins, and campgrounds. The Gauley River National Recreation area also has a campground.

GETTING THERE AND AROUND

AIR

Yeager Airport (CRW, 100 Airport Rd., Charleston, WV, 304/344-8033, https://yeagerairport.com) is located about 70 miles (112 km) northwest of New River Gorge. **Raleigh County Memorial Airport** (BKW, 176 Airport Rd., Beaver, WV, 304/255-0476, https://flybeckley.com) is 50 miles (80 km) south of the park. Both airports have rental cars.

CAR

No public transportation goes through the park; you will need a car to get around. New River Gorge is a 5-hour drive (310 mi/500 km) southwest from Washington DC, a 3.5-hour drive (200 mi/320 km) west of Shenandoah National Park, and a 5-hour drive (290 mi/465 km) north of Great Smoky Mountains National Park. Two highways reach the park: Route 19 crosses the park between Hico and Beckley via New River Gorge Bridge, and I-64 bisects the park near Sandstone. A myriad of narrow dirt and gravel roads weave into the park. For the best route-finding, plug specific names of destinations into GPS navigation and use the park map available at visitors centers.

RAIL

Amtrak (www.amtrak.com) runs the Cardinal line three days per week from Chicago and New York that goes through the park. It stops at Hinton and Prince. Thurmond is a flag stop.

BUS

Greyhound (800/231-2222, www.greyhound.com) goes to Beckley.

TOURS

The **Autumn Colors Express** (844/724-5399, www.autumncolorexpresswv.com, Thurs.-Sun. late Oct., from $180) offers full-day rail tours of the park during peak fall foliage season. Options include coach, dome, and private suites. Tours launch from Huntington or Charleston, West Virginia.

GATEWAY ARCH NATIONAL PARK

Missouri

WEBSITE:
www.nps.gov/jeff

PHONE NUMBER:
314/655-1600

VISITATION RANK:
24

WHY GO:
Learn about
westward
expansion
and slavery.

KEEPSAKE STAMPS ▼▼▼

▲ GATEWAY ARCH

Rather than a park of natural wonders, **GATEWAY ARCH NATIONAL PARK** is a historical landmark in an urban setting. The 630-foot (192-m) silver arch on the west bank of the Mississippi River commemorates one of the main routes for westward expansion during the 19th century. From Missouri, Lewis and Clark launched their Corps of Discovery upriver, opening the gateway for the riverboats, pioneers, and homesteaders who followed them. It's also a memorial to Thomas Jefferson, who initiated the exploration.

The park's Old Courthouse saw its share of history, particularly concerning enslaved Black people. Its steps served as a site for auctioning enslaved people and its courtrooms for hearing cases about emancipation. The most notable case upheld the institution of slavery, which pushed the country into the Civil War.

PLANNING YOUR TIME

You can visit the park grounds 5am-11pm daily year-round, but various attractions have shorter hours. Summer (May-Aug.) and school holidays (Mar.) draw the biggest crowds; visit in early morning or evening for fewer people. To avoid big crowds, go in spring or fall; for the fewest people, visit in winter. The arch is illuminated at night except during bird migrations in early May and late September.

To avoid waiting in lines, purchase tickets for the Arch Tram and riverboat cruises up to two hours in advance online (877/982-1410, www.gatewayarch.com). Combo tickets will save you a few dollars.

Daytime temperatures range 80-90°F (27-32°C) in summer, usually accompanied with high humidity and mugginess. Winter dips to hover around freezing with a few inches of snow that melts off quickly.

ENTRANCES AND FEES

Entry to the park costs $3 per person. Kids 15 years and younger are free. Entry fees are waived for federal lands passholders. Attractions and tours in the park have additional fees, which vary by activity.

The main entry to the park is through the **West Entrance** (11 N. 4th St.). Visitors coming from riverboats or Leonor K. Sullivan Boulevard use the sloped cobbled pathways on either side of the Grand Staircase below the Arch as the **East Entrances.** From Laclede's Landing, the **North Entrances** are on 1st and 2nd Streets.

Entry to the Arch itself is via a secure checkpoint, with the same rules in place as airport checkpoints. Be sure to arrive a half hour before you need to get on the tram with a prepurchased ticket.

▼ PARK GROUNDS IN SPRING

VISITORS CENTERS

Gateway Arch Visitor Center (11 N. 4th St., 877/982-1410, www.gatewayarch.com, 8am-10pm daily summer, 9am-6pm daily winter) contains the ticket office, a movie theater, the Arch Café, the park store, and a gift shop. From here, rangers lead free walks on the grounds several times daily.

SIGHTS

ARCH TRAM

The only way to go up into the Arch is via the **Arch Tram** (877/982-1410, www.gatewayarch.com, 9am-8pm daily summer, 9am-6pm daily winter, $12-16 adults, $8-13 ages 3-15). Tours usually take 45-60 minutes, depending on how much time you spend at the top on the observation platform. Tours start with a multimedia presentation before loading onto the tram. Trams run every 10 minutes, taking four minutes to go up and three minutes to come down. Getting from the top of the tram to the observation platform requires walking up six flights of stairs, and no seating is available in the observation area. Views from the top take in St. Louis and the states of Missouri and Illinois. Exit from the Arch via its legs.

RIVERFRONT TRAIL

Along the Mississippi River, the paved **Riverfront Trail** (0.7 mi/1.1 km, 20 min, easy) is shared by walkers and bicycles. Views include riverboats and the city skyline.

WHERE TO STAY

INSIDE THE PARK

No lodgings are available inside the park, but two cafés are on-site. On the riverboat dock, the **Paddlewheel Café** (50 S. Leonor K. Sullivan Blvd., 877/982-1410, www.gatewayarch.com, 11am-4pm Thurs.-Sun. summer, shorter hours Apr.-Oct.) serves sandwiches, shrimp, and ice cream. In Gateway Arch Visitor Center, the **Arch Café** (314/300-8710, www.cafearch.com, 9am-5pm daily) serves farm-to-table and organic meals.

OUTSIDE THE PARK

Plentiful accommodations and dining options are available in **St. Louis.**

GETTING THERE

AIR

St. Louis Lambert International Airport (STL, 10701 Lambert International Blvd., 314/890-1333, www.flystl.com) is 14 miles (23 km) from Gateway Arch. Car rentals are available.

CAR

From Missouri

To get to Gateway Arch National Park, follow I-44, I-55, I-64, or I-70 into downtown St. Louis. Once downtown, use the following exits and directions to reach the park:

From I-44 east and I-55 north, use exit 292 (Lumiere Place Blvd., Washington Ave., Eads Bridge). From the left lane, make a U-turn to reach Pine Street.

From I-64 east, take exit 40 (last Missouri exit). Turn left onto Gratiot Street and then 4th Street.

From I-70 east, use exit 249B (Tucker Blvd.) and go left onto Market Street.

From Illinois

From Illinois, take I-55, I-64, or US 40 to cross the Mississippi River on the Poplar Street Bridge. After crossing, stay on I-64/US 40 west to turn off at exit 40A (Stadium/Tucker Blvd.), going straight and then right onto Walnut Street.

RAIL

The **MetroLink** (www.metrostlouis. org) light-rail goes every 20 minutes from St. Louis Lambert International Airport to the Gateway Arch (28 min). Debark at 8th and Pine Station or use Laclede's Landing and walk less than 10 minutes to the park entrances.

BUS

The **MetroBus** (www.metrostlouis. org) has multiple routes downtown with stops near the park. The 99 Downtown Trolley, which is actually one of the buses in the downtown core, has a stop on 4th Street and Pine near the park entrance.

Top 3

GATEWAY ARCH

1 ADMIRE THE ARCH

Completed in 1965, the Arch is huge. Each leg is 54 feet (16.5 m) wide, with its base buried 60 feet (18 m) into the ground. The legs are the same distance apart as the arch is high (630 ft/192 m). The stainless-steel exterior hides cement and structural steel. A tram carries sightseers up inside the arch.

You can admire the immense Arch from various locales in the park. Stroll the grounds (5am-11pm daily year-round) on tree-lined pathways to see it close up and at a distance. Accessible paved paths with interpretive signs loop past ponds north and south of the Arch and run the length of the riverfront.

A 35-minute **documentary** (Tucker Theater, 877/982-1410, www.gatewayarch. com, on the hour 10am-7pm daily summer, 9am-5pm daily winter, $7 adults, $3 kids, $4 America the Beautiful passholders), called Monument to the Dream, narrates how the Arch was built.

2 SEE THE OLD COURTHOUSE

OLD COURTHOUSE

Built in 1839, the **Old Courthouse** (11 N. 4th St., 8am-4:30pm daily, free) is a tribute to classic government buildings of the era, with three tiers of balconies overlooking the rotunda inside. Rangers lead daily free tours (times vary), but you can tour the building and four exhibit galleries on your own. The courthouse is closed for renovation 2022-2023.

Two landmark court cases decided here were central to determining the course of U.S. history. In 1847, Dred Scott and his wife sued for freedom from slavery, but the U.S. Supreme Court ultimately ruled that Black people were not citizens and therefore could not sue, which led to the Civil War. In 1873, Virginia Minor and her husband sued for women's right to vote, which finally came to fruition 47 years later.

3 TOUR THE MUSEUM

The museum under the Arch features six themed galleries with exhibits you can touch. Kids enjoy hands-on activities, and computerized simulations give insight into history. Exhibits focus on Indigenous and Creole cultures, colonial St. Louis, Thomas Jefferson, explorers and pioneers, the Riverfront Era, and building the Arch.

RIVERFRONT TRAIL

TAXIS

St. Louis has taxis, ride-sharing, and car services.

BICYCLES

Part of the **Great Rivers Greenway** (https://greatriversgreenway.org), a paved bicycle trail (12.5 mi/20 km one-way), hugs the west bank of the Mississippi River and levee wall. Less than 1 mile (1.6 km) follows the Riverside Trail through Gateway Arch National Park, but you can use the route to ride to the park from North Riverside Park near Old Chain of Rocks Bridge. You can also access the route at multiple locations in between.

PARKING

Gateway Arch has no on-site parking. Near the entrances, there is **metered accessible parking** on Memorial Drive between Walnut Street and Market Street and between Chestnut Street and Pine Street. Multiple **parking garages and surface lots** are within a few blocks of the entrances. You can also drop off or pick up passengers in two locations on 4th Street between Market Street and Chestnut Street in front of the Old Courthouse. Find parking for RVs and cars on Leonor K. Sullivan Boulevard between the Poplar Street Bridge and the levee.

GETTING AROUND

The only way to get around is on foot. No shuttles operate on the grounds, which are around 0.7 mile (1.1 km) long by 0.2 mile (0.3 km) wide. Electric-powered mobility assistance devices are allowed, and wheelchairs are available to borrow from the information desk inside Gateway Arch.

TOURS

One-hour **riverboat cruises** (877/982-1410, www.gatewayarch.com, times vary, daily Mar.-Nov., $21-35 adults, $11-20 ages 3-15) tour the Mississippi on replica historic paddle-wheel steamboats. A National Park Service ranger or the captain narrates the tour. A variety of themed riverboat tours (times, dates, and prices vary) offer different ways to enjoy the cruise: dinner, brunch, lunch, holidays, music, theatrical, and drag shows.

For a unique way to see Gateway Arch and the riverfront, you can fly above in a **helicopter** (www.gateway-helicoptertours.com, 11am-5pm daily Apr.-Nov., starts at $48 pp, 2-person minimum) that fits 2-3 passengers. The three-minute flights are weather-dependent. No reservations are needed, just go below the Arch to the helipad on the riverfront to buy tickets.

HOT SPRINGS NATIONAL PARK

Arkansas

WEBSITE:
www.nps.gov/hosp

PHONE NUMBER:
501/620-6715

VISITATION RANK:
14

WHY GO:
Soak in historic
hot springs.

KEEPSAKE STAMPS ▼▼▼

▲ BUCKSTAFF BATHHOUSE

More than 4,400 years ago, rainwater soaked deep into the earth here, more than 1 mile (1.6 km) down. Coming into contact with a hot fault, the water heated, boiling to the surface again. In today's **HOT SPRINGS NATIONAL PARK**, this hot water gushes at 700,000 gallons (2.6 million) per day, a unique phenomenon in the eastern United States.

In the heyday of the Edwardian era, this once luxurious spot attracted the rich and famous to Arkansas to enjoy the health benefits of the minerals in these waters—and the most sumptuous cluster of natural hot spring bathhouses in North America. The historic architecture, with buildings of marble surrounded by fountains, speaks to the affluence of those times. Today, the buildings house museums, the visitors center, and even a brewery, but are still lauded for their architectural distinction.

PLANNING YOUR TIME

This urban park is just an hour's drive from Little Rock. The small park has two sections. **Bathhouse Row** covers a few downtown blocks at the base of Hot Springs Mountain and can be toured on foot. **Hot Springs Mountain** contains scenic drives, hiking trails, and a campground.

The bathhouses are open year-round, with peak visits March-November. Soaking in hot springs loses its appeal during the hot humid summer with triple-digit heat outdoors. However, that is when visitor services are in full swing and outdoor tours are available. **September-May** offers a more tempting and less crowded time to plunge into the hot water. In winter, when the thermometer plummets below freezing, the baths offer a cozy respite.

ENTRANCE AND FEES

The national park is in the town of **Hot Springs** and has no official entrance. There is no entrance fee.

VISITORS CENTER

Located on Bathhouse Row, **Fordyce Bathhouse Visitor Center** (369 Central Ave., 501/620-6715, 9am-5pm daily year-round, free) claims the most elegant bathhouse from the early 1900s. It even had a bowling alley in the basement and a third-floor music room with a grand piano and a gym.

Rangers lead **guided tours** (daily, free) of the restored building, pointing out stained-glass ceilings and a ceramic fountain. The tour takes in 23 rooms replicated with furniture of the period, including treatment rooms that featured massage and electrotherapy. The history museum has exhibits, films (one shows what the bathing routine entailed), and pictures of its operation from 1915 to 1962.

SIGHTS

BATHHOUSE ROW ENVIRONS

The minerals in the hot springs were believed to have health benefits, thus many **drinking fountains** line Bathhouse Row and the Grand Promenade. Many visitors bring water bottles to fill and take home. **Whittington Spring** (Whittington Ave.) and **Happy Hollow Spring** (Fountain Ave.) are cold-water springs treated with ozone filtration.

North of Bathhouse Row, a cluster of paths connects a gazebo and lawns. **Hot Water Cascade** tumbles into a collection pool, where you can dip your hand in to check the temperature. The large gray **Tufa Rock** was created from the buildup of minerals brought to the surface in thermal waters, which then evaporated to leave the hardened mass

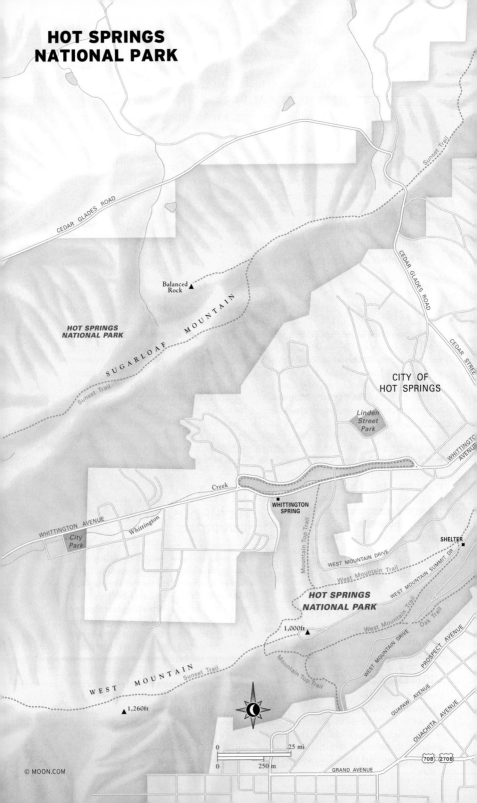

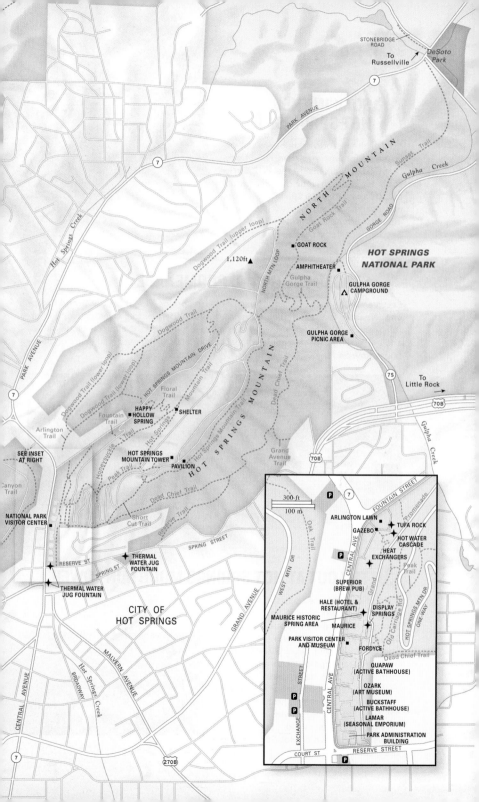

STONEBRIDGE ROAD

To DeSoto Park
To Russellville

PARK AVENUE

7

Sunset Trail

Gulpha Creek

NORTH MOUNTAIN

GORGE ROAD

HOT SPRINGS NATIONAL PARK

Goat Rock Trail

Dogwood Trail (upper loop)

NORTH MTN LOOP

1,120ft

GOAT ROCK

AMPHITHEATER

Gulpha Gorge Trail

GULPHA GORGE CAMPGROUND

Dogwood Trail

Dogwood Trail (lower loop)

Dogwood Trail (lower loop)

HOT SPRINGS MOUNTAIN DRIVE

Floral Trail

Mountain Trail

Dead Chief Trail

GULPHA GORGE PICNIC AREA

75

To Little Rock

70B

Gulpha Creek

PARK AVENUE

Hot Springs Creek

7

Arlington Trail

Fountain Trail

Honeysuckle Trail

HAPPY HOLLOW SPRING

SHELTER

Hot Springs

HOT SPRINGS MOUNTAIN

HOT SPRINGS MOUNTAIN TOWER

PAVILION

Peak Trail

Grand Avenue Trail

HOT SPRINGS MOUNTAIN DRIVE

70B

SEE INSET AT RIGHT

Canyon Trail

Dead Chief Trail

Reserve Trail

Short Cut Trail

NATIONAL PARK VISITOR CENTER

RESERVE ST

Spring Street

THERMAL WATER JUG FOUNTAIN

Spring St

THERMAL WATER JUG FOUNTAIN

CITY OF HOT SPRINGS

CENTRAL AVENUE

Hot Springs Creek

MALVERN AVENUE

BROADWAY

GRAND AVENUE

7

270B

Inset

300 ft
100 m

P 7

FOUNTAIN STREET

ARLINGTON LAWN

GAZEBO

TUFA ROCK

HOT WATER CASCADE

Promenade

P

HEAT EXCHANGERS

Peak Trail

SUPERIOR (BREW PUB)

WEST MTN DR

Oak Trail

CENTRAL AVE

Grand

HALE (HOTEL & RESTAURANT)

DISPLAY SPRINGS

MAURICE HISTORIC SPRING AREA

MAURICE

PARK VISITOR CENTER AND MUSEUM

FORDYCE

Old Carriage Rd

HOT SPRINGS MTN DR

ONE-WAY

QUAPAW (ACTIVE BATHHOUSE)

Dead Chief Trail

OZARK (ART MUSEUM)

BUCKSTAFF (ACTIVE BATHHOUSE)

EXCHANGE STREET

P

P

LAMAR (SEASONAL EMPORIUM)

CENTRAL AVE

PARK ADMINISTRATION BUILDING

COURT ST

RESERVE STREET

P

Top 3

1 SOAK IN THE HOT SPRINGS

Two of the historic bathhouses still offer soaks for weary visitors. For a traditional soak, walk inside the 1912 **Buckstaff** for a dip in your own individual tub. **Quapaw Baths & Spa** offers a more modern spa experience with covered indoor thermal pools and a steam cave. Both charge fees that vary based on services.

QUAPAW BATHS & SPA

2 STROLL THE GRAND PROMENADE

Between Bathhouse Row and the base of Hot Springs Mountain, the **Grand Promenade** passes features fed by hot spring water: thermal fountains, drinking fountains, and display springs. This was the place to be seen. It also has picnic tables and game tables (bring your own checkers or chess). Rangers lead tours on Bathhouse Row and the Grand Promenade.

GRAND PROMENADE

3 TOP OUT AT HOT SPRINGS MOUNTAIN TOWER

Rising like a forested oasis in the middle of the town of Hot Springs, Hot Springs Mountain is topped by **Hot Springs Mountain Tower** (401 Hot Springs Mountain Dr., 501/881-4020, https://hotspringstower.com, 9am-8pm daily May-early Sept., shorter hours Sept.-June, fee). An elevator whisks visitors to the top of the 216-foot-tall (66-m) tower where observation decks yield 360-degree views of the town of Hot Springs and the Ouachita Mountains.

VIEW FROM HOT SPRINGS MOUNTAIN TOWER

ONE DAY IN HOT SPRINGS

Thanks to its small size, you can easily experience the park in one day. Start at the **Fordyce Bathhouse Visitor Center** to get oriented and take a tour. Then walk the National Historic District of **Bathhouse Row** and the **Grand Promenade** and go for a soak in one of the bathhouses. Afterward, drive to the top of Hot Springs Mountain and climb the **Hot Springs Mountain Tower** to take in the views. Return to Bathhouse Row and relax at the **Superior Bathhouse Brewery.**

behind. **Tufa terraces** also line the hillside, where you can depart for a side trail (0.3 mi/0.5 km one-way) that takes off at Stevens Balustrade and returns to Grand Promenade at Hot Water Cascade.

BATHHOUSE ROW

A National Historic Landmark, **Bathhouse Row** has eight bathhouses, leftover hallmarks of 20th-century opulence. The actual row is about 0.25 mile (0.4 km) long, an easy walk along Central Avenue. Most are open to the public. From north to south, the bathhouses include:

Superior is the smallest bathhouse, built in 1916, with a sunporch and brick pilasters. Its services—massage, hydrotherapy, and mercury—were the least

expensive. Today it houses a brewery and pub.

Hale, the oldest bathhouse on the row, was built in 1892. Two subsequent remodels changed its architecture to Mission Revival style, with its original redbrick covered in white stucco. Today, it is a hotel with a restaurant.

Maurice opened in 1912 with a roof garden and basement pool. It is not open to the public.

Fordyce, the largest and most elegant bathhouse, opened in 1915 with the most services—from chiropody to ice thermal water and electrotherapy. It now serves as the visitors center.

Quapaw, which opened in 1922, is the longest bathhouse on the row. Topped with a mosaic tile dome, the Spanish Colonial Revival building now

BATHHOUSE ROW

OZARK BATHHOUSE

houses modern spa services where visitors can bathe in water from the hot springs.

Ozark, built in Spanish Colonial Revival architecture, opened with less extravagant services for the middle class. Today it has art galleries (free) open afternoons Friday-Sunday.

Buckstaff is the best-preserved traditional bathhouse. Built in 1912 with a marble interior, it is fronted by Doric columns and classical architecture. Today, visitors soak in individual tubs and get massages.

Lamar, which opened in 1923, reflects Spanish-style architecture with stucco, brick, and stone. It contains **Bathhouse Row Emporium** (501/620-6740, 9am-5pm daily Apr.-Sept., 10am-5pm Mon.-Fri., 9am-5pm Sat.-Sun. Oct.-Mar.), which sells books, bath souvenirs, bottles to fill with water from the hot springs, and hot beverages made with springwater.

SCENIC DRIVES

NORTH MOUNTAIN DRIVE

North of Bathhouse Row on Central Avenue, follow Fountain Street northeast for **North Mountain Drive.** The short yet scenic drive travels 3 miles (4.8 km) to Hot Springs Mountain. In 0.25 mile (0.4 km), turn right to begin the one-way climb along seven hairpin switchbacks to reach the summit loop. A right turn immediately reveals a picnic area, restrooms, an overlook, and a pavilion. Turn left onto a side spur to the parking lot for **Hot Springs Mountain Tower,** the main attraction. To return to Fountain Drive, leave the summit loop at its northeast end and descend 1 mile (1.6 km, one-way) for fewer switchbacks.

WEST MOUNTAIN DRIVE

West Mountain Drive offers a scenic tour with access to nearby trails. From Bathhouse Row, drive north for 0.25 mile (0.4 km) and turn left onto Whittington Avenue. A left turn follows West Mountain Drive along a one-way loop around the east flank of the mountain and past three overlooks to its tiny summit. Exit the loop by heading south on West Mountain Drive, which ends at Prospect Avenue, south of Bathhouse Row.

RECREATION

HIKING

Sunset Trail (10 mi/16.1 km one-way, 4-5 hrs) leads from Gulpha Gorge Campground to the summit of West Mountain Summit Overlook. The trail crosses several roads that break it into shorter hiking segments and connect it with other hiking trails. The most popular section is the 2.8 miles (4.5 km) from Black Snake Road to West Mountain Summit Overlook, which has the best sunset-viewing location.

On West Mountain, the **West Mountain Trail** (2.4 mi/6.4 km rt, 1.5 hrs) features stone steps and a stone footbridge with ironwork rather than a dramatic destination. Catch it from the Mountain Top Trailhead above Prospect Avenue to return on the Mountain Top Trail.

From the north overlook on Hot Springs Mountain, the **Goat Rock Trail** (2.2 mi/3.5 km rt, 1.5 hrs) drops down switchbacks to small meadows that lead to a stone stairway. The trail climbs 40 feet (12 m) to the novaculite Goat Rock Overlook with views of Indian Mountain.

HOT SPRINGS

Quapaw Baths & Spa

For a modern-day spa experience, **Quapaw Baths & Spa** (413 Central Ave., 501/609-9822, https://quapawbaths.com, 10am-6pm Wed.-Mon., fees vary) offers four large indoor hot pools covered by a stained-glass ceiling. Private baths (individuals or couples) include hydrotherapy plus a variety of herbal additions to enhance your relaxation. After soaking, unwind further in a small steam cave. The spa has a full menu of facials, massages, and body treatments. Proper swim attire is required, and visitors are provided with a robe and slippers. Reservations are requested; guests ages 14-18 must be with an adult.

Buckstaff

For a traditional Hot Springs soak, **Buckstaff** (509 Central Ave., 501/623-2308, www.buckstaffbaths.com, 10am-3pm Tues.-Sun. summer, limited hours other seasons, fees vary) has individual tubs in separate men's and women's facilities. Add on a Swedish massage, loofah mitt, or paraffin hand treatment. Reservations are not accepted for the baths and massages. Manicures, pedicures, and facials require reservations. Kids must be at least 10 years old.

WHERE TO STAY

INSIDE THE PARK

In the historic Hale Bathhouse, **Hotel Hale** (341 Central Ave., 501/760-9010, www.hotelhale.com, from $290) opened a nine-room boutique inn in 2019. Rooms are modern, with thermal mineral soaking baths. Two restaurants offer meals: Fine dining is in **Eden** (dinner Thurs.-Sun., brunch Sat.-Sun.); lighter meals are available at **Zest** (breakfast Fri.-Sat., lunch Tues.-Sat., dinner Wed.-Thurs.).

In the Superior Bathhouse, **Superior Bathhouse Brewery** (329 Central Ave., 501/624-2337, www.superiorbathhouse.com, 11am-9pm Sun.-Mon. and

HOT SPRINGS NATIONAL PARK

THE TRADITIONAL BATHING ROUTINE

At Hot Springs, the traditional bathing routine followed the protocols of European spas.

1 In the bath hall, soak in a private tub for 20 minutes in 100°F (38°C) water. Optionally, scrub with a loofah.

2 Climb into a steam cabinet, with your head inside for two minutes or outside for five minutes.

3 In a sitting tub, soak in 108°F (42°C) water for 10 minutes.

4 Apply heat packs for up to 20 minutes on any achy spots.

5 Cool down with a two-minute shower of cold water.

6 Finish with a full-body Swedish massage.

7 Leave refreshed.

Wed.-Thurs., 11am-10pm Fri.-Sat.) turns hot spring water into thirst-quenching adult beverages and serves pub-style food.

Gulpha Gorge Campground (305 Gulpha Gorge Rd., 40 sites, year-round, $34) can accommodate tents and RVs. All campsites have picnic tables, pedestal grills, full hookups, and fire rings. Facilities include restrooms with flush toilets, potable water, and a dump station. Make reservations (www.recreation.gov) six months in advance.

OUTSIDE THE PARK

The town of **Hot Springs** has chain and independent motels, B&Bs, and inns that surround the national park. The vicinity also has several campgrounds.

GETTING THERE

AIR

Six airlines serve Little Rock National Airport, known as the **Bill and Hillary Clinton National Airport** (LIT, 1 Airport Dr., 501/372-3439, www.clintonairport.com). It's just an hour's drive west to the park via I-30 and US 70. Car rentals are at the airport.

TRAIN

Amtrak (LRK, 1400 W. Markham St., 800/872-7245, www.amtrak.com) serves Little Rock.

BUSES

Intercity Transportation (501/960-5162, http://intercitytransportation.com) runs **buses** from the Little Rock airport to Hot Springs National Park.

CAR

From Little Rock, go west on I-30 to exit 111. Take US 70 west to reach the town of Hot Springs. In town, US 70 becomes East Grand Avenue. Turn right onto Spring Street, which becomes Reserve Street in about 0.5 mile (0.8 km). At Central Avenue, turn right to reach the visitors center. The total distance is 56 miles (90 km, 1 hr).

GETTING AROUND

BUSES

City buses serve the town and the national park of Hot Springs. Routes begin and end at the Transportation Plaza downtown.

PARKING

Parking is limited on Central Avenue along Bathhouse Row. You'll find easier parking for free in the city lot on Exchange Street. To get here, drive south on Central Avenue to Court Street (also called Reserve St.) and turn right. Continue one block west and turn right onto Exchange Street (one-way). Off-street parking is available on the right and in a parking garage on the left.

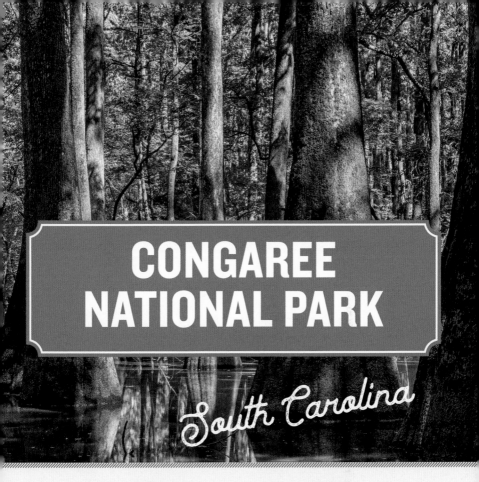

CONGAREE
NATIONAL PARK

South Carolina

KEEPSAKE STAMPS ▼▼▼

WEBSITE:
www.nps.gov/cong

PHONE NUMBER:
803/776-4396

VISITATION RANK:
52

WHY GO:
See the largest
old-growth
hardwood forest.

▲ CYPRESS FOREST AND SWAMP

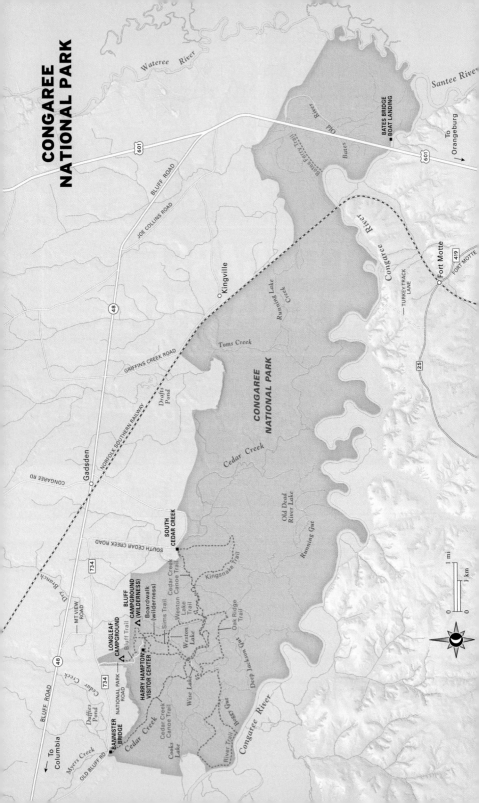

CONGAREE
NATIONAL PARK

Wateree River

Santee River

To Orangeburg

BATES BRIDGE BOAT LANDING

Old River

Bates Ferry Trail

Bates

BLUFF ROAD

JOE COLLINS ROAD

601

Fort Motte

419

FORT MOTTE

Congaree River

TURKEY TRACK LANE

48

Kingville

Running Lake

Creek

25

GRIFFINS CREEK ROAD

Toms Creek

Drafts Pond

CONGAREE NATIONAL PARK

Cedar Creek

NORFOLK SOUTHERN RAILWAY

Gadsden

Old Dead River Lake

CONGAREE RD

Running Gut

SOUTH CEDAR CREEK

SOUTH CEDAR CREEK ROAD

Kingsnake Trail

Cedar Creek Canoe Trail

734

Weston Lake Loop Trail

Oak Ridge Trail

MT VIEW ROAD

BLUFF CAMPGROUND (WILDERNESS)

Boardwalk (wilderness)

Sims Trail

Weston Canoe Trail

Deep Jackson Gut

1 mi

1 km

LONGLEAF CAMPGROUND

Bluff Trail

Weston Lake

River Trail

0

0

Dry Branch

NATIONAL PARK ROAD

HARRY HAMPTON VISITOR CENTER

Wise Lake

Bates Gut

734

48

Cedar Creek

Cedar Creek Canoe Trail

Cooks Lake

River Trail

Congaree River

To Columbia

BLUFF ROAD

OLD BLUFF RD

Cedar Creek

BANNISTER BRIDGE

Duffies Pond

Myers Creek

601

There's nothing like it on the planet. **CONGAREE NATIONAL PARK** contains the most ancient stands of old-growth cypress left in the world. The forest populates a floodplain of the Congaree and Wateree Rivers, which swell with water several times each year to overflow their banks. In doing so, they deposit a nutrient-rich silt that helps sustain the immensely tall trees—loblolly pine, tulip trees, sweet gum, bald cypress, white pine, sycamore, and laurel oak. The park contains the tallest of 15 species of trees, plus six national champion trees for their overall size.

Swamps are one of the hallmarks of the bottomlands that support the forest. The wetlands nurse birds galore, as well as otters, turtles, alligators, snakes, frogs, and catfish. While the rivers served as travel routes for the Congaree people, it's the swamps that saved this habitat from several centuries of plunder for timber and ranching. The result is a unique national park that is also a National Natural Landmark and an International Biosphere Reserve.

PLANNING YOUR TIME

Congaree sits smack in the middle of South Carolina, about a 30-minute drive south of Columbia. Despite its relatively urban locale, this park is wilderness—swamps mean no roads. To see the old-growth forest requires hiking or paddling. Flooding may occur without warning, especially in Cedar Creek and the Congaree River. Check weather and conditions before entering the park.

While visitors come year-round, **spring** (Mar.-June) and October see the most people. Spring can be wet. Summers are hot, humid, fraught with frequent thunderstorms, and a general bug-fest, with swarms of 21 species of mosquitoes.

Fall (Sept.-Nov.) is a favorite time to visit—the air is crisp, and the foliage stunning. Autumn colors peak late October-early November. Winter (Nov.-Feb.) brings unpredictable floods that can submerge trails.

ENTRANCE AND FEES

The main entrance to the park is on Old Bluff Road, 1 mile (1.6 km) before the visitors center. There is no entrance fee.

VISITORS CENTER

The **Harry Hampton Visitor Center** (Old Bluff Rd., 9am-5pm daily) is the place to get oriented in the park, with exhibits, a film, information, backcountry permits, and a gift shop. Ranger-led programs depart from the visitors center.

RECREATION

HIKING

Brown blazes and numbers mark the park's trails. Due to frequent flooding, be prepared for mud, standing water, and downed trees. The difficulty of several trails can vary due to flooding and bridge washouts that may require fording creeks; check on conditions at the visitors center.

Start on the Boardwalk Loop to reach the **Weston Lake Loop** (#3, 4.8 mi/7.7 km rt, 2-3 hrs, easy). The trail passes cypress knees and waterbirds along Cedar Creek.

Crossing Cedar Creek, the **Oakridge Trail** (#4, 9.8 mi/15.7 km rt, 3-4 hrs, easy-difficult) loops through large oaks where you might see wild turkeys. From the west end of the Oakridge Trail, the **River Trail** (#5, 10.1 mi/16.3 km rt,

Top ③

① TOUR THE BOARDWALK

Adjacent to the visitors center, elevated and low boardwalks loop through old-growth forest. The **Boardwalk Loop** (2.4 mi/3.9 km, 1.5 hrs, easy) is a flat trail great for wheelchairs, strollers, and small kids. A self-guided brochure explains the fascinating aspects of this unique environment. Along the trail, cypresses tower more than 130 feet (40 m) into the air. At ground level, hundreds of cypress "knees" (parts of their root system) jut aboveground, and you'll see unbelievably massive loblolly pines.

Because the canopy shuts off so much light, there is almost no understory. The boardwalk goes to Weston Lake, once an oxbow of the Congaree River but now isolated as the riv-

BOARDWALK LOOP

er has changed course. You'll see—and more often, hear—a wide range of wildlife, including owls, waterfowl, and several species of woodpecker, including the rare red-cockaded woodpecker.

② PADDLE CEDAR CREEK CANOE TRAIL

Paddlers can float the flatwater **Cedar Creek Canoe Trail** (15 mi/24 km) from Bannister's Bridge to the Congaree River. Bring your own boat or rent gear in Columbia. Be aware of fluctuating water levels and log jams. In spring and fall, rangers guide **canoe tours** (3 hrs, limited schedule, $70) with canoes, PFDs, and paddles provided. **Reservations** (877/444-6777, www.recreation.gov) are required and open on the first day of the previous month.

CEDAR CREEK

③ WATCH THE SYNCHRONOUS FIREFLY LIGHT SHOW

During mating season, synchronous fireflies light up the forest. Exact dates are always a last-minute calculation based on weather and other conditions, but the annual **Firefly Festival** usually runs for two weeks (mid-May-early June). The park designates one trail as the **Firefly Trail,** and the boardwalk is open only for visitors with mobility needs. Due to limited parking, tickets can only be acquired by lottery (ww.recreation.gov, mid-Apr., $20/vehicle). Check online before April for plans for the coming festival, which may include shuttles from nearby Columbia to the park on select nights.

BALD CYPRESS KNEES

5 hrs, moderate-difficult) loops along the Congaree River. Departing from the east end of the Oakridge Trail, the out-and-back **Kingsnake Trail** (#6, 11.7 mi/18.8 km rt, 6 hrs, moderate) attracts birders to habitat along Cedar Creek.

CANOEING AND KAYAKING

Recognized as the first Blue Trail for paddling in the country, the **Congaree River Blue Trail** (50 mi/81 km) flows from Columbia along Congaree National Park. This multiday paddle route spends the last 20 river miles (32 km) winding through the old-growth forest of the park. Before launching, request a **permit** (803/776-4396 or www.nps.gov/cong, free) at least 48 hours in advance for camping on sandbars. Check river levels ahead of your trip.

WHERE TO STAY

INSIDE THE PARK

There are no lodges or restaurants inside the park. The only accommodations are two walk-in tent-only campgrounds where your vehicle stays in the parking lot. They have picnic tables and fire rings, but no water (bring your own). **Reservations** (877/444-6777, www.recreation.gov) are required up to six months in advance. **Longleaf Campground** (year-round, $10-20) has 14 walk-in campsites and a restroom. **Bluff Campground** (year-round, $5) has six campsites that require a 1-mile (1.6-km) hike from the parking lot; there is no restroom.

OUTSIDE THE PARK

Twenty miles (32 km) northwest, **Columbia** has the closest lodgings and the most restaurants. Nearby **Gadsden** has a few dining options but no lodgings.

GETTING THERE AND AROUND

AIR

Charlotte Douglas International Airport (CLT, 5501 Josh Birmingham Pkwy., Charlotte, NC, 704/359-4013, www.cltairport.com) is in North Carolina, two hours north via I-77. **Charleston International Airport** (CHS, 5500 International Blvd., Charleston, SC, 843/767-7000, www.iflychs.com) is in South Carolina, two hours southeast via I-26. Both airports have rental cars.

CAR

From Charlotte, drive south on I-77 for 95 miles (153 km) to Columbia. Take exit 5 to SC 48 east (Bluff Rd.) and continue 8 miles (13 km). Veer right onto Old Bluff Road and go 4.5 miles (7.2 km) to the park entrance.

From Charleston, drive northwest on I-26 to exit 145B. Continue north on US 601 to SC 48 (Bluff Rd.), where the road heads west. Turn left onto South Cedar Creek Road, then turn right onto Old Bluff Road to the park entrance.

The nearest town, Columbia, has no public transportation to the park but does have rental cars and taxis.

EVERGLADES NATIONAL PARK

Florida

WEBSITE:
www.nps.gov/ever

PHONE NUMBER:
305/242-7700

VISITATION RANK:
27

WHY GO:
See the largest subtropical wetland in the United States.

KEEPSAKE STAMPS ▼▼▼

Shingle Creek, an inconspicuous stream behind an elementary school in Orlando, is the humble origin of one of the world's most-treasured wetland ecosystems. Those headwaters merge into the Kissimmee River, which flows into Lake Okeechobee to discharge into **EVERGLADES NATIONAL PARK**—a vast expanse of marshes, swamps, islands, forests, and waterways encompassing mainland Florida's southernmost points. Despite the best efforts of voracious real estate developers, most of the Everglades remain wild—although decades of attempts at "taming" the land, along with nearby population growth, have dramatically (and in some cases, permanently) altered the ecosystems for the worse. Rising sea levels are also changing this unique landscape, which is currently about one-third saltwater and two-thirds freshwater.

These swamps, forests, and waterways of the Everglades are the traditional lands of the Miccosukee and Seminole peoples. This ecosystem teems with diversity, which is one of the reasons it's been named an International Biosphere Reserve and World Heritage Site.

PLANNING YOUR TIME

The Everglades are a relatively undisturbed wetlands that sprawls across three counties at the southern tip of Florida. With three entrances unconnected by park roads in three different cities, you'll need a car for the long drives in between. Facilities are few and far between.

Miami accesses the northeast part of the Everglades for Shark Valley and is often the only part that many visitors see. **Homestead** is the gateway to the southern Everglades, with a scenic drive and abundant outdoor activities: hiking, canoeing, kayaking, camping, and boating. On the west coast, **Everglades City** is the launch point for the remote Ten Thousand Islands.

You can see one section of the park in one day. But to immerse into the Everglades demands 5-7 days. From the south entrance, the drive to Shark Valley (49 mi/79 km, 1.25 hrs) or the Gulf Coast Visitor Center (58 mi/93 km, 2 hrs) takes time.

Visitation peaks November-April. The best time to visit is **December-March,** the dry season. Temperatures linger in the mid-70s (around 24°C), bugs are less overwhelming, and trees are filled with migratory bird species.

In summer's wet season, the heat amps up into the 90s (32°C and above) with a sweltering humidity of 90 percent. Hurricane season is mid-May to November. Voracious mosquitoes and biting flies peak in July; wear repellent, long-sleeve shirts, and long pants.

ENTRANCES AND FEES

The park's main entrance, southwest of **Homestead,** goes to Ernest F. Coe Visitor Center on the Main Park Road (FL 9336). Shark Valley Visitor Center (Tamiami Trail/US 41), west of **Miami,** serves as the park's north entrance. A remote entrance at **Everglades City** goes to the Gulf Coast Visitor Center.

The entrance fee is $30 per vehicle ($25 motorcycle, $15 individual) and good for seven days. You can **buy your pass online** (www.recreation.gov).

VISITORS CENTERS
Shark Valley Visitor Center

On the busy Tamiami Trail linking Miami and Naples, the **Shark Valley Visitor Center** (36000 SW 8th St., 305/221-8776, 8:30am-5pm daily Dec.-Apr., 9am-5pm daily May-Nov.) offers a

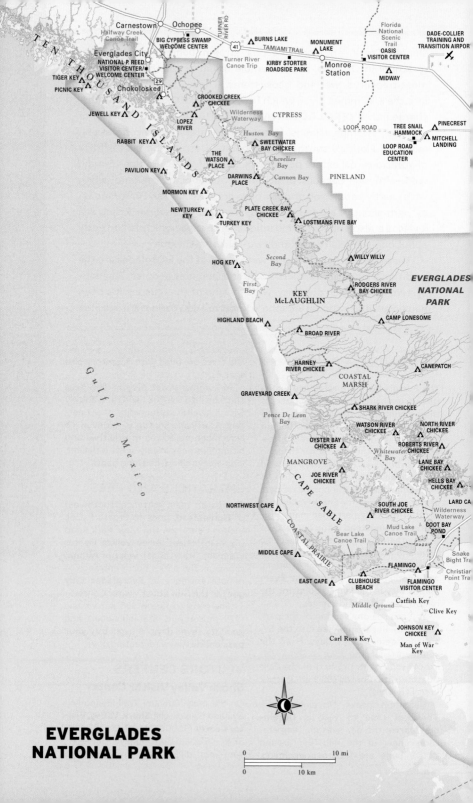

EVERGLADES
NATIONAL PARK

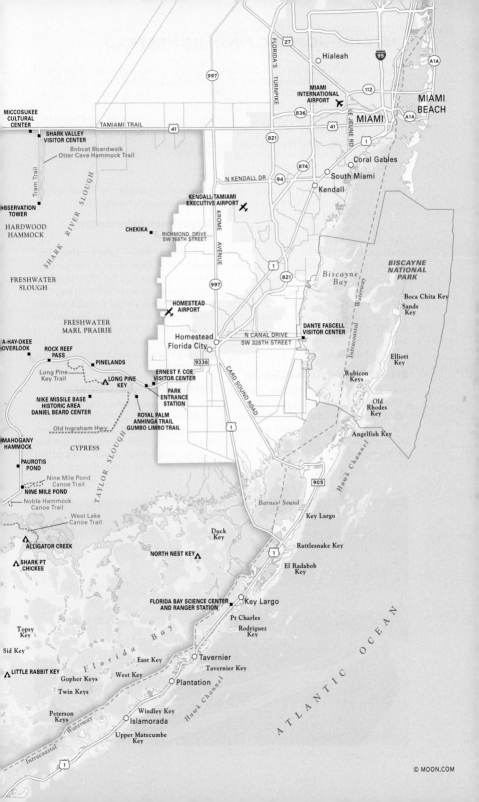

ISLAND-HOPPING FROM HOMESTEAD

Homestead makes a good base for exploring three parks: Everglades, Biscayne, and Dry Tortugas National Parks. From Homestead, short drives go to the Ernest F. Coe Visitor Center in Everglades (11 mi/18 km, 18 min) and Dante Fascell Visitor Center at Biscayne (10 mi/16 km, 21 min).

From the south entrance of Everglades, drive southeast on the Overseas Highway to **Key West** (127 mi/204 km, 3 hrs). Hop a boat to reach **Dry Tortugas National Park.** Camp overnight or stay in Key West.

one-stop shop for the Everglades experience. The visitors center has exhibits and films. Outside are two short trails (one accessible), guided walking tours, and two-hour tram tours (reserve in advance, 305/221-8455, www.sharkvalleytramtours.com). There's also a popular 15-mile (24-km) bike trail loop with bike rentals at the tram station. Plan to arrive early, as parking lots fill quickly. Through 2024, you may encounter construction as the park adds parking and improves the tram trail; check online for potential closures.

Ernest F. Coe Visitor Center

The **Ernest F. Coe Visitor Center** (40001 SR 9336, Homestead, 305/242-7700, 8am-5pm daily mid-Dec.-mid-Apr., 9am-5pm daily mid-Apr.-mid-Dec.) is at the main park entrance. It has exhibits and films that detail the flora, fauna, and history of the Everglades,

plus special works by local artists. A bookstore sells field guides.

Royal Palm Information Station

The **Royal Palm Information Station** (4 mi/6.4 km west of the park entrance on Main Park Rd., 305/242-7237, 8am-4pm daily) is the starting point for two of the park's most popular walking trails: the Anhinga Amble Trail and the Gumbo Limbo Trail. Ranger-led tours depart from the visitors center for walking trails, wading through sloughs, or bicycling.

Flamingo Visitor Center

The **Flamingo Visitor Center** (1 Flamingo Lodge Hwy., 239/695-2945, 8am-5pm daily mid-Nov.-mid-Apr., hours vary mid-Apr.-mid-Nov.) is at the end of the park's main paved road, about an hour south of Ernest F. Coe Visitor

SHARK VALLEY TRAIL

Top ❸

❶ WATCH WILDLIFE

AMERICAN CROCODILE

The one animal instantly associated with the Everglades is the **American alligator,** a stealthy predator growing up to 16 feet (5 m). Backwater paddlers are frequently surprised when they discover that they've come within inches of one of these prehistoric marvels. Gators tend to hug the shoreline and prefer the tree cover. Look on the Anhinga Trail below mangroves and in Shark Valley.

Carnivorous **American crocodiles** tend to nest around Cape Sable and Flamingo, where they are threatened by salinity from rising sea levels entering freshwater bays. These relics headline the park's endangered species, along with **manatees, Florida panthers, wood storks,** and **snail kites.**

The most abundant wildlife are **birds.** Dozens of species call the Glades home, including **anhingas, spoonbills, egrets, flamingos,** and **bald eagles.** During migration season, hordes more nonnative species arrive. Spot them best on wetland hiking trails and paddling trips. Free ranger-led bird-watching programs depart from Flamingo Visitor Center.

❷ CANOE AND KAYAK THE GLADES

The best way to experience the Everglades is in a canoe or kayak. Kayaks are better suited to the narrow waterways, and you'll appreciate the navigational flexibility when paddling through mangrove tunnels. You can go self-guided on paddle trips or join **ranger-led tours** via the visitors centers at Flamingo, Shark Valley, and Gulf Coast (daily in winter, reservations required). **Rentals** are available at Flamingo Marina, Gulf Coast Visitor Center, and Everglades City. Winter is the best time to canoe and kayak, when the waters are calmer and the weather mild.

Beginner paddlers can explore calm backwater sloughs and lakes on several canoe trails located on Main Park Road near Flamingo. Advanced paddlers have options there too. But the king of paddle trips is spending 7-10 days touring **Ten Thousand Islands** on the western coast. Several Seminole-style **chickees** (backcountry permit required) are located throughout the park, providing an elevated and roofed camping area right on the water.

SHARK VALLEY TRAIL

❸ BIKE SHARK VALLEY

Pedal along the utterly flat paved loop of the **Shark Valley Trail** (15 mi/24. km, 2-3 hrs), where you can encounter wildlife, including alligators. At the south end, climb the observation tower to view the expanse of sea grass from the highest point in the Everglades. Rent bikes (first come, first served) from **Shark Valley Tram Tour** (305/221-8455, www.sharkvalleytramtours.com, 8:30am-4pm daily). Through 2024, you may encounter construction projects to mitigate flooding on the trail; check online for potential closures.

Best Hike

ANHINGA TRAIL

DISTANCE: 0.8 mile (1.3 km) round-trip
DURATION: 30 minutes
ELEVATION CHANGE: negligible
DIFFICULTY: easy
TRAILHEAD: Royal Palm Visitor Center

The paved and boardwalk **Anhinga Trail** strolls through a classic Everglades sawgrass marsh. The flat wheelchair-accessible trail goes from the visitors center to loop through lush wetlands with overlooks, interpretive signs, and two short spurs. Even during the hottest summer months, you're likely to see a decent array of wildlife, especially alligators. During the winter months, bird-watching is incredible, with egrets, herons, cormorants, and anhingas. Abundant winter wildlife includes turtles, fish, and snakes. Rangers guide walks daily on this trail.

Center. Inside are educational displays and backcountry permits. Outside are short trails and a marina with boat tours and rentals of canoes, kayaks, boats, and bicycles.

Gulf Coast Visitor Center

On the park's remote northwest coast, the **Gulf Coast Visitor Center** (815 Oyster Bar Ln., Everglades City, 239/695-3311, 8am-5pm daily) gives visitors access to the waterways and tiny islands of the Ten Thousand Islands. The center's main building has nature exhibits, films, and backcountry permits.

SCENIC DRIVE
MAIN PARK ROAD

There's only one road in and out of Everglades National Park, so dedicate a full day to the journey from the park entrance and **Ernest F. Coe Visitor Center** to **Flamingo Visitor Center.** A handful of pullovers along **Main Park Road** (38 mi/61 km) offer stops to walk along a boardwalk, have a picnic, or just stare off into the vast expanse of the Everglades. Mileages given are from the entrance station.

▼ SUNSET OVER THE EVERGLADES

ONE DAY IN THE EVERGLADES

Get oriented at the **Ernest F. Coe Visitor Center,** and then drive the **Main Park Road** through the Everglades, taking in the sights, wildlife, and boardwalk trails through wetlands. Then cruise down to the **Flamingo Marina** for a **boat tour** through the backwaters of Florida Bay.

Long Pine Key

At **Long Pine Key** (5.8 mi/9.3 km), walk the unnamed 0.5-mile (0.8-km) multipurpose trail, which offers a diverse look at the area's ecology.

Rock Reef Pass

The sign just before **Rock Reef Pass** (11 mi/18 km) says "Elevation: Three Feet." This is practically mountainous for the Everglades, since most of this flat, swampy park is at or below sea level. The altitude of Rock Reef Pass makes for a unique ecological combination of pine forest and marshes filled with dwarf cypress trees. A short **boardwalk** tours an ecosystem that is a dry tinderbox in winter and a foot-deep swamp in summer's rainy season.

Pa-hay-okee Overlook

The elevated wheelchair-accessible boardwalk at **Pa-hay-okee Overlook** (14 mi/22 km) offers expansive vistas onto the grassy infinity of the Everglades. In the busy season, the parking lot packs full, and crowds on the boardwalk create cattle-chute movement. Visit before 9am for fewer people.

Mahogany Hammock

Mahogany Hammock (21 mi/34 km) is a boardwalk-through-the-Glades experience. The self-guided loop trail (0.5 mi/0.8 km rt, 15 min, easy) tours dense mahogany trees that provide shade from the canopy, usually full of migratory birds. You'll also see the largest mahogany tree in the United States.

RECREATION

HIKING

Due to seasonal flooding and wetland environments, many trails in the Everglades are paved or boardwalks. Those

ANHINGA TRAIL

GUMBO LIMBO TRAIL

that are not may be muddy and, in some places, flooded in summer.

Located 2 miles (3.2 km) west of Long Pine Key, **Pineland Trail** (0.4 mi/0.6 km rt, 15 min, easy) is a paved trail through slash pine and palmettos. Although the trail is wheelchair-accessible, roots have heaved up the pavement in places.

From the Royal Palm Visitor Center, the wheelchair-accessible **Gumbo Limbo Trail** (0.4 mi/0.6 km rt, 20 min, easy) tours under the shade of gumbo-limbo trees and royal palms. Amid ferns and air plants, look for birds and wildlife on this interpretive path.

The mangrove-lined waterfront **Bayshore Trail** (2 mi/3.2 km rt, 1 hr, easy) launches from the Flamingo Campground and jaunts along Florida Bay with interpretive signs. Check on trail status first at a visitors center. From the Flamingo Visitor Center, the **Eco-Pond Trail** (0.5 mi/0.8 km rt, 20 min, easy) loops with interpretive signs around a freshwater pond full of waterfowl and songbirds.

From Shark Valley Visitor Center, the wheelchair-accessible **Bobcat Boardwalk** (0.5 mi/0.8 km one-way, 20 min, easy) loops through classic sawgrass fields and swamp trees thick with migrating and nesting birds December through May.

BIKING

Off the Main Park Road, the **Long Pine Key Nature Trail** (13 mi/21 km rt, 2-3 hrs) is a loop that goes on double-track through palmettos and pines from the campground to Pine Glades Lake. It connects with the paved (and

MANGROVE AT NINE MILE POND

KAYAK THE GULF COAST.

trafficked) Main Park Road to return. The **Snake Bight Trail** (3.2 mi/5.2 km rt) goes to a boardwalk (dismount here) to see a small bay known as a bight within Florida Bay. Check on maintenance status before riding either of these trails.

Five miles (8 km) east of Shark Valley, a grassy gravel **canal road** (6.4 mi/10.3 km rt) parallels Shark Valley Slough where you can see alligators, turtles, and in winter, birds.

For biking, bring water for the heat. In summer, ride in the morning to avoid afternoon lightning. Rangers lead several bicycle tours, including a nighttime meteor shower ride and moonlight rides, plus daytime rides; some require reservations at visitors centers. **Shark Valley Tram Tours** (305/221-8455, www.sharkvalleytramtours.com) and **Flamingo Marina** (239/695-1095 or 855/708-2207, www.flamingoeverglades.com) have bike rentals.

CANOEING AND KAYAKING

Everglades was made for paddlers! Mangrove tunnels, freshwater sloughs, bays, and islands offer a breadth of habitats to explore, often loaded with birds and wildlife. Rangers guide multiple canoe trips from the visitors centers at Flamingo, Shark Valley, and the Gulf Coast. For some, you must bring your own canoe or kayak; other tours provide canoes. Make required reservations by calling the visitors centers.

For self-guided trips, inquire about water levels at visitors centers before launching, especially during the winter dry season.

Flamingo

Experienced paddlers can explore the twists and turns of the popular **Hell's Bay Canoe Trail** (3-5.5 mi/4.8-8.8 km), a challenging run that announces its intentions with a comically difficult put-in and a trail that can take up to six hours to navigate completely. The difficult **West Lake Canoe Trail** (7.7 mi/12.4 km one-way) runs mainly through open waters but also squeezes through some impressive mangrove tunnels that are occasionally claustrophobic.

Beginner options include the **Nine Mile Pond Canoe Trail** (5.2 mi/8.4 km) through mangrove tunnels and several wider marshes. It's best explored during the summer when water levels are high. **Noble Hammock Canoe Trail** (2 mi/3.2 km) is a short loop through mangroves. From Flamingo Marina, paddlers can also explore the waters of **Florida Bay** and its numerous keys.

Ten Thousand Islands and Wilderness Waterway

Paddling options abound in this wild country, with trips ranging 1-10 days. Check conditions at visitors centers and pick up nautical charts for navigation. Use the park's online Wilderness Trip Planner for assistance in planning overnights at 45 locations: on raised platform chickees above water, sandy beaches, or ground sites between mangroves. Some locations have toilets. Permits are required ($21, plus $2 pp/day). **Reservations** (www.recreation.gov) are available three months in advance. You can also get walk-in permits at Gulf Coast and Flamingo Visitor Centers.

The massive **Ten Thousand Islands** covers an extensive coastline in southwestern Florida. It contains mangrove swamps, tiny keys, grassy marshes, sandy beaches, mud bars, and tropical hardwood hammocks, nearly all of which are undeveloped. Running along Cape Sable and the western edge of the Glades, this region includes the **Ten Thousand Islands National Wildlife Refuge** (239/657-8001, www.fws.gov/refuge/ten_thousand_islands) and Everglades National Park.

Serious canoers and kayakers go for the **Wilderness Waterway** (99 mi/159 km, 7-10 days), which gets paddlers into some of the most isolated backwaters of the Everglades. Winter is best for this adventure. To have prevailing winds aid your paddling, launch at Everglades City in Chocoloskee Bay and finish at Flamingo Marina. **Everglades Adventures** (605 Buckner Ave. N., Everglades City, 239/294-8249, https://evergladesadventures.com) runs shuttle services between Everglades City and Flamingo Visitor Center to get you back to your starting point.

Rentals and Tours

Flamingo Marina (239/695-1095 or 855/708-2207, www.flamingoeverglades.com) rents kayaks and canoes. Canoe rentals are also available at the **Gulf Coast Visitor Center**, but you may have better luck at private operators, as these rentals run out quickly during winter.

Everglades Adventures (605 Buckner Ave. N., Everglades City, 239/294-8249, https://evergladesadventures.com) guides ecofriendly daytime and sunset tours. The company also rents

▼ BIRDS AND MANGROVES IN THE EVERGLADES

FLAMINGO AREA

canoes and kayaks. **Shurr Adventures** (32016 Tamiami Trail, Miami, 239/300-3004, www.schurradventures.com) leads kayak tours through Ten Thousand Islands. It also offers backcountry mangrove tours.

BOATING

In such a water-filled park, boating is the way to tour much of the southern and western parts of the park. Boaters entering waters within the national park must have a **permit** (free, obtainable after completing an online education course) and a **park pass** (www.recreation.gov). Navigational aids are also on the park's website.

Flamingo Marina (239/695-1095 or 855/708-2207, www.flamingoeverglades.com, year-round) has a boat launch, overnight slips for boats with power and water hookups, pump-out services, fuel, showers, and rentals of fishing pontoons, skiffs, and houseboats. Boat rentals are also available in Everglades City.

Wilderness Boat Camping

Boaters can access backcountry campsites that are chickees along the Wilderness Waterway and in Florida Bay, sandy beach sites, or standard ground sites. The three beach sites at **Cape**

Sable are the largest, accommodating around 150 people. They're as beautiful as they are rustic and often uncrowded. Get nautical charts for navigation.

Permits ($21, plus $2 pp/day) are required for overnight trips. **Reservations** (www.recreation.gov) are available three months in advance. Walk-in permits are available at the Gulf Coast and Flamingo Visitor Centers. Check the Wilderness Trip Planner online to aid with campsite selection and dock locations.

FISHING

Numerous fishing charters are available. Most charters offer the choice between flats and deepwater fishing excursions. Most are geared toward small groups (2-5 people). You will need a Florida fishing license.

Everglades Kayak Fishing (239/682-9920, www.evergladeskayakfishing.com) and **Captain Tony Polizos** (239/695-2608) operate out of Everglades City.

WHERE TO STAY
INSIDE THE PARK

There are no lodges in the park. Overnight options on the Main Park Road include camping, eco-tenting, and houseboats.

Flamingo Adventures (855/708-2207, www.flamingoeverglades.com) has **eco-tents** (from $50) with a queen or two double beds on a platform; restrooms are shared. It's all set up for you with bed linens and electricity, and outside, storage bins, a picnic table, and grills. If you'd rather sleep on water, you can rent a fully equipped two-bedroom docked **houseboat** (from $300) with bed and bath linens, a shower, and an outfitted galley; you bring food and personal items.

Two traditional campgrounds welcome tent campers and RVs. Facilities include solar-heated showers, RV dump stations, picnic tables, grills, drinking water, and amphitheaters for evening ranger programs. Near Flamingo Visitor Center, **Flamingo Campground** (855/708-2207, flamingoeverglades.com, year-round, $23-45) has 234 drive-up sites, 40 walk-in sites, 41 RV

BIG CYPRESS NATIONAL PRESERVE

You can get a taste of **Big Cypress National Preserve** (www.nps.gov/bicy) when driving from Shark Valley to Everglades City. This immense freshwater swamp supports diverse wildlife: alligators, crocodiles, fish, turtles, birds, and the elusive Florida panther.

Big Cypress has two visitors centers for maps, information, permits, and bookstores. Ask about schedules for ranger-led programs that include walks, talks, and paddle trips. The **Nathaniel P. Reed Visitor Center** (33000 Tamiami Trail E., Ochopee, 9am-4:30pm daily), also called the Welcome Center, has indoor and outdoor exhibits. The **Oasis Visitor Center** (52105 Tamiami Trail E., Ochopee, 9am-4:30pm daily) has small educational and art exhibits.

Scenic Drives

Two gravel scenic drives depart the Tamiami Trail (US 41). Road guides for each are online (www.nps.gov/bicy); check conditions at visitors centers before driving. The **Loop Road** (27 mi/43 km) tours south through dense forests of dwarf cypress, slash pine, and wildlife. Starting at H. P. Williams Roadside Park, **Turner River Loop** (17 mi/27 km) goes north, an outstanding option for bird-watchers.

Recreation

At **Kirby Storter Roadside Park** (US 41/Tamiami Trail, sunrise-sunset daily, free), an interpretive boardwalk trail (1 mi/1.6 km rt, 30 min, easy) provides views of the swamp and vast expanses of marshlands. Bird-watching is excellent.

Launch canoes and kayaks from the **Turner River Canoe Access** (entry point at US 41 west of Turner River Rd.). Paddling season is November-March.

Where to Stay

Big Cypress National Preserve campgrounds (877/444-6777, www.recreation.gov, from $24) near Ochopee take reservations: **Midway Campground** (52870 Tamiami Trail E., year-round), **Monument Lake Campground** (50215 Tamiami Trail E., mid-Aug.-mid-Apr.), and the primitive **Burns Lake Campground & Backcountry Access** (18495 Burns Rd., mid-Aug.-mid-Apr.).

On Tamiami Trail, Ochopee has a couple of restaurants and lodging options.

Getting There

The **Tamiami Trail** (US 41), east of Naples (36 mi/58 km, 45 min), bisects southern Big Cypress National Preserve. From Shark Valley Visitor Center in Everglades, drive 20 miles (32 km, 25 min) east to Oasis Visitor Center. From Everglades City, drive 6 miles (10 km, 8 min) northwest to the Welcome Center.

BIG CYPRESS NATIONAL PRESERVE

sites, and 3 walk-in group sites. Reservations are accepted up to six months in advance for November-April stays. Nearest the southern entrance, **Long Pine Key Campground** (mid-Nov.-Apr., $25-35) has 108 drive-up sites and one group site. Sites are first come, first served.

A food truck visits the **Flamingo Marina** (11:30am-5pm Wed.-Sun.), and the **Flamingo Marina store** (7am-7pm daily) has convenience foods.

OUTSIDE THE PARK

Accommodations, restaurants, and services are in **Miami, Homestead,** and **Everglades City.** Camping is available in Big Cypress National Preserve.

GETTING THERE

AIR

The nearest airport is **Miami International Airport** (MIA, 2100 NW 42nd Ave., 305/876-7000, www.miami-airport.com), about an hour's drive north. It is also the primary point of entry for travelers entering the United States from South America and the Caribbean. Car rentals are available.

CAR

From Miami, a 40-mile (64-km, 1 hr) drive goes to the Tamiami Trail (US 41) to reach the Shark Valley Visitor Center, a busy spot that's the northwest entry to Everglades. About 36 miles (58 km, 45 min) southwest of Naples via the Tamiami Trail (US 41) is the town of Everglades City, home to the Gulf Coast Visitor Center, the best point for exploring the western half of the Everglades.

From Miami, it's 50 miles (81 km, 1 hr) south via FL 997 or FL 821 to reach Ernest F. Coe Visitor Center at the southern entrance to Everglades.

From Key West, take the Overseas Highway (US 1) through Florida City before dropping into Homestead. The 127-mile (204-km) drive takes three hours.

GETTING AROUND

There is no public transportation within the park.

TOURS

From Homestead, the **Homestead Trolley** (www.cityofhomestead.com, weekends and holidays late Nov.-Apr., free) runs guided tours to the Everglades.

Tram Tours

The most popular tour is the **Shark Valley Tram Tour** (305/221-8455, www.sharkvalleytramtours.com, 9am-4pm daily Jan.-Mar., 9:30am-4pm daily May-mid-Dec., fee) departing from the Shark Valley Visitor Center. Park naturalists, who point out sharks and gators, guide two-hour tours in covered, open-air buses with pull-behind cars. Midway through the tour, you'll stop at a 45-foot-high (14-m) observation platform to see the Everglades from above. Reservations are strongly recommended.

Ranger Tours

Ranger-led tours (daily, free) depart the visitors centers for short walks that vary from easy trails (some wheelchair-accessible) to "Slough Slogs," bird-watching, or nighttime starlight tours. Other tours travel by bicycle, canoe, or boat. Tour schedules change seasonally; winters run full schedules of programs while summers have reduced tours.

Boat Tours

Narrated 90-minute boat tours depart **Flamingo Marina** (352/701-6581 or 855/708-2207, www.flamingoeverglades.com, fee). The **Back Country Boat Tour** (four times daily late Nov.-mid-Apr.) motors up a canal, creek, and two bays on a pontoon boat. The **Florida Bay Boat Tour** (1-3 times daily, late Nov.-early May) circles Florida Bay on a double-deck catamaran. Purchase tickets for both online or at the marina store.

From Everglades City on the Gulf Coast, **Everglades Florida Adventures** (855/793-5542, www.evergladesfloridaadventures.com, 2-4 times daily year-round, fee) guides 90-minute catamaran tours in the Ten Thousand Islands. Purchase tickets online or at the Gulf Coast Visitor Center.

BISCAYNE
NATIONAL PARK

Florida

WEBSITE:
www.nps.gov/bisc

PHONE NUMBER:
305/230-1144

VISITATION RANK:
33

WHY GO:
Explore a national
park that is
95 percent water.

KEEPSAKE STAMPS ▼▼▼

▲ BISCAYNE'S UNDERWATER
GARDENS

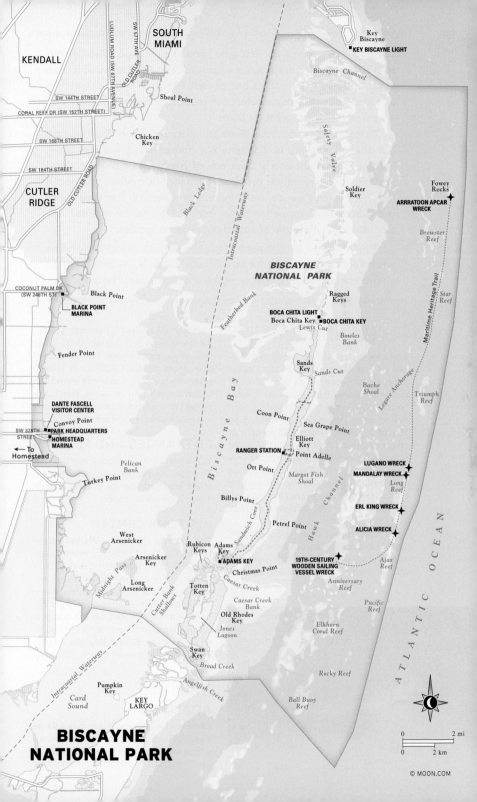

KENDALL

SOUTH MIAMI

LUDLUM ROAD (SW 67TH AVENUE)
SW 57TH AVE
OLD CUTLER ROAD

SW 144TH STREET
Shoal Point
CORAL REEF DR (SW 152ND STREET)
SW 168TH STREET
Chicken Key
SW 184TH STREET

CUTLER RIDGE

Key Biscayne
KEY BISCAYNE LIGHT

Biscayne Channel

Safety Valve

Soldier Key

Fowey Rocks
ARRRATOON APCAR WRECK

Brewster Reef

Star Reef

Black Ledge

Intracoastal Waterway

BISCAYNE NATIONAL PARK

COCONUT PALM DR (SW 248TH ST)
Black Point
BLACK POINT MARINA

Fender Point

Featherbed Bank

Ragged Keys

BOCA CHITA LIGHT
Boca Chita Key **BOCA CHITA KEY**
Lewis Cut
Bowles Bank

Sands Key
Sands Cut

Bache Shoal

Legare Anchorage

Triumph Reef

Maritime Heritage Trail

DANTE FASCELL VISITOR CENTER
Convoy Point
SW 328TH STREET **PARK HEADQUARTERS**
HOMESTEAD MARINA
← To Homestead

Pelican Bank

Coon Point

Sea Grape Point

Elliott Key
RANGER STATION
Point Adelle

Ott Point

Margot Fish Shoal

LUGANO WRECK
MANDALAY WRECK

Long Reef

ERL KING WRECK

ALICIA WRECK

Turkey Point

Billys Point

Sandwich Cove

Petrel Point

Hawk Channel

West Arsenicker

Arsenicker Key

Rubicon Keys
Adams Key
ADAMS KEY
Christmas Point

Caesar Creek

19TH-CENTURY WOODEN SAILING VESSEL WRECK

Ajax Reef

Anniversary Reef

Pacific Reef

A T L A N T I C   O C E A N

Long Arsenicker

Midnight Pass

Cutter Bank Shallows

Totten Key

Caesar Creek Bank

Old Rhodes Key
Jones Lagoon

Elkhorn Coral Reef

Swan Key
Broad Creek

Rocky Reef

Intracoastal Waterway

Card Sound

Pumpkin Key

KEY LARGO

Angelfish Creek

Ball Buoy Reef

Biscayne Bay

0   2 mi
0   2 km

BISCAYNE NATIONAL PARK

© MOON.COM

Located between Key Biscayne and Key Largo, **BISCAYNE NATIONAL PARK** is a tropical water world—with more water than land. Its mainland contains one of east Florida's longest stretches of saltwater mangrove swamp, but most of its islands can only be accessed by canoe, kayak, or boat.

Threatened by rising sea levels and warming water, the immense but shallow estuary of Biscayne Bay houses sea grass meadows, manatees, and an utterly clear mix of fresh- and seawater. Coral reefs full of living polyps provide a base for 500 species of colorful fish. The ecosystem contains incredible diversity: flamingos, ibis, red-footed boobies, pelicans, sea turtles, sharks, barracudas, up-side-down jellyfish, and about 20 endangered species.

The Tequesta people once made the largest island their home while relying on the sea for sustenance. Later, it became home to shipwreck scavengers, sponge makers, and pineapple farmers.

PLANNING YOUR TIME

Biscayne National Park is south of Miami on the Atlantic side of the Florida cape. Once proposed as part of Everglades National Park, Biscayne is easy to pair with visiting that larger neighboring park. Although the water portion of Biscayne (which is 95 percent of the park), Boca Chita Key, and Elliott are open 24 hours daily, other keys are only open for day use. While you can drive to the park's mainland and the visitors center, the bay and islands are only accessible by boat. No bridges or ferries go to the islands.

Temperatures float around 82°F (28°C) in summer, accompanied by humidity and afternoon thunderstorms. Water clarity and minimal waves make summer (May-Sept.) the best season for snorkeling but spring (Mar-June) sees the most visitors. The thermometer drops to 68°F (20°C) in winter, when dry weather can break from time to time with rain or wind. Hurricane season is June-November. Mosquitoes are year-round inhabitants.

ENTRANCES AND FEES

The islands are only accessible by boat. The park entrance is near the Homestead Bayfront Marina in **Homestead.** There is no entrance fee.

VISITORS CENTER

The **Dante Fascell Visitor Center** (9700 SW 328th St., Homestead, 305/230-7275, 9am-5pm daily) is near Convoy Point on the mainland. The center has exhibits, films, a local art gallery, and information. Guided boat tours depart from the visitors center, and you can launch paddle crafts for self-guided exploration. **Elliott Key** has a ranger station that is staffed intermittently.

SIGHTS

ADAMS KEY

Close to the visitors center, tiny **Adams Key** (day-use only) contains mangroves where you can swim, paddle, or snorkel. The island has a picnic area, a short

SEA TURTLE

Top **3**

1 SNORKEL SHIPWRECKS

Accessible only by boat, Biscayne is lined with shallow-water shipwrecks that delight snorkelers and divers. Six shipwrecks line the **Maritime Heritage Trail** on the Atlantic side of the park. Looking more like skeletons than ships, the wrecks date mostly from the late 1800s and early 1900s. Pick up maps at the visitors center to locate the shipwrecks and their mooring buoys. **Biscayne National Park Institute** (786/465-4058, www.biscaynenationalparkinstitute.org) guides tours.

SNORKELERS EXPLORE ELKHORN REEF.

2 PADDLE MANGROVES

Biscayne Bay is rimmed with mangroves in one of the longest mangrove forests on Florida's east coast. These unique forests thrive in saltwater and in turn keep the water clean while creating a rich habitat for birds and aquatic life, including manatees. Paddling a kayak, canoe, or paddleboard into the mangroves is the best way to explore these wonders, even for beginners, who should stick to the rim of the bay. Rent paddle craft at the visitors center or take a guided paddle tour with **Biscayne National Park Institute** (786/465-4058, www.biscaynenationalparkinstitute.org).

3 VISIT BOCA CHITA KEY

The most visited island, small **Boca Chita Key** has an idyllic harbor and a lighthouse that dates from the 1930s. If a park ranger is available, you can access the observation deck for big views full of water, islands, and Miami. Reach this island on the north end of the keys by boat, and camp overnight. **Biscayne National Park Institute** (786/465-4058, www.biscaynenationalparkinstitute.org) guides weekend tours to the island.

BOCA CHITA KEY

TOTTEN KEY

trail, and a dock, but it once housed the Cocolobo Club, a getaway for the rich and famous. Reach this island on the south end of the keys by boat.

ELLIOTT KEY

North of Key Largo, **Elliott Key** is the park's largest island at about 7 miles (11 km) long. It offers swimming, paddling, camping, picnicking, and a hiking trail. Historically, the Tequesta Indians used it periodically, but its early settlers grew pineapples, collected sponges, and sought spoils from wrecked ships.

RECREATION

HIKING

From the visitors center, cross a bridge to reach the jetty to **Convoy Point** (7am-5:30pm daily, 0.6 mi/1 km rt, 20 min, easy) to see the bay.

On Elliott Key, the **Spite Highway Nature Trail** (6 mi/9.7 km one-way, 3 hrs, easy) travels the length of the island, crossing through subtropical forest that harbors butterflies. Access to the key is by boat; camping is available.

CANOEING, KAYAKING, AND PADDLEBOARDING

Beginner paddlers should stick to the mangrove rims of Biscayne Bay, but

experienced paddlers can tackle the 7-mile (11-km) crossing to the keys to camp on Boca Chita Key or Elliott Key.

Secluded **Jones Lagoon,** a shallow waterway with tiny islets between **Totten** and **Old Rhodes Keys,** offers sheltered paddling routes to see fish, sharks, and birds. **Hurricane Creek** is a paddling destination that has snorkeling in mangroves on Old Rhodes Key. Consult with the visitors center on paddle routes before launching. Winter is the best time for these two trips.

Paddle craft are not available for rent in the park; plan to bring your own

SPADE FISH

or rent in Homestead or Miami. Paddlers can launch free from the visitors center parking lot. Pick up a free parking permit to leave your car overnight while camping. **Biscayne National Park Institute** (786/465-4058, www.biscaynenationalparkinstitute.org) guides kayaking and paddleboarding trips to Jones Lagoon or mangrove and sea grass meadows.

DIVING AND SNORKELING

If you have a boat, you can snorkel shallow coral reefs and shipwrecks on your own or go on deeper dives. Otherwise, board a guided snorkeling trip with **Biscayne National Park Institute** (786/465-4058, www.biscaynenationalparkinstitute.org). **Tropic Scuba** (305/205-7829, www.tropicscuba.com) has charter snorkeling and scuba diving trips.

BOATING AND FISHING

To boat in the park, motorboats must launch from marinas in nearby **Miami-Dade County Parks** (www.miamidade.gov): **Homestead Bayfront Park** (9698 SW 328th St., Homestead, 305/230-3033) and **Black Point Marina** (24775 SW 87th Ave., Miami, 305/258-4092). Anglers will need a Florida fishing license to go after tarpon, grouper, snapper, and bonefish. For facilities, mooring, and docking details on boating and fishing, check online (https://ocean.floridamarine.org/boating_guides/biscayne_bay/).

WHERE TO STAY

INSIDE THE PARK

The park has no lodgings or services. First-come, first-served **camping** (tents only, $25-35) is available on two islands. Boaters can overnight in the two harbors ($35). Camping and docking fees are paid by smartphone app (www.recreation.gov). The campgrounds have picnic tables, grills, and toilets.

Boca Chita Key has a grassy shoreline campground. Bring your own water. **Elliott Key** has waterfront and forested sites plus drinking water and cold showers. Contact **Biscayne National Park Institute** (786/465-4058, www.biscaynenationalparkinstitute.org)

for transportation to the islands. For paddlers, overnight parking by permit (free) is at the visitors center.

OUTSIDE THE PARK

The closest accommodations and restaurants are in **Homestead** and **Florida City.** Just over 30 miles (48 km) away, **Miami** adds plentiful options.

GETTING THERE AND AROUND

The nearest international airport is **Miami International Airport** (MIA, 2100 NW 42nd Ave., 305/876-7000, www.miami-airport.com), which also has car rentals.

To reach the Dante Fascell Visitor Center in Homestead, drivers have three options:

From the Florida Turnpike: Take exit 6 (Speedway Blvd.) and turn left onto SW 328th Street (North Canal Dr.). Turn left and drive 4 miles (6.4 km) to the park entrance.

From the north on US 1: At Homestead, turn east onto SW 137th Avenue (Speedway Blvd.) and continue 5 miles (8 km). At SW 328th Street (North Canal Dr.), turn left and drive 4 miles (6.4 km) to the park entrance.

From the south on US 1: At Homestead, turn right onto SW 344th Street (Palm Dr.) and continue 4 miles (6.4 km). Turn right on SW 328th Street (North Canal Dr.) and drive east for 4 miles (6.4 km) to the park entrance.

The **Homestead National Parks Trolley** (www.cityofhomestead.com, late Nov.-Apr., free) provides guided tours from Homestead to Biscayne and Everglades National Parks.

BOAT TOURS

Biscayne National Park Institute (786/465-4058, www.biscaynenationalparkinstitute.org, reservations recommended) guides interpretive boat or sailing tours. Three-hour trips go to Boca Chita Key. The institute also guides higher-activity, full-day tours that combine sightseeing the islands with snorkeling and paddling. Several other companies operate boat or sailing charters; consult with the visitors center for licensed concessionaires.

DRY TORTUGAS NATIONAL PARK

Florida

WEBSITE:
www.nps.gov/drto

PHONE NUMBER:
305/242-7700

VISITATION RANK:
55

WHY GO:
Explore the underwater habitat of coral and sand islands.

KEEPSAKE STAMPS ▼▼▼

▲ FORT JEFFERSON AND MOAT

DRY TORTUGAS
NATIONAL PARK

Palaski Shoal

Sunken wreck

Northkey Harbor

Sunken wreck

East Key

Sunken wreck

Middle Key

Research Natural Area Boundary

Hospital Key

Northwest Channel

Texas Rock

Middle Ground

Iowa Rock

Bush Key

Long Key

Southeast Channel

Tortugas anchorage

DRY TORTUGAS NATIONAL PARK

Brilliant Shoal

Research Natural Area Boundary

Garden Key

LIGHT

FORT JEFFERSON

FORT JEFFERSON VISITOR CENTER

Bird Key anchorage

White Shoal

Brick wreck

D R Y   T O R T U G A S

LIGHT

Loggerhead Key

Windjammer wreck

Research Natural Area Boundary

Loggerhead Reef

Southwest Channel

1 mi

1 km

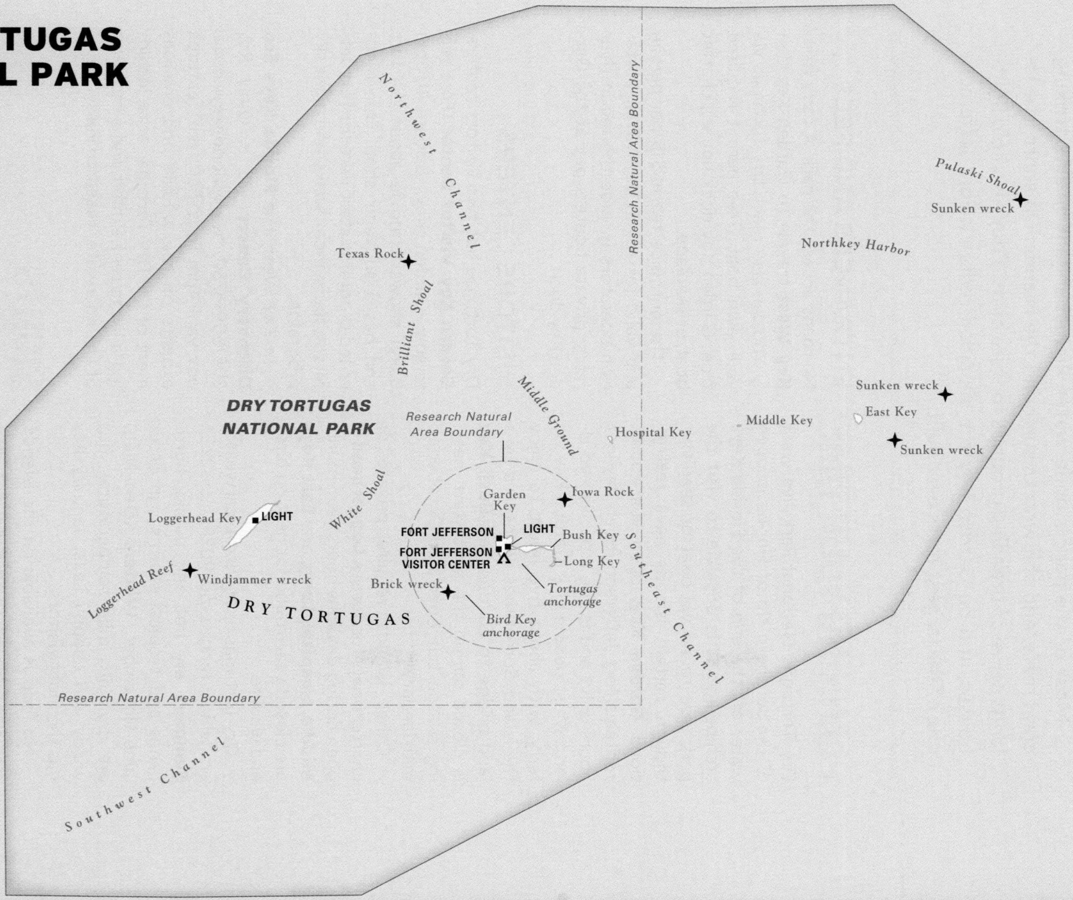

© MOON.COM

West of Key West lies a cluster of seven islands composed of coral and sand. Originally named Las Tortugas ("the Turtles") by Spanish explorers, they eventually became the Dry Tortugas on mariners' navigational charts to indicate the lack of freshwater. Today, these islands, shoals, and waters make up **DRY TORTUGAS NATIONAL PARK.**

Most of the park is underwater. Rich abundant sealife, striking coral reefs, and shipwrecks surround the islands. On shore, the islands serve as breeding grounds for rare birds. They also hold lighthouses, and on Garden Key the six-sided redbrick Fort Jefferson, one of the largest forts ever built.

PLANNING YOUR TIME

Dry Tortugas National Park lies west of the southern tip of Florida in open water off the end of the Florida Keys archipelago. It is possible to visit the park year-round via boat or seaplane, though certain islands have restrictions. **Garden Key,** open year-round, contains Fort Jefferson (open daylight hours only) and is the most visited island. Most people visit Garden Key via ferry, with about five hours to enjoy the island. Sometimes connected by a land bridge to Garden Key, **Bush Key** is closed during the sooty tern nesting season but open mid-October to mid-January.

Other islands require private or charter boats for access. **Loggerhead** is open during daylight hours year-round. **Middle, Hospital, Long,** and **East Keys** are closed year-round for nesting birds and wildlife.

Dry Tortugas has subtropical weather, which ranges 60-90°F (16-32°C). **Summers** are hot and humid; hurricanes and tropical storms can occur June-November. **Winters** (Dec.-Mar.) are dry with mild temperatures, but windy and choppy seas. January-July has the most visitors.

No food is available on the islands. Overnighters and private boaters must bring food and water when visiting Dry Tortugas. You must also pack out your garbage. The ferry has breakfast and lunch included for day visitors, and snacks are available.

ENTRANCES AND FEES

No roads access the park. A ferry from **Key West** travels to Garden Key daily. You can also reach Dry Tortugas via your own boat (free permit required from Garden Key dock house), charter boat, or seaplane.

The entrance fee is $15 per person and valid for seven days. Transportation operators include the fee in their rates; private boaters pay at the Garden Key dock.

VISITORS CENTERS

Dry Tortugas has two visitors centers. **Garden Key Visitor Center** (Fort Jefferson, Garden Key, 8:30am-4:30pm daily) shows a movie about the fort and has a souvenir shop. Free ranger-led programs start here for Fort Jefferson tours, moat walks, and night sky programs.

In Key West, the **Florida Keys Eco Discovery Center** (35 E. Quay Rd., 305/809-4750, www.floridakeys.noaa. gov, 9am-4pm Tues.-Sat., free) features exhibits on the wildlife and environment of the Dry Tortugas area, including a living reef exhibit and a mock-up of an underwater research vessel.

SIGHTS
GARDEN KEY

The **Fort Jefferson Harbor Light,** established in 1825, is still operational today. In 1876, the lighthouse tower was erected northeast of the boat dock. It's a favorite among photographers.

Top ❸

① SNORKEL CORAL REEFS

Dry Tortugas has one of the richest coral communities in the Florida Keys, although warmer sea waters and diseases are taking a toll. The warm, shallow waters boast a cornucopia of kaleidoscopic tropical fish, conch shells, lobster, sponges, sea fans, sea anemones, staghorn coral clusters, and the occasional sea turtle. On Garden Key, you can snorkel directly off **Fort Jefferson Beach,** in reef-protected waters, near the moat walls, and around the coaling dock ruins. Snorkeling gear is included for ferry riders; otherwise, bring your own.

FORT JEFFERSON

② TOUR FORT JEFFERSON

Fort Jefferson (open daylight hours), the well-preserved six-sided fort on Garden Key, is the centerpiece of these remote islands. Nicknamed the "American Gibraltar," it was built in 1846 to control navigation strategically in the Gulf of Mexico, though construction was never completed. During and after the Civil War, it served as a Union-affiliated military prison. By the 1880s, the U.S. Army had abandoned the facility.

Within the fortified walls of the historic citadel are the officers' quarters, soldiers' barracks, a cistern, magazines, and cannons. From November to May, parts of Fort Jefferson are closed to the public while masonry crews work on much-needed preservation projects. An estimated 16 million red bricks were handmade for the fort. You can do a self-guided stroll through the fort or take a ranger tour.

MOAT AROUND FORT JEFFERSON

③ EXPLORE THE MOAT WALL

Built as added protection, 0.5 mile (0.8 km) of moat and **moat wall** surrounds Fort Jefferson. You can stroll portions of the moat wall for views of the water and the fort exterior, or take a ranger tour on the moat wall. While no swimming is permitted in the moat, you can snorkel around outside portions of the moat wall. For a unique underwater experience, overnighters on the island snorkel the moat wall after dark to see nocturnal sea creatures (bring a light).

Near Garden Key, **Bush Key** and **Long Key** are both surrounded by tempting white-sand beaches. You can walk the beaches around Bush Key mid-October to mid-January, when they may be accessible via a land bridge. During the rest of the year, this key is closed to protect nesting sooty terns. Long Key is closed year-round for nesting birds and wildlife. With binoculars, you can view birds and wildlife on both, even during closures.

LOGGERHEAD KEY

Accessible only by private boat or charter, **Loggerhead Key** features the **Loggerhead Lighthouse,** with the existing tower erected in 1858. The park is day-use only, with public pathways open to visitors, but all buildings are closed.

RECREATION

BIRD-WATCHING

Garden Key has excellent bird-watching. More than 200 varieties of birds are spotted annually, especially March-September when nearby **Bush Key** serves as the nesting ground for migratory birds (bring binoculars for viewing). April-May, more than 85,000 brown noddies and sooty terns nest on Bush Key. In spring, look for herons, raptors, and shorebirds; in summer, look for frigatebirds and mourning doves. The fall and winter months bring hawks, merlins, peregrine falcons, gulls, terns, American kestrels, and belted kingfishers. Other birds might include cormorants, masked boobies, black noddies, mangrove cuckoos, and white-crowned pigeons.

Sea-Clusive Charters (1107 Key Plaza, Ste. 315, Key West, 305/744-9928, www.seaclusive.com/index.asp) features tailored excursions led by professional bird guide Larry Manfredi. While on board, you might also spot sharks, dolphins, and if you're lucky, gigantic sea turtles. The cruises can accommodate 8-11 passengers.

BOATING AND KAYAKING

Skilled kayakers can explore the islands; however, the strong currents are only suitable for experienced sea kayakers. By advanced reservation, you can bring kayaks aboard the ferry **Yankee Freedom** (800/634-0939, www.drytortugas.com). Also bring a life vest, an anchor, a bailer, extra paddles, drinking water, waterproof bags for gear, and required safety equipment.

Garden Key and **Loggerhead Key** are both accessible by private boat, though docking on Garden Key can be problematic. It's best to anchor in the harbor and use a dinghy to reach the island's dinghy beach. Overnight anchoring is allowed between sunset and sunrise in the designated anchorage area with a sand-and-rubble bottom. On Loggerhead Key, the dock is only open to government vessels, but visitors are allowed to land south of the boathouse.

FISHING

Anglers can fish from the public dock on Garden Key and the beach west of the dock. Fishing from a boat is only permitted within a 1-mile (1.6-km) radius of Garden Key. Several local fishing charters operate multiday trips to the area; guides are allowed to fish in and around Dry Tortugas.

Contact charter companies for trips: **Andy Griffiths Charters** (6810 Front St., Stock Island, 305/296-2639, www.fishandy.com) or **Dream Catcher Charters** (5555 College Rd., Key West, 305/292-7712 or 888/362-3474, www.dreamcatchercharters.com).

CORAL

DIVING CORAL REEFS

DIVING AND SNORKELING

Reefs and shipwrecks await snorkelers and divers. Off Loggerhead Island, snorkelers can see fish and coral in **Little Africa Reef** while divers can explore early-20th-century **Windjammer Wreck** (check with the park for current status of the mooring ball). Off Bird Key is the 19th-century **Bird Key Wreck** in 4-9 feet (1.2-2.7 m) of water. **Sea-Clusive Charters** (1107 Key Plaza, Ste. 315, Key West, 305/744-9928, www.seaclusive.com/index.asp) offers multiday diving excursions.

WHERE TO STAY

INSIDE THE PARK

Dry Tortugas National Park has no public lodgings. Camping is the only option for overnighting on Garden Key. A short walk from the public dock leads to a primitive **campground** (10 sites and a shared overflow area, $15, first come, first served, 3-night maximum) with picnic tables, barbecue grills, and composting toilets. Campers must bring their own water, pack out all garbage, and make ferry reservations.

OUTSIDE THE PARK

Accommodations, restaurants, and services are available in **Key West.**

GETTING THERE AND AROUND

Travelers can reach Key West by flying into the **Key West International Airport** (EYW, 3491 S. Roosevelt Blvd., 305/809-5200, www.eyw.com). Dry Tortugas National Park lies approximately 70 miles (113 km) west of Key West and is only accessible by ferry or private boat from Key West.

Ferries and seaplanes access Garden Key, but not the other islands where personal boats, kayaks, and canoes can go. To reach Garden Key by ferry, schedule a day trip on the 110-foot (33-m) catamaran **Yankee Freedom** (100 Grinnell St., 800/634-0939, www.drytortugas.com, 8am-5:30pm daily), which docks in the Historic Seaport at Key West Bight. Reservations are recommended and required for overnighting on Garden Key.

If traveling to Garden Key by private vessel (free permit required from Garden Key dock house), docking restrictions limit use of the public dock (closed 10am-3pm and sunset-sunrise). On Loggerhead Key, you can only land vessels south of the dock and boathouse.

ISLANDS

A handful of national parks lie isolated on remote U.S. islands. The Hawaiian Islands offer the easiest access for visitors. On the Big Island, lava leaps from the Kīlauea Crater at Hawai'i Volcanoes National Park. Maui's upcountry is the place to watch the day begin or end from the 10,023-foot (3,055-m) summit of Haleakalā Crater.

East of Puerto Rico, Virgin Islands National Park sits nestled in the Caribbean Sea. More than 60 percent of the island of St. John is national park, with sandy beaches, coral gardens, and peaceful hiking paths.

Hidden deep in the South Pacific, the National Park of American Samoa comprises a handful of tiny islands in the Samoan archipelago. Tenacious visitors can discover its treasures—unique rainforests, coral communities, and traditional Samoan culture.

◄ POOLS OF 'OHE'O, HALEAKALĀ NATIONAL PARK

ISLANDS

Ni'ihau
Kaua'i
O'ahu
Honolulu
Moloka'i   Maui
HAWAI'I   **Haleakalā NP**
Hawai'i
Hawai'i Volcanoes NP

PACIFIC OCEAN

National Park of American Samoa
Tutuila   Ofu   Ta'ū
Pago Pago

AMERICAN SAMOA

PACIFIC OCEAN

United States

Japan

NORTH PACIFIC OCEAN

Haleakalā National Park
Hawai'i
Hawai'i Volcanoes National Park

Philippines

EQUATOR

Indonesia

National Park of American Samoa

Samoa
American Samoa
Australia   Fiji   Tonga   Tahiti

SOUTH PACIFIC OCEAN

New Zealand

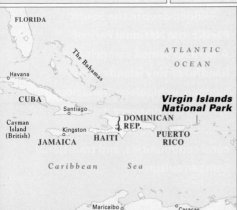

FLORIDA

Havana

ATLANTIC OCEAN

The Bahamas

CUBA
Santiago

Virgin Islands National Park

Cayman Island (British)
Kingston   **DOMINICAN REP.**
JAMAICA   HAITI   **PUERTO RICO**

Caribbean Sea

Maricaibo   Caracas

VENEZUELA

ATLANTIC OCEAN

PUERTO RICO

San Juan

Charlotte Amalie

Virgin Islands National Park

U.S. VIRGIN ISLANDS

Caribbean Sea

The National Park ISLANDS

HALEAKALĀ, MAUI

Most visitors go to Haleakalā for sunrise, but there are also trails that tour the colorful crater and a portion of the park that spills to the coast at Kīpahulu (page 711).

HAWAI'I VOLCANOES, HAWAI'I

The 13,679-foot (4,169-m) summit of Mauna Loa looms above the shorter Kīlauea, an active volcano in the process of building new land (page 721).

VIRGIN ISLANDS

Surrounded by turquoise seas, the island of St. John includes historic plantations, snorkeling beaches, boating, and opportunities for hiking amid tropical forests (page 731).

AMERICAN SAMOA

This tropical paradise has rainforest hiking trails, sandy beaches, coral reefs for snorkeling, and the customs of the 3,000-year-old Samoan culture (page 740).

1: THE SUMMIT AREA, HALEAKALĀ, MAUI
2: HIKING IN HAWAI'I VOLCANOES, HAWAI'I
3: FOUREYE BUTTERFLYFISH, VIRGIN ISLANDS

Best OF THE ISLANDS

Sunrise over Haleakalā: Watch the sun come up and then spend the day hiking across the crater floor (page 715).

Crater Rim Drive: See the volcanic forces that created the Hawaiian archipelago (page 725).

Trunk Bay: Lounge under coconut palms on this white-sand beach flanking clear turquoise water for snorkeling (page 735).

Vai'ava Strait: One of American Samoa's National Natural Landmarks was created by volcanoes (page 744).

PLANNING YOUR TRIP

HAWAI'I

Hawai'i Volcanoes is located on the Big Island of Hawai'i, while Haleakalā is on the island of Maui. Both islands have airports.

The prime tourist season for the Hawaiian Islands starts two weeks before **Christmas** and lasts until **Easter.** It picks up again in early June and ends in late August. Everything is heavily booked, and prices are higher. Hotel, airline, and car reservations are a must. You can generally save money and avoid a lot of hassle if you travel in the off-season (September-early December and late-April-late May). **Hurricane season** is June-November.

VIRGIN ISLANDS

There are no airports on St. John. Travelers must fly into St. Thomas Cyril E. King Airport on Charlotte Amalie and then take a car barge or ferry to St. John.

December-March is the dry season with the best sailing winds and most comfortable temperatures. However, the island sees its highest number of visitors April-June, August, and October-December.

Hurricane season runs June-November, with the peak from August to October.

AMERICAN SAMOA

Tutuila Island has the only international airport. All visitors must have a valid passport, a return ticket, and confirmation of funds. A visa may be required. **October-May** is the monsoon season with tropical storms, but that's also when there are the most visitors (Mar.-May, Oct.-Nov.). Go June-September for cooler, drier weather.

▲ NATIONAL PARK OF AMERICAN SAMOA

HALEAKALĀ NATIONAL PARK

Hawai'i

KEEPSAKE STAMPS ▾▾▾

WEBSITE:
www.nps.gov/hale

PHONE NUMBER:
808/572-4400

VISITATION RANK:
29

WHY GO:
Watch the sun rise over a volcanic summit.

▴ HALEAKALĀ CRATER

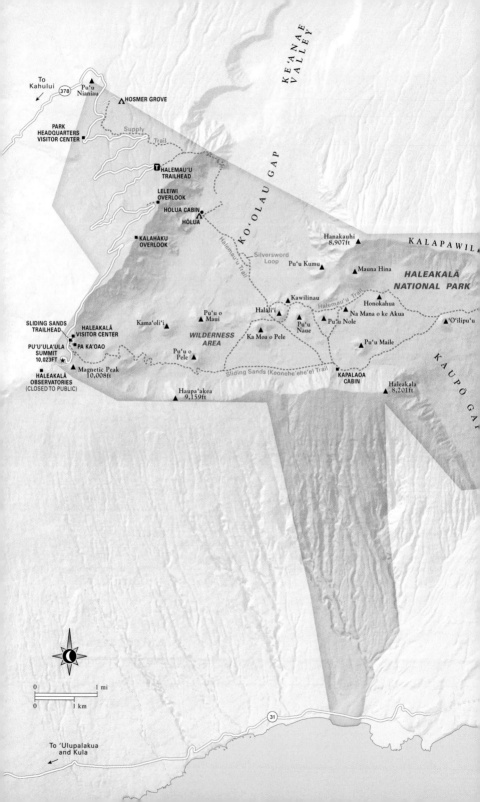

To
Kahului

378

Pu'u
Nianiau

HOSMER GROVE

KE'ANAE
VALLEY

PARK
HEADQUARTERS
VISITOR CENTER

Supply

Trail

HALEMAU'U
TRAILHEAD

LELEIWI
OVERLOOK

HOLUA CABIN
HŌLUA

KO'OLAU GAP

Silversword
Loop

KALAHAKU
OVERLOOK

Hanakauhi
8,907ft

KALAPAWIL

Pu'u Kumu

Mauna Hina

HALEAKALĀ
NATIONAL PARK

Kawilinau

Halali'i

Honokahua

Na Mana o ke Akua

'O'ilipu'u

SLIDING SANDS
TRAILHEAD

HALEAKALĀ
VISITOR CENTER

PU'U'ULA'ULA
SUMMIT
10,023FT

PA KA'OAO

Magnetic Peak
10,008ft

HALEAKALĀ
OBSERVATORIES
(CLOSED TO PUBLIC)

Kama'oli'i

Pu'u o
Maui

WILDERNESS
AREA

Ka Moa o Pele

Pu'u
Naue

Pu'u Nole

Pu'u Maile

Pu'u o
Pele

Sliding Sands (Keonehe'ehe'e) Trail

KAPALAOA
CABIN

KAUPŌ GAP

Haupa'akea
9,159ft

Haleakala
8,201ft

0   1 mi
0   1 km

31

To 'Ulupalakua
and Kula

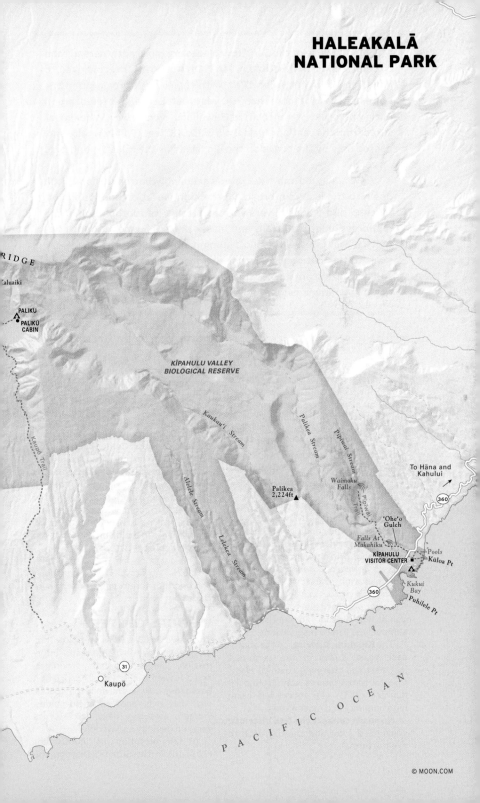

HALEAKALĀ
NATIONAL PARK

RIDGE

aluaiki

PALIKU

PALIKŪ
CABIN

KĪPAHULU VALLEY
BIOLOGICAL RESERVE

Kaukau'i Stream

Palikea Stream

Pīpīwai Stream

Kaupo Trail

Alelele Stream

Lelekea Stream

Palikea
2,224ft ▲

Waimoku
Falls

Pīpīwai
Trail

To Hāna and
Kahului

360

'Ohe'o
Gulch

Falls At
Makahiku

KĪPAHULU
VISITOR CENTER

Pools
Kūloa Pt

Kukuí
Bay

360

Puhilele Pt

31

Kaupō

P A C I F I C   O C E A N

Meaning "House of the Sun," few places are more aptly named than this volcano in **HALEAKALĀ NATIONAL PARK.** It is believed to have been dormant since 1790, with the summit area around the crater inactive for more than 300 years before that, yet radiocarbon dating recorded use by Native Hawaiians even earlier. When measured from the seafloor, Haleakalā is 30,000 feet (9,144 m) tall—surpassed only by the peaks on the Big Island as the tallest mountains on earth.

Views plunge from the crater's seemingly barren volcanic rock down to the lush rainforest. On the high-elevation pumice slopes, graceful and fragile silversword maintains its foothold while the rainforest hides waterfalls and glassy pools. The most popular activity is visiting the volcano's summit for sunrise—but there's far more to this national park than simply the light of dawn. Sunsets and stargazing are just as spectacular. Any time of day, the mountain's sheer immensity provokes awe.

PLANNING YOUR TIME

Two sections of Haleakalā commandeer Maui's southeast. Peak visitation (Feb.-Sept., Dec.) splits between them based on seasonal weather. The **Summit District** houses Haleakalā Crater. The summit of Haleakalā is 20-30 degrees (12-18°C) cooler than the coast, and the weather is unpredictable. You can leave an 80-degree (27°C) beach to arrive at the crater in 50-degree (10°C) weather with wind and rain.

Rain and even snow can fall year-round, but **summer** (May-Sept.) typically sees better conditions. There are **no visitor services at the summit—** bring food, drinks, warm layers, sunglasses, a hat, and sunscreen. At this high elevation, the solar radiation is strong, and visitors may feel light-headed or out of breath due to reduced oxygen at high altitude. For sunrise at the summit, you'll need reservations.

The **Kīpahulu District,** on the southeast coast, tucks in the rainforest just past the charming town of Hana. Coastal temperatures stay around 70 degrees (21°C) year-round but bring high humidity and mosquitoes.

No roads connect the two districts; you'll need a car and one day each to explore both.

ENTRANCES AND FEES

Access to the **Summit District** is via HI 378 (open year-round), a paved and curvy road; severe weather may temporarily close the road. The entrance station is located prior to the park headquarters and the turnoff to Hosmer Grove Campground. The Park Headquarters Visitor Center is less than 1 mile (1.6 km) farther along the road.

Access to the **Kīpahulu District** is via HI 360 (the Road to Hana) and HI 31 (open year-round). The paved Road to Hana is fraught with potholes and bumps, making it very rough to drive. The official Kīpahulu entrance is at the visitors center.

The entrance fee is $30 per vehicle ($25 motorcycle, $15 individual) and good for three days. Admission includes both districts.

VISITORS CENTERS

The park has three visitors centers. They each have exhibits, maps, information, ranger program schedules, and a Hawaii Pacific Parks Association bookstore (www.hawaiipacificparks.org) that sells maps and field guides. Rangers also give daily talks (times vary) on geology and wildlife.

At an elevation of 7,000 feet (2,134 m) in the Summit District, the

Top ③

1 WATCH SUNRISE FROM HALEAKALĀ CRATER

SUNRISE AT HALEAKALĀ NATIONAL PARK

A Haleakalā sunrise is a unique experience. But it requires advance planning, **reservations** (877/444-6777, www.recreation.gov, available 60 days in advance, $1 per vehicle), and waking up at 2am-3am.

The biggest crowds go for the highest point at **Puʻu ʻUlaʻula** (Red Hill Summit) at a glass-sided observation area (24 hours daily) on the official summit of Haleakalā (10,023 ft/3,055 m). **Haleakalā Visitor Center** (9,740 ft/2,969 m) is the second-highest viewing point. Two lower-elevation viewpoints offer less crowded alternatives: **Leleiwi Overlook** (8,840 ft/2,694 m) and **Kalahaku Overlook** (9,324 ft/2,842 m, only accessible downhill).

Most mornings are clear enough to see the sunrise over the crater. But call the **Hotline for Haleakalā Summit** (808/944-5025, ext. 4) for current conditions. Bring warm clothes for the near- or below-freezing temperatures and beach chairs for sitting. The reservation allows Summit District access 3am-7am. Reservations are not required after 7am.

2 DRIVE UP THE VOLCANO

The sheer climb up **Haleakalā Road** (HI 378, 10 mi/16.1 km) wows with each curve from the park entrance to the summit as the air thins with elevation. At **Leleiwi Overlook** (milepost 17.5, 8,840 ft/2,694 m), walk to see the massive crater from this vantage point (0.5 mi/0.8 km rt, 20 min, moderate). You'll peer down at the huge floor and sheer multihued cliffs. At **Kalahaku Overlook** (milepost 18.7, 9,324 ft/2,842 m), view the crater from the interpretive observation platform. The road terminates at the summit and **Haleakalā Visitor Center,** where a slow meander at altitude is needed to climb to the highest point in the park at 10,023 feet (3,055 m). Native Hawaiians view the summit area as sacred.

3 FIND PARADISE AT THE POOLS OF ʻOHEʻO

The **Pools of ʻOheʻo** (near the Kīpahulu Visitor Center) in ʻOheʻo Gulch are the stuff of a dreamy paradise. Tucked in the rainforest, waterfalls drop into placid pools. Also called the Seven Sacred Pools (there are actually more), they are closed to swimming, but you can still enjoy their serenity.

Walk the **Kuloa Point Trail** (0.5 mi/0.8 km rt, 30 min, easy) that loops past the famed pools, taking in the ocean views on the promontory and archaeological sites. Respect these pools, which are sacred to Native Hawaiians, and go in the early morning to avoid crowds. Access to the pools may close periodically for safety; check online or stop at the visitors center first for updates.

THE POOLS OF ʻOHEʻO

KĪPAHULU COAST

Park Headquarters Visitor Center
(808/572-4459, 8am-4pm daily) has exhibits on the cultural and natural history of the park.

Also in the Summit District, the **Haleakalā Visitor Center** (sunrise-noon daily) is located at 9,740 feet (2,969 m), 10 miles (16 km) up the park road from the Park Headquarters Visitor Center. Geology exhibits detail the history of the volcano. A ranger-guided walk takes place most days (10am and 11am). From the parking lot, take in the **Pa Ka'oao Trail** (0.4 mi/0.6 km rt, 20 min, moderate) with views toward the crater.

The **Kīpahulu Visitor Center** (808/248-7375, 9:30am-5pm daily) is on the coast in the southeast portion of the park. Exhibits offer insights into the Hawaiian culture.

RECREATION
HIKING
Hike Maui (808/784-7982, www.hikemaui.com) is the only company that offers commercially guided hiking tours in the park, both at the summit and at Kīpahulu.

Summit District
The **Hosmer Grove Nature Trail** (0.5 mi/0.8 km rt, 30 min, easy) is at the park's lower boundary just after the entrance. The trail loops through a dense grove of sweet-smelling pine and fir. To extend the trip, hike the **Supply Trail** (4.6 mi/7.4 km rt, 3 hrs, strenuous) to the crater rim. To reach the trailhead, turn left on the road toward the campground.

The Haleakalā Crater is a vast wilderness with Maui's best hiking. Temperatures can range 30-80°F (-1°C to 27°C) over the course of a single day, and the high elevation can tax lungs.

In the thin air of 9,800 feet (2,987 m) from the summit visitors center, **Keonehe'ehe'e Trail** (8 mi/12.9 km rt,

SILVERSWORD PLANTS ON HALEAKALĀ SUMMIT TRAILS

4-5 hrs, strenuous) descends to the crater floor. This barren, windswept trail lacks shade en route to the cinder cones. The rough part comes with the climb (2,500 ft/762 m) back up to the visitors center.

For a more oxygenated excursion at 7,990 feet (2,435 m), **Halemau'u Trail** (7.5 mi/12.1 km rt, 4-5 hrs, strenuous) meanders through scrub brush before reaching the edge of a giant cliff to peer down into the Ko'olau Gap, where the volcano exploded outward. The well-defined trail descends switchbacks with drop-offs to Holua Cabin (reservations needed to camp overnight) before climbing out, for an elevation gain of 1,000 feet (305 m).

Kīpahulu District

The **Pipiwai Trail** (4 mi/6.4 km rt, 2 hrs, moderate) follows boardwalks and footbridges through a tropical rainforest before ascending through bamboo so thick it blocks out the sun. The path emerges at the base of ribbonlike 400-foot (122-m) Waimoku Falls. Plan to camp overnight at the Kīpahulu Campground to hit the trail before the day-trippers arrive. The trail departs from the Kīpahulu Visitor Center.

Native Hawaiian guides lead cultural interpretive hikes through the **Kipahulu 'Ohana** (Hana, 808/248-8673, http:// kipahulu.org, 2-3.5 hrs, $49-79, reservations required), a living farm and traditional wetland growing taro inside the park. Sample foods such as poi,

BAMBOO FOREST ON PIPIWAI TRAIL

Best Hike

DISTANCE: 11.5 miles (18.5 km) round-trip
DURATION: 7-8 hours
ELEVATION CHANGE: 2,500 feet (762 m)
EFFORT: strenuous
TRAILHEAD: Halemau'u (lower trailhead) and Keonehe'ehe'e (summit trailhead)

SLIDING SANDS SWITCHBACK LOOP

The **Sliding Sands Switchback Loop** combines the best segments of hiking inside the crater of Haleakalā. Park at the Halemau'u trailhead, then hitch a ride up to the Haleakalā Visitor Center, near the summit for the Keonehe'ehe'e (Sliding Sands) Trailhead. The Sliding Sands Trail plunges down switchbacks to the crater floor. At all junctions, follow signs to the Holua Cabin and Halemau'u Trail. You'll pass intriguing features en route: silverswords, colorful slopes, cinder cones, and a deep volcanic pit. At the turnoff to Holua Cabin, stay on the Halemau'u Trail for a leg-burning ascent of switchbacks back up to the car.

For a smaller but still demanding taste of the vast crater, park at the visitors center to drop down the Sliding Sands Trail about 2 miles (3.2 km) to a distinct rock formation. You'll need to climb over 1,200 feet (366 m) back up on the return.

For either excursion, be prepared for hiking at altitude and changeable weather. Bring plenty of water.

breadfruit, and bananas. The walk also takes in historic sites and the Pools of 'Ohe'o.

BACKPACKING

Backcountry campsites and cabins require **reservations** (877/444-6777, www.recreation.gov), available six months in advance.

Two **campsites** ($8-9) are in Haleakalā Crater. The Holua campsite, in a cold and dry locale, is accessible via a 3.7-mile (6-km, one-way) hike down Halemau'u Trail. Set in a lush forest with wetter weather, the Paliku campsite requires hiking 9.3 miles (15 km) from the Sliding Sands Trail at the summit.

You can also hike to three rustic **backcountry cabins** ($75) at Holua,

SLIDING SANDS TRAIL

ONE DAY IN HALEAKALĀ

With only one day, aim to drive to the **summit of Haleakalā.** On the road between the Park Headquarters and Haleakalā Summit Visitor Centers, stop to admire the views from roadside overlooks. At the summit, you can stroll to the highest point in the park at 10,023 feet. With an advance reservation, you can **watch the sunrise** from the summit.

Kapalaoa, and Paliku. They have basic cooking facilities and bunk beds.

BIKING

Watching the day begin from Haleakalā Crater, followed by feeling the crisp air in your face as you weave through cow-speckled pastures via bicycle, is full of adrenaline magic. To bike from the summit, you must make **advance reservations** for sunrise access and provide **your own bicycle and transportation.**

Bike tours down Haleakalā start at 6,500 feet (1,981 m), outside the national park. If you want to include sunrise at Haleakalā Crater, that means waking up early, with pickups at 2am. (After watching the sun rise, it's back in the van for the drive down to the bike start.) Tours without sunrise usually visit the summit at around 10am and then descend to the start of the bike tour.

To rent a bike or book a tour, contact **Maui Sunriders** (71 Baldwin Ave., Pai'a, 808/579-8970, www.mauisunriders.com) or **Bike Maui** (810 Ha'iku Rd., Ste.

120, Haiku, 808/575-9975, www.bike-maui.com).

STARGAZING

Haleakalā's elevation and lack of light pollution make the summit a prime location for stargazing. Bring a pair of binoculars or rent them from a local dive shop. Star maps, available at the Haleakalā visitors centers and online, can help you identify the constellations. Nights can be cold on the summit; bring layers to stay warm and a camp chair.

To observe the night sky through big telescopes with astronomy experts, book a tour with **Maui Stargazing** (808/298-8245, www.mauistargazing.com). The five-hour tour starts at sunset. Their scopes are big enough to see deep-space celestial objects. As a bonus, they bring outerwear and hot chocolate to keep you warm.

BIRD-WATCHING

One of the best bird-watching places is at **Hosmer Grove** on the loop trail. Even

▼ VIEW FROM HALEAKALĀ SUMMIT

WILDFLOWERS

if you don't see native honeycreepers (birds whose bills have adapted to extract nectar from native plant species), the treetops chirp with birdsong different from anywhere else on the planet.

Higher up toward the summit, bird-watchers should look for two endangered species: the 'u'au (Hawaiian petrel), which burrows in areas near the **summit visitors center**, and the nene (Hawaiian goose), which is Hawaii's state bird, can be spotted along park roadways and the grasslands surrounding **Paliku Cabin.**

WHERE TO STAY

INSIDE THE PARK

The park has two tent campgrounds (year-round, $5, 3-night maximum) with picnic tables, barbecue grills, and vault toilets. Make **reservations** (877/444-6777, www.recreation.gov) six months in advance.

Hosmer Grove Campground is in the Summit District (6,800 ft/2,072 m). It has potable water and grassy sites. Nights can get close to freezing. Access to the summit sunrise is included in the reservation.

With cliff and ocean views on Maui's southern shore, **Kīpahulu Campground** can be humid. It has mostly grassy sites with some hidden beneath lauhala trees. Drinking water is available at the visitors center.

OUTSIDE THE PARK

Most accommodations in **Makawao, Pai'a,** and **Kula** are conveniently located within an hour's drive of Haleakalā summit. Near the Kīpahulu coast, the closest services are in **Hana.**

GETTING THERE AND AROUND

AIR

Kahului Airport (OGG, 1 Kahului Airport Rd., 808/872-3830, www.airports. hawaii.gov) has direct flights from a host of mainland cities. Car rentals are at the airport.

CAR

To reach the Summit District from Kahului, take HI 37 to HI 377 where it meets HI 378. The Summit District of Haleakalā National Park is located at the end of HI 378. The curvy drive has multiple switchbacks and will take about 2.5-3 hours to reach the summit. The last gas en route is in Pukalani.

To reach the coastal Kīpahulu District, you'll have to drive the Road to Hana. From Kahului, take HI 36 to HI 37, then to HI 31. Kīpahulu is 11 miles (18 km) past Hana. The narrow, curvy, and partially unpaved drive will take approximately four hours one-way. Fill up on gas before you go; the last gas on the way to Hana is in Pai'a. Plan to depart Hana early in the day so that you won't be driving the rough road in the dark.

There is no public transit—and no gas station—within the park.

TOURS

Several tour companies guide trips to Haleakalā summit for sunrise, sunset, or daytime visits, as well as excursions to Kīpahulu. Vehicles range from buses to minivans, and all tours include narration. The following guide companies are licensed in the park: **Polynesian Adventures** (877/930-1740, www.polyad.com), **Temptation Tours** (800/817-1234 or 808/877-8888, www. temptationtours.com), **Roberts Hawaii** (808/539-9400, www.robertshawaii.com), and **Valley Isle Excursions** (808/871-5224, www.tourmaui.com).

HAWAI'I VOLCANOES NATIONAL PARK

Hawai'i

KEEPSAKE STAMPS ▼▼▼

▲ KĪLAUEA SUMMIT ERUPTION

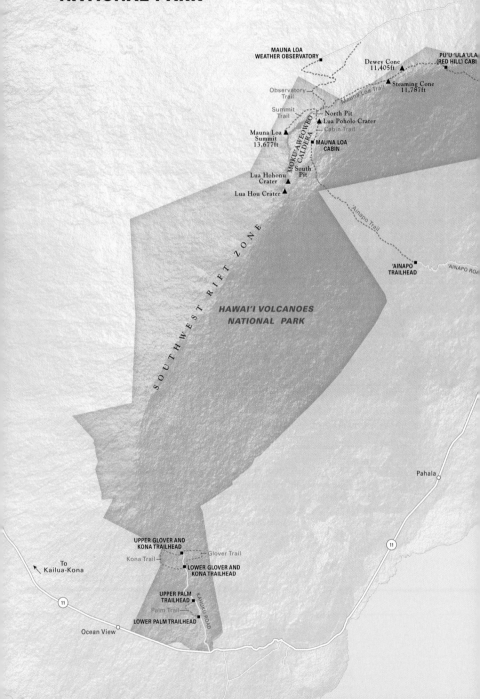

HAWAI'I VOLCANOES NATIONAL PARK

MAUNA LOA
WEATHER OBSERVATORY

Dewey Cone
11,405ft

PU'U 'ULA'ULA
(RED HILL) CABI

Steaming Cone
11,787ft

Observatory
Trail

Mauna Loa Trail

Summit
Trail

North Pit
Lua Poholo Crater
Cabin Trail

Mauna Loa
Summit
13,677ft

MOKU'AWEOWEO CALDERA

MAUNA LOA
CABIN

Lua Hohonu
Crater

South
Pit

Lua Hou Crater

'Ainapo Trail

SOUTHWEST RIFT ZONE

HAWAI'I VOLCANOES
NATIONAL PARK

'AINAPO
TRAILHEAD

'AINAPO ROA

Pahala

11

UPPER GLOVER AND
KONA TRAILHEAD

Glover Trail

To
Kailua-Kona

Kona Trail

LOWER GLOVER AND
KONA TRAILHEAD

11

UPPER PALM
TRAILHEAD

KAHUKU ROAD

Palm Trail

LOWER PALM TRAILHEAD

Ocean View

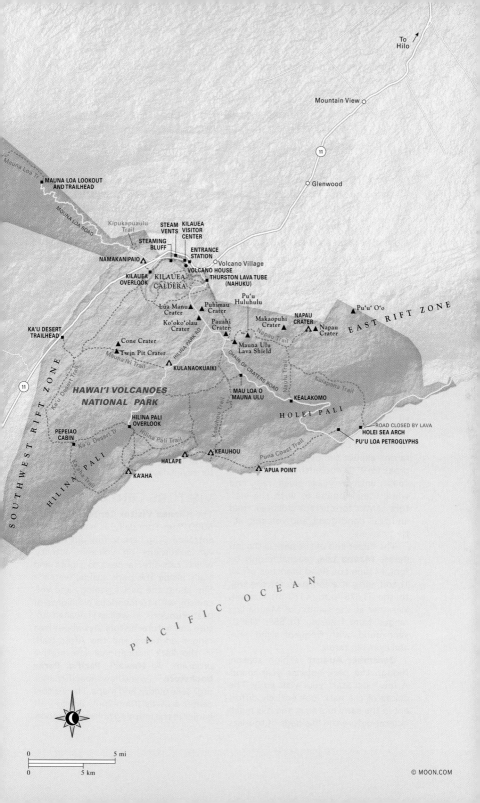

To Hilo

Mountain View

11

Glenwood

MAUNA LOA LOOKOUT
AND TRAILHEAD

Kipukapuaulu
Trail

STEAM
VENTS

KILAUEA
VISITOR
CENTER

STEAMING
BLUFF

ENTRANCE
STATION

NAMAKANIPAIO

Volcano Village

VOLCANO HOUSE

KILAUEA
OVERLOOK

KILAUEA
CALDERA

THURSTON LAVA TUBE
(NAHUKU)

Pu'u
Huluhulu

Pu'u 'O'o

KA'U DESERT
TRAILHEAD

Lua Manu
Crater

Puhimau
Crater

Ko'oko'olau
Crater

Pauahi
Crater

Makaopuhi
Crater

NAPAU
CRATER

EAST RIFT ZONE

Napau
Crater

SOUTHWEST RIFT ZONE

Cone Crater

Twin Pit Crater

Mauna Iki Trail

Mauna Ulu
Lava Shield

KULANAOKUAIKI

Napau Trail

Naulu Trail

HAWAI'I VOLCANOES
NATIONAL PARK

11

MAU LOA O
'MAUNA ULU

CHAIN OF CRATERS ROAD

Kalapana Trail

KEALAKOMO

HOLEI PALI

HILINA PALI
OVERLOOK

PEPEIAO
CABIN

Keauhou Trail

Hilina Pali Trail

Puna Coast Trail

ROAD CLOSED BY LAVA

HOLEI SEA ARCH

PU'U LOA PETROGLYPHS

HILINA PALI

HALAPE

KEAUHOU

KA'AHA

'APUA POINT

PACIFIC OCEAN

0   5 mi

0   5 km

© MOON.COM

This volcanic landscape fumes steam, pumps sulfur, seethes lava, and lights up a fiery display like something out of Dante's *Inferno*. Kīlauea's volcanic activity shows the birthing process of the still-growing Hawaiian Islands. High above Kīlauea, the behemoth Mauna Loa is the largest active volcano on earth. Together, they make up **HAWAI'I VOLCANOES NATIONAL PARK.**

Because of its scientific and scenic value, the park has been named an International Biosphere Reserve and a World Heritage Site. It became newsworthy as well in 2018, when Kīlauea erupted, ramping up its activity to historically devastating levels. Molten lava broke free from fresh cracks in the earth and flowed into local neighborhoods, destroying more than 700 homes. Accompanying earthquakes ravaged park roads, buildings, and trails. Today, many of these have been repaired and reopened, but the landscape of the park has changed forever. Many Native Hawaiians see living with Pele, the primordial force of the volcanoes, as part of their lives, their culture, and their history.

PLANNING YOUR TIME

Located on the Big Island of Hawaii, the park extends north and south off HI 11. Most visitors head south for the heart of the park: **Kīlauea Caldera.** At the 4,091-foot (1,246-m) caldera rim, expect temperatures 12-15 degrees (6-9°C) cooler than the tropical coast, with overcast skies, rain, and wind. Check online or with the visitors center for current closures, road and trail conditions, and volcanic activity levels.

The upper end of the park is the immense **Mauna Loa,** reachable only by foot. Mauna Loa Road branches off HI 11 and ends at a footpath for the trek to the 13,678-foot (4,170-m) summit. Weather at the summit of Mauna Loa ranges from freezing to 55°F (13°C) year-round, with frequent wind, rain, and even blizzards.

December-August is high season, though the park appeals year-round. A few tips: Start your visit early. The colors of the park look entirely different in the early morning, and it is much quieter before the busloads of tourists arrive. Also, pack a lunch; services within the park are minimal.

ENTRANCE AND FEES

The park entrance is on **HI 11** (near milepost 28), west of Volcano Village. The entrance fee is $30 per vehicle ($25 motorcycle, $15 individual) and good for seven days.

VISITORS CENTER

The **Kīlauea Visitor Center** (808/985-6000, 9am-5pm daily) is near the park entrance. Stop here to find out the latest conditions on volcanic activity, which can alter access to sights and trails inside the park. Inside, watch a film about the park's geology and volcanism, with tremendous highlights of past eruptions, as well as Hawaiian culture and natural history. Ask about free ranger-led tours and the After Dark in the Park educational interpretive program. A **Hawai'i Pacific Parks bookstore** (www.hawaiipacificparks.org) sells guides and maps. The visitors center crowds 10am-2pm; aim to visit earlier in the morning or late afternoon.

Top ❸

❶ VIEW KĪLAUEA CALDERA

KĪLAUEA CRATER PLUMES

Continuously active since 1983, the huge **Kīlauea Caldera** and its collection of smaller craters dominate the heart of the park. It's an ever-changing otherworldly landscape. During the 2018 and 2020 eruptions, Halema'uma'u Crater changed: Its lava lake drained, then the crater collapsed and filled with water. Next, lava filled the lake, turning it to steam, and the lava hardened again into a crust. Even when quiet, Kilauea still emits a distinctive sulfur smell and has underground earthquakes. During eruptive phases, it can steam and sputter lava, which is best viewed at night. See the caldera from overlooks on Crater Rim Drive or the Crater Rim Trail.

❷ GAZE OUT FROM MAUNA LOA

At 75 miles (121 km) long and 64 miles (103 km) wide, snowcapped Mauna Loa (13,678 ft/4,170 m) occupies the entire southern half of the Big Island. The summit of Mauna Loa contains the giant **Moku'aweoweo Caldera.** Visitors can drive up the 11-mile (18-km) **Mauna Loa Road** to a lookout at 6,600 feet (2,012 m), but only hikers can reach the summit. This remote mountaintop bastion is the least-visited part of the park but visible from many locations.

❸ TOUR CRATER RIM DRIVE

Crater Rim Drive (11 mi/18 km, 2-3 hrs) arcs around Kīlauea Caldera past steam vents, sulfur springs, and tortured fault lines that always seem on the verge of swallowing the landscape. Along the way, peer into the mouth of Halema'uma'u Crater, home of the fire goddess Pele.

Start at the **Kīlauea Visitor Center** to get oriented. On the north rim, the **Kīlauea Overlook** offers views into the caldera. Afterward, stop at the **steaming vents** pullout, where even the parking lot steams.

To explore the south portion of Crater Rim Dive, return past the visitors center and turn south just before the park entrance. At **Kīlauea Iki Overlook,** the crater floor resembles a desolate desert landscape. Next, stop to walk through the **Nāhuku-Thurston Lava Tube.** Finish at the overlook of the brownish-red cinder cone **Pu'u Pua'i** (Gushing Hill).

KĪLAUEA IKI VOLCANIC CRATER

ONE DAY IN HAWAI'I VOLCANOES

You can see the park's greatest hits in one long day by driving **Crater Rim Road** and **Chain of Craters Road.** Stop at the visitors center and then walk along the **Crater Rim Trail.** Visit the **Nāhuku-Thurston Lava Tube** and hike the **Kīlauea Iki Trail.**

SIGHTS

VOLCANO ART CENTER GALLERY

In the original 1877 Volcano House, the **Volcano Art Center Gallery** (808/ 967-8222, https://volcanoartcenter.org, 9am-5pm daily) contains one of the finest art galleries in the state. Featured artists exhibit in a variety of media: metal, painting, sculpture, jewelry, photography, and mixed media.

Join **Aloha Fridays** (times vary, free) for demonstrations of traditional Hawaiian ukulele, hula, language, chants, and lei-making. Other programs including cultural forest walks, hula performances, and "talk stories" at the center's **Niaulani Campus** (19-4074 Old Volcano Rd., Volcano, 808/967-8222, http://volcanocenter.org), five minutes east of the gallery outside the park entrance.

NĀHUKU (THURSTON LAVA TUBE)

South of the Kīlauea Iki Overlook is the remarkable **Nāhuku** (Thurston Lava Tube, 0.5 mi/0.8 km rt, moderate). A one-way paved path drops steeply into a vibrantly green fern forest filled with native birds. The lighted lava tube tunnel takes about 10 minutes to walk through. At the other end, a fantasy world of ferns and moss reappears, and the trail climbs back to the parking lot.

SCENIC DRIVES

CHAIN OF CRATERS ROAD

At the south end of Crater Rim Drive, the **Chain of Craters Road** (38 mi/61 km rt, 1.5 hrs) drops 3,700 feet (1,128

▼ HAWAI'I VOLCANOES NATIONAL PARK

VIEW FROM CHAIN OF CRATERS ROAD

m) in elevation down the *pali* (cliff) to the coast. En route, the road traverses lava that was laid down in 1974; remnants of the old road can still be seen in spots.

Several craters line the road. **Luamanu Crater** is a deep depression lined with green vegetation. At **Puhimau Crater,** walk to the viewing stand to peer over the crater's edge. Next, you'll pass **Ko'oko'olau Crater, Hi'iaka Crater,** and **Pauahi Crater.** At 9.9 miles (15.9 km) is **Kealakomo Lookout,** a picnic area with unobstructed views of the coast. The road then heads over the edge of the *pali* and diagonally down to the flats. The last section of road runs close to the sea, where cliffs rise up from the pounding surf. The road ends near the **Holei Sea Arch,** which you can see by walking a short distance on the road past the closed gate.

HILINA PALI ROAD

Two miles (3.2 km) down Chain of Craters Road, **Hilina Pali Road** (18 mi/29 km rt, 2 hrs) shoots southwest over a narrow, roughly paved road to **Hilina Pali Overlook,** on the edge of the rift. Expansive views stretch over the benched coastline. This rough but passable road is closed beyond Kulanaokuaiki Campground.

MAUNA LOA ROAD

Mauna Loa Road (22 mi/35 km rt, 1.5 hrs) is a narrow, curvy, and potholed one-lane road that leads to the **Tree Molds** (scattered potholes of entombed tree trunks), the **Kipuka Puaulu** bird sanctuary, and the trailhead for Mauna Loa summit. From its terminus at Mauna Loa Lookout (6,662 ft/2,030 m), you can overlook Kīlauea below on a clear day. Traveling this road leaves 99 percent of the tourists behind. Find the road 2.5 miles (4 km) south of the park entrance on HI 11.

RECREATION

HIKING

Kīlauea Summit

With multiple trailheads, the **Crater Rim Trail** is a long trail arcing around the north, east, and south rims of Kīlauea Caldera. Check on trail status before hiking. The most popular sections explore westward and eastward routes (5 mi/8 km rt, 2.5 hrs, easy) from the visitors center or Volcano House. Begin with unparalleled views of the vast Kīlauea Caldera before heading west to **Steam Vents** and **Steaming Bluff** (1.2 mi/2 km rt), where water heated by the volcano rises from cracks in the earth, and farther to **Kīlauea Overlook** (3.2 mi/

Best Hike

KĪLAUEA IKI TRAIL

DISTANCE: 4.8 miles (7.7 km) round-trip
DURATION: 3 hours
ELEVATION CHANGE: 400 feet (122 m)
EFFORT: moderate
TRAILHEAD: Kīlauea Iki Overlook

In 1959, lava spewed 1,900 feet (579 m) into the air from a huge crack in the Kīlauea crater wall. Seventeen separate lava flow episodes followed, creating a lake of lava known as **Kīlauea Iki** (Little Kīlauea). From the Kīlauea Iki Overlook, the **Kīlauea Iki Trail** drops from the rim into the crater, which is filled with lush tropical rainforest and the heaved and cracked solidified lake (you can walk on it!). Due to crowded parking lots, plan to hike at 7am. You can also park at the Devastation Trailhead to hike via the Byron Ledge Trail to connect with Kīlauea Iki Trail (adds 2.2 mi/3.5 km rt).

5.2 km rt) before returning. Or instead, go eastward to tiptoe along the **Waldron Ledge** before cruising the rim of **Kīlauea Iki** to the Kīlauea Iki Trailhead (3.4 mi/5.5 km rt) and back.

From the visitors center, the paved and boardwalk **Haʻakulamanu Trail** (1.2 mi/2 km rt, 30 min, easy), also called **Sulphur Banks,** explores smelly fumaroles surrounded by red-brown earth covered in yellow-green sulfur.

Behind Volcano House, the wheelchair-accessible paved **Earthquake Trail** (0.8 mi/1.3 km rt, 30 min, easy) leads to the **Waldron Ledge** for superb views of Kīlauea Caldera. Nearby, the **Halemaʻumaʻu Trail** (1.6 mi/2.6 km rt, 1 hr, moderate) descends through lush mosses and rainforest to the crater floor, but then you must climb back up! Pick up a trail guide for interpretive stops.

From the Puʻu Puaʻi Overlook, the paved **Devastation Trail** (1 mi/1.6 km rt, 30 min, easy) heads across a field ravaged by the Kīlauea Iki eruption and one of the most photographed areas in the park.

When hiking on trails around Kīlauea Summit, use caution: Keep your distance from sinkholes, steep cliffs, unstable ground, and cracks. Volcanic gases (vog), which can lead to hazardous air quality, shift direction quickly with winds; check on vog status at the visitors center.

Chain of Craters Road

The **Puʻu Huluhulu Trail** (2.5 mi/4 km rt, 2 hrs, moderate) climbs 210 feet (64 m) to the summit of a steaming volcanic crater with 360-degree panoramic views. Start the hike from the Mauna Ulu Trailhead.

The **Puʻu Loa Petroglyphs Trail** (1.4 mi/2.3 km rt, 1 hr, easy) follows a boardwalk encircling many of the 23,000 ancient petroglyphs considered sacred to Hawaiians. Some rocks are entirely covered with designs, while others have only one or two small symbolic marks.

Guides

Friends of Hawaii Volcanoes National Park (808/985-7373, http://fhvnp.org) tour guides are retired park rangers and wildlife biologists. Tours are on demand, and transportation is not provided. Other guided hikes are led by **Native Guide Hawaii** (808/982-7575).

BACKPACKING

A **permit** ($10) is required for camping at backcountry campsites and cabins. Obtain permits in person from the Backcountry Office (Crater Rim Dr., 808/985-6178, 8am-4pm daily) the day prior to your hike, or reserve one in advance online. Check on drinking water availability; you may need to carry enough for your trip.

Halapē

From the Hilina Pali Overlook on Hilina Pali Road, the **Hilina Pali Trail** (9.8 mi/15.8 km rt, 2-3 days) descends across hot, dry, rugged terrain. It drops straight down the *pali* with multiple switchbacks to a junction, where the hot, steep left fork yo-yos up and down to **Halapē,** a sugary beach and sheltered lagoon with backcountry campsites and restroom facilities.

Mauna Loa

It's a grueling climb to the 13,678-foot (4,170-m) summit of the island's largest volcano. Be prepared for altitude sickness and changes in weather—rain or even snow. Staying hydrated is imperative. There are two trail options.

From the terminus of Mauna Loa Road, the **Mauna Loa Road Trail** (38 mi/61 km rt, 6,600 ft/2,012 m elevation gain, 3-4 days) ascends to the **Pu'u 'Ula'ula cabin** (Red Hill, 7.5 mi/12.1 km one-way, 4-6 hrs). The next day, climb 11.6 miles (18.6 km) to the **Mauna Loa summit cabin** (8-12 hrs one-way) on the caldera's rim. They have bunks and composting toilets.

A shorter but still ultra-strenuous trail to the summit goes from Mauna Loa Observatory trailhead outside the park, a two-hour drive via Saddle Road. The **Mauna Loa Observatory Trail** (12.8 mi/20.6 km rt, 1,975 ft/602 m elevation gain, 7-9 hrs) climbs up the volcano's north slope to the rim of the Moku'aweoweo Caldera (the summit). The Mauna Loa summit cabin is at 5.9 miles (9.5 km).

BIKING

Bring your bicycle along to cruise the paved **Crater Rim Drive** (11 mi/17.7 km), the moderate **Hilina Pali Road** (18 mi/29 km rt), or the challenging **Mauna Loa Road** (22 mi/35 km rt). The classic challenge follows the **Summit to Sea** (36 mi/58 km rt)—the path of the Mauna Ulu eruption on the Chain of Craters Road. Cycling maps are available from the visitors center.

You can also take a guided bike tour with **Bike Volcano** (808/934-9199, www.bikevolcano.com).

WHERE TO STAY

INSIDE THE PARK

Volcano House (1 Crater Rim Dr., 808/756-9625, www.hawaiivolcanohouse.com, from $279) is the only hotel inside the park. Dating from the 1940s, it has the feel of a country inn, but with updated decor and facilities. From its rim location, you can see the glow of the crater from your window. Inside, **Uncle George's Lounge** (11am-10pm daily) and **The Rim at Volcano House** (breakfast, lunch, and dinner daily) have priceless views of the crater.

North of the caldera, **Nāmakani-paio Campground** (HI 11, 808/756-9625, www.hawaiivolcanohouse.com,

PU'U LOA PETROGLYPHS, CONSIDERED SACRED BY NATIVE HAWAIIANS

reservations recommended) has spartan A-frame cabins (from $80) that sleep up to four people with a double bed and two single bunks. Linens, soap, towels, a blanket, and an electric light are provided, but there are no electrical outlets. The campground is a large grassy area surrounded by trees. Rent a tent ($55) or bring your own ($15, no hookups). Cabins and campsites have picnic tables, fire pits, and shared restrooms with showers.

South of the caldera off the Chain of Craters Road, **Kulanaokuaiki Campground** (Hilina Pali Rd., $10) has nine first-come, first-served sites. Facilities include picnic tables and a vault toilet, but no drinking water.

Kīlauea Military Camp (Hilina Pali Rd., 808/967-8333, http://kilaueamilitarycamp.com) is where military families vacation. Several eateries, including **Crater Rim Café** (5pm-8pm Fri.-Sat., 7am-9:30am Thurs.-Sun.), are open to the public.

OUTSIDE THE PARK

Volcano Village has accommodations and restaurants. Most are on Old Volcano Road, the inner road that parallels HI 11 through town.

GETTING THERE AND AROUND

AIR

Most direct mainland-Big Island flights land at the **Ellison Onizuka Kona International Airport** (KOA, Keahole Airport Rd., 808/327-9520, http://airports.hawaii.gov/koa) on the island's west side. It's a two-hour drive to the park via HI 11. Some planes land on the east side at **Hilo International Airport** (ITO, Kekuanaoa St., 808/961-9300, http://airports.hawaii.gov/ito). From Hilo, the park is roughly 40 miles (64 km) south via HI 11. Both airports have car rentals.

CAR

From Kailua-Kona, drive southeast on HI 11 for 96 miles (155 km, 2.5 hrs) to the park entrance. From Hilo, take HI 11 southwest for 29 miles (47 km, 45 min).

Once inside the park, part of the caldera is encircled by 11 miles (18 km) of the paved **Crater Rim Drive.** From Crater Rim Drive, the paved **Chain of Craters Road** leads through lava flows down the *pali* to the coast.

Due to overcrowded parking lots, plan to arrive by 7am. The park updates online the status of popular parking lots (visitors center, Kīlauea Iki, Puʻu Puaʻi, Devastation Trailhead, and end of Chain of Craters Rd.) so you can plan your itinerary accordingly. Always have alternatives in mind.

BUS

Hele-On Bus (808/961-8744, www.heleonbus.org) connects Hilo with the Kīlauea Visitor Center and Volcano Village. Once inside the park, there is no public transit.

TOURS

Bus Tours

Bus tours depart from Big Island locations to tour the national park. Hilo-based tours include **Roberts Hawaii** (808/539-9400, www.robertshawaii.com) and **KapohoKine Adventures** (93 Banyan Dr., inside Grand Naniloa DoubleTree by Hilton, Hilo, 808/964-1000, www.kapohokine.com). From the Kona side, **Hawaii Forest and Trails** (808/331-8505, www.hawaii-forest.com) offers a 12-hour round-trip adventure of the main park sights.

LAVA FLOWING INTO THE OCEAN

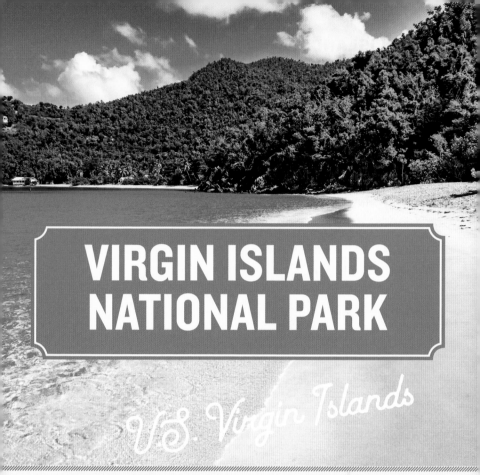

VIRGIN ISLANDS NATIONAL PARK

U.S. Virgin Islands

KEEPSAKE STAMPS ▼▼▼

WEBSITE:
www.nps.gov/viis

PHONE NUMBER:
340/776-6201,
ext. 238

VISITATION RANK:
46

WHY GO:
Snorkel and dive
amid coral reefs.

▲ VIRGIN ISLANDS NATIONAL PARK

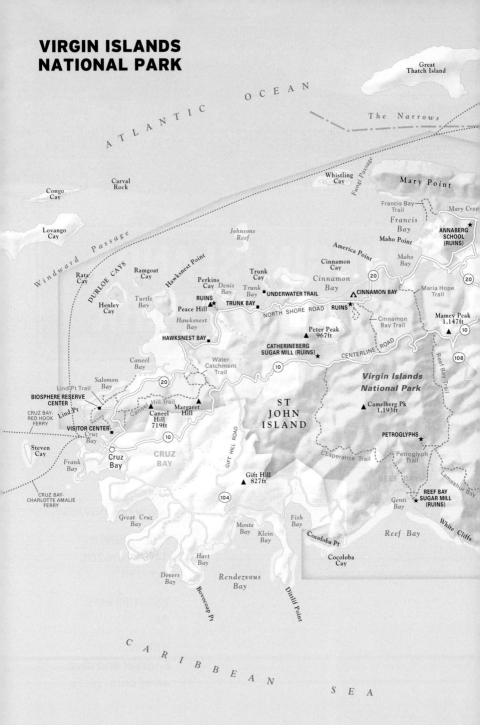

VIRGIN ISLANDS NATIONAL PARK

ATLANTIC OCEAN

The Narrows

Great Thatch Island

Mary Point

Congo Cay

Carval Rock

Whistling Cay

Fangs Passage

Francis Bay Trail

Mary Cree

Francis Bay

ANNABERG SCHOOL (RUINS)

Lovango Cay

Johnsons Reef

Maho Point

Maho Bay

America Point

Cinnamon Cay

Rata Cay

Ramgoat Cay

Hawksnest Point

Cinnamon Bay

Maria Hope Trail

20

Windward Passage

DURLOE CAYS

Turtle Bay

Perkins Cay

Denis Bay

Trunk Cay

UNDERWATER TRAIL

CINNAMON BAY

20

108

Henley Cay

Peace Hill

TRUNK BAY

Trunk Bay

RUINS

Cinnamon Bay Trail

Mamey Peak 1,147ft

Hawksnest Bay

NORTH SHORE ROAD

10

HAWKSNEST BAY

Peter Peak 967ft

CATHERINEBERG SUGAR MILL (RUINS)

CENTERLINE ROAD

Reef Bay Trail

Caneel Bay

Water Catchment Trail

Virgin Islands National Park

20

Salomon Bay

Lind Pt Trail

Caneel Hill Trail

10

Camelberg Pk 1,193ft

BIOSPHERE RESERVE CENTER

Lind Pt

Caneel Hill 719ft

Margaret Hill

ST JOHN ISLAND

CRUZ BAY-RED HOOK FERRY

VISITOR CENTER

Cruz Bay

PETROGLYPHS

CRUZ BAY

10

Petroglyph Trail

Steven Cay

Cruz Bay

L'Esperance Trail

Lameshur Bay

Frank Bay

Gift Hill 827ft

REEF BAY

Genti Bay

REEF BAY SUGAR MILL (RUINS)

CRUZ BAY-CHARLOTTE AMALIE FERRY

104

White Cliffs

Great Cruz Bay

Monte Bay

Fish Bay

Reef Bay

Klein Bay

Cocoloba Pt

Hart Bay

Cocoloba Cay

Devers Bay

Rendezvous Bay

Bovocoap Pt

Distill Point

CARIBBEAN SEA

© MOON.COM

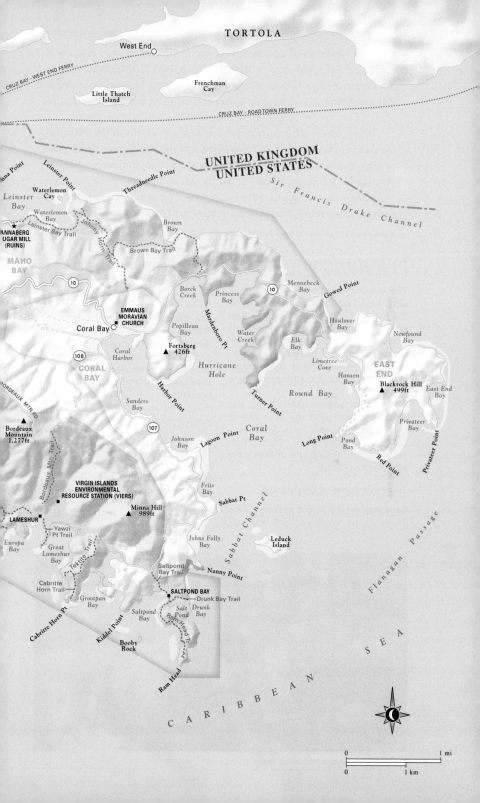

Dreamy white-sand beaches, brilliant turquoise water, and coral reefs are the hallmarks of **VIRGIN ISLANDS NATIONAL PARK,** which covers more than 60 percent of the small island of St. John. Offshore, the island hosts a tropical marine reserve with 302 species of fish, diversity that contributes to the park's utter beauty.

Along peaceful hiking paths, ruins of sugar works and plantation houses remain for visitors to explore. But even older are the petroglyphs, evidence that the Indigenous Taino people once thrived in this island paradise. In 2017, two devastating back-to-back hurricanes struck the island. While full park operations have since resumed, some rebuilding may continue into 2023.

PLANNING YOUR TIME

The island of St. John is mountainous, with two laid-back hamlets outside the national park boundary. **Cruz Bay,** on the far western end of the island, is where ferries and boats from neighboring islands arrive. **Coral Bay** is a sprawling settlement along a wide horseshoe-shaped bay on the far eastern end of the island.

The **dry season** (Dec.-Mar.) has weather perks, with the best sailing, but visitation peaks in waves (Apr.-June, Aug., Oct.-Dec.). Mosquitoes swarm after storms and in **hurricane season** (Aug.-Oct.).

ENTRANCE AND FEES

Cruz Bay serves as the park entrance. There is no entrance fee; however, there are amenity fees for **Trunk Bay** ($5) and for overnight mooring ($26).

VISITORS CENTER

The **Cruz Bay Visitor Center** (8am-4:30pm daily) has exhibits on the human and natural history of St. John, and a three-dimensional map helps you get your bearings. Park rangers can answer questions and hand out maps and brochures.

SIGHTS

HAWKSNEST BEACH

Hawksnest Bay is home to glorious **Hawksnest Beach,** a long wide strip of pale sand fringed by a canopy of mature trees and sandwiched between rock promontories. Hawksnest is the

BLUE TANG FEEDING ON CORAL IN VIRGIN ISLANDS NATIONAL PARK

TRUNK BAY

Top ③

1 SWIM IN TRUNK BAY

Trunk Bay (8am-4pm daily, $5 pp) is St. John's most magnificent beach and its most popular, a vision of fluffy white sand, sea grape trees, and coconut palms. Named for the leatherback turtles that nest here, Trunk Bay is a long beach—even at its most crowded you will find some quiet. Facilities include a snack bar and restrooms. An underwater snorkel trail lies along Trunk Cay, just offshore.

2 SNORKEL WATERLEMON CAY

Waterlemon Cay is home to the best coral reef snorkeling in St. John, but it is not for beginners. To reach the tiny offshore islet requires a walk (1.6 mi/2.6 km rt, 1 hr, easy) from **Leinster Bay Beach** east on an old Danish road to **Waterlemon Bay** and then a 0.2-mile (0.3-km) swim. A shallow reef fringes the protected side of the cay, deepening to 20 feet (6.1 m) with an intricate diversity of coral life and sea stars.

3 EXPLORE THE ANNABERG RUINS

The ruins of the **Annaberg Sugar Mill** are the best place to learn about the colonial-era life of planters and enslaved people on St. John. The site includes the ruins of a windmill, a sugar factory, a mill round, a rum still, and quarters for the enslaved workers. A 0.25-mile (0.4-km, one-way) paved trail with interpretive signs meanders through the grounds.

In the 1840s, the Danish government built two schools nearby. A display describes the history of the **Annaberg School ruins.** Find the site a short distance from the road en route to the Annaberg Plantation. Climb the steps for the best views.

closest beach you can drive to from Cruz Bay.

At the top of the headland between Hawksnest and Trunk Bays is **Peace Hill,** a grassy knoll and windmill ruin with beautiful views.

CINNAMON BAY

Cinnamon Bay is home to an excellent beach, extensive ruins, a hiking trail, and some of St. John's best water sports. The long and winding shore gives way to expansive **Cinnamon Beach,** where the fine white sand creates a wide, shallow bank ideal for snorkeling on the reef about 40 feet (12 m) from shore.

Explore the remains of the bay's 1680 colonial settlement at the **Cinnamon Bay ruins,** across the street from the

beach. A self-guided walk (1 mi/1.6 km, 30 min, easy) leads through the ruins of a sugar factory, an estate house, bay rum stills, and a small Danish cemetery.

MAHO BAY BEACH

Maho Bay is a long narrow beach well protected from surf, which makes it a good destination for stand-up paddleboarding and swimming. Facilities include three new pavilion and restrooms.

FRANCIS BAY

Francis Bay is a great place for swimming and home to the best bird-watching on St. John, especially at **Francis Bay Pond.** A small coral reef at the western end of **Francis Bay Beach** is perfect for beginning snorkelers. The **Francis**

Best Hike

REEF BAY

DISTANCE: 5.2 miles (8.4 km) round-trip
DURATION: 3.5 hours
ELEVATION CHANGE: 900 feet (274 m)
EFFORT: strenuous
TRAILHEAD: Reef Bay Trailhead on Centerline Road

The **Reef Bay Trail** descends steeply to the shore at Reef Bay. At about halfway on the rocky and sometimes slippery forest trail, a spur visits Taino **petroglyphs** from about 1300-1450. On the main trail, you'll also pass the remains of four different sugar factories, including the extensive Reef Bay ruins, and some of the oldest and tallest trees in the park. **Reef Bay** was the site of one of the most productive sugar plantations on St. John. The remains of the **Reef Bay Sugar Mill,** now home to bats, consist of a well-preserved mill building, handsome stone smokestack, and cattle round. Large copper pots used in the manufacture of sugar lie on the ground outside of the building. At Reef Bay, you can swim or snorkel (bring your own gear). The tough part is the climb back up to the trailhead.

Bay Trail (1 mi/1.6 km rt, 30 min, easy) passes through a crumbling plantation house before reaching an overlook with a view of the pond, then ending at the beach.

LEINSTER BAY

Calm **Leinster Bay Beach** is covered with packed coarse yellow sand and fringed by shade trees. It's a decent place to swim and snorkel. From the beach, hike 0.25 mile (0.4 km, one-way) up the **Johnny Horn Trail** to reach plantation house ruins once associated with the Annaberg estate.

SALTPOND BAY

Remote and uncrowded, **Saltpond Bay** is located near the end of Route 107. After a 10-minute hike to the beach, you can snorkel the underwater landscape around the jagged rocks in the middle of the bay. The site offers picnic tables and pit toilets and is accessible by public transportation.

SCENIC DRIVE

NORTH SHORE SCENIC DRIVE

From Cruz Bay, the **North Shore Road** (Rte. 20, 6.8 mi/10.9 km one-way, 20 min) enters Virgin Islands National Park in a few minutes. The road curves in and out along the north coastline of the park for quintessential St. John views: powder-white beaches, pristine coral reefs, and awesome overlooks. You'll pass Hawksnest Beach, Trunk Bay, Cinnamon Bay, and Maho Bay. The route terminates at Leinster Bay Beach and the Annaberg ruins.

RECREATION

HIKING

The **Cinnamon Bay Trail** (2 mi/3.2 km, 1 hr, strenuous) is an uphill trek that follows an old Danish road all the way to Centerline Road. The trail passes through ruins and land that would have been cultivated with sugarcane during the plantation era, now all secondary forest.

The **Yawzi Point Trail** (0.6 mi/1 km, 30 min, easy) follows the headland separating Little Lameshur and Great Lameshur Bays. The trail cuts through a dry forest before reaching the point. People suffering from a tropical skin disease were sent to a quarantine camp here in the 18th and 19th centuries.

The extreme southeastern tip of St. John is a narrow finger of land called **Ram Head** (2.4 mi/3.8 km rt, 1.5 hrs, moderate), a dramatic place with views of the Caribbean Sea and the irregular foothills of southern St. John. The trail starts from the Saltpond Bay parking lot.

From behind the Cruz Bay Visitor Center, the **Lind Point Trail** (2.3 mi/3.7

RUINS OF THE ANNABERG SUGAR MILL

km rt, 1 hr, moderate), a forested loop, is the only way to reach secluded **Honeymoon Beach.** Enjoy the powdery white sand for pleasant views of Lovango, Mingo, and Henley Cays.

SNORKELING

Snorkeling is the most popular activity on St. John. On the north shore, the **Trunk Bay Underwater Trail** is a good reef for beginners. The 650-foot (62-m) underwater snorkel trail lies between a series of buoys off the southwestern tip of Trunk Cay. It's a short swim out to the trail, and the area is normally protected from currents and wind. Use reef-safe sunscreen to protect the coral.

Jumbie Beach has a shallow, maze-like reef along the eastern side, where you may see lobsters and nurse sharks.

On the south shore, **Saltpond Bay** has good reef snorkeling around the two jagged rocks that break the surface of the bay. At **Great Lameshur Bay,** the snorkeling is best along the eastern shore. **Little Lameshur Bay** has snorkeling for beginners just off the western end of the beach.

Maho Bay has offshore sea grass beds that provide food for green turtles, especially in the early morning and late afternoon. **Leinster Bay,** near Annaberg, has nice sea grass beds where you may see sea stars, conchs, and turtles. **Brown Bay,** accessible only on foot, has a sea grass bed just offshore.

Mangroves provide a fascinating glimpse into an important marine habitat. The best place for mangrove snorkeling is **Princess Bay,** along Route 10 (East End Rd.).

Rent snorkel gear from **Crabby's Watersports** (Cocoloba Shopping Center, Coral Bay, 340/626-1570), **Concordia Eco-Resort** (Concordia, 340/690-0561), **Arawak Expeditions** (Mongoose Junction, 340/693-8312, www.arawakexp. com), and **Low Key Watersports** (1 Bay St., Cruz Bay, 340/693-8999, http:// divelowkey.com). **Virgin Islands Ecotours** (Honeymoon Beach, 340/779-2155, www.viecotours.com) offers a three-hour hike and snorkel on the grounds of Caneel Bay Resort.

DIVING

St. John has several dive sites, including two off Cruz Bay. The *Maj. Gen. Rogers,* a 1940 army freighter, was sunk in 1972 to become an artificial reef. The excellent reefs around **Grass Cay** and **Mingo Cay** are good for beginning divers. There is a dizzying array of sealife

ANCIENT PETROGLYPHS ALONG THE REEF BAY TRAIL

at **Witch's Hat** on the southern tip of Steven's Cay, just off Cruz Bay.

South shore dives include **Cocoloba,** an easy, sandy reef dive, and **Maple Leaf,** a large offshore reef east of Reef Bay. The most famous east-end dive site is **Eagle Shoal,** between Ram Head and Leduck Island. Access to Eagle Shoal is limited.

Low Key Watersports (Cruz Bay, 340/693-8999, http://divelowkey.com) offers daily dive trips.

KAYAKING

Kayaking is popular off St. John's north shore, where you can paddle up to beaches or out to offshore islets, like Whistling Cay, Waterlemon Cay, or the Durloe Cays.

Hurricane Hole (Borck Creek, Princess Bay, and Water Creek) is a critical mangrove ecosystem best explored by kayak or stand-up paddleboard. From Coral Bay, it takes about an hour to paddle into it. Check on its status first as the U.S. Coast Guard may still be removing some 50 boats sunk or washed into the mangroves from the hurricanes. Bring a snorkel to explore the enchanting world amid the knobbed knees and underwater roots of the mangrove trees.

On the north shore, rent kayaks at **Virgin Islands Ecotours** (Honeymoon Beach, 340/779-2155, www.viecotours.com). For Coral Bay, **Crabby's Water Sports** (Cocoloba Plaza, 340/626-1570, www.crabbyswatersports.com) rents single and two-seater kayaks.

Outfitters guiding paddle trips include **Arawak Expeditions** (Mongoose Junction, 340/693-8312, www.arawak-exp.com) and **Virgin Islands Ecotours** (Honeymoon Beach, 340/779-2155, www.viecotours.com).

REFLECTING POOL ON THE REEF BAY TRAIL

NUMEROUS BEACHES OFFER RELAXATION.

WHERE TO STAY

INSIDE THE PARK

Rebuilt after the hurricanes, the ocean-front **Cinnamon Bay Resort** (1 Great Cinnamon Bay, St. John, 669/999-8784, www.cinnamonbayvi.com, 2-night minimum, 7-night minimum for holidays) opened with new facilities in late 2021. You can stay in eco-tents (from $180), wood platform sites with a rain cover (with tent, sleep gear, and cookware added on or self-supplied, from $55), or cottages (from $220). Shared bathhouses have showers (no hot water) and flush toilets. The **Rain Tree Café** (daily, hours vary seasonally) serves breakfast, lunch, and dinner. A camp store has to-go foods and some groceries.

OUTSIDE THE PARK

St. John's hotels and villas are among the priciest in the Virgin Islands. A few moderate hotels in **Cruz Bay** offer affordable options.

GETTING THERE AND AROUND

AIR

There is no airport on St. John. The closest airport is on **St. Thomas** (SST, Cyril E. King Airport, Airport Rd., Charlotte Amalie West, 340/774-1629, www.viport.com). **Varlack Ventures** (340/776-6412) operates ferries between St. Thomas and Cruz Bay. Ferries leave Charlotte Amalie daily (10am, 1pm, and 5:30pm, $13 one-way).

TAXIS

Taxis are widely available on St. John, especially in Cruz Bay and at the popular north shore beaches. Try **C&C Taxi Service** (340/693-8164) or **Star Fish Tours & Taxi Service** (340/998-6139). Some taxis provide island tours.

CAR RENTALS

Numerous rental companies based around Cruz Bay only rent 4WD sport-utility vehicles suitable for the island's roads. You must be able to drive on the left side of the road; if you are uncomfortable with that, take taxis. There are three gas stations on St. John, one on Centerline Road and two on the road between Cruz Bay and the Westin Resort.

BUSES

The air-conditioned **VITRAN buses** (340/693-8001, $1) run hourly from Cruz Bay to Coral Bay and Saltpond Bay, along Centerline Road.

TOURS

Cruz Bay Watersports (340/776-6234, http://cruisebaywatersports.com) offers catamaran trips for sunsets, snorkeling, and beach visits. A number of operators offer one-day sailing trips around St. John. Contact the activity desk at your lodging for availability and pricing.

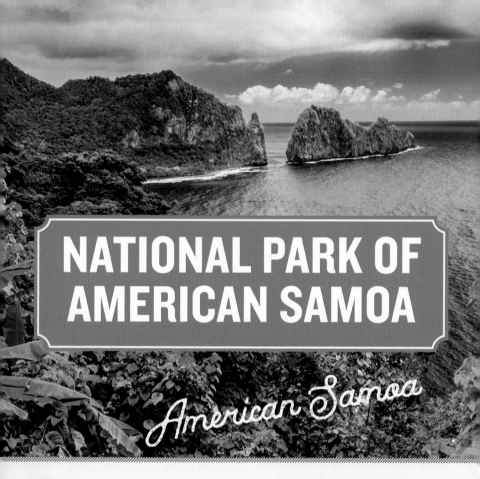

NATIONAL PARK OF AMERICAN SAMOA

American Samoa

WEBSITE:
www.nps.gov/npsa

PHONE NUMBER:
684/633-7082, ext. 22

VISITATION RANK:
62

WHY GO:
Visit a tropical
rain forest and
coral reefs.

KEEPSAKE STAMPS ▼▼▼

▲ VAI'AVA STRAITO

Located south of the equator, the remote **NATIONAL PARK OF AMERICAN SAMOA** is the southernmost national park in the United States. It's anchored by three islands in the Samoan archipelago, where lush mountain rainforests cling to the volcanic landscape broken up by tropical beaches. Underwater, a prolific marine ecosystem contains 950 species of fish and 250 species of coral in one of the planet's largest living coral communities.

The National Park of American Samoa also preserves historic military sites from World Wars I and II, when Tutuila Island served as a base for U.S. troops. More importantly, it honors the traditional Samoan culture, which has thrived for 3,000 years on Samoa. Contrary to other U.S. national parks, which are owned by the federal government, the National Park of American Samoa leases land from the local people.

PLANNING YOUR TIME

ocated in the South Pacific (north of Fiji, Tonga, and Tahiti), American Samoa sits east of the international date line, far south of the equator. The national park is split across three of the Samoan Islands.

Tutuila Island has the largest and most visited national park tract. The town of **Pago Pago** serves as the main base for the park; Pago Pago International Airport is at the south end of the island. Other villages are outside Pago Pago, and roads can be rough. The village of Vatia is inside the park, while Fagasa and Afono are close to the park boundaries. Bring a sense of adventure and a good dose of self-sufficiency (for snorkeling, bring your own gear), as services are few.

Sixty miles (97 km) east are the tiny Manu'a Islands of **Ta'ū** and **Ofu,** reachable by boat and air. On Ta'ū Island, the main access points are the boat harbor at Faleasao and Fiti'uta Airport. The village of **Ofu** is the main access point for Ofu Island.

Spring (Mar.-May) and **fall** (Oct.-Nov.) are the best times to visit. October-May is the monsoon season, which sees tropical storms. Temperatures range 75-85°F (24-29°C), but oppressive humidity can make it feel much hotter. Rain is frequent, the mosquitoes are ubiquitous, and acute solar radiation can intensify sunburns. Humpback whales migrate to the islands in September and October.

The Samoan people follow *fa'asamoa,* a distinct set of cultural mores. Ask permission to take photos and use beaches, observe evening prayer time with silence, and respect Sundays with quiet and in some locations no swimming or hiking. Clothing, including swimwear, should be modest.

ENTRANCES AND FEES

For entry into American Samoa, visitors must have a passport, return ticket, and confirmation of funds. Upon arrival, nationals from Great Britain, Australia, New Zealand, and Canada may receive 30-day entry permits. Visas are required for all other international travelers.

There is no national park entrance fee and no official entrance station.

VISITORS CENTER

The **national park visitors center** (8am-4:30pm Mon.-Fri.) is in Pago Pago across from the Pago Way Service Station. Exhibits focus on the island's natural history and Samoan culture. Rangers can advise on hiking trail conditions and trip planning. Kids can pick up Junior Ranger activity books. Field guides and natural history books are

NATIONAL PARK OF AMERICAN SAMOA

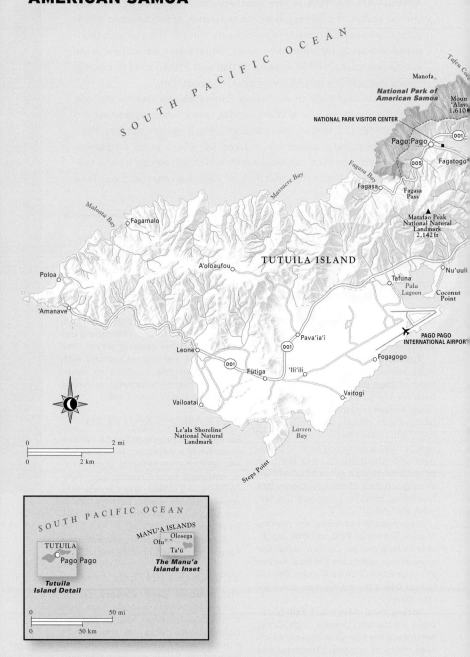

SOUTH PACIFIC OCEAN

Tafeu Cove

Manofa

National Park of American Samoa

Moun 'Alav: 1,610

NATIONAL PARK VISITOR CENTER

Pago Pago

001

005

Fagatogo

Fagasa Bay

Fagasa

Fagasa Pass

Massacre Bay

▲ Matafao Peak National Natural Landmark 2,142 ft

Maloata Bay

Fagamalo

TUTUILA ISLAND

Nu'uuli

Tafuna

Pala Lagoon

Coconut Point

A'oloaufou

Poloa

'Amanave

Pava'ia'i

001

✈ PAGO PAGO INTERNATIONAL AIRPORT

Leone

Fogagogo

001

Fūtiga

'Ili'ili

Vaitogi

Vailoatai

Le'ala Shoreline National Natural Landmark

Larsen Bay

0 _____ 2 mi

0 _____ 2 km

Steps Point

SOUTH PACIFIC OCEAN

MANU'A ISLANDS

TUTUILA

Pago Pago

Ofu Olosega

Ta'ū

The Manu'a Islands Inset

Tutuila Island Detail

0 _____ 50 mi

0 _____ 50 km

Pola Island
Vai'ava Strait National Natural Landmark
Craggy Point
Cape Matatula
Vatia Bay
Afono Bay
Masefau Bay
Onenoa
Tula
Vatia
Amalau Valley
Masefau
Sa'ilele
'Aoa
Maugaloa
Ridge
Afono
006
Faga'itua
Amouli
Au'asi
Afono Pass
Pago Pago Harbor
Aua
North Pioa Mountain 1,718ft
Alega
001
Faga'itua (bay)
001
Utulei
Rainmaker Mountain National Natural Landmark
'Aunu'u
Faga'alu
001
Fatumafuti
Breakers Point
Fatu Rock

'AUNU'U ISLAND NATIONAL NATURAL LANDMARK

Taema Bank

Nafanua Bank

To Manu'a Islands, see inset below

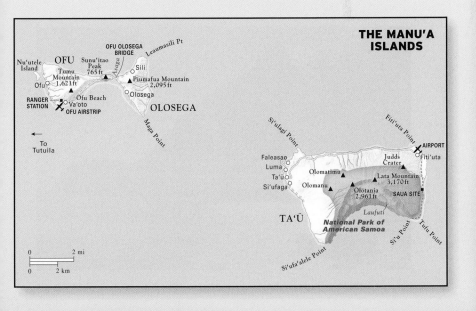

THE MANU'A ISLANDS

Nu'utele Island
OFU
OFU OLOSEGA BRIDGE
Leaumasili Pt
Sunu'itao Peak 765ft
Asaga
Sili
Tumu Mountain 1,621ft
Piumafua Mountain 2,095ft
Ofu
Ofu Beach
Olosega
RANGER STATION
Va'oto
OLOSEGA
OFU AIRSTRIP
Maga Point

To Tutuila

Si'ulagi Point
Fiti'uta Point
AIRPORT
Faleasao
Judds Crater
Fiti'uta
Luma
Olomatimu
Ta'ū
Lata Mountain 3,170ft
Si'ufaga
Olomanu
Olotania 2,961ft
SAUA SITE
TA'Ū
Laufuti
Si'o Point
National Park of American Samoa
Tufu Point
Si'ufa'alele Point

0   2 mi
0   2 km

Top ③

VAI'AVA STRAIT

① SEE VAI'AVA STRAIT

One of the most iconic sights in the national park is **Vai'ava Strait,** a National Natural Landmark on Tutuila Island. Steep, forested, and rocky cliffs plunge into the sea at a gap in between Pola Island and the mainland. Waves cut between the rocks to form the strait while the erosion-resistant volcanic rocks still stand on either side as a geological marvel. The scenic strait is near Vatia Village on the north coast of the park. For the best views, drive to the pullout 4.1 miles (6.6 km) beyond the village of Aūa. You can also see it from the beach at the end of the Lower Sauma Ridge Trail.

② VISIT AUNU'U ISLAND

Located 1 mile (1.6 km) off Tutuila Island, **Aunu'u Island** is a National Natural Landmark with its origins in volcanic basalt and tuff. To go to the island, drive to 'Au'asi on the eastern end of Tutuila Island and take the Aunu'u Island ferry. Aunu'u Beach has outstanding snorkeling (bring your own gear) in protected coral reefs with a white-sand beach. The island is small enough that you can walk from the dock to the beach.

③ SNORKEL OFU BEACH

On remote Ofu Island, the long white-sand **Ofu Beach** is one of the best places for snorkeling in American Samoa. Its protected reef lies in easily accessible shallow water, with a diverse range of coral and fish. Clear water yields outstanding visibility for spotting tropical fish and brilliant coral. Bring your own snorkel gear.

OFU BEACH

Best Hike

MOUNT ʻALAVA ADVENTURE TRAIL

DISTANCE: 5.6 miles (9 km) round-trip
DURATION: 3.5 hours
ELEVATION CHANGE: 400 feet (122 m)
EFFORT: strenuous
TRAILHEAD: in Vatia, across from Lower Sauma Ridge Trailhead

For hikers who enjoy challenges, the **Mount ʻAlava Adventure Trail** navigates a steep ascent of a ridge via 56 ladders (steep steps with ropes) and 783 stairs. The reward is reaching the summit of the tallest peak in the park and a Samoan fale (pavilion). Views include Pago Pago and Vaiʻava Strait. Hike down via the trail to Vatia Village and back on the road to make a loop.

sold in the **Hawaii Pacific Parks Association** (www.hawaiipacificparks.org) bookstore.

TUTUILA ISLAND

NATIONAL NATURAL LANDMARKS

Tutuila Island has several National Natural Landmarks. Even though most are outside the national park boundary, they are part of the national park system for their unique geology and flora. Many are on private land; you can view them but they may not be accessible. **Vaiʻava Strait** and **Aunuʻu Island** are the two most easily recognized geological marvels.

Two rainforest-draped landmarks stand on either side of Pago Pago Harbor, both created from molten magma. **Matafao Peak** (2,142 ft/652 m) is the highest mountain on Tutuila. Opposite the harbor sits **Rainmaker Mountain.** Route 001 around the west side of the harbor hugs the base of Matafao; driving from the village of Aūa to Āfono Pass yields a good view of Rainmaker.

South of Pago Pago International Airport on Route 001, a side trip from Leone Village down Taputima Road leads across private land (ask permission) to **Leʻala Shoreline.** It contains tropical flora, rock sculpted by wave action, and two types of volcanic layers.

HIKING

Many trails are primitive or unimproved and cross private land; request permission before hiking. Due to rain, trails are frequently slippery and muddy. Look for large fruit bats in trees or flying, even in daytime.

The **Lower Sauma Ridge Trail** (0.4 mi/0.6 km rt, 30 min, moderate) visits archaeological sites. The short trail with interpretive signs cuts through rainforest until it reaches a beach. At the beach, look across Vatia Bay for views of Vaiʻava Strait **National Natural Landmark** and try to spot Pola Island, where seabirds nest.

The **World War II Heritage Trail** (1.7 mi/2.7 km rt, 1 hr, moderate) passes several World War II historic sites before entering a rainforest loaded with birds. Near the end of the trail, you'll encounter steep steps with rope handrails. The trailhead is between Fagaʻalu and

MATAFAO PEAK

OFU ISLAND

SAMOAN CEREMONY

to Leolo Ridge, where a rocky outcrop overlooks coral lagoons and the three Manu'a Islands. Look for the trailhead near the Ofu Harbor. Though the trail is outside the national park boundary, it is park-maintained and yields views inside the national park.

Utulei on the coast road; a sign next to the IBM Laundromat denotes the path. Park at the nearby public parking lot next to the harbor.

MANU'A ISLANDS

The remote islands of **Ta'ū** and **Ofu** are 60 miles (97 km) east of Tutuila Island. The islands contain half of the National Park of American Samoa, which lines their southern shores. These small undeveloped islands are home to traditional Samoans who live on farms or in tiny villages. There are no amenities or services.

HIKING

Island trails are rugged, primitive, and undeveloped. Due to rain, they are often muddy and slick. Consider hiring a local guide, or check with the park service for options.

On Ta'ū, the **Si'u Point Trail** (5.7 mi/9.2 km rt, 3 hrs, moderate) tours a coastal tropical forest on an old dirt roadbed—an extension of the main paved road in Fiti'uta—and passes a cultural history site.

Ofu Island has the **Tumu Mountain Trail** (5.5 mi/8.8 km rt, 3 hrs, strenuous), which climbs an old road to the top of the highest point on the island at 1,621 feet (494 m). From the summit, it follows another trail 0.25 mile (0.4 km)

WHERE TO STAY

INSIDE THE PARK

The National Park Service offers a **homestay program** for those who want to immerse themselves in Samoan life. Participants live in a Samoan village, learn local customs, and help with sustenance gardening, collecting fruit, and fishing. Each host sets an independent fee for stays; the transaction is between you and the host, without park service involvement.

OUTSIDE THE PARK

Outside the park, **Pago Pago** has the most lodging options. On the **Manu'a Islands,** lodging is extremely limited: homestays are best for Ta'ū; Ofu has **Vaoto Lodge** (684/655-1120, www.vaotolodge.com).

GETTING THERE AND AROUND

The most accessible airport is **Pago Pago International Airport** (PPG, Pago Pago, http://americansamoaport.as.gov) on Tutuila Island. Car rentals are available. From Pago Pago, **Samoa Airways** (684/699-9126 or 684/699-9127, http://samoaairways.com) offers several flights per week to **Fiti'uta Airport** (FAQ) on the island of Ta'ū or a twice-weekly flight to **Ofu Airport** (OFU) on the island of Ofu.

To get around **Tutuila Island,** take a taxi or the independently operated **Aiga buses** (Mon.-Sat.), which run often though not on any set schedule. From Fagatogo market, buses travel to Vatia Village within the national park and to the island's remote corners. Buses are labeled with their destinations; simply flag one down for pickup. The islands of Ta'ū and Ofu have no public transportation or taxis. Ofu is small enough to walk almost everywhere.

ESSENTIALS

THE HISTORY OF
THE NATIONAL PARKS

INDIGENOUS PEOPLES

Indigenous people inhabited many of the U.S. national parks more than 10,000 years ago. Archaeological evidence points to many millennia of use—both permanent and seasonal—from the coastal lands of Olympic to the shores of Indiana Dunes on Lake Michigan and the warmer climes of the Everglades.

When the idea of national parks took hold in the United States, it coincided with another movement already afoot: to displace Indigenous people from their traditional lands, remove their means of livelihood, and corral them onto reservations. Yellowstone was not just the first national park; it was also the first national park to remove the people already living there (in this case, the Sheepeaters or Shoshone). The story is similar in many of the biggest and most popular parks: the Cherokee in Great Smoky Mountains, Miwok of Yosemite, Blackfeet and Kootenai of Glacier, and the Hopi, Havasupai, Navajo, and others of the Grand Canyon.

Some parks are trying to forge partnerships with Indigenous peoples in an effort to share their cultures. Grand Canyon has created the first **Inter-Tribal Cultural Heritage Site** at Desert View Watchtower, which features demonstrations by Indigenous artisans. Likewise, Glacier Bay has the **Tlingit Huna House,** the Xunaa Shuká Hít, which shares traditional woodcraft and dances. But other issues persist, such as hunting and fishing rights, water rights, archaeological artifact ownership, sacred sites, and land claims.

To hear Indigenous people speak about their history in the national parks and cultural ties to the parks, listen to **Parks Podcast** (www.parkspodcast.com). Yellowstone, Grand Canyon, and Acadia launched the series, with more parks to come.

THE FIRST NATIONAL PARK

No country in the world recognized any land as a national park until President Ulysses S. Grant signed a bill in 1872 to create **Yellowstone National Park.** Some countries had nature preserves and lands with national protection, as did the United States, but none set aside national parks for the preservation of unique features and enjoyment by the people.

Yellowstone benefited from champions of preservation such as John Muir and George Bird Grinnell, who laid the groundwork, while artists and photographers documented its features. Expedition leader Ferdinand Hayden in 1871 recommended a national park, an idea suggested to him by a Northern Pacific Railway lobbyist who saw the potential earnings from train ridership. Hayden's report to Congress included details of Yellowstone's uniqueness, but also stated that the land was unsuitable for farming or mining, rendering it useless for development. It ignored the many Indigenous groups who had lived in and relied on resources in the park. With Hayden's recommendations also came a warning: to avoid the fate of Niagara Falls, a national treasure surrounded by private development.

Creating the boundaries of the first national park was a function of bureaucracy. When Yellowstone was created in 1872, the states in which it now resides—Wyoming, Idaho, and Montana—did not yet exist. So, the federal government designated a big square on the map without concern for topographical features.

The federal vision fell far short—providing no funding, no agency to run Yellowstone, and no protection for its natural features and wildlife, only appointing an unpaid superintendent who visited the park just twice. The park floundered, overrun by poachers and squatters.

Six years later, Congress finally appropriated money to "protect, preserve, and improve" Yellowstone. With a new mandate, the second superintendent, Philetus Norris, built a few primitive roads, constructed a station at Mammoth Hot Springs, and hired the park's first gamekeeper to battle poachers. But then political machinations swapped in a series of ineffectual superintendents, and in its second decade, Yellowstone ran wild. Vandals destroyed natural features, poachers slaughtered wildlife, loggers harvested timber, squatters threw up shelters and camps for tourists, and hot springs facilities were erected as laundries and baths.

The public loved the idea of Yellowstone, but Congress trashed its annual funding in 1886 due to ineffective management. The solution to Yellowstone's problem turned out to be the **U.S. Army**, which erected Fort Yellowstone to enforce regulations.

Bison issues propelled Congress to further action. Huge bison slaughters outside the park fed the booming fur and meat business; the federal government encouraged them as a means to subdue Indigenous people who relied on bison for food and to force them to move onto reservations. Inside Yellowstone, poachers likewise jeopardized the survival of bison. With eviction from the park as the maximum punishment, the army had no strong clout. Finally, a journalistic outcry about the bison slaughters forced Congress to pass the **National Park Protection Act** in 1894 to protect birds, animals, and natural features in Yellowstone. Violators faced fines and jail.

As the first national park, Yellowstone eventually paved the way for other U.S. national parks. Yosemite and Sequoia National Parks followed in 1890, and Mount Rainier gained parkhood in 1899. With the idea of national parks taking off, the first two decades of the 1900s saw the frenzied addition of 12 more national parks—Crater Lake, Wind Cave, Mesa Verde, Glacier, Rocky Mountain, Lassen Volcanic, Hawai'i Volcanoes, Haleakalā, Denali, Grand Canyon, Zion, and Acadia.

THE NATIONAL PARK SERVICE

Managing the growing number of national parks became problematic. While U.S. Army units ran Yellowstone and Yosemite, other parks relied on various agencies for oversight. The addition of national monuments, mineral springs, memorials, military parks, and historical sites compounded the problem by taking the total number of federal preservation lands to 35.

By 1910, several national organizations, including the Sierra Club, lobbied for a new federal agency to take over the national parks. The U.S. Forest Service opposed the concept, arguing in favor of the timber industry that relied on public lands. But Stephen Mather, a conservationist, and Horace Albright, a young lawyer, launched a campaign to create the National Park Service.

Finally, 44 years following the creation of Yellowstone National Park, President Woodrow Wilson put his signature on the 1916 **Organic Act** to establish the **National Park Service.** The act directed the agency to preserve the scenery, natural and historic objects, and wildlife. The act also required the agency provide for the enjoyment of those things in a way that preserved them for future generations.

The new agency was placed under the Department of the Interior, an entirely different branch of the federal government from the Department of Agriculture that oversaw the U.S. Forest Service. To this day, that differentiation in federal management separates the purpose of the national parks and national forests and the way they can be used.

THE PARKS TODAY

National parks were steadily added to the system over the century following the creation of the National Park Service. Today, the NPS oversees 63 national parks and administers more than 400 public lands.

Many of our parks have gained recognition beyond the country's boundaries. The United Nations Educational, Scientific and Cultural Organization

(UNESCO) has named 15 of the parks as World Heritage Sites and 19 as Biosphere Reserves.

Our national parks protect some of the country's most scenic and unique places. From the first rays of sunlight to hit the country in Acadia to the ice-draped highest peak on the continent in Denali, these national prizes yield visions of raw, uncontrolled beauty. Glacier's ice-scoured mountains, Grand Canyon's deep chasm, and Yosemite's vertical walls remind us of the earth-shaping forces that wrought our landscape. Bison herds wandering in Yellowstone let us connect with our roots, as do the cliff dwellings in Mesa Verde. For those where city lights drown out the stars, the parks are places where the Milky Way still sparkles in the night sky. These parks offer renewal for the human spirit and a regeneration of that deep connection to how we, as humans, fit in the world.

ROAD RULES

CAR AND RV RENTAL

Most car rental companies have locations at major international airports. To reserve a car in advance, contact **Budget** (U.S. 800/218-7992, outside U.S. 800/472-3325, www.budget.com), **Dollar Rent A Car** (866/434-2226, www.dollar.com), **Enterprise** (855/266-9289, www.enterprise.com), or **Hertz** (U.S. and Canada 800/654-3131, international 800/654-3001, www.hertz.com).

To rent a car, most companies require drivers to be at least 21 years old and have a valid driver's license. Companies may also tack on additional fees for those under age 25. You will also need liability insurance, which you can purchase through the rental company. Private auto insurance also tends to cover rental cars, but check with your insurance company to verify.

The **average cost** of a rental car is $50 per day or $210 per week; however, rates vary greatly based on the season, distance traveled, and availability. Weekend and summer rentals cost significantly more. Generally, it is more expensive to rent from car rental agencies at an airport because of added fees. To avoid excessive rates, first plan travel to areas where a car is not required, then rent a car from an agency branch in town to further explore more rural areas. Rental agencies occasionally allow vehicle drop-off at a different location from where it was picked up for an additional fee.

Another option is to rent an **RV.** You won't have to worry about camping or lodging options, and many facilities, particularly farther north, accommodate RVs. However, RVs are difficult to maneuver and park, limiting your access to some trailheads and sights in national parks. Be aware that some national park roads ban RVs or restrict length. They are also expensive, both in terms of gas and the rental rates. Rates during the summer average $1,300 per week and $570 for three days, the standard minimal rental. **Cruise America** (800/671-8042, www.cruiseamerica.com) has branches throughout the United States.

Electric vehicle charging stations are starting to make a few inroads into the parks. Research availability before your trip; stations aren't as common as they are in cities.

ROAD CONDITIONS

Road closures are not uncommon, especially in winter in mountain parks. Traffic jams, accidents, mudslides, fires, and snow can affect interstate and local highways at any time. Before heading out on your adventure, check road conditions online with the state highway department and the national park.

In an emergency, **dial 911** from any phone. The American Automobile Association, better known as **AAA** (800/222-4357, www.aaa.com), offers roadside assistance free to members; others pay a fee.

Be aware of your car's maintenance needs while on the road. The most frequent issues result from **summer heat.** If the car gets hot or overheats, stop for a while to cool it off. Never open the radiator cap if the engine is steaming. After the engine cools, squeeze the top radiator hose to see if there's any pressure in it; if there isn't, it's safe to open. Never pour water into a hot radiator because it could crack the engine block. If you start to smell rubber, your tires are overheating, and that's a good way to have a blowout. Stop and let them cool off. When descending steep mountain roads, use lower gears for the engine to force a slowdown rather than riding your brakes and wearing them down. During **winter,** a can of silicone lubricant such as WD-40 will unfreeze door locks, dry off humid wiring, and keep your hinges in shape. Mountain parks may require chains or traction devices for winter access.

MAPS AND GPS NAVIGATION

Always travel with a printed map or guide; do *not* rely solely on GPS navigation, which is notoriously unreliable inside the national parks. Some park travelers relying on GPS get led to the wrong location, into dead ends, or onto closed roads, snowbound passes, or defunct roads. Carry printed up-to-date road maps and learn how to read them. Check seasonal access and weather conditions for all driving routes prior to travel.

Upon entering any national park and paying the park entrance fee, you'll be offered a free park map. These maps are good for paved road navigation and locating services, but they are not detailed enough for backcountry trails or rough 4WD roads. For topographical maps, download maps from **National Geographic** (www.natgeomaps.com) or order them from the **USGS** (http://store.usgs.gov).

INTERNATIONAL DRIVER'S LICENSES

If you are visiting the United States from another country and planning to drive, you need to secure an International Driving Permit from your home country before your arrival. (You won't be able to get one once you're here.) You must also bring your government-issued driving permit.

Visitors from outside the United States should check the driving rules of the states they will visit at www.usa.gov. Among the most important rules is that traffic runs on the right side of the road in the United States. Note that many states have bans on using handheld cell phones while driving. If caught, expect to pay a hefty fine.

HEALTH AND SAFETY

HOSPITALS AND EMERGENCIES

Most national parks are tucked into remote locations where emergency services take longer to respond. Hospitals, emergency rooms, and urgent care facilities are often located outside the national parks in nearby towns several hours away. The larger parks with huge visitation numbers may have an urgent care clinic.

If you are injured in a park, **dial 911** or the park phone number for emergencies. If cell service is not available, flag down a ranger or passing motorist to get help instead. Due to the remote locations of many national parks, do not rely on having cell phone service to call for help.

WILDERNESS SAFETY

For hikers, backpackers, mountain bikers, climbers, and river travelers, be prepared to handle emergencies on your own. Be competent in administering first aid, self-rescuing, and providing your own evacuation. Only rely on calling for help in life-threatening situations or where severe injuries prevent you from being able to get out on your own.

HEAT EXHAUSTION AND HEATSTROKE

Being out in the elements can present its own set of challenges. Heat exhaustion and heatstroke can affect anyone during the hot summer months, particularly during a long strenuous hike in the sun. Common symptoms include nausea, light-headedness, headache, or muscle cramps.

DEHYDRATION

Many first-time hikers to high-mountain or arid parks are surprised to find they drink more water than at home. Wind, sun, altitude, and lower humidity can add up to a fast case of dehydration. It manifests first as a headache. Before launching at a trailhead, consult with rangers about current reliable water sources.

While hiking, drink lots of water—even more than you normally would. With children, monitor their fluid intake. In desert parks, plan to carry and drink 1 gallon (3.8 l) of water per person per day. It's also a good idea to take electrolytes with your fluids, to keep the body's water and sodium levels from getting out of whack.

HYPOTHERMIA

Exhausted and physically unprepared hikers are at risk for insidious hypothermia. The body's inner core loses heat, reducing mental and physical functions. Watch for uncontrolled shivering, incoherence, poor judgment, fumbling, mumbling, and slurred speech. Avoid becoming hypothermic by staying dry. Don rain gear and warm moisture-wicking layers rather than cottons that won't dry and fail to retain heat. Get hypothermic hikers into dry clothing and shelter. Give them warm non-alcoholic and noncaffeinated liquids.

If the victim cannot regain body heat, get into a sleeping bag with the victim, both stripped for skin-to-skin contact.

POISON OAK, IVY, AND SUMAC

Poison oak, ivy, and sumac are vines or shrubs that inhabit forests. Common in Western states, poison oak has three scalloped leaves. Found across the United States except for tropical islands and Alaska, poison ivy has three spoon-shaped leaves and grows along rivers, lakes, and oceans. With 7-13 leaflets, poison sumac grows in wet, swampy zones in the North and Florida. Contact with these plants may cause a rash and itching, which can be transferred to your eyes or face via touch. Your best protection is to wear long sleeves and long pants when hiking, no matter how hot it is. Tecnu can cleanse your skin after exposure to poison oak and poison ivy. Calamine lotion can help ease the rash and itching.

GIARDIA

Lakes and streams can carry parasites like *Giardia lamblia*. If ingested, it causes cramping, nausea, and severe diarrhea for up to six weeks. Avoid giardia by boiling water (for 1 min, plus 1 min for each 1,000 ft/305 m elevation above sea level) or using a one-micron filter. Bleach also works: Add 2 drops per quart (2 drops/l) and wait 30 minutes. Tap water in campgrounds, hotels, and picnic areas has been treated; you'll taste the chlorine.

ALTITUDE

Some visitors from sea-level locales feel the effects of altitude at high elevations in mountain parks of the Rockies and the Sierra. Watch for light-headedness, headaches, or shortness of breath. To acclimate, slow down the pace of hiking and drink lots of fluids. If symptoms spike, descend in elevation as soon as possible. Altitude also increases UV radiation exposure: To prevent sunburn, use a strong sunscreen and wear sunglasses and a hat.

▶ BLACK BEAR, YELLOWSTONE

WILDLIFE SAFETY TIPS

While you may see bison, elk, moose, deer, pronghorn, wolves, coyotes, or bears, remember that wildlife is just that . . . wild. Though bison, elk, or even bears may appear tame, they are not, and injuries are common. Here are a few tips to remain safe.

Do not approach wildlife. Crowding wildlife puts you at risk and endangers the animal, often scaring it off. Seemingly docile bison and elk have suddenly gored people crowding too close. Stay at least **100 yards away** (91 m, the length of a football field) from bears and wolves. For all other wildlife, stay at least **25 yards (23 m) away.**

For spying wildlife up close, use a good pair of **binoculars** or a **spotting scope.** Use telephoto lenses for photography.

Take safe selfies. Bison gorings are becoming more prevalent; many are related to people trying to take selfies. Maintain a safe distance, and snap photos of wildlife far in the background.

Do not feed any animal. Because human food is not part of their natural diet, they may suffer at foraging on their own. As they rely on people for handouts, they become aggressive, endangering both human visitors and themselves.

Follow instructions for food storage. Bears, wolves, and coyotes may become more aggressive when acquiring food, and ravens can strew food and garbage, making it more available to other wildlife.

Let the animal's behavior guide your behavior. If an animal appears twitchy, nervous, or points eyes and ears directly at you, back off: You're too close. If you behave like a predator stalking an animal, the creature will assume you are one.

If you see **wildlife along a road,** use pullouts to drive completely off the road. Use the car as a blind to watch wildlife, and keep pets inside. Watch for cars, as visitors can be injured by inattentive drivers whenever a wildlife jam occurs.

WILDLIFE

BEARS

Many of the national parks are home to **black bears** and **grizzly bears.** Bears are dangerous around food, be it a carcass in the woods, a pack on a trail, or a cooler in a campsite. Proper use, storage, and handling of food and garbage prevent bears from being conditioned to look for food around humans and turning aggressive.

On the trail, pick up any dropped food, including wrappers and crumbs, and pack out all garbage. When camping, use low-odor foods, keep food and cooking gear out of sleeping sites in the backcountry, and store them inside your vehicle in front-country campgrounds.

Bear Bells versus Pepper Spray

On trails in grizzly country (Alaska, Washington, Idaho, Montana, and Wyoming), you'll hear jingle bells, sold in gift shops as **bear bells.** While making noise on the trail does prevent surprising a bear, bear bells are not a substitute for human noise on the trail in the form of talking, singing, hooting, and hollering.

Most hikers in grizzly country carry an 8-ounce (237-ml) can of **pepper spray,** which deters bear attacks without injuring the bears or humans. Spray it directly into a bear's face, aiming for the eyes and nose. Carry it on the front of your pack where it is easily reached. If confronted with a bear, you won't have time to dig it out of your pack.

MOUNTAIN LIONS

Because of their solitary nature, it is unlikely you will see a mountain lion, even on long trips in the backcountry. These large cats rarely prey on humans, but they can—especially small kids. Hike with others, keep kids close, and make noise on the trail. If you do stumble upon a cougar, do not run: Remain calm and gather your group together to appear bigger. Look at the cat with peripheral vision, rather than staring straight on, and back away slowly. If the lion attacks, fight back with rocks, sticks, or by kicking.

HANTAVIRUS

Hantavirus infection is contracted by inhaling dust from deer mice droppings. When camping, store food in rodent-proof containers. If you find rodent dust in your gear, disinfect the gear with water and bleach (1.5 cups bleach to 1 gal water/240 ml to 3.8 l). If you contract the virus, which results in flu-like symptoms, seek immediate medical attention.

SPIDERS, MOSQUITOES, AND TICKS

Spiders, mosquitoes, and ticks can carry diseases such as West Nile virus and Rocky Mountain spotted fever. Protect yourself by wearing long sleeves and pants and use insect repellent in spring-summer, when mosquitoes and ticks are common. If you are bitten by a tick, carefully remove it by the head with tweezers, disinfect the bite, and then see a doctor. Some spiders, such as the brown recluse, carry poison in their bites. If symptoms are severe (breathing difficulty, nausea, sweating, and vomiting), seek medical attention immediately.

SNAKES

Rattlesnakes are ubiquitous in prairie and desert parks across the West. When hiking, keep your eyes on the ground and an ear out for the telltale rattle—a warning to keep away. Should you be bitten, seek immediate medical help.

TRAVEL TIPS

ENTERING THE UNITED STATES

PASSPORTS AND VISAS

International travelers entering the United States must have **passports** and in some cases **visas.** Check online (https://usa.gov/enter-us) for a list of countries with **visa waivers.**

In most other countries, the local U.S. embassy should be able to provide a **tourist visa.** The application fee for a visa is US$160, plus you'll need to pay an issuance fee. While a visa may be processed in as little as 24 hours on request, plan for at least a couple of weeks, as there can be unexpected delays, particularly during the busy summer season (June-Aug.). For information, visit https://travel.state.gov.

Travelers from countries in the **Visa Waiver Program** must have an **e-passport** and register in advance online (www.cbp.gov/travel/international-visitors/esta). You'll only need to show documentation at your international port of entry. Once in the United States, you will not need to show documentation when traveling between states except for commercial flights.

One exception applies to **citizens of Canada** and countries in the **Western Hemisphere Travel Initiative,** who may use passport cards, Trusted Traveler Program cards (https://ttp.dhs.gov), or enhanced driver's licenses.

MONEY AND CURRENCY EXCHANGE

International travelers should exchange currency at their major port of entry. As you travel, use ATM cards to get more cash. Smaller denominations ($50 and under) work best. Using a credit card while traveling will give you the best exchange rates.

EMBASSIES AND CONSULATES

If you should lose your passport or find yourself in some other trouble while visiting the United States, contact your country's offices for assistance. The website of the **U.S. State Department** (www.state.gov) lists the websites for all foreign embassies and consulates within the United States. Also, a representative can direct you to the nearest embassy or consulate.

CUSTOMS

Before you enter the United States from another country by sea or by air, you'll be required to fill out a customs form. Those driving into the country will make verbal declarations at their point of entry. Check with the U.S. embassy in your country or the **Customs and Border Protection** website (www.cbp.gov) for an updated list of items you must declare.

In general, the United States does not allow plants, drugs, firewood, or live bait to cross borders. Some fresh meats, poultry products, fruits, and vegetables are restricted, as are firearms. Pets are permitted to cross the border with a certificate of rabies vaccination dated within 30 days prior to crossing. Bear sprays are not allowed on airplanes in checked or carry-on luggage and are considered firearms in Canada; they must have a U.S. Environmental Protection Agency-approved label to go across the border.

If you require medication administered by injection, you must pack your syringes in a checked bag; syringes are not permitted in carry-ons coming into the United States. Also, pack documentation describing your need for any narcotic medications you've brought with you. Failure to produce documentation for narcotics on request can result in severe penalties in the United States.

LEAVE NO TRACE

To keep the national parks pristine, visitors to these parks need to take an active role in maintaining them.

Plan ahead and prepare. Hiking in the backcountry is inherently risky. Three miles (4.8 km) hiking at the high elevations in Wyoming may be much harder than the same distance through your neighborhood park back home. Choose appropriate routes for mileage and elevation gain with this in mind, and carry hiking essentials.

Travel and camp on durable surfaces. In front-country and backcountry campgrounds, camp in designated sites. Protect fragile plants by staying on trails even in mud, refusing to cut switchbacks, and walking single file. If you must walk off the trail, step on rocks, snow, or dry grasses rather than wet soil and delicate plants.

Leave what you find. Flowers, rocks, and fur tufts on shrubs are protected park resources, as are historical and cultural items. For lunch stops and camping, sit on rocks or logs where you find them rather than moving them to accommodate comfort.

Properly dispose of waste. Pack out whatever you bring, including all garbage. If toilets are not available, pack out toilet paper. Urinate on rocks, logs, gravel, or snow to protect soils and plants from salt-starved wildlife, and bury feces 6-8 inches (15-20 cm) deep at least 200 feet (61 m) from water.

Minimize campfire impacts. Make fires in designated fire pits only, not on beaches. Use small wrist-size dead and downed wood, not live branches. Be aware: Fires and collecting firewood are not permitted in some places in the parks.

Respect wildlife. Bring along binoculars, spotting scopes, and telephoto lenses to aid in watching wildlife. Keep your distance. Do not feed any wildlife, even ground squirrels. Once fed, they become more aggressive.

Be considerate of other visitors. Particularly be aware of cell phones and how their use or noise cuts into the natural soundscapes of the parks.

For more Leave No Trace information, visit www.LNT.org.

PASSES, PERMITS, AND FEES

Many national park passes are available for purchase online. Entrance fees must be paid in person at the individual park entrances; some unstaffed entrances may be cash-only.

ENTRY FEES

Entrance fees range from free to $35 or more per vehicle; entry fees for motorcycles, bicyclists, and individuals on foot are slightly reduced. Once paid, most entrance fees are good for seven days.

ANNUAL PASSES

The **Annual Pass** (www.recreation.gov, $80) admits entrance to all national parks and federal fee areas for up to one year. Most national parks also offer their own **Annual Pass** ($50-70) granting access to the one park for up to one year. All U.S. fourth graders (https://everykidoutdoors.gov) are eligible to receive a free annual pass.

SENIOR PASS

U.S. citizens or permanent residents age 62 and older have two pass options: an **Annual Senior Pass** ($20, $10 processing fee), good for one year, or a **Lifetime Senior Pass** ($80, $10 processing fee), which is valid for life. To purchase either pass, apply online (https://store.usgs.gov/recreational-passes) or bring proof of age (state driver's license, birth certificate, or passport) in person to any national park entrance station (processing fee waived at park entrances). In a private vehicle, the card admits four adults, plus all children under age 16. Four annual senior passes can be traded in for the lifetime senior pass.

Both senior passes grant the passholder discounts on fees for federally run tours and campgrounds; however, discounts do not apply to park concessionaire services like hotels, boat tours, and bus tours.

ACCESS PASS

Blind or permanently disabled U.S. citizens or permanent residents can request a lifetime **National Parks and Federal Recreational Lands Access Pass** (https://store.usgs.gov/recreational-passes, free, $10 processing fee) for access to all national parks and other federal sites. The pass admits the passholder plus three other adults in the same vehicle; children under age 16 are free. Passholders also receive a 50 percent discount on federally run tours and campgrounds. Proof of medical disability or eligibility is required for receiving federal benefits.

MILITARY PASS

U.S. military personnel, veterans, and Gold Star Families can get a lifetime **National Parks and Federal Recreational Lands Access Pass** (https://store.usgs.gov/recreational-passes, free) for access to all national parks and other federal sites. The pass admits the passholder plus three other adults in the same vehicle; children under age 16 are free. Passholders also get 50 percent discounts on federally run tours and campgrounds. Passes must be acquired in person at entrance stations; proof of service is required.

FEE-FREE DAYS

Admission is free on Fee-Free Days: Martin Luther King Jr. Day (Jan.), the first day of National Park Week (Apr.), National Park Service Anniversary (Aug.), National Public Lands Day (Sept.), and Veterans Day (Nov. 11).

VOLUNTEER PASS

Those volunteering in national parks or other federal lands can get an annual pass to all national parks by reaching 250 service hours. Service hours may be accrued in one year or across several years.

RESERVATIONS

During the busy summer months, accommodations can be hard to come by. It's common for national park lodgings to be fully booked **up to 13 months in advance.** Cancellations sometimes provide last minute limited options. Most campground reservations are handled by www.recreation.gov, available **six months in advance** and often booked within minutes.

CAMPING WITHOUT RESERVATIONS

Don't have reservations for camping? Here are a few tips for snagging a campsite in summer.

Make a base camp and stay put rather than shuffling campgrounds every day or so. You'll spend a little more time driving to some destinations, but you'll experience the park more with the time you save from searching campground after campground only to be confronted with "Full" signs.

On any day you plan to move camp, change locations in early morning to get a campsite before campgrounds fill up. Make getting your next campsite the first priority rather than sightseeing.

At first-come, first-served campgrounds, plan to begin prowling for a site an hour or more before the fill times mentioned on the park's website.

WILDERNESS PERMITS

If you're planning a backcountry excursion, follow all rules and guidelines for obtaining **wilderness permits** for specific parks (www.nps.gov). Rules vary between parks, especially regarding fees, reservations, and procedures for picking up permits. Park-specific backcountry offices will have information on any health, trail, bear, or other alerts in the area. Check online for individual park *Backcountry/Wilderness Trip Planners* for assistance. For your safety, let someone outside your party know your route and expected date of return.

ACCESSIBILITY

While some national park structures have been fitted with ramps and wider doors, many historic or remote structures remain inaccessible. However, most campgrounds designate specific campsites that meet the Americans with Disabilities Act standards.

There are many resources to help travelers with disabilities plan their trip. Check on the specific park's website and the NPS app for services pertinent to that park. Many parks have facilities, programs, and trails designed for those with wheelchairs and physical or mobility challenges. Most park brochures are also available in large print or braille, and some in audio format. Park videos often have captioned versions. Trained service dogs are permitted in many parks, but check on requirements; some parks with prevalent grizzly bear populations discourage them in the backcountry.

TRAVELERS OF COLOR

National parks draw visitors of all ethnicities and races. While the parks have not always been inclusive places, they are public lands, meant for everyone to enjoy, and a great place to start adventuring outdoors. Here are some resources to help you prepare for your trip.

Misha Euceph hosts **Hello, Nature** (www.rei.com/blog/podcasts/hello-nature), an eight-episode podcast that visits popular national parks, exploring who the parks are for. During the episodes, Euceph shares her experiences as a person of color.

Other resources provide how-to guides for launching into outdoor pursuits such as hiking, camping, and backpacking, which are the backbone of many national park adventures. **Diversify Outdoors** (www.diversifyoutdoors.com) is a coalition of bloggers and social media personalities who are passionate about the outdoors and strive for equity, inclusion, and access for all. **Melanin Base Camp** (www.melaninbasecamp.com) features outdoor athlete bloggers, trip reports, and gear reviews. **Latino Outdoors** (https://latinooutdoors.org) has bilingual educational resources in their How-To Vamos Outdoors.

COVID-19 AND THE NATIONAL PARKS

The coronavirus pandemic has had a significant impact on the United States, including the regions covered in this guide, and the situation is constantly evolving. Now more than ever, Moon encourages its readers to be courteous and ethical in their travel. Be respectful to local residents and mindful of the situation in your chosen destination when planning your trip.

With the exception of federal laws, no one size fits all regarding COVID-19 protocols in national parks. It is imperative to look up **current requirements** and **local restrictions** on specific park websites and the NPS app. The most important ones are listed under "Alerts." If you're traveling to or from an area that is currently a COVID-19 hot spot, you may want to reconsider your trip.

Moon encourages travelers to **get vaccinated** if their health status allows and to take a **coronavirus test** with enough time to receive the results before departure if possible. Some destinations may require proof of vaccination or a negative COVID test result before arrival, along with other tests and a **self-quarantine period** after arrival. Check local requirements and factor these into your plans.

If you plan to fly, check with your **airline** and the **local health authorities** for updated travel requirements. Some airlines may be taking more steps to help you travel safely, such as limiting occupancy; check their websites before buying your ticket. Flights may be more infrequent, with increased cancellations.

Pack **hand sanitizer,** a **thermometer,** and plenty of **face masks.** Federal rules as of 2022 require masks inside buildings (visitors centers, hotels, and restrooms), on public transportation, and in crowded outdoor spaces. Masks are required for all visitors, even those who are vaccinated.

Assess the risk of entering **crowded spaces,** joining **tours,** and taking **public transit.** Research **special requirements** that may be in effect with visitor services: shuttles, campgrounds, ranger programs, hotels, restaurants, reservations, and permits.

Be flexible and patient. Many parks have reduced staff due to COVID-19 rules for housing their seasonal workers. Some tours and venues may require **reservations,** enforce **capacity limits,** or operate during **different hours** than the ones listed. Always have a **backup plan** in case of site closures or event cancellations.

When trying to maintain **social distancing** on trails, be cautious about stepping off trails. Look for durable surfaces and avoid trampling fragile alpine or wetlands plants or wildflowers.

LGBTQ TRAVELERS

The national parks are generally LGBTQ-friendly, but in the small rural towns surrounding the parks, don't expect to find much in the way of overt gay culture or nightlife. For perspective on visiting the national parks from two gay travelers, tune in to the podcast **Gaze at the National Parks** (https://gazeatthenationalparks.com). Avid hikers Dustin Ballard and Michael Ryan share their on-the-trail adventures in many of the U.S. national parks, adding new destinations each season.

TRAVELING WITH CHILDREN

The National Park Service has designed ways to pique the interest of kids through educational activities online (www.nps.gov, under "Learn About the

Park"), in-park activities, and visitors center hands-on exhibits.

Hiking with kids can either be a nightmare or a hoot. To make it more fun, take water and snacks along to prevent hunger and thirst from sapping their energy. Take extra layers to keep kids warm if the weather turns. Help them connect with the environment while hiking by asking them about what they see and why things are the way they are. If you make hiking a fun experience for them, they'll want to do it again.

JUNIOR RANGER PROGRAMS

Junior Ranger Programs (www.nps. gov/kids/jrRangers.cfm) mix educational activities with experiences for families to do in the park. Most activities target ages 6-12. Pick up Junior Ranger activity guides ($3-5 or free) at any visitors center. Kids complete the self-guided activities and receive a Junior Ranger badge after stopping at a visitors center to get sworn in.

TRAVELING WITH PETS

Pets are allowed inside national parks, but only in limited areas: campgrounds, parking lots, and roadsides. They are not allowed on most trails and beaches, in the backcountry, or at most park lodges or motor inns. When outside a vehicle or in a campground, pets must be on a leash or caged. Be kind enough to avoid leaving them unattended in a car anywhere. Be considerate of wildlife and other visitors by keeping your pet under control and disposing of waste in garbage cans. Some national parks (such as Grand Canyon) provide kennel services for a fee.

FIREARMS

Federal law allows legally carried firearms into the national parks. However, they are prohibited in visitors centers, ranger stations, fee-collection buildings, and other facilities. Those places are marked with signs at all public entrances. Discharging firearms in the park is illegal except when presented with "imminent danger."

WI-FI AND CELL SERVICE

Cellular service and internet connectivity within the national parks tend to be limited. In general, plan to be out of reach while you travel in the parks, where service is unavailable on many roads, trails, campgrounds, picnic areas, and lodges. National park visitors centers, ranger stations, and campgrounds rarely have Wi-Fi. Some park lodges may offer limited Wi-Fi for overnight guests, but connectivity will often be very slow.

MOBILE APPS

The National Park Service has a free **NPS smartphone app** covering each national park. Download the app before you begin your trip because cell service and internet are limited inside the parks. Some sections can be saved for offline use. The app has information on alerts, visitors centers, hikes, geyser predictions, road closures, ranger programs, self-guided tours, and interactive park maps. Even with the app, your first stop for accurate up-to-date information should always be a national park visitors center and the national park website.

INDEX

TUV

WXYZ

LIST OF MAPS

PHOTO CREDITS

1: © Michael Ver Sprill | Dreamstime.com; 3: © Becky Lomax (1-4), © Jason Busa | Dreamstime.com (5), 4-5: © Kalyan V. Srinivas | Dreamstime.com; 8-9: © NPS/Tim Rains; 9: © Sreejith Sankaradasa Kurup | Dreamstime.com; 10: © Dfikar | Dreamstime.com; 11: © Stephen Moehle | Dreamstime.com; 12: © Munst64804 | Dreamstime.com (top), © Becky Lomax (bottom); 13: © Hannator92 | Dreamstime.com; 14: © Nicholas Motto | Dreamstime.com; 15: © NPS/Sandy Groves (top), © Hotshotsworldwide | Dreamstime.com (bottom); 17: © NPS/Erin Whittaker; 18: © Becky Lomax; 21: © Michael Ver Sprill | Dreamstime.com; 22: © Becky Lomax; 24: © Nature Picture Library / Alamy Stock Photo; 25: © Noppakun | Dreamstime.com; 26: © Becky Lomax (top & bottom); 27: © NPS/Jacob W. Frank; 28: © NPS/Patrick Myers; 29 © Lawrence Weslowski Jr | Dreamstime.com (top), © Liao Qiongna | Dreamstime.com (bottom); 31: © Björn Alberts | Dreamstime.com; 31: © Valentin Armianu | Dreamstime.com; 32: © Marcy Yoshida; 33 © Becky Lomax (top); Scott Griessel | Dreamstime.com (bottom); 34 © Tobkatrina | Dreamstime.com; 37: © NPS/Neal Herbert; 38-39: © NPS/Jacob W. Frank; 41: © NPS/Ken Conger (left), ©NPS (middle), ©NPS/Neal Herbert (right); 42: © Galyna Andrushko | Dreamstime.com; 43: © NPS/Jim Pfeiffenberger; 44: © Alan Gregory (top), © NPS/Ken Conger (middle), © NPS/Tim Rains (bottom); 45: © Bennymarty | Dreamstime.com; 49: © Roussien | Dreamstime.com (top), © Pamela Johnson | Dreamstime.com (bottom); 51: © NPS/Jacob W. Frank; 52: © NPS/Tim Rains; 53: © NPS/Neil Blake; 54: © NPS/Emily Messner; 55: © NPS/Lian Law (top) © NPS/Tim Rains (bottom); 56: © NPS/Alex Vanderstuyf; 57: © NPS/Jacob W. Frank; 59: © NPS/Jacob W. Frank; 60: © NPS/Tim Rains; 61: © NPS/Katie Thoresen; 62: © Galyna Andrushko | Dreamstime.com; 66: © Galyna Andrushko | Dreamstime.com (top), © NPS/Jim Pfeiffenberger (bottom); 70: © NPS/Bill Thompson; 71: © NPS/E. Booher; 74: © NPS/E. Booher; 75: © NPS/Karen Tucker; 76: © NPS; 77: © NPS; 80: © NPS (top) © NPS/M. Fitz (bottom); 81: © NPS; 83: © Alan Gregory; 86: © Alan Gregory; 87: © Alan Gregory (top), © Alan Gregory (bottom); 88: © NPS/Bryan Petrtyl; 89: © Alan Gregory; 90: © Alan Gregory; 91: © © Alan Gregory; (top), © Alan Gregory; (bottom); 92: © Alan Gregory; 93: © Michele Cornelius | Dreamstime.com; 97: © NPS (top); © Martinmark | Dreamstime.com (bottom); 98: © Lembi Buchanan | Dreamstime.com; 99: © NPS; 100: © NPS (top), ©NPS (bottom); 101: © NPS; 102: © NPS/DevDharm Khalsa; 103: © NPS/Penny Knuckles; 106: © NPS/Zak Richter; 107: © NPS/Zak Richter (top), © Joshanon1 | Dreamstime.com (bottom); 108: © NPS/Mike Thompson; 109: © NPS/Neal Herbert; 110-111: © Haveseen | Dreamstime.com; 113: © Joshua Daniels | Dreamstime.com (left), ©Maria Luisa Lopez Estivill | Dreamstime.com (middle), © Becky Lomax (right); 114: © Nstanev | Dreamstime.com (left), © Becky Lomax (right); 115: © Becky Lomax; 116: © Martin Molcan | Dreamstime.com (top), © Nickolay Stanev | Dreamstime.com (middle), © Björn Alberts | Dreamstime.com (bottom); 117: © Becky Lomax; 121: © Kailyn Enriquez | Dreamstime.com; 123: © Becky Lomax (top) © Becky Lomax (bottom); 126: © Djschreiber | Dreamstime.com; 127: © Snyfer | Dreamstime.com; 127: © Kevin Wells | Dreamstime.com; 129: © Becky Lomax; 130: © Becky Lomax (top) © Becky Lomax (bottom); 131: © Bertl123 | Dreamstime.com; 132: © Becky Lomax; 133: © Becky Lomax; 134: © Christopher Arns; 135: © Srongkrod Kuakoon | Dreamstime.com (left), © Becky Lomax (middle), © Richard Billingham | Dreamstime.com (right); 136: © Becky Lomax; 137: © Becky Lomax; 138: © Miles Eldon; 139: © Lorcel | Dreamstime.com; 140: © Luckyphotographer | Dreamstime.com; 144: © Demerzel21 | Dreamstime.com; 146: © Peter Mautsch / Maranso Gmbh | Dreamstime.com; 147: © Becky Lomax; 148: © NPS; 149: © NPS; 150: © Becky Lomax; 151: © Patrick Poendl | Dreamstime.com; 152: © Becky Lomax; 153: © Michal Balada | Dreamstime.com; 157: © Bukki88 | Dreamstime.com (top), © Jenna Blough (bottom); 159: © Alan Gregory; 160: © Jenna Blough (top) © Jenna Blough(bottom); 162: © Alan Gregory; 164: © Claire White | Dreamstime.com; 168: © Jenna Blough; 169: © Nytia Henriot | Dreamstime.com (top), © Jenna Blough (bottom); 170: © Jenna Blough; 171: © Jenna Blough; 172: © Jenna Blough; 173: © Jenna Blough (top), © Nyker1 | Dreamstime.com (bottom); 174: © Sandra Foyt | Dreamstime.com; 175: © Jenna Blough; 176: © Jenna Blough (top), © Lunamarina |

588: © NPS/Jeff Manuszak; 589: © Darren Dwayne Frazier | Dreamstime.com (top), © NPS/Katrina George (bottom); 590: © NPS/Katrina George; 591: © Valariej | Dreamstime. com; 593: © Michael Thompson | Dreamstime.com; 597: © kgcphoto / istockphoto.com; 598: © Posnov / istockphoto.com; 599: © Daniel Hosie / istockphoto.com; 600: © Patrick Barron | Dreamstime.com; 604: © NPS (top), © NPS (bottom); 605: © George Burba | Dreamstime.com; 606: © Caleb Lawson | Dreamstime.com; 607: © Patrick Barron | Dreamstime.com; 608-609: © Asboard90|Dreamstime.com; 611: © Dndavis | Dreamstime. com (left), © Natalia Bratslavsky | Dreamstime.com (middle), © NPS/G.Gardner (right); 612: © Adventures on the Gorge; 613: © Becky Lomax; 614: © Mona Meraseau (top), © Daveallenphoto | Dreamstime.com (middle), © Kottapsm | Dreamstime.com (bottom); 615: © Asboard90 | Dreamstime.com; 619: © NPS; 620: © Sean Pavone | Dreamstime.com; 621: © Lightscribe | Dreamstime.com; 623: © Cvandyke | Dreamstime.com; 625: © Alex Grichenko | Dreamstime.com; 626: © Donald Fink | Dreamstime.com; 627: © Anthony Heflin | Dreamstime.com; 628: © Anton Foltin | Dreamstime.com; 629: © Anthony Heflin | Dreamstime.com; 630: © Alex Grichenko | Dreamstime.com; 631: © Melinda Fawver | Dreamstime.com; 632: © Becky Lomax; 636: © Becky Lomax; 637: © Becky Lomax (top), © Becky Lomax (middle), © Becky Lomax (bottom); 639: © Becky Lomax (top), © Becky Lomax (bottom); 640: © Becky Lomax; 641: © Becky Lomax; 642: © NPS; 646: © NPS; 647: © Wangkun Jia | Dreamstime.com (top), © Wangkun Jia | Dreamstime.com (bottom); 648: © NPS; 649: © ScenincMedia | Dreamstime.com; 650: © Jon Bilous | Dreamstime.com; 653: Adventures on the Gorge (top), Mitgirl | Dreamstime. com(bottom); 654: © Mona Meraseau (top), Edward Lange | Dreamstime.com (bottom); 655: © Michael Bowen | Dreamstime.com; 656: © Sean Pavone | Dreamstime.com; 657: © Kenneth Keifer | Dreamstime.com; 658: © Adventures on the Gorge; 659: © Steveheap | Dreamstime.com; 660: © F11photo | Dreamstime.com; 662: © NPS; 664: © Iandewarphotography | Dreamstime.com (top), NPS (bottom); 665: © Legacy1995 | Dreamstime.com; 666: © Allilev | Dreamstime.com; 670: © Sandra Foyt | Dreamstime. com (top), © Josh Kroese | Dreamstime.com (middle), © Itsadream | Dreamstime.com (bottom); 671: © NPS; 672: © Sandra Foyt | Dreamstime.com; 673: © Zrfphoto | Dreamstime. com; 675: © Mark Norton | Dreamstime.com; 678: © Tashka | Dreamstime.com (top), Pierre Leclerc | Dreamstime.com (bottom); 679: © Caleb Lawson | Dreamstime.com; 680: © William C. Bunce | Dreamstime.com; 684: © Andy | Dreamstime.com; 685: © NPS/R. Cammauf (top), © Dietmar Rauscher | Dreamstime.com (bottom); 686: © John Anderson | Dreamstime.com; 687: © Peter Etchells | Dreamstime.com; 688: © NPS/R. Cammauf (top), © NPS (bottom); 689: © NPS/R. Cammauf; 690: © Sandra Foyt | Dreamstime.com; 691: © NPS/T.Taylor; 692: © Chiyacat | Dreamstime.com; 694: © NPS/ Shaun Wolfe; 696: © NPS / Rob Waara; 697: © NPS (top), © NPS/Judd Patterson (bottom); 698: © NPS (top), © NPS/Rob Waara (bottom); 700: © Bennymarty | Dreamstime.com; 703: © Varina and Jay Patel | Dreamstime.com (top), © NPS/Brett Seymour (bottom); 704: © NPS/John Dengler; 705: © NPS/Brett Seymour; 706-707: © Industryandtravel | Dreamstime.com; 709: © Mikko Ryynänen | Dreamstime.com (top), © MNStudio | Dreamstime.com (middle), © Susanna Henighan Potter (bottom); 710: © Eddydegroot | Dreamstime.com; 711: © MNStudio | Dreamstime.com; 715: © Estabienn | Dreamstime. com (top), © Dayton344 | Dreamstime.com (bottom); 716: © Fairytaleportraits | Dreamstime.com; 717: © Anne M. Fearon-wood | Dreamstime.com (top), © MNStudio | Dreamstime.com (bottom); 718: © Nyker1 | Dreamstime.com; 719: © MNStudio | Dreamstime.com; 720: © Anne M. Fearon-wood | Dreamstime.com; 721: © NPS/Janice Wei; 725: © Chee-onn Leong | Dreamstime.com (top), © MNStudio | Dreamstime.com (bottom); 726: © Alexander Demyanenko | Dreamstime.com; 727: © NPS/J. Wei; 729: © NPS; 730: © NPS; 731: © Jocrebbin | Dreamstime.com; 734: © Joni Hanebutt | Dreamstime. com; 709: © Susanna Henighan Potter; 711: © Susanna Henighan Potter; 735: © Jiawangkun | Dreamstime.com; 737: © Jiawangkun | Dreamstime.com; 738: © Susanna Henighan Potter (top and bottom); 739 © Svecchiotti | Dreamstime.com; 740: © Sorin Colac | Dreamstime.com; 744: © NPS (top), NPS (bottom); 745: © NPS; 746: © NPS; 747: © NPS; 748-749: © Miroslav Liska | Dreamstime.com; 755: © Becky Lomax; 758: © NPS/ Penny Knuckles

TEXT CREDITS

Alaska

Text for the Alaska national parks adapted from *Moon Alaska*, first edition, by Lisa Maloney

California

Text for Death Valley National Park adapted from *Moon Death Valley National Park*, first edition, by Jenna Blough

Text for Joshua Tree National Park adapted from *Moon Palm Springs & Joshua Tree*, first edition, by Jenna Blough

Text for Redwood National and State Parks and for Channel Island National Park adapted from *Moon Coastal California*, fifth edition, by Stuart Thornton

Text for Pinnacles National Park adapted from *Moon Northern California*, seventh edition, by Elizabeth Linhart Veneman & Christopher Arns, and from *Moon Monterey & Carmel*, fifth edition, by Stuart Thornton

Pacific Northwest

Text for Crater Lake National Park adapted from *Moon Oregon*, 11th edition, by Judy Jewell & W. C. McRae

Text for the Washington national parks adapted from *Moon Washington*, 10th edition, by Matthew Lombardi

Southwest

Text for the Arizona national parks adapted from *Moon Arizona & the Grand Canyon*, 13th edition, by Tim Hull

Text for the Colorado national parks adapted from *Moon Colorado*, ninth edition, by Terri Cook

Text for Great Basin National Park adapted from *Moon Nevada*, eighth edition, by Scott Smith

Text for the Texas national parks adapted from *Moon Texas*, ninth edition, by Andy Rhodes

Text for the Utah national parks adapted from *Moon Utah*, 12th edition, by W. C. McRae & Judy Jewell

Rocky Mountains

Text for the Colorado national parks adapted from *Moon Colorado*, ninth edition, by Terri Cook

Text for the South Dakota national parks adapted from *Moon Mount Rushmore & the Black Hills*, third edition, by Laural A. Bidwell

Great Lakes and Northeast

Text for Acadia National Park adapted from *Moon Maine*, seventh edition, by Hilary Nangle

Text for Cuyahoga Valley National Park adapted from *Moon Cleveland*, second edition, by Douglas Trattner

Text for Isle Royale National Park adapted from *Moon Michigan*, sixth edition, by Paul Vachon

Text for Voyageurs National Park adapted from *Moon Minnesota*, fourth edition, by Tricia Cornell

The South

Text for Great Smoky Mountains National Park adapted from *Moon Great Smoky Mountains National Park,* first edition, by Jason Frye

Text for Shenandoah National Park adapted from *Moon Blue Ridge Parkway Road Trip,* first edition, by Jason Frye

Text for Mammoth Cave National Park adapted from *Moon Kentucky,* second edition, by Theresa Dowell Blackinton

Text for Congaree National Park adapted from *Moon South Carolina,* sixth edition, by Jim Morekis

Text for Everglades National Park adapted from *Moon Sarasota & Naples,* second edition, by Jason Ferguson

Text for Biscayne National Park and Dry Tortugas National Park adapted from *Moon Florida Keys,* third edition, by Joshua Lawrence Kinser

Islands

Text for Hawai'i Volcanoes National Park adapted from *Moon Big Island of Hawai'i,* eighth edition, by Bree Kessler

Text for Virgin Islands National Park adapted from *Moon U.S. & British Virgin Islands,* sixth edition, by Susanna Henighan Potter

ACKNOWLEDGMENTS

A huge thank-you goes out to all past and present members of the National Park Service. It's through their labors that we have access to such treasures. For many in the park service, their work is a devotion to the park they love.

I thank my parents for introducing me to the national parks. Before I was born, my father worked summers at Mount Rainier National Park. On one of my parents' first dates, he took my mom bushwhacking to see a secret cluster of ancient trees. After they were married, my parents led us kids to the giant trees, which later became known as Grove of the Patriarchs (after the trail and bridge were installed). As grandparents, my folks took their small grandchildren to hug the no-longer-secret trees. After my father passed away, my mother, along with all of the kids and grandkids, returned to our grove to honor his memory amid those sacred trees. Experiencing the national parks is one of the greatest gifts parents can give their children. Big thank yous go to all my family and friends who travel the parks with me. Marcy Yoshida, Barb Penner, Alan Gregory, and KT Duncan also helped me with parts of this book.

I thank the regional writers who contributed mounds of their expertise. Their valuable insight into their "home" parks provided the backbone of this project; without it, this book could not be. In a time when national parks are changing rapidly, my editor Leah Gordon handled an inordinate amount of alterations to the text well after deadlines. I owe her immense gratitude for her support and dedication to helping make details as up-to-date as possible. Likewise, a huge appreciation goes to Karin Dahl for updating maps with a new park and even closures in some and Lucie Ericksen for sourcing such evocative photos.

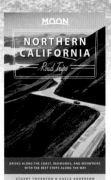

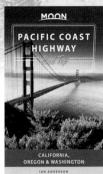

ROAD TRIP GUIDES FROM MOON

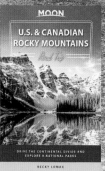

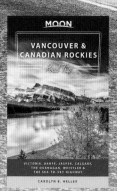

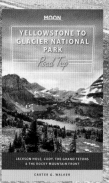

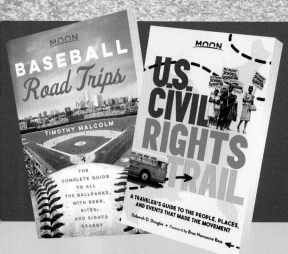

MAP SYMBOLS

═══	Expressway	○	City/Town	✈	Airport	⚲	Golf Course
═══	Primary Road	◉	State Capital	✗	Airfield	🅿	Parking Area
═══	Secondary Road	✪	National Capital	▲	Mountain	▰	Archaeological Site
┅┅	Unpaved Road	★	Point of Interest	✦	Unique Natural Feature	⛪	Church
───	Feature Trail	•	Accommodation			⛽	Gas Station
─ ─ ─	Other Trail	▼	Restaurant/Bar	⚐	Waterfall	◉	Glacier
┈┈┈	Ferry	■	Other Location	▲	Park		Mangrove
═══	Pedestrian Walkway			🚩	Trailhead		Reef
▮▮▮	Stairs	⋀	Campground	🎿	Skiing Area		Swamp

CONVERSION TABLES

°C = (°F - 32) / 1.8
°F = (°C x 1.8) + 32
1 inch = 2.54 centimeters (cm)
1 foot = 0.304 meters (m)
1 yard = 0.914 meters
1 mile = 1.6093 kilometers (km)
1 km = 0.6214 miles
1 fathom = 1.8288 m
1 chain = 20.1168 m
1 furlong = 201.168 m
1 acre = 0.4047 hectares
1 sq km = 100 hectares
1 sq mile = 2.59 square km
1 ounce = 28.35 grams
1 pound = 0.4536 kilograms
1 short ton = 0.90718 metric ton
1 short ton = 2,000 pounds
1 long ton = 1.016 metric tons
1 long ton = 2,240 pounds
1 metric ton = 1,000 kilograms
1 quart = 0.94635 liters
1 US gallon = 3.7854 liters
1 Imperial gallon = 4.5459 liters
1 nautical mile = 1.852 km

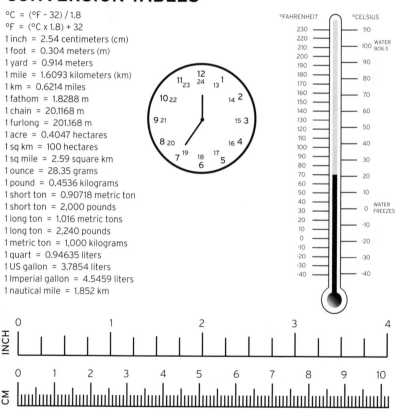

MOON USA NATIONAL PARKS

Avalon Travel
Hachette Book Group
1700 Fourth Street
Berkeley, CA 94710, USA
www.moon.com

Editor: Leah Gordon
Acquiring Editor: Nikki Ioakimedes
Fact-Checker: Ashley M. Biggers
Copy Editor: Christopher Church
Graphics and Production Coordinator: Lucie Ericksen
Cover Design: Kimberly Glyder Design
Interior Design: Megan Jones Design
Map Editor: Karin Dahl
Cartographers: Moon Street Cartography, Mike Morgenfeld, John Culp
Indexer: Rachel Kuhn

ISBN-13: 978-1-64049-621-7

Printing History
1st Edition — 2018
3rd Edition — October 2022
5 4 3 2 1

Front cover photo: Sequoia National Park, California © Larry Geddis / Cavan Images/ GettyImages
Back cover photos (top to bottom): Upper Rose River Falls, Virginia © NPS/Brett Raeburn; Yosemite, California © F11photo | Dreamstime.com; Maho Bay Beach, Saint John, Virgin Islands National Park, U.S. Virgin Islands © Jimschw1 | Dreamstime.com

Printed in China by R.R. Donnelley

Yosemite

Olympic

CAPITOL REEF

Rocky Mountain

Cuyahoga Valley

HOT SPRINGS

MOON

KOBUK VALLEY

Crater Lake

BRYCE CANYON

BIG BEND

Acadia

GATEWAY ARCH

National Park of American Samoa

GATES OF THE ARCTIC

Channel Islands

ZION

GUADALUPE MOUNTAINS

Theodore Roosevelt

NEW RIVER GORGE

Virgin Islands

GLACIER BAY

Pinnacles

GREAT BASIN

CARLSBAD CAVERNS

Wind Cave

MAMMOTH CAVE

Hawai'i Volcanoes

WRANGELL-ST. ELIAS

Redwood National & State Parks

SAGUARO

WHITE SANDS

Badlands

SHENANDOAH

Haleakalā

KATMAI

Lassen Volcanic

PETRIFIED FOREST

GREAT SAND DUNES

Glacier

GREAT SMOKY MOUNTAINS

DRY TORTUGAS

LAKE CLARK

Joshua Tree

GRAND CANYON

MESA VERDE

Grand Teton

Voyageurs

BISCAYNE

KENAI FJORDS

Death Valley

North Cascades

CANYONLANDS

Yellowstone

Isle Royale

EVERGLADES

DENALI

Sequoia & Kings Canyon

Mount Rainier

ARCHES

Black Canyon of the Gunnison

Indiana Dunes

CONGAREE